AMERICAN ORIENTAL SERIES
VOLUME 53

ESSAYS IN MEMORY OF E. A. SPEISER

AMERICAN ORIENTAL SERIES

VOLUME 53

AMERICAN ORIENTAL SOCIETY

NEW HAVEN, CONNECTICUT

1968

ESSAYS IN MEMORY

OF

E. A. SPEISER

EDITED
BY
WILLIAM W. HALLO

AMERICAN ORIENTAL SOCIETY
NEW HAVEN, CONNECTICUT
1968

Also published simultaneously as

JOURNAL OF THE AMERICAN ORIENTAL SOCIETY
VOLUME 88
NUMBER 1

COMMITTEE FOR THE
SPEISER MEMORIAL ISSUE

W. F. ALBRIGHT
J. J. FINKELSTEIN
MOSHE GREENBERG
SAMUEL NOAH KRAMER
W. W. HALLO, *Chairman*

PRINTED IN THE UNITED STATES OF AMERICA
J. H. FURST CO., BALTIMORE, MARYLAND

TABLE OF CONTENTS

ILLUSTRATIONS

E. A. SPEISER
(1902–1965)

IN MEMORY OF E. A. SPEISER

MOSHE GREENBERG

EPHRAIM AVIGDOR SPEISER was born on January 24, 1902 in Skalat, Galicia (then in Austrian Poland, now in the Ukrainian SSR). He graduated from the Gymnasium of Lemberg (Lvov) in 1918, and came to the U. S. in 1920 where, under J. A. Montgomery and Max Margolis he earned an M. A. degree at the University of Pennsylvania in 1923 (thesis published as "The Hebrew Origin of the First Part of the Book of Wisdom"), and a Ph. D. at the Dropsie College in 1924 (thesis: "The Pronunciation of Hebrew according to the Transliterations in the Hexapla").[1] A Harrison Research Fellow in Semitics at the University of Pennsylvania from 1924-26, he then went to the Near East as a Guggenheim Fellow and Annual Professor of the Baghdad School of the American Schools of Oriental Research for the 1926-27 season. He surveyed northern Iraq (producing "Southern Kurdistan in the Annals of Ashurbanipal and Today"), and discovered and made preliminary excavations at Tepe Gawra. He also taught comparative Semitics at Jerusalem's Hebrew University in 1927. Later, as field director of the Joint Excavation of the ASOR and the University Museum in 1930-32 and 1936-37 he thoroughly explored Tepe Gawra and nearby Tell Billa, establishing a reputation for scientific excavation on the part of the Baghdad School (BASOR 183.5). The results were published in *Excavations at Tepe Gawra,* Vol. I (1935). His association with the ASOR continued as non-resident director of the Baghdad School from 1934-47, and as a vice-president of the Schools from 1948 to his death.

In 1928 Speiser joined the faculty of the University of Pennsylvania as assistant professor of Semitics; three years later, at the age of 29, he became full professor. During the thirties he systematically published and integrated the data being uncovered at Tepe Gawra and Tell Billa into a new picture of the ethnic, linguistic and cultural composition of early Mesopotamia (*Mesopotamian Origins* [1930]). An abiding interest in the Nuzi tablets generated many studies, among which are the text publications of "New Kirkuk Documents Relating to Family Law" (1932) and (with R. H. Pfeiffer) *One Hundred Selected Nuzi Texts* (1936). Investigation of the Hurrian component at Nuzi and elsewhere led to a survey of "Ethnic Movements in the Near East in the Second Millennium B. C." (1933) and to the organization of linguistic data culminating in the still standard *Introduction to Hurrian* (1941).

After the U. S. entered the Second World War, Speiser was called to Washington to serve as the chief of the Near East Section, Research and Analysis Branch of the Office of Strategic Services. At the termination of the war and his service he was awarded a Certificate of Merit whose citation laid particular emphasis on his ability to anticipate where information would be needed well in advance of events. Reflecting this phase of his activity is his book on *The United States and the Near East* (1947, 1950), an insightful survey of the lands and peoples of the modern Near East in the light of their backgrounds.

Returning to academic life, Speiser took on the chairmanship of the Department of Oriental Studies at the University of Pennsylvania in 1947, a responsibility he discharged to his death. In 1954 he was appointed the first A. M. Ellis Professor of Hebrew and Semitic Languages and Literatures. Now his synthetic interests, always lively, came increasingly to the fore. Mesopotamian culture received his attention in the translations of "Akkadian Myths and Epics" in Pritchard's *Ancient Near Eastern Texts* (1950, 1955) and in such studies as "The Idea of History in Ancient Mesopotamia." Linguistic studies kept pace: articles on Akkadian lexicography and comparative Semitic morphology issued from his

[1] Full citation of all bibliographical items will be found on pp. 587-603 of J. J. Finkelstein and M. Greenberg, eds., *Oriental and Biblical Studies: Collected Writings of E. A. Speiser* (Philadelphia: University of Pennsylvania Press, 1967). (Attention may be called here to supplementary items listed by J. A. Brinkman in *Catholic Biblical Quarterly* 30.282 f. and by W. W. Hallo in JAOS 88/3 [in Press].) That volume contains a fine appreciation of Speiser by J. J. Finkelstein (pp. 605-616), to which this notice is but an adjunct.

pen. An outcome of his earlier work on Nuzi legal texts was a growing emphasis on the importance of law as a central feature of Mesopotamian civilization and a key to its understanding. Characteristic was his assertion that "A direct study of [Hammurabi's laws] can be far more revealing than scores of books *about* Hammurabi's Babylonia."[2]

From 1955 on, Speiser's longstanding attachment to biblical studies (after Montgomery's death in 1949 he annually taught the course in a book of the Bible) was harnessed to the Jewish Publication Society's Bible translation project. He became a member of its translation committee, and his intense work for the next ten years on this project—he once estimated that fully a third of his time was devoted to it—overflowed in a series of learned and popular articles on biblical themes through the decade. At the same time he was both editing and contributing to the first volume of the *World History of the Jewish People, At the Dawn of Civilization* (1964), covering the Near Eastern background of biblical history. His last book, an introduction, translation and commentary to *Genesis* in the Anchor Bible (1964) was the fruition of this lifelong interest. "Sooner or later," he once wrote, "the intellectual fortunes that we amass in peripheral areas get to be wisely invested in the Bible."[3]

Such a broad conception of Near Eastern civilization could not fail to inspire both colleagues and students. Speiser was a mainstay of the departmental seminar in "Interconnections of Oriental Civilizations" that for years bound together diverse men and fields in an absorbing, common effort at enlarging horizons. Students in increasing numbers came to study under him, and his response to them was unstinting. To the end, and even amidst the pains of his last illness, he maintained a gruelling teaching schedule, which in some years amounted to 12 hours a week and more. His lectures were models of lucidity and pointedness, based on full, carefully prepared notes which bear the marks of periodic revision, not only for substance but for language, wit and style.

He was generous in attention to individuals: colleagues and students found him ready to help in personal and scholarly problems; with his worldly wisdom and academic expertise, he was repeatedly called upon for both types of advice. He had a sharp tongue and (as he was fond of saying) "did not suffer fools gladly." If he misprized a man, he did not mind letting him know it; yet upon those he regarded as deserving he bestowed unmeasured attention. His close combing of work submitted to him for criticism by veteran scholars as well as novice students was a standing kindness to men in the field. He was for a time an editor of this Journal, and served on the editorial committee of the ASOR; but his direct and indirect contribution to standards of scholarship and writing far outrun these specific services.

Speiser's eminence in his field was nationally recognized. He had been president of the American Oriental Society and a member of its Executive Board; vice-president of the American Association for Middle East Studies, and of the Linguistic Society of America; he was a fellow of the American Academy for Jewish Research. The Hebrew Union College honored him with a Doctor of Hebrew Letters and later named him to the Board of Overseers of its Archeological School in Jerusalem. His reputation in humanistic circles earned him membership in the American Philosophical Society and on the Advisory Board of the Guggenheim Foundation. In 1959 the American Council of Learned Societies awarded him a prize for outstanding scholarly achievement in the humanities. And in 1964 the University of Pennsylvania named him University Professor, a title reserved for distinguished scholars who have contributed to more than one discipline.

Speiser exerted a rallying influence on those who worked with and under him. He looked for and found coherence, and was able to impart the sense of it to others. He had a gift for bringing out one's strengths and spurring one to his best effort—chiefly through his own example of excellence and his ability to teach of what excellence consists. The many students who, by his death on June 15, 1965, had come to study under him felt he was the embodiment of healthy scholarship.

For those who knew him, the memory of E. A. Speiser is a call to style and standards, to integrity and breadth of outlook, to the acceptance of responsibility for the advancement of knowledge.

[2] *Oriental and Biblical Studies*, p. 538.

[3] Cited by Finkelstein from a letter, *ibid.* 606.

IŠME-DAGAN AND ENLIL'S CHARIOT[1]

MIGUEL CIVIL
UNIVERSITY OF CHICAGO

THE CHARIOT, both as a cultic implement used in processions and as an element in mythological tales, such as Ninurta's *Angin dimma,* has a traditional place in Sumerian religion. The bridge between the real chariot and the mythical one is the model chariot, which may be an humble clay object or a piece of jewelry, kept in a sacred place. In some of the passages quoted below it is not possible to decide whether they refer to the actual vehicle or to its model.

The oldest sacred chariot on record[2] is probably the one of Ningirsu, which was an object of special veneration on Gudea's part[3] and whose coach house had been built before by Entemena[4] and again by Urukagina.[5] The archives of the Lagaš dynasty often mention food at offerings to the sacred chariots or at the "chariot's place" (ki-^{giš}gigir),[6] as well as on occasion of the vehicles' comings and goings,[7] which can be processions or simply trips of the sovereign. Chariots of various deities such as Bau,[8] Sataran,[9] Ningirsu,[10] and Ninlil, are known from the times of the Ur III dynasty. The construction of the last one gave the name to a still unplaced year of Ur-Nammu or Šulgi.[11] Offerings continue to be made to the chariots,[12] particularly on the 6th or 7th day of the month, when they are presented mostly sheep.[13] The Isin kings followed the tradition, and Enlil's chariot is mentioned in the 16th and 19th years of Išbi-Erra.[14]

It is in this context that the hymn published here must be placed. In this new hymn, Išme-Dagan is introduced as the builder of a chariot (^{giš}gigir-maḫ)[15] for Enlil, and the ensuing blessings for the king, which include his mystical cohabitation with Inanna, are described. Very few year-formulae of Išme-Dagan have been recovered, but it is likely that this event was commemorated in a now lost date, since the construction of a ^{giš}mar-šum for Ninlil did deserve a special commemoration,[16] and chariots are thus celebrated elsewhere.[17] Noteworthy is the long inscription of a Cassite king, probably Kadašman-

[1] Abbreviations are those of CAD, supplemented by R. Borger, Handbuch der Keilschriftliteratur I. Presargonic Lagaš inscriptions are quoted according to Sollberger's Corpus. Additional abbreviations: Ag = Curse of Agade, Falkenstein, ZA 57 43 ff. BF = Bird-Fish Debate (in SDD). FI = Farmer's Instructions (according to my own ms.). SDD = M. Civil, Sumerian Debates and Dialogues (to be published as Texts from Cuneiform Sources V). UK = Silver-Copper Debate (in SDD). Numerical references preceded by an asterisk and enclosed in brackets refer to the critical signs copied at the end of the article. Thanks are due to Professor Samuel Noah Kramer for his kind permission to publish CBS 6136 and for an excellent photo of the tablet. Detailed information about the terminology of the chariot and its parts will be found in A. Salonen, Landfahrzeuge des alten Mesopotamien (AASF 72/3) to which the reader is referred for the technical terms not explicitly discussed in this article.

[2] Archeological representations are of course much older. Some notes, now partly outdated, on "Prozessionswagen der babylonischen Götter" were published by A. Salonen in StOr 13/2.

[3] Cyl A vi 17 ff.; vii 13 ff.; xxviii 15; B ix 15; xiii 18 f.; xvi 15.

[4] Ent 22 i 6, 9.

[5] Ukg 10 ii 3.

[6] DP 43 i 1 f.; 53 ix 22; RTC 47 v 7.

[7] DP 53 i 13 f.; xi 2 ff. [from Nina to Lagaš]; 197 i 6 ff.; Nikolski 23 i 6 ff.; TSA 1 xii 12 ff.; RTC 47 i 5.

[8] HSS 4 3 ii 10; ix 9; 52: 3.

[9] ITT 2/2 3569: 3.

[10] HSS 4 52: 1; RTC 308 r. 2.

[11] Sollberger, AfO 17 15 (= Šulgi 3); F. R. Kraus OrNS 20 397 (= Ur-Nammu d).

[12] TCL 2 5501 ii 20; Jones-Snyder, SET 142: 3; ITT 2/1 833 (p. 30 "au puits"); 2/2 3100: 1; 3/2 6546.

[13] Or 47 ff. 357: 3 f.; 372: 3 f., 14; 378: 4 f.; Or 18 pl. xiv 38: 2 ff.; StOr 9 20: 3 ff.; AnOr 1 135: 3 ff.; Boson, Tavolette 162: 3 f.; 202: 4 f.; 345: 2 ff.; etc. As Prof. W. W. Hallo kindly points out to me, these texts refer to an aspect of the lunar cultic activities and it is likely that gigir is here short for u$_4$-sakar$_x$(SAR) ^{giš}gigir "chariot's crescent," a part of the wheel discussed by Salonen, Landfahrzeuge 116 f., and a very apt designation for the moon crescent itself, rather than a cultic chariot.

[14] BIN 9 198: 11; 429: 14.

[15] ^{giš}gigir-maḫ is, according to Ḫḫ V 8, a specific name for Enlil's chariot, found also in 4R 12: 23, r. 9.

[16] UET 1 219 = RA 33 26 no. 50, 51; for Išme-Dagan's year-names see Edzard, Zwischenzeit 76[372].

[17] UCP 10/1 51 no. 13, 14, 52 no. 23; Sumer 5 81 no. 31.

Enlil II,[18] to perpetuate the memory of a ^{giš}gigir-maḫ for Enlil built during his reign.

Sources. CBS 6136 is a four column tablet with large, but often carelessly written, signs. On the obverse the right column is 20% narrower than the left one; the difference in width is less pronounced on the reverse. My reconstruction assumes, taking into account the high number of indented lines, a total length of 96 lines. If this estimate turns out to be erroneous it will be almost certainly by excess.

No duplicates of CBS 6136 have as yet been identified.

Literary type and contents. According to its subscription, the text is a tigi for Enlil, composed in the usual way of a sa-gíd-da (of about 64 lines) and a sa-gar-ra (of some 31 lines). This literary genre and the sa-notations have been studied by Falkenstein in ZA 49 95 ff., 101 ff.; see also W. W. Hallo, BiOr 23 241.

The first part (sa-gíd-da) is an address to the chariot itself, praising individually each one of its parts with an appropriate laudatory phrase based on the shape or function of the part. The second part (sa-gar-ra) shifts from the physical description to a symbolic mythical level and describes a procession or festival with Enlil riding his chariot, surrounded by Ninurta and the Anunnas. Agricultural implements are somehow included in the festival.[19] At the end, there is a prayer of Ninurta to Enlil in favor of the royal wheelwright, who, as a reward for the construction of the chariot, will become the mystical spouse of Inanna.

The hymn belongs thus to Römer's type A II a (SKI 5 ff.), and has a close parallel in a long text which describes how Lipit-Ištar built a plow to be used in a festival inaugurating the agricultural season.[20]

Due to limitations in space, the edition of this hymn is not accompanied by the usual philological and lexical commentary, but some technical terms of special interest are discussed in a lexical appendix. The general vocabulary of the royal hymns is rather well known thanks to Römer's SKI and the anterior studies of Falkenstein, where the interested reader will find information about the more usual words of the Sumerian hymnology.

TEXT

^{giš}gigir-maḫ ^{d}en-líl en-geštu$_2$-ga [21] a-a-dingir-re-e-ne-ke$_4$
é-kur èš-maḫ-a-na dím-me-za bí-in-dug$_4$
^{d}iš-me-^{d}da-gan sipa-gal-zu mu-dùg sa$_4$-a-me-en
šà-ama-sa$_7$ ù-tu mas-su-kalam-ma-ka
me-kù-sikil-zu pa-è-ak-dè á-bi mu-un-da-an-ág
šu mu-ra-túm gá-la nu-mu-e-ta-dag-ge
[ ] ⸢x⸣ [22]-na mi-ni-in-sa$_7$-ge-en
[ ] ⸢x⸣ [23]-ta ba-an-gub-bé-en
[ ] ⸢x x⸣ [24]-ma-2-bi níg u$_6$-di gál-me-en
^{giš}šu-kár-zu dalla-maḫ im-è ^{giš}tir-^{šim} ^{giš}erin-na-gin$_x$
^{giš}ma-gíd-zu [25] a-gàr ab-sín gál-tak$_4$-a ḫé-gál še-gu-nu
[su]-din-zu dungu pan [26]-zu
⸢x⸣-an-ki [27] gú téš lá-a-me-en
$^{[giš]}$erin$_2$-zu-ta ^{giš}rab-maḫ-zu nu-è erim$_2$ šu-ri-ri-me-en

[18] F. el-Wailly, Sumer 10 52; Seux, RA 59 13.

[19] The passage contains a clear allusion to the Hoe-Plow Debate, see discussion in SDD.

[20] STCV 75 and 79, plus four unpublished duplicates, one of them an OB bilingual. Edited in SDD as an appendix to the Hoe-Plow Debate.

[21] There is a half-preserved sign [*1], which is certainly not -ke$_4$, after -ga, but it may very well belong to the first line of col. ii.

[22] [*2].

[23] [*3].

[24] [*4].

[25] Gloss [*5] under ^{giš}ma-gíd, perhaps *⸢ni⸣-ir-ki!*, but if so, hardly fits the word it glosses (see lexical notes), and furthermore two at least of the other glosses seem to be Sumerian.

[26] Although sír would make sense, cf. dungu-sír = *erpetu šapītu* CT 16 19: 33 f.; the sign [*6] is almost certainly pan.

[27] [*7] -an-ki (over erasure) preferable, but -an-na is also possible.

15 [^{giš}kak-s]a$^{?}$-lá-zu sa-pàr-šè ná-a [ ] ⸢x⸣ [28]-lá-a-me-en
[ ] ⸢x⸣ [29]-záḫ
17–27 *broken*
⸢x⸣ [30][ ]
sag-ki-[zu] a ⸢x⸣[ ]
30 á-šita$_4$-z[u] ḫi-li d[u$_8$]
^{giš}KAK-a-za [32] kár ⸢x⸣ [33][ ] a-gi$_6$ sur-sur
é-su-lum-ma-zu usan$_3$ b[ar-uš-bi] [34] anše zi-zi-i [35]
^{giš}DUB-zu [36] sa-šú-⸢uš⸣-gal-[x] erim$_2$-DU nu-[ ]
gaba-gál-zu me-maḫ nam-⸢x⸣ [37] gal-bi kin-kin
35 ^{ú}KI.KAL-zu ur-s[ag (x)] téš-ba du$_7$-du$_7$
gáb-íl-zu gud-áb-da-k[e$_4$] níg-dugud íl-íl
šà-sù-zu guruš dun-d[un] gú-da lá-[ ]
da-da-zu ki [ ] téš-a [ ]
gìr-gub-zu [ ] ⸢x⸣ [38][ ]
40 ⸢giš.x⸣ [39][-zu]
41–61 *broken*
62 u$_4$-b[a]
lugal-a-ni ⸢x⸣ [40][ ]
kù-babbar guškin n[a$_4$]
65 sa-gíd-[da-àm]
kéš [41]-gal-ni šu-du$_7$ [ ] gìr-ni gub-gu[b]
ama-^{d}nin-líl nitada[m-ma-ni] gú-da mu-ni-[in-lá]
^{d}nin-urta ur-sag [ ]
^{d}a-nun-na k[i] egir-ra-a-ni dù[g]
70 ^{giš}gigir nim-gin$_x$ gír-gír-re [gù-dé]-ur$_5$-ša$_4$-bi [42] dùg-ga-à[m]
dùr^{ùr}-a-ni erin$_2$-na lá-a [ ]
^{d}en-líl ^{giš}gigir-zu maḫ-a-ni [ ]-zalag-ga-ni na-UD-[UD]
gizkim-ti ⸢x⸣ [43][ ] ^{d}nin-[ ] ḫar-ra-a[n]
ki-ur$_5$-šag$_5$-g[e]
76 lugal [ ]
76–80 *broken*
81 *unidentifiable traces* [44]
[x x x] ⸢x⸣ [45] ^{giš}šu-kár gán-[x]
[x x] um-ta-è-a-àm [46]
[^{giš}a]l-e ^{giš}apin-e ⸢giš nam⸣-erin$_2$ a-da-mìn ḫa-mu-ra-an-e
85 lugal-e inim-^{d}en-líl-lá-šè gizzal ba-ši-in-ak
^{d}nin-urta-ke$_4$ ^{giš}apin-kù-ge si nam-mi-in-sá ⸢gán⸣-zi na-uru$_4$^{ru}
gur$_7$-du$_6$-gur$_7$-maš-^{d}en-líl-lá-ke$_4$

---

28 [*8].
29 [*9].
30 See note 21.
31 [*10].
32 Gloss za-ra underneath ^{giš}KAK.
33 [*11].
34 Restoration based on Angin 99 (quoted in the lexical notes sub é-su-lum-ma), and on the constant association of the usan$_3$ with bar-uš: e. g. DP 492; BE 30 8 iii pass.; Gud cyl A xiii 18; SRT 14: 9; STVC 115 ii 5′.
35 Gloss [*12] i-zì-zi-[(x)], doubtful, under zi-zi-i.
36 Gloss i under giš (see lexical notes sub ^{giš}DUB).
37 [*13].
38 [*14].
39 [*15].
40 [*16].
41 The sign is certainly KÉŠ, not EZEN.
42 Reconstruction based on Ḫḫ V 13: ^{giš}gigir-gù-dé-ur$_5$-ša$_4$ = *MIN* (*narkabtu*) ^{d}*Ninurta*; also on Angin II 24′: ^{giš}gigir-zu gù-dé-ur$_5$-ša$_4$-bi: *nar-kab-ta-ka ana ri-gim ra-me-me-šá.*
43 [*17].
44 [*18].
45 [*19].
46 This line could be indented and part of line 82.

gú-gur-gur-ru-dè numun-zi na-mu-gar
⌜šul⌝[47] ur-sag é-kur-za-gìn-na sag-íl-la mu-un-ku$_4$
en-^{d}n[in-urt]a-ke$_4$ ^{d}en-líl-ra sizku[r m]u-na-ab-bé
^{d}iš-me-^{d}da-gan ⌜sipa⌝ šu-du$_7$ x x[48] gìr-za sì-ga-ra
lugal ^{giš}gigir-ra ma-ra-an-dím-ma-ra igi-zi bar-mu-un-še
^{d}inanna dumu-gal-ki-ág-zu nitadam-šè sum-mu-an
u$_4$-ul-šè gú-da ḫa-mu-ri-in-lá
ḫi-li níg-ku$_7$-ku$_7$-da úr[49]-kù
nam-ti-diri-na u$_4$ ḫa-ba-ni-in-sù-du
sa-gar-ra-àm
tigi-^{d}en-l[íl-l]á-kam

TRANSLATION

Oh lofty chariot, Enlil, the lord of intelligence, the father of the gods,
Spoke about your construction, in the Ekur, his sublime shrine.
You have been given an auspicious name by Išme-Dagan—the all-wise shepherd,
Born of a beautiful womb, the leader of the country—
He gave orders so that your holy and pure *me* could become famous.
He applied (his) hand to you(r construction, and) has not stopped since.
In his [. . .] he has made you beautiful,
You have been placed with [. . .] by him.
[. . .] the two [. . .],[50] you are a sight to behold.
Your furnishings are outstanding, like the cedar forest.
Your pole, a field with open furrows, abundance of late grain.
Your *sudin*, a cloud, your bow(?) [. . .], (with which) you join heaven and earth.
From your yoke, your huge stock, there is no escape, you clamp down the evildoer,
Your [rope-fastened] pegs are laid like a net, you . . . [. . .]
(lacuna)
[Your] front [. . .]
Your furnishings, [. . . fu]ll of charm [. . .].
Your axle, . . . [. . .] pours a flood.
Your rope-box, [its] whip [and goad] rouse up the donkeys.
Your pole pin, a large net [. . .] does not [release] the evildoer.
Your front guard, the sublime *me* of [. . .] greatly seeks.
Your platform, warriors [. . .] fighting together.
Your side beams, an ox and a cow carrying a heavy load.
Your cross beams . . . [. . .] embracing [. . .]
Your side board . . . [. . .] together [. . .]
Your foot board, [. . .]
(lacuna)
The[n . . .]
His king, . . . [. . .]
Silver, gold, (precious) sto[nes . . .]
(sa-gíd-da)
(Enlil) completed his great harnessing, he stepped in [. . .]

[47] [*20].
[48] [*21].
[49] There is an erased sign between úr and kù; for úr-kù cf. UET 6/1 11: 2; CT 42 4 ii 6 f.; TuMNF 3 25 r. 14 ff.; SRT 1 v 31 f.
[50] Perhaps umbin is to be restored in this line.

He emb[raced] Ninlil, the Mother, [his] wife.
Ninurta, the Hero, [. . . in front]
The Anunnas . . . , after him [. . .]
The chariot shines like lightning, its bellowing [noise] is a pleasure.
[. . .] his donkeys harnessed to the yoke.
Enlil, his mighty chariot, his shining [. . .], is bright.
The secret sign [. . . of] Nin[. . .], the trip [. . .]
The place which rejoices the liver [. . .]
The King [. . .]

(lacuna)

[. . .] the field implements [. . .]
Which came out from [. . .]
Let the hoe (and) the plow, the implements of the working people, have a contest before you.
The King paid attention to Enlil's instructions,
Ninurta put the holy plow in good order, and plows the fertile field.
So that the silos and granaries of Enlil
May be piled high, he drops the fertile seed.
The youthful Hero proudly enters the resplendent Ekur.
The lord Ninurta offers a prayer to Enlil:
"Towards Išme-Dagan, the accomplished shepherd . . . , who has performed (this) service for you,
Towards the King who has built you the chariot, cast a pious glance!
Give to him, as spouse, Inanna your beloved eldest daughter,
Let them embrace forever!
Delight, sweetness, holy limbs,
May last a long time in his abundant life."
(*sa-gar-ra*)
It is a *tigi* of Enlil.

LEXICAL NOTES

á-šita$_4$ (30) "implements"

Written also á-šu-du$_7$ in Ag 93 and EWO 321 (see below); this writing is to be explained by ŠITA$_4$ = šutul Proto-ea 246, although á-ŠITA$_4$ has vocalic ending in context as well as in the gloss ašte (Nabnitu IV 328; Antagal F 177). Akk.: *ḫišiḫtu* (lex. ref. CAD 6 204a s. v.), *takaltu* (Antagal III 191; Ḫḫ V 192, 193 [á-šita$_4$-UM]; and *ūturtu* (Ḫḫ VI 10).

Parts of the plow: ^{giš}apin-zu á-šita$_4$-bi ḫa-ra-ab-kéš "have the implements of your plow put together" FI 15 (the late version differs: ^{giš}šudun-zu tùn-dím-zu [. . .]: *ni-ir-ka i-na ta-ka-[al-ti-ka* . . .]; agricultural implements in general: WZJ 9 237: 321 (text A [checked] has á-šita$_4$; H and I have á-šu-du$_7$); parts of the loom: giš á-šu-du$_7$-a túg-gada ù na$_4$-esi HSS 4 6 viii 1 f.; UET 3 1504 x 29; of a litter: á-šu-du$_7$-a ^{giš}ma-a-al-tum BIN 9 453: 4; insignia of kingship: á-šita$_4$ (var. á-šu-du$_7$-a)-nam-lugal-la-ka-na im-ma-ra-an-ba-ba Ag 93; varia: UET 3 322; 745 r. 3′.

Cf. šu-du$_7$ with the meaning "fully equipped" said, e. g. of wagons (BIN 8 127: 1) or plows (Ḫḫ V 117), as well as šita$_4$ = *šuklulu* S$_b$ II 234. In Angin 53: áb-dab-a-ni ŠITA$_4$ bí-in-lá, the late version II 2′ reads ^{giš}šudun instead of ŠITA$_4$. In *á(text GÀR)-šita$_4$: *puzra* CT 16 42: 14 f. the text must in all probability be emended to *á-úr. Note also á-šita$_4$ = *qarnu* MSL 6 7, note to line 27a.

da (38) "side(board)"

^{giš}da-da-(a)-gigir = *marḫaṣu* Ḫḫ V 37, MSL 6 8, revised (from texts S$_9$ and BM 64377 [unpubl.]; ST must read da!-da-gigir [from photo] and the entry ^{giš}SAL-la-dagal-gigir must be eliminated). Fore: MSL 6 38: 9 has ^{giš}ta-ta (var. dal-d[al])-mar-gíd-da. The sides could be made of, or covered with, goat and sheep skins: BIN 9 192: 5; 193: 9.

For ^{giš}da "board" cf. e. g. RA 16 19 i 8 (2 cubits), 20 ix 14 (10 cubits); TU 121 iii 3 (6 cubits); etc. The translation "Abflussrohr" AHw 611, an etymological speculation, is unacceptable.

^{giš}**dù-a** (31) "axle."

^{giš}KAK^{da}-a-gigir = *qarnu, zarû, manzazu* Ḫḫ V 26, 28, 30a(!), MSL 6 7, revised and confirmed by BM 64377 (unpubl.); additional ref. in CAD 21 70a *zarû* A. A reading zara$_x$, as given by the gloss, is also possible, cf. fore. MSL 6 37:33; RTC 239 ii 3′; BIN 8 127 (quoted sub ^{d}KI. KAL): etc. kak-za-ra UET 3 Index 186 (copy in one of the passages, 348:1, has -a-ra, which appears also in ITT 3/2 6542:2, but probably -*za- is intended in both cases) is perhaps to be read kak$^{\text{za-ra}}$,[51] and there is still the possibility that the late gloss da ought to be dismissed as incorrect. For dà-a < dù-a, cf. Ḫḫ XI 134; Izi C i 15; etc.

^{giš}**DUB** (33) "pole pin" (?)

Obviously connected with Ḫḫ V 68 ff. (in line 70 the text of ST: ŠID-kak-šà-ga, is preferable in view of Angin 60 quoted below). The only way to explain the gloss i in our text is to consider it as a phonetic var. of the NA$_4$ (= i$_4$) of the source N of Ḫḫ V, and that should be taken as an indication that the reading is kišib ("seal"), not as a phonetic gloss of the sign DUB itself.[52]

^{giš}DUB alone does not seem to occur with this meaning, but we have DUB-kak^{urudu} DP 481 i 3; ITT 1 1275 (p. 17); and DUB-kak-bar-ra DP 481 ii 1 (identical with Ḫḫ V 68) followed by e-ni-lá; níg-urudu-kalag-ga DUB-kak-šà-ga-ka bí-in-lá Angin 60, the late version (CT 15 42 K 4864 +) has ^{giš}ŠID-[. . .].

The association with "seal" on the one hand and with pegs (kak) on the other, suggests a cotter or key to keep the pegs or dowels in place; our line 33 seems to confirm that the function of the ^{giš}DUB was to keep things in place. The same meaning fits also ^{giš}ŠID-umbin-mar-gíd-da = *kanasarru* Ḫḫ V 99, very likely "pole pin."

It is uncertain whether DUB-sa-kak^{zabar} TU 126 ii 2 is related with these terms; DUB^{guškin} in RA 17 212 is certainly something else.

é-su-lum-ma (32) "a box to keep the whips and goading stick."

^{giš}é-zú-lum-gigir = *laḫaruška* Ḫḫ V 17; ^{giš}é-zú-lum-ma = *laḫaruššu* Ḫḫ VII A 64; ^{kuš}é-zú-l[um-ma] = *laḫaruška* Ḫḫ IX 102 (revised text in MSL IX, now preceded by *bīt kabābi* and *bīt ulluli*); *laḫaruška* = *bīt qanē* Malku II 200; cf. also ^{giš}su-lu-mar-gigir (var. su-l[um) fore. MSL 6 36:20; ^{giš}šu-mar-gigir in the Ras Shamra forerunner, ibid. 36:9 is the same word. The derivation from *é-zú-limmu suggested in RA 21 142 and MSL 6 6 (on the strength of Ḫḫ VII A 161: ^{giš}al-zú-a-ba) is unwarranted, since the older texts write consistently su-lum; and there is no reason to assume any connection between a type of hoe and the present implement; cf. also the writing su-lu-mar, above; also šul-lum-mar WVDOG 43 42 iii II.

The meaning of é-su-lum-ma is clear from: ^{kuš}usan$_2$ bar-uš é-su-lum-ma-ka bí-in-sù "he (Ninurta) put away in the e. the whip and the goad" Angin 99. The passage kù ab-gaz-za-mu kù ba-ab-si-il-lá-mu zú-lum-mar-ra ⌜x⌝: *šá* ⌜*la*!⌝-*ḫa-ru-uš-ki pi-ti* "my silver broken into pieces, my silver given in trust, which could break open (?) the z." SBH 19 r. 1 raises the question of the relationship between é-su/zú-lum-ma and su/zú-lum-mar. The last expression is a verbal compound as shown by the form su-lum nu-mu-un-mar in UET 6/2 286:3 (below).

^{giš}illar-gin$_x$ edin-ki-nu-zu-gá nam-ba-e-dè-šub-bu-dè-en
mu-in-na-šeš-mu-ne-ka nam-ba-an-ku$_4$-ku$_4$-dè-en
su-lum-mar-du$_{10}$-sa-mu-ne-ka kir$_4$ nam-ba-an-ku$_4$-ku$_4$-dè-en

"Do not let me be thrown, like a throwing stick, into the steppe, a place unknown to me,
Do not let me enter the . . . of straw of my brothers,
Do not let me put the nose into the s. of my friends"

These lines of the end of Lugalbanda's prayer to Utu (Lugalbanda and Ḫurrum 166 ff.) are commented, as it were, by two recently published proverbs:

[51] This possibility is not contradicted by the existence of the genitive compound kak-za-ra-(ak).

[52] There is a possibility, nevertheless, that DUB (= kišib) could be read metonymically, or should we say metagraphically, *na/i, since na$_4$ alone can mean also "seal," cf. CAD A/1 61a *abnu* 10 a. The writings na$_4$, zá, and i(a)$_4$, of course, are simply different attempts to render a sound non-existent in the Akkadian phonemic system.

in-nu in-ga?-dab	I gathered (?) straw,
in ma-an-dug$_4$ (for *kú?)	He fed(?) me (more) straw.[53]
su-lum nu-mu-un-mar	I was not tethered,
su-lum-mar ma-an-dab	He held me with a s.
	UET 6/2 286
nam-tar-mu ga-àm-dug$_4$	I want to tell my fate:
su-lum-mar-àm	It is a s.
a-rá-mu ga-àm-dug$_4$	I want to tell my ways:
kir$_4$-lú ba-an-šeš-e	It bothers (lit. makes feel bitter) one's nose.
	UET 6/2 292

Note the parallelism straw/su-lum in the Lugalbanda passage and the first proverb; these sentences represent a popular way to say "to live a donkey's life."

The only passage from lexical sources which might be of some help is Nabnitu XXI 209; zú-lum^{lum}-[ma]r! = *ḫarāšu ša imēri*; for the usual interpretation of this entry see CAD 6 95a *ḫarāšu* A;[54] the second lum is not written in gloss size, but there is no serious objection to interpreting it as a gloss, since the size confusion is found elsewhere in Nabnitu. Quite possibly the gloss was introduced to avoid the confusion with ḫum = *ḫarāšu* of A V/1:3. If this interpretation of Nabnitu XXI 209 is correct, the resulting meaning for the substantive su-lum would be something like "tethering rope" or "tethering ring," a meaning which fits quite well the passages adduced above. Verbs used with the compound su-lum-mar are kéš in: [. . .]-su-lum-mar-re-da-kam su-lum-mar-re kéš-da (unpubl. and unnumbered Ur fragment in the British Museum, courtesy S. N. Kramer), and its opposite bad, in: gar-ra šeš-mu zu-lum-ma-ra [x]-⌜x⌝-NE-bad ba-u$_5$ CT 15 29:25, and an equivalent of *petû* in the passage from SBH 19 r. 1, quoted above. The meanings "to tie" and "to open" are compatible with the translation of su-lum just proposed. Another reference for su-lum-mar is: [. . .] su-lum-mar (var. -gar) nu-gar BF 29, in a half-broken passage. We must mention also the late divine name ^{d}KA^{zu}-lum-gar^{mar} = ^{d}*é-a* CT 25 33:16, which appears also in the Theodicy 277 (W. G. Lambert, BWL 88). According to Diri IV 304 and Ea VI 203, the logogram KI.SAG.DU has a reading sulummar with a translation *tubullû* "climbing-belt" to harvest dates (Meissner, Sachau Festschrift 22 ff.; W. G. Lambert, BWL 328). It is another writing of the same word with another specialized meaning (from "loop of rope" to "climbing-belt").

The é-su-lum-ma thus takes its name not from the whips but from ropes to tether the animals that were also kept there; it could be made, according to the lexical references, from wood, leather, or reeds. As for its physical shape, one could imagine something like the quiver seen on the front part of chariots and wagons in archeological representations. As a matter of fact the *laḫaruška* was used also to keep arrows; cf. STT 2 366:9 "they placed the bow in the bow case they filled the l. with shining arrows" (*laḫarušak undalli qanī ebbūtu*), see E. Reiner JNES 26 196, and cf. ref. from Malku II 200, above.

^{giš}**erin$_2$** (14, 71) "yoke."

Akk. *ṣimittu* (ref. CAD 21 198 s. v.).

While the meaning yoke for ^{giš}erin$_2$ is reasonably certain and confirmed by the form of the original pictogram, the difference between ^{giš}erin$_2$ and the much more frequent ^{giš}šudul/n = *nîru* is not altogether clear. By translating "crosspiece of a yoke," CAD loc. cit. seems to imply that ^{giš}šudul is a more general term. However, both in plows and in chariots and wagons, the pole on which the yoke rests is considered part of the plow or vehicle and has specific names, and it is perfectly clear from STVC 75 ii 4 ff. and dupl. that ^{giš}sudul designates only the "crosspiece," made by joining two pieces (^{giš}šudul á-2-bi) fastened by dowels secured with rope tied around (^{giš}kak-sa-lá). The contrast ^{giš}šudul/^{giš}erin$_2$ is thus hardly the one between a whole implement and one part of it. From the Lagaš-Girsu Presargonic texts one gets

[53] A word play on in, "straw" and "insult," is likely.

[54] The connexion with *ḫarāšu*, if correct, makes attractive an explanation (at least on the level of popular etymology) of the difficult *laḫaruška/laḫaruššu* as **lū aḫruš-ka/šu* "let me tie you/him down," that would also provide a solution for the unparalleled alternation *-ška/-ššu*.

the impression that ^{giš}erin$_2$ is associated with wagons and chariots, and ^{giš}šudul with the plow: ^{giš}erin$_2$-mar (DP 413, 414, 446, 486, 502; VAS 14 162; TSA 26, 31; etc) but always šu$_4$-dul$_5$ (written also šá-dul$_5$ DP 492 vii 10; TSA 28 i 1; 31 i 1 ff., vii 4 ff.) for the plow (DP 410, 413, 436, 446; TSA 28, 31; etc.). Also, ^{giš}erin$_2$ appears to be associated mostly with equids and ^{giš}šudul with oxen. There are however exceptions, and if we have a ^{giš}erin$_2$ for a wagon in BIN 8 127:4 (Sargonic), we have also a ^{giš}šudul for a wagon (pulled by oxen) in AS 16 7 iii 10′ (OB), and one for a chariot in BIN 9 437:17 (Isin). A šu$_4$-dul$_5$ for oxen is mentioned in Gud cyl. B xv 20, while line 12 has a šá-dul$_5$ for donkeys; cf. also: anše ki-^{giš}šudul-šè . . . ú íl-í[l-(i)] UK B$_3$ 30. In the case of the plow, ^{giš}erin$_2$ is rare, see the series ^{giš}apin, ^{giš}erin$_2$, ^{giš}ninda$_2$ in TCL 5 6036 xv 18 ff.; xvii 5 ff.; xviii 11 ff. In WZJ 9 237:316 ^{giš}apin-^{giš}šudul-erin$_2$-bé-e (cf. Van Dijk, SGL 2 137; Falkenstein, ZA 64 81), erin$_2$ is the oxen team plus the plowmen (see my discussion to Hoe-Plow debate, line 91 in SDD).

gáb-íl (36) "main beams on both sides of the chariot body."

Lex.: ^{giš}gáb-íl-gigir = *kabbillu* Ḫḫ V 33; = *bubūtu* V 53; with fore. MSL 6 37:31 f.; 40:14 f.; *kabbillu* has an Akk. synonym *tillu* Malku II 205. The word gáb-íl belongs to formations of the type ga-b-$\sqrt{\ }$ and ga-n-$\sqrt{\ }$, frozen verbal forms used as active participles, the first one for transitive verbs, the second one for intransitive verbs, and means simply "carrier."

From Akk. *bubūtu* (ref. CAD 2 302b *bubūtu* B) it is clear that there are two gáb-íl in a vehicle, one on each side, and that alone makes Salonen's translation "axle" (Landfahrzeuge 102) very suspect. Our line seems to confirm that there are two gáb-íl in a chariot: "an ox and a cow carrying heavy loads." One could think of the two lateral beams forming the body of the chariot, on which rest the cross-beams (šà-si/šà-sù) mentioned in the following line 37.

The word gáb-íl is otherwise well known with the meaning basket: fore. Ḫḫ VIII-IX MSL 6 195:192; 188:79a-b (^{gi}gáb-íl-si-ga, ^{gi}gáb-íl-maḫ); it is used for fish: DP 285 i 4; TSA 48 iv 1; RTC 34 ii 1; ITT 3/2 6160:1 (capacity = 120 sila$_3$); Riftin 64: 5 f. and pass.; and in connection with scales, probably to weigh wool: DP 509 iv 5. The meaning "basket" is likely too in W. G. Lambert, BWL 243: 47 ff.: gá-e gú-e gáb-íl-mu *ba(tablet: ZU)-ab-ri-ri "as for me, my carrying basket rests on my shoulders (lit. neck)." I would also consider the entries Izi V 110 (ga-ab-íl) and the others given in CAD 21 7 a for gáb-íl = *zabbilu*, not as belonging to *zabbilu* B, but to *zabbilu* A "basket."

gaba-gál (34) "front guard of the chariot"

See CAD 5 1 b *gabagallu*; and for gaba-gál as a literary term Falkenstein ZA 56 49. Salonen, Landfahrzeuge 88 is to be modified according to MSL 6, Ḫḫ V 18 ff.: ^{giš}še-ir-gaba-gál-gigir, ^{giš}gaba-gál-gigir = *irtu*; these entries must be added to the lexical section of *irtu* in CAD 7 183; for line 18, cf. še-ir-DU$_8$-na (older NIR-DU$_8$-na) quoted sub ma-gíd.

^{giš}**kak-sa-lá** (15, restored) "dowel or peg, secured with a rope."

This word has been tentatively restored in line 15, because the traces fit and the presence of sa-pàr makes a word play on sa very likely. The term appears in STVC 75 ii 2 and 7:

^{giš}dam-bi téš-bi im-mi-in-u$_5$ ^{giš}kak-sa-lá (var. -sal-la) bí-in-tuku
^{giš}šudul á-2-bi im-mi-in-lá ^{giš}kak-sa-lá bí-in-tuku
"He ties together the two arms of the yoke, he puts there a peg secured by a rope"

In the lexical sources, ^{giš}kak-sa-lá (of a plow) appears in fore. to Ḫḫ V MSL 6 43:30; 174:51; but the main text (Ḫḫ V 161 f.) has (kak)-sal-la as in the variant above; the Akk. equivalent of sa-lá or sal-la is *mussiru*.

^{ú}**KI.KAL** (35) "platform of the chariot."

Reading not directly attested; possibly ḫirin/ḫurin, from ^{giš}al-e ^{ú}KI.KAL$^{\text{bu-ri-in}}$ šu-šè al-gá-gá "the hoe controls the h. weeds" Hymn to the Hoe 106 (the gloss has a variant ḫi-rí-in-na); this reading is confirmed by CT 39 12:17 (quoted with additional references CAD 6 197b *ḫirinnu* A): *šumma ina* PÚ.LÁ URU ^{ú}KI.KAL$^{\text{hi-ri-in}}$ IGI;[55] the preceding line has the same text with ^{ú}KI.KAL without gloss, showing that a reading *^{ú}ki-kal is also possible, cf. in that connexion ú-ki-kalag-ga "hard ground weeds" UK C 25. Finally, a new source quoted below gives the reading sas.

^{giš} ^{ú}KI.KAL-gigir = *sassu* Ḫḫ V 32 (with fore. MSL 6 36:10); the unpubl. duplicate BM 64377 gives for this line the gloss sa-as, but being an

[55] Cf. also ḫi-ri-im KI.KAL = *piṭru* Diri IV 266.

CBS 6136 obv.

CBS 6136 rev.

unreliable school tablet with many errors, the gloss needs confirmation. The determinative ú in Ḫḫ V 32 (cf. MSL 6 7) is not an error since it is also found in our text, in the Agade text BIN 8 127: 2, and in related meanings as in ^{gada} ^{ú}KI. KAL UET 3/1 81 s. v.

1 ^{giš}mar-gíd-da šu-du$_{7}$-a 1 ^{giš}šubur ^{ú}KI.KAL^{SAR} ^{giš}za-ra nu-tuku ^{giš}erin$_{2}$ nu-tuku "one fully equipped cart, 1 š. (= *majāltu* Ḫḫ V 67) with platform (but) without pole (and) without yoke" BIN 8 127: 1 ff.; [ur-sag-7] ^{giš}KI.KAL-gigir [bí-in-lá]: [*7 qar*]*-ra-du ina sa-*[*as-si* . . .] Angin II 5′, corresponds to the OB version line 55: ušum-ur sag-dúr-ra (= *kussû, littu* Ḫḫ V 40 f.) bí-in-lá; [. . .] x ^{giš}KI.KAL-gigir i-zi ḫu-luḫ z[i-zi]: [. . . *sa-as-s*]*i a-gu-ú gal-ti sa-at-*[*bi-u*] K 9008: 3′ f. (RA 51 109; cf. Landsberger WZKM 57 12[50]).

$^{\text{(ú)}}$KI.KAL designates also the "sole" of sandals or boots (Ḫḫ XI 130; TU 283: 1, 3; BIN 9 383: 2: 428: 9; 469: 2 f.; etc.) and a type of linen cloth: ^{gada} ^{ú}KI.KAL.

B. Landsberger, JNES 8 275[83]; Salonen, Landfahrzeuge 95; for the plant see Landsberger, MSL I 224.

^{giš}ma-gíd (11) "chariot pole"

Written also ^{giš}mu-gíd-gigir = *mašaddu* Ḫḫ V 46, var. adds -da after gíd, (followed by su-din and erin$_{2}$ as in our text).

Frequent in Presargonic Lagaš texts as part of a chariot (DP 479 i 3), of wagons (DP 411 i 1; 413 i 3 ff.; 414 i 1 f.; 420: 2; etc.), and also of the vehicles called ^{giš}níg-šu-(k)[56] (cf. ^{giš}níg-šu-gi = *narkabtu* Ḫḫ V 3; BWL 242 iii 29) (DP 413 i 1; 414 i 2; 418 iii 5; 427 ii 1; Nik 282 i 2) and ḪAR.ḪA-da-(k) (DP 413 i 2; 414 i 3; 418 iii 4; Nik I 282 i 1; etc.). It is made from wood of gul-bu (DP 418 iii 4; 413 i 2; 427 ii 1; 482 i 4), še-du$_{10}$ (DP 414 i 1; 419 i 3; 482 i 2; Nik 282 i 2; ITT 2/2 5725: 3, 6) and mes-babbar (DP 482 i 2; Nik 282 i 1). According to DP 482, parts of the ma-gíd were the mud and the nir-du$_{8}$-na (cf. še-ir-du$_{8}$-na-(k)[57] in Angin 56, replaced in the late version [II 6′] by še-ir-tab-ba = *liwītu*).

Older references, such as UET 2 25 i 5, mean perhaps only "beam." maš-DI-tum in RTC 222 ff. (Gelb, MAD 3 185 s. MŠD?) is in all likelihood an eating or drinking utensil.

^{giš}rab (14) "neckstock," or a similar implement.

Our line comparing, in agreement with A 1/4: 4 f.: šudul DUL = *nî*[*ru*], *rappu*, the yoke with the ^{giš}rab, suggests that this often discussed term (see simply Falkenstein, ZA 49 127 f.; Sjöberg, ZA 54 57, with previous literature) means after all a kind of pillory, and confirms the meaning "to clamp down" for šu--ri-ri = *lâṭu*. For a further discussion, see SDD, lexical index s. giš-gú and giš-šu.

sag-ki (29) "front of the chariot"

As part of the chariot, sag-ki seems to be found only in late descriptions of the Big Dipper constellation (CT 33 1 ff. i 18; AFO 4 75 r. 4; Salonen, Landfahrzeuge 83 f.).

su-din (12)

Akk. *suddinnu* "bat" Ḫḫ V 47, between mu-gíd and erin$_{2}$ as in our text; N 959 (NB school tablet) has a var. sun-din; also in fore. MSL 6 36: 19, with a var. šu-din.

The translation "Kummet" (Salonen, Hippologica 105 f.) is difficult to accept because the pieces of the harness are treated in Ḫḫ XI (see forthcoming additions in MSL IX); it must be something on the pole or yoke, preferably on the latter because of the, admittedly not very clear, rest of line 12.

šà-sù (37) "cross beams of the chariot body"

This translation assumes that šà-sù is the same as ^{giš}šà-si. This term is applied to a part of a wagon: ^{giš}šà-si-mar VAT 4778 ii 2 (Or 16 3), and more often to a part of the implement ^{giš}ri-gi$_{4}$-bí-lú (in all probability the same as ^{giš}ar-gi$_{4}$-bil-lu): DP 410 i 5, iii 7: 414 ii 3; 418 iii 1; 433 iii 4; 436 iv 7; 446 ii 5; TSA 26 iv 2; VAS 14 57 iii 2 (made of the woods asal or gul-bu).

The translation "cross beam" for ^{giš}šà-si is based on the well-documented meaning "rail of a door frame" of this term (apparently missing in Salonen, Die Türen): according to TCL 5 6036 xii 2, 12, 21, each door of 6 x 2 cubits mentioned in this text had six rails 2 cubits long; in RA 16 19 v 20′ f. there are only four for the same

[56] Cf. ^{giš}níg-šu-gi = *narkabtu* Ḫḫ V 3; Lambert, BWL 242 iii 29; ^{giš}níg-šu umbin!-na na$_{4}$ guškin-ta dar-a PBS 10/2 6 iii 30 (cf. Castellino, ZA 52 19); níg-šu ^{giš}gigir ḫar-ra-an-na sì-ga-me-èn MBI 3 ii 6 (Šulgi hymn); Hallo, JAOS 88 83: 19 and 87.

[57] Another example of šer$_{7}$ = NIR in main dialect texts. Unpublished Ur III economic texts from Nippur write also pèš-NIR-gu instead of the usual pèš-še-ir-gu.

type of door (^{giš}ig-é-sig$_5$) and are made of apple wood, while in the case of TCL 5 6036 they were made of poplar (xvii 14) as in RA 16 19 i 34; in UET 3 826 iii 7 f. they are made of ^{giš}ù-suh$_5$. To judge from AnOr 1 86 : 9 f.: 2 kuš-gud-babbar ⌜šà⌝-si ^{giš}gu-za-šè the term indicates also leather slats, or the like, in a chair, but the text of this isolated passage is uncertain.

OF DICE AND MEN

GEORGE F. DALES
UNIVERSITY MUSEUM, PHILADELPHIA

PROFESSOR SPEISER HAD A KEEN INTEREST IN AND AN APPRECIATION FOR international relations, both modern and ancient. He possessed an intuitive feel for the motivations behind and for the practical mechanics of the cultural, social and economic interactions between peoples and states. His archaeological and historical writings often were punctuated by seemingly modest statements concerning these complex matters—statements which have pointed the way to new and important avenues of research. Such a statement appeared more than thirty years ago in his report on the Tepe Gawra excavations.[1] In describing a unique playing die attributed to Gawra level VI, Akkadian period, he suggested that it was "ultimately of Indian origin." When that was written the spectacularly unexpected discovery of the Harappan civilization of the Indus Valley had but recently been revealed to the world,[2] and C. J. Gadd's fascinating description of "Indian style" seals found at Ur[3] was fresh from the press. Amidst the archaeological excitement and fervor of the 1920's and early 30's there was no lack of attempts at what we now call comparative archaeology, but it is a small monument to Speiser's perspicacity that he could spot correctly the "international" significance of a simple die.

Naturally, during the thirty some years since the Gawra publication, more information has been forthcoming concerning the question of Mesopotamian-Indus relations. But unhappily the picture is far from precise. Too many of the "facts" are indeed but inferences. The purpose of this paper is to review the various types of evidence available and to introduce some new material which reflects direct contact between the Indus and Mesopotamian regions during the periods from about 2400 to about 1900 B. C.

Just what is the evidence behind the sugges-

[1] E. A. Speiser, *Excavations at Tepe Gawra*, Vol. I (1935).

[2] Sir John Marshal, *Mohenjo-daro and the Indus Civilization* (1931).

[3] C. J. Gadd, "Seals of Ancient Indian Style found at Ur," *Proceedings of the British Academy*, 18 (1932).

tions of influences and contacts between the Sumero-Akkadians of Mesopotamia and the "Harappans"[4] of South Asia? It can be classified for convenience into the following types, arranged in descending order of certitude:

(1) actual material objects—the products of one civilization found in archaeological contexts in the other.

(2) stylistic and typological details which suggest more than coincidental similarities between the two cultures.

(3) references in ancient written records. Inasmuch as the Harappans have not favored us with such material we can seek such information only in Mesopotamia.

(4) suppositions concerning the ofttimes assumed role of the Mesopotamians in the origin and development of Harappan civilization.

The latter point is the least tangible and the most difficult to verify. The subject has been discussed in detail several times previously.[5] Here, it will only be restated that there is no evidence to support theories of wholesale migrations of peoples and goods from Mesopotamia to South Asia. The knowledge of certain fundamental concepts and techniques—for example, writing and some metallurgical techniques—may have been learned from contact with the early Mesopotamians, or their neighbors in southern Iran, but Harappan civilization itself was a product of its own internal genius and development. It must remain a moot question as to whether *without* the initial advances and stimuli of Mesopotamia, Harappan civilization would have sprung up at all. But we need to know much more about the mechanics of civilization-making in general before discussions of specific examples can be meaningful.

However, we are on *some* common ground with both the southern Mesopotamians and the Harappans when we observe that both riverine civilizations suffered from a common lack of basic raw materials and natural resources. There could have been no Ur or Nippur in Mesopotamia nor a Mohenjo-daro or Harappa in the Indus basin without a considerable amount of trade and exploitation of the hinterlands. A fascinating question is just how extensive the search for these basic materials was and to what degree—if any—they involved direct contact between the Near East and South Asia.

This brings us to the evidence of the ancient written word. Here, because of the as yet total absence of Harappan archives,[6] the only potential source of information is the rich store of Sumero-Akkadian cuneiform documents from Mesopotamia. There, among the tens of thousands of economic, historical and religious documents, are sporadic but tantalizing references to distant lands. But there is considerable difficulty in linking the names in the documents with actual geographic entities. There has been a special academic interest for more than a decade in locating the lands called Magan, Meluhha and Dilmun because of the economic, commercial and religious importance attached to them by the Sumerian and Akkadian scribes from about 2400 to about 1900 B. C. Mesopotamian contact with these lands in-

[4] The name "Harappan" is merely a modern convenience derived from the present day name of the site in the Punjab where the Indus civilization was first recognized. We know not a single word of their language, much less what they called themselves.

[5] Sir Mortimer Wheeler, *Civilizations of the Indus Valley and Beyond* (1966) and *The Indus Civilization* (Supplement to the Cambridge History of India, 2nd ed., 1960); W. A. Fairservis, "The Harappan Civilization—New Evidence and More Theory," *American Museum Novitates*, No. 2055 (1961); J.-M. Casal, "Les debuts de la civilisation de l'Indus à la lumière de fouilles récentes," in *Comptes rendus des séances de l'année 1960* (Académie des Inscriptions et Belles-Lettres, 1961), pp. 305-316; A. Ghosh, "The Indus Civilization: Its origins, authors, extent and chronology," in *Indian Prehistory: 1964* (Deccan College Postgraduate and Research Institute, Poona, 1965), pp. 113-156; G. F. Dales, "A Suggested Chronology for Afghanistan, Baluchistan, and the Indus Valley," in *Chronologies in Old World Archaeology*, Chicago (1965), pp. 257-284.

[6] That the Harappans knew the art of writing is generally agreed but the only extant examples are short, as yet undeciphered, inscriptions on stamp seals, pottery and other small objects. No hint of a library or even of a lengthy text has as yet been found in a Harappan context. Perhaps their main corpus of writings was put onto soft materials such as leaves or wood which have perished. One can speculate that if there *is* any validity to the theories of commercial and cultural contacts between the Harappans and Mesopotamia, there may be undiscovered archives containing bilingual records on clay tablets. In light of the negative evidence so far from excavations at major sites such as Harappa, Mohenjo-daro, Chanhu-daro and Lothal, I would suggest that such records might be found at the alleged Harappan seaports such as Sutkagen-dor and Sotka-koh. See note 12 below.

volved ships and journeys of considerable distance and risk. Various locations from Egypt to India have been suggested for these three important lands. The arguments have been fully set out and discussed in a number of other articles [7] and need not be rehashed here. For our purpose, suffice it to note that many of the commodities listed as imports into southern Mesopotamia from Magan, Meluhha and Dilmun *could* have come from the southern Iran, southern West Pakistan and Indus regions. The scribal inferences alone are not sufficiently detailed to insure the positive identification of these lands. But, coupled with the bits of archaeological evidence that are slowly being collected, there is good reason to suspect that at least one of the three names refers to Harappan territory. Just how intimate the contacts were in reality is an unknown factor at this point, as is the nature of the contacts.

But let us now consider the archaeological evidence. First off is the picture formed by the geographical distribution of Harappan settlements. There is virtually no trace of Harappan penetration into the mountainous regions of Baluchistan to the west of the lower Indus Valley. There are very few archaeological hints suggesting direct relations between the Harappans and Afghanistan although there are relatively easy land routes between the two regions which have been heavily trafficked throughout the historical periods. The only parallels which are suspiciously similar come from the French excavations at Mundigak in southeastern Afghanistan.[8] There a small sculptured male head [9] has certain stylistic similarities to the few examples of extant Harappan sculpture from Mohenjo-daro, (especially the fillet around the head). Also there is a peculiar type of ceramic object [10] called a trap or cage for small animals which is found at Mundigak and Mohenjo-daro and Chanhu-daro, but that is the extent of the recognizable contacts. Further north we see no appreciable signs of Harappan penetration or influence in the western Punjab and up in the direction of Peshawar and the Khyber Pass. To the north, Harappan sites are known as far as the foot of the Simla Hills (Rupar). Very important was the discovery of Harappan material at the site of Alamgirpur, about 28 miles northeast of Delhi. This is, so far, the only known site demonstrating the penetration of "mature" Harappan culture into the Ganges-Jumna basin. In the southeast we see a heavy concentration of Harappan sites in the peninsular area north of Bombay called Gujarat or Saurashtra.[11] There are over 80 Harappan sites in this relatively small area alone but there are no signs of penetration or influence into west-central India, nor do we have even a hint of Harappan activities along the southwestern coast of India. It is to the west, along the Makran Coast of West Pakistan, that the scattered bits of archaeological evidence lead us. A University of Pennsylvania expedition in 1960 verified the presence of "mature" Harappans along the coast as far west as the Dasht Valley, the present border between Pakistan and Iran.[12] The fortified sites of Sutkagen-dor in the Dasht Valley and Sotka-koh in the Shadi-Kaur Valley north of Pasni must have played key roles in Harappan commercial activities. Both sites could have served as way stations for coastal seatrade. Also, located as they are near the mouths

---

[7] See especially A. Leo Oppenheim, "The Seafaring Merchants of Ur," *JAOS*, 74 (1954), pp. 6 ff.; W. F. Leemans, "Foreign Trade in the Old Babylonian Period," *Journal of the Economic and Social History of the Orient*, III (1960); M. Birot, review of Leeman's "Foreign Trade . . . ," *JESHO*, V (1962), pp. 91 ff.; S. N. Kramer, *The Sumerians* (1963) and "Dilmun: Quest for Paradise," *Antiquity*, 37 (1963), pp. 111-115 and "The Indus Civilization and Dilmun, The Sumerian Paradise Land," *Expedition*, 6 (1964), pp. 44-52; M. E. L. Mallowan, "The Mechanics of Ancient Trade in Western Asia," *Iran*, III (1965), pp. 1-8; B. Buchanan, "A Dated Seal Impression Connecting Babylonia and Ancient India," *Archaeology*, 20 (1967), pp. 104-107 and "A Dated 'Persian Gulf' Seal and its Implications," in *Studies in Honor of Benno Landsberger* (Chicago, 1965), pp. 204-209; Annual preliminary reports of Danish expeditions to the Persian Gulf region in *KUML* (Årbog for Jysk Arkaeologisk Selskab, Aarhus); C. J. Gadd, "The Dynasty of Agade and the Gutian Invasion," *Cambridge Ancient History*, Vol. I, Chap. 19 (Revised edition, 1963); I. Gershevitch, "Sissoo at Susa," *Bull. of the School of Oriental and African Studies*, 19 (1957), pp. 317-320; T. Jacobsen, "The Waters of Ur," *Iraq*, 22 (1960), pp. 174-185.

[8] J.-M. Casal, *Fouilles de Mundigak* (Memoires de la Delegation archéologique française en Afghanistan, 17, 1961).

[9] *Ibid.*, pls. XLIII-XLIV, pp. 76 and 255.

[10] *Ibid.*, fig. 84, pp. 145-146; E. Mackay, *Further Excavations at Mohenjo-daro*, pl. LIV, pp. 16 ff.

[11] See especially S. R. Rao, "Excavation at Rangpur and other Explorations in Gujarat," *Ancient India*, 18 and 19 (1962 and 1963), pp. 5-207.

[12] G. F. Dales, "Harappan Outposts on the Makran Coast," *Antiquity*, 36 (1962), pp. 86-92 and "A Search for Ancient Seaports," *Expedition*, 4 (1962), pp. 2-10.

of the only valleys which offer reasonably easy access, they commanded the gateways between the sea and inland Makran.[13]

Exploration along the Arabian Sea coast of Iran is the next logical stage in the search for Near East-South Asian connections. It would be indeed a coincidence if the modern border between Pakistan and Iran also was the western "international" border of the Harappan empire. On the other hand, if it should prove to be that no Harappan sites exist west of the Dasht Valley, it would be an interesting case study for the geographical determinists.

There are some tantalizing indications that middlemen were involved between the Mesopotamians and Harappans. They may have been enterprising merchants of the so-called Kulli culture[14] which inhabited large areas of southern Baluchistan. The relationships—chronological, cultural and economic—between the Harappans and these enigmatic Kulli people remain one of the most fascinating problems in South Asian archaeology. The extremely limited amount of archaeological evidence available so far suggests that Kulli culture was at its height just prior to the advent of Harappan civilization and that there was some overlap with the Harappan period. Just how much overlap there was is a moot question. Recently, pottery having distinctive Kulli and other Baluchistan characteristics, was excavated from burial cairns on the island of Umm an-Nar off the coast of Abu Dhabi in the southern Persian Gulf.[15] This attested presence of the Kulli-ites in the Persian Gulf region suggests that they may have been intimately involved in the assumed communications between the Harappans and Mesopotamians. But there may have been other peoples involved. Danish excavators[16] have since 1952 been uncovering the remains of a unique culture in the Persian Gulf which was at least partly contemporaneous with the time span concerned in the subject of this paper—namely from about 2500-1900 B. C.

Especially significant among the Persian Gulf finds are the stamp seals of a style unique to this region.[17] Circular in shape, with a pierced boss on the back side, these seals display a few iconographic details reminiscent of Kulli painted pottery, but most importantly, some of them are engraved with Harappan script. Because of their distinctive shape and style, Wheeler has dubbed them generically "Persian Gulf seals."[18]

A happy discovery was made recently, not in the field but in the vast collection of cuneiform documents in the Yale University Babylonian collection. A tablet representing a mercantile agreement of the Larsa period, dated precisely to the tenth year of Gungunum, King of Larsa, and bearing the impression of a typical "Persian Gulf" seal has been published by Drs. Hallo and Buchanan.[19] This single bit of evidence provides a crucial anchor point for dating the Persian Gulf finds. But more than that, it gives important inferential dating evidence for the Harappans. A Persian Gulf-type seal was discovered in western India at the Harappan harbour town of Lothal.[20] Unfortunately it was a surface-find but given the weight of the other indications of Harappan—Near East contacts during the centuries before

[13] Their present locations, some miles from the seacoast, is apparently the result of geomorphological changes in the coastal region since Harappan days. That such changes might even have been partially related to the decline of Harappan prosperity is a possibility. See references in note 12 plus R. L. Raikes, "The Mohenjo-daro Floods," *Antiquity*, 39 (1965), pp. 196-203.

[14] Although somewhat outdated, the best general description of the Kulli culture is by S. Piggott, *Prehistoric India* (1950). See also G. F. Dales, "A Suggested Chronology for Afghanistan, Baluchistan, and the Indus Valley," in *Chronologies in Old World Archaeology* (1965), pp. 257-284.

[15] *KUML* for 1962, 1964 and 1965 (see note 7). Also T. G. Bibby, "A Forgotten Civilization of Abu Dhabi," *British Petroleum Magazine*, 13 (1964), pp. 28-32.

[16] See yearly reports in *KUML* beginning with 1952. Also P. V. Glob and T. G. Bibby, "A Forgotten Civilization of the Persian Gulf," *Scientific American* (October 1960), pp. 62-71; and *Illustrated London News* for January 4, 1958, January 11, 1958, August 27, 1960 and January 28, 1961.

[17] See references in notes 7 and 16 plus G. Bibby, "The 'Ancient Indian Style' Seals from Bahrain," *Antiquity*, 32 (1958), pp. 243-246; C. J. Gadd, "Seals of Ancient Indian Style found at Ur," *Proceedings of the British Academy*, 18 (1932), pp. 3-22; Sir M. Wheeler, *The Indus Civilization* (2nd ed. 1960), pp. 90-93.

[18] *Antiquity*, 32 (1958), p. 246.

[19] William W. Hallo and Briggs Buchanan, "A 'Persian Gulf' Seal on an Old Babylonian Mercantile Agreement," in *Studies in Honor of Benno Landsberger* (1965), pp. 199-209; B. Buchanan, "A Dated Seal Impression Connecting Babylonia and Ancient India," *Archaeology*, 20 (1967), pp. 104-107.

[20] See especially S. R. Rao, "A 'Persian Gulf' Seal from Lothal," *Antiquity*, 37 (1963), pp. 96-99 and "Shipping and Maritime Trade of the Indus People," *Expedition*, 7 (1965), pp. 30-37.

and after 2000 B. C., it is more than probable that the Lothal seal belonged to the period of Harappan occupation. If nothing more, its very presence in India does furnish us with some concrete evidence of communication between the two regions. Less tangible, but equally as suggestive, is the comparative evidence of stylistic and typological similarities between Harappan and Mesopotamian artistic and decorative elements. Sir Mortimer Wheeler [21] has presented a comprehensive description of the most significant of these similarities—e. g. certain distinctive types of beads, the trefoil pattern, the spread-wing eagle motif, the representation of humans disguised as animals, and the " Gilgamesh motif " which depicts a savage looking man standing triumphantly between two upright animals.

Granted, there are profound dissimilarities also —e. g. in the type of seal (cylinder as opposed to stamp), architecture, sculpture, etc.—but these are what mark the crucial differentiation between separate societies and cultures. The scattered *similarities* are the more difficult to explain. In this particular instance there are enough distinctive ones to suggest convincingly that some degree of mutual contact must have existed. It is most significant that those similarities which do exist can be dated from the Mesopotamian end between the latter part of the Sumerian Early Dynastic period and the end of the Larsa period, just where the other types of dating evidence point.[22]

This brings us finally to the evidence suggested by the title of this paper. Mention has already been made of the terracotta die " of Indian origin " discovered by Professor Speiser in his Tepe Gawra excavations. Its number dots are arranged consecutively on opposite sides so that 2 is opposite 3, 4 opposite 5, and 6 opposite 1.[23] Speiser's " Indian " attribution for the Gawra die suggested a basic synchronism between the Mesopotamian Old Akkadian period and the " mature " Harappan period of South Asia.

Since Speiser's publications, only a few other cubical dice have been reported from Mesopotamian sites. The most significant discovery was that of " broken clay dice " in a " hoard " found in a pottery vessel buried beneath an Akkadian period house floor at Tell Asmar in the Diyala region of central Iraq.[24] It was in this and other " hoards " from Akkadian houses at Tell Asmar that etched carnelian beads, bone inlays, stamp seals, a cylinder seal, and a distinctive type of knobbed pottery—all these with strong Harappan stylistic parallels—were found.[25] Two dice were found at Ur. One of bone [26] has lightly incised dots, now partly obliterated, but whose order is certainly not like modern dice. It was dated by Woolley to the 1st Dynasty of Ur (i. e. Early Dynastic III). The second die is of grey clay.[27] Its dots are arranged 1 opposite 2, 3 opposite 6, 4 opposite 5. It was found loose in the soil of Pit X in the Royal Cemetery and could date to anytime from Early Dynastic III to the Ur III period. A single die of baked clay with 1 (or x) opposite 2, 3 opposite 6 and 4 opposite 5 was found at Nippur but in a context too late to be relevant here (Kassite).[28] Games were certainly popular throughout Mesopotamian and Near Eastern history but the use of cubical dice seems to have been a rare and late innovation.[29] The archaeological evidence—albeit scanty—directs our attention instead to South Asia and to the Harappan period for the possible origin of the cubical type of dice.[30] Like the Tepe Gawra die, many of the Harappan examples are made of

[21] *Op. cit.* (note 17).

[22] For the radiacarbon dates relevant to Harappan civilization see, D. P. Agrawal, " Harappan Culture: New Evidence for a Shorter Chronology," *Science*, 143, pp. 950-952; B. B. Lal, " A Picture Emerges—an Assessment of the Carbon-14 Datings of the Protohistoric Cultures of the Indo-Pakistan Subcontinent," *Ancient India*, 18 and 19 (1962 and 1963), pp. 208-21; G. F. Dales, " A Suggested Chronology for Afghanistan, Baluchistan and the Indus Valley," in *Chronologies in Old World Archaeology* (1966), pp. 257-284; For the newest dates from the " latest mature Harappan " level at Mohenjodaro see Robert Stuckenrath and G. F. Dales, " University of Pennsylvania Radiocarbon Dates X," *Radiocarbon* 9 (1967).

[23] None of the dice described here—except one—has the dots arranged in the order of modern dice on which the opposite numbers always add up to seven.

[24] Henri Frankfort, " Tell Asmar, Khafaje and Khorsabad: Second Preliminary Report of the Iraq Expedition," *Oriental Institute Communications*, No. 16 (Chicago, 1933), p. 48.

[25] *Ibid.*, pp. 47-53.

[26] Sir C. L. Woolley, *Ur Excavations*, Vol. IV: *The Early Periods*, p. 44 and fig. 7, a.

[27] *Ibid.*, pp. 44, 79 and fig. 7, b.

[28] D. E. McCown and R. C. Haines, *Nippur I* (Oriental Institute Publications, Vol. 78, 1967), pl. 153, 11.

[29] In Egypt they were not common until Graeco-Roman times, although isolated examples have been found at Thebes and Amarna dating to the New Kingdom (mid-16th century B. C. at the earliest). See W. C. Hayes, *The Scepter of Egypt*, Part II (1959), p. 405.

[30] W. N. Brown, " The Indian Games of Pachisi, Chaupar, and Chausar," *Expedition*, 6 (1964), pp. 32-35.

terracotta and the number dots are arranged in non-modern order.

Sir John Marshall in his Mohenjo-daro excavation report states that "many" dice were found at the site, although he publishes only four examples.[31] They are made of terracotta and the opposite numbers are arranged 1/2, 3/4, 5/6. Ernest Mackay, who continued the Mohenjo-daro excavations,[32] reported that dice were found at "all levels"[33] of the Harappan city. Published examples include three terracotta dice, one with the opposite dots arranged 1/3, 2/4, 5/6 (Pl. CXL, 19); one with the dots arranged 1/2, 3/4, 5/6 (Pl. CXL, 20) and another with identically arranged dots but inlaid with tiny beads (Pl. CXLII, 84). Three stone dice are also published: one of yellow agate with dots arranged 1/2, 3/6, 4/5 (Pl. CXL, 63); one of white limestone with dots arranged 1/3, 2/5, 4/blank (Pl. CXLII, 85); and one of light grey stone with dots placed 1/2, 3/5, 4/6 (Pl. CXLII, 86). From the Harappan period levels at the city of Harappa itself, seven examples have been published,[34] two of stone, four of terracotta and one of faience. Four of these have the opposite dots arranged 1/2, 3/4, 5/6; two have them placed 1/2, 3/5, 4/6; and a unique terracotta example has the dots arranged in modern order—i. e. with the opposite dots adding up to seven.

At the northeasternmost Harappan site, Alamgirpur—not far from Delhi—one terracotta cubical die was found in the limited excavations.[35] The photograph shows three sides of the die with the number dots two, four and six but the remaining three sides are not described. Similarly, near the southeastern extremity of the Harappan domain, a single terracotta die was uncovered in the Harappan levels at Lothal,[36] the presumed seaport site where the "Persian Gulf" stamp seal was found. Its dots are arranged 1/2, 3/5, 4/6. As for the two remaining major Harappan sites which have been subjected to excavation, no cubical dice were published from Chanhu-daro (Sind)[37] or from Kalibangan (Rajasthan) where excavations are still in progress. Thus at the two major Harappan cities alone, an overwhelmingly larger number of cubical dice has been found than has been uncovered in the numerous and extensively excavated contemporaneous sites in all of Mesopotamia.

From the sportive lightheartedness inferred by these gaming pieces, we move to a different class of object whose use and significance is more enigmatic. Whether they were of religious significance, as their features seem to suggest, must remain an open question until the unlikely day when we can begin to understand something about Harappan religious practices. I am referring specifically to a most distinctive type of male terracotta figurine. These figures, fashioned in-the-round, depict a nude male body, perhaps ithyphallic, with extremely obese stomach, prominent buttocks, shoulder-holes for the attachment of movable arms and stubby tail. Most of the examples have animal-like faces and deep holes in the navel and rump. Now there is absolutely no stylistic similarity between the majority of Near Eastern and Harappan clay figurine. Thus to find examples of such a peculiarly distinctive type of representation in both areas suggests strongly some common contacts—or at least common awareness.

Hundreds—perhaps thousands—of clay figurines have been excavated from Mesopotamian sites. They are well enough documented so that a reasonably comprehensive classification of them—by type, style and period—has been possible. Figurines of "foreign" origin or inspiration can be recognized with reasonable assurance. The novel type of nude male figurines under consideration here is emphatically not a characteristic Mesopotamian creation. Neither *male* nudity, male obesity, nor animation are found among Sumero-Akkadian figurines of this date. On the other hand, the practice of combining human and animal features was common throughout Mesopotamian history. This will be further discussed below.

The Mesopotamian examples, only three in

31 *Mohenjo-daro and the Indus Civilization* (1931), pl. CLIII, 7-10 and pp. 551-552.

32 *Further Excavations at Mohenjo-daro* (1938), pp. 559-560.

33 This means, in fact, only approximately the upper two-thirds of the total 75 feet of occupational remains. Recent tests at the site have shown that at least 25 feet of the lowest and earliest levels of the city are below the present ground water level and have been untouched for practical purposes by the excavators.

34 M. S. Vats, *Excavations at Harappa* (1940), pl. CXX, 46-48 and 51-54.

35 *Indian Archaeology—Review for 1958-59,* pl. LXII, p. 52.

36 S. R. Rao, "Further Excavations at Lothal," *Lalit Kalā*, No. 11 (April 1962), pl. XVII, fig. 61.

37 E. J. H. Mackay, *Chanhu daro Excavations, 1935-36* (1943).

number, come from the current series of excavations at the holy city of Nippur in southern Iraq.[38] All were found in the "Scribal Quarter" part of the city—one was a surface find but two of them were discovered in private houses dated definitely to the Sumerian Ur III period (approx. 2100-2000 B. C.)

The most complete of the three examples (fig. 1) was found on the floor of a house in the fifth level shoulders, which are far out of proportion to the rest of the body, are pierced through to allow the attaching of movable arms. The penis is broken but marks on the belly suggest that the figure was ithyphallic. A stubby tail is crudely but clearly indicated. The face is, fortunately, almost intact. It is that of a bearded human male.

The second dated figurine from Nippur[40] was also found in association with an Ur III house in

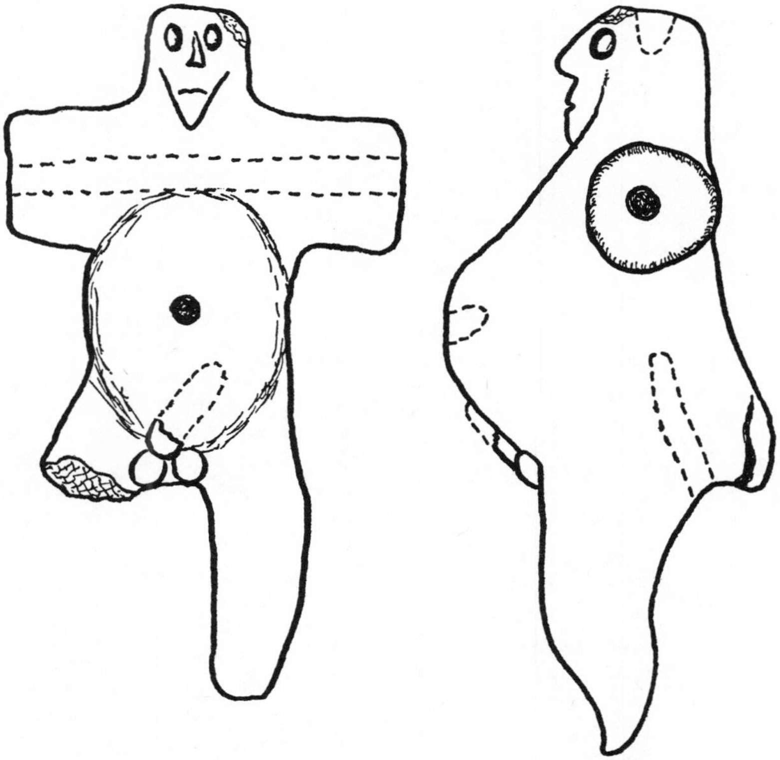

FIGURE 1. Nippur.

of the so-called TB area of Nippur.[39] It is very crudely executed. The grossly protuberant belly has a deep hole at the navel. There is a deep hole in the arms and another down through the top of the head (for attaching a headdress?). The

the TB area. The legs and head are missing but otherwise it is unmistakably on the same type of fat male figurines. The shoulders are pierced for movable arms. Unhappily the published photograph is too unclear and the description too brief to furnish us with further details. One unusual feature is the depiction of bands crisscrossing the chest and belly.

[38] D. E. McCown and R. C. Haines, *Nippur, I*, Oriental Institute Publication LXXVIII (1967).

[39] *Ibid.*, pl. 128, 9—incorrectly and incompletely described as a "seated figure: perforated from anus through top of head, holes in arms, top of head chipped at left front." It is now in the University Museum, Philadelphia, number 53-11-69.

[40] *Ibid.*, pl. 144, 8 and p. 94 where it is grouped with chariot models— ". . . suggestive of a chariot because of its 'axle,' but it could also be a remnant of a manikin with movable arms and head."

The third and remaining Nippur example[41] was found on the surface of the same area of Nippur and is certainly of the same type. Only the torso is preserved but the genitals are visible in the photograph as is the deep navel hole.

Thus we are confronted with a small group of atypical figurines in southern Mesopotamia, found in contexts dating to the period of presumed Sumerian international seafaring activities. Is it merely coincidental that we find almost identical fat male figurines at Harappan sites where they are typologically and stylistically at home? The basic concept of animated figurines with movable heads and arms is widely manifested among Harappan figurines as is the popularity of grossly exaggerating the roundness of the human body. There is a large corpus of Harappan figurines, both male and female, whose bodies are blown up into round balls.

The most important Harappan example is from Chanhu-daro in the southern Indus Valley (fig. 2).[42] This rather carefully made figurine is intact except for its head and lower legs. Also, the end of the penis is missing but enough remains to suggest that the representation is ithyphallic. The body profile is virtually identical to that of the Nippur example. A stubby tail is depicted and the heavy shoulders are pierced for movable arms. It differs from the Nippur example in that the navel and arms are not pierced. Unfortunately the head is missing but traces of a red painted "necklace" remain.

Quite a few fat male figurines have been published from Mohenjo-daro. They are of added importance because several of them, while having human bodies, also have animal heads and tails.[43] Both Marshall and Mackay interpreted these objects as representing some sort of abortive female figures. Of one, Marshall[44] says it is "obviously represented as pregnant and the extreme exaggeration of the buttocks suggests steotopygy." Mac-

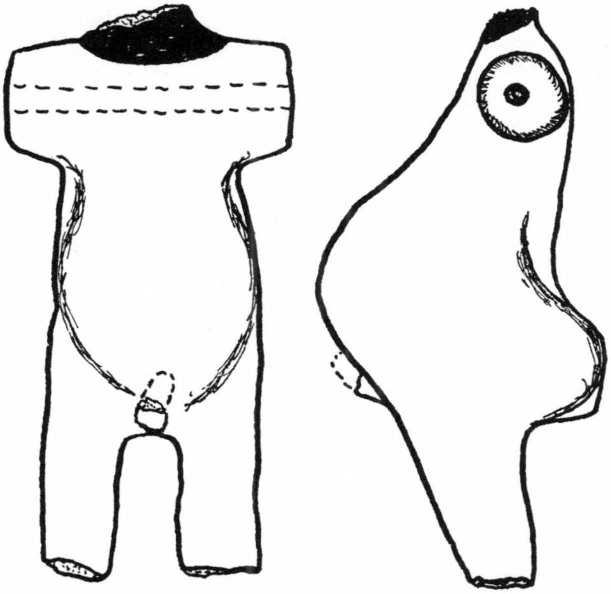

FIGURE 2. Chanhu-daro.

[41] *Ibid.*, pl. 128, 7 and p. 89—described only as a "seated figure."

[42] E. J. H. Mackay, *Chanhu-daro Excavations 1935-36* (1943), pl. LIX, 2 and pp. 166-167—part of the Boston Museum of Fine Arts collection presently on loan to the University Museum, Philadelphia.

[43] Sir John Marshall, *Mohenjo-daro and the Indus Civilization*, pls. XCV, 24; CXVIII, 15; CLIII, 38; pp. 344 and 549. E. J. H. Mackay, *Further Excavations at Mohenjo-daro*, pls. LXXIV, 13; LXXVIII, 3 and 12; LXXXI, 5, 8 and 14; pp. 294-295, 314-315. They are apparently not common at Harappa but some of the "pregnant women" may in fact be this type. See for example, M. S. Vats, *Excavations at Harappa*, pl. LXXVI, 28-30.

[44] *Op. cit.*, p. 549, Pl. CLIII, 38.

kay,[45] in describing his finds at Mohenjo-daro, states that "they were obviously intended to represent human forms with animal heads . . ." He too felt that the swollen bodies represent pregnancy. Now, with more examples available for study—especially the well preserved Chanhu-daro and Nippur ones—we can say with a high degree of certainty that some of the objects are basically human males with some animal attributes. Just as in Mesopotamian art, the combining of human and animal attributes was an important aspect of Harappan iconography, seen not only in the figurines but in the scenes engraved in the stone stamp seals. There one sees curious groups of human figures wearing horned headdresses and long animal tails. Its purpose and significance for the Harappans will probably never be known to us. Even in Mesopotamia with its voluminous surviving corpus of religious and mythological written records plus its abundant artistic remains, the true significance of human-animal representations is still far from modern understanding. For example, the Sumerians often depicted humans dressed up as animals but performing human activities such as playing musical instruments. Such representations are seen on stone religious plaques of the Early Dynastic period and most strikingly in the inlaid scenes on a wooden harp from the so-called "Royal" tombs at Ur. Even the magnificant gold bull's head surmounting the harp is sporting a heavy curly beard of lapis lazuli. In this matter it would be presumptuous to insist on any definite relationship or influence between the Harappans and Mesopotamians, but in light of the other evidences for mutual contacts during this period from about 2500-1900 B. C., the possibility cannot be overlooked.

The ultimate significance of inquiries such as this is not just to play intellectual games with bits and pieces of ancient castoffs and debris. The aim, very seldom attainable, is to reconstruct the life and times which produced the tattered remains we so arrogantly "discover." This is especially true with objects such as we have discussed in this paper. The objects themselves, when treated collectively, make a convincing case for Near East-South Asian contacts. But what we would really like to know is the nature and extent of these relations. Just how cognizant were the citizens of each region of the peoples and culture of the other? What degree of *dependence*—if any—was involved?

The importance of seafaring activities for both the Harappans and Mesopotamians is strongly indicated, if not proved, by the archaeological and written evidence. On the Harappan end we have only the mute archaeological indications, including the distribution of what appear to have been major seaport towns. The Mesopotamian written records, on the other hand, point out specific goods and materials which were being imported from some distant lands—probably in part at least from the Harappan region. Partial explanation for why virtually no Mesopotamian objects or products have been found in Harappan sites comes from these Sumero-Akkadian documents. Because southern Mesopotamia has no raw hard materials, it was necessary to import all the wood, stone and metals for the needs of the civilization. "International" trade was therefore a vital concomitant of the practical endeavors of the southern Mesopotamians. In return, the Mesopotamians had only soft and consumable items to exchange. Among these were garments, wool, "perfumed" oil, and leather products—items which have left no trace in the archaeological record.

Finally, a potentially significant chronological "coincidence" should be noted. Or was it a coincidence? From the Mesopotamian economic texts we learn that by the end of the Larsa period "international" trade came to a virtual standstill. This is usually explained in terms of internal Mesopotamian difficulties. But the end of the Larsa period is also the lower limit for the finding of Harappan objects and influences in southern Mesopotamia. And this is apparently, on the basis of the carbon-14 chronology for South Asia, the end of the mature Harappan period, precipitated, we think, by natural disaster and floods. Were these events which just coincidentally occured in these distant regions or was there some very serious effect of the decline in one area on the fortunes of the other? Could the unexpected disasters in the southern Indus Valley have deprived the Mesopotamians of vital raw materials for the maintenance of their complex, but highly vulnerable, empire? These questions can probably never be satisfactorily answered, but they are worth asking as long as we are engaged in the

[45] *Op. cit.*, p. 294.

search for a better understanding of the mechanics, the advantages, and the liabilities of international relations.

The continued discovery of such mundane objects as dice and figurines alone can provide the material verification for such inquiries.

LE PAYS DE CANAAN

R. DE VAUX
ÉCOLE BIBLIQUE ET ARCHÉOLOGIQUE FRANÇAISE,
JERUSALEM

C'EST LE REGRETTÉ E. A. SPEISER qui releva le premier le mot *kinaḫḫu* au sens de "pourpre rouge" dans les textes de Nuzi et mit ce mot en relation avec le nom de Canaan et avec le nom postérieur de la Phénicie.[1] Cette découverte a donné un nouvel élan aux recherches sur l'origine du nom de Canaan et sur sa signification géographique. Cet essai dédié a sa mémoire cherchera seulement à donner l'état de la question et à proposer les solutions qui paraissent les plus probables.

I. Le nom.

Dans les textes akkadiens, le nom de Canaan apparaît pour la première fois, au début du xve siècle av. J. C., dans l'inscription de la statue d'Idrimi, qui s'enfuit au "pays de Kinani";[2] un peu plus tard, le nom revient trois fois dans les tablettes d'Alalakh.[3] Au siècle suivant, onze lettres d'Amarna mentionnent le pays de *Kinaḫni* (cinq fois dans des lettres venant de Byblos et de Tyr), ou *Kinaḫḫi* (sept fois dans des lettres du roi de Babylone, du roi du Mitanni et du Pharaon), ou *Kinaḫi* (une fois dans une lettre d'Alashia-Chypre),[4] une fois le gentilice *kinaḫaiu*, les Cananéens.[5] La même forme *Kinaḫḫi* se rencontre dans une lettre écrite en akkadien par Ramsès II à Ḫattušil III.[6] A la même époque, un texte akkadien de Râs Shamra parle du pays de *Kinaḫi*.[7] Mais les documents égyptiens emploient la forme *Knʿn*, avec l'article (sauf une fois), "le Canaan." Le nom désigne le pays de Canaan, l'adjectif qui en dérive, *knʿn.w* est plus rare et designe les habitants de ce pays. Le mot revient dans six textes, le plus ancien date d'Aménophis II (Cananéens),[8] le plus récent est de la XXIIe Dynastie (Canaan).[9] Dans une liste ugaritique de Râs Shamra, un individu est qualifié de *knʿny*, "Cananén."[10] L'hébreu dit *K[e]naʿan*, et *Knʿn* se lit encore sur les monnaies de Laodicée-de-Phénicie (Beyrouth) au iie siècle av. J. C.[11]

La comparaison de ces différentes graphies ne peut laisser aucun doute:[12] le mot est d'origine

[1] E. A. Speiser, "The Name Phoinikes," *Language*, XII (1936), pp. 121-26; *One Hundred New Selected Nuzi Texts = AASOR*, XVI (1936), pp. 121-22.

[2] L. 18-19, S. Smith, *The Statue of Idrimi*, Londres, 1949, p. 14, cf. p. 73.

[3] Alalakh 48, 5; 154, 26; 181, 9, D. J. Wiseman, *The Alalakh Tablets*, Londres, 1953, p. 46.

[4] *EA* 8, 15. 17. 25; 14 II 26; 30, 1; 35, 15; 109, 46; 131, 61; 137, 76; 148, 46; 151, 50; 162, 41 et AO 7095 = *RA*, XIX (1922), p. 100.

[5] *EA* 9, 19.

[6] E. Edel, "KBo I 15 + 19, ein Brief Ramses' II. mit einer Schilderung der Kadešschlacht," *ZA*, 49 (1950), p. 208, 1. 29.

[7] Texte cité dans J. Nougayrol, *Iraq*, XXV (1963), p. 123; publié dans *Ugaritica V*, nº 36.

[8] E. Edel, "Die Stelen Amenophis' II. aus Karnak und Memphis," *ZDPV*, LXIX (1953), pp. 132 et 167-73; W. Helck, *Urkunden der 18. Dynastie* (*Übersetzung zu den Heften 17-22*), Berlin 1961, p. 38.

[9] G. Steindorff, *JEA*, XXV (1939), pp. 31-32.

[10] Gordon 311, 7.

[11] G. F. Hill, *Catalogue of the Greek Coins . . . Phoenicia*, pp. 1-li et 32. Sur l'attribution à Beyrouth, cf. en outre R. Dussaud, *Syria*, XXV (1948), p. 314, n. 3; H. Seyrig, *Antiquités Syriennes*, IV, Paris, 1953, p. 122, n. 4.—Peut être faut-il ajouter une mention de *knʿn* à El-Hofra, A. Berthier–R. Charlier, *Le sanctuaire punique d'El Hofra à Constantine*, Paris, 1955, nº 102 = H. Donner–W. Röllig, *Kanaanische und aramäische Inschriften*, Wiesbaden, 1962-64, nº 116, mais la lecture n'est pas assurée: au lieu de *'š knʿn*, "Cananéen," on lirait mieux *'š kn 'l*, "préposé à."

[12] S. Moscati, "Sulla storia del nome Canaan," *Studia Biblica et Orientalia*, III, Rome, 1959, pp. 266-69.

ouest-sémitique et il se prononçait avec un *'ayin* (ainsi en ugaritique et en hébreu) et les Égyptiens l'ont transcrit correctement. Il était certainement prononcé avec un *'ayin* à Byblos et à Tyr, mais les lettres d'Amarna qui proviennent de ces deux villes l'écrivent *Kinaḫni* parce que l'akkadien avait perdu le *'ayin* et que, très spécialement dans les gloses cananéennes d'Amarna, le *'ayin* est transcrit par *ḫ*. Les formes *Kinaḫḫi* des autres lettres d'Amarna et *kinaḫḫu* des textes de Nuzi peuvent s'expliquer par une assimilation; elles ne se rencontrent que dans des textes écrits hors de Canaan. La forme *Kinaḫi* d'Alashia et de Râs Shamra akkadien est une graphie simplifiée, qui est également celle du gentilice *kinaḫaiu*. Mais souvent aussi l'écriture akkadienne ne tient pas compte du *'ayin*; cette alternative est représentée par la forme *Kinani* de la statue d'Idrimi et des tablettes d'Alalakh.[13]

La forme authentique du nom est donc *Kn'n* et elle est attestée soit directement soit à travers la graphie akkadienne *Kinaḫni* dans les régions qui seront plus tard la Palestine et la Phénicie et qui étaient le pays de Canaan. Dans ces régions, l'influence linguistique des Ḫurrites a été pratiquement nulle et il ne faut pas chercher à expliquer le nom par le ḫurrite comme on a parfois voulu le faire, soit en partant de la forme *kinaḫḫi*,[14] soit en considérant seulement la terminaison *-ni*, *-na* comme un suffixe ḫurrite ajouté à un mot sémitique.[15]

En restant dans le domaine sémitique, plusieurs étymologies du nom ont été proposées. Dans son *Thesaurus*, il y a plus d'un siècle, W. Gesenius l'expliquait comme la "terre basse" et, malgré des oppositions assez vite exprimées, cette explication a été largement acceptée.[16] Elle peut se recommander de certains textes bibliques, spécialement de Num 13:29: l'Amorite habite la montagne, le Cananéen habite le bord de la mer et la vallée du Jourdain. Mais la racine *kn'* n'est employée en hébreu qu'au *nifal* au sens d'être soumis ou humilié, au *hifil* au sens d'humilier; en araméen, le *qal* signifie "plier, abaisser," ce qui, d'après certains usages de l'arabe, semble être le sens fondamental de la racine, jamais "être bas."

Lorsque le mot *kinaḫḫu* eut été reconnu dans les textes de Nuzi avec le sens de "teinture pourpre," on a interprété Canaan comme le "pays de la pourpre."[17] E. A. Speiser avait été plus prudent: *kinaḫḫu* est mentionné avec diverses marchandises dont la première est le bois de cèdre, qui provenait de la côte syrienne; de la même région venait la pourpre et on appelait celle-ci à Nuzi du nom de son pays d'origine, Canaan, mais il ne cherchait pas à expliquer le nom de Canaan.[18] E. A. Speiser

[13] Sur ce traitement du *'ayin* ouest-sémitique en akkadien, cf. déjà Ed. Dhorme; "La langue de Canaan," *RB*, XXIII (1914), pp. 368-69 = *Recueil Ed. Dhorme*, Paris, 1951, pp. 482-83. Récemment, S. Moscati, "Preistoria e storia del consonantismo ebraico antico," *Accademia Nazionale dei Lincei, Memorie*, VIII, v, 8 (1954), pp. 421-23.—On comparera ugaritique *'pr*, égyptien *'pr. w* = akkadien *ḫap/biru*, ou hébr. *Ya'akob*, égyptien *Y'qb-hr* = akkadien *Yaḫqub-il* et *Yaqub-il*.

[14] J. Lewy, "Influences ḫurrites en Israël," *Revue des Etudes Sémitiques*, 1938, pp. 49-54; W. F. Albright, "The Role of the Canaanites in the History of Civilization," *Studies in the History of Culture* (W. H. Leland Volume), Menasha, Wis., 1942, p. 25, n. 50.

[15] B. Maisler, "Canaan and the Canaanites," *BASOR*, 102 (apr. 1946), pp. 7-12; W. F. Albright, réédition de l'étude citée note 14 dans *The Bible and the Ancient Near East* (*Albright Volume*), New York, 1961, p. 358, n. 50 (= réédition Anchor Books, 1965, pp. 477-78, n. 50); A. Goetze, *JCS*, XVI (1962), p. 52; cf. *JCS*, X (1956), p. 35.

[16] Encore F. M. Abel, *Géographie de la Palestine*, I, Paris, 1933, pp. 254 et 318.

[17] Surtout W. F. Albright, *l. c.* notes 14 et 15. Il est allé jusqu'à postuler un mot sémitique entièrement perdu **kn'*, qui aurait signifié "murex."

[18] Dans les travaux cités note 1. En revanche, il expliquait le nom de la Phénicie comme le pays de la "pourpre," φοῖνιξ, et il admettait avec d'autres linguistes que ce mot grec était d'origine purement indo-européenne. Cette dernière opinion est peut-être à réviser. Le mycénien du linéaire B possède un mot *po-ni-ki-ja* ou *po-ni-ke-a* avec le sens de "peint ou teint en rouge." D'après M. Ventris-J. Chadwick, *Documents in Mycenaean Greek*, Cambridge, 1959, pp. 91 et 405, c'est probablement un emprunt sémitique. M. Astour, *JNES*, XXIV (1965), pp. 348-349, en a rapproché le nom propre hébreu *Puwwah*, gentilice *Puni*, Nomb. 26: 33; en arabe, *fuwwa* désigne la garance, plante d'où l'on tire la teinture rouge, et à Râs Shamra *pwt* apparaît en parallèle avec "lin." "Phénicien" et "Punique" dériveraient donc d'une racine sémitique. L'hypothèse a été acceptée par C. H. Gordon, *Ugaritic Handbook*, Rome, 1965, glossaire, nº 2028 et 2031. Mais ce n'est qu'une hypothèse, cf. récemment H. A. Hoffner, "Ugaritic *pwt*: A Term from the Early Canaanite Dyeing Industry," *JAOS*, 87 (1967), pp. 300-3, et il faudrait expliquer pourquoi la Phénicie a été appelée, non pas du nom de la pourpre précieuse dont elle avait la spécialité, mais du nom de son substitut à bon marché, la garance qui poussait aussi bien en Grèce qu'en Syrie-Palestine, cf. V. Loret, "Orcanette et garance," dans *Kêmi*, III, 1930-35, pp. 23-32. Mais c'est un problème qui ne nous concerne pas directement ici.

pensait que *kinaḫḫu* désignait une variété de la pourpre rouge et ce sens est entré dans les dictionnaires,[19] mais des doutes ont été récemment exprimés.[20] Quoi qu'il en soit, *kinaḫḫu*, désignant une couleur ou une matière colorante rouge, avec ou sans relation avec la pourpre, ne se rencontre nulle part en dehors de Nuzi, et l'hébreu, l'ugaritique, l'akkadien de Râs Shamra appellent la pourpre par d'autres noms.[21] Canaan n'est certainement pas le "pays de la pourpre."

Dans la Bible, "Canaan" (collectif) et "Cananéen" signifient parfois "marchand," spécialement "marchand de Phénicie," ainsi Ez 16:29; 17:4; Zach 14:21; Prov 31:24; Job 40:30. On en a conclu que Canaan signifiait le "pays des marchands." [22] Cette hypothèse serait appuyée par la première mention égyptienne des Cananéens dans les stèles de Karnak et de Memphis qui relatent la première campagne asiatique d'Amenophis II: [23] la liste du butin compte 640 prisonniers "cananéens" après les *mariannu* (l'aristocratie militaire) et leurs femmes et avant les fils et filles de princes et les chanteuses des princes. Cela signifierait que le nom ne désigne pas les habitants d'un pays mais les membres d'une classe sociale, celle des riches marchands de Syrie-Palestine. Mais le chiffre des prisonniers cananéens est le plus élevé de la liste [24] et Canaan est déjà attesté comme un nom de pays avant Aménophis II dans l'inscription d'Idrimi et les tablettes d'Alalakh. Si les "cananéens" de ces stèles sont des marchands—ce qui n'est pas prouvé—, la désignation est dérivée du nom du pays, et non pas le contraire. La même conclusion vaut pour l'usage biblique, qui est tardif. De plus, la racine *kn'* n'a nulle part en sémitique un sens qui se rapporte au commerce. Il est vrai que l'hapax *kin'ah* de Jer 10:17, "paquet" ou "ballot" d'émigrant, est traduit "marchandises" par Symmaque et le Targum, mais, même si ces traductions ont touché juste, le mot désignerait proprement le ballot des marchands ambulants qu'on appelait "cananéens," et ce serait encore un sens dérivé.

L'hypothèse la plus récente [25] revient à l'étymologie ancienne, mais elle l'explique autrement: Canaan serait le pays où le soleil "s'incline," l'Occident.[26] Ce serait la traduction ou l'équivalent, en sémitique de l'Ouest, de l'akkadien Amurru, qui signifie le "pays de l'Ouest." Mais ce n'est pas une traduction, car Canaan et Amurru sont des pays différents, comme on va le voir. Si Canaan est seulement un équivalent d'Amurru et signifie aussi l'Occident, le nom aurait été donné d'abord au pays par des étrangers qui habitaient plus è l'Est; ce sont les Mésopotamiens qui ont appelé le pays de l'Ouest MAR.TU en sumérien et Amurru en akkadien. Mais tout indique que Canaan est une appellation indigène; l'explication est donc peu vraisemblable.

Si le mot est un terme géographique, il n'est pas nécessaire—et il est peut-être impossible—de lui trouver une étymologie, et nous le laisserons inexpliqué. Si vraiment les Ḫurrites de Nuzi appelaient *kinaḫḫu* la teinture pourpre, c'est parce qu'elle était un produit importé de *Kinaḫḫi*, Canaan, de même que nous appelons mousseline un tissu fabriqué à Mossoul. Si la Bible appelle les marchands des "cananéens," c'est parce que les Cananéens-Phéniciens avaient acquis une sorte de monopole du commerce d'importation en Israël.[27]

II. Le pays de Canaan d'après les textes non bibliques.

Il n'est pas aisé de déterminer ce que représente ce pays de Canaan dans les documents cunéiformes et égyptiens. Souvent, il n'est cité qu'en

[19] W. von Soden, *Akkadisches Handwörterbuch*, I, Wiesbaden, 1965, s. v.

[20] M. Dietrich-O. Loretz, "Der Vertrag zwischen Suppiluliuma und Niqmandu," *Die Welt des Orients*, III, 3, 1966, pp. 225-32: le mot pourrait désigner seulement une teinte de rouge, sans référence à la pourpre.

[21] *Ibid.* Cf. aussi R. Gradwohl, *Die Farben im alten Testament*, Berlin, 1963, pp. 66-73, qui maintient cependant, p. 68, que le nom de Canaan vient de celui de la pourpre.

[22] B. Maisler (Mazar), "Canaan and the Canaanites," *BASOR*, 102 (Apr. 1946), pp. 7-12. L'hypothèse est acceptée comme une alternative par W. F. Albright dans sa réédition de "The Role of the Canaanites . . . ," (cf. note 15), n. 50.

[23] Pour le texte et le commentaire, cf. note 8.

[24] Il ne faut pas lui comparer une autre liste du butin donnée à la fin de la stèle de Memphis avec des chiffres beaucoup plus forts: elle est d'une origine différente, cf. Edel, *l. c.*

[25] M. Astour, "The Origin of the Terms 'Canaan,' 'Phoenicians,' and 'Purple'," *JNES*, XXIV (1965), pp. 346-350.

[26] Cf. les sens de *kn'* en hébreu et en araméen mentionnés ci-dessus. Les parallèles arabes que cite M. Astour sont insuffisants: "plier ses aîles pour descendre" (un grand oiseau) dérive du premier sens de *kana'a*, "se replier, se rétracter"; "s'incliner vers l'horizon" (une étoile), "tomber" (la nuit) dérive du second sens du même verbe: "se rapprocher."

[27] Cf. S. Moscati cité note 12.

passant et sans référence géographique, et ses limites ont pu changer avec les époques et selon les circonstances historiques. Il convient de ne garder que les textes explicites et de les prendre dans l'ordre chronologique.

D'après l'inscription de la statue d'Idrimi, la première station du fugitif au pays de Canaan est Ammia.[28] Cette ville est plusieurs fois mentionnée dans les lettres d'Amarna et elle se localise sur la côte ou près de la côte, une vingtaine de kilomètres au nord de Byblos.[29] Un demi-siècle plus tard, si les "Cananéens" faits prisonniers par Aménophis II sont bien des habitants du pays de Canaan, le terme pourrait avoir une grande extension géographique, car la campagne d'Amenophis avait atteint Qadesh et le pays de Niyi, les marais de l'Oronte dans la région d'Apamée. Mais aussi, ces prisonniers peuvent venir d'une des régions soumises par le Pharaon, un pays de Canaan dont le texte ne nous indique pas la position.

Au siècle suivant, les archives d'Amarna apportent des informations qu'il est difficile de combiner entre elles. Certaines lettres permettent de situer en Canaan les villes de Ḫinnatuna (Ḥannaton de la Bible) et d'Akshapa (Akshaf de la Bible) dans la région d'Acre, de Ḥaṣor en Galilée, de Sidon, Tyr et Byblos sur la côte phénicienne;[30] on rejoint ainsi la donnée de la statue d'Idrimi. Mais d'autre lettres paraissent attribuer à Canaan un sens beaucoup plus large. Un roi du Mitanni (?) donne à son messager vers l'Égypte une lettre de recommandation auprès des "rois de Canaan," serviteurs du Pharaon.[31] Rib-Addi de Byblos oppose à la docilité antérieure des "rois de Canaan" l'activité rebelle des fils d'Abdi-Ashirta, princes d'Amurru.[32] Aménophis IV rappelle à l'ordre Aziru d'Amurru: il doit se soumettre s'il veut rester en vie, le Pharaon ne désire pas sévir contre "tout le pays de Canaan."[33] Dans ces textes, le nom semble s'appliquer à toutes les possession asiatiques de l'Égypte, mais cette conclusion n'est pas certaine.[34] Une dernière lettre donnerait à Canaan une extension encore plus grande: Aménophis IV-Akhenaton a demandé à Abdimilki de Tyr des nouvelles de Canaan, et celui-ci répond en transmettant des informations sur Danuna, Ugarit, Qadesh et sur le conflit entre Aziru d'Amurru et Biryawaza de Damas.[35] Le pays de Danuna est une quantité incertaine,[36] mais on ne peut lui trouver aucune place en Syrie[37] et le plus vraisemblable est qu'il était quelque part en Cilicie orientale. Il est impossible d'étendre aussi loin le pays de Canaan et Danuna n'a jamais appartenu à l'Égypte. De plus, la lettre d'Abdimilki date des dernières années d'Amenophis IV, à un moment où Qadesh avait rompu avec l'Égypte.[38] Quant à Ugarit, la ville pouvait être encore sous le contrôle égyptien, mais n'était pas pour autant considérée comme "cananéenne." Il y a, parmi les nouveaux textes de Râs Shamra, une lettre adressée d'Ugarit à Ramsès II et qui

[28] S. Smith, *The Statue of Idrimi*, ll. 18-23, cf. pp. 72-73.

[29] Peut-être Amyun au sud de Tripoli, R. Dussaud, *Topographie historique de la Syrie antique et médiévale*, Paris, 1927, p. 117, n. 1; S. Smith, *l. c.*, p. 73; H. Klengel, *Geschichte Syriens im 2. Jahrtausend v. u. Z.*, I, Berlin, 1965, p. 175 et n. 9.—Si, comme on l'admet parfois (encore W. Helck, *Beziehungen Ägyptens zy Vorderasien im 3. und 2. Jahrausend vor Chr.*, Wiesbaden, 1962), Ammia est identique à Ambia et si Ambia est localisé à Enfé sur la côte au sud de Tripoli, la conclusion est la même.

[30] *EA* 8, 17; 131, 57-61; 137, 73-76; 148, 39-46; *RA*, XIX (1922), p. 100.

[31] *EA* 30, 1. De son côté, Burnaburiash de Babylone dit au Pharaon: "Canaan est ton pays et ses rois sont (tes serviteurs)," mais c'est pour se plaindre que ses marchands aient été attaqués à "Ḫinnatuna de Canaan," *EA* 8, 13-25. Cela ne prouve pas que Canaan ait eu une grande étendue. De fait, le même Burnaburiash se plaint une autre fois que ses caravanes aient été rançonnées par Biryawaza de Damas et par Pamaḫu, le commissaire du Pharaon, *EA* 7, 73-77: c'est pourtant un pays qui appartient au Pharaon. Canaan n'est pas mentionné alors: est-ce un hasard, ou est-ce parce que la pays de Damas ne fait pas partie de Canaan?

[32] *EA* 109, 44-48.

[33] *EA* 162, 39-41.

[34] Cf. S. Moscati, *I predecessori d'Israele*, pp. 47, 50; I. J. Gelb, *JCS*, XV (1961), p. 42.

[35] *EA* 151, 49-53.

[36] En dernier lieu, l'étude aventureuse de M. Astour, "The Danaans-Danunians," dans ses *Hellenosemitica*, 1965, pp. 1-112, où l'on trouvera les références aux travaux antérieurs. Cf. spécialement R. O'Callaghan, *Orientalia*, XVIII (1949), pp. 193-97; W. F. Albright, *AJA*, LIV (1950), pp. 171-72; E. Laroche, *Syria*, XXXV (1958), pp. 263-75.

[37] A. Goetze, *JCS*, XV (1961), p. 50, le localise dans l'actuel Hatay au nord d'Ugarit. Mais cette région faisait alors partie du territoire de Mukish-Alalakh, qui s'étendait jusqu'à la mer, J. Nougayrol, *Palais Royal d'Ugarit*, IV, pp. 10-15; M. Liverani, *Storia di Ugarit*, Rome, 1962, pp. 48-49; 70-71; H. Klengel, *Geschichte Syriens* . . . , I, 1965, p. 252.

[38] Cf. K. A. Kitchen, *Suppiluliuma and the Amarna Pharaos*, 1962, p. 14; E. F. Campbell, *The Chronology of the Amarna Letters*, 1964, pp. 71-72.

rend compte d'un paiement fait par les gens d'Ugarit aux chefs des "gens de Canaan" (*mât ki-na-ḫi*) par devant l'envoyé spécial du Pharaon en pays hittite.[39] La ville d'Ugarit était alors en dehors de Canaan et il n'y a aucune preuve qu'elle y ait jamais été incluse. De tout cela on peut conclure que le roi de Tyr ne donne pas des nouvelles de Canaan, mais que, de Canaan où il est, il envoie au Pharaon les nouvelles qui peuvent l'intéresser.[40]

Abdimilki mentionne aussi Amurru. A cette époque, contrairement à une opinion souvent exprimée et malgré l'apparence de certaines lettres citées plus haut,[41] Amurru et Canaan désignaient des pays différents. D'après les lettres d'Amarna, complétées par les textes de Boghazköi et ceux de Râs Shamra,[42] Amurru était alors le nom d'une région de la Syrie centrale[43] qui fut d'abord soumise à l'Égypte. Des princes locaux, Abdi-Ashirta puis Aziru s'y taillèrent un royaume, l'État d'Amurru, qui se rendit indépendant et devint finalement le vassal des Hittites. Les limites de cet État ont varié avec l'avance ou le recul d'Abdi-Ashirta et de son fils mais elles peuvent être généralement définies ainsi pour la fin de l'époque d'Amarna:[44] au Nord, Amurru était bordé par les royaumes d'Ugarit, de Qaṭna et de Nuḫašše, vassaux des Hittites; à l'Est et au Sud-Est par ceux de Qadesh, devenu vassal des Hittites, et de Damas, resté sous le contrôle de l'Égypte; au Sud, il était limitrophe des possessions égyptiennes, sa frontière partait de la mer au Nord du territoire de Byblos dans la région de Tripoli et rejoignait le territoire de Damas dans la vallée du haut Oronte.

Cette géographie politique se modelait approximativement sur l'organisation administrative que l'Égypte avait établie dans son empire asiatique. Elle semble l'avoir divisé, peut-être déjà sous Thutmès III, en trois provinces, qui avaient chacune un chef-lieu où résidait ordinairement le *râbiṣu* ou *šakîn mâti*, le commissaire du Pharaon.[45] Au Nord s'étendait une province dont le nom n'est pas explicité par les textes, mais qui s'appelait sans doute la province d'Amurru, puisqu' elle correspondait à la région de ce nom et qu'elle tomba finalement tout entière aux mains des princes d'Amurru; son chef-lieu était Ṣumur, la Simyra de l'époque hellénistique, qui est maintenant identifiée très vraisemblablement avec Tell Kazel, au nord du fleuve Éleuthère.[46] A l'Est et au Sud-Est se trouvait la province d'Upè, dont la ville principale était Damas mais dont le centre administratif était Kumidi, l'actuel Kâmid el-Lôz dans la Beqa' au Nord de l'Hermon. Au Sud, s'étendait la province de Canaan. Une lettre du roi d'Alashia (Chypre) mentionne, entre deux lacunes, la "province de Canaan";[47] sa capitale était Gaza, qui avait été la base de départ des expéditions de la conquête et qui resta naturellement la résidence du commissaire égyptien: nous en avons le témoignage déjà sous Aménophis II,[48] puis sous Aménophis IV.[49] Après qu'Amurru eût fait sécession, il ne resta que les deux provinces d'Upè et de Canaan, qui subsistèrent au moins jusque sous Ramsès II: une lettre de ce Pharaon relative au voyage de la princesse hittite qu'il devait épouser parle successivement du commissaire du pays d'Upè et du commissaire du pays de Canaan.[50] Cette province de Canaan s'étendait sur la côte depuis la frontière d'Amurru au Nord jusqu'à la frontière d'Égypte au Sud, elle comprenait toute la Palestine mais elle ne dépassait pas la limite du Jourdain. Les posses-

---

[39] Cf. Note 7.

[40] Cf. déjà A. F. Rainey, *IEJ*, XIV (1964), p. 101; *BiblArch*, XXVIII (1965), pp. 105-06.

[41] *EA* 109 et 162.

[42] Les textes sont rassemblés par S. Moscati, *I predecessori d'Israele*, pp. 101-09, à compléter par les textes de Râs Shamra publiés par J. Nougayrol, *Le Palais Royal d'Ugarit*, IV, 1956, très spécialement pp. 284-86.

[43] Au xviiie siècle déjà, deux lettres de Mari parlent d'un pays d'Amurru qui est situé au Sud de Qaṭna et, semble-t-il, au nord de Ḥaṣor; les textes d'Alalakh qui mentionnent Amurru sont moins explicites mais ils s'accordent avec cette localisation, cf. G. Dossin, *RSO*, XXXII (1957), pp. 37-38; J.-R. Kupper, *Les nomades en Mésopotamie au temps des rois de Mari*, Paris, 1957, pp. 179-80.

[44] I. J. Gelb, *JCS*, XV (1961), p. 42; H. Klengel, "Aziru von Amurru," *Mitteilungen des Instituts für Orientforschung*, X (1964), pp. 55-83, cf. pp. 67-69.

[45] W. Helck, *MDOG*, 92 (1960), pp. 1-13, spéc. pp. 6-8; Id., *Die Beziehungen . . .* , pp. 258-60; M. Liverani, *Introduzione alla storia dell'Asia anteriore antica*, Rome, 1963, pp. 221-22; H. Klengel, *l. c.*, pp.60-61.

[46] M. Dunand-N. Saliby, "A la recherche de Simyra," *Annales Archéologiques de Syrie*, VII (1957), pp. 3-16; M. Dunand, A. Bounni, N. Saliby, *ibid.*, XIV (1964), pp. 3-14.

[47] *EA* 36, 15: *piḫati ša kinaḫi*.

[48] Lettres de Ta'annak, nº 5 et 6.

[49] *EA* 287 et 289.

[50] E. Edel, "Weitere Briefe aus der Heiratskorrespondenz Ramses' II," *Geschichte und Altes Testament* (Festschrift Alt), 1953, pp. 29-63.

sions égyptiennes à l'Est du lac de Tibériade dépendaient de la province d'Upè (Damascène) et, malgré les interventions militaires de Ramsès II en Moab et en Edom,[51] l'Égypte n'avait pas pris pied dans la Transjordanie du centre et du Sud.

Les mentions de Canaan dans les documents égyptiens postérieures à l'époque d'Amarna complètent ces informations. Vers la fin du xiiie siècle, un texte, décrivant l'" extrémité " de Canaan, énumère plusieurs stations entre la frontière égyptienne et Raphia et Gaza;[52] il s'agit évidemment de l'extrémité méridionale de Canaan. A la même époque, un autre texte parle d'esclaves cananéens du Ḫuru.[53] Il apparaît que Ḫuru a alors été employé comme un équivalent de Canaan. Un maître scribe a parmi ses titres celui de " messager du Pharaon auprès des princes des pays étrangers du Ḫuru depuis Silè (à la frontière d'Égypte) jusqu'à Upè (la Damascène)";[54] vers 1100 av. J.C., Wenamon s'embarque sur la mer du Ḫuru pour aller à Byblos et, de là, il envoie en Égypte un messager qui revient au pays de Ḫuru.[55] Ces textes mettent dans le Ḫuru toute la côte palestinienne et phénicienne jusqu'à Byblos mais aussi la Damascène; ils semblent indiquer qu'après Ramsès II les provinces d'Upè et de Canaan avaient été fusionnées et que les possessions égyptiennes d'Asie étaient appelées indifféremment Ḫuru ou Canaan. Cela pourrait expliquer que, dans la stèle de victoire de Merneptah, les noms des villes palestiniennes et d'Israël soient encadrés par les noms de Canaan et de Ḫuru.[56] Cela n'est pas contredit par la dernière mention égyptienne de Canaan, qui est postérieure à l'établissement des Philistins et d'Israël: une statuette a été inscrite au nom d'un " messager royal en Canaan et en Philistie."[57] On peut ajouter enfin que les textes égyptiens établissent entre Ḫuru et Amur la même distinction que nous avons noté dans les textes cunéiformes entre Canaan et Amurru; ce sont deux pays distincts: l'Onomasticon d'Amenopé oppose le vin du Ḫuru à celui d'Amur et, beaucoup plus tard, dans le Décret de Canope, Amur et Ḫuru de l'égyptien correspondent à Syrie et Phénicie du grec.[58]

III. Le pays de Canaan dans les textes bibliques.

C'est dans la Bible que le pays de Canaan est le plus souvent nommé, et déjà pour l'époque des Patriarches. Mais, à la différence des témoignages extrabibliques, aucun texte n'est contemporain de la situation qu'il décrit, c'est-à-dire de l'installation des Israélites en " Canaan," et les textes les plus explicites sur la géographie de ce pays sont aussi les plus tardifs dans leur rédaction. De plus, l'usage a varié et il a été influencé par les circonstances historiques.

Il y a cependant un trait permanent: jamais le pays de Canaan ne s'étend à l'Est du Jourdain. Le passage du Jourdain marque l'entrée en Canaan, Nomb 33:51; 34:2; 35:10; cf. Deut 32:49; Jos 5:12. Les territoires de Ruben et de Gad sont limités à l'Ouest par le Jourdain et ils sont en dehors du pays de Canaan, Jos 22:10-11, 25, 32. Un seul texte, Gen 50:10-11, fait exception en parlant de " Cananéens " à l'Est du Jourdain, mais c'est parce qu'il veut assimiler la tradition aberrante d'une tombe de Jacob en Transjordanie.

Nous avons vu que le Jourdain était également la limite de la province égyptienne de Canaan. Il est raisonnable de penser que les Israélites en s'installant dans le pays ont connu cette désignation administrative et on peut se demander s'ils n'y ont pas conformé leur vocabulaire. En fait, les deux textes bibliques les plus détaillés donnent au pays de Canaan les mêmes limites que nous avons établies pour la domination égyptienne à la fin du xiiie siècle av. J. C. Le premier, Nomb 34:2-12, trace les frontières du pays de Canaan, " héritage " d'Israël, et l'autre, Ez 47:15-20; 48:1, décrit les limites du pays à partager entre les tribus de l'Israël futur. Dans ces deux textes, la limite méridionale va de l'extrémité de la Mer Morte au Torrent d'Égypte, la Méditerranée est

[51] K. A. Kitchen, " Some New Light on the Asiatic Wars of Ramesses II," *JEA*, L (1964), pp. 47-70.

[52] Pap. Anastasi I, 27; trad. dans *ANET*, p. 478b.

[53] Pap. Anastasi III A 5-6 = IV 16, 4; trad. dans R. A. Caminos, *Late-Egyptian Miscellanies*, Londres, 1954, pp. 117 et 200.

[54] Pap. Anastasi III, 1, 9-10; R. A. Caminos, *l. c.*, p. 69.

[55] *ANET*, pp. 26a, 28a.

[56] *ANET*, p. 378a.

[57] G. Steindorff, " The Statuette of an Egyptian Commissioner in Syria," *JEA*, XV (1939), pp. 30-37. L'inscription serait de la XXIIe Dynastie.

[58] A. H. Gardiner, *Ancient Egyptian Onomastica*, Oxford, 1947, pp. 180* et 187*, Cependant, cf. G. R. Hughes, *JNES*, X (1951), p. 259, n. 12, d'après lequel, au lieu de *'Imr*, il faudrait lire *'Iš(w)r* (Syrie) dans le texte démotique du Décret de Canope.

la limite occidentale et le Jourdain sert de limite orientale, comme dans les textes qui viennent d'être cités. Quant à la frontière septentrionale, l'incertitude des noms et de leur localisation a permis d'envisager deux tracés. Certains exégètes, voulant rester plus près du territoire qu' Israël a réellement occupé, proposent une ligne allant de l'embouchure du Nahr el-Qasimiyé aux sources du Jourdain et à l'Hermon;[59] les autres mettent cette limite beaucoup plus au Nord, et il faut certainement leur donner raison.[60] Les points de la frontière communs aux deux textes sont: la Mer, Lebo Hamat, Ṣedad, Ḥaṣor-ʿEnân. Ils dessinent une ligne normale si l'on identifie Lebo Hamat avec Lebwé sur le Haut-Oronte; Ṣedad avec Ṣadad au Nord de l'Hermon; Ḥaṣor-ʿEnân avec les puits de Qaryatein à mi-chemin entre Damas et Palmyre. Le premier point à partir de la mer Méditerranée est le mont Ḥor dans les Nombres, Ḥethlôn dans Ézéchiel. Dans ce contexte, le mont Ḥor doit correspondre au massif le plus septentrional de la chaîne du Liban, le Djebel Akkar; Ḥethlôn peut être identifié avec Ḥeitelâ au Nord-Est de Tripoli, au pied du Djebel Akkar et juste au Sud du fleuve Éleuthère. Avant de descendre à Lebwé dans la Beqaʿ, la frontière suivrait ainsi l'Éleuthère, qui est une limite naturelle: elle sépare aujourd'hui le Liban de la Syrie et, d'après ce que nous avons dit de la position de Simyra, elle séparait autrefois Canaan du pays d'Amurru. Dans les deux textes, Ḥaṣor-ʿEnân marque l'angle Nord-Est de Canaan et la frontière descend ensuite au Sud pour rejoindre par une courbe le lac de Tibériade d'après les Nombres, le Jourdain au Sud de ce lac d'après Ezéchiel. La Damascène est ainsi inclue, implicitement dans les Nombres, explicitement dans Ézechiel: la limite septentrionale passe entre le territoire de Damas et celui de Hamat, Ez 47:17, 48:1.

Ces deux descriptions diffèrent tellement dans la formulation et pour certain détails qu'elles sont certainement indépendantes l'une de l'autre. Mais elles s'accordent tant entre elles pour l'essentiel et contre la réalité historique de leur époque qu'elles doivent remonter à une source ou à une tradition commune. Ez 47:16-18 se réfère aux territoires de Hamat, de Damas, de Gilead et du Hauran (dont c'est la seule mention dans la Bible). Ce sont tous des noms de provinces assyriennes établies entre 733 et 720 av. J. C.; la forme de la tradition donnée par Ézéchiel est donc postérieure à cette date. Mais ces noms sont absents de la description des Nombres; la tradition ou la source commune est donc antérieure à la fin du viiie siècle av. J. C. Cependant cette description ne représente pas, comme on l'a parfois dit, l'empire d'Israël à l'époque de David et de Salomon, car elle inclut la Philistie et elle exclut la Transjordanie au Sud du lac de Tibériade. Il est très vraisemblable que, malgré leur rédaction tardive, les descriptions de Nomb 34:2-12 et Ez 47:15-20 gardent le souvenir de ce que Canaan signifiait pour les Israélites au moment de leur installation: c'était le Canaan des Égyptiens, tel que nous l'avons décrit, après la fusion des provinces d'Upè et de Canaan.[61]

Le même souvenir se retrouve dans d'autres textes. Jos 13:2-5, en décrivant le pays "qui reste encore," marque l'écart entre le territoire que les tribus vont se partager et le Canaan qu'elles auraient dû conquérir.[62] Celui-ci s'étend au Nord jusqu'à Lebo Hamat, comme dans Nomb 34 et Ez 47, et jusqu'au territoire de l'Amorite; ce territoire paraît être ici (et pour la seule fois dans la Bible, semble-t-il) le pays d'Amurru qui bordait au Nord la province égyptienne de Canaan. Ce sont les mêmes limites, au Nord et au Sud, qu'indique un texte ancien, Nomb 13:17, 21: les envoyés de Moïse vont reconnaître le pays de Canaan depuis le désert de Ṣin jusqu'à Lebo Hamat.[63] L'expression "depuis Lebo Hamat jusqu'au Torrent d'Égypte" restera pour signifier

[59] Depuis J. P. Van Kasteren, "La frontière septentrionale de la Terre Promise," *RB*, IV (1895), pp. 23-26, jusqu'à M. Noth, *Das vierte Buch Mose. Numeri* Göttingen, 1966, pp. 215-216.

[60] B. Maisler (Mazar), "Lebo Hamath and the Northern Boundary of Canaan," *BJPES*, XII (1945-46), pp. 91-102 (hébreu); J. Simons, *The Geographical and Topographical Texts of the Old Testament*, Leyde, 1959, pp. 98-103; Y Aharoni, *The Land of the Bible. A Historical Geography*, Londres, 1967, pp. 61-70 et carte A, p. 60. Cf. aussi la carte IX 4b dans *Atlas of Israel*, Jerusalem, 1956-64 (hébreu).

[61] C'est ce qu'avait déjà vu Mazar, *l. c.*, pp. 93-96, et dans l'ouvrage collectif, *Views of the Biblical World*, Jerusalem, I, 1958, pp. 238-39 et la carte.

[62] D. Baldi, "La Terra Promisa nel programme di Giosue," *Liber Annuus Studii Biblici Franciscani*, I, 1950-51, pp. 87-106; F. M. Abel, "La prétendue caverne des Sidoniens et la localisation de la ville de ʿAra," *RB*, LVIII (1951), pp. 47-53.

[63] Cf. la carte 50 dans Y. Aharoni, *Carta's Atlas of the Bible*, Jerusalem, 1964 (hébreu).

les points extrêmes du pays sous Salomon, 1 Rois 8 : 65, et sous Jéroboam II, 2 Rois 14 : 5.

Ces conclusions vont contre une opinion assez commune,[64] d'après laquelle le nom de Canaan aurait été d'abord appliqué à la seule Phénicie, puis aurait été étendu dans la Bible à la région côtière en général, à la vallée du Jourdain, à la Cisjordanie du Nord et du centre, enfin à toute la région située à l'Ouest du Jourdain. Nous avons vu que les textes extrabibliques n'autorisaient certainement pas une telle conclusion ; quant aux textes bibliques, il est beaucoup plus vraisemblable que les Israélites ont d'abord reçu le terme avec le sens qu'il avait à la veille de leur établissement. L'étendue du terme se restreignit quand on identifia Canaan avec le pays conquis et non pas avec le pays "promis," ainsi Gen 10 : 19, ou, au contraire, quand on limita les Cananéens aux régions du grand Canaan qui n'avaient pas été soumises, ainsi Jos 17 : 11-13 ; Juges 1 : 27-33, ou enfin quand l'habitat propre des Cananéens se fut réduit à la Phénicie : les marchands furent appelés "Cananéens" parce qu'ils venaient de Phénicie ; Tyr et Sidon sont les "forteresses de Canaan," Is 23 : 1-14 ; Sidon est le premier-né de Canaan, Gen 10 : 15 ; 1 Chr 1 : 13 ; "Sidonien" équivaut à "Cananéen," Deut 3 : 9 ; Juges 18 : 7 ; 1 Rois 11 : 5, 33 ; 2 Rois 23 : 13, de même que "Sidoniens" et "Phéniciens" alternent chez Homère. Au iie siècle av. J. C., lorsque Beyrouth s'appelait Laodicée-en-Phénicie, la légende sémitique de ses monnaies l'appelle "métropole en Canaan" (c'est le seul exemple du nom dans les inscriptions de Phénicie). A la même époque, la Septante traduit quelquefois Canaan par Phénicie et, dans le Nouveau Testament, la Cananéenne de Mat 15 : 22 correspond à la Syro-Phénicienne de Marc 7 : 26.

[64] B. Maisler, *Untersuchungen zur Geschichte und Ethnographie Syriens und Palästinas*, Giessen, 1930, pp. 52-74; S. Moscati, *I predecessori d'Israele*, p. 67; M. Noth, *Die Welt des Alten Testaments*[4], Berlin, 1964, pp. 45-48.

AN OLD BABYLONIAN HERDING CONTRACT AND GENESIS 31 : 38 f.

J. J. FINKELSTEIN
YALE UNIVERSITY

IN THE FINAL CONFRONTATION BETWEEN JACOB AND LABAN, after the latter had caught up with his fleeing son-in-law, Jacob gives vent to his feelings at his mistreatment by Laban, especially with regard to his long term of service as Laban's shepherd, in the following words (v. 38 f.): 'It is now twenty years that I have been with you—your ewes and your she-goats never miscarried, nor did I myself consume the rams from your flock. The ones fallen prey to wild beasts I did not charge to you (lit.: bring to you)—I myself *made good the loss,* whether it was snatched by day or by night.'

The italicized phrase does not in this instance imply a guess at the meaning of the Heb. verb *ʾaḥaṭṭennah,* for the translation is clearly demanded by the context. The problem is rather that of the use of the verb *ḤṬʾ*, here in the *piʿēl,* in a way which is not documented anywhere else in the Bible. It is of course well understood that the root sense of the verb is "to err, to miss"—hence *ḥēṭʾ* usually as "sin (of omission)"—with the factitive *piʿēl* denoting "purification, cleansing, lustrating, etc." and the *hithpaʿēl* denoting the reflexive of the same actions, i. e. "to purge, purify oneself, etc." But these usages all fall within the sacral or cultic sphere ; none is analogous to the profane usage in the passage under review.

It happens, however, that this is one of those instances where the Mesopotamian—or common ancient Near Eastern—cultural background of the episode can be pinpointed with precision. It was characteristic of E. A. Speiser that he was able to sense that this was the case—witness his reference to the herding provision of the Laws of Hammurapi Par. 266—in his commentary on the passage.[1] He could not have known that the anomalous use of the verb *ḤṬʾ* to denote Jacob's assump-

[1] *Genesis* (The Anchor Bible, 1964), 247.

tion of liability for the loss provides the tell-tale link to the story's background, since it occurs in an unpublished Old Babylonian tablet of the time of Samsuiluna, YBC 5944 of the Yale Babylonian Collection,[2] the text of which follows:

92 *laḫrātu* (U_8.ḪI.A)[a]
20 *immerū* (NITÁ.ḪI.A)[b]
22 *lillidū* ($SILA_4$.D[U.ḪI.A])
24 *ḫurapū*(?) ($SILA_4$ [.NIM?])
33 *enzātu* (UD_x[=ÙZ].ḪI.A)
4 *uriṣū* (UD_x.MÁŠ.G[AL])[c]
27 *lalīʾū* (UD_x.TUR)
ŠU.NIGIN 1 mēʾat + 50 + 8 U_8.ḪI.A[d]
ŠU.NIGIN 64 *enzātu*ḪI.A
ša IdEN.ZU-*ša-mu-uḫ*
a-na Da-da-a SIPAD
ip-qí-du
a-na pí-ḫa-t[*im*]
i-za-a[*z*]
ù ḫa-li-iq-[*tam*]
i-ri-a-ab
I*Ni-id-na-tum ka-pa-ra-šu*
ú-da-pa-ar-ma[e] *a-na ḫi-ṭì i-za-*[*az*][f]
5 ŠE.GUR I*Da-da-*[*a*]
Ì-ÁG-E

IGI dEN.ZU-*e-ri-ba-am*
IGI *Ḫa-bi-ya*
IGI *Na-ra-am-ì-lí-šu*
ITU Šu-nigin-na u₄ -18- kam/mu
Sa-am-su-i-lu-na lugal-[e]

'92 ewes, 20 rams, 22 breeding lambs, 24 [spring(?)] lambs, 33 she-goats, 4 male goats, 27 kids—total: 158 sheep; total: 64 goats, which Sinšamuḫ has entrusted to Dadā the shepherd. He (i. e. Dadā) assumes liability (therefore) and will replace any lost (animals). Should Nidnatum, his (i. e. Dadā's) shepherd boy, absent himself,[e] he (i. e., Nidnatum)[3] will bear responsibility for any (consequent) loss, (and) Dadā will measure out 5 *kōr* of barley.'

Three witnesses; date: Samsuiluna year 1(?), fourth month,[g] 16th day.

NOTES TO THE TEXT

a. For the readings, Akkadian equivalents, and translations of the logograms denoting the different categories of sheep and goats in lines 1-7, cf. Oppenheim and Hartman, "The Domestic Animals of Ancient Mesopotamia" in *JNES* IV (1945), 152 ff., and Landsberger, *MSL* VIII/1 under the respective Sumerian entries together with his extended notes and Excursus I, pp. 55 ff.

b. Written thus, without UDU.

c. May also be read *mašgallu*(*m*), *ibid.* p. 30 line 216 and p. 58.

d. To be read *immerātu* here rather than *laḫrātu*, since the term includes the rams as well, and is thus parallel to the term used to denote all the goats, including the males, UD_x = *enzu* "she-goat."

e. Cf. sub *duppuru* in the dictionaries; it is paralleled by *nadū* "to neglect (one's contracted duties)."[4]

f. In citing this passage, CAD 3 187 omits *i-za-*[*az*] which is clear on the tablet and on Feigin's copy, thus fundamentally misconstruing the legal point of the stipulation.

g. The month name is a curious writing for what must be ŠU.NUMUN.A = *Duʾuzu* (*Tammuz*); note eme.sal nimen for NIGIN, which may have led to this writing.

Some difficulties within the text itself will have to be clarified before we turn to the light it sheds on the biblical episode. It emerges, in the first place, that the shepherd Dadā does not himself, or all by himself, engage in the actual herding of the flocks. In his capacity of shepherd (*rēʾum*) he seems to function more like a shepherd contractor, the one who contracts with the owners of flocks, but who "sub-contracts" with or otherwise employs "shepherd boys" (*kaparrum*) who do the actual herding.[5] This was known from Old Babylonian sources, especially letters, in which it is clear that the *reʾum* was more than a shepherd in the strict sense, since he often held the "franchise"—so to speak—over large districts or even cities. This is now confirmed by a new text of the Edict of Ammiṣaduqa in which the shepherds (SIPAD.MEŠ) are on a par with the *iššakku* (ENSÍ)-farmers—who were not themselves the

---

[2] The tablet will appear as No. 7 in *YBT* 12, a forthcoming volume of Old Babylonian texts from the reign of Samsuiluna copied by the late S. I. Feigin.

[3] The wording does not preclude the possibility that Dadā is the one who would be responsible for any loss resulting from Nidnatum's absence, but this interpretation would not account for the interruption of the statement of Dadā's responsibilities at line 17, and its resumption in line 19 with the repetition of the name of Dadā.

[4] Cf. below, note 13.

[5] Cf. E. Grant, *The Haverford Symposium on Archaeology and the Bible*, p. 234 no. 5, which is another herding contract between the same owner and Dadā, dated in Samsuiluna 11. Read *ip-qí-du* after the name I*Da-da-a* in line 13. The *kaparru*'s in that contract are Kabta-bānī and Ilī-tūram (lines 14 ff.); no liability clauses of any kind are stated in that document.

agricultural laborers—and the *šusikku*'s who stood in some financial relationship to the palace.[6]

The present contract involves three rather than two parties. Dadā the shepherd assumes overall liability (*piḫatum*) for the flock which is legally under his charge or custody (*paqādum*), and is therefore responsible for the replacement (*ri'ābum*) of any lost animals. Such loss (*ḫaliqtum*) must be understood as due to circumstances constituting neglect on the shepherd's part, thus excluding loss due to the action of wild carnivores (except under circumstances where the loss might have been preventable) or to death by disease or even natural causes—as provided for in the L(aws of) H(ammurapi), Par. 266. While these forms of liability are assumed by Dadā with respect to the owner of the flock, Nidnatum the shepherd "boy" is made explicitly liable for any loss (*ḫīṭum*) occasioned by his wilful neglect of his duties, i. e., by being absent from his job. On the basis of LH 267, where the loss (*ḫiṭītum*) due to *pissatum* "mange(?)"[7] is assessable against the negligent (*ēgū*) shepherd, it may be posited in this case as well that Dadā will have to make good such loss to Sinšamuḫ, the owner, but the contract specifies explicitly that Nidnatum, whose behavior was directly responsible for the loss resulting from his negligence, will be obliged to make it up to Dadā. The latter must nevertheless pay Sinšamuḫ 5 *kōr* of barley. This ought not to be interpreted as an additional penalty—presumably for having retained such an irresponsible *kaparrum*—but rather as a refund of the larger part of the wage which must have been part of the agreement even though not stipulated in writing, which, according to LH par. 261, would have amounted to 8 *kōr* of barley per year.

Ḫiṭum in the sense of "loss, damage" is not limited in usage to flocks and herds, but occurs also in connection with the produce of fields and orchards. When the word is thus used, the implication is usually present that the "loss, damage, deficiency" was caused through neglect by the person in whose legal custody the property had been at the time such damage or loss was sustained. It cannot denote such loss or injury as resulted through circumstances which the shepherd could not reasonably have been expected to prevent, such as those illustrated by LH 266. Apart from *pissatum*, however, neither the "codes" nor the contracts ever specify the kind of damage for which the shepherd would be liable.

We may now return to the Jacob-Laban story. It is apparent that in Chs. 30-31 we have the most detailed record of the law and lore of shepherding to be found in the Bible. There is nothing specifically "Israelite" in the story, and it would be reasonable even *a priori* to assume that its background would be common to all of the ancient Near East. It is nevertheless particularly striking to find imbedded within the Hebrew narrative elements of the precise terminology current in Old Babylonian herding contracts. Furthermore, the point of Jacob's particular agreement and stipulations in his relation to Laban stands out *only* when the normally prevailing arrangements

[6] This new text of the Edict of Ammiṣaduqa will be published shortly by the present writer. It duplicates in part the fragmentary edict text of Samsuiluna published by Kraus in the Landsberger Festschrift, *AS* 16 225 ff., as amended by him in his important new study *Staatliche Viehhaltung im altbabylonischen Lande Larsa* (*MKNAW*, Afd. Letterkunde, N.R. 29/5) p. 13 note 3. The official status of the *šusikkum* was already known from Par. 10 of the Edict of Ammiṣaduqa (Kraus, *SD* V 24 f., 118 f.). While these texts, and particularly those discussed by Kraus in *Viehhaltung*, are concerned with state-owned herds and flocks, it is nevertheless apparent that even a shepherd (n a . g a d a or s i p a d) who contracted with private flock owners was not usually the one who did the actual herding. While Kraus (ibid. 13) appears to accept Landsberger's understanding of *susikkum* as "plucker" (MSL VIII/1 37, cf. CAD B *sub baqāmu and* (*bīt*) *buqūmi*) or "shearing-master," I intend to show elsewhere, on the basis of unpublished evidence, that the Akkadian for SU.SI.IG is *šusikkum* and that the person so designated is concerned not with shearing live animals, but with the disposition of the carcasses of dead animals, of large cattle as well as of sheep and goats.

[7] For discussion and earlier literature, see Lautner, *Personenmiete* (*SD* I) 97 n. 319, also, *Driver and Miles BL* I 459 f. Szlechter, in *Tablettes juridiques . . . Genève*, 104, would ascribe the term to *PSS* "destroy, wipe out" and therefore as a general term for "loss" (occurring within the sheepfold, as contrasted to *ḫaliqtum*, which would then denote losses from outside the fold). This seems to me unlikely, as it would render *ḫiṭīt pissatim* a genitive construct in which both constituents are synonymous. The phrase must mean "damage, loss" due to a *particular* cause, represented by *p.* That *ḫiṭītum* in this usage means strictly "loss, damage," note the phrase *ana ḫiṭītim ša ibaššū* PN LUGAL-E BA-NI-IB-GI$_4$-GI$_4$ "PN (the shepherd) will compensate the owner (or king) for any loss that may occur," Riftin, *Staro-vavilonskie . . . dokumenty etc.* No. 59: 8 ff.; *YBT* VIII 60: 8 ff.; 92: 8 ff.; 106: 8 ff., all Larsa documents.

in such contracts are kept in mind. These conditions may now be reviewed in detail.

1. Jacob offers to accept as his wages dark-colored (*ḥūm* "brown"?) sheep and variegated goats (30:32). What was Jacob's purpose in proposing such unusual terms for his employment? Did he expect to get a greater share of the flocks under such an arrangement as compared with the prevailing division between owner and shepherd or was it an offer to work for less than the prevailing share? Circumstances point unmistakably to the second view. In the Near East, the sheep are usually white and the goats black. Among the modern day shepherds the "white" and the "black" are synonymous with "sheep and goats" or "Kleinvieh."[8] In the Nippur herding contracts of the Achaemenid period the same phrase is used: *piṣâti u ṣalmâti* (var. *ṣalindu*)[9] "white and black" to denote all the small cattle together composed of sheep and goats of either sex and various age designations, which in the earlier periods are usually summarized as U_8.UDU.ḪI.A = *ṣēnu*. The percentage of dark-colored sheep and variegated goats would therefore have been very small. But Jacob's offer can best be evaluated against the background of the prevailing terms known from the cuneiform herding contracts. Our information in this respect, however, is surprisingly scanty and ambiguous. It is surprising because it is certain from LH 264 that the contracts between owner and shepherd provided for fixed proportions for each on the basis of an expected percentage of new births, and the division of other products,[10] presumably consisting of wool, milk products, and skins (of dead animals). Yet the extant contracts of the period almost never go into such details, specifying only the liability of the shepherd for loss and/or *pissatum* (-loss). There does exist one Diyala contract from Ashjaly, UCPSP X p. 131, No. 58, where this proportion is stipulated, and on the basis of the copy, Landsberger and others have concluded[11] that the proportion is 60:40, i.e., out of every hundred new births, 60 head will go to the owner of the flock, 40 to the shepherd. If this reading of the pertinent lines is correct, and the instance taken as typical, then there would be no question about Jacob's having agreed to a compensation substantially lower than the common rate. But the lines were difficult to interpret to begin with, and a collation, made by the present writer a few years ago, reveals that lines 9 ff., read as follows: *i-na* UDU.ḪI.A *ša i-ṣa-ba i-na* 1 *me-at* 60[12] + 20 *šu-ši-i i-na-ad*⟨*-di*⟩*-in ù a-na ḫa-li-iq-tim i-za-az*[13] "of the sheep which (constitute the) increase,[14] he (the shepherd) will give (to the owner) 80 out of 100,[15] and he (i.e., the shepherd) will be responsible for any loss." The proportion, in other words, is not 60:40 but 80:20, which in fact approaches more closely to the proportion of 9:1 which prevails for the most part among the sheep-herding Arabs of the modern Near East as reported by recent investigators.[16] The Neo-Babylonian and Achaemenid herd-

[8] Dalman, *Arbeit u. Sitte in Palästina* VI 180.

[9] Landsberger, *AfO* X 158.

[10] The negligent herdsman must make up to the owner the appropriate proportion of new births (*talittum*) and products (*biltum*, i.e., wool and dairy products) "in accordance with his contract" (*ana pī riksātišu*).

[11] Apud Lautner, *Personenmiete* 91 n. 305; *Driver and Miles BL* I 457.

[12] The horizontal wedge copied by Lutz is an erasure, and is to be ignored.

[13] Other corrections resulting from collation are: line 3, name: *I-si-da-na*; line 5, end: *a-na* UDU.ḪI.A *re-im*; line 13: *i-na-ad-di-ma* (*nadû*, the usual verb to denote delinquency in such documents, for which the text discussed in the present article substitutes *duppuru*).

[14] The reading of the word is certain, but the problem is that the expected form should have been *ūṣabā*. Landsberger, however, called my attention some time ago to the form *ya-ṣa-ab* (Sum. d a ḫ . ḫ e . d a m) in *a.-i.* II i 45, i.e., a West Semitic form, which may well lie behind the form *iṣabā*.

[15] The proportion must be expressed here in some idiomatic way, since *šu-ši-i* would otherwise appear to be redundant. Prof. Sachs suggests to me the possibility "that the scribe read 1, 20 *šu-ši-i* as the Akkadian words for 'one (and) one-third sosses' (= 80)."

[16] T. Ashkenazi in *Tribus Semi-nomades de la Palestine du Nord* (Paris 1938) reports (p. 164): 'Pour ses services, un berger reçoit 8 à 10 agneaux par 100 têtes de menu bétail. . . . Il est responsable du bon état du troupeau, de sa croissance ou de sa mortalité" (cf. LH 264). If the average increase is calculated at 80 lambs per 100 ewes per annum (see note 18) the share of the shepherd on this basis would amount to 15-18 lambs out of 80, or roughly 20 percent. H. Charles in *Tribus Moutonnières du Moyen-Euphrate* (Documents d'Études Orientales de l'Institute Français de Damas Vol. VIII) p. 117, reports the wage of the shepherd as one-tenth of the increase, but that he receives certain expenses in addition. Dalman, *op. cit.*, 215, records an instance where the shepherd receives 25 percent of the new-born lambs, but is then not entitled to compensation for any other expense. Such expenses, for clothing and other equipment, are assumed by the owner(s) of the flock in the cases reported by Ashkenazi and Charles.

ing contracts operate on a different principle. In these documents a guaranteed return is stipulated, based on the number of bearing ewes and she-goats in the flock, by which the shepherd-contractor is obliged to deliver to the owner of the flock 66⅔ lambs per 100 ewes per annum and one kid per she-goat according to some contracts but 66⅔ per 100 according to other contracts. In addition, the shepherd must deliver a stipulated quota of wool, goat-hair, cheese, butter, skins and sinews —the latter two items based on the stipulated expectation of ten animal deaths per hundred head.[17]

The stipulation of 66⅔ lambs per 100 ewes is particularly interesting, as it almost certainly is based on the theoretical or premissed birth rate —and perhaps even survival rate for the new births—of 100 percent, as is clearly indicated in those instances where the shepherd is obliged to deliver one kid per she-goat. One would naturally deduce from this that, at least as far as lambs are concerned, the shepherd gets as his share 33⅓ percent. Yet in fact this is an unrealistic calculation, for a birth-rate—not to mention survival rate —of one to one of young to adults would have amounted to extraordinary good fortune, since the prevailing expectation was an increase in new births of only 80 percent or, in some instances, even less.[18] Jacob says as much to Laban in the quotation cited above; it was due to his presence and his dedication that Laban's ewes and she-goats never miscarried, i. e., that they had 100 percent successful births. That this was the case, and that Laban himself acknowledged that this rate of increase was extraordinary and the result of special grace, is proved by 30:27, when Laban is prompted to make a generous gesture upon Jacob's notifying him that he is ready to return to his homeland: "Laban replied to him: 'Please— I have grown rich;[19] for Yahweh has blessed me

[17] These texts, largely from the Murashu archive, were treated by Augapfel, *Babylonische Rechtsurkunden* etc. 82-86; S. v. Bolla, *Untersuchungen zur Tiermiete und Tierpacht im Altertum* (Münchener Beiträge zur Papyrusforschung etc., Vol. 30 [1940]) 120 ff.; Cardascia, *Les Archives de Murašû* 155 f.

[18] Kraus, *Viehhaltung* 24 ff., has established that for official purposes the standard calculation was 80 lambs per 100 ewes. Cf. also *ibid.* 50 f., and Neugebauer and Sachs *MCT* 130 f., with note 295 l (VAT 8522), although calculations of 70 and 75 per 100 are also known. As it must be assumed that the percentage of surviving new births in the Neo-Babylonian period was not different from the OB period, this would leave the NB shepherd about 17 percent of the new births computed on the basis of 80 per 100 ewes, and proportionately less if the basis was 70 or 75 per 100.

[19] I assume that *NḪŠ* here is cognate with Akk. *naḫāšu* "to flourish, prosper," which may be denominative of *nuḫšu* "abundance, prosperity" (cf. Sum. ḫ é . g á l), which is the only way in which Laban's reply makes sense. This suggestion was made long ago by J. Sperber, *OLZ* 16 (1913) 389, and was cited by Ges.-Buhl (16th ed.) s. v., but has since been ignored by most translations and commentaries which continue to derive the verb in this occurrence from *naḥēš* "to perform divination" etc. (as in Gen. 44: 5, 15), which is out of place in the present context. The translations based on the divination notion must assume that Laban's reply amounts to a confession that at some earlier time Laban, presumably puzzled by his extraordinary good fortune, performed divination only to ascertain the source of this benevolence and that it was through this process that he learned of the true reason for his prosperity: Jacob's presence in his household. To my knowledge, divinational procedures are invoked only when the future is to be determined, i. e., whether some contemplated action will meet with success or failure, or when the recent experience of the client/"patient" (either private person, or the king, or the temple) has been so unfavorable as to suggest divine displeasure, the aim of the procedure then being to pinpoint the source of that displeasure. When a person is enjoying good fortune he is not inclined to inquire after the reason for it; he will invariably assume, if he is moved to reflect on it at all, that it is the just reward for his proper conduct, his own abilities, or that he is the object of divine grace. The ancients would no more be inclined to look a gift horse in the mouth than the moderns. Further, *NḪŠ* denotes only manipulative divinatory procedures, the result of which would have been couched in a reply that amounted to little more than "yes" or "no," or "favorable/unfavorable." It would have been extremely laborious if not impossible with such procedures to pinpoint Jacob as the source of Laban's good fortune (in a manner analagous to the procedure described in I Sam. 14 36 ff., where, characteristically, it was invoked because of the manifestation of divine displeasure). The only way in which Laban could have been made aware through some external agency that it was Jacob who was the cause of his good fortune would have been through a message type of oracle, i. e., by a dream or by prophecy; neither of these oracular media could be covered by the action *NḪŠ*. From the narrator's point of view it was rather the case that Laban intuitively sensed that his good fortune was due to Jacob's presence, and in a moment of gratitude, prompted by Jacob's announcement that he would like to return home, candidly acknowledged the latter's role in the increase of his wealth. That this occurrence of *NḪŠ* would be, on the present argument, the only one in the Bible to be ascribed to **NḪŠ* = *naḫāšu* remains a difficulty (whether the name *Naḥšôn* may be explained by the same root is a matter of dispute) but in view of the unmistakably Mesopotamian elements otherwise

on your account.'" Laban, in other words, had hardly expected that his flocks would increase at the rate they did, which was presumably at 100 percent or better.[20]

In other words, the 66⅔ stipulation of the Neo-Babylonian contracts, while obviously arrived at on the basis of an ideal of 100 percent increase, in realistic terms resulted in a proportion for the shepherd of considerably less, on the average, than even the 20 percent which was his normal due in the Old Babylonian period. For if the increase amounted, on the average, to 80 lambs per 100 ewes, the shepherd would, on this basis, have taken only about 13 lambs for himself, or 16 percent of the increase. This discrepancy between the Old and Neo-Babylonian practices cannot easily be accounted for. One might surmise that the difference would have been made up by the proportion of by-products to which the Neo-Babylonian shepherd was entitled, and about which we hear nothing in the Old Babylonian contracts. On the other hand, the Old Babylonian shepherd was entitled to an annual wage of 8 *kôr* of barley (LH 261) while the Neo-Babylonian shepherd is entitled to no direct wage—at least none is stipulated in the contracts. Furthermore, LH and the Old Babylonian herding contracts which are preserved, all concern private enterprise, i. e., the herds and flocks are the property of private individuals, and the shepherds with whom they contract are also "free agents" in contrast with the Neo-Babylonian contracts in which the flocks and herds are temple-owned, and the shepherds are thus more or less in the position of "state employees." There are no means by which such factors can be safely counterbalanced, but it would not be too risky a surmise if it is supposed that on total balance the remuneration to the shepherds of the Old and Neo-Babylonian periods, including all forms of benefits in addition to their percentage of the new-born lambs, would have been roughly the same, or that in value such remuneration equalled a total of about 20 percent of the increase. It is a fair conclusion, that the abnormally colored or marked animals that would have constituted Jacob's share under his agreement would not have amounted to 20 percent of the flocks even if Laban had not resorted to deceit to deprive Jacob of his share.

2. Natural loss. Here we may include losses resulting from attacks by wild beasts, and deaths due to disease. Jacob is silent about the latter category, which must certainly have constituted a significant factor in the calculations, and it should therefore be assumed that such loss was outside Jacob's liability. The Old Babylonian texts dealt with by Kraus make an explicit allowance of a 15 percent annual attrition rate for the older animals (ewes and rams),[21] the carcasses of which must nevertheless be accounted for, and the Neo-Babylonian contracts, which calculate a ten percent attrition rate (based apparently on the entire flock) also require that the carcasses be accounted for. Jacob is very eloquent, however, in delineating his liability for animals lost as the prey of wild beasts. That he makes such a point

---

present in the story, and the perfect sense it supplies to the passage and to the episode as a whole, the rendering proposed here appears to me the most plausible one.

[20] If the possibility of multiple births is allowed for, which was probably extremely rare in the ancient Near East (see Kraus, *Viehhaltung* 50 f.). In this connection, it should be noted that the sense of *maṯ'îmôṯ* in Song of Songs 4:2 is not that each ewe is accompanied by a pair of twin lambs, none being bereft (*šakūlāh*), but rather that each ewe is "matched" with its lamb beneath it. The image is one of symmetry, not of prolificness, as is clear from the subject of the image, the teeth of the beloved, which are white and perfectly aligned; each of the upper teeth is exactly aligned with and matched by its lower counterpart, without any unsightly gap. This usage of the denominative of the word for "twin" is well understood by A. Robert and R. Tournay in their translation and commentary *Le Cantique des Cantiques* (Paris, 1963) 161, who cite the similar sense of the Qal denom. *tô'ᵃmîm* in Ex. XXVI 24, XXXVI 29. The passage discloses, at all events, that a lamb for each ewe, or 100 percent increase, was the cherished ideal and implies also absence of losses due to death.

There is, to be sure, the passage at the beginning of Tablet VI i of the Gilgamesh epic where Ishtar blandishes the hero with a series prospective blessings, promising among other things that "your she-goats will cast triplets (*takšē*), your sheep twins (*tu'āmi*, line 18). But in this context it is clearly implied that, far from being a frequent occurrence, it was so rare as to be interpreted as a manifestation of special divine benevolence. On the mundane level, such occurrences would have been so infrequent as to have no significant effect on the statistics of new births in proportion to the number of bearing females.

[21] See Kraus, *Viehhaltung* 14, 59 ff. The term for this category is (KUŠ) RI.RI.ga = *miqittum* "fallen," i. e., "cadavers." As Kraus notes, it is not clear why only older animals are allowed under this category, since the mortality rate among the lambs might have been expected to be just as high.

of it must be understood as implying a certain reproof to Laban since this kind of liability went against the prevailing custom—as Speiser already observed—or, more precisely, the "statutory" prescriptions found in the cuneiform corpora, e. g., LH 266, which frees the shepherd from liability for animals lost as a result of an epidemic (*lipit īlim*) or as prey to lions, upon his declaration of these circumstances on oath, to the owner of the herd.[22]

It may well be assumed that such extraordinary conditions of work were not accepted by Jacob voluntarily, but were imposed upon him by Laban at the beginning of his service, when he had little bargaining power. These harsh conditions are underscored by Jacob's further reproach that he bore the liability for such losses whether they occurred by day or by night. This cannot be empty rhetoric. It implies that some compromise arrangement for equalizing the liability would have been more equitable: losses to wild animals in the daytime might legitimately have been borne by the shepherd, on the ground that greater vigilance could have prevented it,[23] whereas attacks on the fold at night by lions or wolves would have been almost impossible to defend against. Laban's rapacity—and the point of Jacob's specification of it—lay in his burdening of Jacob with liability for losses to wild beasts under any and all circumstances.

3. In the light of the above, one may wonder whether Jacob's final complaint about the conditions of his work—exposure to the blazing sun during the day and to the icy blasts of the steppe at night—might not have been something more than the mere rhetoric of the "Faithful Shepherd." From the analogues among the modern bedouin sheepherding practices cited above, it appears that it is customary for the owner of the flocks to supply the shepherd with appropriate clothing for winter and summer, unless the proportion of new births to which the latter was entitled was sufficient for him to acquire these necessities from his own resources. The latter condition was certainly not fulfilled by the terms of Laban's contract with him, so that Jacob's final reminder of the physical conditions under which he served his father-in-law for twenty years may have been as pointed as the rest of his statement.

It is, at all events, clear from all the foregoing that only a thorough appreciation of the herding agreements of the Ancient Near East, and their distinctive phraseology, together with their modern analogues, can bring home the full force of the Jacob-Laban relationship, as described by the former's eloquent account of it, when the two came to the parting of their ways.

---

[22] At this point one must note the possibility that *YBT* I 28 rev. 26 ff. may represent a hypothetical case similar to LH 266, as Clay was himself aware (*ibid.* p. 27), even though his reading and interpretation of the relevant lines are in need of revision. It is questionable whether gu$_4$-nigin-na (lines 27, 33) means "ox of the fold" (or "herd), the more likely meaning being "straying, wandering" (Civil, *AS* 16 p. 8; Deimel *ŠL* 483: 50, also Civil, by private communication). Lines 29-31, however they are to be understood, must nevertheless be read: gaba-ri nam-lugal-la-ni-šè íb-ri-ri(!). In view of the difficulties otherwise posed by this entire text (see *JAOS* 86 p. 357), it will probably prove impossible to unravel the mysteries in this section, but the following are some tentative suggestions: a) gaba-ri is possibly not to be understood here in the sense of "equivalent" (Clay, Civil), since in the next section the scribe uses the less ambiguous gu$_4$-gu$_4$-gim "ox like ox" in the required sense of "equivalent." b) The final verb would be related to RỊ.RI-ga: *miqittu* "fallen, loss," and recalls LH 266 lines 80-81: *mi-qi-it-ti tarbaṣim be-el tarbaṣim i-ma-aḫ-ḫar-ma* (*!*) (cf. variant from ŠU of stela in Sm. 26). c) I suggest that gaba-ri here may stand for *maḫāru* "accept." The general sense of the case would be that the owner of the ox would be required to accept the loss himself, although, admittedly, I cannot derive this sense directly from the syntax. Note also that the case leaves unstated who had been in charge of the ox, a herdsman (thus parallel to LH 266) or someone who hired it (thus parallel to LH 244). For a related lawsuit from Nuzi, cf. Hallo, *JAOS* 87 (1967) 64 fn. 1.

[23] In the Mesopotamian private records and administrative texts losses to wild animals do not form any specific category; they are presumably subsumed under the rubric of *ḫaliqtum* "lost," i. e., unaccounted for, and therefore the responsibility of the shepherd, or under the category of LÁL.DŬ = *ribbatum* ("arrears," i. e., shortages, to be made good by the shepherd) in the administrative records, when the shepherd may be presumed to be responsible for the loss, or, if the shepherd was to be absolved from responsibility—e. g., loss to wild animals occurring at night—this category, which would not have been large, would have been subsumed within the 10 percent or 15 percent natural loss of the older animals that was routinely credited to the shepherd. In either case, it must be presumed that the prevailing practice differed to some degree from that prescribed by the laws of Hammurapi, and that this difference worked to the disadvantage of the shepherd.

ZU EINIGEN HETHITISCHEN WORTBEDEUTUNGEN

JOHANNES FRIEDRICH
BERLIN

GERN HÄTTE DER VERFASSER DAS GEDÄCHTNIS DES VEREWIGTEN DURCH EINEN GRÖSSEREN ARTIKEL, vielleicht aus der gemeinsam umkämpften churritischen Grammatik, geehrt. Verschiedene Umstände gestatten das leider nicht, daher müssen die folgenden, hoffentlich auch nicht ganz nutzlosen, Kleinigkeiten zum hethitischen Lexikon genügen, um den guten Willen zu beweisen.

1. *tarra-* und *tari̯i̯a-*

Um die Bedeutung des Mediums *tarra-* ist schon mehrfach gerungen worden: der Verf. dachte in seinen Staatsverträgen I (1926) S. 153 an "besorgt sein, sich kümmern," Sommer HAB (1938) S. 192[5] an "imstande sein, können;—bezwingen(?)," Güterbock Oriens 10 (1957) S. 359 an "müde werden," Otten MDOG 94 (1963) S. 20 f. an "versorgen." Wenn der Verf. jetzt die Uebersetzung "sich anstrengen, sich Mühe geben;—besorgt sein um, sorgen für" vorschlägt, so zieht er dabei das gleich zu nennende Verbum *tari̯i̯a-* und das davon weitergebildete *tari̯i̯ašḫa-* herein, das in dem Vokabular KBo I 42 I 19 das akkadische *mānaḫtu* "Anstrengung, Mühe, Sorge" übersetzt.

Die ergiebigste Belegstelle ist nach wie vor § 2 des Kupanta-KAL-Vertrages (Verf., Staatsverträge I S. 106-109). Muršilis Vater Šuppiluliuma hatte dem Mašḫuiluwa, dem Vater des Kupanta-KAL, seine Tochter zur Gattin gegeben, hatte aber sonst keine Zeit, sich sehr um seinen Schutz zu kümmern: E 9 *A.BU.I̯A-ma ta-me-e-da-ni* KUR-*e e-eš-ta* E 10 *na-aš Ú.UL tar-ra-ad-da-at na-aš-ši* EGIR-*an Ú.UL ti-i̯a-at* "mein Vater aber war in einem anderen Lande und bemühte sich nicht und kümmerte sich nicht um ihn."[1] Anders nach dem Regierungsantritt des Muršili: D 12 *nu-uš-ši* EGIR-*an ti-i̯a-nu-un* D 13 *nu-uš-ši* EGIR-*an pa-a-un* "ich kümmerte mich um ihn und sorgte für ihn."[2] Ein weiterer willkommener Beleg ist jetzt das unveröffentliche 2764/c II 13-18 bei Houwinck ten Cate JNES 25, 1966, S. 171. Der sehr fragmentarische Text lässt immerhin erkennen, dass vorher die Gašga Feindseligkeiten unternommen hatten. Daraufhin Muršili: (13) GIM-*an-ma* LUGAL-*uš ki-e* [*ud-da-a-ar* . . . . . ***iš-****ta-ma-aš-šu-un*] (14) *nu tar-ra-aḫ-ḫa-at nam-ma* [. . . . . . .] (15) *nu* ERÍN^{MEŠ} ANŠU.KUR.RA^{MEŠ} *ni-ni-i*[*n-ku-un* . . .] "als ich, der König, aber diese [Worte . . . . hörte], strengte ich mich entsprechend (*nu* . . . *namma*) an [. . . . .] und bot Fusstruppen (und) Wagenkämpfer [auf . . . .]." Wenig ergiebig sind die zwei schon von Güterbock Oriens 10, 359 behandelten Belege, KUB XIII 9 I 6-8, wo Tutḫalija IV. angeredet wird: "Unser Herr, du bist ein Kriegsheld(?), aber im Rechtsstreit zu entscheiden gibst du dir keine Mühe (*Ú.UL tar-ra-at-ta* Z. 8)"[2a] und KUB XV 1 II 14 f. "was ich jetzt zu erledigen mich nicht bemühe (*ar-ḫa a-ni-i̯a-u-u̯a-an-zi Ú.UL tar-ra-aḫ-ḫa-ri*)." Desgleichen KUB XV 32 I 2 f. . . . . *nu ku-it ku-it me-ḫur* ^{LÚ}E[N] (3) *tar-ra-at-ta* "um welche Zeit auch der (Haus-) Herr sich bemüht."

Aus "sich Mühe geben" entwickelt sich die Bedeutung "für etwas sorgen," und so kommt man in KBo XII 38 IV 7 f. . . . SUM-*un* (8) URU$^{\text{DIDLI.ḪI.A}}$ 70 *tar-ra-u-u̯a-zi* zu Ottens Uebersetzung (MDOG 94 S. 21) ". . . gab ich 70 Ortschaften (mit dem Auftrag) zur Versorgung" (*tarrau̯a*(*n*)*zi* Inf. I). Und das Partizip *tarrant-* heisst "angestrengt" oder kann mit Güterbock Oriens 10, 359 durch "müde" übersetzt werden: KBo XV 34 II 14 *nu ma-a-an* ^{LÚ}EN É$^{\textit{TIM}}$ *Ú.UL tar-ra-an-za* "wenn der Hausherr nicht müde (ist)," (kann er am nächsten Morgen noch ein Kultfest veranstalten).

Wichtig für die Abrundung der Bedeutung "sich anstrengen" ist die Tatasche, dass das Verbum *tari̯i̯a-* (*dari̯i̯a-*) mit Goetze in Sturtevants Glossary als *-i̯a-*Ableitung (wie *u̯eššii̯a-* neben *u̯eš*(*š*)- "kleiden" usw.) zu unserem Verbum gehört,[3] also auch "sich anstrengen, sich Mühe

[1] Wörtlich "trat nicht hinter ihn."

[2] Wörtlich "ich trat hinter ihn und ging ihm nach."

[2a] So übersetze ich im Gegensatz zu Otten ZA NF 16, 236 (2. Pers. Sing. Praesens, nicht Praet.).

[3] In seinem Ḫattušiliš (1925) S. 100 hatte Götze *dari̯i̯a-* noch mit "anrufen" übersetzt.

geben" bedeutet (so auch Güterbock Oriens 10, 358 f.). So vor allem KUB XXI 27 IV 38 f. "Ḫattušili hat sich für die Person des Gottes angestrengt (*A.NA* ZI DINGIR^{LIM} (39) *še-ir da-ri-i̯a-at*)." Ferner an den schon von Gurney AAA 27, 100, und Güterbock Oriens 10, 358 f. genannten Belegstellen. Vgl. vor allem noch das Kompositum *anda darii̯a-* KBo IV 12 I 7: ((6) mein Vater legte mich dem Mittannamuwa (7) in die Hand,) *na-aš-mu-kán an-da da-a-ri-i̯a-at* "und der bemühte sich um mich, sorgte für mich." Das Partizip *tarii̯ant-* heisst mit Güterbock Oriens 10, 358 ebenfalls "angestrengt, erschöpft" (KBo II 8 I 26. III 6 III 64. KUB XII 63 I 9. XXIV 3 II 35. 36). Den Schlussstrich unter die Grundbedeutung "sich anstrengen" zieht, wie hier nochmals erwähnt sei, das weitergebildete *tar(r)ii̯ašḫa-*, das im Vokabular KBo I 42 I 19 akkadisch *mānaḫtu* "Anstrengung, Mühe, Sorge" übersetzt.[4]

Sowohl *tarra-* wie *tarii̯a-* haben kausativische Weiterbildungen auf *-nu-*, die sich aber in der Bedeutung etwas unterscheiden: *tarranu-* heist "in Sorge (Kummer) versetzen,"[5] so KUB XXII 37 II 10. XXXIII 9 III 12. BoTU 6 II 4 und vor allem im Kompositum *arḫa tarranu-* KBo III 1 I 6. 16. 26 *nu ut-ne-e ar-ḫa tar-ra-nu-ut* "und er versetzte das Land in äusserste (*arḫa*) Bedrängnis." *tarii̯anu-* (*darii̯anu-*) dagegen heisst mit Güterbock Oriens 10, 358 f. "bemühen, belästigen;—(einen Gott oder Menschen) zur Fürsorge veranlassen, um Fürsorge anflehen." "Belästigen" vor allem KUB XVII 29 II 11. 13 (übersetzt bei Güterbock Oriens 10, 358), "(einen Menschen) angehen, bitten" KUB XIV 3 II 56 (Sommer AU S. 10 f. 128), "(einen Gott) anflehen" KUB VII 60 III 13. BoTU 4 A III 10. 13.

2. *šap-, šapii̯āi-*

Bei Laroche DLL S. 85 sind zwei Verba neben einander genannt, das luwische *šappa-* "écorcer, entwinden," verglichen mit heth. *šippāi-*, und *šapii̯āi-* "récurer, scheuern." Man darf aber wohl beide in ein Verbum zusammenfassen, wie es auch im HW des Verf. geschehen ist, und übersetzen "(Unreinheit von einem Gegenstande) abkratzen, abschaben; (Baumstämme) von Rinde befreien;—(allgemein) abwischen, säubern." Wir haben demnach in der 3. Pers. Sing. Praes. *ša-ap-zi* "er wischt (die Hände des Königs) ab" (vgl. H. El. I^2 § 213a) KUB XXV 36 I 13, 3. Pl. Praes. *š[a-ap-p]a-an-zi* KUB XXXIX 6 I 9. 45 I 10, in der 3. Sing. Praet. das "luwische" 𒑱 *šap-pa-at-ta* "er schälte (die Stangen) ab" KUB VIII 50 III 16 (im neuassyrischen Gilgamesch-Epos Tafel X Kol. III Z. 42 entspricht akkadisch *kapāru* "abschälen"; so schon Verf. ZA NF 5, 56 und Goetze JCS 1, 319[71]), in der 2. Sing. Imp. *šapii̯ai* "säubere" KUB XII 58 I 8 (parallel *parkunu-* "reinigen"), im Genetiv des Verbalsubstantivs *šap-pu-u̯a-aš* "des Abschabens" KUB XXXIX 45 I 11 (Otten Welt des Orients 2, 478 Z. 11), im Partizip *šapii̯ant-* "abgewischt" KUB XII 58 IV 3. 6 (parallel wieder *parkunu-* "reinigen"). XXXIII 69 III 10 ("abgekratztes Salz"), im Iterativ *šap-pí-eš-k-* "wiederholt abwischen" KUB XIII 4 IV 42. Verwandt ist wohl *šippāi-* "schälen, abschaben."

3. *šii̯a-?*

šii̯a- "sich zeigen," im HW im Anschluss an andere Forscher angenommen, im Nachtrag dazu angezweifelt, existiert sicher nicht.[6] Vielmehr ist mit Güterbock ZA NF 10, 62 nur ein Medium zu *šāi-, šii̯a-* "drücken" anzusetzen. Also BoTU 4 A II 5. 14. 16 3. Sing. Praes. *šii̯ari* und 3. Sing. Praet. *šii̯ati* "(das Blut) drückt(e) sich (hervor), spritzt(e) (hervor)"[7]) und KUB VIII 1 II 3 3. Plur. Praes. UR.MAḪ$^{ḪI.A}$ *ši-i̯a-an-da-ri* "Löwen werden (aus dem Dickicht) hervorbrechen" (nur ungenaue, nicht mit Weidner a. a. O. falsche Uebersetzung von akkad. *innamdaru* "sie werden wüten" (von *nadāru*)).

4. *uleš-*

Der Verbalstamm sei in dieser Form angesetzt, denn das im HW angegebene *ulāi-* KUB XXIX 1 I 34 ist in Lesung und Deutung doch zu unsicher, um mit herangezogen zu werden. Eine 3. Pers. Praet. *ulešta* begegnet BoTU 23 A I 32 f. *nu* ^{I}*Zi-da-an-ta-a[š A.]NA* ^{I}*Ḫa-an-ti-li [kat-ta]-an* (33) *[ša-ra-]a ú-li-eš-ta . . . . nu-kán* ^{I}*Mur-ši-li-in ku-e[n-nir]* "Zidanta schlich sich von unten herauf an Ḫantili heran, ... und sie töteten

[4] Belegt auch als *tarrii̯ašḫaš* KUB XXIV 3 I 48, als *darii̯ašḫaš* KUB XXXI 127 I 25.

[5] Güterbock Oriens 10, 359 "ermüden."

[6] Weidners "sich zeigen" < "gesehen werden" AfK 1 S. 61 war wohl ursprünglich als IGI-*i̯a-* von IGI "Auge" aufgefasst.

[7] *parā šii̯ati* KUB XXXVI 101 II 9 in zerstörtem Zusammenhang.

den Muršili." Ferner *ulišta* (unter Auslassung des unergiebigen Beleges KUB VI 34, 20) im Telipinu-Mythus KUB XVII 10 I 12 f. *ᵈTe-li-pí-nu-ša pa-it mar-mar-ri an-da-an* (13) *ú-li-iš-ta še-e-ra-aš-ši-ša-an ḫa-li-en-zu ḫu-u̯a-i-iš* " und Telipinu ging (und) schlüpfte (tauchte) in den Sumpf(?), und über ihm wucherte(n) (lief(en)) Wasserlinse(n)."[8] Ferner in dem Mythus vom Königtum im Himmel (KUB XXXIII 120; Güterbock, Kumarbi S. 7), wo ein homoerotischer Akt zwischen Kumarbi und Anu in die Worte gefasst ist (Z. 25 f.) LÚ-*na-tar-še-it-kán A.NA ᵈKu-mar-bi* ŠÀ-*ŠU an-da* ZABAR[9] (26) *ma-a-an ú-li-iš-ta* " seine Mannheit (sein Sperma) schlüpfte in das Innere Kumarbis wie Erz." Dass das durch den Mund geschieht, ergibt sich aus dem Folgenden, wo Kumarbi das zu sich Genommene wieder ausspeit (Z. 39 f. nach Lesung und Ergänzung von Schulers *ḫa-at-ta-an-za* LUGAL-*uš* KA × U-*kán pa-ra-a al-la-pa-aḫ-ḫa-aš* UŠ$_{12}$(!)[10] [LÚ-*na-tar-ra*] (40) [*a*]*n*[-*d*]*a im-mi-i̯a-an* " der kluge König spie aus dem Munde Speichel und Sperma vermischt aus "). Für das Verbum *uleš-* scheint nach den drei Belegstellen die Uebersetzung " schlüpfen, schleichen " angebracht.

Nachtrag zu 2:

Den Verbalstamm šap- wird H. G. Güterbock demnächst in der Revue Hittite behandeln und möchte ihm die Bedeutung " to hit, beat " geben. Ich habe meine Darstellung unverändert gelassen und überlasse dem Leser die Entscheidung zwischen Güterbock und mir.

[8] Zur Bedeutung von *ḫalenzu* s. Otten Baghdader Mitteilungen 3, 94 f.

[9] Lesung von Goetze JAOS 69, 181.

[10] Nach von Schuler Zeichen ŠL 17, 3, an der Bruchstelle beschädigt (in Boğazköy sonst anscheinend nicht belegt).

AN OLD BABYLONIAN LIST OF AMORITES

I. J. GELB
THE UNIVERSITY OF CHICAGO

Introduction

IT IS A WELL KNOWN FACT that in the Ur III period persons bearing the designation MAR.TU (= Amorite) have names which are frequently noncommittal linguistically, such as names with the suffix *-ānum* in *Ḫumrānum* or *Nukrānum*, while in the Old Babylonian period persons who bear good West Semitic names, such as *Šamšu-'iluna* or *Jašma'-Haddu*, do not bear the designation MAR.TU in the great majority of cases. This has led some scholars to the assumption that only the names of the Ur III period are to be called " Amorite," while the names of the Old Babylonian period represent a different ethno-linguistic unit, which they have called " East Canaanite " because of its alleged close relationship to the " West Canaanites " of Palestine and parts of Syria.

In my article " The Early History of the West Semitic Peoples," *JCS* XV (1961) pp. 27-47, especially pp. 33 f., I not only expressed my conviction that the degree of linguistic relationship between the Ur III Amorites and the West Semites of the Old Babylonian period has been seriously underestimated by all the scholars who have written on the subject, but also concluded that for all practical intents and purposes the two groups are identical and represent the same people, namely the Amorites. This conclusion was based to a large extent on the study of West Semitic names of persons bearing the designation MAR.TU in the early Old Babylonian texts from Isin (*BIN* IX) and from Tell Asmar (unpublished). For many of the problems discussed in this article, see also Giorgio Buccellati, *The Amorites of the Ur III Period* (Naples, 1966, issued at end of 1967).

Tablet TA 1930, 615

The aim of this brief note is to make known the unique and most important of these unpublished Tell Asmar texts, namely TA 1930, 615. This tablet belongs to the Iraq Museum in Baghdad, but is now, together with the other Tell Asmar tablets, on loan to the Oriental Institute, Chicago. The text lists the names of twenty-nine individuals, all bearing good West Semitic names and the designation MAR.TU. The tablet was excavated at Tell Asmar, ancient Eshnunna, on February 6, 1931 at the locus P 31, 1, with the notation " burnt palace or beneath it." According to *OIP* XLIII Pl. II, the locus P 31, 1 was in the area of the southeastern corner of the so-called " Gimil-Sin temple." From *OIP* XLIII pp. 46 f., we learn that the great conflagration which destroyed the temple took place " in one of the reigns immediately succeeding that of Bilalama, probably that of Isharramashu." This would place our tablet about forty years after the fall of the Third Dynasty of Ur. For the general chronological situation see also *OIP* XLIII pp. 196 f.

The mottled, light to dark brown tablet, measuring 83 × 61 × 22 millimeters, is well preserved, and the reading of the two-column text offers little difficulty. The small, destroyed portions of its top and left side can be easily reconstructed from the context; the only doubtful point concerns line 43 at the end of Reverse i, which could represent a line of writing or an empty space. Individual lines are separated by rulings, at times quite indistinct. Sections are separated by open space in three cases, after lines 43, 44, and 47.

Transliteration and Translation

i	1.	[*1 dumu? Ab-da-El*]	[1 son? of ʿAbd-ʾEl],
	2.	[*1 dumu?* PN]	[1 son? of PN],
	3.	[*1 dumu? X*]-⌜*x*⌝[a]-*El*	[1 son? of . . . .⌝-ʾEl,
	4.	[*1 du*]*mu Mu-ti-me-El*	[1 s]on of Mutī-me-ʾEl,
	5.	[*1 š*]*eš Šu-mu-um*	[1 br]other of Śumum,
	6.	[*1 du*]*mu Ma-aš-da-kum*	[1 s]on of Maśdakum,
	7.	[*1 š*]*eš Ì-lí-ma-da*	[1 br]other of ʾIlī-maʿda?,
	8.	7	7
	9.	[*ba-a*]*b-tum Ab-da-El-me*	[the sec]tion of ʿAbd-ʾEl.
	10.	*1 dumu Ik-zu-El*	1 son of Jiksû-ʾEl,
	11.	*1 dumu Na-ma-El*	1 son of Naʿma-ʾEl,
	12.	[*1*] *dumu I-me-ri-nu-um*	[1] son of ʾImmerānum?,
	13.	[*1*] *dumu Na-*gi_4*-a-nu-um*	[1] son of Nāgihānum,
	14.	[*1 du*]*mu I-ba-um*	[1 s]on of Jibâʾum,
	15.	[*1 dumu*] ⌜*Za?-i*⌝?[b]*-nu-um*	[1 son of] ⌜Zāji⌝num?,
ii	16.	[*1 dumu* PN]	[1 son of PN],
	17.	⌜*1 dumu Ku?-na*⌝?[c]-[*nu?-um*]?	⌜1 son of Kûnānum]?,
	18.	*1 dumu Ḫu-na-nu-um*	1 son of Ḥunnānum,
	19.	9	9
	20.	*ba-ab-tum Ik-zu-El-me*	the section of Jiksû-ʾEl.
	21.	*1 dumu Mi-il-ki-la-El*	1 son of Milkī-la-ʾEl,
	22.	*1 Ú-ga-zum*	1 ʾUgāzum?,
	23.	*1 Ša-la-nu-um*	1 Śaʾlānum
	24.	*1 Mu-ut-Ga-bi-id*	1 Mut-Kabid,
	25.	*1 dumu Ib-li-nu-um*	1 son of Jiblimum?,
	26.	*1 dumu Ba-lu-zum*	1 son of Palūsum,
	27.	*1 dumu I-la-n*[*u?-um*]?	1 son of ʾIlān[um]?,
	28.	*1 šeš Za-ma-*[*ra*]?-*nu-*[*um*]	1 brother of Ḏama[rā]nu[m]?,

Rev. i	29.	*1 Ú-da-*[*ma*]? *šeš* NI-[. . . .]	1 Hûdâ-[ma]? brother of NI-[. . . .],
	30.	*1 dumu* E-[. . . .]	1 son of E-[. . . .],
	31.	*10*	10
	32.	*ba-ab-tum M*[*i-il-k*]*i*-[*la-E*]*l-me* [d]	the section of M[ilk]ī-[la-'E]l.
	33.	*nigín-ba 26* [e] MAR.TU	Total: 26 Amorites,
	34.	*e*[f]*-lu-tum-me*	deputies.
	35.	*1* MAR.TU	1 Amorite,
	36.	*ba-ab-tum Ba-ša-nu-um*	the section of Bâšānum,
	37.	*a-ab-ba-ta*	from the Sea.
	38.	*gìr* [d]*Innin-e-ru-um-ma-za-ri*	Control of Innin-êrum-maṣṣarī.
	39.	*1 dumu Mu-ut-Na-nu-um*	1 son of Mut-Nanum,
	40.	*1 šeš Ma-ni-um*	1 brother of Manijum,
	41.	*ba-ab-tum Ab-da-El-me*	the section of 'Abd-'El.
	42.	[. . . .]	[from . . . .]
	43.	[. . . .]?	[. . . .]?
Rev. ii		(small space)	
	44.	[*nigín-ba 3*] *daḫ-ḫu-me*	[Total: 3] supernumeraries.
		(large space)	
	45.	*šu-nigín 30 lá 1* MAR.TU	(Grand) Total: 29 Amorites
	46.	[*ur*]*u?*[g]KI*-a tuš*[h]*-a-me*	residing in the [cit]y.
	47.	[*gì*]*r Lú-ša-lim*	[Contr]ol of Lu-šalim.
		(large space)	
	48.	[*iti N*]*i-ig-mu-um ud 22-kam*	[Month of N]iqmum, 22nd day,
	49.	[*mu* . . .].[i]	[the year when . . .].
	50.	[. . . .]	[. . . .]
	51.	[. . . .]	[. . . .]

Photographs of TA 1930, 615 are reproduced on page 45.

The early Old Babylonian date of the text agrees well with its system of writing, in which signs with a voiced consonant stand for voiceless phonemes. Cf. *Mu-ut-Ga-bi-id /Mut-Kabid/* (line 24), *Ba-lu-zum /Palūsum/* (line 26), etc. Similar conclusions can be drawn from the single-consonant writing of *I-me-ri-nu-um /'Immerānum?/* (line 12), *Ḫu-na-nu-um /Ḥunnānum/* (line 18), *e-lu-tum /ellūtum/* (line 34), and *-ma-za-ri /maṣṣarī/* (line 38).

The text is written in Sumerian, not Akkadian. This is clear from the occurrence of *a-ab-ba-ta* "from the Sea" (line 37) *nigín-ba* "its total" (lines 33 and [44]), ⌜*ur*⌝*u?* KI*-a tuš-a-me* "(Amorites) residing in the city" (line 46), *ba-ab-tum* PN*-me* "(the men of) the section of PN" (lines 9, 20, 32, 36, and 41; instead of Akkadian *ba-ba-at* PN), and by the plural suffix

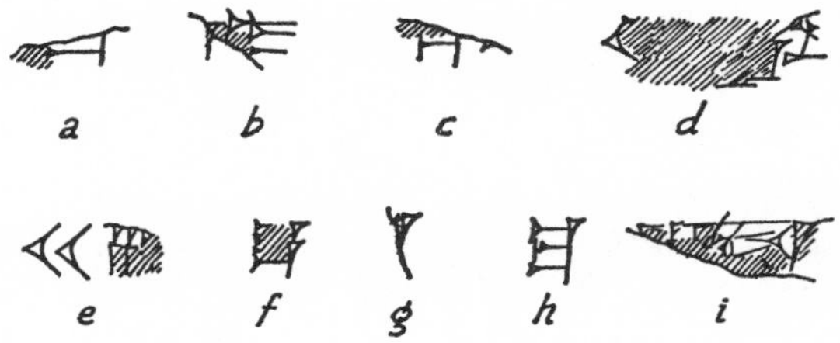

-me in the above cases as well as in *e-lu-tum-me* "deputies" (line 34) and *daḫ-ḫu-me* "supernumeraries" (line 44).

Contents

The whole text can be subdivided into four parts, as reconstructed just below:

1)	*1 dumu/šeš*	PNs		*7*	*bâbtum*	PN-*me*
	1 dumu	PNs		*9*	*bâbtum*	PN-*me*
	1 dumu/šeš	PNs; PNs		*10*	*bâbtum*	PN-*me*
			nigín-ba	*26*	MAR.TU	*e-lu-tum-me*
2)	*1* MAR.TU			*1*	*bâbtum*	PN *a-ab-ba-ta*
						gìr PN
	1 dumu/šeš	PNs		*2*	*bâbtum*	PN [. . . .-*ta*]?
			[*nigín-ba*	*3*]		*daḫ-ḫu-me*
3)			*šu-nigín*	*29*	MAR.TU	[*ur*]*u*?^{KI}*-a tuš-a-me*
						[*gì*]*r* PN
4)						**Date**

The first part (lines 1-34) lists three groups of 7, 9, and 10 individuals, each group assigned to a *bâbtum* "section." The family relationships of each individual are noted as *dumu* PN "son of PN," *šeš PN* "brother of PN," or simply as PN (only in lines 22-24). Instead of *dumu*, the reconstruction *šeš* is also possible in lines 1-3. A unique formulation is found in PN *šeš* PN (line 29). The individuals listed after the word *bâbtum* are also the first ones named in each section.

All individuals listed in the three sections of the first part of the text are subsumed as *26* MAR.TU *e-lu-tum-me* (lines 33-34). The reading of the sign *e*, while partially shaded, is practically assured. For the interpretation of *e-lu-tum-me* see below.

The second part of the text (lines 35-44) lists three individuals assigned to two sections. One unnamed Amorite was assigned to the *bâbtum* of *Bâšānum*. While MAR.TU is a common personal name in the Ur III texts, such an interpretation is impossible in our text, where all persons are Amorites. The Amorite or the section is said to come *a-ab-ba-ta* "from the Sea" and was under the control of the Akkadian *Innin-êrum-maṣṣarī*. Two individuals, designated as *dumu/šeš* PN, were assigned to the *bâbtum* of *'Abd-'El*, who is also listed in line 9 of the first section. Line 42, with barely preserved traces of signs, and line 43, now completely missing, may have contained a geographic term designating the origin of the individuals in the second section, parallel to *a-ab-ba-ta* "from the Sea," occurring within the first section.

All individuals in the two sections of the second part of the text are subsumed as [*3*] *daḫ-ḫu-me* "[3] supernumeraries" (line 44).

The first two lines of the third part (lines 45-46) read *šu-nigín 30 lá 1* MAR.TU [*ur*]*u*?^{KI}*-a tuš-a-me* "the (grand) total: 29 Amorites residing in the city." The broken sign at the beginning of line 46 is not longer (despite its appearance on the photo!) than the compound sign *šu-nigín* just above. The preserved traces of the sign fit the reading *uru* very well.

The assigning of all individuals listed in the text was done under the control of the Akkadian *Lu-šalim* (line 47).

The fourth part (lines 48-51) gives the date "22nd day of Niqmum," a well known month in the calendar of the Diyala Region in the Old Babylonian period. Unfortunately nothing is preserved of the year date except traces at the end of line 49, possibly to be read as *il*.

Of the twenty-nine individuals, only three are listed by their real names (lines 22-24), one man in addition to his name bears the connotation "brother of PN" (line 29), and one individual is called simply MAR.TU (line 35). All other individuals are simply connoted as *dumu* PN "son of PN" or *šeš* PN "brother of PN."

Of the twenty-nine Amorites, twenty-six are called MAR.TU *e-lu-tum-me* (lines 33-34) and three *daḫ-ḫu-me* (line 44).

The only attested meaning of *daḫ-ḫu* in Sumerian contexts known to me is "additional," "supplementary," or "supernumerary," not "replacement" or "substitute." Thus the *3 máš daḫ-ḫu* ^{d}*Gu-la* "3 supplementary goats (for) Gula" (Jacobsen, *CTC* 8:11) are issued in addition to other animals destined for Gula (lines 9 f.). Cf. also *6 udu 2 máš* which are *daḫ-ḫu lugal* (Lau, *OBTR* ii 8); *še-ba* "barley rations" and *še-ba daḫ-ḫu* (Contenau, *CHÉU* 28:1 f., and similarly *YOS* IV 284:1); and PNs *libir-àm* and *daḫ-ḫu-me* in a text listing rations for prisoners of war (*TCL* V 6039 *passim*, and similarly in *UET* III 1391 liii). The meaning "addition" or "reserve" was given to this word by Jacobsen, *OIC* 13 p. 57. This meaning is confirmed by the equation of Sumerian *daḫ* with Akkadian *aṣābu* and *ruddû* "to add," found in lexical texts (*ŠL* 169, 2 and 6). It is, of course, possible that from the original meaning "additional," "supernumerary," a secondary meaning "substitute," "replacement" could have developed by the Old Babylonian period. This meaning, favored by Ungnad, *ZA* XXXI (1917/18) pp. 56-57, and, in later years, by Landsberger, *JCS* IX (1955) pp. 122 and 127, is supported by the equation of *daḫ* with *ri'ābu* "to replace" in a lexical text (*ŠL* 169, 5). Even such a derived meaning as "assistant" is possible, to judge from the equation of *daḫ* with *râṣu* and *rîṣu* "help(er)" (*ŠL* 169, 7 and 8). The different classes of soldiers/workers are indicated by the sequence *erín*, *daḫ*, and SI (*dirig*$_{x}$) often found in military rolls, such as *CT* VI 15-18, Grant, *Cuneiform Documents in the Smith College Library* No. 271, and in unpublished texts from Khafaje (see *OIC* 13 p. 57).

The word *e-lu-tum* appears to be Akkadian *ellūtum*, plural of *ellum*. The meanings of *ellum* given in the Akkadian dictionaries are: "clean," "pure," "holy," "sacred," "free of claims," "free man," and "noble." None of these meanings seem to fit our context. On the other hand, *ellum* together with *namrum* are frequent synonyms of *ebbum*. The latter word, translated as "trustworthy" (*CAD* E p. 4a) or "verlässlich" (von Soden, *AHWB* p. 180b), is used in a specialized sense, particularly in the Mari texts, for persons charged with taking census. This may very well be the meaning of *e-lu-tum-me* in our text. The translation "deputy" is based on my understanding of the semantic evolution of the word, from "pure" that is, purified in a sacred sense or sworn in, to "trustworthy," "entrusted," or "deputized" to perform certain sensitive tasks which otherwise easily invited graft, such as census-taking for the purpose of taxation or conscription.

To judge from the meanings of the two words just discussed, our text deals probably with the appointment of twenty-six *ellūtum* and three *daḫḫu* delegated to perform certain duties involved in conscription and/or taxation, as amply illustrated by Mesopotamian texts from the Pre-Sargonic period on. It can be taken for granted that our Amorites performed or were to perform these duties among their own, that is, among the Amorite people living in certain unspecified parts of the country.

Three more points connected with the Amorites need stressing here:

The derivation of Amorite(s) *a-ab-ba-ta* "from the Sea" (line 37), that is, from the Sea-Land or from a land across the Sea, yields for the first time evidence for the Amorites originating not in the West but in the south-eastern part of Mesopotamia, near the Persian Gulf. This was the nomadic area par excellence throughout the whole of ancient Mesopotamian history.

As will be seen from the next sections, all the Amorites listed in our text bear good Amorite names (with the possible exception of *Ì-lí-ma-da*). What that implies is that our Amorites represented an unassimilated ethno-linguistic unit, still uninfluenced by the dominant Babylonian ethnos.

These Amorites, assigned to five different *bâbtum* (lines 9, 20, 32, 36, and 41), resided in the city (line 46), in this case probably Eshnunna. Since the five *bâbtum* are named after individuals, the word *bâbtum* cannot denote as large a section as "a quarter of a city" (as interpreted in *CAD* B p. 10a and von Soden, *AHWB* p. 94b), but small encampments, each probably restricted to individuals belonging to a certain tribal grouping.

Personal Names

Of our text's thirty-one personal names, twenty-nine are Amorite. The other two names, both following the term *gìr* "under the control," are Akkadian, and thus represent the Akkadian ruling class.

The first of the Akkadian names, ^{d}*Innin-e-ru-um-ma-za-ri* (line 38) is to be interpreted as *Innin* + *êrum-maṣṣarī* "Innin + êrum is my guard(ian)," based on parallels of the type *Ì-lí-*

ma-za-ri "my god is my guard(ian)" (Istanbul Museum 31172, Old Babylonian; A 21982, Old Babylonian). The compound divine name *Innin* + *êrum* is of the *Nintul-arṣatum* type (*MAD* III p. 66). For names composed with the root *ʿWR* "to be watchful" see *MAD* III p. 59 and von Soden, *AHWB* p. 247a. A PN *I-nin-e-ru-um* occurs on Iraq Museum 43613, Sargonic.

Lú-ša-lim, the second Akkadian name (line 47), written *Lú-ša-lim* and *Lú-šá-lim* in Old Akkadian, is to be interpreted as *Lu-šalim* "may he be well," similar to *Lu-damiq*, *Lu-dannat*, *Lu-dârî*, etc. (*MAD* III pp. 155 f.).

Twenty-six of the twenty-nine Amorite names are listed below. Not listed are two completely destroyed names (lines 2 and 16) and two names with only the first sign preserved (line 29). The notes following the list are limited to names whose interpretation requires further justification.

Ab-da-El	/*ʿAbd-ʾEl*/	(lines [1], 9, 41)
Ba-lu-zum	/*Palūsum*/	(line 26)
Ba-ša-nu-um	/*Bâšānum*/	(line 36)
Ḫu-na-nu-um	/*Ḫunnānum*/	(line 18)
I-ba-um	/*Jibâʾum*/	(line 14)
Ib-li-nu-um	/*Jiblimum*/?	(line 25)
Ik-zu-El	/*Jiksû-ʾEl*/	(lines 10, 20)
I-la-n[*u*?-*um*]?	/*ʾIlānum*/	(line 27)
Ì-lí-ma-da	/*ʾIlī-maʾda*/?	(line 7)
I-me-ri-nu-um	/*ʾImmerānum*/?	(line 12)
⌜*Ku*?-*na*⌝?-[*nu*?-*um*]?	/*Kûnānum*/?	(line 17)
Ma-ni-um	/*Manijum*/	(line 40)
Ma-aš-da-kum	/*Maśdakum*/	(line 6)
Mi-il-ki-la-El	/*Milkī-la-ʾEl*/	(lines 21, ⌜32⌝)
Mu-ut-Ga-bi-id	/*Mut-Kabid*/	(line 24)
Mu-ut-Na-nu-um	/*Mut-Nanum*/	(line 39)
Mu-ti-me-El	/*Mutī-me-ʾEl*/	(line 4)
Na-gi$_4$*-a-nu-um*	/*Nāgihānum*/	(line 13)
Na-ma-El	/*Naʿma-ʾEl*/	(line 11)
Ša-la-nu-um	/*Śaʾlānum*/	(line 23)
Šu-mu-um	/*Śumum*/	(line 5)
Ú-da-[*ma*]?	/*Hûdâ-ma*/?	(line 29)
Ú-ga-zum	/*ʾUgāzum*/?	(line 22)
⌜*Za*?-*i*⌝?-*nu-um*	/*Zājinum*/?	(line 15)
Za-ma-[*ra*]?-*nu-*[*um*]	/*Ḏamarānum*/?	(line 28)
[*X*]-⌜*x*⌝-*El*	/. . . .-*ʾEl*/	(line 3)

With the PN *Ab-da-El* /*ʿAbd-ʾEl*/ cf. *Ab-te-Il* /*ʿAbd-ʾIl*/ MAR.TU at Isin (*BIN* IX 316:13).

With *Ba-lu-zum* /*Palūsum*/ cf. *Ia-ap-lu-zum* (*JCS* XIV 24 No. 49:4), *Pa-al-zu-um* (*JCS* IX 65:18), *Pu-ul-zu-na-*ᵈIM /*Pulsuna-Haddu*/ (unpublished), and, for the root consonants, Ugaritic *Bil-zi-ia* = *PLSJ* (*MRS* VI p. 253), etc.

I know of no parallels to our *Ib-li-nu-um*, unless this is a scribal misunderstanding for *Ib-li-mu-um*, comparable with *Ja-ab-li-mu-um* (*CT* XLV 6:5 +) and *Bu-ul-ma-na-*ᵈIM (*ARM* I 41:18, 30). The root *BLM* or *PLM* is unknown to me.

Ik-zu-El MAR.TU occurs also in TA 1930, 244. My interpretation of the first element as *Jiksû-* is based on the existence of *KSW* (besides *KSJ*) "to cover," "to bind" in other Semitic languages, such as South Arabic and Akkadian.

Ì-lí-ma-da is the only name in the list of twenty-nine Amorites which may be Akkadian. Cf. MA.DA-*ì-lí* or *Ma-da-ì-lí* among Ur III names in *MAD* III p. 169. Note, however, DINGIR-*ma-di* (*ARM* IX 291:42), *Ì-lí-ma-di* (*JCS* XIII p. 116 No. 33:19), *Ì-lí-ma-di-a-aḫ* (*RA* LII p. 214 No. 1:8), *Ì-lí-ma-da-ḫi* (*RA* LIII p. 83 No. 14:7), and *Ì-lí-ma-da*!-*ḫa* (*VAS* VIII 14:4) occurring with many other Amorite names in the Old Babylonian period.

I do not know of a better interpretation of *I-me-ri-nu-um* than as /*ʾImmerānum*/, considering the writing with *ri* as a scribal error. Names based on this noun are common in Semitic languages.

Ma-ni-um MAR.TU and *Ma-ni-Il* MAR.TU are found in Ur III texts cited in *MAD* III p. 179.

For the infix *-ak-* in *Ma-aš-da-kum* cf. *Ša-ap-ra-kum* at Mari (*RA* XLIX p. 18 v 11) and *Ša-ba-ar-kum* MAR.TU in Ur III (*PDTI* 335:7).

For the divine name *Kabid* in *Mu-ut-Ga-bi-id* /*Mut-Kabid*/ cf. *I-bi-iš-Ka-bi-id* /*Jîbiś-Kabid*/ in an unpublished Old Babylonian text from Kisurra.

For the divine name *Nanum in Mu-ut-Na-nu-um* /*Mut-Nanum*/ cf. *Jâtir-Nanum* (*passim* at Mari), and, for the structure, *Mut-Kabid* (just above) or *Mut-Dagān* (*passim* at Mari).

I prefer to interpret *Na-gi*$_4$*-a-nu-um* as /*Nāgihānum*/ from the root *NGH* "to shine," because of the spelling with *Ḫ* in *Na-ki-ḫu-um* (*TIM* III 31:17 +), *Na-ki-ḫi-im* (*TIM* III 77:5a), and ᶠ*Ni-ig-ḫa-tum* (*ARM* II 66:3), rather than as /*Naqijānum*/ from the root *NQJ* "to be pure."

The reconstruction of *Ú-da-*[. . . .] to *Ú-da-*[*ma*]? is based on comparison with *Ú-da-ma*

Reverse

Right edge

Obverse

TA 1930-615. Reverse is inverted to show alignment with the Right edge.

MAR.TU in a text from Isin (*BIN* IX 414:5). Very doubtful.

I know of no parallels to the name spelled *Ú-ga-zum*, perhaps /*Juqāṣum*/.

Language of Personal Names

The linguistic data deduced from the analysis of the Amorite personal names of TA 1930, 615 fit in every respect the interpretation of the Amorite language as presented in my brief study "La lingua degli Amoriti," *Accademia Nazionale dei Lincei. Rendiconti della Classe di Scienze morali, storiche e filologiche* Serie VIII, volume XIII (1958) pp. 143-164. A much larger work on the Amorite language, prepared with the help of computers, is now in preparation. Note the following:

A before *'e* is preserved in *Mi-il-ki-la-El* /*Milkī-la-'El*/, but is assimilated to *e* in *Mu-ti-me-El* /*Mutī-me-'El*/, as elsewhere in Amorite.

The careful differentiation of the two phonemes *š* and *ś* in Amorite areas, such as Mari or Chagar Bazar, is not followed regularly in Babylonian areas, as in our *Ša-la-nu-um* /*Śa'lānum*/, *Šu-mu-um* /*Śumum*/, and *Ba-ša-nu-um* /*Bâšānum*/.

As many as six names have the name of the god *'El* as the second element: *'Abd-'El, Jiksû-'El, Milkī-la-'El, Mutī-me-'El, Na'ma-'El*, and . . . .-*'El*. Other divine names occurring in our text are *Kabid* in *Mut-Kabid*, and *Nanum* in *Mut-Nanum*.

Nominal formation, *jaqtul* (hypocoristica): *Jibâ'um* and *Jiblimum*?

Nominal formation, *-ān*: *Bâšānum, Ḫunnānum, 'Ilānum?, Kûnānum?, Nāgihānum, Śa'lānum, Ḏamarānum?*, and perhaps *'Immerānum*.

Nominal formation, *-ak-*: *Maśdakum*.

Noun, active participle, *qātil*: *Nāgihānum* and *Zājinum*?

Noun, passive participle, *qatūl*: *Palūsum*.

Noun, passive participle: *qatil*: *Manijum*.

Noun, passive participle, *qatl*: *Bâšānum* and *Śa'lānum*.

Noun, nominative singular + mimation, *-um*: *passim*.

Noun, construct state, zero ending: *'Abd-'El, Mut-Kabid*, and *Mut-Nanum*.

Noun, predicate state, *-a*: *Na'ma-'El* and perhaps *'Ilī-ma'da*.

Noun, pronominal suffix first person singular, *-ī*: *Milkī-la-'El, Mutī-me-'El*, and perhaps *'Ilī-ma'da*.

Verb, prefix third person masculine singular, *ji*: *Jibâ'um, Jiblimum?*, and *Jiksû-'El*. The spelling with *ji-*, instead of *ja-*, is not an outcome of the Barth-Ungnad law, but due to the influence of the Akkadian milieu.

Particle *-la-*: *Milkī-la-'El*.

Particle *-ma-*: *Mutī-me-'El*.

Conclusion

In concluding I should like to comment on the fate of scholarship in our field, as due to the haphazards of discovery. As noted at the beginning of this article, it has been fashionable, until quite recently, to separate the Ur III Amorites, that is, the ethno-linguistic unit as reconstructed on the basis of names of persons bearing the designation "Amorite," from the so-called East Canaanites, that is, the West Semites of the Old Babylonian period, who generally do not bear the designation "Amorite." Now the tablet here published offers the missing link between the Ur III and Old Babylonian periods, by providing us with a list of persons bearing good West Semitic names plus the designation "Amorite," thus proving beyond the shadow of any doubt that both the Ur III and Old Babylonian West Semites belonged to one and the same ethnic grouping, namely Amorites. I venture to say that had this unique text become known some forty years ago, the term "East Canaanite" would never have entered scholarly circles and the wasteful arguments and controversies of the ensuing years would have been avoided. It must be said to the credit of Édouard Dhorme that his clear-cut distinction between the Amorites of the Ur III and Old Babylonian periods, on the one hand, and the later Canaanites, on the other, was just as valid in his day as it is now. See Dhorme's "La langue de Canaan" and "Les Amorréens à propos d'un livre récent," first published in a series of articles in *Révue biblique* 1913, 1914, 1928, 1930, and 1931, later republished in *Recueil Édouard Dhorme* (Paris, 1951) pp. 81-165 and 405-487.

REFLEXES OF SARGON IN ISAIAH AFTER 715 B. C. E.*

H. L. Ginsberg
Jewish Theological Seminary of America

Isaiah's attitude toward Assyria is treated, along with other matters, in a paper which I titled 'From Isaiah's Diary.'[1] As 'Isaiah's Diary' I designated the block of text Isa 1-12 because it is arranged, in principle, chronologically (the deviations are few and accountable) and consequently reads, in the light of history, like a prophet's journal. It ends with the year 715.

All the passages which I believe to be Isaian reflexes of Sargonic history after 715 are contained in what may be called 'the Book of Pronouncements' (*maśśǭ'*[ōṯ], formerly rendered 'burden[s]'), comprising chs. 13-23 *minus* 17:12—18:7[2] *plus* 30:6-7. There is no chronological sequence here, as can be seen from the fact that the 'pronouncement' 14:28 ff. is dated in the year of the death of King Ahaz, which was in no case earlier than 726, while the 'pronouncement' ch. 17 antedates (though surely not by many months) the fall of Damascus in 732.[3] Often, however, the content becomes a very sure guide to a dating when examined by the light that is shed by our present knowledge of late eighth century history. In a larger work I shall endeavor to show that (apart from the obvious case of ch. 20) at least four prophecies in these chapters were occasioned by developments in the career of King Sargon II of Assyria, but here I shall limit myself to two cases for which the evidence is overwhelming.

1. From the Year 712

The connection of the prophetic narrative ch. 20 with the Assyrian expedition of 712 to Ashdod is vouched for by the text, and is not disputed. That the 'pronouncement' 22:1-14 is likewise connected with the Ashdod-led and Egypt-backed South Palestinian rebellion of 713-2 is only a minority view,[4] but it can be reinforced with telling new arguments.

I have observed elsewhere,[5] giving detailed proofs and credit to predecessors whose ideas I borrowed or adapted, that

(1) V. 1 may be paraphrased, 'Why this exhibition of sorrow,[6] O city famed for gaiety?' Verses 1-3 are Isaiah's sarcastic consolation of Jerusalem in an *anticipated* mourning and v. 4 his genuine grief over the, likewise future, disaster which shall be the occasion for that mourning.

---

* On the transliteration of Hebrew in this paper: The open quality of the vowels *e* and *o* is only marked when they are long; the closed quality, only when they are short. The short quantity of vowels is not noted diacritically except in the case of ḥaṭephs; simple shwas, silent and vocal alike, are without notation.

[1] 'Ọz lḎǭwīḏ (Biblical Studies Presented to David Ben Gurion on his 77th Birthday [Publications of the Israel Society for Biblical Studies XV]), Jerusalem 1962, pp. 335-50 (Hebrew).

[2] This passage comprises two ahs (*hōi*) whose proper location is with the four *ah* chapters 28-31, say (in view of the resemblance of 17:12-14 to ch. 29) between chs. 29 and 30. If the in every way isolated 'ah' 10:1-4a is similarly prefaced to the somewhat related section 28:1 ff., we obtain a heptad of ahs. (On 5:8-24 as an original heptad of ahs, see Mordecai M. Kaplan Jubilee Volume, New York 1953, English Section, 259 end [JBL 69 (1950): 53-54)].

[3] For our purpose, it is more important to realize that the order in which the Pronouncements appear is not chronological than to find out what it is. The latter, however, is comparatively simple: we have two series of prophecies, each following the order Mesopotamia, the West, Egypt. (Cf. Y. Kaufmann, *Tōlḏōṯ hǫ'ĕmūnǭ hayyiśr'ēlīṯ* III, pp. 169-70.)

[4] O. Procksch, Jesaia I, 1930, pp. 276-7, 287, 293-4 (especially these last two pages), cites Ewald and Kleinert as predecessors in preferring a dating in the reign of Sargon to one in the reign of Sennacherib. Procksch himself specifies the beginning of the revolt of 713-2, in which Ashdod was joined not only, apparently, by other Philistine states but also by Edom and Judah. Y. Kaufmann, op. cit. III, 170-1, comes closer to the truth in surmising an actual show of force against Judah by the Assyrians who were engaged in crushing the rebellion.

[5] *Op. cit.* (see n. 2 end), pp. 251-2.

[6] At that time I knew only the biblical *locus classicus* Isa 15:3//Jer 48:38. I have since noted that, only two years before the date I assign to Isa 22, the people of Musasir in Armenia were driven by Sargon to such a frenzy of grief that they 'went up on the roofs of their houses and wept bitterly' (D. D. Luckenbill, Ancient Records of Assyria II, p. 94 bottom).

(2) Verses 5-13 recall a *recent* ʻ day of tumult, and din,[7] and dismay ʼ on which the people addressed—government circles in Jerusalem—bethought them of everything but the God of whose long-standing resolve that crisis was but the execution (8b-11). If they had listened to YHWH, they would have wept and mourned then, but instead they made their slogan, ʻ Eat and drink, for tomorrow we die ʼ (vv. 12-13).

(3) And that, says v. 14, is why YHWH decreed then the catastrophe which shall give them cause for the future mourning with which the chapter opened.

Obviously it is observation 2 and the verses it is based on that require to be examined closely for indications of historical background. Most important are vv. 7-11; here is a translation of them:

7a Then were your [7a] choicest lowlands
b filled with chariots and horsemen,[8]
6b with trains of horsemen in pairs.[9]
7c They stormed at Judah's [10] gate
8 and pressed beyond [11] the [10] screen.
Your [12] thoughts turned on that day
to the arms in Forest House
9a and your minds to the City of David,
b in which were many breaches.

[10] So you counted Jerusalem's houses, and pulled houses down to strengthen the wall with. [9c] You further collected the waters of the Lower Pool, [11] and made a reservoir between the two walls for the waters of the Old Pool.

11c But you gave no thought
to him who planned [13] it,
d no mind to him
who long since devised [13] it.

The basic assumption of our rendering of vv. 7-8a is that the enemy has by no means assailed the gate of Jerusalem. Not the least objection to such an interpretation is that it is scarcely conceivable that the authorities would have put off the preparations of 8b-11 until they had come to such a pass, and that they simply could not have proceeded with such preparations once things had come to such a pass. This consideration alone argues for our inference that the gate of 7c, no less than the screen of 8a, is located at the border of Judah, not in the wall of Jerusalem. Further, to begin with, how could chariots get within storming distance of Jerusalem? And to continue, how many *ʻămọ̄qīm* are there in Jerusalem's neighborhood? In the sense of ʻ valley,ʼ the Hebrew *ʻẹ́meq* can designate only a fairly flat and broad valley, and the only one of that description in the vicinity of Jerusalem is the Valley of Rephaim to the south. On the other hand, a common meaning of *ʻẹ́meq*, and possibly the only one it ever has in the plural, is ʻ plain ʼ or ʻ lowland ʼ (see 1 Ki 20:23, 25, 28; Cant 2:1; 1 Chr 12:15; 27:29).

It so happens that we have knowledge of a historical situation, within the period spanned by Isaiah's prophetic activity, such as we have shown

[7] I render *mbwsh* thus here because in 18: 2, 7 *qw qw wmbwsh* can hardly mean anything but ʻ gibberish and jabbering ʼ (cf. *qw* ʻ muttering, murmuring,ʼ 28: 10, 13; Ps 19: 5). For unintelligibility is the natural complement of remoteness and inaccessibility (cf. Deut 28: 49; Jer 5: 15) and, current exegesis notwithstanding, the notions of remoteness and inaccessibility alone are expressed by all the other terms which describe the people which dwells in the land ʻ beyond the rivers of Ethiopia,ʼ ʻ whose land is cut off (not ʻ through ʼ) by streams.ʼ [For *mmuššọ̄k* ʻ distant in space,ʼ cf. *nimšak* ʻ to be distant in time,ʼ Isa i3: 22; Ezek 12: 25, 28. *Mwrṭ* cannot be miswritten twice for *mmrṭ* but must be from *yrṭ*, for which Job 16: 11 (if correct) and the Arab. *wrṭ* suggest a meaning something like ʻ thrust away.ʼ That *nōrā* here means ʻ distant ʼ was surmised already by Ibn Janāḥ (who also ascribed this sense to it in Isa 21: 1) ; note that the Arab. *waraʼa* means ʻ to repel.ʼ The expression *mn hwʼ* I suspect of being miswritten for a single word from a root cognate with the Arab. *nhw* ʻ to prohibit.ʼ *Wọ̄họ̄lʼọ̄*, finally, means, here as everywhere else, ʻ and beyond.ʼ

[7a] Probably the masculine plural *ʻmqykm* is to be read (haplog.).

[8] Rd. *wpršym*, with others.

[9] This clause is (a) impossible where it stands and obviously either a parallel or a variant to 7b and (b) linguistically suspicious in any case and doubtless to be emended in the light of 21: 7a (which see) to *rkb ṣmd pršym*.

[10] These two elements are in the opposite positions in the Hebrew; their transposition in the translation serves the purpose of clarity.

[11] As in the Ugaritic cliché *tgly ḏd il wtbu* . . . ʻ she passes beyond *ḏd il* and enters . . .ʼ. We interpret *wygl* as a scriptio defectiva for *wyglw* in view of l. 7c, just as everybody reads the plural for *wtbṭ* (I simply regard this too as a scriptio defectiva for the plural) in l. 8b because of vv. 9-11.

[12] See the preceding note.

[13] A reference to 37: 26//2 Ki 19: 25 is ample justification for these renderings. For good measure, cf. the synonymous parallelism *ʻśy//yṣ* in Isa 5: 19; 25: 1; 32: 6-7. Similarly, *pʻl* (*//ḥšb*) means ʻ to devise ʼ in Micah 2: 1, and YHWH's *pọ́ʻal* and *maʻăśē yọḏáyim* are nothing but his plan in Isa 5: 12b.

to be presupposed by our passage. Very much of a gateway into Judah is the Valley of Elah (1 Sam 7:2, 19; 21:10—Arab. Wādi-s-Sanṭ) from Azekah (Arab. Tell Zakariyye) upward (eastward), constituting as it does a tongue of relatively low land which extends far into the hill country and is joined by wadis from everywhere in the interior of northern Judah; and the position and function of the fortress Azekah, which was situated on an elevation at the outer end of this inlet of law-lying land, was sufficiently analogous to those of the entrance screens of the Tabernacle (Exod 26:36-37) and the Tabernacle Enclosure (Exod 27:16)[14] to make its metaphorical designation as 'the entrance screen of Judah' easily comprehensible. And this Azekah—which by the way lay about fifteen miles due east of Ashdod—was attacked and captured by the Assyrian expeditionary force which crushed the Ashdod-led revolt in the year 712.[15] How long after the fall of Azekah King Hezekiah remained defiant, we cannot say. If its fall preceded that of Ashdod, the Assyrians may not immediately have pressed their advantage against Judah, and the latter may not have sued for peace immediately. In any case, the attack on and/or the capture of Azekah is surely the background of Isa 22:1-14.[16]

2. From the Year 705

According to Isa 14:3-4a, the poem that follows, vv. 4b-21, was composed by the author in anticipation of the death of 'the king of Babylon.' In view of Sargon's notorious Babylonism, whose manifestations included a three years' residence in Babylon and the stressing of both his Babylonian titles and of his benefactions to the inhabitants and temples of the southern metropolises in an account intended for foreigners (the Cyprus Stela), it would not be remarkable if Isaiah regarded Babylon (a city whose name was presumably far more familiar to him [see Gen 10:10; 11:1-9] than Calah [see Gen 10:11, 12] let alone Dūr-Sharrukīn, of which he probably never heard), as the center of the Assyrian empire. In fact, it is my belief, which I shall endeavor to justify elsewhere, that he does so regard it in 21:1 ff. But in the first place, Isaiah never designates the empire (which is not the same thing as the royal residence) as Babylon or its ruler as king of Babylon (just as he never designates the king of Egypt as king of Zoan or the like, or the king of Aram as king of Damascus, or the king of Israel-Ephraim as king of Samaria). And in the second place, every line of the poem protests against its being interpreted as a vision of the future. It sounds like nothing so much as a spontaneous reaction to a death which, gratifyingly, has taken place. We shall see that it is actually an ode on the death of Sargon. As for vv. 3-4a, they are clearly an editorial touch of exilic or post-exilic date, and so are vv. 22-23. So, for that matter, are vv. 1-2, which most naturally imply the exile of the whole of Israel, of the south as well as the north, and are suggestively reminiscent of Zech 1:17b; 2:12-13. To be sure, the contrast between the spirit of v. 2 and that of vv. 4b-21 makes their juxtaposition so grotesque that, with a sense of humor, one can enjoy it; but vv. 4b-21 must be appraised independently of what precedes and of what follows it.

How applicable this poem is to the death of

[14] The natural and other features of Israel from north of Jerusalem to south of Hebron are excellently represented in combination, on a scale of 1:250,000, on Map 20 in the Israel Army's Historico-Geographic Atlas of Palestine (אטלס גיאוגרפי—היסטורי של ארץ ישראל, no date).

[15] See H. Tadmor, JCS 12 (1958): 80-83.

[16] In 701, to be sure, Sennacherib took Lachish, which is likewise a 'gate-screen of Judah,' and a large slice of western Judah to boot. But the following considerations militate against the old hypothesis (still adhered to by Kissane) that our passage reflects those events. (1) There is very likely some connection between the denunciation of those in charge of the destinies of Judah in vv. 1-14 and the bitter condemnation of 'Shebna who is in charge of the household' in vv. 15 ff. But as can be seen from v. 22, this Shebna's tenure of that office preceded that of Eliakim son of Hilkiah; and since the crisis of 701 fell in the incumbency of Eliakim (2 Ki 18:18—19:2//Isa 36:3—37:2), the one that occurred during or close to Shebna's incumbency necessarily occurred before 701. (2) In 701, Jerusalem itself was besieged. Our passage, on the other hand, though it speaks of the 'day of tumult, and din, and dismay' as something past, mentions only preparations for a siege precipitated by reports from the lowlands. (3) In our passage, Isaiah accuses his hearers of not having turned to YHWH and of not having heeded his call to mourning during the crisis. As is well known, they did do both these things at the height of the crisis in 701: Hezekiah sent his ministers to Isaiah in rent garments and in sackcloth to beg him to intercede with YHWH, and Isaiah sent back a message of hope and comfort (2 Ki 19:1-35//Isa 37:1-35). At last, his expectation that a chastened Judah would turn back to YHWH was realized.

Sargon, was noted by Winckler [17] at the beginning of the century and has been stressed again by writers in recent decades.[18] I find most persuasive the argumentation of Orr. Orr first stresses, as we have, that the author is obviously looking back upon a specific accomplished fact and then notes, as did already Winckler, the remarkable parallelism between, on the one hand, Isa 14: 18-19 and, on the other, both the actual fate of Sargon (he was killed, and from all appearances, abandoned in battle, a fate not known to have overtaken any earlier king of Akkad or Assyria) and the way the fact is referred to in the cuneiform text K 4730: ‘Sargon . . . was not buried in his house.’ (The gist of the preserved part of that document is that [Sargon's son and successor] Sennacherib ordered the soothsayers to ascertain the sin for which the deceased had suffered such a fate.[19])—One might add that our poem stresses that this fate befell a cruel and mighty conqueror, something which, in all of the period in the history of western Asia during which the Hebrew Scriptures were produced, happened only once: in the summer of the year 705.—Orr then goes on to reason that if the poem was composed on the death of Sargon it cannot be from anybody's pen but Isaiah's, since it is practically inconceivable that there should have been flourishing at the same time as Isaiah another, but completely unknown, Hebrew poet capable of producing such a literary gem, and he quotes with approval the judgment of his father that it is ‘the oldest and perhaps the most powerful ballad in the literature of the world.’ [20] (A more exact term would be *ode*—H. L. G.) Orr therefore concludes as follows:

[17] H. Winckler, Die Keilinschriften und das Alte Testament[3], 1903, pp. 47 ff.

[18] The following have come to my attention: B. Bonkamp, Die Bibel im Lichte der Keilschriftforschung, 1939, p. 425 (cited but not accepted by E. J. Kissane, The Book of Isaiah I, 1941, p. 167); A. Gelin apud Robert and Tricot, Initiation Biblique[3], 1954, p. 151 (cited, but not accepted, by O. Eissfeldt, Einleitung in Das Alte Testament[2], 1956, p. 385); Avigdor Orr, A. Biram Jubilee Volume (Hebrew), Jerusalem, 1956, pp. 84-87.

[19] Why that fate was regarded as a punishment is indicated by Isaiah; see a few notes further on. Isaiah also states clearly for what offense the punishment was meted out, v. 20a. The answer of the soothsayers of K 4730 to this question has not been preserved (for an ingenious surmise, see H. Tadmor, Eretz Israel V, 150-163; English Summary, p. 93*), but one thing is certain: it bore no resemblance to that of Isaiah.

> That Isaiah's authorship of the dirge can be disproved by merely literary and stylistic criteria is really out of the question. Of course it is difficult to prove that the diction of the dirge is characteristic of Isaiah, but that argument carries no weight so long as it has not been proved that it is characteristic of anybody else—and it has not been. The ideological arguments are no better. No theorizing by any scholar about what Isaiah might be expected to say on the occasion of Sargon's death can cancel the actual words that he did utter in our dirge. No matter what view of Isaiah's ideology one may adopt, since there can be no question about his loyalty to his people, for whose sorrows he grieved, there must always remain room in his teaching for this sigh of relief over the fall of the oppressor.

The only fault I find with the foregoing is its diffidence. The ideology and the diction of the ode are not merely compatible with Isaian authorship; they are positive arguments in its favor. I also dissent strongly from Orr's exclusion of vv. 20-21 from the original ode; they are an organic part of it.

As regards ideology, who but Isaiah could have felt so strongly that Sargon's fate was a punishment for wrongs done to all nations, and that the moment was one for rejoicing for the whole world, as not even to hint specifically at his own people? Nahum, a century later, was aware that the fall of Nineveh was cause for rejoicing for all nations (Nah 3: 19b); but he conveys the impression that only the wrongs done to Israel constituted ‘plotting evil against YHWH’ (Nah 1: 11) on the part of Asyria, and he only dwells on the comforting implications of its fall for his people (Nah 2: 1, 3). To condemn him for it, is not a little Pecksniffian; but to fail to be moved by our ode to admiration of Isaiah's fidelity to his championship of the rights of all people (10: 7) and to his hope for the crushing of Assyria as a liberation of all nations (14: 24-27 [21])

[20] Elias Auerbach, Wüste und Gelobtes Land II, p. 99. Auerbach, by the way, no doubt unaware of the manner of Sargon's death, identified the tyrant of Isa 14 with Tiglath-pileser.

[21] In order that the pronominal suffixes of *m'lyhm* and *škmm* (so read!) may have an antecedent, and in order that v. 27, which purports to be giving an explanation of something, may really explain something, v. 25b must be placed between vv. 26 and 27.

I should like to note here that Isa 10: 5-15 and 14: 24-27 are undisputedly Isaian passages, and that the implication of the former is that Assyria has no right to destroy the identity of any nation (10: 7b) by means of population shifts (v. 13 end—the Karatepe inscriptions have established the fact that *hōrīḏ* means ‘to exile [masses]’); that even to conquer and plunder is not a little Philistine. Even a non-Hebraist may, if he makes the necessary allowance for the inadequacy of the translator, gain a fair idea of both the literary excellence and the breadth of vision of the poem from the following translation.[22]

4b How is the taskmaster vanished,
tyranny ended!
5 Broken is the staff of the godless,
the rod of oppressors;
6 that smote peoples in wrath,
with stroke unceasing,
that belabored nations in fury,
unsparingly beating!

7 All earth is calm, untroubled,
and shouts for joy.
8 Even pines rejoice at your fate
and cedars of Lebanon:
'Now that you have lain down,
there shall none come up to fell us.'

9 Sheol below with a start
prepared for your coming;
rousing for you the shades
of all earth's chieftains,
making to rise from their thrones
all kings of nations.

10 All speak up and say to you,
'Even you have been stricken as we were,
have become just like us!
11 Your pomp is brought down to Sheol
and the strain of your lutes!
Maggots are to be your bed
and worms your coverlet!'

12 How are you fallen from heaven,
O Luminous, son of Dawn![23]
How are you felled to earth,
O vanquisher of nations!

13a Once you thought in your heart,
b 'I will scale the sky!
c I will set my throne
d above El's stars!
14 I will mount the back of a cloud—
I will match 'Elyon:
13e I will sit[24] in the Assembled Gathering[25]
f in Highest Heaven!'[26]
15 Instead, you are brought down to Sheol,
to Lowest Pit.[27]

is permitted her only in the case of Aram and Ephraim (10: 6, cf. 8: 4; 9: 16 [*ḥōnēp̄*], 18 [YHWH's *'eḇrō̄*]); and that otherwise even punitively to invade is permitted her only in the case of Judah (10: 12; cf. 8: 8a). An appreciation of the implications of 10: 5-15 and 14: 24-27 is incompatible with a predisposition to deny the Isaianity of other universalistic prophecies—and/or crudely to minimize their universalism.

[22] Emendations already in BHK[3] will not be specially noted in footnotes. Neither will my transposition of clauses in vv. 13-14 and in v. 19 be noted otherwise than by their rearrangement in the translation.

[23] No doubt an echo of ancient mythology; future finds may furnish us with evidence similar to the famous Ugaritic parallel to Isa 27: 1.

[24] In other pre-Hellenistic biblical scenes of the heavenly assembly (1 Ki 22: 19; Isa 6: 1-2; Zech 3: 8; 4: 14), only YHWH sits (by the way, he may stand to pronounce judgment, Ps 82: 1), no doubt in order to obviate any false conclusion that there are gods besides YHWH. (It would seem from Dan 7: 9-10 that even the possibility of such misunderstanding no longer occurred to Jews at the time when those verses were written.) In the ancient pagan literatures, on the other hand (Mesopotamian, Ugaritic, and Greek literature), assemblies of entire pantheons of seated gods are a commonplace, and our v. 13e would seem to reflect an awareness of the fact.

[25] Read *bpḫr mw'd* after Ugar. *pḫr m'd* (that this is actually miswritten *phr m'd* in one instance [CATC I = Gordon 137, l. 20—contrast l. 14] is only a coincidence). Even supposing the locality was conceived of as a mountain (see next note), the designation 'Mount of Assembly' owes its existence to textual corruption.

[26] Surely 'sky' is precisely what *ṣpwn* means in Job 26: 7, where between its being governed by the verb *nṭy* (which so frequently governs *šmym*, the commoner word for 'sky') and its standing in antithesis to 'earth' it admits of no other interpretation. Our passage offers a bit of additional evidence: *yarkṯē ṣōp̄ōn* stands in antithesis to *yarkṯē bōr*, and the polar opposite of the nether world is the sky, Amos 9: 2; Ps 139: 8. Nothing is gained by resisting this logic. True enough, the Ugaritic *pḫr m'd* (like the Greek pantheon) holds its sessions on a mountain, and a mountain named Ṣpn plays an important part in the Ugaritic epics. But the mountain on which the Ugaritic *pḫr m'd* meets is not Ṣpn but Ll (see refs. above in n. 25).

[27] The expression occurs again in Ezek 32: 23, in a context which makes it clear that this, the lowest—and without a doubt least desirable—level of the nether world was reserved for those who were slain in battle (and, presumably, not decently buried) and for those who died uncircumised (Ezek 32: 19, 21, etc.); cf. O. Eissfeldt, Studies in Old Testament Prophecy Presented to Professor Theodore H. Robinson, Edinburgh 1950, pp. 73-81. It is suggestive that Assyria and her multitudes are specifically named as denizens of 'Lowest Pit' in Ezek 32: 22. For a variant of 'Lowest Pit,' see below, v. 19.

Such notions were not confined to Israel. The Sidonian kings Tabnit and Eshmunazor both wish that anyone who disturbs their sarcophagi may suffer the like deprivation of 'rest with the shades'—'and may he not be buried in a grave,' adds Eshmunazor (l. 8), which

16 They who behold you stare,
they peer at you closely:
'Is this
the man who shook the earth,
who made realms tremble,
17 who made the world like a waste
and wrecked its [28] towns,
who chained to his palace gate [29]
18 all the kings of nations?'
Yet they were all laid in honor
each in his house,[30]
19a while you were left lying unburied
b like loathsome carrion,[31]
e like a trampled corpse
c in [32] the clothing of slain gashed by the sword
d who descend to the depths [33] of the Pit.
20 You shall not have a tomb like [34] those others;
because you destroyed countries,[35]
you murdered peoples! [35]

Let nevermore be remembered
the breed of evildoers!
21 Prepare a shambles for his sons
for the guilt of their father.[36]
Let them not arise to possess the earth;
then the world's face shall be covered with towns.[37]

The poem, then, fits the unique event of the year 705 B. C. E. as admirably as was claimed above, is literarily as worthy of Isaiah (and Isaiah as uniquely worthy of it) as was claimed above, and—with its constant 'peoples,' 'nations,' 'the earth,' 'the world,' 'realms,' 'countries,' and 'towns,' and never a special word (perfectly understandable and legitimate though it would have been) about 'Israel,' 'Jacob,' 'Judah,' 'Jerusalem,' or 'Zion'—reads as much like a perfect sequel to Isa 10:5-15; 10:24-27 as was claimed above. As for lexical-stylistic considerations, they could hardly in any case outweigh the foregoing other evidence. But as a matter of fact, the diction is still another powerful argument for the Isaian authorship of the poem. For while a few Isaianisms would hardly embarrass any theory of authorship seriously, it is to be hoped that nobody will try to explain away eight exclusively Isaian features of style or diction and five other features which while not exclusively Isaian are characteristically Isaian, all in a composition of 17½ short verses! Compare:

no doubt explains why he will have no rest with the shades. No doubt that is also what is meant by the wish of the two Nērab priests of the moon-god that anyone who disturbs their sarcophagi may die 'an evil death.' These Phoenician and Aramaic inscriptions can be read in the originals in Donner and Röllig, Kanaanäische und aramäische Inschriften I, pp. 2-3, 45, and in German translation ibid. II, pp. 17, 20, 275, 276. As for Sargon's own cultural sphere, there is the well known passage in the Twelfth Tablet of the Gilgamesh Epic in which a person who has, exceptionally, been allowed to return from the nether world to earth is asked, among other questions, 'Have you seen him whose corpse was cast out upon the steppe?' and replies 'I have; his spirit finds no rest in the nether world' (ANET, p. 99, col. a.). As will be seen in v. 19, the case of 'him whose corpse was cast out upon the steppe" is indeed the case of the person apostrophized in the text.

[28] Rd. *'ryh*, with pronominal suffix referring to tēḇēl. BHK^3's hesitation is due to its sharing the common misunderstanding of v. 21; see below.

[29] For MT, which is substantively insipid and linguistically suspicious, I read אִסְרֵי לפתח ביתֹה.

[30] I. e. 'tomb'; so also no doubt in K 4730, quoted above, n. 19.

[31] According to BHK^3, Aquila and Jerome and a variant in LXX connect the noun in the original with postbiblical *nṣl* 'decomposing dead flesh.'

[32] Reading *blbwš* (haplog.).

[33] Though BHK^3 adds a query, the emendation to *'dny* 'the sockets of' is plausible in view of 'Lowest' in v. 15, on which see above n. 27.

[34] I have disposed of Dahood's alleged Heb. *ḥdw/y* (=Ugar. ditto) 'to see' in a paper contributed to a *Festschrift* which will probably appear shortly before or after the volume for which the present manuscript is destined.

[35] MT's second person pronominal suffixes are so perplexing that LXX changes them to first person ones. Anything is better than the absurd statement that it was his own country that the tyrant destroyed and his own people that he murdered and—after all that has gone before!—that it is for this that the tyrant has met with the evil death that will guarantee perpetual suffering to his spirit. But LXX's solution is not good enough. To have understood what vv. 4b-19, 21—with their *peoples*, *nations*, *kings*, *realms*, *earth*, and *world*—are all about is to be driven to the conclusion that in v. 20a *'arṣḵō̦* is miswritten for *'ărō̦ṣōṯ* and *'ammḵō̦* for *'ammīm*.

[36] Rd. *'ăḇīhē̦m*; the preceding verses have dealt exclusively with a single 'man' (v. 16) and his hubris and tyranny.

[37] Rashi, Ibn Ezra, and Redaq all know this interpretation, which is supported by the masoretic vocalization of *ml'w* as a qal and which, Rashi had the acumen to note, is required by v. 17. So also Ehrlich, who cites neither predecessors nor, what is more unfortunate, v. 17.

	Isa 14: 4b-21	*The Rest of Isa 1-33*	
4b	*ngś//rhb* [38]	3:5	ditto
	šbth mrhbh	30:7	*rhb hm šbt* [39]
4b-5	*nōḡēś . . . šbr šéḇeṭ*	9:3[4]	*šéḇeṭ hannōḡēś . . . ḥtt* [40]
5	*nōḡēś . . . mōšlīm*	3:12	*nōḡśọw//mọšlū bō* [41]
5-6	*šéḇet . . . nky*	10:24; 30:31	*šéḇeṭ nky*
	šbr šéḇeṭ	14:29	ditto [42]
7	*nwḥ, šqṭ*	30:15	ditto
9	*'ōrēr//hēqīm*	23:13	*hēqīmū//'ōrrū* [43]
11	*hūraḏ š'ōl . . . hemyaṯ*	5:14	*š'ōl . . . wyọraḏ hămōnọh* [41]
12	*npl//gd'*	9:9[10]; 10:33; 22:25	ditto [44]
20	*šḥt . . . zéra' mrē'īm*	1:4	*zéra' mrē'īm . . . šḥt* [45]
		11:9	*r'//šḥt*
21	*umọl'ū pnē ṯēḇēl*	27:6	ditto [46]

[38] The parallelism *ngś//rhb*, recurring only in 3: 5, is one of the exclusively Isaian features of the poem. As is well known, *mrhbh*, conjectured long ago in our passage in the light of the LXX and of 3: 5, is now brilliantly confirmed by 1QIs[a]. It is nevertheless contested by H. M. Orlinsky in JQR 43 (1953) :333-37, and an etymology for the masoretic *mdhbh* is seriously proposed by him in VT 7 (1957): 202-3. His reasoning, however, can only be explained by his celebrated feud with 1QIs[a], which reaches its climax in the sweeping assertion that the scroll contains not a single reading that is more original than that of MT, (*Tarbiz* 24 [1955-6]: 8).

Incredible as it may sound, Orlinsky denies that the Septuagint read *mrhbh*, on the even more incredible ground that 'The term ἐπισπουδαστής reflects no known or assumed meaning of רהב.' Yet this is an assumption which many modern scholars share with, among other authentic Semites, Paul of Tella, who translated the text of the fifth column of the Hexapla into Syriac, thus producing the Syro-Hexaplar Version, in the years 616-617 C.E. It so happens that just in our passage and in Isa 21: 3 Paul rendered the Greek **spoudaz* by means of Syr. *ḥpṭ*; but in the seven other passages which are preserved in Codex Ambrosianus (ed. Ceriani) he rendered the verb *spoudazein* by the saph'el or the estaph'al of *rhb*, and in Koh 7: 9[10] he did the same for *speudein*. Another proof of the correspondence *speud(az)ein* = *rhb* is that sometimes the very Hebrew word which the Septuagint rendered by the one the Peshitta independently rendered by the other; so at Job 31: 5; Koh 8: 2-3; Esth 8: 14. As for modern scholars, has Orlinsky never consulted Buhl, Brown-Driver-Briggs, or Koehler? They all, s. v. *rhb*, compare the Aramaic-Syriac *rheḇ*, which means 'to hasten, hurry (intrans.)' in the p'al and estaph'al and 'to urge, press (trans.)' in the saph'el (so also the postbibl. Heb. *sirheḇ*). As a matter of fact, a sense close to 'to press or drive'—namely, 'to rule or dominate'—was 'assumed' for *rhb* already by the Targum to Isa 3: 5. (How close the two senses really are can be seen from the fact that the plural of *nōḡēś* 'oppressor or task-master' means 'rulers, authorities' in Isa 3: 12; 60: 17.)

Orlinsky endeavors to dispose of the evidence of the Hebrew of Isa 3: 2 with the same desperation as he endeavors to dispose of the evidence of the Septuagint of 14: 4b, but the curious reader may look that up for himself. So, too, of his 'constructive' article in VT 7 (1957): 202-3, in which he tells us what the MT reading *mdhbh* does mean, I will only say that he produces not a single parallel from a root *dhb* but only alleged parallels with the radical consonants *d'b* or even *db'* and in the process interprets with complete confidence the crux (and near-certain corruption) *db'k*, Deut 33: 25.

[39] *Šbt* associated with *rhb* only in Isaiah, though to be sure just this last *rhb* verse in Isaiah (*not* 3: 5 and 14: 4b) *is* 'obscure.'

[40] As a matter of fact, the received text of this passage has *maṭṭē* as well as *šéḇeṭ* in common with 14: 4b-5, but I am persuaded that in 9: 3[4] *mōṭaṯ* or *mōṭōṯ* is to be read instead.

[41] A juxtaposition found only in Isaiah.

[42] *Šbṭ* is not found with *šbr* outside Isaiah, though *mṭh* is.

[43] A parallelism found only in Isaiah. (22.33, with some emendation and rearrangement, yields the sense: This very land of Kittim, which (zẹ̄) Sidonians founded, whose towers they erected, whose ramparts they raised up, is a people that has ceased to be. Assyria has turned it into a ruin.)

[44] At this point I should have compared the elements common to 14: 16 and 13: 13, but I am coming to feel more and more that ch. 13, though it borrows some Isaian (and some Zephanian) diction, is post-Isaian (and post-Zephanian). Details in a larger work.

[45] The phrase *zéra' mrē'īm* is found only in Isaiah.

[46] A phrase found only in Isaiah.

AKKAD DYNASTY INSCRIPTIONS FROM NIPPUR

ALBRECHT GOETZE
YALE UNIVERSITY

THE FIFTH AND SIXTH SEASONS of excavations at Nippur (1955/56 and 1957/58) conducted jointly by the Oriental Institute of the University of Chicago and the Baghdad School of the American Schools of Oriental Research brought to light a few inscriptions of the Akkad Dynasty (ca. 2430-2250 [1]). Their publication [2] forms the subject of this article.

1. Rīmuś

(a) Fragments of inscribed vases of Rīmuś [3] are frequent and have not only been found in Nippur [4] but also in numerous other places in both northern and southern Mesopotamia.[5] Even now such fragments can be picked up in Nippur on the surface or on the old dumps.

Thureau-Dangin in his Die sumerischen und akkadischen Königsinschriften (SAK) (= Vorderasiatische Bibliothek I, 1907) has distinguished three variants of such vases: [6] one — called " Vase A " — with a three line inscription, one — " Vase B " — with a six line inscription, and one — " Vase C " — with a thirteen line inscription. The fragments here presented belong to examples of either A : 5N-T567 [7] and 6N-T1033a [8] or B/C : 6N-T1033 [9]; C is represented by 2N-445.[10]

There is nothing new the fragments have to contribute.

(b) The fragment 6N-T264 [Now NBC 10736] (55 × 51 mm from SB 67 in the Inanna temple) is probably also to be attributed to Rīmuś and contains Ur III copies of 2 inscriptions of his. The preserved text reads as follows:

obv.	[*a-na*]	" to
2	[^{d}. . . . .]	. . . . . .[a]
	[*Rí-mu-uś*]	Rīmuś,
4	[*śàr*]	king of
	Kiši[^{ki}]	Kiš,
	iśruk [b]	dedicated (this)."
6	!	
	a-[*na*]	" To
8	^{d}*Inan*[*na*]	Inanna
rev.	*Rí-m*[*u-uś*] [c]	Rīmuś,
	ś[*àr*]	king of
10	*A-kà-d*[*è*]	Akkad,
	ì-nu Gir-[*śu*^{ki}] [d]	when he
12	*en-a-*[*ra-am*] [e]	defeated Girsu,
	in śall[*at*] [f]	from the booty
14	[*Gi*]*r-śu*[^{ki}] [g]	of Girsu
	[*iśruk*] [h]	dedicated (this)."

[a] Either Enlil or Inanna; cf. Vase B. — [b] a.mu-ru. — [c] Another reading and supplementation is hardly possible. One may object that Rīmuś takes nowhere else the title *śàr A-kà-dè*^{ki}; what with the scarcity of the available material, this would be an ***argumentum e silentio*** that carries no conviction. — [d] Cf. l. 14. — [e] See AO 5475 (RA 8 200) obv. i 7. — [f] *nam.ra.aka*; see Vase C 11 and UET I 10 11. — [g] Cf. l. 11. — [h] [*a.mu*]*-r*[*u*]; see Vase C 13 and UET I 10 13.

The second inscription must refer to the beginning of the king's reign, when the whole of Mesopotamia was in revolt and had to be re-subjugated.[11] [12]

[1] This is calculated according to the chronology to which I adhere and which assumes that Hammurapi of Babil reigned 1848-1806 B.C.

[2] A bibliography of previously published texts is given by I. J. Gelb, Mat. for the Assyrian Dict. 2^{2} (1961) 193 ff. (with additions 216 f.). See furthermore H. Hirsch, AfO 20 (1959/60) 1-82.

[3] Whatever the meaning of the name is, the final *-ś* contains the suffix of the third person singular.

[4] H. V. Hilprecht in the preface of BE I/1 (1893) p. 19 counts sixty-one pieces from the first two seasons. See also BE I/2 (1896) p. 8.

[5] Such as Uruk, Ur, Sippar, Khafājah, Tell Brak.

[6] Hilprecht (BE I/1 p. 20) had in addition set up one with an inscription of eleven lines; it is however represented only by a single (mutilated) example.

[7] Beginning with the king's name.

[8] The same.

[9] What is preserved starts with the name; but the beginning is mutilated. As the vertical line at the left margin shows, the inscription continued after the title.

[10] Mentioned in Gelb's bibliography. Examples of A are pictured in V. K. Šileiko, Votivnyja Nadpisi (1915) p. 9 f.; F. J. Stephens, YOS IX pl. XLIII; H. V. Hilprecht, BE I pl. V; of B in BE I pl. IV; of C in BE I pl. III and XX.

[11] C. A. Gadd, Dynasty of Agade and the Gutian Invasion (CAH revised edition I Chapter XIX, 1963) 20 ff.

[12] There may be some interest in referring back to Hugo Winckler, RA 2 (1888) 62 and Altor. Forsch. I/5 (1897) 376.

2. Narām-Sīn

Small mace head 6N-128 from the temple of Inanna.[13]

	^{d}*Na-r[a-am-]* ^{d}*Sīn*	"Narām-Sīn,
2	*śàr* *ki-ib-ra-tim*	the king of the four
4	*ar-ba-im* *a-na*	quarters (of the world), to
6	^{d}*Inanna* *in Nippur*^{ki} [a]	Inanna in Nippur
8	*iśruk* [b]	dedicated (this mace)."

[a] *En.l[íl*^{ki}*]* — [b] *a.mu-ru.*

See the parallels PBS XV 18 (vase dedicated to Enlil found in Nippur) and UET VIII 11 (mace head dedicated to Ištarān found at Ur).

3. Śar-kali-Śarrī

(a) Stamped half-brick, weathered: 6N-T1123; copy omitted. Found at the south end of the street which runs along the west side of the Ziggurat.

i	*Śar-kà-lí-śàr-rí*	"Śar-kali-śarrī,
2	*śàr* *A-kà-dè*^{ki}	king of Akkad,
ii	*bāni*	he who built
2	*bīt* ^{d}*En-líl*	the temple of Enlil."

Stamps with which such inscriptions were produced exist: BE I 3 (reverse with handle) see pl. II fig. 3; also H. V. Hilprecht, Explorations in Bible Lands (1903) p. 33. On the circumstances of find see J. P. Peters, Nippur 2 (1897) p. 374 (cf. plate I). To the best of my knowledge, however, actual bricks with the impression of the stamp have not been recorded before, although there is no doubt that examples must have been encountered.

(b) 6N-T658, an Ur III copy of an inscription of Śar-kali-śarrī; 52 × 72 mm, from SB 76.

i	^{d}*En-líl*	"Enlil,
2	*śàr*	the king
	ì-li	of the gods, —
4	^{d}*Śar-kà-lí-śàr-rí*	Śar-kali-śarrī,
	mār da-dì-śu [a]	his beloved son,
6	[gap of ca. 4 ll.]	
	[*maḫ-rí-iš*]	before
	[^{d}*En-líl*]	Enlil,
ii	*a-bí-śu* [b]	his father,
2	*a-na Nippur*^{ki}	to Nippur
	è-la-kam	he will come,
4	*al-śu*	upon him
	i-za-ad [c]	he will take (his) stand.[d]
6	*ma-na-ma*	Whoever
	e-TI[. . . .] [e]	will . . . . (and)
8	*bīt* ^{d}*E*[*n-líl*]	destroy
	u-śa-z[*a-ku-ni*] [f]	Enlil's temple,
10	MU.[. . . .]	will . . . . . .
	[x x x x]	the inscription(?),
12	[. . . . .]	to another (?)
	[*śum*]	'the name
iii	[*Śar-kà-lí-*] *śa*[*r?-rí*]	'of Śar-kali-śarrī
2	*śu-ṣí-e?*[*-ma*] [g]	'take off and
	śu-mi[*-me*]	'my name

[13] I assume this is the mace head mentioned by D. Hansen in Chronologies in Old World Archaeology (1965) 209.

[14] See H. Hirsch, AfO 20 (1959/60).

4	*śu-ku$_x$-[un]* [h]	'put on (in its stead).'
	i-qá-ab-[bi-]	will say,
	ù [i]	
6	*ù lu in* [x?]	or 'in
	na-ap-se$_x$-ni-śu [k]	a hiding place
	a-ra-b/pu-šu [l]	I will put(?) (it)' —
8	*^{d}En-líl*	may Enlil,
	śàr	the king
10	*ì-li*	of the gods,
iv	[. . . . . . .]	[. . . . .]
2	[. . . . . . .*-a*]*r*?-	[. . . . .].
	[x-*m*]*a*	[. . .].
	[*ù*?] [m]	and may he
4	[*zē*]*r-śu* [n]	his seed
	[. . . . . -]*na*	. . . .
6	[. . . . . -]*śu*	. . . . his . . . .
	li-il-	pluck
	qù-ut	up.
8	!	!
	DU.DU-*ta* [o]	. . . .
	*sar-*x	. . . . . .
10	*^{d}Śar-kà-lí-*	Śar-kali
	śàr-rí	śarrī".

(a) The interchange here of *mār da-dì-śu* with *mār* DA.TI-*^{d}En-líl* in BE I 2, where Enlil was not mentioned before, proves anew (if this was still necessary) that the father of the king was not called Dati-Enlil. Barton, Royal Inscriptions of Sumer and Akkad (1919) 146 f. still had carried that over from Thureau-Dangin, SAK (1907) 164 f., although the notion had long since been rejected (see F. Weissbach, Reall. der Ass. 2 (1934) 196). See furthermore I. J. Gelb, MAD 3 (1957) 103; H. Hirsch, AfO 20 (1959) 28 fn. 295; CAD 3 (1959) 20a.

(b) The complementation is taken from F. M. Th. Böhl, Med. uit de Leidsche Verzameling van Spijkerschrift-Inscripties 1 (1933) 12. One might be tempted to restore in the preceding gap a short report on the defeat of an enemy who is obligated to appear in the future before his overlord and his god.

(c) For *i-za-ad* (with final *d*, instead of expected *z*) compare *li-zi-id* UET I 275 iv 10. Perhaps the *d* is not a simple mistake of the younger copyist (see Landsberger, OLZ 1931 131), but gives a hint at the prehistory of the final *Z* of the verb.

(d) This is merely an attempt at a literal translation. The real sense might be that the Akkad king will hold the vassal to account.

(e) Form of *etēqum*? No parallel is available.

(f) On this verb see most recently D. O. Edzard, AfO 19 (1959) 22 f. The object *bītum* appears here for the first time. It seems to favor the translation "remove, destroy" which Edzard proposes (von Soden "flach hinwerfen lassen"; Gelb "to damage").

(g) Cf. *śumi-śu-me pi$_5$-śi$_4$-iṭ-ma śumīmi śu-ku$_8$-un i-qá-bi-ù* UET I 276 i 19 ff. Instead of the imperative "erase" the other imperative "cause to leave (*waṣā'um*)" is found in our passage.

(h) The sign is *gú* not otherwise recorded with a syllabic value in Old Akkadian.

(i) See above under (g) and in addition PBS V 36 rev. iv 1 ff.

(k) The nomen loci must belong to the verb *pasānum* (*paṣānum*) that is well known in the meaning "to cover, to veil" from the Middle Assyrian Laws (§§ 40 f.). The first meaning is probably the basic one; for "conceal, hide" see B. Landsberger, ZA 41 (1933) 220. It is confirmed in Behistun 159 by the Old Persian version (*apa-gaudaya-*). In passages like ours it is quite customary to curse the man who hides the inscription so that nobody can see it anymore; see the quotations collected by W. J. Hinke, A New Boundary Stone of Nebuchadrezzar I (1907) 48 f. Accordingly *napśēnum* should fall in the semantic field of *ašar la amāri* "place where (the inscription) cannot be seen," *puzru* "hiding place" etc.

(l) The verb *rapāsum* has not been clarified as yet (cf. Landsberger, MSL I 171 f.). Do we have to do here not with *rapāsum, irpis* (*i*-class), but with a different verb that belongs to the *u-class*?. At any rate, the context seems to require a *verbum ponendi*. The subjunctive seems to mark the promising oath (see von Soden, Grundriss der Akk. Gramm. § 185^d).

(m) Suggested by the open space at the end of the line.

(n) The normal sequence in Akkad inscriptions is *iśdam nasāḫum* — *zēram laqātum*, but *zērum* seems assured in l. 4 here. Hence the context must be altogether different.

(o) This is obviously a subscription which states more definitely from where the inscription was taken by the copyist. Edzard, AfO 19 (1959) 18 ff. has collected the wording of such subscriptions; none coincides with ours, so that the meaning remains doubtful. It seems that DU.DU = *su$_8$* or *súg* = Akk. *uzuzzum* "stand" is pertinent.

(c) Two Old Akkadian tablets — 6N-T112 [now NBC 10619] and 6N-T662 (45 × 89 mm and 79 × 107 mm respectively) both from SB 76 [15] — contain at the end the same new date formula of Śar-kali-śarrī:

mu : Śar-kà-lí-śar-rí
Puzur-Eš$_4$-tár,śakkana
é.^{d}En.líl.dù-da
bí-gub-ba-a
mu.ab-ús-a

"year (when): Śar-kali-śarrī —

[15] Both tablets were written in the same month: *iti ^{d}Inanna-ka* and in both of them the remark follows: *Nam-maḫ, en$_x$.si-ke$_4$ igi-bí-šè* "Nam-maḫ, the ensi, (was) witness thereof."

5 N-T 567

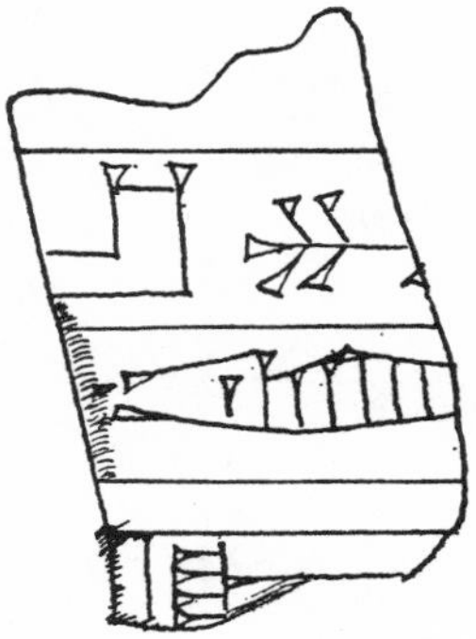

6 N-T 1033 a

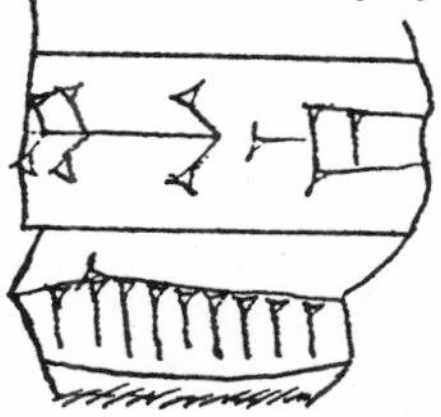

6 N-T 1033

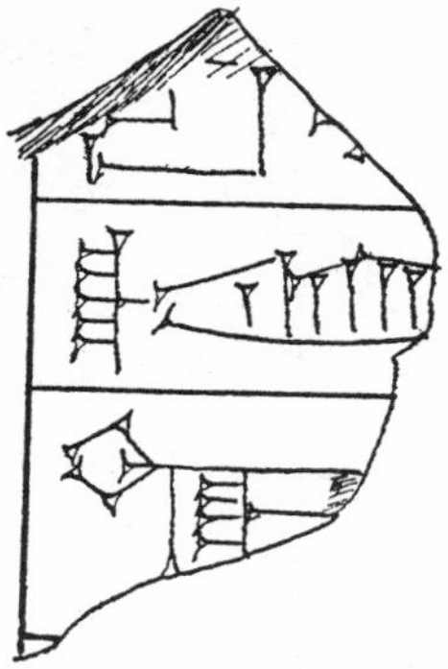

6N-T264

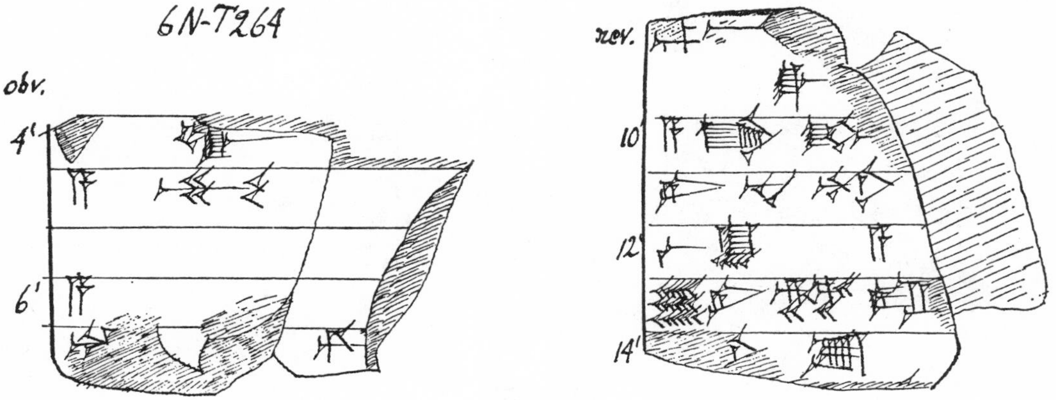

6 N-T 658

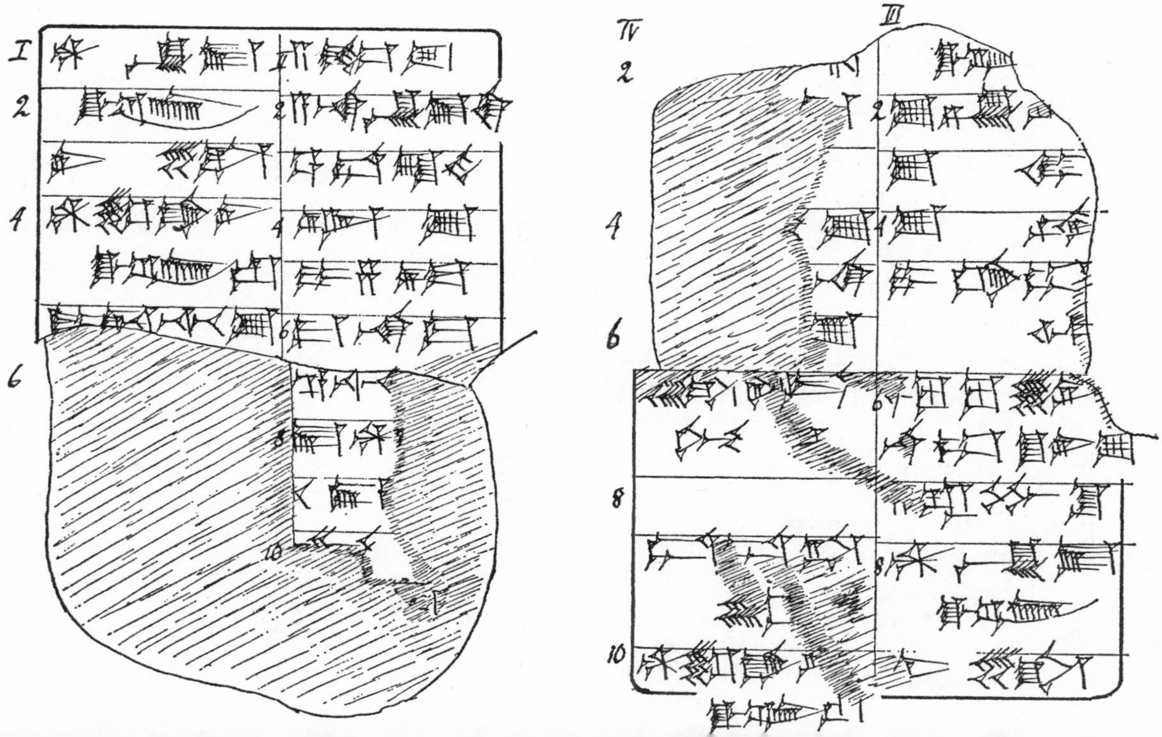

6N-T112

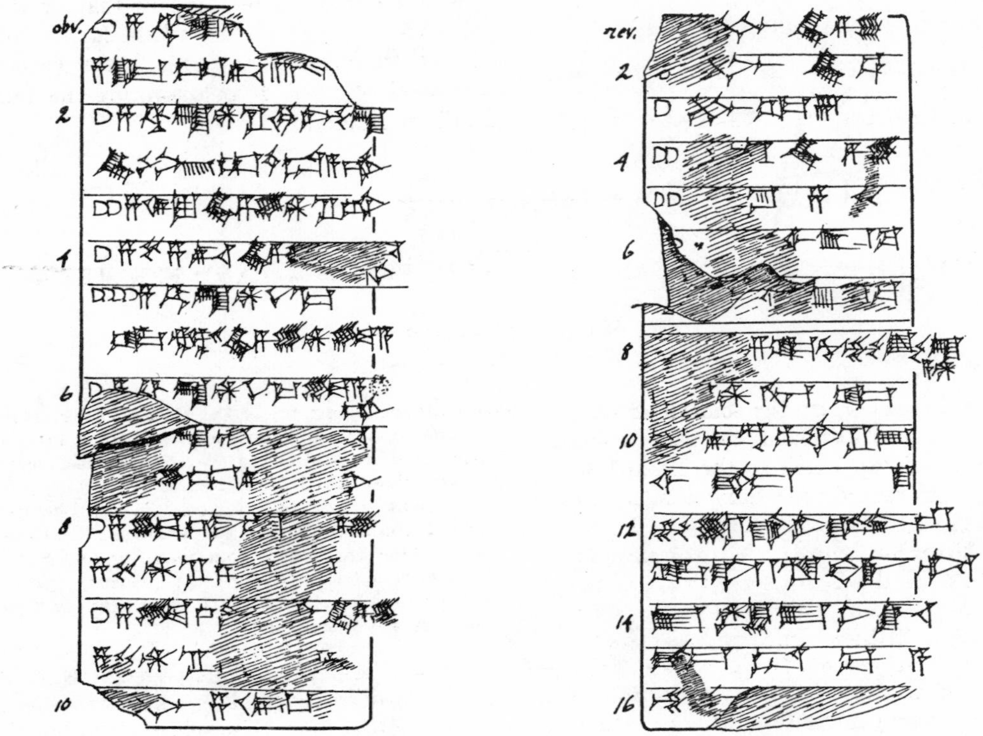

6N-T662

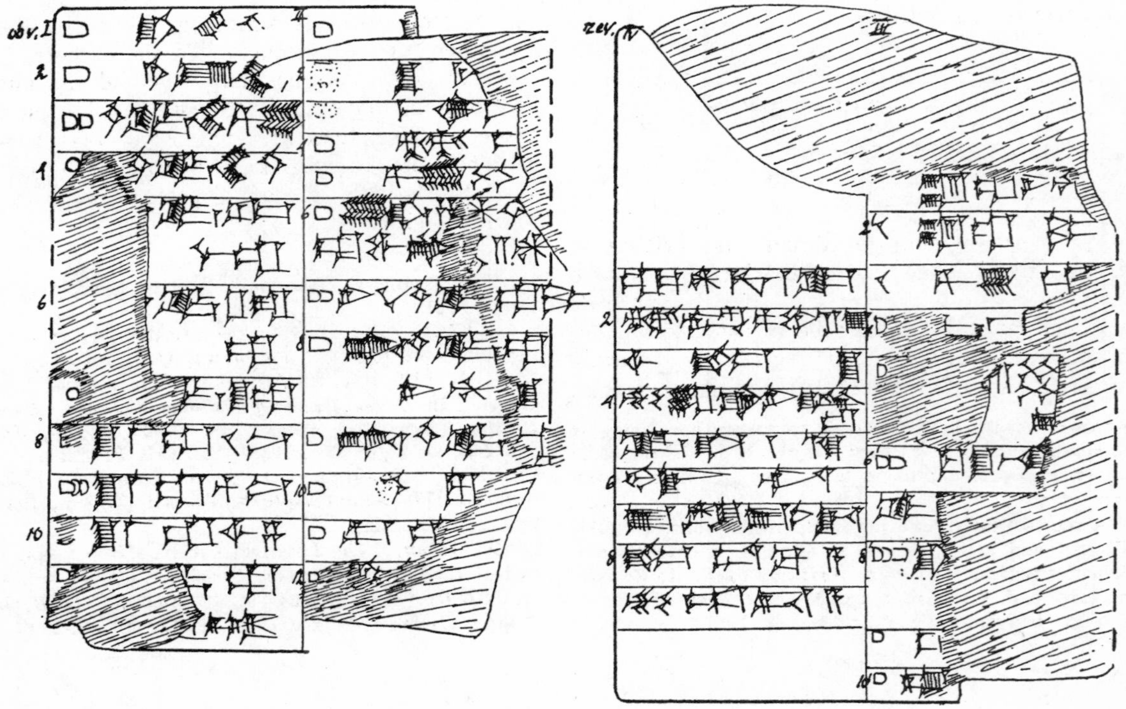

Puzur-Eštar,[16] the general,[17]
assisted him
at the building of the temple of Enlil —

[16] Is this the same man as the recipient of the letter AO 4419 (RA 23, 1926, 25)?

[17] On the title see A. Goetze, JCS (1963) 7 f.

the following year."

For the whole date compare that of RTC 187 (=SAK 226 sub d): *Śar-kà-lí-śar-rí úś-śi*$_{11}$ *bīt* ^{d}*En.líl in Nippur*^{ki} *iś-ku-nu* "year (when) Śar-kali-śarrī laid the foundation for the temple of Enlil in Nippur."

IDEALISM AND PRACTICALITY IN NUMBERS 35:4-5 AND EZEKIEL 48

MOSHE GREENBERG
UNIVERSITY OF PENNSYLVANIA

TO ONE FAMILIAR WITH the sometimes cavalier operation of biblical criticism, the salient feature of E. A. Speiser's approach to the Bible was his predisposition to regard everything carefully, even material that seemed on the face of it to be the product of error or fantasy. With his profound understanding of the Near East this predisposition resulted time and again in evoking new information from hitherto uncommunicative texts. The priestly writings of Israel were particular beneficiaries of his attention; repeatedly they were shown to harbor genuinely ancient, even pre-Israelite practices and terminology. The following study of two problematic passages in that literature is inspired by his example and dedicated in gratitude to his memory.[1]

I. The Pasture Lands of the Levites

> In framing an ideal we may assume what we wish, but should avoid impossibilities.
> —Aristotle, *Politics*, Bk. II: Ch. 6 (1265a)

The penchant for schematizing, so evident in the priestly writings of ancient Israel, has been felt to bespeak a visionary mentality distant from mundane realities. It has been invoked as evidence for an exilic provenance. Of the scheme of Levitical cities (Num. 35; Josh. 21) Wellhausen wrote:

> It would hardly have occurred to an author living in the monarchical period, when the continuity of the older history was still unbroken, to look so completely away from all the conditions of the then existing reality; had he done so, he would have produced upon his contemporaries the impression merely that he had scarcely all his wits about him. But after the exile had annihilated the ancient Israel, and violently and completely broken the old connection with the ancient conditions, there was nothing to hinder from planting and partitioning the *tabula rasa* in thought at pleasure, just as geographers are wont to do with their map as long as the countries are unknown.[2]

Since Wellhausen, Palestinologists have made notable progress in finding a historical-geographical anchorage for this scheme,[3] although they, along with others who regard it as an early element in Israelite tradition,[4] concede the utopian character of a good part of it. To the historian, the unreal aspect is annoying; he deprecates it as unhelpful for his quest. To the exegete, however, it poses the question, How did the author intend to be understood? Nowhere is this question more pressing than at Num. 35:4-5—a passage admitted on all hands to be "utopian" (i.e. fantastic)—the rule allocating pasture lands to the Levitical cities:

[1] A representative offering of Speiser's biblical studies will be found in the section so entitled of *Oriental and Biblical Studies: Collected Writings of E. A. Speiser*, edited by J. J. Finkelstein and Moshe Greenberg (Philadelphia: University of Pennsylvania, 1967).

[2] J. Wellhausen, *Prolegomena*, trans. Black and Menzies, p. 161.

[3] S. Klein, "The Cities of the Priests and Levites and the Cities of Refuge" (Hebrew), *Qobeṣ* of the *JPES*, 1935, pp. 81 ff.; W. F. Albright, "The List of Levitic Cities," in *Louis Ginzberg Jubilee Volume: English Section* (New York, 1945), pp. 49-73; A. Alt, *Kleine Schriften*, ii (München, 1953), 294-315; B. Mazar, "The Cities of the Priests and the Levites," *Congress Volume, Oxford 1959* (*Supplements to VT*, vii [Leiden, 1960]), pp. 193-205.

[4] M. Haran, "The Levitical Cities: Utopia and Historical Reality" (Hebrew), *Tarbiz* 27 (1958), 421-439; cf. *JBL* 80 (1961), 45-54; Y. Kaufmann, *The Book of Joshua* (Hebrew) (Jerusalem, 1959), pp. 270-282.

[4] The town pasture that you are to assign to the Levites shall extend a thousand cubits outside the town wall all around.
[5] You shall measure off two thousand cubits outside the town on the east side, two thousand on the south side, two thousand on the west side, and two thousand on the north side, with the town in the center.[5]

As Gray and others have pointed out, the only interpretation that this allows without forcing is a figure of this shape:

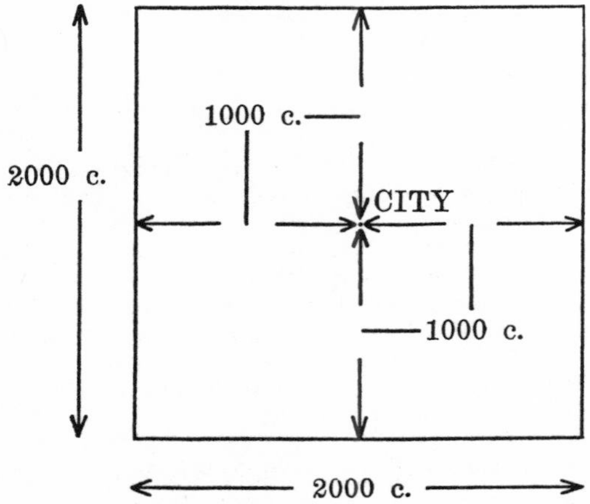

"It necessarily follows that the writer . . . forgot to allow for the dimensions of the city."[6] Wellhausen set forth trenchantly the objections to our passage.

The regulation that a rectangular territory of two thousand ells square should be measured off as pasture for the Levites around each city (which at the same time is itself regarded only as a point . . .) might, to speak with Graf, be very well carried out perhaps in a South Russian steppe or in newly founded townships in the western States of America, but not in a mountainous country like Palestine, where territory that can be thus geometrically portioned off does not exist, and where it is by no means left to arbitrary legal enactments to determine what pieces of ground are adapted for pasturage and what for tillage and gardening; there too, the cities were already in existence, the land was already under cultivation, as the Israelites slowly conquered it in the course of centuries.[7]

Such scoffing appears less in place today, or at least will have to be extended to a far larger field, in the light of the liberal doses of theory that appear sprinkled throughout ancient Near Eastern law collections. Impractically rigid and merely paradigmatic formulations are not infrequently found there alongside what seems to be case law. What, for example, could be more impracticable than the codification in Hammurabi and Eshnunna of prices and wages, as though these items might be eternally fixed through all time?[8] The rules of talion in Hammurabi and the Pentateuch must similarly be regarded as theoretical.[9] Especially significant for our purpose is the implicitly paradigmatic nature of some laws—valid as formu-

[5] The translation is that of *The Torah . . . A New Translation* (Philadelphia: The Jewish Publication Society of America, 1962). On the philological problems, cf. G. B. Gray, *Numbers* (*ICC*) ad loc. and Haran, *Tarbiz*, p. 430, n. 15. The LXX '2000' in vs. 4 is a harmonistic, inferior reading; cf. S. D. Luzzatto, *Commentary to the Pentateuch* (Hebrew), ed. P. Schlesinger (Tel Aviv, 1965), pp. 493 f. *sabib* means 'on every side' as in Ezek. 45: 2b. A summary of various interpretations is in J. Greenstone, *Numbers* (Philadelphia, 1939), pp. 353 f.

[6] Gray, p. 468. Haran's conception (*Tarbiz*, p. 430 fn. 15) allows for a city in the center of the area. He takes *qir ha'ir* to mean the built-up part of the town, since *qir* never means "town wall" (Heb. *ḥoma*). He then makes the starting point of the 1000 cubit lines the center of this built-up part. Thus the city area would consume part of the 1000 cubits on every side; but since Israelite towns were small [see details in Noth, *The Old Testament World*, Eng. trans. p. 147], free space would always remain around the town in the 2000 cubit square for pasture land. Haran's idea is plausible in itself, but a starting point in the center of the built-up part is hardly consonant with the expression *miqqir ha'ir waḥuṣa*, which sounds as though the starting point of measurement is at the limit of the town's *qir*, not its center. Perhaps *qir ha'ir* is an ellipsis for *qir ḥomat ha'ir* (cf. Josh. 2: 15) "the (outer) side of the city wall"; Ben-Yehuda's *Thesaurus* properly defines *qir* as "the side (or surface) of a wall (*ḥoma*)." So we are still faced with the problem of the legislator's having "forgotten" the dimensions of the city.

[7] *Prolegomena*, p. 159. Similarly A. Bentzen, *Introduction to the OT*, ii (Copenhagen, 1948), 70: "The descriptions are given quite theoretically. The town is regarded as a mathematical point without any idea of concrete geographical situations. This is presumably best understood as the work of an 'author' living outside Palestine."

[8] J. Miles (*The Babylonian Laws*, i [Oxford, 1952], 474) found that, where controls are available, the rents for boats in Hammurabi appear to be "not compulsory, but exemplary."

[9] Ibid., 408, 426; "Crimes and Punishments," in *Interpreters Dictionary of the Bible*, p. 742. B. Landsberger cast doubts on the validity and seriousness of some of Hammurabi's laws in his "Die babylonischen Termini für Gesetz und Recht," *Symbolae . . . Koschaker* (Stud. et Doc. ad Iura Or. Ant. Pert. [Leiden, 1939]), pp. 219-234; especially relevant are the rulings listed there in n. 11 (p. 221) that "make the impression of theory."

lated in specific circumstances only, though their limited applicability is not expressly stated. Such a law is that of the goring ox in Eshnunna 53 and Exod. 21:35: if an ox not known to be a gorer gores another ox the owners must divide between themselves the worth of the living and of the dead ox. Goetze has seen the principle behind this ruling: in view of the unforeseeability of the accident and the risk assumed by the victim's owner when he let his ox mingle with others, the owner of the gorer is not made to bear the entire loss. "It is the intention of the legislator to divide the loss as evenly as possible."[10] As was anciently noticed, however, the ruling achieves its intention only when the two live oxen are of equal worth; should there be a disparity in their values, the procedure indicated by the law cannot result in an evenly shared loss (indeed if the victim is, say, half the value of the gorer its owner will actually be enhanced).[11] This law, then, is strictly applicable in one case only; in all others the principle derivable from this paradigm must be applied; namely, that when an innocent ox gores another, the two owners divide the loss equally—or, in other words, the gorer's owner is liable only to half-damages.[12]

Now the provision of a rectangular strip of pasture land around each Levitical city appears to belong to paradigmatic law. What is important is the principle that the landless class of Levites (e. g. Num. 18:23 f.) be furnished such a strip of ground around each of its towns on which to graze its animals. How to deal with natural obstructions and the like that might interfere with laying out the area as prescribed is no business of this statement, whose purpose is to formulate the principle. Yet there is this difference between the goring ox paradigm and that of the pasture land: in the former, one case, at any rate, exists in which the paradigm is applicable as stated, but in the latter no case can be imagined in which the town in the center is a mere mathematical point. Did the author "forget" the dimensions of the town? How can his paradigm be generalized?

The earliest explication of Num. 35:4-5 is found in the Tannaitic regulations about the Sabbath limit (2000 cubits from the place a man lives, beyond which he was forbidden to go on the Sabbath)

> . . . R. Akiba expounded it thus: "You shall measure off two thousand cubits outside the town on the east side, etc." (vs. 5)—but the other verse (vs. 4) says, "a thousand cubits outside the town wall all around"! . . . How are the two to be harmonized? One thousand cubits defines the pasture land; two thousand, the Sabbath limit [i. e. the town limit with respect to Sabbath movement]. R. Eliezer, son of R. Yose the Galileean, says: One thousand cubits for pasture, the second thousand for farmland and vineyards [both, then, refer to the Levite's territory, and there is no reference here to the Sabbath limit] (*Mishna, Soṭa* 5.3).

Both regard the total depth of the strip prescribed in Num. 35:4-5 as 2000 cubits (erroneously, it seems to us).[13] Moreover, though a difference appears between R. Akiba and R. Eliezer concerning the grounding of the Sabbath limit on that passage, all authorities agreed that the limit was in fact 2000 cubits deep. In view of the relatedness of these two topics, it is of interest to us to inquire how the Tannaim drew the Sabbath limit around a town, for presumably that will represent as well how they understood the drawing of the Levites' pasture land.

> How is the shape of a town regularized [so as to facilitate drawing its Sabbath limits]? If the town is oblong, it is left as is [and the limit is measured from its real boundaries]. If it is a circle, it is squared. If it is square [but its sides do not parallel true north, south, east and west] it is not squared again [to make it so]. If it is wide on one side and narrow on the other, both sides are made equal [i. e. it is turned into a rectangle]. If a house projected like a stage, or two houses [on

---

[10] *The Laws of Eshnunna* (*AASOR* 31 [1956]), p. 138; almost the same is Doughty's formulation in *Arabia Deserta* i, 351 (reference from Driver, *Exodus*): "The custom of the desert is that of Moses, 'If any man's beast hurt the beast of another man, the loss shall be divided.'"

[11] Consider the following examples:

Gorer's worth (owned by A)	Victim's worth (owned by B)	Cadaver's worth; victim's depreciation	Proceeds of sales to each owner	A's Loss	B's Loss
100	200	20; —180	60	40	140
200	200	20; —180	110	90	90
200	100	10; — 90	105	95	gain of 5

[12] See Mechilta to Exod. 21:35 (ed. Lauterbach, iii, 95 f.) and Rashi ad loc. The formulation of the law (reminiscent of Solomon's judgment) evidently intends to underscore the idea that both parties are to contribute to the settlement equally.

[13] Like the LXX, the Tannaim took the cubit measurement of both vss. 4 and 5 to refer to the depth of the strip outside the town walls. Unlike the LXX, they did not harmonize the difference between the measurements.

By a singular exegesis of R. Eliezer's opinion, Maimonides (*Code, Laws of the Sabbatical and Jubilee Year*, 13.2) concluded that the Pentateuchal law prescribed a strip of land 3000 cubits deep for the Levites' pasture!

different sides of the town] projected like a stage, a straight line is drawn including them and the 2000 cubits are measured from that line outward. If the town was shaped like a bow or a *gamma* [the interior] is considered full of houses and courtyards and the 2000 cubits are measured from these [imaginary boundaries] outward.[14]

When a circular city is to be squared, it is turned into the shape of a square tablet (ABCD). The Sabbath limits are then drawn square like another square tablet (EFGH). When the depth of the Sabbath limit is measured, one does not measure 2000 cubits diagonally from an angle of the town square to an angle of the Sabbath limit square (BK), for that would reduce the corners of the Sabbath limit. But the corners are drawn by laying a tablet 2000 cubits square diagonally from the angle of the town square (IFJB).[15]

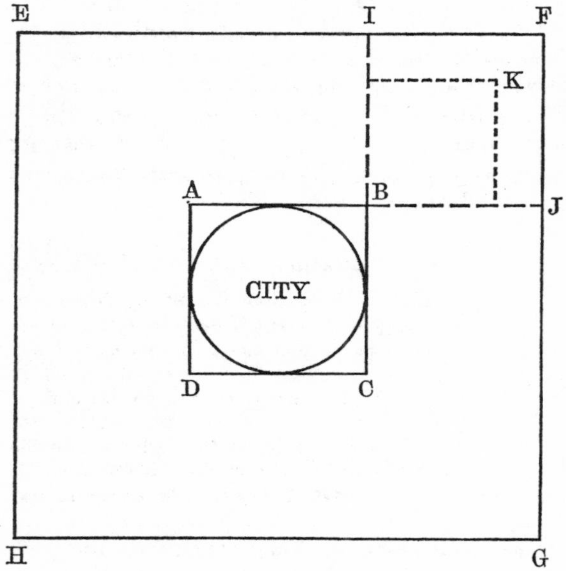

The Tannaim thus regarded the Sabbath limit area as a rectangle whose sides were preferably lined up with the compass points; its depth was 2000 cubits from the extreme limits of the town on each of its four compass points—expressed by the squaring or rectangling of the town. Now, since the Sabbath limit took its reference from the pasture land of the Levitical cities,[16] this discussion provides, in fact, the earliest detailed commentary on the biblical passage. Its agreement with the modern view of the shape intended by Num. 35:4-5—a square with the town in the center—encourages one to ask whether it has any light to shed on our question: why the biblical author treated the town as a point. Indeed it does.

The first lesson of the Tannaitic discussion (and only a sampling has been given here) is, how very complicated the description of this area becomes once the town at its center is given dimensions and treated as a changeable quantity. The simplicity of the expedient adopted in Num. 35:4-5 to describe the relation of the area to the town is highlighted by comparison. The depth of the pasture land, say the verses, is to be 1000 cubits from the town limits on all sides, laid out in such a way that, given a town of 0 dimensions it would form a 2000 cubit square around it. What if the city had dimensions and was irregular to boot? Then an analogous procedure was to be followed: from the easternmost point of the town extend a line due east for 1000 cubits, and from the extreme points of the town's south, west and north extend corresponding lines of 1000 cubits toward the other compass points. Then draw a square (or rectangle) whose sides would be perpendicular to these lines at their end points; thus[17]

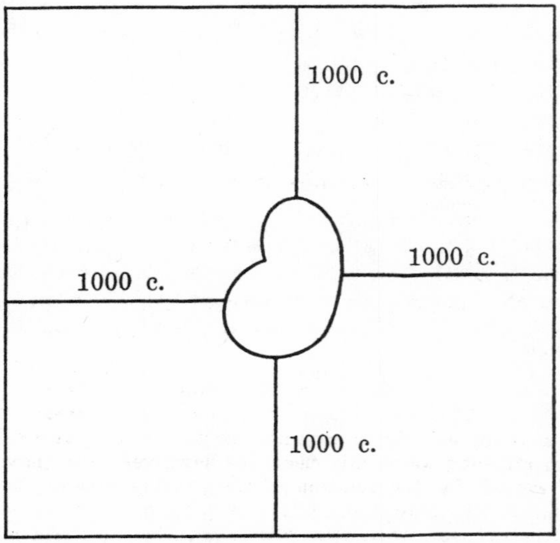

[14] Baraita in *Bab. Erubin*, 55a; with variants in *Tosefta Erubin* 4.1-6 (on which see S. Lieberman, *Tosefta Kifshuta*, iii, 366 f.). Cf. Soncino Talmud, ad loc. for drawings.

[15] Baraita in *Bab. Erubin*, 56b.

[16] Hence the discussion of the former merges into a discussion of the latter (ibid.; cf. *Tosefta, Arakin*, 5.19).

[17] This solution to the practical question of generalizing the prescription of Num. 35: 4-5 was suggested to me some years ago by my brother, Daniel A. Greenberg.

As in the goring ox paradigm, the specific terms in which the law is formulated are inapplicable to any other situation, but from them a principle may be extracted and generalized. The principles here are: a depth of 1000 cubits from the town limits in each direction; a square (or rectangular) area whose sides are aligned with each of the compass points. (The 2000 cubit measurement of the four sides is paradigmatic and given only to bring home the square shape; without it, the direction to extend the pasture "a thousand cubits outside the town wall all around" could have been misconstrued to mean a circular area.) The complicated Tannaitic prescriptions for the Sabbath limit furnish the answer to our question; far from having "forgotten" the dimensions of the town, the biblical author will be seen to have omitted them as an unnecessarily complicating factor. His postulation of a town of 0 size turns out to be the most economical way of giving directions for the layout of the pasture land.

At the same time it is the most practical. His purpose was to provide a strip of land around each town with a constant measurement. Had he been truly an impractical visionary, he might have prescribed following the contours of the town at a depth of 1000 cubits all around it. But the difficulty of carrying out such a prescription for an irregularly shaped town (as many, if not most are) would effectively preclude its ever having been carried out by the Israelite peasantry. It must have been practicality that urged on the Tannaim too the rectangular conception of the Levite pastures and the Sabbath limit area, in contrast with the strange shapes concocted by more recent commentators to the biblical text.[18]

Since the Tannaim were prescribing boundaries in Palestine, not in South Russia or the western United States, they gave thought to what to do with intervening mountains, gullies, houses, graves, and the like.[19] What occurred to them on this head was not beyond the imagination of the priestly author of Num. 35. To be sure, there is no evidence that the early author ever worked matters out so finely for the Levitical pasture lands. But in view of the later discussion, critics' dimissal of Num. 35:4-5 as fantastic for having failed to spell out such details does little justice to the inventiveness of legalists. It is having it both ways to reproach a man for fantasy and deny him the capacity to work out his problem imaginatively.

A final note: it is of interest that Old Babylonian geometrical texts have been found posing problems similar to those we have been discussing. Questions of inclosing square fields within larger squares or enlarging circular cities by larger concentric circles are treated, at times with drawings. Thus neither the idea of treating territory as abstract geometric shapes nor the knowledge of the requisite mathematical operations was absent from Near Eastern antiquity.[20] That abstract shapes were applied in reality to settlements will be shown later.

II. Ezekiel's Allocation of Tribal Territory

> **The allocation of land in the age to come will be different from the allocation in this age. In this age, if one has a grain field, he has no orchard; if an orchard, he has no grain field. But in the age to come everyone will have holdings in the highlands, in the foothills, and in the valleys.[*]**
>
> **—*Bab. Talmud, Baba Batra* 122a**

Gray (*Numbers*, p. 466) considered the geometrical treatment of the Levitical cities, "impossible in the actual land, [paralleled] in Ezekiel's *ideal* division of W. Palestine into a series of exact parallelograms (Ezek. 48)." On that scheme Julius Bewer wrote, "It takes no account of the physical and topographical realities. Parallel lines are drawn at equal intervals (cf. 47:14) between the N. and S. borders from E. to W. to mark the territory of each tribe without regard to the contour of the land and its widening toward the S., or to the territorial needs of differ-

[18] E. g. J. L. Saalschütz, *Das mosaische Recht*, i (Berlin, 1846), 101. Saalschütz raises the question of the size of the city in relation to the pasture around it, pertinently observing that the lawgiver must have had regard for the relation of the grazing area to the needs of its inhabitants. In our discussion, we have postulated that, while the 2000 cubits are exemplary, the 1000 are meant to be the fixed depth of the pasture strip everywhere. It may be supposed that the lawgiver had in view a town of average size, for which he reckoned this to be adequate grazing land.

[19] *Mishna, Erubin*, 5.4; *Gemara*, ad loc.

[20] See Anne D. Kilmer, "The Use of Akkadian *DKŠ* in Old Babylonian Geometry Texts," in *Studies Presented to A. Leo Oppenheim* (Chicago, 1964), pp. 140-146.

ent tribes." The overall shape is thought to be a parallelogram, wholly unrealistic.[21]

Now it is true that the oracle fills Palestine from north to south with strips running across it from its eastern to its western borders, and that the tribes are thereby to divide the land "equally" (47:14). But nothing is said of the width of each tribal portion, so that Davidson's more circumspect judgment is to be preferred that "[there is no] indication whether the greater or lesser breadth of the country from the Jordan to the sea was taken into account."[22] Apart from that qualification, however, Bewer's comment represents the current opinion on the scheme. Is it justified?

The vagueness about the dimensions of the tribal portions contrasts with the precision regarding both the disposition of the holy district (45:1-8; 48:8-22) and—what is relevant to our present interest—the location of each tribe. Allowance is made for Jerusalem's eccentric position: seven tribes are ranged north of it, five to its south. To that extent, then, as even critics admit, the scheme accords with reality.[23]

At this point, it is necessary to consider the tendency of the larger unit of which Ezek. 47-48 forms the climax. Kaufmann[24] has aptly called chapters 40-48 "a messianic Priestly Code," designed to bring up to date provisions of the Torah that had by then become obsolete, and (we may add) to set aright wrongs in Israel's past life. With regard to the land, significant new rulings are laid down. Land tenure, for example, is to be based (as it was originally) on inalienable tribal allotments. These are to be made, not by lot and human surveyors (cf. Josh. 18:1-10), but by the explicit decree of God (47:13 f.; 48:29). The resident alien's landlessness, a longstanding disability that encroached seriously on the old ideal "the same rule shall apply to you and to the alien resident in your midst" (Num. 15:16), is remedied by allowing him to obtain holdings in the territory of his host tribe (47:22-23). Special provision is made for the king's property and for lands he might distribute to his sons and servants: formerly, the king confiscated private property for such purposes; in the future, crown lands—part of a special thirteenth portion, over and above the twelve tribal portions—will be at his disposal, "and he shall not take any of the inheritance of the people, thrusting them out of their property" (46:18; cf. vs. 16 f. and 45:8). The boundaries of the future settlement will accord with the ancient oracle promising Cisjordan only to the patriarchs. The transjordan tribes will be resettled on the west bank, the northern boundary of settlement extended into southern Syria.

Concord and unity will reign among the tribes. Ezekiel envisioned the end of the dual kingdoms of Judah and Israel: "I will make them one nation in the land . . . and one king shall be king over them all; and they shall no longer be two nations, and no longer be divided into two kingdoms (37:22)." Perhaps to promote integration, the tribe of Judah is relocated north of Jerusalem, in the heartland of the former northern kingdom. Benjamin, on the other hand, is moved south to adjoin Simeon. Unequal shares in the land might sow resentment, and so it is laid down (47:14) that the tribes shall take possession of the land "equally" (lit. "each like his brother").

So far, then, the provisions of the land apportionment can be seen to stem from a realistic view of political, geographical, and religious determinants. In the provision for equal shares an important assumption is made: the equal size of the tribal populations and their similar needs in land. But inasmuch as the make-up of the future restored tribes was entirely unknown, since the bulk of them had scattered beyond recall, such a convenient assumption is hardly censurable as a working basis for a theory of restoration. Where the scheme seems to take flight from reality is in the astonishing north-to-south array of tribes in strips across the country, so different from the historical tribal division recorded in the book of Joshua, and so apparently heedless of the terrain of Palestine. This array gives the whole a fantastic appearance. Has it a grounding in some reality?

Let us look more closely at what is implied in the notion that the tribes will have equal shares in the land. Tradition recorded an apportionment made in Joshua's time; was there a lesson to be learned from it for the future? Josh. 17:14-18 tells how the Josephides complained of their share to Joshua: it was wooded highlands and therefore

---

[21] Bewer, *Ezekiel*, (*Harper's Annotated Bible Series*, No. 9), ii, 80, at 48:1-7; Cooke, *Ezekiel* (*ICC*), ii, 524; Fohrer, *Ezechiel* (*HAT*), p. 260; May, in *IB* vi, 332.

[22] *Ezekiel* (*CB*), p. 387; note too May's "apparently."

[23] Smend, *Ezechiel* (*KHAT*), p. 392.

[24] *Toldot ha'emuna*, vii, 566 ff.; *The Religion of Israel*, p. 443 ff.

inadequate for a tribe of their size. Joshua advised them to clear the land and it would suffice for them, but more or different land is what the tribe wanted. How could such cause for complaint be averted in the future?

The 10th century Palestinian Arab geographer Al Muḳaddasi ("the Jerusalemite") gives what in all essentials has remained to this day the standard gross geographic description of Palestine and Syria:

The country, physically, may be divided into four zones. The first zone is that on the border of the Mediterranean Sea. It is the plain-country, the sandy tracts following one another, and alternating with the cultivated land. Of towns situated herein are Ar Ramlah, and also all the cities of the sea-coast. The second zone is the mountain-country, well wooded, and possessing many springs, with frequent villages and cultivated fields. Of the cities that are situated in this part are: Bait Jibrîl, Jerusalem, Nâbulus, Al-Lajjûn, Kâbul, Kadas, the towns of the Bikâ' and Antioch. The third zone is that of the valleys of the (Jordan) Ghaur, wherein are found many villages and streams, also palm-trees, well cultivated fields, and indigo plantations. Among the towns in this part are Wailah, Tabûk, Sughar, Jericho, Baisân, Tiberias, Bâniyâs. The fourth zone is that bordering on the Desert. The mountains here are high and bleak, and the climate resembles that of the Waste; but it has many villages, with springs of water and forest trees. Of the towns therein are Maâb, 'Ammân, Adhra'âh, Damascus, Hims, Tadmur, and Aleppo.[25]

In a word, Palestine-Syria may be described as comprising four longitudinal zones, of which three are included in Cis-jordan: the coastal plain, the western highlands, and the central (Jordan) valley.[26]

Now if one wished to apportion the country from southern Syria to the tip of the Dead Sea into equal shares, the only way to do it would be to take cuts across the three longitundinal zones, thus providing each share with a bit of coastal plain, a bit of highlands and a bit of the central valley. To be sure, the equalization would be only approximate, but it would be closer by this than by any other ready method. Far from disregarding reality, then, the scheme of Ezek. 48 adopts the only way the topography of Palestine allows to parcel the land into roughly similar shares.

III. Artificiality in Territorial Arrangements in Antiquity

The passages we have studied in Numbers and Ezekiel are designs for the future, according to their plain sense. Schematization and idealization are to be expected in them. How far from reality such schematization was depends on the amount of abstraction in topographical layouts that the Israelite found about him, and that is virtually unknown to us. Evidence of city planning has become available in recent decades. "Macalister could still write that the typical Israelite settlement from the age of the monarchy was built without rational order and plan. It is now clear that this notion was based on the spotty work of early archeologists. Wherever connected areas of considerable size have been exposed, a latticework of streets intersecting at right angles, or nearly at right angles, has been found."[27]

From all over the Near East evidence exists for the patterned shape of ancient cities.

Normally the wall of a Mesopotamian city is arranged in wide curves or in rectilinear, mostly quadrilateral, and often symmetrical designs. . . . Square, rectangular, and round cities are typically new foundations; these forms clearly represent abstractions, natural only in planned cities. . . . It has been repeatedly asserted that both rectangular and round city plans have as their prototype such military encampments as those represented on Assyrian reliefs. . . . In fact, symmetrical enclosures forming simple geometric figures are the customary way in which migrating tribes or armies arrange their camps.[28]

A remote yet intriguing analogue to the tribal reapportionment of Ezek. 47-48 can be found in Athens, a generation after Ezekiel, among the reforms of Cleisthenes. Aiming to abolish undue

---

[25] M. J. de Goeje, *Bibliotheca Geographorum Arabicorum* (Leiden, 1870, 1873), vol. iii, p. 186; cited by G. Le Strange, *Palestine under the Moslems* (reprinted Beirut, 1965), p. 15, whence the above translation is taken.

[26] D. Baly, *The Geography of the Bible* (London, 1957), pp. 8 f.; see the graphic map in *Eretz Israel* 2 (Jerusalem, 1953), facing p. 25; cf., finally, the lucid exposition of G. A. Smith, *Historical Geography of the Holy Land*[25] (London, 1931), pp. 46-54, which includes the biblical terminology for geographical divisions of the country, attesting to native awareness of these areas.

[27] Avi-yonah and Yeivin, *The Antiquities of Israel* (Hebrew) (Tel Aviv, 1955), p. 99; cf. the more qualified opinion by McCown, in article "City," *IDB* I, 636a; a contrary opinion in G. E. Wright, *Biblical Archaeology*, p. 186—but the town plan in Avi-yonah, p. 99 (Megiddo) and the remarks of Kenyon, *Archaeology in the Holy Land*, pp. 252 f. (on Beth-Shemesh) and 254 (Tell el Far'ah) speak for at least some planning.

[28] A. L. Oppenheim, *Ancient Mesopotamia* (Chicago, 1964), pp. 133 ff.

local and family influence on politics, and to enfranchise new citizens many of whom were resident aliens (cf. Ezek. 47: 22 f.), Cleisthenes revolutionized the tribal system in a way that evokes the wonder of modern historians: "A system more artificial than the tribes and trittyes of Cleisthenes it might well pass the wit of man to devise." [29]

Taking the map of Attica as he found it, consisting of between one and two hundred demes or small districts, Cleisthenes distinguished three regions: the region of the city, the region of the coast, and the inland. In each of these regions he divided the demes into ten groups called *trittyes*, so that there were thirty such trittyes in all. . . . Out of the thirty trittyes he then formed ten groups of three, in such a way that no group contained two trittyes from the same region. Each of these groups constituted a tribe, and the citizens of all the demes contained in its three trittyes were fellow tribesmen. . . . The ten new tribes, based on artificial geography, took the place of the four old tribes, based on birth. . . . And the deme, a local unit, replaced the social unit of the clan. This scheme of Cleisthenes . . . might seem almost too artificial to last. The secret of its permanence lay in the fact that the demes, the units on which it was built up, were natural divisions, which he did not attempt to reduce to a round number.[30]

The reform of Cleisthenes and Ezekiel's resettlement scheme have in common: tribes, geographical regions whose nature (if we have interpreted Ezekiel rightly) is crucial for the scheme, and resident aliens that must be integrated. How differently each dealt with these variables is most instructive. The Athenian had a democratic ideal before him, the Judahite, an ideal of concord and justice, ultimately based on religion. The motive for integrating the resident alien illustrates the difference. For the former, it was a matter of reshaping the balance of political power; for the latter, the fulfillment of an ideal of equal treatment under the law. Even more characteristic: for the Athenian, the locality was fundamental, the tribe an artificial, political creation. For the Judahite, the tribe was fundamental and the locality artificially molded to serve it.[31] On the score of artificiality, however, Cleisthenes' historically attested reform makes the visionary tribal apportionment of Ezekiel seem the essence of simplicity and naturalness.

* * * * *

The priestly writers, like the legislators, were fond of ideal formulations. But to understand them it is necessary to credit them with more than extravagant imagination, reckless of reality. "In framing an ideal we may assume what we wish, but should avoid impossibilities." In the two items we have studied the priestly writers have hewn to Aristotle's injunction.

[29] E. M. Walker in *CAH*, iv, 143; I am grateful to my teacher and colleague Lloyd W. Daly for bringing Cleisthenes' reform to my attention.

[30] J. B. Bury, *A History of Greece*[3] (London, 1951), pp. 211 f.

[31] On the significance and persistence of familial groupings in Israel, cf. Speiser, "'People' and 'Nation' of Israel," *JBL* 79 (1960), 157-163.

OIL PLANTS IN HITTITE ANATOLIA

HANS G. GÜTERBOCK
ORIENTAL INSTITUTE, UNIVERSITY OF CHICAGO

IN THE RITES aimed at bringing back the vanished god several kinds of fruit are used for "Analogiezauber." Beside such examples as the fig, which holds "a thousand seeds," or the raisin, which has wine in its interior,[1] the olive is mentioned as holding oil. It is, however, not the only such fruit: there is ^{GIŠ}*ša(m)ma(m)ma*, which is also said to hold oil, and ^{GIŠ}*liti-/leti-*, which seems to be of a similar nature. Since all three occur side by side in the same texts, neither *šamama* nor *liti-* can be the Hittite reading of the Akkadogram ^{GIŠ}*ZÉ-ER-DU*,[2] "olive." The prob-

[1] Thus, GIŠGEŠTIN.È.A (=UD.DU.A), e.g. KUB XXXIII 68 ii 13 (*RHA* 77, 128); 74 i 5 (ibid. 164, line 14); XVII 12 iii 10 f.; 13 ii 5 f. (ibid. 144, partly restored). One would expect fresh grapes rather than dried ones! In KUB XVII 10 ii 19 the word is lost, restoration without È.A (*RHA* 77, 93) is possible but not certain.

[2] Akkadian *sirdu*, but in Boğazköy always written with *zé* (KUB XXXVII 2 with *si* in obv. 18 is Babylonian import according to Köcher's note in the introduction).

lem, thus, is to determine the meaning of the two Hittite words.

For ^{GIŠ}*šamama* the translation "sesame" has been proposed and entered in the dictionary.[3] The present writer has for a long time held a different opinion which he will set forth in the following pages. The scholar to whose memory this issue is dedicated was always interested in problems of material culture, especially such that were connected with the spread of a term. In addition, another contribution to this issue is dealing with the problem of the very existence of sesame in the ancient Near East, so that it may not be out of place here to bring the Hittite evidence into the debate. While the decision as to whether *šamaššammu* is sesame or not must be left to others, I shall here use the traditional translation "sesame" for the sake of convenience.

The ideogram of Akkadian *šamaššammu*, ŠE.GIŠ.Ì, occurs in Hittite texts.[4] It clearly refers to the seed: it is strewn on bread (KBo VIII 91 rev. 3 f.), or the word is used to designate a special kind of bread: NINDA.ŠE.GIŠ.Ì "sesame bread," NINDA.LÀL.ŠE.GIŠ.Ì "honey bread with sesame."[5]

Much more frequent is the term for the oil, Ì.GIŠ.[6] Again we may leave aside the question of whether this is sesame oil or some other kind as well as the problem of the Akkadian reading, *ellu* or *šamnu* (see the discussion in the dictionaries just quoted). We may safely do so since there is nothing in the Hittite texts which would link Ì.GIŠ with the word primarily to be discussed here, ^{GIŠ}*šamama*.

A typical passage from the invocation rituals is KUB XVII 13 col. ii:[7]

(1-4) Behold, [olives are lying here.] Just as [the olive] holds oil in its 'heart,' thus [hold thou, o Mother-goddess,] the king, queen, princes and the land of Hatti in friendliness in thy heart and soul!

(5-8) Behold, raisins are lying here. Just as the [raisin] holds wine in its 'heart,' thus hold thou, (etc.).

(9-12) Behold, ^{GIŠ}*šamama* are lying here. Just as the ^{GIŠ}[*š.*] holds oil in its 'heart,' thus hold thou, (etc.).

(13 f.) [Beho]ld, *le*[*tiš* is lying here. Just as the *letiš* . . . . .] evil [. . . . (continuation broken).

These stereotype passages from invocations may be tabulated as follows:

KUB XVII 13 ii

RHA 77, 143 f. (above)

[olive]	— oil
raisin	— wine
šamama	— oil
le[*tiš*]	— [. . .]

KUB XXXIII 74 + . . . , i

RHA 77, 164 f.

fig	— 1000 seeds
raisin	— wine
olive	— oil
letiš	— to *lilarešk-* heart and soul
šammamma	— [. . . .]

HT 100 + . . .

RHA 77, 163

fig	— sweet
liti	— to *lilarešk-*
raisin	— wine
olive	— oil

KUB XVII 12 iii 8 ff.

Oriens XV 350

fig	— 1000 seeds
raisin	— wine

KUB XXXIII 75 ii 16 ff.

RHA 77, 146

fig	— 1000 seeds
olive	— [oil]

---

[3] First used by Goetze in *ANET*, p. 127, translating KUB XVII 10 ii 15; advocated by H. Otten, *Hethitische Totenrituale* (1958) (abbr. *HTR*), p. 134; accepted by J. Friedrich, *Hethitisches Wörterbuch* (*HW*) 2. Ergänzungsheft, pp. 22 and 31.

[4] References given by E. Laroche, *RHA* XIX/68 (1961) 45.

[5] KBo VIII 89 obv. 12; Bo 2040 rev. 16 in *HTR* 134.

[6] Friedrich, *HW* 277 without reference; Deimel, ŠL 231, 157 without ref. to Boğazköy; see *CAD* s. v. *ellu* B, *AHw* s. v. *ellu*(*m*) II. A few random references to Boğazköy texts follow: KUB IX 6 i 6-11 (Otten, *LTU* p. 37); XII 15 vi 10, 18 (cf. KUB XI 31 i 21, which writes simple Ì in analogous context); XXV 42 iii 11; KBo XV 47 rev. 7 with dupl. 48 iv 6; 52 vi 33.

[7] Transliterated by E. Laroche in *RHA* XXIII/77 (1965) 143 f. For all texts transliterated there we simply refer to *RHA* 77.

KUB XXXIII 68 ii 6-16

RHA 77, 128

fig	— 1000 seeds
šamama	— (different, see below)
raisin	— wine
olive	— oil

In some texts there is more variety in the wording of these spells. In the Telipinu text, first version (KUB XVII 10 ii 15 ff., *RHA* 77, 92 f.), this particular group reads as follows (the preceding and following spells are not relevant here):

(15) *kaša* ^{GIŠ}*šamamma kitta* [. . .
(16) *šakuwan eštu.* There follow:

the fig	— being sweet
the olive	— holding oil
the [raisin] [8]	— holding wine; then:

(22) *kaša* ^{GIŠ}*liti kitta*
nu ŠA ^{d}*Telipinu* [. . .
(23) *iškiddu.*

Here again, *šamama,* olive, and *liti* occur side by side; but whereas the passage about the olive has the well-known form, we are told that something should be *šakuwan* [like] [9] *šamama.* Unfortunately the adjective/participle *šakuwant-* is still far from clear,[10] so we cannot—at least not yet—use it to determine the character of *šamama.*

For *liti* we learn from this passage that it has something to do with anointing (*iškiddu* "let it anoint"); and since it has here (as also outside the texts so far listed) the determinative GIŠ, we may safely consider it as falling into the same class as ^{GIŠ}MA "fig," ^{GIŠ}GEŠTIN "grape, raisin," ^{GIŠ}*SERDU* "olive," and ^{GIŠ}*šamama,* in other words, take it as the name of a tree and its fruit.[11] It is for this reason that we listed *liti-* as an oil-bearing fruit in our introduction. Unfortunately the verb *lilarešk-* [12] is unknown. While a general or derived meaning like "to appease, propitiate" may be guesssed at, it is hard to determine the concrete meaning of the verb said of the fruit *liti-*, except that the verb *išk-* "to anoint," used in connection with the same fruit in the Telipinu spell, may perhaps indicate in what direction one might look.[13]

Turning to other ritual texts, we find *šamama* included in various lists of ingredients. These are as follows:

1. KUB XII 26 iii 11-14

BAPPIR	'beer bread'
BULÙG	malt
GA.KIN.AG	cheese
UZU.Ì	suet
^{GIŠ}*ZÉ-ER-TUM*	olive
^{GIŠ}MA	fig
^{GIŠ}GEŠTIN.È.A	raisin
^{GIŠ}*ḫa-aš-ši-ik-kań*	. . . .
^{GIŠ}*ša-am-ma-ma*	. . . .

2. KUB XXIX 1 iv 4 ff.

Ì.ŠAḪ	lard
LÀL	honey
GA.KIN.AG	cheese
EM-ṢÚ	rennet(?)
(SÍG BABBAR	white wool)
(SÍG MI	black wool)
BAPPIR	'beer bread'
BULÙG	malt
^{GIŠ}*ša-ma-ma*	. . . .
^{GIŠ}GEŠTIN.È.A	raisin
^{GIŠ}*le-e-ti*	. . . .
^{GIŠ}*šu-wa-i-tar*	. . . .
(KUŠ.GUD	cowhide)
MUN	salt

[8] For the restoration, raisin or grape, see above, n. 1.

[9] For this restoration see below, n. 13.

[10] Cf. *HW* 178. The passage closest to ours is *RHA* 77, 161 B ii 5, where the god is invited to "eat the smooth, hot, *šakuwant-*[. . .]"—the name of the food being lost! Should this *šakuwant-* turn out to be the same as the participle "seen, visible" one might think of "conspicuous, beautiful, pleasing" or the like.

[11] It is hard to understand why W. von Soden listed this word from this text in *AHw* under *littu*(*m*) III "stool"—albeit with the question "dazu?" Equally unjustified is Otten's transliteration as Akkadogram, *HTR* 134. That it is a Hittite *-i* stem is shown by the occurrence of the nominative form in *-iš*, KUB XXXIII 74 i 8 (*RHA* 77, 165, 17), common gender, as against endingless neuter in *-i* in the other texts. See already Laroche, *RA* 52 (1958) 188 (*HW*, 2. Erg. 17).

[12] Ingeniously reconstructed from broken texts by Laroche, *RHA* 77, at the passages quoted and p. 144 (note 13 below). Is this, despite the *-r-*, to be connected with the verb *lila*(*i*)-, *HW* 2. Erg. 17?

[13] Another broken text, KUB XXXIII 38 col. i (*RHA* 77, 144), seems to have a comparable combination of spells: *lilareš*[*kiddu*] calls for the restoration of *liti*, and *šakuwan* recalls *šamama* in the Telipinu text just discussed. What follows (in lines 6-8) shows that that text should indeed be restored in the form of a comparison (n. 9 above).

Otten, *HTR* p. 134, quotes the following from unpublished ritual texts:

3. 634/b, 6 f.
(measured by *se'a*)

^{GIŠ}MA	fig
[. . . .]	
^{GIŠ}*ša-am-ma-ma*	. . . .

4. 139/d i 8 ff.
(measured by handful)

[. . . .]	
^{GIŠ}GEŠTIN.È.A	raisin
^{GIŠ}*ZERTUM*	olive
^{GIŠ}*NU*[*RMU*]	pomegranate
[. . . .]	
^{GIŠ}*ša-am-ma-ma*	. . . .
^{GIŠ}*le-e-ti*	. . . .

5. 110/e obv. 5

[. . . .]	
[^{GIŠ}GEŠ]TIN.È.A	raisin
^{GIŠ}*ZERTUM*	olive
^{GIŠ}*ša-ma-ma*	. . . .
^{GIŠ}*ḫa-ši-ig-ga*	. . . .

6. KUB XII 64, 1-4

[. . . .]	
^{GIŠ}*ḫa-aš-ši-i*[*g-ga*]	. . . .
^{GIŠ}*ša-ma-ma*	. . . .
NINDA *EM.ṢÚ*	sour bread
BULÙG BAPPIR	malt and 'beer bread'

In the ritual for the dead, *šamama* occurs in lists introduced by the heading "all fruit" in the sense of "fruit of all kinds." These are:

7. KUB XXXIX 7 ii 16 f., repeated ibid. 63 f. (*HTR* pp. 36, 40)

^{GIŠ}*IN-BI*$^{\text{ḪI.A}}$ (*ḫumanda*)	(all) fruit
^{GIŠ}MA	fig
^{GIŠ}GEŠTIN.È.A	raisin
^{GIŠ}*ZÉ-ER-TUM*	olive
^{GIŠ}*ša-ma-am-ma-an-za*	*š*.s (Luwian plural)
(var.: No. 8: ^{GIŠ}*ša-am-ma*[-. . .]; ii 64: ^{GIŠ}*ša-ma-ma*)	
^{GIŠ}ḪAŠḪUR	apple
^{GIŠ}ḪAŠḪUR.KUR.RA	'mountain apple' (= ?)

8. KUB XXXIX 21 i 10 f. (*HTR* p. 88)

IN-BI$^{\text{ḪI.A}}$ *ḫuman*	all fruit
^{GIŠ}[. . . .]	. . . .
. . . .	
^{GIŠ}ḪAŠḪUR.KUR.RA	'mountain apple'
^{GIŠ}*ša-am-ma-m*[*a*]	. . . .

9. There is another list which requires some comment. In KBo X 34 col. i, ^{GIŠ}*šamama* occurs in lines 18 and 24, but the seeming third occurrence in line 14 is a copying mistake of mine which should be corrected. The tablet has *ša-ma-iz-na-aš*, as clearly visible on the photograph.[14] The passage, lines 11-25, is divided by horizontal rules into four lists.

The *first* of these deals with different kinds of bread, the last of which is honey bread. The phrase which follows, *kuišša para* (or *kuitta para*, depending on the gender), literally "each one out," is often used in such listings in the sense of "und zwar, namely, including the following items," or the like. It is here followed by a list of words in the genitive indicating the materials from which the breads are made; whether this refers to several of the bread names which precede it or only to the last, NINDA.LÀL, remains open. The materials enumerated are:

ZÍZ "wheat,"[15] *ḫaršanila-*, *euwan-*, *parḫuena-*, GÚ.TUR "peas," GÚ.GAL.GAL "chickpeas (? or: beans?)," *ša-ma-iz-na-*, ^{GIŠ}*ḫa-aš-ši-ig-ga-*, and *ša-ap-ša-ma-*.

The *second* section (15-18) lists "all fresh (and) dried fruit" ^{GIŠ}*IN-BU ḫuman RA-AṬ-BU ŠA-BU-Ú-LU* "namely, of each a little: fig, raisin, olive, *paizzinna-*, *warawara-*, apple, 'mountain apple,' ^{GIŠ}*zu-u-pa*,[16] ^{GIŠ}*dammašḫuel*, pomegranate, grape (here without È.A!), ^{GIŠ}*ša-ma-ma*."

In the *third* listing, the decisive first word (line 19) is not clear; does it begin with [DU]G? Does it refer to juice? At the end of the paragraph we

[14] Against an "emendation" of *iz* into *ma* (i.e., assuming a "mistake" of the scribe which my miscopy would have "corrected") is the occurrence of [. . . *š*]*a-am-ma-iz-zi-li-iš* in line 25, where *iz* before *zi* is in order. I am unable to offer an interpretation for either of these groups of signs. An "emendation" of *am-ma* to *ne* is, again, contradicted by the simple *ma* of line 14. Besides, **šamamanaš* would be the only example for the omission of GIŠ and for an *-n* stem!

[15] I cannot go into details here; but since ZÍZ is the most common bread cereal of the Hittites, and since the texts never have GIG for "wheat," whereas real wheat is archaeologically attested even for pre-Hittite times in central Anatolia, I think that ZÍZ, in Hittite texts, cannot be limited to the meaning "emmer wheat."

[16] Since Akkadian *zūpu* "origanum" (or "hyssop," *HW* 2. Erg. p. 34 without reference) is not a fruit but an herb, written with SAR, attested only once in a late text and suspect of being a loan from Aramaic (see *CAD* for this information), it cannot be meant here. We therefore take ^{GIŠ}*zupa* as Hittite name, in the neuter plural form, of a fruit.

read *memal ŠA* GIŠ*IN-BI* "meal of fruit;" is this an item by itself or a description of what precedes? The list itself, again in the genitive, is: "of apples, of figs, of raisins, of pomegranates, of [GIŠ]*ḫatalkešna-*, of *euwan-*."

The *fourth* is a list of "roasted" items (*[š]anḫunta*). They are: *[ḫarš]aniliš*, *euwan*, *parḫuenaš*, GÚ.GAL.GAL, [GÚ.TUR], GIŠ*ša-ma-ma duwarnanda* "broken *š*.s," GIŠ.KÍN.ḪI.A *duwarnanda* "broken *k*. s." [17] After a short break there follows "[. . . *š*]*ammaizziliš* (see n. 14 above), filled."

From these lists we learn the following about *šamama*:

a) It is consistently written with GIŠ, the determinative commonly used for trees and fruit of trees.

b) While in the first few lists it is associated with other ingredients as well as with fruit, it is expressly subsumed under the heading *INBU* in lists Nr. 7 and 8. In list 9 it appears among "fresh and dried fruit" and again under the heading "roasted ones," but is not found among the ingredients used for breads.

c) The last section of list 9 speaks of "broken" *š*. This brings us to another passage which requires some discussion. In KUB XXXIII 68 ii 7 ff. (*RHA* 77, 128) we read:

(7) *nu* GIŠMA *maḫḫan andurza LIM* NUMUN-*an ḫarzi*
(8) *ziga ŠÀ-it aššu ud-da-a-na-za ḫark*
GIŠ*ša-ma-ma* (9) *maḫḫan duwarnizzi*
nu pár-aš-te-ḫu-uš (10) *peššiezzi*
kardiya-tta-ma-at-kan šara danzi /
(11) *ziga* dU *idalu ud-da-a-ar arḫa peššiya*
(12) *nu-za aššu ud-da-a-ar da-a* /

Despite the difficulties of this text we may venture the following translation:

Just as the fig has a thousand seeds inside,
(thus) hold thou (o god) good words(?)[18] in thy heart!
Just as he[19] breaks the *šamama* and throws away the *p*.s (= shells?),
and they lift it up to thy heart,
(thus) throw thou, o Storm-god, away the evil words
and take the good words!

(The next sections use the well-known similes of the raisin holding wine and the olive holding oil, as tabulated above; there follows the section with GIŠ.KÍN discussed in n. 17 above.)

It was this passage in conjunction with the observations mentioned before which made me think of some kind of nut: *šamama* is the fruit of a tree, it contains oil, and something is thrown away[20] when it is broken. This leaves open the question of which kind of nut or nut-like fruit *šamama* may be: walnut, hazelnut, pistachio, almond; all grow in Asia Minor.

In view of the difficulties encountered in the interpretation of this passage (XXXIII 68 ii 7 ff.) it is better not to put too much emphasis on what may be the cracking of shells! There is, however, another observation to which the lists give rise:

d) The sequence of fruits and other ingredients is by no means fixed, a fact which makes all conclusions based on sequence alone rather hazardous. Now Otten's main argument was the "Nebeneinander beider Begriffe" (*HTR* 134), viz., the combination of *ḫaššikka* — *šamama* (XII 26, our No. 1; add Nr. 6) or *šamama* — *ḫaššikka* (110/e, No. 5) on the one hand, and NINDA.LÀL *ḫaššiggaš* and NINDA.LÀL ŠE.GIŠ.Ì on the other.[21] However, we observed that *šamama* is not

---

[17] GIŠ."ḪAR" must here be the name of a fruit (or tree). For GIŠ.KÍN = *kiškanû* see *AHw* s.v.; another occurrence seems to be KUB XXXIII 68 ii 18 (*RHA* 77, 128 f.) with (Hittite?) complement -ri: "Whoever speaks evil to the dear Storm-god about the king and queen, *nan* GIŠ.KÍN-*ri du-ud-du-uš-x*[. . .-*d*]*u*? (I cannot restore or translate this); whoever speaks a harsh word to you, o [Storm-]god, give ⟨him⟩ a [. . . .] 'mountain apple'; whoever [. . . .] a sour [. . . .] to the Storm-god, give him a sour apple, o Storm-god!" Here the mention of two other kinds of fruit in the next clauses makes *kiškanû* more likely than GIŠ.ḪUR = *uṣurtu*.

[18] Assuming a mistake for *ud-da-a-ar*, as lines 11 and 12 actually write. An ablative here seems out of place.

[19] Who is meant? The officiating priest? Or the patron of the ritual? For the general subject Hittite normally uses the 3d pers. plur., as found here in line 10. To take *šamama* here as subject (verb form in the sing. would be in order after a neuter plur.) would imply intransitive use of the active form of *duwarna(i)*- ("as the *š*.s pop and shed the *p*.s"), a use for which there is to my knowledge no other example.

[20] Apart from the hard shell, one might think of the fleshy outer shell of a walnut (if this is what the *šamama* is). Is there any connection between *par(a)šteḫa-* and *paršdu-* "sprout, shoot"?

[21] In Bo 2040 rev. 15 f. In the duplicate, KUB XXVII 19, 3, only the first term is preserved; there is space of undetermined length available for the restoration of

among the ingredients used for bread (or honey bread alone) in our text No. 9, first section. But just there, at the end of the list (KBo X 34 i 14) and following *ḫaššiggaš*, we find a word (in the genitive) *šapšamaš*!

Now it seems obvious that, once it had been noted that *šamama* contains oil, the similarity of sound between *šamama* and Akkadian *šamaššammu* played its part in the proposal that *šamama* be sesame. But the assonance is not very close, especially in view of the fact that the Hurrian form is *šumišumi*.[22] *šamama* lacks the second *s* found in all other forms of this international word. It seems to me that the *šapšama-* of KBo X 34 i 14 has a much better chance of being the Hittite name of the sesame, for the following reasons:

1) The assonance with *šamaššammu, šumišumi* is closer;
2) it does not have the determinative GIŠ;
3) in contrast to *šamama* it is used for honey bread, and
4) its position after *ḫaššikka-* corresponds exactly to that of ŠE.GIŠ.Ì in Otten's text.[23]

What, then, is [GIŠ]*liti-/leti-*? Also a fruit, different from both *šamama* and the olive, and one whose product can be used for anointing. Thus the almond offers itself as a candidate, since almond oil is known for its cosmetic use. It is clear that this is no more than a possibility; the evidence is not sufficient really to determine the nature of *liti-*.

If we may sum up our conclusions, even though they are only tentative, we have the following oil producing plants in the Hittite texts:

[GIŠ]*SERDU*,	the olive;
[GIŠ]*šamama*,[24]	a kind of nut;
[GIŠ]*liti-*,	perhaps the almond;
ŠE.GIŠ.Ì,	probably read *šapšama-* in Hittite, "sesame" according to the traditional translation.

the second. The parallel text KUB XXXII 128 i 5 simply says "all (kinds of) honey bread" without naming them. The wording in *HW*, 2. Erg. 22: "wechselt in Paralleltexten mit (dem) Idgr." puts more into Otten's statement than what the facts warrant.

[22] Known from the Ras Shamra vocabulary: Thureau-Dangin, *Syria* XII (1931), text No. 8 on pp. 234 ff. and Pl. L-LII, col. ii 11 on p. 238, corresponding to *Ḫḫ* II 124 (*MSL* V p. 61). *HW* 325 and *HTR* 134, n. 3, quote secondary literature.

[23] It must be stated that at the time of Otten's writing the tablet KBo X 34 had not yet been excavated, so that he could not know about *šapšama-*.

[24] In all places known to me ending in *-a*. According to the participle *duwarnanda* in KBo X 34 i 24 we are safe in taking this for neuter plural. Once there occurs a Luwian plural in *-anza* (above, list 7). Other occurrences, which have no immediate bearing on the discussion, are:
KUB XXXI 79, 3 (letter about transport by boat) may be restored as [. . . . . AD].KID [GIŠ]*ša-ma-ma na-aš up-p*[*í* . . .] "[(so and so many containers) of wick]erwork (filled with) *šamama*: dis[patch] them!"
KUB XXXIII 34 obv. 8 (*RHA* 77, 127): [GIŠ]*ša-ma-ma-kán wa-ar-aš-t*[*a*] "he harvested *š*.s."
KUB XXXIV 80 obv. 9: *naš* [GIŠ]*ša-ma-am-ma ki-i-ša-ru* "let him become, turn into, *š*." The parallel paragraphs have "let him turn into a fish" and "into the river Maraššandaš," respectively. Does line 10 contain the verb [*li-*]*le-e-ia-ru* from *lilai-*, discussed in n. 12 above?

INDIVIDUAL PRAYER IN SUMERIAN: THE CONTINUITY OF A TRADITION

WILLIAM W. HALLO [1]
YALE UNIVERSITY

I. A Sumerian Psalter?

SINCE THE FIRST PSALM STUDIES of Hermann Gunkel at the beginning of this century, the exegesis of the Biblical Psalter has accorded an ever more prominent place to the comparison of the hymns and prayers of the cuneiform tradition of ancient Mesopotamia.[2] As early as 1922,

[1] Originally presented, under the title of "The Psalter of the Sumerians," to the Philip W. Lown Institute of Advanced Judaic Studies, Brandeis University, November 2, 1966.

[2] For exhaustive bibliographies of current psalm exegesis, cf. the periodic surveys in *Theologische Rundschau* n.F. 1 (1929, by M. Haller), 23 (1955, by

Stummer ventured to point out numerous "Sumero-Akkadian parallels to the structure of Biblical psalms"[3] in a study which, admittedly, found little favor with Assyriologists.[4] In the 1930's at least three different monographs reverted to the theme, Cumming comparing "The Assyrian and Hebrew Hymns of Praise," Widengren "the Akkadian and Hebrew Psalms of Lamentation,"[5] and Castellino both "The lamentations and the hymns in Babylonia and in Israel."[6] All these studies retain their usefulness but, with the exception of Castellino's, they suffer from a common defect: they tend to exempt the Mesopotamian material from the very Gattungsforschung which, following Gunkel, they accept as axiomatic for Hebrew psalmody.

This is the more strange since the Akkadian material comes provided with its own generic classifications, and with specific indications of its cultic Sitz im Leben. Often enough, it is cited by title only, and incorporated within elaborate cultic calendars or ritual prescriptions and thus clearly secondary in importance to its context.[7] Indeed, Gunkel[8] and Mowinckel[9] relied on these aspects of the Mesopotamian material to justify a parallel approach to the Psalms, and Begrich[10] had drawn elaborate comparisons between the individual laments of the Bible and the private prayers of Mesopotamia as early as 1928.

In the 1940's and 1950's, the comparative study of the Psalms turned most of its attention, perhaps understandably, to the newly discovered Ugaritic texts which were evidently so much closer to the Psalms in language, style and imagery than any other Ancient Near Eastern parallels yet unearthed. Patton's monograph on the "Canaanite parallels in the Book of Psalms" was followed by the briefer treatments of Coppens and O'Callaghan, and a number of penetrating contributions by Albright.[11] Yet the fact remains that the Ugaritic texts adduced in all these studies are neither hymns nor prayers, and thus can only indirectly serve to illuminate the categories of Biblical psalmody as such.

The present decade has, happily, witnessed a reassertion of the relevance of the Mesopotamian material while recognizing the need to confine the assessment of parallels within comparable Gattungen, at least to begin with. Thus E. R. Dalglish's valuable study of "Psalm 51 in the light of Ancient Near Eastern Patternism"[12] is a deliberate attempt to meet the methodological standards first demanded of Stummer's book forty years earlier: to compare this unique subspecies of individual lament with the comparable penitential categories in cuneiform. Bernhardt has reviewed the entire history of Psalm exegesis with special reference to the so-called "royal psalms," and evaluated these in the light of the Ancient Near Eastern ideology of kingship without, however, limiting himself to a specific cuneiform genre.[13] More recently still, Mitchell Dahood's commentary on Psalms 1-50 in the Anchor Bible has returned to the Ugaritic parallels with a vengeance, in part out of an understandable disenchantment with the excesses of the older Mesopotamian comparisons.[14]

But to say that recent Psalm criticism has more accurately recognized the limits of the comparative method is not to imply that it has everywhere reached them. For if the rich spectrum of Mesopotamian religious poetry was not monolithic in terms of its genres, neither was it a single unchanging canon throughout the nearly three millennia of its attested existence. Quite the contrary, I believe we can distinguish at least four different cuneiform "canons" within Mesopotamia, each

J. J. Stamm). For a comprehensive historical survey, cf. K.-H. Bernhardt, *Das Problem der Altorientalischen Königsideologie* (= VT Supp. 8, 1961) chs. 1-3.

[3] Bernhardt, *op. cit.*, 83 n. 5.

[4] Cf. the review by B. Landsberger, OLZ 28 (1925) 479-483.

[5] Bernhardt, *loc. cit.*

[6] *Le lamentazioni individuali e gli inni in Babilonia e in Israele* (1939).

[7] "No adequate study of literary types in the vast Akkadian liturgy has yet appeared" although "as compared with the Psalter, the Babylonian texts promise a much larger body of definite results, as in many cases not only the liturgical texts are preserved in writing, but also the order of the ceremony in which they were sung or recited." W. G. Lambert, AfO 19 (1959-60) 47. Cf. already S. Langdon "Calendars of liturgies and prayers," AJSL 42 (1926) 110-127.

[8] Cf. e. g. Gunkel-Begrich, *Einleitung in die Psalmen* (1933) § 1.3-§ 1.5.

[9] Cf. now D. R. Ap-Thomas, "An appreciation of Sigmund Mowinckel's contribution to Biblical studies," JBL 85 (1966) 315-325.

[10] Bernhardt, *loc. cit.*

[11] *Ibid.*

[12] (Leiden, 1962), with notes by A. Falkenstein. Cf. the review by Castellino, VT 15 (1965) 116-120.

[13] *Op. cit.* (note 2).

[14] M. Dahood, *Psalms* I (1-50), (The Anchor Bible, New York, 1966). Cf. the review by D. A. Robertson, JBL 85 (1966) 484-6.

the product of a very different age and set of religious presuppositions, and each thoroughly transformed before it was accepted into the next canon. Of these, only the two latest ones have hitherto been systematically invoked in any comparative study of the Biblical Psalter: on the one hand, that is, the Akkadian canon which, originating in Old Babylonian times, was expanded and organized in Middle Babylonian times and enshrined in the great libraries of the neo-Assyrians and, on the other hand, the late bilingual Sumero-Akkadian tradition of Middle Babylonian times which, elaborated in those same libraries, received its final form in the epigonic schools of Seleucid and Parthian Babylonia long after the demise of a native Akkadian body politic.[14a]

But there were at least two other recognized bodies of cuneiform literature which preceded these. One of these is the Old Sumerian canon whose beginnings go back, it would seem, almost to the beginnings of writing itself, and which may well have been gathered into an official corpus under the Sargonic kings of Agade. Much of this literature is only at this moment beginning to yield to the spade of the excavator and the cryptographic skills of the decipherer, and it is still too early to assess its true import.[15]

But there is a more substantial body of Sumerian literature, which I would like to call neo-Sumerian and which, at least since the Second World War, has absorbed the attention of ever more Assyriologists. This literature, chiefly created under the dynasties of Agade, Ur III and Isin I, was organized into a scholarly curriculum in the Old Babylonian period. It attained a high degree of literary excellence and to some extent survived the destruction of the Old Babylonian schools to influence, as I think, also the literary products of later ages. Up to now, this neo-Sumerian literature has been almost completely neglected by comparative Biblical studies, at least as far as the comparative study of the Psalms is concerned. Yet I hope to show that we now know it well enough to attempt to compare it, not only with the Akkadian and bilingual religious poetry of later Mesopotamia, but also with Biblical psalmody.

In order to do so within the bounds of the methodology already set forth, it is necessary in the first place to essay a generic classification of neo-Sumerian religious poetry. Only then will it be possible to match the resulting categories with the corresponding genres in the later material, whether Babylonian or Biblical. Finally, a single genre from the several canons will be subjected to closer scrutiny in order to weigh specific comparisons and contrasts in the balance.

The concise bibliography of neo-Sumerian literature compiled by Maurice Lambert may serve as a starting-point for our classification.[16] His survey recognizes fifteen separate genres. Two of these, myths and epics, fall outside the purview of religious literature in the narrow sense at issue here, i. e. hymns and prayers. This is also true of the three types of wisdom literature which Lambert distinguishes[17] even though, of course, a few examples of wisdom compositions may be found among the neo-Sumerian hymns just as they found their way into the Hebrew Psalter. A similar ambiguity surrounds the so-called love-poems on the one hand, and on the other the "catalogue texts" which have an analogue in Ps. 68 if Albright's interpretation of the latter text[18] is correct. Finally, we must eliminate from consideration the genre of "Learned and Scientific Texts" which are largely or wholly prose in form and non-literary (i. e. monumental or archival) in origin. That leaves us with seven genres of neo-Sumerian religious poetry, to wit: lamentations, hymns to gods, hymns to temples, liturgies, royal hymns, compositions devoted to the "philosophy of history," and those on religious philosophy,—seven prima facie components of an assumed neo-Sumerian psalter. Let us see whether they warrant the label, first collectively on the basis of their common treatment and canonical arrangement, and then individually on the basis of their distinguishing characteristics.

To begin with, then, can we speak of the seven genres, taken together, as a canonical[19] collection

---

[14a] Cf. e. g. the numerous parallels considered by G. R. Driver, "The Psalms in the light of Babylonian research," *apud* D. C. Simpson, ed., *The Psalmists* (1926) 109-175.

[15] Hallo, JAOS 83 (1963) 167; M. Civil and R. D. Biggs, "Notes sur des textes sumériens archaïques," RA 60 (1966) 1-16.

[16] "La littérature sumérienne . . . ," RA 55 (1961) 177-196, 56 (1962) 81-90, 214.

[17] For a more detailed subdivision, cf. E. I. Gordon, Bi. Or. 17 (1960) 124.

[18] HUCA 23/1 (1950-51) 1-39.

[19] I am concerned here only with the literary sense of the term, not its religious or cultic connotations.

in the sense of the Biblical Psalter? The usual criteria here would seem to be an authoritative text, a reasonably fixed number and sequence of individual compositions, and the grouping of these compositions into recognizable books or subdivisions.[20] Recent discoveries at Qumran have warned us not to apply these tests too rigorously even to the Biblical Psalter, and the evidence is even more tenuous in the case of the Sumerian texts. But it does suffice to show that some of them, at least, are met there as well. Duplicate exemplars of single compositions, for instance, show a large measure of agreement even when found at widely scattered sites, not only in wording but also in textual details that may be described as "masoretic" such as line counts, strophic structure, classification and so forth. Or again, compositions of the same genre, or of closely related genres, were often collected on single tablets in an order which seems to have been more or less fixed. We are not yet in a position to restore this order in anything like its entirety, nor the major groupings of the corpus as a whole, but the analogy of the later canonizations of cuneiform literature suggests that the Old Babylonian schools were busy fixing both order and grouping. In short, we will not be adjudged terribly premature if we already operate with the hypothesis that the religious poetry of the neo-Sumerian tradition constituted the materials of what, in effect, may be described as a complete Psalter from the literary point of view.

Let us now turn more specifically to the individual genres as isolated above, beginning with the hymns, a category which by virtue of its importance gave its name to the entire Biblical Psalter, and which survived it as a living form in the Hodayoth of Qumran and the psalms of Sirah if not of Solomon. The same category is also well-represented in the neo-Sumerian corpus, in all of its diversity. There are, first of all, the hymns to various deities, corresponding to the Biblical hymns to God in several respects. For one thing, they are the most numerous of the hymns. More important are the structural parallels, the natural consequence of the essential nature of hymns, which, by their very definition, were "laudatory." Thus the invocation of the deity in the vocative is followed (or, in the Sumerian, initially preceded) by one or more epithets in apposition to the divine name, and by long recitals of the deity's attributes, and of his achievements—past, present and future—in mythology and history, whether these are properly objects of praise, or awe or outright terror. The public recital which provided the setting for the hymn is frequently alluded to in its very text by repeated exhortations to the soloist or chorus to sing the deity's praises or to respond to them antiphonally. The typical hymn concludes with a final doxology phrased in one of a relatively limited number of stereotyped formulas. All these characteristics apply equally to the Biblical as to the neo-Sumerian examples of the genre.

The more specialized hymnal genres of the Psalter are also represented in Sumerian. Thus the "Zion songs" may be likened to the more elaborate hymns to temples and sacred cities in the neo-Sumerian corpus, while the "royal hymns"[21] resemble that class of Sumerian hymns to a deity which include, or conclude with, a prayer on behalf of a specific king. These hymns have been described as "royal hymns in the wider sense," and had a place in the public worship of the temples. They must be distinguished from Sumerian royal hymns in the stricter sense, in which the king's praises are put into his own mouth in the first person, or addressed to him in the second. Such hymns have no liturgical annotations or classifications; they have few references to the deity nor pray to him on behalf of the king, but rather emphasize the king's merits. Presumably they belonged in the courtly ceremonial rather than in the temple service, and it is harder to find their analogue in the Biblical Psalter, though a relatively secular poem such as Ps. 45 might be cited for comparison.

Conversely, it is difficult to find a precise Sumerian equivalent to the much-debated accession hymns of the Psalter. For while the ideology of Mesopotamian kingship may have somehow influenced the latter, it is there applied to God in a fundamentally different sense. This is true also in large measure of such minor Biblical categories as "pilgrim songs," congregational thanksgivings, "legend" and "wisdom" psalms. "Liturgies" on the other hand, are represented in the neo-Sumerian corpus by a number of examples.

Turning next to the congregational laments,

[20] Cf. Hallo, IEJ 12 (1962) 21-26.

[21] Cf. W. H. Ph. Römer, *Sumerische 'Königshymnen' der Isin-Zeit* (1965) and my review, Bi. Or. 23 (1966) 239-246.

this relatively minor Psalm genre, to which most of the Book of Lamentations should be added, corresponds to the rather substantial body of lamentations over the destruction of cities in the neo-Sumerian corpus. In both cases, it is clear that real historic events, and more specifically national disasters, inspired the compositions. But both tended to sublimate the events into vague and involved allusions to the flight of the divine presence or the breakdown of cultic processes. As a result, there is sometimes uncertainty in both as to just what historic event is intended, the more so as there seems to have been no great reluctance about applying older allusions to more recent events. On the Mesopotamian side, it is clear from the number of Sumerian examples; from their intricate strophic structure and liturgical glosses; and from their survival in other forms into later periods, that the public laments represented a thoroughly institutionalized, temple-centered response to the recurrent trauma of wholesale destruction which was visited on the Mesopotamian city-states and empires throughout their history.[22]

What then of the prayers of the individual which form the largest single quotient of the Biblical psalter? Oddly enough, individual, or at any rate private, prayer is very poorly represented in Sumerian literature.[23] In part this may be because the official cult concentrated on the king, and had little use for the private individual, who relied more often than not on a popular religion to which the official religious literature bears little direct testimony, or on the intercession of his personal protective deity with the great gods of the official pantheon. Indeed, our chief examples of private prayer in early Mesopotamia come not from canonical texts at all, but from the monuments.[24] The ubiquitous seal cylinders of the neo-Sumerian and adjacent periods typically show the private seal owner led before the great god by his personal deity. And the typical purpose of private votive objects (as of royal ones) was to forward to the deity the prayer which doubled as the name of the object by leaving the object, with its inscription, on permanent deposit in the cella of the temple, close to the niche which held the statue of the deity. Such inscribed votive objects were, then, considered as taking the place of the suppliant, and relieving him of the need to proffer his prayer in his own person, orally and perpetually. This is stated in so many words by many of the votive inscriptions, and is implied also by the fact that the most expensive type of votive, the statue, clearly depicts the worshipper, not the deity. Other types of votive objects such as steles, bowls, and replicas of tools and weapons from the petitioner's daily life, were simply more modest means to attain the same end. But even such objects were made of semi-precious stones or precious metals and thus beyond the means of most worshippers, and there was consequently the need for a less costly method of written communication with the divine. Apparently, then, it is out of this essentially economic context that there gradually arose a canonical literary genre as a vehicle of individual prayer. At first it took a form which was less literary, or canonical, than economic, or archival. For the formal choice fell upon the letter, a form abundantly familiar to the neo-Sumerian scribes for straightforward economic purposes. Presently, the bare outlines of the archival letters were elaborated to create what constituted, in content if not in form, true prayers, albeit in prose, and ultimately they freed themselves entirely from the style of the letter to develop into poetic parallels of the Biblical laments of the individual. It will be my purpose to examine this particular genre, its literary history, and its later affinities, more closely.

II. The Neo-Sumerian Letter-Prayers

Let me begin my presentation of the genre with a translation of one of its shorter and more familiar examples (B_6):[25]

Speak to my king with varicolored eyes who wears a lapus lazuli beard
Say furthermore to the golden statue "born" on a favorable day,
(to) the "sphinx" raised in the holy sheepfold, summoned in the pure heart of Inanna[26]

[22] Cf. R. Kutscher, *a-ab-ba hu-luh-ha: the history of a Sumerian congregational lament* (unpubl. Ph. D. thesis, Yale, 1966); J. Krecher, *Sumerische Kultlyrik* (1966); T. Jacobsen, PAPhS 107 (1963) 479-482.

[23] Cf. A. Falkenstein, "Das Gebet in der sumerischen Ueberlieferung," RLA 3 (1959) 156-60, where prayers contained within other literary genres are also listed.

[24] Cf. Hallo, "The royal inscriptions of Ur: a typology," HUCA 33 (1962) 1-43 esp. pp. 12-14.

[25] Cf. below, (V), for a bibliography of the genre and previous treatments.

[26] For an Ur III example of a lapus lazuli "sphinx" cf. UET 3: 415: 2.

(to) my lord, the prince of Inanna:
"You in your form are a child of Heaven,
Your command like the command of god is never equalled (var.: is not rebutted by the foreign lands)
Your words are a storm-wind (to be) rained down from heaven, having none to count them (var.: shepherd them)
Thus speaks Uršagga your servant:
'My king has watched over my person,
I am a citizen (lit.: son) of Ur,
If my king is (truly) of Heaven,
Let no one carry off my patrimony,
Let no one destroy the foundations of my father's house.'
May my king know it."

This brief but fairly representative example may suffice for the moment to indicate that, formally, our genre belongs to the category of Sumerian letters. As such, its literary analogues are of several kinds. There are, first of all, the preserved examples of royal correspondence in which the reigning king (not, as here, the statue of the deified king) is addressed by, or addresses himself to, one of his servants. Such letters are known to us so far only in the form of literary imitations of assumed originals allegedly emanating from the chancelleries of Ur and Isin.[27] As such they share some of the flourishes and other stylistic characteristics of our genre. Secondly, the school curriculum has preserved a small number of private letters, in Sumerian as well as Akkadian, as mundane in style as in content, which served as models of everyday correspondence for apprentice scribes.[28] Their purely fictional character may be judged by the fact that one of them is supposedly written by none other than a monkey.[29]

If, however, we wish to find the origin of our genre in the "real" world, we have to go back of all these literary letters of the Old Babylonian period to the archival documents of the neo-Sumerian period. Several hundred Ur III letters are known, and in their most characteristic form they constitute drafts, or orders to pay in kind, drawn on the great storage-centers of the royal economy in favor of the bearer, usually the representative of the king or of some high royal official.[30] Such documents, while letters in form, are orders in function, and have therefore been aptly designated as letter-orders.[31] The texts we are here considering, while essentially identical to them in form, function as prayers. I therefore propose to call them letter-prayers.[32] The seven or eight separate examples in ten to twelve copies of the genre recognized until recently[33] can now be more than doubled by newly published exemplars from Ur and by unpublished material from the Yale Babylonian Collection.[34]

Let us first consider the structure of the newly-named genre. It begins with a salutation to the divine addressee which employs the basic terminology of the archival letters: to my god speak, thus says[35] NN, your servant (so I; cf. B_{14}, B_{19}, M, O, P), but usually elaborates on it in two significant ways. In the first place it nearly always modifies the adressee's name with a longer or shorter succession of laudatory epithets in the form of appositions (F, G, J). In the second place, it frequently adds a second salutation, including further epithets and ending 'to him say furthermore' (B_1, B_8, C_2, D, H, K, L).[36] On one occasion there is even a third salutation ending 'to him (say) for the third time,' (B_{16})[37] while other letters content themselves with additional epithets or predicates at this point (B_6, B_{17}, C, E).

The message itself now follows, and its length varies considerably. In the longest example so far attested (H), it runs to about 45 lines, or five

---

[27] Cf. F. R. Kraus, "Altmesopotamische Quellensammlungen zur altmesopotamischen Geschichte," AfO 20 (1963) 153-155.

[28] See below (V), *sub* B_{19}, M, O, and P for Sumerian examples. For Akkadian examples, cf. F. R. Kraus, "Briefschreibübungen im altbabylonischen Schulunterricht," JEOL VI/16 (1959-62) 16-39. To all appearances, the pitifully executed Akkadian examples come from a much more rudimentary stage of the curriculum.

[29] Below, V, sub B_{14}.

[30] Cf. E. Sollberger, *The Business and Administrative Correspondence under the Kings of Ur* (= TCS 1, 1966).

[31] A. L. Oppenheim, AOS 32 (1948) 86 *ad* H 24 *et passim*; Hallo, *HUCA* 29 (1958) 97-100. For neo-Babylonian letter-orders, cf. Oppenheim, JCS 5 (1950) 195 *ad* UET 4: 162-192.

[32] This term seems preferable to F. Ali's "letters of petition" (Ar. Or. 33: 539), or Falkenstein's "Gottesbrief" which is difficult to translate. The genre is here taken to include letters to deities, as well as those to kings and other mortals couched in the elaborate style of some of the letters to deities.

[33] A. Falkenstein, OLZ 36 (1933) 302; "Ein sumerischer Gottesbrief," ZA 44 (1938) 1-25; "Ein sumerischer Brief an den Mondgott," *Analecta Biblica* 12 (1959) 69-77; J. J. A. van Dijk, *La sagesse suméro-accadienne* (1953) 13-17.

[34] See below, V.

[35] na-ab-bé-a. So always except in J which has nu-ub-bé-a! Once na-bé-a in PBS 1/2: 93: 3 (= B_{14}).

[36] ù-ne-dè-dah; for the reading cf. Falkenstein, ZA 44: 11 but note now the apparent ù-di!-a-dè-dah in L.

[37] ù-na (var. ne)-de-peš.

times the length of the salutation. But in other instances, the message is little longer than the salutation, and in a number of cases it is shorter. Indeed, there are two instances where, at least as far as preserved, the texts ends with the salutation (E, C) and one of these even lacks the phrase "thus speaks NN" (E). The body of the letter has no recognizable structural subdivisions like the salutation. However, most of its sentiments can be classified as expressing (1) complaint (2) protests (3) prayers and (4) formal reinforcements of the appeal, though not necessarily in that order.

The conclusion of the letter-prayers (when preserved) may occasionally consist of a vow to repay the kindness besought in the body of the text. More often it consists of a brief stereotyped formula either borrowed from the language of secular letters or peculiar to the genre itself. We will consider the various formulations in due course. For now, let us turn to the contents of the various letter-prayers, following the structural outline already presented.

To begin with the addressees, they include five of the great gods, and two goddesses. No discernible principle governs the choice of the male deities, but two of them appear to be from the circle of Nergal, the lord of the netherworld, if not Nergal himself (C, G), which seems to bespeak a special concern with the threat of death. The others are Utu (D_2), Nanna (E), Enki (H), and Martu (J). The goddesses invoked can be described more consistently. They are both healing goddesses, in one case (B_{17}) Nintinuga, and in two or three others (F, D_4) Ninisina.[38] In at least two of these cases, the choice of addressee is clearly dictated by the contents of the letter, for they are petitions for relief from sickness.

The letters addressed simply to "my god" (I)[39] or "(my) king" (B_1, B_6, B_8, K) pose more of a problem since, on the one hand, gods were sometimes addressed as "my king" even within the context of the letter-prayers (J) and, on the other hand, the deified (and/or deceased) king could be addressed as "my god." In at least one case, it is clear that the letter-prayer is addressed to King Šulgi of Ur (B_1), and there is another text which, though not formally a letter-prayer, has been described as a letter or prayer to the deified Rim-Sin of Larsa.[40] But where neither royal name nor divine name is mentioned, it is difficult to decide the exact status of the recipient, whether addressed as "god" or "king." Perhaps the question is of secondary importance, for both were petitioned in similar terms (albeit for different ends?), and in similar guise (i. e. in the form of their cult statue; cf. B_6, K).

For the sake of completeness, I will mention here also two "letter-prayers" addressed neither to gods nor to kings but to private persons, or at most to officials (B_{16}, L). One of them is from a priest of Enlil to his son, the other from a scribe to his relative or colleague (gi-me-a-aš). Both are stylistically identical with the authentic letter-prayers, and not with the simple literary "practice-letters" between private persons (B_{19}, M, O, P). Perhaps they represent an intermediate stage in the development from secular letter-order to letter-prayer.[41]

The epithets applied to the various addressees in all these letter-prayers are drawn freely from all the rich storehouse of attributes available for embellishing Sumerian religious and monumental texts in general. But the choice was not wholly a random one, for in most instances there was a decided emphasis on those qualities of the addressee which were crucial for the substance of the petition that followed in the body of the letter. Thus the letters which prayed for the restoration of health praised the healing goddess for her therapeutic skills (B_{17}, D_4, F); one which asked for legal redress stressed the unalterableness of the divine command (B_6); one of those concerned with scribal problems (H) addressed Enki as the lord of wisdom. In one of the two "private" letter-prayers, a father apostrophizes his son, among many other things, as "the son who is available for his god, who respects his father and mother (var. mother and father)" (B_{16}).[42]

Our next question concerns the character of the presumed writers of the letter-prayers, as far as these may be identified by their personal names or professional titles. This is not always possible, for a name like Uršagga in B_6 (above) is com-

[38] Kraus, JCS 3 (1949) 78 n. 30 recognizes a whole sub-genre of letters to healing deities.

[39] Cf. also JCS 8: 82; CT 44: 14.

[40] Falkenstein, *Analecta Biblica* 12 (1959) 70, n. 1 *ad* TRS 35.

[41] Note that some of the same personal names occur in different kinds of literary letters. Cf. B_{16} and $B_{7,8}$, B_{16} and B_{19}, K and M.

[42] dumu dingir-ra-(a)-ni-ir gub-ba / a-a-ama-a-ni (var. ama-a-a-ni)-ir nì-te-gá.

mon enough, the virtual equivalent of our "Goodman" or Everyman. Whether the Gudea of I is a private person or one of several city-rulers of that name is not clear. Here as in other cases (J), there is only indirect evidence for the question. However, by far the largest number of letters are clearly written by scribes (C, F, G, H, K, L). Even where the writer claims a more specialized title in the salutation (B_1), he may still refer to himself as a scribe in the body of the text. This state of affairs is readily explained when we remember the origin of the letter-prayers genre in the context of the scribal schools. As in the case of the "school essays," the scribe found in his own life and circumstances the materials for exercising his stylistic talents.

One of these scribal letter-prayers (C) is even penned by a woman scribe—and thus becomes, incidentally, a rare bit of evidence for the existence of such women at this time. It is not the only letter-prayer from a woman (cf. B_{17}) but it is the only one which reveals her status, not only professionally but socially, for it seems (the passage is however broken) that she is further identified as a daughter or retainer of Sin-kašid, king of Uruk. As a matter of fact, we possess one example of a letter-prayer written by a king himself—in this case Sin-iddinam of Larsa, a later contemporary of Sin-kašid (D_4). It may be noted in passing that the Akkadian tradition of (royal) letter-prayers is first attested, at Mari, only a generation or two after this.[43] So much for the writers, real or fictitious, of the letter-prayers. Let us now consider their actual messages: the petitions which were the subject of the letters, and the sentiments employed to convey them.

The complaint with which the body of the letter often begins may refer to either the causes or the consequences of one's suffering. One of the favorite stylistic devices is to describe one's life as "diminishing" (B_1)[44] or as "ebbing away in cries and sighs" (B_{17}).[45] One petitioner seems already to foresee his bones carried off by the water to a foreign city (K).[46] Another form of complaint is to stress the loss of friends and protectors: "those who know me, my friends, are on a hostile footing with me" (B_{17});[48] "those who know me no longer approach me, they speak no word with me, my own friend no longer counsels me, he will not set my mind at rest" (H below).[49] The loss of protection or patronage is expressed both plainly: "I have no protector" (B_{17}, B_1, L)[50] and metaphorically: "like a sheep which has no faithful shepherd, I am without a faithful cowherd to watch over me" (I);[51] "I am an orphan" (lit. the son of a widow, B_1)[52] which recalls Gudea's moving plaint to Gatumdu: "I have no mother—you are my mother; I have no father—you are my father."[53]

The petitions of the letter-prayers concern, in the first instance, the same problems as their complaints. Relief from sickness is thus one of them; in the letters to healing goddesses, it is phrased typically as "may she remove from my body (interrupt) whatever sickness demon may exist in my body"[54] (B_{17}, D_4), and is followed by the hope for restoration of complete health: "may you place my feet in the station of life" (B_{17});[55] "may Damu your son (oh healing goddess) effect my cure" (D_4).[56] Letters addressed to deified kings typically seek divine or royal protection where other friends and protectors fail: "oh my king, may you be my protector" (B_1, B_8; cf. B_6).[57] But some of the same texts go further and their petitions may be more specific than their complaints had been. One seeks to be confirmed in the claims to his patrimony (B_6, above); another prays for his freedom, perhaps from debt-slavery (B_1).[58] This is also true of the two letter-prayers addressed to private persons. In one, a

[43] G. Dossin, *Syria* 19 (1938) 125 f. Cf. also van Dijk, *Sagesse* 13 f.; E. A. Speiser, "Omens and Letters to the Gods," AOS 38 (1955) 60-67 = *Oriental and Biblical Studies* (1967) 297-305; and below nn. 96 f.

[44] zi-mu ba-e-tur; the variant (YBC 6458) has, however, ba-i.

[45] im-ma-si im-ma-diri-ga-ta zi al-ir-ir-re. For a slightly different translation, cf. Römer, SKIZ 113, end. Cf. also H 23 below.

[46] gìr-pad-du-mu šà-uru-kúr-ra-šè a nam-ma-an-tùm.

[48] zu-a kal-la-mu gìr-kúr mu-da-an-gin; var. ba-an-dib-bé-eš (cf. Civil, Iraq 23: 167).

[49] Cf. the same topos in the individual laments of the Psalter, e. g. Ps. 31: 12, 38: 12, 41: 10, 55: 13-15.

[50] lú-èn-tar-(re) la-ba-(an)-tug (nu-un-tug).

[51] udu-gim sipa-gi-na nu-tug na-gada-gi-na nu-mu-un-túm-túm-mu. Cf. A. Sjöberg, Bi. Or. 20 (1963) 46 f.

[52] dumu-nu-mu-(un)-zu-me-en.

[53] Cyl. A iii 6 f.; cf. Ps. 27: 10.

[54] á-zág su-mà gál-la su-mà íb-ta-an-zi; var. gá-la ha-ba-⌈an-dag⌉-ge (SEM 74: 14). Cf. van Dijk, *Sagesse* 15 f.

[55] *Ib.*

[56] dDa-mu dumu-zu nam-a-zu-mu hé-ak (SEM 74: 16).

[57] lugal-mu èn-(mu) hé-tar-re; var. hu-mu-un-tar-re.

[58] ki-ama-mu(var.-bi)-šè hé-im-mi-íb(ib)-gi$_4$-gi$_4$.

father seems to be pleading with his son for support in his old age (B_{16}); in another, a scribe asks his colleague or relative for preferment to a higher post and other favors (L). Thus the letter-prayers were clearly the vehicle for expressing a variety of human needs.

In addition to the complaint and the petition, the body of the letter-prayer is usually reinforced by protestations of past merits and present deserts on the part of the suppliant. He argues his moral innocence or ignorance, his cultic piety, his unswerving loyalty to the god, or simply his high political or social status: "I do not know my guilt" (B_8);[59] "I do not know my sin, of my sin I have no knowledge" (K);[60] "I observed (all) your festivals and offerings"[61] or, negatively phrased, "my proper devotions (?) I have not withheld from you" (J),[62] or both together: "I performed (or sent) the regular prayers, the sacrifices and the offerings generously (mah-bi) to all the gods, I did not withhold anything from them" (D_4).[63] To emphasize his loyalty, the penitent may insist "I do not speak hostile (foreign) words" (I),[64] perhaps even that he has not sworn by a foreign king (G).[65] On the contrary, he asserts, "I am a citizen of Ur" (B_6),[66] or "I am a scribe" (H, B_1).[67] One letter lists the past military and other service of the writer in detail (B_1). Apparently the recital of past achievements or present rank is supposed to qualify their bearer for future favors.

To persuade the deity to act on his behalf, however, the penitent does not rely solely on his own past merits and present status. Rather, in time-honored fashion, he seeks to persuade the deity or king to act, as it were, "for the sake of thy name," as well as to sway him by promise of future benefits. The element of "suasion" is typically (and somewhat provocatively) phrased as the protasis of a conditional sentence: "If my queen is truly of heaven" (B_{17}, D_4); "if my king is truly of heaven" (B_6).[68] Note that the latter expression also occurs in the letters to living kings.[69] The vows of the letter-prayers are even less subtle: if his or her petition is granted, the writer says, "I will surely be your slave-girl, will serve as court sweeper of your temple, will serve in your presence" (B_{17})[70] or "dwell in your gate and sing your praises . . . and proclaim your exaltation" (H; cf. D_4, J),[71] preferably in public.[72] Perhaps the most persuasive offer that the petitioner can dangle before the deity's eyes is to endow him or her with yet another epithet, based on their latest kindness: "When I have been cured, I will rename my goddess the one who heals(?) the cripples" (B_{17}, cf. also G 46).[73]

So much for the body of the letter-prayers. Their conclusion is much briefer, but it includes, in at least two instances, another important clue to the cultic situation of the entire genre, for reference is made there to "(my) letter which I have deposited before you" (H [variant], G). This, together with the fact that it is a statue which is actually addressed (B_6) shows clearly that our letters reflect a practice of leaving petitions in the temple, at the feet of the cult statue or at least in is own cella.[74] But the brief concluding formulas are also crucial for assigning the genre its proper place in Sumerian literary history. For of these formulas some, like "may my king know it"[75] (B_6), "it is urgent" (B_{10})[76] or "do not be

[59] šul-a-lum nu-zu.

[60] nam-tag-mu nu-zu nam-tag-mà geštú la-ba-ši-gál.

[61] ezen-sizkur-zu-uš x ba-gub-bu-da-gim. (SEM 74 = D_4?)

[62] nì-ša$_6$-ga-tuku-mu la-ba-e-ši-kèš.

[63] dingir-re-e-ne-ir mah-bi inim-ša$_6$-ša$_6$-gi-nam-ma / sizkur-ra nidba (PAD ^{d}INNIN)-bi i-kin-en / nì-nam nu-mu-ne-kéš.

[64] dingir-mu lú-kúr-di nu-me-en (Falkenstein, OLZ 1962: 373.)

[65] lugal-kúr-ra mu-ni nu-mu-un-pà-dè.

[66] dumu urí^{KI}-ma-me-en.

[67] dub-sar-me-en.

[68] Falkenstein, ZA 44: 22.

[69] E.g. Šulgi to Irmu 3, 30; L. B. 2543 (unpubl.).

[70] ù gá-e geme-zu (var.-ni) (hé)-me-en é-za-a (var. é-a-ni) kisal-luh-bi hé-me-en igi-zu (var.-ni)-šè hé-gub Cf. Gadd, *Ideas of Divine Rule* 27 n. 3, who compares Ps. 84: 10 [= 84: 11 in the Hebrew version].

[71] KA-tar-zu ga-si-il (D_4); palil?-e? KA-tar-zu hé-si-il-e me-tés numun hé-i-i (J).

[72] Cf. e.g. Ps. 22: 23; 26: 12; 35: 18 and below, note 92.

[73] Van Dijk, *Sagesse* 15 f. (line 20).

[74] After hearing the present paper at its original presentation (above n. 1), Prof. Jacobsen pointed out that the excavations in the Diyala region uncovered a clay tablet in an unopened envelope lying near the base of a cult statue. As he recalled, the envelope bore only the ascription "to DN." Note also that the late (?) copy of a votive inscription of Sin-iddinam published by van Dijk, JCS 19 (1965) 1-25 includes two "letters" confided by the king to the statue of his father for transmittal to Utu.

[75] lugal-mu hé-en-zu; cf. BIN 2: 53: 3 which, according to Falkenstein, ZA 44: 24 and *Anal. Bibl.* 12: 70 n. 2, is also (an extract from) a letter to a god, although that seems hard to prove.

[76] a-ma-ru-kam. For the expression, cf. Sollberger, TCS 1, p. 99 (49).

negligent" (O),[77] are clearly borrowed from the older clichés with which the secular letter-orders and royal letters of Ur and Isin closed. Others, as befits our genre, are more florid: "at the command of Enlil may (my) eyes behold your face (B_{17})."[78] But the most common conclusion: "may the heart of my god (or king) be appeased" (B_1, G, H, I) helps to identify our genre as the lineal antecedent of the post-Sumerian penitential psalms, to which we may now turn.

III. The Post-Sumerian Penitential Psalms

The Sumerian penitential psalm, or ér-šà-hun-gá,[79] is first attested by a single example from Nippur dated to the Middle Babylonian period. The text in question, published and edited by Langdon as long ago as 1917, was recently re-edited by the late Father Bergmann.[80] It does not actually carry any generic designation, but it ends with the typical closing of the later, labelled eršahunga's: "may your heart be appeased like that of a natural mother, like that of a natural father." This is, in expanded form, also the typical ending of the earlier letter-prayers, but since the Middle Babylonian example is not otherwise cast in the form of a letter, we may see it as an early example, or at least a forerunner, of the eršahunga.[81] Its significance for our purpose lies, then, in the fact that it provides the missing link between the neo-Sumerian letter-prayers of the Old Babylonian period, and the fully developed post-Sumerian penitential psalms of the first millennium, whose very name (literally lament for appeasing the heart, i. e. of the god) reflects its concluding formula.

At first glance, the comparison may seem far-fetched. The late genre is, to begin with, wholly poetic in style, as attested not only by the language, parallelisms and other internal features, but also by the fact that its lines, in distinction from the earlier letter-prayers, are now fixed in their division and as to their number for each separate composition. In the second place, the new genre has lost all formal traces of any epistolary origins, with one possible exception, namely the use of the phrase "your servant" to refer to the penitent, whether he otherwise presents himself in the third or in the first person.[82] Thirdly, it is couched in the emesal-dialect of Sumerian, once erroneously translated as the "woman's language"[83] but more properly described as a kind of whining or wailing tone used by women or goddesses neither exclusively nor universally, but by them only in certain contexts, and also by certain men, notably the singers called gala (*kalû*) and in the context of lamentation.

In these formal or external respects, then, the post-Sumerian penitential psalms clearly represent a new genre as compared to the neo-Sumerian letter-prayers. Indeed, if we were to confine ourselves to their formal characteristics, we might be forced to conclude that they were simply the later successors to the neo-Sumerian eršemma-psalms. The eršemma, however, survived in its own right and under its old designation, albeit chiefly as a subsection of longer compositions. And when we consider the penitential psalms from the point of view of contents and phraseology, a different picture emerges. For this aspect of their description, we may rely largely on Dalglish's summary.[84] The typical eršahunga, then, begins with a long hymnic introduction in which the deity invoked is apostrophized by a succession of epithets designed, in Dalglish's words, "to remind them of their special attributes, whose exercise may have caused the distress of the worshipper or may be the cause of salvation later to be invoked in the prayer." As such, they of course immediately recall the salutations of the letter-prayers.

The complaint section of the eršahunga in-

[77] gú-zu na-an-šub-bé-en. With this closing cf. za-e nam-ba-e-še-ba-e-dè-en-zé-en in the Ibbi-Sin correspondence: CADE 48b and Hoffner, JAOS 87 (1967) 302.

[78] du_{11}-ga ^{d}En-lil-lá-ka (var.-kam!) múš-me-zu igi hé-bí-du_8 (var. ba-ab-du_8). Cf. UET 6: 173 iv 6 f.: du_{11} ^{d}nin-in-si-na mùš lugal-mà-kam igi-bi bí-ib-du_8, which thus is clearly also the conclusion of a letter (in spite of Kramer's reservation, ib., p. 4), presumably to a king.

[79] Cf. S. Langdon, OECT 6 (1927) pp. iii-x; RA 22 (1925) 119-125. The Akkadian equivalent is given variously as *unnînu* (?) (ŠL 2: 579: 392), *eršahungû* (AHw 245 f.) or *šigû* (see refs. Dalglish, *op. cit.*, 34 f.).

[80] PBS 10/2: 3, ed. by E. Bergmann, ZA 57 (1965) 33-42.

[81] J. Krecher, ZA 58 (1967) 28 regards it as "den Eršahunga-Liedern nahestehend und also wahrscheinlich aus der frühen Kassitenzeit (?)."

[82] Cf. the references and literature cited by Dalglish, *op. cit.* (note 12) 31 f. n. 58. The same usage appears to apply to the Akkadian "literary prayers of the Babylonians"; cf. W. G. Lambert, AfO 19 (1959-60) 47 f.

[83] SAL is here rather "thin, attenuated." Cf. now J. Krecher, "Zum Emesal-Dialekt des Sumerischen," *Falkenstein AV* (1967) 86 n. 1.

[84] Op. cit. (above, n. 12), pp. 21-35. To Dalgish's list add now probably CT 44: 14 and 24.

cludes, like that of the letter-prayers, a description of the penitent's distress, a confession of his sin, and a final cry of woe. The description of his distress is less specific here than in most of the letter-prayers, and even the allusions to sickness are more often meant metaphorically than literally. But the other two elements often employ the phraseology of the letter-prayers almost verbatim. Sins are typically committed in multiples of seven in both genres,[85] and in both there is an emphasis on the penitent's ignorance of his sins, or of his specific transgressions.[86] The cry of desperation in both may resemble the bleating of an animal or the moans of a woman in childbirth,[87] though the later genre adds a few characteristic interjections of its own.

Another typical portion of each penitential psalm is the petition, or prayer in the narrower sense. Since the distress is described vaguely as an unknown sin or sins, or the resulting affliction, the petition too is, naturally, less explicit than in the letter-prayers. Even so, expressions such as "free me from my sin," "remit my punishment,"[88] or "rescue me from destruction"[89] can be found in both genres.

The votive formula which is so marked a part of the letter-prayers recurs with little change in the eršahunga's; both thus differ from the more or less unconditional thanksgiving formulas of other late genres. Compare for example the previously quoted "If Damu your son effects my cure, then I will surely sing your praises"[90] with the later "Absolve my sin and I will sing your praises."[91] Both genres, too, stress the favorable "publicity" which will redound to the deity.[92]

Finally, we may return to the starting point of our comparison by considering the concluding formula of the penitential psalm. In its fullest form it includes seven different formulations, but of these, only the last two recur in virtually every instance, namely: "may your heart be appeased like that of my natural mother and father."[93] Thus we have here the closing formula of many letter-prayers expanded only to include the specific equation between personal god and parent which had been merely implicit earlier.[94]

In spite of certain formal and substantive differences, then, the post-Sumerian eršahunga's in striking measure perpetuate the tradition of the neo-Sumerian letter-prayers, and Falkenstein's assessment that they derive from Akkadian conceptions needs to be reviewed.[95] The formal differences no doubt reflect a change in the cultic situation: instead of commissioning a scribe to deposit a clay tablet in letter form at the feet of the divine statue, the later penitent commissioned the gala-singer to recite his prayer orally. Perhaps it was feared that gods could no longer read Sumerian, for while letters continued to be addressed to them[96] or deposited before their statues,[97] they no longer served as prayers but as royal reports or oracular inquiries respectively; and they were now written in the vernacular, like the letter-prayers to the gods of Anatolia,[98] Egypt[99] and elsewhere.[100]

The substantive changes too are readily ex-

[85] Cf. e. g. I 8 f. (Kramer, TMH nF 3 p. 21) with IV R 10: 45 ff.: na-ám-tag-ga imin-a-rá-imin-na. Note also Jacobsen, JCS 8: 86 (CNM 10099) (end): dingir-mu nam-tag-ga-mu imin-[. . .].

[86] Cf. e. g. K (above, n. 60) with IV R 10:42: na-ám-tag-ga nì-ag-a-mu nu-un-zu-àm = *anni epušu ul idi*.

[87] Cf. e. g. B_{17} (above, note 45) with K. 3153 (OECT 6: 21-3; BA 5: 578 f.): ib-si ši-mu zi-ir-ra = *maṣi napišti itašuš*.

[88] Cf. the gate called šul-a-lum-du_8-du_8 (H 49, below) with the eršahunga-passages cited CADE 170a.

[89] Cf. H 51 f. (below) with PBS 10/2: 3: 7 (Bergmann, ZA 57: 34): nam-da-ad-gu-ud šu-bar-zi sag-ki!-tum ZA. GI.

[90] Above, notes 56 and 71.

[91] OECT 6: 43: 49; cf. Bergmann, ZA 57: 41.

[92] Cf. H 53 (below) with PBS 10/2: 3r8 (ZA 57: 41 f.): ukù-e pà-hé-ni-ib-bé ka-na-mé hé-ma-zu.

[93] Dalglish, *op. cit.*, p. 32.

[94] On this equation, see also Hallo, JCS 20 (1966) 136 f., n. 53.

[95] "Nach meiner Auffassung trotz sumerischer Sprache sind die ér-šà-hun-gá-Kompositionen aus akkadischen Vorstellungen herausgewachsen," *apud* Dalglish, *op. cit.*, 34, n. 72.

[96] Most notably the famous report of Sargon's eighth campaign; cf. A. L. Oppenheim, "The city of Assur in 714 B. C.," JNES 19 (1960) 133-147, who lists the other examples of the genre. Previously Ungnad, OLZ 21 (1918) cc. 72-6. Cf. also H. Tadnor, JCS 12 (1958) 82.

[97] Referring to Knudtzon, *Assyrische Gebete an den Sonnengott*, Jastrow stated long ago: "Aus Andeutungen in den Texten selbst geht . . . hervor, dass man die aufgeschriebene Frage vor dem Gottesbild niederlegte": *Die Religion Babyloniens und Assyriens* 2 (1912) 175; cf. also W. W. Struve, ICO 25/1 (1962) 178.

[98] According to Goetze, *Kleinasiatische Forschungen* 1 (1930) 220, the "second plague prayer" of Muršili (ANET 394-6?) was in the form of a "Gottesbrief." (Ref. courtesy H. Hoffner, Jr.)

[99] G. R. Hughes, "A Demotic letter to Thoth," JNES 17 (1958) 1-12, with other examples of the genre.

[100] Cf. the Jewish custom of depositing "letter-prayers" in the Western Wall, which survives to this day.

plained in terms of historically attested changes in the Babylonian Weltanschauung as these have been delineated by Jacobsen.[101] Where the earlier Babylonians worried chiefly about the divine origin of natural misfortunes and manmade disasters, the later ones were more concerned with their own sins, known or unknown, as the causes of their afflictions. The petition of the individual accordingly witnessed a corresponding shift in emphasis: the deity was now entreated to remove, not the affliction, but the sin; not the symptom but the assumed underlying cause. It is, however, not my purpose to dwell on these differences, important though they certainly are as indices of developmental stages in the history of Mesopotamian religion. From the point of view of *literary* history, it is the similarities between the earlier and the later genre that are most impressive. They entitle us to regard the neo-Sumerian letter-prayers as the lineal antecedents of the post-Sumerian penitential psalms, and to throw them into the balance in any comparison with the individual laments of the Biblical Psalter.

IV. A New Sumerian Letter-Prayer (H)

A. Texts [102]

YBC 4620 (=A): complete in 56 lines

YBC 7205 (=B): "rectilinear" extract tablet,[103] ll. 1-15.

YBC 8630 (=C): "rectilinear" extract tablet;[103] ll. 36-end.

B. Structure

The letter-prayers have no structural labels,[104] but the present text, by virtue of its great length, shows a clear strophic structure based on meaning units and the occurrence or recurrence of certain formulas. There is also the evidence, in exemplar A, of the line count. While the total (56) is correct, the subtotals are too low by two for the obverse (31 for 33) and too high by two for the reverse (25 for 23). Unless they were slavishly copied from a model (in which case it is hard to see why the disposition of the lines would have been altered), this seems to imply that the formulas of lines 2 and 7 were not counted as separate lines, while the long lines 39 and 40, which in A are written over 1½ lines and in C over two separate lines, were in fact counted separately. On this assumption, and with one minor transposition (moving the couplet 18 f. after line 27), the poem consists of eleven five-line stanzas plus a concluding "doxology" of one line.

C. Transliteration of A.[105]

i

^{d}en-ki en-zà-dib-an-ki-a nam-ma-ni **zà nu-di**
ù-na-a-du$_{11}$
^{d}nu-dim-mud nun(1)-gištú-dagal-la(2) **an-da nam-ba-an-tar**
me-zi hal-ha(3) a(4)-nun-ke$_4$-ne **a-rá-bi ság** [**nu-di**]
gal-zu-mah u$_4$-è-ta u$_4$-šú-uš **igi-gál ba-ab-sè-**[**ga**?]
en-nì-zu lugal-engur-ra dingir-sag-du-ga-mu-ú[r]
ù-ne-dè-dah

ii

⌜^{d}EN.ZU-*ša-mu-úh*(5) dub-sar dumu Ur-^{d}nin-[...]
ìr-zu na-ab-bé-a
u$_4$ šu mu-⌜e⌝(6)-du$_{11}$-ga(7) nam-lú-ulù-uš mu-e-ni-[n-...]
mu-pà-da-zu-šè! IM-šub li-bí-ak ab-ba-gim [...]
ezen-sizkur-zu-uš(8) gìri-mu la-ba-ni-sil lul-aš ì-du-un-na

iii

e-ne-éš (9)nì-a-na(10) bí-ak-a(11)-mu di nam-tag(12)-ga(13)-mu
nu-[til?]

[101] Cf. for the present his "Ancient Mesopotamian religion: the central concerns," PAPhS 107 (1963) 473-484.

[102] Copies to be published in a forthcoming YOS volume.

[103] Cf. Gordon, S.P. p. 8.

[104] On these cf. my remarks Bi.Or. 23 (1966) 241 f.

[105] With a few minor restorations based on B and C; these are not indicated as such.

ù(14)-nam-tar-ra(15)-ke$_4$(16) mu-DU(17) ki-lul-la ìl-la-en izkim
na-ma-ab(18)-kin
dingir-kúr-ra nam-tag(19) (20)hu-mu-túm(21) zá-bi nu-mu-da-pà
u$_4$-la-la-má é-bi an-né bí-du$_{11}$-ga
sag-sìg-šè nam-tag-mu nu-me-a gaba im-ma-da-ri-e[n]

v(b)

⸢bappir⸣-ra-bala-⸢bàn⸣-da-gim kišib-e ba-ab-dáb-bé-en
⸢níg-šu-kaskal-la⸣ giš-šudun-bi-TAR-a-gim har-ra-an-na ba-gub-bé-en

(iv)

ki-ná ú-u$_8$-a-a-e ba-ná-en a-nir mu-un-si-il
alan-ša$_6$-ga-mu gú ki-šè ba-lá gìri-šè ba-tuš-en
[. . .].PA.AH-mu ki ba-ni-in-íl uktin-mu ba-kúr
[. . .] ù-nu-ku gìri-mu-a ab-sì zi-mu ba-da-zal
u$_4$-zalag-ga u$_4$-HI-da-gim im-ma-an-ak ki-túm-mu ba-an-zé-ir

v(a)

dub-sar-me-en nì-mu-zu-zu a-na-mà uh-šè ba-ku$_4$-re-en
šu-mu sar-re-dè ba-DU ka-mu inim-bal-bal im-ma-an-lá
ab-ba nu-me-en gištú-mu ba-dugud igi-du$_8$-mu ba-⸢gil⸣-gil

vi

guruš-ad-hal é-lugal-a-ni íb-ta-è-a-gim sag ki-a· mu-túm-túm
lú-zu-a-mu na-ma-te-gá inim-ma na-ma-ab-bé
ku-li-mu ad nu-mu-da-gi$_4$-gi$_4$ šà-mu la-<ba>-še$_4$-dè
lú-in-na su-lum-mar-šè ba-ku$_4$-re-en nam-tar-mu ba-kúr-e-en
dingir-mu za-ra nir-im-ta-gál-en lú-šè nam-mu

vii

guruš-me-en a-gim ki-lul-la nam-ma-bàra-⸢gè⸣-en

lower edge

reverse gùd-ús é-mu la-la-bi nu-mu-⸢gi-gi⸣
é-dù-dù-a-mu sig$_4$-e nu-ub-tag-⸢ge$_4$-a⸣
giš-ù-tur-tur (22) ki-píl-là-mú-a-gim(23) gurun(24) la-ba-íl
giš-suhhuš gú(25)-má(26)-da-mú-a-gim pa-mu la-ba-sìg-sìg

viii

tur-ra-(27)me-en(28) u$_4$-mu nu-me-a ur$_5$-šè nam-ba-du-un
sahar-ra nam-bí-ib-bala-e-en
ki ama-a-a(29) nu-gub-ba(30) ba-e-dab-bé-en
a-ba-a a-ra(31)-zu-mu mu-ra-ab-bé-e
ki im-ri-a-mu gú nu(32)-si-si-iš zà mu-e-tag-ge-en
a-ba-a kadra-mu (eras.: mu) ma-ra-ni-íb-ku$_4$(33)

ix

^{d}dam-gal-nun-na nitalam ki-ága-zu
ama-mu-gim ha-ra-da-túm ír-mu hu-mu-ra-ni-ib-ku$_4$-⸢ku$_4$⸣

^dasal(34)-alim-nun-na dumu-abzu-ke₄
a-a-mu-gim ha-ra-da-túm ír-mu hu-mu-ra-ni-ib-ku₄-ku₄
45)   ír-šà-ne-ša₄-mu hu-mu-ra-[ab]-bé
                              ír-mu hu-mu-ra-ni-ib-ku₄-ku₄(35)

x

u₄-da nam-tag (36)ga-mu-ra-túm(37) ⌈erím⌉-ta (38)KU-mu-da(39)
(40)ki-kiruda-⟨⟨da-da⟩⟩-mà(41) igi (42)ù-ba-e-ni-bar(43) (44)ama₅-mu
    šu-te-ba-ab(45)
ki-kukkú-ga-mu u₄-šè   (46)ù-mu-e-ni-ku₄(47)
ká-šul-a-lum-du₈-du₈-za(48) ga(49)-túš   KA-tar-zu ga-si-il
50)   nam-tag-mu(50) gu-gim ga-mu-ra-si-il
                              nam-mah-zu ga-⌈àm⌉(51)-du₁₁

xi

ki-nam-tag-dugud-da šu-nigin-zu   ár   ga-à[m-...](52)
ka-garáš-a(53)-ka   šu-bar   zi sag-ki-tùm(54)-mu [...](55)
ukù-e pa ga-ni-ib-è   kalam-e   hé-zu-z[u](56)
dingir-mu ní-te-gá-zu   gá(57)-me-en
55)   ù-na-a-du₁₁ (58)mu-ra-gub-ba-mu(59) arhuš(60) tuk-ma-r[a](61) (62)

xii

[š]à dingir-mu ki-bi ha-ma(63)-gi₄-gi₄

25
56

D. Variants (other than line divisions).

1.	B: en-mah	33.	C inverts the next two couplets, thus:
2.	B adds: -ke₄		43, 44, 41, 42.
3.	B: -hal-la	34.	C: asal-lú-⌈HI⌉-
4.	B: ^da-	35.	C omits line 45.
5.	B: -*ùh*	36–37.	C: hu-mu-ra-ab-tù[m]
6.	B omits	38–39.	C: KU-ma-a[b]
7.	B adds: -ta	40–41.	C: ki-⌈ru⌉-da-mu
8.	B: šè !	42–43.	C: ⌈i⌉-ni-in-bar
9–10.	B: a-na-àm	44–45.	C: arhuš tuku-mu-⌈da-ab⌉
11.	B: -ka-	46–47.	C: mi-ni-in-KU?
12–13.	B omits	48.	C omits
14.	B omits	49.	C: ga-an-
15.	B: -mu	50.	C omits
16.	B: omits	51.	C: -an-
17.	B: ⌈e-ne⌉ ?	52.	C omits line 51
18.	B: -ni-in-	53.	C omits
19.	B: -a (?)	54.	C: -túm-
20–21.	B: ha-ma-tùm	55.	C: ⌈UN-x-y⌉
22–23.	C: NE-gim ba-gub	56.	C omits l. 54
24.	C: gurum_x(GAM)	57.	C: gá-e-
25.	C: omits	58–59.	C: ⌈im⌉-ma-ra-sar
26.	C: má-gíd-	60.	C: giš-
27–28.	C: -mu	61.	C: -ta
29.	C adds -m]u	62.	C inserts a line: [...]-⌈mu-ra⌉
30.	C: -⌈be-en⌉ ?		hu-mu-⌈un-gál⌉-[...]?
31.	C omits	63.	C: -ma-ab-
32.	C: nu-mu-un-[...]		

E. Translation

i

1. (1) To Enki, the outstanding lord of heaven and earth whose nature is unequalled
(2) Speak!
2. (3) To Nudimmud, the prince[(1)] of broad understanding who determines fates together with An,
3. (4) Who distributes the appropriate divine attributes among the Anunnaki, whose course cannot be [reversed]
4. (5) The omniscient one who is given intelligence from sunrise to sunset,
5. (6) The lord of knowledge, the king of the sweet waters, the god who begot me,
(7) Say furthermore!

ii

6. (8) (This is) what Sin-šamuh the scribe, the sone of Ur-Nin[. . .],
7. (9) your servant, says:
8. (10) Since[(2)] the day that you created me you have [given] me an education.
9. (11) I have not been negligent toward the name by which you are called, like a father [. . .].
10. (12) I did not plunder your offerings at the festivals to which I go regularly.

iii

11. (13) (But) now, whatever I do, the judgment of my sin is not [. . .]
12. (14) My fate[(3)] has come my way, I am lifted onto a place of destruction, I cannot find an omen.
13. (15) A hostile deity has verily brought sin my way, I cannot find(?) its side.
14. (16) On the day that my vigorous house was decreed by Heaven
15. (17) There is no keeping silent about my sin, I must answer for it.

iv

16. (20) I lie down on a bed of alas and alack, I intone the lament.
17. (21) My goodly figure is bowed down to the ground, I am sitting on (my) feet.
18. (22) My [. .]. is lifted from (its) place, my features are changed.
19. (23) [. . .] restlessness is put into my feet, my life ebbs away.
20. (24) The bright day is made like an "alloyed" day for me,[106] I slip into my grave.

v

21. (25) I am a scribe, (but) whatever I have been taught has been turned into spittle(?) for me
22. (26) My hand is "gone" for writing, my mouth is inadequate for dialogue.
23. (27) I am not old, (yet) my hearing is heavy, my glance cross-eyed.
24. (18) Like a brewer(?) with a junior term(?) I am deprived of the right to seal.
25. (19) Like a wagon of the highway whose yoke has been broken(?) I am placed on the road

---

[106] Cf. "Man and his God" (Kramer, VT Suppl. 3: 175) line 69. Van Dijk also calls my attention to Ur Lament (Kramer, AS 12: 36) 190: u_4-HI-da ba-da-an-tab, and the new variant from Ur (UET 6/2: 137: 73): u-mud!-e ba-da-an-ku_4. This, and parallel expressions like our line 48 or Reisner, SBH pl. 77: 20 f., suggest a meaning "day of darkness" and possibly a reading u_4-mu_x-da for our expression; for mud = dark(ness), cf. u_4-mud = *ūmu da'mu* (CADD 74c), ^{d}Nanna i-mud = *^{d}Sin adir* (CADA/1: 103b). Note also an-usan-da = *da'ummatu* (CADD 123b), where USAN (USÁN) may have the reading mud_x (cf. USÀN = NUNUZ + ÁB × SA and MÙD = NUNUZ + ÁB × KAŠ).

vi

26. (28) Like an apprentice-diviner who has left his master's house I am slandered ignobly.
27. (29) My acquaintance does not approach me, speaks never a word with me,
28. (30) My friend will not take counsel with me, will not put my mind at rest.
29. (31) The taunter has made me enter the tethering-rope, my fate has made me strange.
30. (32) Oh my god, I rely on you, what have I do to with man?!

vii

31. (33) I am grown-up, how am I to spread out in a narrow place?
32. (34) My house (is) a plaited nest, I am not satisfied with its attractiveness.
33. (35) My built-up houses are not faced with brick(?)
34. (36) Like little (female) cedars planted in a dirty place, I(?) bear no fruit.
35. (37) Like a young date palm planted by the side of a boat,(4) I produce no foliage.

viii

36. (38) I am (still) young, must I walk about thus before my time? Must I roll around in the dust?
37. (39) In a place where my(5) mother and father are not present I am detained,
38. who will recite my prayer to you?
39. (40) In a place where my kinsmen do not gather I am overwhelmed,
40. who will bring my offering in to you?

ix

41. (41) Damgalnunna, your beloved first wife,
42. (42) May she bring it to you like my mother, may she introduce my lament before you
43. (43) Asalalimnunna, son of the abyss,
44. (44) May be bring it to you like my father, may he introduce my lament before you.
45. (45) May he recite my lamentation to you, may be introduce my lament before you.

x

46. (46) When I(6) have verily brought (my) sin to you, cleanse(?) me from evil!
47. (47) When(7) you have looked upon me in the place where I am cast down, approach my chamber!(8)
48. (48) When(9) you have turned my dark place into daylight,[107]
49. (49) I will surely dwell in your(10) gate of Guilt-Absolved, I will surely sing your praises!
50 (50) I will surely tear up my(11) sin like a thread, I will surely proclaim your exaltation!

xi

51. (51) As you reach the place of heavy sin, I will surely [sing your] praises.
52. (52) Release me at the mouth of the grave, [save me] at the head of my tomb!
53. (53) (Then) I will surely appear to the people, all the nation will verily know!
54. (54) Oh my god, I am the one who reveres you!
55. (55) Have mercy on(12) the letter which I have deposited before you! (13)

---

[107] Cf. Kramer, Two Elegies 1. 89.

xii

56. (56) May the heart of my god be restored!

F. Translation—Principal Variants

(1) B: the lofty lord
(2) So B. A: On
(3) So B. A: The X of fate
(4) C: by a long-boat
(5) C omits
(6) C: he
(7) C omits
(8) C: have mercy on me!
(9) C omits
(10) C omits
(11) C omits
(12) C: Hear
(13) C: (which) I have written to you

G. Abridged Glossary [108]

ad-gi$_4$-gi$_4$ (30): von Soden, AHw s. v. *malāku* Gt (*mitluku*); van Dijk, SGL 2: 98.
ad-hal (28): CADB s. v. *bārû*.
a-gim (33): von Soden, AHw s. v. *kīam*.
an-da nam-tar (3): Falkenstein, SGL 1: 99 f. *ad* STVC 34 iii 7.
a-rá (4): Römer, SKIZ 108 *ad* SRT 12: 21.
arhuš-tuku (47[var.], 55): Römer, SKIZ 264 n. 13.
e-ne-éš (13): CADI s. v. *inanna*.
gaba-ri (17): von Soden, AHw s. v. *mahāru*.
gal-zu (5): CADE s. vv. *eršu* A, *emqu*.
gil-gil (27): CADE s. v. *egēru*.
gìr-sil (12): CADH s. v. *habātu* A [v. D.].
giš-suhhuš (37): MSL 5: 117: 288 and 142: 28.
giš-ù (36): Falkenstein, GSGL I 72; SAHG 153: 32.
gùd-ús (34): Falkenstein, SGL 1: 71; ZA 57: 121 f.
gú-ki-šè-lá (21): Falkenstein, ZA 57: 97 f.
gú-si-si (40): Römer, SKIZ 155: 28.
har-ra-an / kaskal (19): Römer, SKIZ 178 f.
igi-gál (5): CADB s. v. *bišītu, bišīt uzni* [v. D.].
igi-gál-sì: van Dijk, SGL 2: 116; Hallo, Bi. Or. 23: 243-4.
im-ri-a (40): Sjöberg, Falkenstein AV 202-9. Cf. also me-a-im-ri-a-mu, MSL 4: 56: 660e and *passim* as late OB PN.

[108] Only the latest discussions are listed, and occasionally an additional reference. No reference is made to words adequately explained in Deimel, *Šumerisches Lexikon*. I am indebted to J. van Dijk for the references marked [v. D.].

IM-šub-àk (11): Jestin, Thesaurus 2: 24. CADA/1: 305c s. v. *ahu, aham nadû* [v. D.].
kadra (40): von Soden, AHw. s. v. *kad/trû*.
ka-garáš (52): von Soden, AHw s. v. *karāšu* II.
KA-tar-si-il (49): Bergmann, ZA 56: 34 *ad* SEM 74: 17. Cf. the syllabic spelling CT 44: 14: ka-ta-ar-zu še-si-li-im.
ki-kukkú-ga (48): Sjöberg, *Nanna-Suen* 76 *ad* TRS 30: 10.
ki-lul-la (14, 33): Castellino, ZA 52: 32.
ki-píl-lá (36): Jacobsen *apud* Gordon, S. P. 461.
kiruda (47): Falkenstein, ZA 56: 128.
kišib-dáb (18): Oppenheim, *Eames*, 129, 242 *ad* P 18.
ki-túm/tùm/tum (24, 52): van Dijk, *Sagesse* 62; Falkenstein, ZA 57: 109.
ku$_4$-(ku$_4$) in sense of "turn into" (25, 31, 48): Hallo and van Dijk, *Exaltation of Inanna*, Glossary, s. v.
lá (26): von Soden, AHw, s. v. *maṭû* II.
la-la with é (16): Sjöberg, Nanna-Suen 174; Krecher, *Sumerische Kultyrik* 141.
la-la-gi$_4$ (34): *ib.*
lú-in-na (31): Jacobsen *apud* Gordon S. P. p. 461.
LUL-aš (12): von Soden, AHw s. v. *ma'diš*; UET 6: 2: 5.
lú-zu-a (29): Civil, *Iraq* 23: 167; JNES 23: 5, *ad* Ludingira 6.
me-zi-hal-ha (4): Falkenstein, ZA 49: 106: 10; VS 2: 8: 26.
nam-mah-du$_{11}$ (50): Hallo and van Dijk, *loc. cit.*, s. v.
nam-mu (32): *ib.*, s. v.; cf. Falkenstein apud MSL 4: 42; Castellino, ZA 52: 34.
níg-šu (19): Civil, JAOS 88: 13, n. 56.
nir-gál with dative (32): Falkenstein, SGL 1: 103 *ad* STVC 34 iii 30.
pa-sìg-sìg (37): cf. pa-sig̃$_7$ = *arta banû* CADṢ 139a.
sag-du (6): CADB s. v. *banû*.
ság-du$_{11}$/di (4): Falkenstein, SGL 1: 44; ZA 57: 93.
sag-sìg (17): van Dijk, SGL 2: 30.
sag-túm-túm (28): Landsberger, MSL 4: 27: 11; Hallo, Oppenheim AV 97 note 23 *ad* OBGT III 173 ff.
sahar-ra-bala (38): Hallo and van Dijk, *loc. cit.*, s. v. sahar-da . . . gi$_4$.

su-lum-mar (31): Civil, JAOS 88:8 f.
šà-ki-bi-gi$_4$-gi$_4$ (56): Civil, Oppenheim AV 89.
šu-bar-zi: ŠL 2:354:121 f. [v. D.].
šu-du$_{11}$ (10): Römer, SKIZ 69, n. 305. AHw s. v. *liptu, lipit qātē* [v. D.].
šul-à-lum (49): CADE s. v. *ennittu.*
šu-te-gá (47): Römer, SKIZ 86 f.
u$_4$-HI-da (24): Hallo, BiOr. 20:139 s. v. níg-SAR/HI-a and above, n. 106.
uktin (22): Falkenstein, *An. Bibl.* 12:72 no. 1; ZA 55:4 n. 8; CAD s. vv. *bunabuttum, ṣubur panī* [note: Goetze, JAOS 65:225:69 reads ukkur.]
ù-na-a-du as noun (55): Hallo, Bi. Or. 20:142 [3]; Civil, JNES 23:7 *ad* Ludingira 7.
ù-nu-ku (23): CADṢ s. v. (*la*) *ṣalālu/ṣalilu.*
ú-u$_8$-a-a-e (20): Krecher, *Sumerische Kultyrik* 114 f.
zà-dib (1): Römer, SKIZ 252.
zà-pà (15): cf. Kramer, TMH 3 p. 21:9.
zà-tag (40): Falkenstein Bi. Or. 22:282 n. 24; Gordon, S. P. pp. 68, 81.

V. List of letter-prayers and other neo-Sumerian literary letters.

The letter-prayers and other neo-Sumerian literary letters were tradited in the schools both singly and in Sammeltafeln, but apparently the order was not entirely fixed. Many of the twenty items in Collection B (see below) occur in different groupings on other Nippur tablets. In BE 31:21, for example, B$_7$ is followed by the catchline of B$_8$ and in STVC 8, B$_{14}$ and B$_{15}$ follow each other without a break; but in SLTN 129, the sequence is B$_7$, (break), B$_{10}$, B$_{14}$.[109] B$_{12}$[110] and B$_{18}$[111] follow each other in SLTN 131, which Falkenstein has described as "einen literarischen Sammeltext,"[112] and B$_{12}$ recurs at the end of a collection of model contracts.[113] At Ur, one tablet (UET 6:173) has the following sequence: B$_{17}$, K, B$_1$, B$_4$, B$_8$. Another (UET 6:174) begins with B$_7$, continues with A, and ends with B$_{17}$. Note also that B$_{14}$ occurs in an Ur catalogue text together with non-epistolary entries.[114] The following list therefore is necessarily arranged in a somewhat arbitrary order.

I. "Royal Correspondence"

A: Letter Collection A: royal correspondence of Ur; cf. for the present F. Ali, *Ar. Or.* 33 (1965) 529 ff. Eight duplicates from the Yale Babylonian Collection will be published in a forthcoming YOS volume.

B: Letter Collection B; cf. Ali, *ibid.* and *Ar. Or.* 34 (1966) 289 f., note *.[114a] Includes the royal correspondence of Isin and the following letters more or less in the style of the letter-prayers.

B$_1$: From Aba-indasa[115] to (Šulgi)
Texts: UET 6:173 ii 2-iii 6; 178; 179; YBC 6458 (unpubl.)

B$_6$: From Ur-šagga to "my . . . king"
Texts: BL 5; ZA 44 pl. I; UET 6:177; YBC 6711 (unpubl.)
Translation: Langdon, BL, p. 15; revised in BE 31, p. 25; Falkenstein, ZA 44:1-25; Kramer, ANET 382; above, 75 f.

B$_7$: From Lugal-murub to (his) king
Texts: BE 31:21:1-18; SLTN 129 left edge and obv.; UET 6:174a; PBS 13:46 iii.
Translation: Langdon, BE 31, p. 48

B$_8$: From Lugal-murub to (his) king
Text: UET 6:173 iv 8 ff.; cf. also BE 31:21 (catchline)

B$_{10}$: From Ur-Enlila to the ensi and sanga
Texts: PBS 13:48 iii; SLTN 129 rev. 1-5; YBC 7175 (unpubl.); unpubl. tablet in private possession in Ohio (ref. courtesy R. McNeill).

---

[109] Gordon, Bi. Or. 17 (1960) 141 (7) regards these texts as "Essay Collection No. 7," but it is clear that all the texts included in it are letters.

[110] Cf. F. Ali, "Blowing the horn for official announcement," Sumer 20 (1964) 66-68.

[111] F. A. Ali, "Dedication of a dog to Nintinugga," *Ar. Or.* 34 (1966) 289-293.

[112] NG 1 (1956) 32.

[113] NBC 7800 (unpubl.); separately also on YBC 12074 (unpubl.).

[114] UET 6: 196: 4! Some of the other entries in this catalogue duplicate or resemble entries in the Yale catalogue of royal hymns. Cf. UET 6: 196: 6 with Hallo, JAOS 83 (1963) 171: 13, also UET 6: 196: 2 and 11 with JAOS 83: 171: 6 and 9 respectively.

[114a] After this article was completed, I obtained a Xerox copy of Ali's dissertation from University Microfilms (Ann Arbor, Michigan); to this I owe three or four corrections or additions in the following list.

[115] Perhaps identical with the Indasu whose defeat by Šu-Sin is recorded in late copies; cf. Edzard, AfO 19 (1959-60) 9-11, but note also J. Laessøe, AS 16 (1965) 195 f.

B_{14}: From Ugudulbi ("the monkey") to Ludiludi his mother
Texts: PBS 1/2:92; 93; STVC 8:1-7; SLTN 129 rev. 66 ff. Cf. also above, note 114.
Translations: Falkenstein, ZA 49:327; van Dijk, *Sagesse* 14; cf. Gordon, *Bi. Or.* 17:141, n. 156.

B_{15}: From Utudug to Ilakni'id
Texts: STVC 8:8; PBS I/:95; cf. Ali, *Ar. Or.* 33:539, n. 45.

B_{16}: From Lugal-murub to Enlil-massu his son
Texts: BE 31:47; UET 6:175; ib. 176; YBC 7170 (unpubl.)

B_{17}: From Inannakam to Nintinugga
Texts: PBS 1/2:94; 134; UET 6:173 i 1'-4'; *ib.* 174e; *ib.* 180.
Translations: van Dijk, Sagesse 15 f.; Falkenstein, SAHG No. 41.

B_{19}: From Inim-Inanna to Enlil-massu.
Text: PBS 1/2:91.

C: From the daughter(?) of Sin-kašid, king of Uruk, to Meslamtaea-Nergal(?) (salutations only)[116]
Text: TRS 58

D: Royal correspondence of Larsa,[117] including the following:

D_2: From [. . .] to Utu
Text: UET 6:182 (?)

D_4: From Sin-iddinam, king of Larsa, to Nin-isina[118]
Texts: UET 8:70; YBC 4705, YBC 4605 (unpubl.); cf. also SEM 74.

II. "Scribal Correspondence"[119]

E: From [. . .] to Nanna (salutations only)
Text: *Anal. Bibl.* 12:71 f.
Translations: Falkenstein, *ib.*, 69-77; Sjöberg, *Nanna-Suen* 104-7

F: From Nanna-mansi to Nin-isina
Text: TRS 60
Translation (in part): Kraus, JCS 3: 77 f.

G: From Nanna-mansi to [. . .]
Text: BE 31:7
Translation: Langdon, *ib.* pp. 21-25

H: Sin-šamuh to Enki
Texts: YBC 4620, 7205, 8630 (above)
Translation: Hallo, above.

I: From Gudea to "my god."
Text: TMH n. F. 3:56
Translation: Kramer, *ib.*, pp. 20 f. Cf. Sjöberg, *Bi. Or.* 20:46 f.

J: From Etel-pi-Damu to Martu
Text: YBC 5631 (unpubl.)

K: From Inim-Enlila to (his) king
Text: UET 6:173:5'-14'

L: From Gudea-Enlila to An-mansi his relative
Text: TMH n. F. 3:57.

M: From [. . .] son of Inim-Enlila to [. . .]
Text: BE 31:29
Translation: Langdon, BE 31, p. 48.

III. "Personal Correspondence"

O: From Sag-lugal-bi-zu to Nur-Kabta
Text: L. B. 1013, to be publ. in TLB III.

P: From ⌜Etel-pi⌝(?)-Enlila to Nudimmud-siga his father (?)
Text: PBS 12:32.

[116] Was there a small collection of Uruk letters between those of Isin and Larsa as in the case of the royal hymns, for which cf. my remarks JCS 17 (1963) 116?

[117] Cf. S. N. Kramer, JAOS 88 (1968) 108, n. 3.

[118] I intend to edit this letter elsewhere.

[119] E, I and J are included here only provisionally.

THE ROOT *ZBL/SBL* IN AKKADIAN, UGARITIC AND BIBLICAL HEBREW

MOSHE HELD
COLUMBIA UNIVERSITY

THIS PAPER CONTAINS a lexicographical study of the Hebrew root *zbl/sbl* in the light of Akkadian *zabālu,* Ugaritic *zbl* and other related materials. It should be stressed at the outset that not all of the material herein presented is entirely new. However, almost none of it is to be found in the standard Hebrew lexicons and commentaries, the most recent ones being no exception.

We shall first briefly turn to Hebrew *zbl* which is attested only six times in the Hebrew Bible.[1] It is not surprising to note, therefore, that the exact meaning and derivation of this rare and poetic root have been a problem to ancient and modern scholars alike. As a verb *zbl* is a *hapax* occurring only in Genesis 30:20 where the MT reads as follows: *hpʿm yzblny ʾyšy ky yldty lw ššh bnym.* The problematic idiom *yzblny ʾyšy* has most recently been studied by the late E. A. Speiser in his translation and commentary on the Book of Genesis.[2] While such an interpretation as "My husband will tolerate me"[3] needs no refutation, the widely accepted renderings "My husband will dwell with me"[4] or the more recent rendering "My husband will recognize me as his lawful wife,"[5] are equally difficult. Indeed, Speiser rightly rejects such interpretations, and offers instead the following translation: "This time my husband will bring me presents."[6] Such a rendering is of course based on Akkadian *zubullû,*[7] well known in the idiom *zubullâ zabālu*[8] "to bring marriage gifts" rarely attested in OB,[9] but common in Assyrian[10] where it is essentially a synonym of Babylonian *bibla wabālu* (*zabālu*).[11]

Speiser's rendering, tempting as it may be, is difficult on several counts. First, our biblical verse has *yzblny* alone, not **zbl yzblny* or **yzblny zbl.* Secondly, such an interpretation isolates our word from the other occurrences of *zbl* in biblical Hebrew; for while there is no denial of the fact that *zbl* in Ps. 49:15 is obscure,[12] surely *zbl* in the idioms *ʿmd [b]zblh,*[13] *byt zbl*[14] and *zbl qdš*[15] must denote "princeship, royalty," as noted by Albright years ago.[16]

This assumption recommends itself particularly in the light of the Ugaritic evidence given below. Thirdly, and of no less importance, *zubullû* in Akkadian never denotes a "present" as such, but rather is restricted to the marriage gifts brought into the house of the bride for the marriage banquet.[17] Characteristically, even the Aramaic-

---

[1] Gen. 30:20; I Kings 8:13 [=II Chron. 6:2]; Isa. 63:15; Hab. 3:11; [Ps. 49:15].

[2] *Genesis* (The Anchor Bible No. 1, 1964), pp. 229, 231.

[3] Koehler, *Lexicon,* p. 250a.

[4] This rendering goes back to the medieval commentators; cf. Targum, Ibn Ezra, Saadia, Ibn Janāḥ and others.

[5] M. David, *VT,* I (1951), pp. 59-60.

[6] Speiser, *op. cit.,* p. 229.

[7] Speiser, *ibid.,* p. 231.

[8] *CAD,* Z, pp. 152-153.

[9] See the OB passage quoted in *CAD,* Z, p. 152a.

[10] Ass. Code, § 30:33-35 *abu ša zubullâ izbilūni kallassu ilaqqia ana mārišu iddan* "The father who has brought the marriage gifts may fetch his daughter-in-law and give her to his son"; *ibid.,* § 31:40-42 *šumma aʾīlu ana bīt emīšu zubullâ izbil u ašassu mētat* "If a man has brought the marriage gifts into the house of his father-in-law but his (prospective) wife has died."

[11] CH § 159:33-39 *šumma awīlum ša ana bīt emīšu biblam ušābilu terḫatam iddinu ana sinništim šanītim uptallis* "If a man who has brought the marriage gifts to the house of his father-in-law and has given the bride price has then looked favorably upon another woman." Cf. *ibid.,* § 160:47-52; § 161:60-64. For other references see *CAD,* B, p. 220.

[12] It is plausible, though by no means certain, that the difficult *mzbl* in this obscure verse has nothing to do with the root *zbl* under consideration. For attempted renderings and emendations see the commentaries and cf. also N. H. Tur-Sinai, *Hallashon wehassefer,* II (1951), pp. 344-346 [reading *mizbāl* = Arabic *mazbala* "dunghill"?]. The recent attempt by M. Dahood (*Psalms,* The Anchor Bible No. 16, 1966), p. 301 [reading *mezē bōleh lō* "consumed by the one who devours for himself"?] is even more labored, farfetched and altogether unacceptable.

[13] Hab. 3:11.

[14] I Kings 8:13 [=II Chron. 6:2].

[15] Isa. 63:15.

[16] *JPOS,* 16 (1936), pp. 17-18; *idem,* "The Psalm of Habakkuk" in *Studies in OT Prophecy* (Edinburgh, 1950), p. 16, n. mm.

[17] See the discussion and bibliography in *CAD,* Z,

Syriac loan *sblnt*[18] preserves the original meaning of *zubullû* and is also restricted to marriage gifts only.[19] The word for "gift, present" in Akkadian is not *zubullû*, but rather *qīštu* or *širiktu*[20] = Ugaritic *ytnt//ušn*;[21] Phoenician *mtt* (Punic *mtnt*);[22] Hebrew *mattānā* (*mattāt*); Aramaic *mattenā*;[23] Arabic *'ṭīya* (*hadīya*) or *hiba*.[24]

The correct rendering of our Genesis idiom would seem to be: "This time my husband will exalt/elevate me."[25] In other words, our *yzblny* is only a poetic synonym of *ynś'ny*[26] or *yrwmmny*,[27] in all probability to be vocalized as a Piel: *yezabbelēnī*. Such an interpretation used to be rejected because "The Assyrian *zabâlu* means commonly 'to carry, bring . . .' and the evidence that it means also 'to lift up,' or 'exalt,' seems . . . . questionable."[28] However, this rendering is now fully vindicated by Ugaritic *zbl*.

Indeed, it is now generally recognized that Ugaritic knows not only such epithets of Baal as *zbl b'l arṣ* "the Prince, Lord of Earth" (attested eight times),[29] or simply *zbl b'l* "Prince Baal" (attested four times),[30] but has also the substantive *zbl* used as an A word in synonymous parallelism with *ṯpṭ* "ruler" (attested eight times),[31] on the one hand, and the idiom *kḫṯ zbl* "throne[32] of princeship/royalty" (attested five times)[33] on the other. Suffice it to quote the following two examples, one from the Baal Epic, the other from the Legend of King Keret. In the description of the combat between Baal and Yamm we read: *ylm*[34] *qdqd*[35] *zbl ym// bn 'nm*[36] *ṯpṭ nhr* "It (the club) strikes the head of Prince Yamm, on the forehead (it strikes) Ruler Nahar."[37] The Keret passage, dealing with the removal of Keret's malady, reads: *ṯb*[38] *bny lmṯbtkm// lkḫṯ zblkm*[39] "Sit, my sons, upon your seats (of kingship), upon your thrones of prince-

pp. 152 f.; cf. now also S. Greengus, JCS, 20 (1966), pp. 55 ff.

[18] M. Jastrow, *Dictionary*, II, pp. 950 f.; J. Levy, *Wörterbuch*, III, pp. 467 f.; C. Brockelmann, *Lex. Syr.*², p. 455.

[19] Driver's assertion that Akkadian *zubullû* has no connection with LH and Syriac *sblnt* (*The Assyrian Laws*, p. 472) is erroneous and must be rejected.

[20] These two well attested substantives may even be employed in synonymous parallelism; cf. e. g., *YOS* 9, no. 35: 148-154 *šulmam u balāṭam ša kīma Sîn u Šamaš dārium*(!) *ana qīštim liqīšūšum ana širiktim lišrukūšum* "May (the gods) grant (Samsuiluna) as a gift, bestow upon him as a present, life and well being which are eternal as the moon and the sun."

[21] IK: 135-136, 277-278 *Udm ytnt il//(w)ušn ab adm* "Udm is a gift of El, a present of the Father of Man."

[22] Donner-Röllig, no. 29: 2; *ibid.*, 99: 1, 2; 102: 2; 104: 1; 112: 1; 113A: 1.

[23] Dan. 2: 6, 48; 5: 17 and frequently in the *Targumim*; only rarely does the Targum employ *mōhabtā*, *mōhabā* (e.g., Prov. 18: 16; 19: 6; 21: 14; 25: 14).

[24] In a majority of cases Saadia renders Hebrew *mattānā* by Arabic *'aṭīya* and only rarely does he prefer *hiba* (< *wahaba* "to give, donate, grant"; e. g., Gen. 25: 6; Num. 18: 6; cf. Prov. 15: 27).

[25] So approximately G. von Rad, *Genesis*⁸ (Göttingen, 1964), p. 255 (= English translation, p. 288).

[26] Cf. II Sam. 5: 12; Est. 3: 1; 5: 11; 9: 3.

[27] Cf. Ex. 15: 2; Isa. 25: 1; Ps. 34: 4; 118: 28.

[28] S. R. Driver, *The Book of Genesis* (Westminster Commentaries), p. 276, n. 1.

[29] VAB, A: 2-4; I*AB, 6: 9-10; I AB, 1: 41-43; *ibid.*, 3: 2-3, 8-9, 20-21; *ibid.*, 4: 28-29, 39-40.

[30] IIIAB, B: 38-43; IIIAB, A: 7-8; Gordon, Text 133: 10 (broken context).

[31] III AB, C: 8-9, 16, 23; III AB, A: 14-15, 16-17, 21-22, 24-25, 29-30.

[32] Ugaritic *kḫṯ* (< Hurrian *kišḫi*; cf. *kaḫšu* "throne" in EA 120: 18) is a poetic synonym of *ks'* and is frequently employed as its B word (cf. VI AB, 4: 24-25 [restored]; III AB, A: 12-13, 19-20; IIAB, 6: 51-52 [reversed order!]; V AB, D: 46-47; I AB, 5: 5-6; *ibid.*, 6: 33-35 [restored]; IVAB, 3: 14-15; II K, 6: 23-24; note also the parallelism of *kḫṯ//hdm* (II AB, 1: 34-36) = *ks'//hdm* (I*AB, 6: 12-14).

[33] IIIAB, B: 23-24, 24-25, 27-28, 29; II K, 5: 24-25.

[34] Ugaritic *hlm* (= Hebrew *hālam*) *-ylm* (= *yalimu*; contrast Hebrew *yahalōm*) is a poetic synonym of *mḫṣ* "to strike" and is attested in the Baal and Aqht Epics only (III AB, A: 14-15, 16-17, 21-22, 24-25; III D, 4: 22-23, 33-34; ID: 78-79). The sequence of *hlm* (= *halama*; cf. III D, 4: 33-34)—*ylm* (= *yalimu*; cf. III AB, A: 16-17, 24-25) is in no way different from the one of *hlk* (= *halaka*; cf. IK: 92-93, 94-95 = 180-181, 182-183)—*ylk* (= *yaliku*; cf. IK: 207-208 and note IIAB, 6: 18-21 !). The latter sequence points to a very interesting isogloss between Ugaritic and the Canaanite dialects.

[35] Ugaritic *qdqd* is a poetic synonym of *riš* "head" and is frequently employed as its B word (III AB, B: 7-8; I*AB, 6: 14-16; IID, 6: 36-37; IIK, 6: 55-57; cf. the identical Hebrew pair in the very same order in Gen. 49: 26; Dt. 33: 16; Ps. 7: 17; 68: 22). Our sequence of *qdqd*(A)—*bn 'nm* (B) is due to metrical considerations; for a similar sequence for the very same reason, cf. *qdqd* (A)—*'l udn* (B) "head-pate" in III D, 4: 22-23, 33-34; ID: 78-79.

[36] For *bn 'nm* "forehead" cf. Ex. 13: 9, 16; Dt. 6: 8; 11: 18; Dan. 8: 5 and see H. L. Ginsberg, *Kitbe Ugarit*, p. 73; *idem*, *ANET*², p. 131, n. 10.

[37] III AB, A: 24-25.

[38] Observe the sequence of *šebet—zebūl* in I Kings 8: 13.

[39] For the correct rendering of the parallel Hebrew idioms see already W. F. Albright, *JPOS*, 16 (1936), pp. 17 f.

ship."[40] In short, Ugaritic *zbl* is the semantic equivalent of Hebrew *nāśīʾ*,[41] in all probability to be vocalized as *zabūl(u)*[42] fully analogous with the Canaanite Qal passive *ḫamūdu* attested in the Amarna letters.[43]

We shall now turn to Hebrew *sāḇal* in the light of Akkadian *zabālu*, giving special attention to the substantive *sēḇel*. It should be stated at the outset that Hebrew *sāḇal* goes hand in hand with Akkadian *zabālu* in virtually all shades of its meaning. The primary meanings of Akkadian *zabālu* "to transport, to carry a load" are well known and are now fully documented.[44] The most widely known occurrence is probably the one in the Gilgāmeš Epic (The Flood Story) where the Babylonian poet states: *3* ŠÁR ERÍN.MEŠ *nāš sussulša* (var. *sussullиša*) *izabbilū šamna* "The ark's basket carriers were transporting 10,800 (units of) oil."[45] Of greater relevance for our study is the fact that Akkadian *zabālu* is very commonly used in connection with transporting clay, bricks[46] and straw.[47] One is immediately reminded of the reference to *teḇen* "straw," *ḥomer* "clay" and *leḇēnīm* "bricks" in Exodus in connection with Israel's forced labor in Egypt (Hebrew *siḇlōt*).[48]

The verb *sāḇal* is attested eight times in the Hebrew Bible. Considering that the verb in Gen. 49:15 is the result of a misvocalization (see below), the only problematic occurrences are in Ps. 144:14[49] and Eccl. 12:5,[50] both of which are beyond the scope of this study. In three cases[51] *sāḇal* means "to carry a load" and is synonymously parallel to *nāśāʾ*.[52] Although such synonymous parallelism is by no means characteristic of Akkadian literature, it is a fact that the same pair, *našû//zabālu*, is well attested.[53] Thus, to quote but one passage from the Annals of Aššurbanipal: *allu tupšikku ušaššīšunūti ušazbila kudurri* "I had them take up the hoe (and) the basket, I had them carry the corvée basket for me."[54]

In two cases[55] Hebrew *sāḇal* is employed in connection with *ḥēṭʾ* "sin" and *awōn* "guilt," fully analogous with such well known Akkadian idioms as *arna*[56]/*ḫīṭa*[57]/*šērta*[58] *zabālu* (= *našû, wabālu, šadādu*) "to bear, suffer sin/punishment." Of some interest at this juncture is Isa. 53:4 where both *nāśāʾ* and *sāḇal* are employed in connection with *ḥolī* "sickness" and *maḵʾōḇ* "pain." While it cannot be denied that Akkadian *zubullu* sometimes denotes the lingering on of a chronic

[40] II K, 5: 24-25.

[41] It may not be out of place to note in passing that the Hebrew *nāśīʾ* has recently been studied by E. A. Speiser in *CBQ*, 25 (1963), pp. 111 ff. While his criticism of the derivation and interpretation of *nāśīʾ* by M. Noth and J. van der Ploeg seems fully justified, it must be stated that this very criticism as well as his own interpretation would have gained much in probability were they based not only on indirect evidence from Akkadian, but on direct and convincing evidence from Ugaritic derived from the usage and meaning of the substantive *zbl*.

[42] Contrast W. F. Albright in *Studies in OT Prophecy* (Edinburgh, 1950), p. 16, n. mm.

[43] EA 138: 126-129 (Rib-Addi): *u yāpu//ḫamūdu ša šapir ištu šarri bēlī lā nadin yâši* "But (something) nice (gloss: desirable) which was sent by the king, my lord, has not been given to me." (This passage is quoted in *CAD*, H, p. 73b and I, p. 325a).

[44] *CAD*, Z, pp. 1 ff.

[45] *Gilg.* XI: 67.

[46] Cf. e.g., *AJSL*, 32 (1916), p. 281: 29-30 *ṭiddam u libittam lizbilūnim* "Let them transport for me clay and bricks"; Streck, *Asb.*, p. 88 x: 88 *nišī mātiya . . . izabbilū libnātēšu* "My people transport its (the temple's) bricks"; VAB, 4, p. 62 ii: 66-68 *libnāti u ṭiddam ina qaqqadiya lu azbil* "I transported on my head bricks and clay."

[47] Cf. e.g., *BE*, 17 (1908), no. 34: 39-40 *ina eriqqi tibna kī azbila* "When I transported hither the straw in the wagon."

[48] Ex. 5: 4 ff.; cf. *ibid.*, 1: 14.

[49] The accepted renderings of *allūpēnū mesubbālīm* as "our oxen are laden" or even "our cattle are heavy with young" (see the commentaries) are hardly convincing. It seems preferable to render our verse as follows: "Our cattle are well cared for; (there is none that breaks out, and none that stampedes, and there is no alarm on our ranges)." Such a translation of the first clause is not too remote from the renderings of the versions (Sept., Targum, Syriac) and would seem to be supported by the Aramaic verb *sabbēl* "to sustain, maintain" (Aḥiqar: 48-49, 71-72, 204) and the substantive *sibbūl* "sustenance, maintenance" (Aḥiqar: 74, 205; cf. A. Cowley, *Aramaic Papyri*, no. 43: 4).

[50] For this difficult verse see H. L. Ginsberg, *Koheleth* (Tel Aviv-Jerusalem, 1961), pp. 132, 137. [*yistabbēl* = *yitnassēʾ*].

[51] Isa. 46: 4, 7; 53: 4.

[52] Observe that the same pair in parallelism is also attested in Aramaic poetry (Aḥiqar 90-91).

[53] Cf. e.g., Borger, *Esarh.*, p. 20 (no. 21): 15-17 (*aššī-ušazbil*); *ibid.*, p. 62: 38-39 (*nāši marri—ēpiš dulli—zābil kudurri*); VAB, 4, p. 240 ii: 53 (*ṣābit allu—nāš marri—zābil* [*tupšikki*]).

[54] Streck, *Asb.*, p. 88 x: 92-93.

[55] Isa. 53: 11; Lam. 5: 7.

[56] Cf. e.g., W. G. Lambert, *BWL*, p. 132: 98 (Šamaš Hymn) *māḫir da'ti lā muštēšeru tušazbal arna* "You make (the judge) who accepts presents and does not provide justice bear punishment" (*CAD* Z, p. 3 f.).

[57] See the references in *CAD*, H, pp. 211 f.

[58] Cf. e.g., W. G. Lambert, *BWL*, p. 202: 5.

disease,[59] this is certainly not the norm in Akkadian. Thus, notwithstanding the self-evident transition of "to bear" into "suffer,"[60] there is no escape from the conclusion that in this particular usage Hebrew *sāḇal* is closely connected with Ugaritic *zbl* "to be sick, to suffer."[61] It will be recalled that in Ugaritic *zbl*[62] and *zbln*[63] denote "sick man" and "malady, sickness" respectively. Suffice it to observe that in the Keret Epic *zbln* "malady" is a B word synonymously parallel (five times) to *mrṣ* "sickness" on the one hand, and is likewise a B word synonymously parallel (twice) to *mdw* "illness"[64] on the other. Thus, the text dealing with King Keret's illness and his subsequent recovery by means of El's magic reads: [*my*][65] *bilm ydy*[66] *mrṣ gršm*[67] *zbln* "Who among the gods can remove the sickness, driving out the illness?"[68] Keret's son, overzealous to succeed his sick father as king, states: *aḫt*[69] *'rš mdw*[70] *anšt 'rš zbln* "You have become a brother of the bed of illness, a companion of the bed of malady."[71] However, it should be borne in mind that in no Semitic language is *zbl/sbl* the norm for "to be sick" and "sickness." The interdialectal distribution for "to be sick" is as follows: Akkadian *marāṣu*; Ugaritic *mrṣ*; Hebrew *ḥālā* (poetic *nimraṣ*); Aramaic *mer'a*; Arabic *mariḍa*. The distribution for "sickness" is: Akkadian *murṣu*; Ugaritic *mrṣ*; Hebrew *ḥolī*, *maḥălā*; Aramaic *mer'a*; Arabic *maraḍ*. It is worth noting, however, that the counterpart of Hebrew *ḥālā* is now attested in Mari, where a *nēštu* "lioness" is said to be *šībat u ḫalât* "old and sick."[72]

Finally, some remarks concerning the noun *sēḇel* "forced labor, corvée work." Our atten-

[59] Cf. e.g., R. Labat, *TDP*, p. 102: 15 *šumma tulī imittišu du'um murussu uzabbal* "If his right breast is dark, his illness will linger on"; for other references see *CAD*, Z, p. 4.

[60] See the remarks of H. L. Ginsberg and S. Lieberman in *Keret*, p. 34.

[61] There is no justification for C. H. Gordon's assumption that Ugaritic has a *zbl* I "princeship" (*UM*, III, no. 594 = *UT*, III, no. 815) and a *zbl* II "invalid, disease" (*UM*, III, no. 595 = *UT*, III, no. 816), nor is there any justification for his seeking a link between the two on the basis of a questionable statement such as: "*zbl* I and *zbl* II may be the same word, for 'The Prince' may refer honorifically to the deity or demon of 'disease'" (*UT*, III, no. 816)!

[62] The word *zbl, zbln* "sick man," "sickness" is attested eleven times in Ugaritic in the Keret Epic only. For *zbl* "sick man" cf. IK: 98-100, 186-188 *zbl//'wr* "sick man—blind man."

[63] For *zbln* "sickness" cf. IK: 16-17 *kṯrm//zblnm* "in . . . . in sickness"; IIK, 5: 20-21, 27-28 (cf. the restored text *ibid.*, 10-12, 14-15, 17-18) *mrṣ//zbln* "sickness-illness"; IIK, 6: 8-9 obscure passage; *ibid.*, 35-36, 50-52 *mdw//zbln* "sickness-illness."

[64] See note 63 above.

[65] For this certain restoration here (as well as in ll. 10-12, 17-18) cf. ll. 14-15 in our text. The interrogative *my* is also attested in I* AB, 6: 23-24 = I AB, 1: 6-7 where render, with Cassuto (*Tarbiz*, 12 [1941], p. 179) and Ginsberg (*ANET*², p. 139b) as follows: "Baal is dead! what becomes of the people, Dagon's son (is dead)! what of the masses?" (Contrast C. H. Gordon, *UM*, III, no. 296 = *UT*, III, no. 424; *UL*, pp. 42, 43; and G. R. Driver, *CML*, p. 109). For the spelling *my* cf. Amarna *miya*(*mi*) (e.g., EA 129: 81; 85: 63-64; 104: 17-19) and Phoenician *my* (e.g., *Klmw*: 10-11, 11-12, 12-13, 13-14, 15). Note that Ugaritic also has the interrogative *mn*(*m*) (e.g., VAB, D: 34-35, 48) = Akkadian *mannu*; Aramaic *man*; Arabic *man*.

[66] The etymology of our word is questionable, but the parallelism with *grš-m* (inf) "to drive out" makes the rendering quite certain. It would seem to be supported also by IIK, 6: 47-48 where the faithless son rebukes his sick father saying: *ltdy ṯšm 'l dl* "You do not chase away those that prey on the poor." Any connection with Akkadian *nadû* "to throw" (C. H. Gordon, *UM*, III, no. 1213 = *UT*, III, no. 1616; G. R. Driver, *CML*, p. 157, n. 16) is open to serious doubts.

[67] The verb *grš* "to drive/chase away/out" is usually an A word in Ugaritic (VIAB, 4; 24-25; IIIAB, A: 12-13; VAB, B: 15-16; *ibid.*, D: 46-47), the only exceptions being our text and IID, 1: 29-30 (= 48-49; *ibid.*, 2: 2-3, 18-19). It is worth noting that *grš* is Canaanite only as is indicated by the following distribution: Akkadian *ṭarādu*; Ugaritic *grš*; Moabite *grš*; Hebrew *grš*; Aramaic *ṭerad*; Arabic *ṭarada*. In one case only (VAB, D: 44-45) does the Ugaritic poet prefer to employ *ṭrd* instead of *grš*.

[68] II K, 5: 20-21.

[69] Ginsberg's rendering of this passage (*Keret*, p. 32; *ANET*², p. 149a) is very convincing, but the connection of our *anš* with Arabic *anisa* (*Keret*, p. 49) is less certain. As a matter of fact, Arabic *anisa* "to be gentle, sociable" seems closer to *anš* in IIID, 1: 16 (= V AB, E: 35) where El says to his daughter: *yd'tk bt kanšt* "I care for you, daughter mine, for you are gentle." However, this passage is not without difficulties and entirely different interpretations have been suggested (e.g., U. M. D. Cassuto, *The Goddess Anath*, pp. 72, 88).

[70] Cf. with Ginsberg (*Keret*, p. 49), Hebrew *'ereś dewai* (Ps. 41: 4) and note also Akkadian *ereš anḫūti* "bed of weariness" (E. Ebeling, *Handerhebung*, p. 8: 9). One wonders whether, in light of this Akkadian idiom, Ps. 6: 7a should not be emended to read: *yāga'tī be⟨'ereś⟩ anḥātī*, or *yāga'tī be⟨yeṣū'ā⟩ anḥāti*. Both parallelism and meter clearly indicate that a word has accidentally been omitted.

[71] II K, 6: 35-36, 51-52.

[72] *Syria*, 19 (1938) p. 125: 13 (quoted in *CAD*, H, p. 54a).

tion should first be directed to two key passages from Mari and Amarna in which the nouns *sablum* (= Hebrew *sēḇel*)[73] and *massu*[74] (= Hebrew *mas*)[75] are attested. These passages are not only of interest in themselves, but serve as a point of departure for some of the following remarks. The Mari passage, contained in a letter by Kibri-Dagan,[76] reads: *aššum sablim*[77] *ša ḫalṣiya* TUR *u* SAL.TUR *ana dannatim kamāsim*[78] *bēlī išpuram* "Concerning the corvée workers from my district my lord ordered me to assemble male and female minors into the fortress."

The Amarna passage, contained in a letter from Megiddo,[79] reads: *anumma anākūma errešu* [gloss: *aḫrišu*[80]] *ina Šunama u anākūma ubbalu* LÚ.MEŠ (*awīlūti*) *massu* MEŠ "now I alone[81] am plowing in the town of Šunama and I alone am bringing the corvée workers."

The noun *sēḇel* is attested three times in the Hebrew Bible and in all three cases the meaning "corvée work," not just "burden" or "labor," is self-evident. The first verse,[82] dealing with Solomon's appointment of Jeroboam as overseer of the corvée workers, reads: *wh'yš yrb'm gbwr ḥyl wyr' šlmh 't hn'r ky 'śh ml'kh hw' wypqd 'tw lkl sbl byt ywsp* "And Jeroboam was a man of action; when Solomon noted him to be a young man fit for (overseeing) forced labor[83] (cf. Akkadian *dulla epēšu*![84]), he put him in charge of all the corvée workers of the house of Joseph." Equally important is the following poetic verse from the Psalms:[85] *hsyrwty msbl škmw kpyw mdwd t'brnh* where we must render: "I removed his back from the corvée basket,[86] his hands are free from the basket."[87]

The last verse,[88] dealing with the protective measures of Nehemiah against the Samaritans, reads: *hbwnym bḥwmh whnś'ym bsbl 'mśym* "Those who rebuild the wall and those who carry the basket are loading."[89] In this verse, *hnś'ym bsbl* is not to be rendered as "they that bore

[73] See already J. R. Kupper, *ARM*, 3, p. 116.

[74] Note that the term *massu* is now also attested in the Alalakh Tablets; cf. e. g., Wiseman, *Alalakh*, no. 269: 18 *idi* LÚ.MEŠ *massi ša ina Muraba illiku* "wages of the corvée workers who have come from Muraba"; for other references see now von Soden, *AHw*, p. 619a.

[75] The biblical terms *mas* and *mas 'ōḇēd* have been studied by I. Mendelsohn in *BASOR*, 85 (1942), pp. 14 ff.

[76] *ARM*, 3, no. 38: 5-7 (quoted in *CAD*, D, p. 89b); cf. *ibid.*, ll. 8-14.

[77] The term *sablum* is also attested (in broken context) in two other Mari letters by Zimri-Lim (*ARM*, 2, 67: 5) and Kibri-Dagan (*ibid.*, 88: 9).

[78] For this idiom cf. *ARM*, 5, 36: 8-10 *mātum ana dannatišu kamsat u bazaḫātūya dunnunā* "The people are assembled in their fortress and my outposts are strong."

[79] *RA*, 19 (1922) pp. 97-98: 10-14; cf. *ibid.*, ll. 22-23, 24-25.

[80] The verb *ḫarāšu* "to plow" (= Ugaritic *ḥrṯ*; Phoenician and Hebrew *ḥrš*) is also attested as a Canaanite gloss to Akkadian *erēšu* in EA 226: 10-12 *anumma errešu* (gloss: *aḫrišu*) *u ibaqqama* "now I am plowing and plucking the sheep."

[81] This translation is corroborated not only by the context of the letter and the form *anāku* + *ma*, but also by the parallel passage (*RA*, 19, pp. 97-98: 24-25) where the Canaanite gloss *yaḫudunni* is attested. Thus, *anākūma* (gloss: *yaḫudunni*) *ubbalu* LÚ.MEŠ *massa* MEŠ must be rendered: "I alone (in contradistinction to the other governors; cf. ll. 15-23) am bringing the corvée workers" (contrast *CAD*, I, p. 321a).

[82] I Kings 11: 28.

[83] Contrast the standard renderings of *'śh ml'kh* such as "industrious," "energetic," "apt agent," and the like (e. g., R. Kittel, *Könige* [HKAT], pp. 99 f.; J. Gray, *I & II Kings* [The OT Library, 1963] p. 273).

[84] See *CAD*, E, p. 207; *ibid.*, D, pp. 173 f. Note that the Hebrew idiom is a verbatim translation of the Akkadian *ēpiš dulli* (*CAD*, E, p. 238b).

[85] Ps. 81: 7.

[86] It would seem that Hebrew *sēḇel* may denote a basket (for carrying earth) as can be inferred from the synonymous parallelism of *sēḇel*//*dwd*. Such an assumption seems to be corroborated not only by the Akkadian semantic equivalents of Hebrew *sēḇel*, namely *kudurru* and *tupšikku*, but also by the etymological equivalent of Hebrew *sēḇel*, namely Akkadian *zabbīlu* "basket (for carrying earth)." While it is true that Akkadian *zabbīlu* is attested only in NB, it can hardly be considered a loan from Aramaic (contrast *CAD*, Z, p. 6b).

[87] For *dwd* "basket" cf. II Kings 10: 7 and Jer. 24: 1, 2.

[88] Neh. 4: 11. It must be admitted that this verse is not free from textual difficulties. These, however, are not directly related to the problem under consideration.

[89] MT *'mśym* is problematic, but the emendation to *ḥmšym* allegedly meaning "prepared" (see the commentaries) is equally difficult. It stands to reason that our *'mś* is but a variant of *'ms* "to load, to carry" (cf. particularly Neh. 13: 15) since our sequence of *nś'*—*'mś* is not very remote from the one of *nś'*—*'ms* in Isa. 46: 3. The verb *'ms*, which is Canaanite only, is well known in Ugaritic (e. g., IID, 1: 31-32; *ibid.*, 2: 5-6, 19-20), Phoenician (e. g., Ašmn'zr: 5-6, 7-8, 21) and Hebrew. Of particular interest here is the usage of *'ms* (//*kll*) in connection with the construction of Baal's palace (II AB, 4-5: 72-73). The two passages may be destined to elucidate one another, despite the fact that at the present both are far from being completely understood.

burdens," "burden bearers"[90] or the like, but rather "basket carriers."[91] Moreover, the very same idiom seems to be hidden in I Kings 5:29 where the MT reads: *wyhy lšlmh šbʿym ʾlp nśʾ sabbāl wšmnym ʾlp ḥṣb bhr* "Solomon had seventy thousand corvée workers and eighty thousand mountain hewers." The majority of biblical scholars are agreed in deleting *nśʾ* as a gloss.[92] Of these, most are inclined to read *sabbāl* alone,[93] a reading allegedly supported by II Chron. 2:1, 17, while others read *sēḇel* alone[94] on the basis of I Kings 11:28. However, neither the deletion of *nśʾ* nor the interpretations of *sabbāl* can in any way be justified. It need only be pointed out to be accepted that the correct and original reading in I Kings 5:29 is neither *sabbāl* alone "porter" nor *sēḇel* alone "labor," but rather *nśʾ sēḇel*. Such a reading is fully corroborated not only by Neh. 4:11, where the text has *hnśʾym bassēḇel*, but also, and this is surely more important here, by such well known Akkadian idioms as *nāš tupšikki/ zābil tupšikki; nāš kudurri / zābil kudurri* "corvée workers," literally "basket carriers." Only a few examples can be mentioned here: *nāši marri*[95] *alli*[96] *tupšikki ēpiš dulli zābil kudurri ina elēli ulṣi ḫūd·libbi nummur panī ubbalū ūmšun*[97] "(The corvée workers) who wield the spade, the hoe, the basket, the forced laborers, the basket carriers spend their time in jubilation, rejoicing, happiness (and) good spirits."[98] These idioms are also well attested in literary texts, the most illuminating case being the joke in which the horse whispers into the ear of a mule while mating with her: *mūru ša tullidī kī yâti lu lasim ana imēri zābil tupšikki lā tumaššalī*[99] "May the foal which you will bear be a swift runner like me; do not make it resemble the ass which has to do forced labor"[100] (literally, "to carry baskets").

It is worth observing that the idiom *zābil tupšikki/zābil kudurri* (literally, "a basket carrier") becomes a stereotyped expression for "forced labor" in general. Thus, *zābil tupšikki elīšunu ukīn* means "I imposed corvée work upon them,"[101] while *zābil kudurri elīšunu aškun* means "I imposed forced labor upon them."[102] Small wonder, therefore, that one finds in Akkadian such expressions as *tupšikka emēdu*[103] / *kudurra emēdu*[104] "to impose forced labor" (literally, "to impose the basket."[105]) These are of course in no way different in meaning from the more general idiom *dulla epēšu/emēdu* "to perform/impose corvée work."[106]

These observations immediately shed light not only on *sēḇel* in the passages discussed above, but also on such verses as Ex. 6:6 where *sblt* is in synonymous parallelism with *ʿbdh*[107] (= Akkadian *dullu*!). Moreover, it would seem that Gen. 49:15 also belongs here. In this verse the correct reading is surely not *wyṭ škmh lisbol* but rather *wyṭ škmh lesēḇel* in synonymous parallelism with *mas ʿoḇēd*. This reading is not only supported by the parallelism of *mas* and *siḇlot* in Ex. 1:11, on the one hand, and the sequence of *sēḇel* and *šeḵem* in Ps. 81:7 on the other, but also by Mari *sablum*

[90] So most recently J. M. Myers, *Ezra-Nehemiah* (Anchor Bible No. 14, 1965), p. 123.

[91] Characteristic is the approach of G. R. Driver (*CML*, p. 142, n. 6) who not only misunderstands and mistranslates *hnśʾym bsbl*ᵉas "carrying loads," but even goes so far as to assume that it is but a wrong gloss on *ʿmśym*. The latter he renders as "bricklayers" and all this doubtful philology is based solely on the Arabic root *ǵammasa* allegedly meaning "to set in cement"!

[92] See the note in *Biblia Hebraica* and cf. e. g., Koehler, *Lexicon*, p. 648b.

[93] So most recently John Gray, *I & II Kings*, p. 147 where the reading *sabbāl* is taken for granted.

[94] Cf. e.g., J. A. Montgomery, *Kings* (ICC), p. 139.

[95] For the "kulturwort" *marru* (> Aramaic-Syriac *marrā*) see now von Soden, *AHw.*, p. 612b. Observe that the sequences *allu—marru* (e.g., VAB, 4, p. 240 ii: 53), *allu—tupšikku* (e.g., Borger, *Esarh.*, p. 20, 19a: 21-23), *marru—tupšikku* (e.g., VAB, 4, p. 62 iii: 12-15) are well attested in Akkadian frequently referring to corvée work.

[96] *AHw.*, p. 37b; *CAD*, A, pp. 356 f.

[97] For the idiom *ūma wabālu* "to spend the time (in joy or sorrow)" see *CAD*, A, p. 20.

[98] Borger, *Esarh.*, p. 62: 38-40; cf. Streck, *Asb.*, p. 88 x: 92-95.

[99] W. G. Lambert, *BWL*, p. 218: 17-18.

[100] Cf. Gen. 49: 14-15.

[101] *AKA*, p. 273 I: 56.

[102] *Ibid.*, p. 277 I: 67.

[103] Cf. e.g., W. G. Lambert, *BWL*, p. 114: 56-57 *ša . . .tupšikku bītāt ilī rabûti immedušunūti* "(An official) who imposes upon them (the citizens of Sippar, Nippur and Babylon) corvée work for the temples of the great gods." For other numerous references see *CAD*, E, p. 143.

[104] Cf. e.g., *AKA*, p. 310 ii: 47 *šeʾam tibna kudurru ēmissunūti* "I imposed upon them (a tribute of) barley, straw and corvée work"; see also *ibid.*, p. 279 I: 73.

[105] One is tempted to note here also the idiom *kudurra epēšu*, but the references given in *CAD*, E, p. 211b are far from convincing.

[106] See the numerous references in *CAD*, E, pp. 207, 142; *ibid.*, D, pp. 173-174.

[107] Cf. Ex. 5: 4 where *sblt* is in parallelism with *mʿśh*.

and Alalakh-Amarna *massu* respectively. In other words, the biblical poet draws his pair of synonyms from two different layers of the NW Semitic dialects, the earlier one represented by *sēḇel* (Mari: *sablum*), the later one represented by *mas* (Alalakh-Amarna: *massu*).

It now becomes abundantly clear that biblical scholarship errs in deleting *nś'* in the expression *nś' sabbāl* in I Kings 5:29 and in reading *sabbāl* alone on the basis of II Chr. 2:1, 17. It should be borne in mind that at least II Chr. 2:1 has the idiom *'īš sabbāl,* not just *sabbāl* alone![108] Once again it need only be pointed out for our ready acceptance that the correct and original reading of our idiom is certainly *'īš sēḇel* which is but a variant of, and in no way different in meaning from, *nś' sēḇel.* Such a reading is not only corroborated by the Akkadian expression ERÍN GI.ÍL = *ṣāb tupšikki* "man of the basket, basket carrier,"[109] but also by the Alalakh-Amarna idiom *awīlūti massi/a* "men of the corvée."[110]

In short, when we render such Akkadian expressions as *nāš/zābil tupšikki/kudurri* into biblical Hebrew, we obtain *nōśē' sēḇel* or **soḇēl sēḇel*; similarly, a rendering into Hebrew of the Akkadian *ṣāb tupšikki* and Alalakh-Amarna *awīlūti massi/a* yields *'īš sēḇel* and *'anšē mas* respectively.

[108] There seems to be no escape from the conclusion that the attestation of *sabbāl* "porter" in biblical Hebrew is altogether doubtful. Thus, in II Chron. 2:17 the word *'yš* has accidentally been omitted as is evident from verse 1 where the reading *'yš sēḇel* is by now self evident. Note that even in a prosaic text the parallel to *ḥṣb bhr* would surely be *'yš sēḇel* not just *sbl* alone. It also stands to reason to read in Neh. 4:4 *kšl kḥ hassēḇel wh'pr hrbh* and to render: "The basket carriers are worn out for there is too much earth (to be carried in the corvée baskets!)." More problematic is II Chron. 34:13 where *sabbālīm* "porters" can hardly be correct. The word may denote here "corvée masters." Note the *mnṣḥym* "overseers" in our verse and cf. *'l hammas* "corvée master" (e.g., I Kings 4:6).

[109] P. Kraus, *Altbab. Briefe,* II (1932), p. 63:5.

[110] Observe that in all its occurrences, both in Alalakh and in Amarna, the idiom is always *LÚ.MEŠ massi/a* = *awīlūti massi/a.*

MILITARY POLITICS IN THE MUSLIM DYNASTIC STATES, 1400-1750 *

J. C. HUREWITZ
COLUMBIA UNIVERSITY

Nearly half of the political systems in the Middle East late in the 1960s were Islamic monarchies. Two of them, in fact, dated back to the period before the European imperial powers engulfed the Muslim world. Military politics in the eight surviving monarchies, in some respects, resembled military politics of the preimperial dynastic states more closely than of the postimperial Middle East Islamic republics of the twentieth century. Even in some of the republican polities, particularly those that have fallen under military rule, there are traces of preimperial influence. Moreover, the popularity of the military coup d'état in the postwar Middle East undoubtedly owes a great deal to the fact that the violent seizure of political power had become an accepted mode of changing political leaders and policies in the Muslim dynastic states. The key to military politics in the preimperial Islamic dynastic states was the failure to fix a policy on succession. It was this ambiguity, as we shall see, that invited military intervention into politics.

The latest possible date at which the general community of Muslim states was still relatively free from the subordinating influence of European imperialism was the turn of the eighteenth century. At that time the present-day area of the Middle East, stretching from Morocco to Afghanistan and Pakistan, comprised four large Muslim dynastic states—the Ottoman (Turkey), the Safavi (Persia), and the Mughal (India) empires, and the 'Alawi kingdom of Morocco. There were, in addition, many small tribal principalities in the Arabian Peninsula and North Africa into

* This paper has been adapted from a chapter in my forthcoming *Middle East Politics: The Military Dimension* (working title), which was completed under the sponsorship of the Council on Foreign Relations and the School of International Affairs at Columbia University, and will be published in 1968.

which the Ottoman and 'Alawi realms faded at their extremities. None of the major Muslim states of the day could be described as subordinate to any single European power or any combination of European powers.

The Ottoman Empire, it is true, had just suffered its first decisive defeat in Europe. The Treaty of Carlowitz (1699), which brought to an end a decade and a half of fierce fighting that had ranged Austria, Poland, Venice, and Russia (the last signing a separate peace) against the massive Muslim Empire, deprived the Padishah of territory north of the Danube that he never regained. Despite its manifest weakness, the Ottoman Empire was not easily shoved out of Europe, so that by the end of the eighteenth century it still clung to most of its possessions there. Neither had Persia been reduced to wardship, despite the political anarchy through which it passed in the half-century preceding the Napoleonic wars. Shielded by geographic isolation, Persia escaped the European expansive pressure—with the exception of Peter I's short-lived occupation of Persian districts in the Caucasus—until tsarist forces began bearing down on the Caucasian principalities just "reconquered" by the emergent Qajar dynasty (1794-1925) that finally reunited the shahdom. Meanwhile, the maritime powers of western Europe at the start of the eighteenth century were still clutching insecurely the margins of India, many European-held ports being significantly out of Mughal reach at the southern tip of the subcontinent. Few observers at the time would have predicted that in less than a century the Mughal Empire would disappear.

The Muslim State System

The Muslim dynasties of the day were military and tribal in origin, as were most Muslim states, large and small, up to that time. Nor was this surprising. Islam itself had emerged from a tribal society, so that the tribal influence became durably imbedded in the Islamic religious political system. More than that, the *dar al-Islam* or territory under Islamic rule encompassed far-flung tribal districts, which kept spawning new military dynasties. This, Persia and Afghanistan well illustrated in the eighteenth century. In Persia after the destruction of the Safavi dynasty, a member of the Afshar tribe, one of the original pillars of that dynasty, proclaimed himself shah. However, although Nadir Shah (1736-47) demonstrated his military brilliance by reuniting the kingdom and expanding its dominions into central Asia and northern India, he failed to launch a dynastic line of his own. On the other hand, one of the Afghan commanders in Nadir Shah's army, Ahmad Khan Abdali (later Ahmad Shah Durrani), seized power in Qandahar, making it the capital of an independent principality. Ahmad Shah's descendants later united Afghanistan under a dynasty that is still ruling the kingdom in the second half of the twentieth century. Moreover, in the 1790s after a half-century of near political anarchy Aqa Muhammad Khan, a chief of the Qajar tribe, another original tribal supporter of the Safavis, reintegrated the kingdom under a new dynasty that lasted through World War I.

As early as the fourteenth century 'Abd al-Rahman ibn Khaldun (1332-1407) attributed the desert beginnings of Muslim dynasties to the military superiority of the beduin tribesmen. They "provide their own defense and do not entrust it to, or rely upon others for it," declared the renowned Arab historical sociologist, whereas the settled townsmen and villagers "have entrusted defense of their property to the governor and ruler who rules them and to the militia which has the task of guarding them."[1] Yet ibn Khaldun acknowledged the inferiority of "desert civilization . . . to urban civilization."[2] The urbanization of a successful dynasty, he continued, first lifts it to heights of glory by yielding "leisure and tranquility in which the fruits of royal authority are enjoyed," and then thrusts it downward to the stage of "waste and squandering," when it "is seized by senility and the chronic disease from which it can hardly ever rid itself, for which it can find no cure, and, eventually, it is destroyed."[3]

Had ibn Khaldun been present at the opening of the eighteenth century, he would probably have labeled the three imperial dynasties as senile. Indeed, Safavi rule in Persia expired in 1722, followed four decades later by the expiry, for all practical purposes, of Mughal rule in India. The Ottoman dynasty at Istanbul, however, con-

[1] Ibn Kahldun, *The Muqaddimah: An Introduction to History*, translated from the Arabic by Franz Rosenthal (New York, 1958) vol. 1, pp. 257-58.

[2] *Ibid.*, p. 308.

[3] *Ibid.*, pp. 354-55, see also *An Arab Philosophy of History: Selections from the Prelegomena of Ibn Khaldun of Tunis*, arranged and translated by Charles Issawi (London, 1950), chap. 6.

trived to limp along with declining energy until it was rescued in 1839-41 by the intervention of the European concert seeking to preserve the balance of power on the continent which might have been upset by the sudden disappearance of the sprawling Muslim empire. These three dynasties together with the 'Alawi dynasty of Morocco were hardly fly-by-night. Safavi and Mughal rule endured for more than two centuries each, and Ottoman rule for more than six centuries, an enviable record in all history. The 'Alawi dynasty of Morocco, meanwhile, entered its fourth century in the mid-1960s, having survived by the skin of its teeth more than fifty years of French overlordship.

Despite the political divisions, the Islamic world in 1700 still viewed itself as one society, and in some respects it was. The sovereign Muslim states were still glued together by the principles and customs of a generalized Islam under the supremacy of a common religious law. Insofar as a Muslim owed wider allegiance than to his tribe, his locality, or his guild, it was to the Muslim *ummah* or community. The *shari'ah* or sacred law protected his personal rights, and each Muslim polity in its total experience seemed a replica of the next. This preserved transdynastic institutions and related activities, most notably those connected with religious law and the court system that served it, which functioned in all states, large and small. The few Muslims who travelled from one dynastic jurisdiction to another up and down the dar al-Islam thus felt thoroughly at home. A trained *qadi* or judge of the sacred law, for example, could find employment anywhere in the dar al-Islam, and sometimes did. In the fourteenth century ibn Khaldun, a native of Tunis could serve as judge in Cairo, the seat of authority of another Muslim state. His contemporary fellow Maghribi, Muhammad ibn 'Abdallah ibn Battutah (1304-77), famous for his travels in Asia and Africa, held comparable offices in India and the Maldive islands.[4]

[4] Phillip K. Hitti, *History of the Arabs from the Earliest Times to the Present* (6th edition; London, 1956), pp. 567-70.

The universality of the sacred law kept alive the theory of a universal Islamic state, implied in the concept of the dar al-Islam, long after the start, in the ninth century, of the political fragmentation of the 'Abbasid Caliphate (750-1258), the last state to embrace almost the entire Muslim community. An Islamic state system, slow to emerge, seemed embryonic by contrast to the European state system. Administrative law varied from state to state. Religious doctrinal quarrels, it is also true, provided criteria for identifying mutually discrete states in both systems.[5] The Safavi dynasty, for example, established the Ja'fari rite of Shi'ah (schismatic) Islam as the state religion of Persia at the start of the sixteenth century. Yet until the twentieth century Persia had no fixed territorial boundaries with its Sunni (orthodox) Muslim neighbors. Those Muslim countries that held on to their sovereignty did not begin to exchange permanent diplomatic missions with one another until the mid-nineteenth century. Nor did anything that even remotely resembled the balance of power in Europe take shape within the Islamic zone before the close of World War II,

The absence of fixed rules of succession lay at the basis of military politics in Islam. No systematic study of the succession process in Islam has yet been made, although many scholars have probed into particular manifestations of it. We are here concerned with the process only in the age of Islamic political degeneration. In many ways, succession in that age was more fluid and elusive than in the classical age of Islam. What follows is an initial attempt to structure a theory on the basis of limited evidence.

The principle of primogeniture, almost uniformly applied in Europe, was not recognized in Islam, least of all among the Muslim dynasties of the seventeenth and eighteenth centuries. All male members of an extended royal family were acceptable candidates for the throne—brothers, nephews, cousins, and uncles as well as sons and grandsons. In theory, the successor was elected. But a mode of orderly election never became institutionalized. As a consequence, Muslim polities, hovering between hereditary and "elective" monarchies, became inured to violent and disorderly succession whenever the reigning monarch's wishes were not honored after his death. The "electoral college" consisted of the wives and the concubines in the harem and their attending eunuchs, the advisory and administrative

[5] See, for example, Majid Khadduri's introduction to his translation of *The Islamic Law of Nations: Shaybani's Siyar* (Baltimore, 1966), pp. 60-65. The best account of the origins of the European state system is Garrett Mattingly, *Renaissance Diplomacy* (London, 1955).

imperial staffs at the palace, the religious leaders (particularly in the Ottoman Empire), and the princes—all acting in varying combinations. Each combination sought alliance with top military commanders, for the ultimate decision favored that candidate with the strongest military support. Military intrusion into politics was thus built into the succession process, and whether or not the soldiers continued playing decisive political roles under the new monarch depended on his capacity or the capacity of the civilian manipulator behind the throne (whether a queen mother in the Ottoman Empire or Safavi Persia or a civilian consortium) to seize and hold the political leadership.

In an effort to assure an orderly succession, the monarch usually designated as crown prince one of his male relatives, most often a son. A powerful dynast took precautions to try to make his choice stick. He might attempt to groom the crown prince for later responsibilities by naming him governor of an important province close to the capital or by having him serve an apprenticeship in the palace. A not infrequent complementary step was the despatch of ambitious princes as governors to provinces remote from the capital. But such precautions were rarely foolproof. Succession crises threatened to wreck, on more than one occasion, each of the four dynasties under review, even the most powerful of them, the Ottoman, in its halcyon phase. The first ten Ottoman sultans from Osman to Süleyeman I (died, 1566), it is generally agreed, were "able and intelligent men rare if not unique in the annals of dynastic succession." [6] Yet even then the dynasty suffered three major crises in the transfer of the crown from one sultan to the next.[7] The Mughal dynasty was in full vigor in the seventeenth century. Yet consider the turmoil of 1657-58, while Shah Jahan, best known for the erection in his reign of the Taj Mahal, still sat on the throne. He had named as heir his oldest son, Dara Shukoh. But the youngest, Awrangzib, was the most ambitious of the four princes, who did not even wait for their father to die. They jumped the gun instead, as false word of the emperor's death reached them from agents at the palace. The war of succession, which lasted more than a year, finally brought Awrangzib to the throne, his three brothers to defeat and death, and Shah Jahan to imprisonment for his remaining eight years.[8]

Before we examine the role of the military in resolving succession crises in Muslim dynasties, we ought first consider the nonmilitary measures devised to check the princely rivalry, if not remove it altogether. How better to remove the rivalry than remove the princely rivals? Muslim dynasties, if they lasted long enough, could be expected to engage in fratricide. In the Ottoman Empire Fatih Sultan Mehmed II (1451-81), the conqueror of Constantinople, actually gave legal sanction to fratricide "by strangulation with a silken bow-string . . . to the end that blood should not be let." [9] The "law" continued in force until after the death of Mehmed III (1595-1603), who had executed nineteen brothers soon after accession and two sons in later years, or about a fourth of the total number of known royal executions in the dynasty's history, nearly destroying the ruling family altogether. After a reign of more than a half-century, Shah Tahmasp I of Safavi Persia left nine living sons on his death in 1576. Within two years only one remained. The bloodletter, the dissolute Shah Isma'il II, wore the crown for only eighteen months.[10]

Following the death of Mehmed III in 1603 the Ottoman dynasty introduced a benign alternative to fratricide. All princes older than seven except the sons of the ruler were locked up in the *kafes* (cage) or special quarters of the Top Kapi palace at Istanbul. There they stayed for life, unless chosen as sultan, receiving little if any formal education as youngsters, permitted female companionship as they reached maturity, but denied the right to have children, leading a purposeless, indolent existence.[11] The institution of the kafes inhibited royal rebellion. But it also guaranteed

[6] Benerd Lewis, *The Emergence of Modern Turkey* (London, 1961), p. 23.

[7] See, for example, A. D. Alderson, *The Structure of the Ottoman Dynasty* (Oxford, 1956), chap. 2.

[8] Iftikhar Ahmad Ghauri, *War of Succession between the Sons of Shah Jahan, 1657-1658* (Lahore, 1964); and *The Cambridge History of India*; vol. 4, *The Mughul Empire*, planned by Lieutenant-Colonel Sir Wolseley Haig and edited by Sir Richard Burn (Cambridge, 1937), chaps. 7-8.

[9] Alderson, *op. cit.*, p. 27; and H. A. R. Gibb and Harold Bowen, *Islamic Society and the West: A Study of the Impact of Western Civilization on Moslem Culture in the Near East*, vol. 1, part 1 (London, 1950), p. 36.

[10] Edward G. Browne, *A Literary History of Persia*: vol. 4, *Modern Times, 1500-1924* (Cambridge, 1930), pp. 98-100.

[11] Alderson, *op. cit.*, chap. 5.

that heir pollution would place on the throne political incompetents lacking the capacity to develop executive leadership. Yet the imperial government, in theory, remained as personal as it had always been, with the sultan as the sole decision taker. The reigning sultan even lost the right to name his successor. The real sultan makers were the self-constituted "civilian-military" coalitions formed by the inmates of the harem and the palace (including at times the *'ulama* or religious elite) with the principal military officers in the capital. In Safavi Persia, meanwhile, the shah adopted the Byzantine custom of maiming the princes. Blindness was viewed in Persia "as an absolute disqualification" for inheriting the crown.[12] In fact, Shah Tahmasp's oldest son, Muhammad Khudabanda, renounced the crown in 1576 because of partial blindness. This condition later enabled him to escape death at the hand of the sanguinary Isma'il. At Isma'il's death, Muhammad Khudabanda, as the sole living brother, ascended the throne and, after a lackluster decade, abdicated under pressure in favor of his son, 'Abbas I, in whose 42-year reign the Safavi dynasty reached its full power and splendor. 'Abbas promptly rendered his two younger brothers politically harmless by blinding them, and later murdered his oldest son and blinded another.[13]

Military Politics in the Dynastic States

Violent succession was the corollary of the refusal to honor the reigning monarch's choice of political heir. Violence could be invoked only with the support of the army, which meant, in effect, the support of army commanders. The struggles for succession were mostly settled by civil war and by coup d'etat, with the outcome as closely related to the structure of the military command as to the prevailing political environment. Yet even when the royal contenders were political misfits, the dynasties were not overturned, since it was much easier to legitimate a new incumbent of an established line than to try legitimating a new dynasty.

The theory of Ottoman succession in the empire's prime, prior to the mid-sixteenth century, seemed to rest on the assumption that a prince who had undergone an apprenticeship would make a better sultan than one who had not, and that the crown would pass from father to the most meritorious son. An Ottoman sultan of that period, moreover, was not a nominal but an executive ruler and served as his own commander in chief. The sultan's way of providing governing experience and determining regal talent therefore lay in appointing his sons viceroys of the major provinces and in giving them field commands in the recurrent wars. The consistently high quality of sultanic leadership in the early centuries attested to the soundness of the selection procedure. It saved the empire at the dawn of the fifteenth century when Timur (Tamerlane) of Samarqand defeated and captured Bayezid I in the battle of Ankara in 1402. Even though it took more than a decade of bitter civil war until the four meritorious princes slugged it out, in the end the sole survivor could, as reintegrator of the Ottoman state, proclaim himself Mehmed I.

While the Ottoman procedure proved useful for locating effective rulers, it also tended to breed wars of succession, chiefly because it failed to provide dignified political employment for the unsuccessful candidates. According to custom fixed by Murad I (1359-89), the third Ottoman emperor, the acceding sultan's brothers, treated as expendable, were simply set aside to enable the new generation of princes to move up the ladder of sultanic candidacy. The alternative for the princely apprentices could hardly have been more sharply delineated: either the highest office in the realm or political oblivion. Little wonder that the selection procedure invited violence.

Those Ottoman princes who gained experience in military statecraft, which was the essence of Ottoman provincial and imperial politics, almost invariably developed ambitions, nurtured by mothers and others who stood to benefit from a prince's triumph. The rebellious spirit among the aspiring princes grew steadily more vigorous as the dynasty aged. When princes rebelled in the lifetime of their father, the sultan had no choice but to dispose the offenders for the sake of holding the state together. In the Ottoman Empire this meant, not blinding the rebels, as was the Safavi practice, but killing them. Bayezid II (1481-1512) began his reign in a civil war with his younger brother, later poisoned two rebellious sons, and finally abdicated against his will at the climax of a three-year war of succession among the three surviving sons. It was the youngest who seized Istanbul in 1512, proclaimed

[12] Browne, *op. cit.*, p. 98.

[13] See *ibid.*, chap. 3 for further details.

himself Selim I, and defeated and executed his older brothers. By the time such monarchs subdued their royal opponents, they had manifestly become seasoned warriors. Thus in 1516-17 Selim the Grim, as he became known to posterity, swallowed up the Mamluk Empire consisting of Egypt and the Arab districts north of the Arabian Peninsula.[14]

The Mughal theory of succession with princes assigned to provincial apprenticeship paralleled the Ottoman, and so too did the consequences. From the death of Jahangir in 1627 the outcome of civil wars invariably determined the inheritor of the crown. Except in tribal districts such as the Pushtu-speaking north (on both sides of the present-day Afghan-Pakistan frontier), the provincial armies were essentially mercenary, and the soldiers (among them non-Muslims) salaried. The princely rivals prepared for the contest (or rebellion, for often an ambitious prince did not bide his time) by hoarding money and jewels in the provincial treasuries to pay the armed forces and to distribute largesse to major political advisers. Those princes triumphed who commanded their own troops, mustered the largest armies with the temptation of well-paid employment and the prospects of booty, and won initial battles, for mercenary soldiers rarely sustained allegiance or devotion to their royal commanders, except in victory. Not uncommonly, the mercenary armies melted away overnight, after a defeat in battle or merely in fear of such a defeat.

Consider, for example, the abortive rebellion of Awrangzib's third son, Akbar, in 1681. For the scheme to usurp the throne, Akbar had assembled some thirty thousand troops. The night before the expected decisive battle Awrangzib ensnared the commander of Akbar's army and killed him. Learning of their commander's death early the next morning, Akbar's officers simply withdrew their contingents without informing Akbar, leaving behind for him "a faithful band of 350 horse."[15] The rebels, civil warriors and coup d'etaters, then as now, sought credentials of legitimacy. Four ʿulama on Akbar's staff issued a statement on the eve of the expected military showdown accusing Awrangzib of forfeiting the throne by violating the shariʿah. Awrangzib himself nearly a quarter of a century earlier had tried to legitimate the deposition of Shah Jahan by having him declared "infirm and intellectually unfit for governing the realm," a condition that required, in defense of the faith, "government by a pious and vigorous man" such as Awrangzib. In later correspondence with the imprisoned Shah Jahan, Awrangzib justified his actions by noting that "kingship means the protection of the realm and the guardianship of the people. . . . A king is merely God's elected custodian and the trustee of His money for the benefit of the subjects."[16]

From the Ottoman and Mughal theory of succession the Safavi and ʿAlawi practices in Persia and Morocco veered away. Nor was this astonishing, since the political systems differed. The Ottomans and the Mughals kicked over their tribal traces in the process of erecting imperial states that expanded the dar al-Islam by absorbing large infidel-populated districts. The Safavis and ʿAlawis, by contrast, preserved the classical Islamic character of their dynastic states by building political systems that made primary use of the inherent military power of martial tribes. Such tribes are prone to dissipate their power in rivalry, and in Muslim history this condition was transcended whenever rival tribes could be enlisted in a sectarian cause.

The Turkman tribes which figured prominently in the founding of the Safavi state had begun to affiliate with a Sufi order that gave rise to a Shiʿah sect at the start of the fourteenth century, under the leadership of Shaykh Safi al-Din (ca. 1250-1334). Shaykh Safi gave the dynasty its name, but the dynasty's founder was his sixth-generational descendant, Shah Ismaʿil I (1501-24).[17] Ismaʿil's sectarian Turkman warriors were collectively known, because of their scarlet headdress, as the Qizilbash (red head) tribes.[18] It was the propagation of the Jaʿfari rite of Shiʿah Islam that united the nine tribes behind Ismaʿil in the opening quarter of the sixteenth century in the conquest of what became the Safavi empire and in the establishment of their sect as the state

[14] Alderson, *op. cit.*, chaps. 2-3 and 8-10; see also Sydney Nettleton Fisher, *The Foreign Relations of Turkey, 1481-1512* (Urbana, 1948), chaps. 3, 4, and 8.

[15] *The Cambridge History of India*, *op. cit.*, vol. 4, p. 252; for disappearing princely armies in 1657-59 when Awrangzib overwhelmed his older brothers see pp. 222-28; see in general, chaps. 6-8 and 10-12.

[16] As cited *ibid.*, pp. 232-33.

[17] Cf. Browne, *op. cit.*, chaps. 1-2.

[18] The Turkman tribesmen constituted the bulk of thte Qizilbash forces, which, however, also included recruits from the towns.

religion. The Qizilbash tribes, at the start of Isma'il's reign, came mostly from Azarbayjan and adjacent eastern Anatolia, and perhaps even from as far west as Syria.[19] They spoke Turkish dialects, as opposed to the Persian and Persian-related dialects spoken by most of the indigenous population elsewhere in the empire.

These seminomadic Turkman warriors accepted Isma'il as their military, political, and religious leader, believing him endowed with divine attributes. From Azarbayjan Shah Isma'il diffused the Qizilbash tribes through the northern and central provinces, giving them large tax-free tracts of choice lands and investing their chiefs with lifetime governorships. Livestock breeders and warriors by profession, the tribesmen also became professional Shi'is spreading the faith throughout the newly fabricated realm. Thus, the Safavi dynasty and the Qizilbash tribes became mutually dependent. Dynastic influence reached into the provinces through the tribes, yet no single tribe could aspire to the crown, for such an ambition was bound to stir the jealous hostility of the remaining Qizilbash tribes. Still, so long as these tribes continued to pull in religious harness, to acknowledge Safavi leadership, and to enjoy a monopoly or near monopoly of military power, they formed a military political aristocracy. Beyond that, the Qizilbash amirs had preempted the provincial governorships from the outset, so that when the early Safavi shahs sent their sons to the provinces, the princes could become no more than nominal governors. From such offices they could hardly gain experience in military-religious rulership.

This system meant, in effect, that in the best of circumstances the Qizilbash chief became a protector and a protagonist of his princely charge, in the hope, it may be assumed, that he would continue his custodial or advisory role when the prince became shah. Thus, military-political competition sharpened, because the Qizilbash tribes were automatically drawn into the process of selecting the new shah and keeping him on the throne. In the final analysis, the Safavi princes faced the same stark alternative that the Ottoman and Mughal princes faced, either the crown or probably maiming or execution, with this major difference: the Safavi prince did not command his own troops but leaned instead on the Qizilbash forces. Yet the dynastic line was assured so long as it could provide male issue and did not have to parry a major threat from outside the Qizilbash system.

The working of the system became manifest at the death of Tahmasp I (1524-76) who was survived by nine mature sons and many grandsons. Four sons and at least one grandson at the time filled nominal but distant provincial governorships. Yet even the favored son, Haydar, kept in the Safavi palace at Kazvin in the expectation that he would inherit the mantle of political and religious leadership, apparently received little or no training for office. Consequently, after proclaiming himself shah with the support of his Qizilbash guardian, Haydar was almost immediately murdered by the partisans of his imprisoned brother Isma'il, who were led by a half-sister with rival Qizilbash (and Circassian) military backing. The irrationally suspicious Isma'il II in his brief reign, as we have seen, nearly destroyed the Safavi house altogether. Of the entire Safavi line, Shah Muhammad Khudabanda (1577-87) alone delegated political and military powers to his son and chosen heir, Hamza, who resided at the palace and who responded to the opportunity by excelling in military command, particularly in war with the Ottoman Empire. Yet it is instructive that the partly blind shah delegated such powers because of his own incompetence. The murder in 1587 of Hamza, who had gone a long way toward establishing his credentials as a meritorious regal candidate, propelled his younger brother 'Abbas to the throne with strong Qizilbash endorsement.[20]

In the dozen years of weak imperial leadership the influence of the Qizilbash tribes steadily expanded, and they were becoming inured to their praetorian role. 'Abbas I (1587-1629), however, set out to contain the tribal influence starting in the first year of his reign by suppressing a Qizilbash uprising. Despite lack of prior training,

---

[19] This is suggested by two of the tribal names, Rumlu (Anatolian) and Shamlu (Syrian).

[20] For details see *Tadhkirat al-Muluk: A Manual of Safavid Administration*, translated from the Persian by V. Minorsky (Cambridge 1943), particularly pp. 5-36 and 187-97; Browne, *op. cit.*, chaps. 2-3; Sir John Malcolm, *The History of Persia, from the most Early Period to the Present Time* (rev. edition; London, 1829), vol. 1, chaps. 12-13; Sir Percy Sykes, *A History of Persia* (3rd edition; London, 1951), vol. 2, chaps. 52-53; and Laurence Lockhart, *The Fall of the Safavi Dynasty and the Afghan Occupation of Persia* (Cambridge, 1958), chaps. 1-3.

'Abbas developed on the throne into a ruler of executive and military talent, taking into his own hands supreme authority. He reorganized the military institution, not by destroying the Qizilbash contingents, but by diluting their ranks with fresh recruits loyal to the crown, called the *shah-i sevan* (the shah's friends).[21] To supplement and counteract the Qizilbash provincial military power, 'Abbas also created new nontribal units paid by the shah and directly reliant on him: the *qullar* (slaves) of the shah, recent converts to Islam mostly of Caucasian Christian origin, trained as musketbearing cavalry, who became the shah's elite troops; Persian-speaking peasants trained as mounted infantry who were issued swords and daggers as well as muskets; and an expanded artillery corps armed with heavy guns. Moreover, as Qizilbash governors died, 'Abbas replaced them with slaves of the palace service whose devotion to the crown was unquestioned. Nevertheless, at the end of his reign, five of every six provincial amirs were still Qizilbash chiefs.[22]

Despite the military and administrative innovations, 'Abbas inhibited the normal development of the dynasty by removing his immediate heirs. For his own lifetime, he built well. He curbed the rebellious tribes; he created a detribalized imperial, as distinct from the tribal provincial, military power; and he enlarged the realm. But on his death in 1629, the tribal groups still enjoyed enough power to reassert their roles as shah sustainers, if not also shah makers. This role they continued playing throughout the life of the Safavi dynasty for nearly a century longer, forming varying coalitions, often with harem inmates, to run the empire from behind the throne. Even after the extinction of the Safavi dynasty, the Qizilbash tribes remained a primary force in the country, for from their ranks came the stillborn Afshar dynasty of Nadir Shar in the middle decades of the eighteenth century and the long-lived Qajar dynasty at its close.

The military-political system of 'Alawi Morocco, like that of Safavi Persia, was tribal. The 'Alawi dynasty was established in the 1660s on the ruins of the century-old Sa'di principalities based as Fez and Marrakesh, which in turn had come into being on a wave of religious resistance to infidel conquest, first by Portugal and later also by Spain, of the Moroccan coast starting as early as 1415. The Sa'di sharifs, or claimed descendants of the Prophet, contrived to organize and defend the Moroccan hinterland against further European encroachment, but to the end the twin states remained rivals. Isma'il (1672-1727), the second ruler of the 'Alawi line of sharifs, finally fused the territory into a single kingdom and drove the Europeans from almost all their coastal strongholds. The secret of the success of the long-lived *mawlay* (master), as the 'Alawi monarchs styled themselves, lay in his reorganization and enlargement of the *gish* (military) tribes.

Isma'il doubled the number of gish tribal federations to four. He infused loyal 'Alawi retainers into the original Sheraga (easterners) federation, taken over from the Sa'dis, and reassembled from scattered localities the Sudanese tribesmen, known as the *'abid al-Bukhari* (Bukhari's slaves) or the Bwakhir, originally brought into Morocco as slave soldiers. Of the two new federations, the Sherada and the Udaya, the second was built around the tribe of his maternal uncles, giving the federation its sobriquet, "uncles of the mawlay." The gish tribes, primarily Arabs or Arabized Berbers and negroes, were settled in the fertile plains west of Fez and Meknes in the north and of Marrakesh in the south. In return for the tax-free use, and sometimes possession, of the land, the tribes were required to provide soldiers to the state at the mawlay's pleasure.

Isma'il failed to fix the succession, and on his death the gish tribes, joined after a while by Berber mountain tribesmen, got out of hand in playing the praetorian game. No fewer than fourteen incumbents sat on the 'Alawi throne in thirty years, as varying combinations of tribal commanders in disorderly rotation selected and deposed Isma'il's sons. Fortunately, the gish tribes did not exhaust the candidates, for Isma'il's sons were said to exceed fifty in number. Stability was not restored until the death in 1757 of Mawlay 'Abdallah, who had reigned at least five times and who was followed by his son, Muhammad III (1757-90). From the death of Muhammad in 1790 through the mid-nineteenth century the gish tribes, particularly the Sherada and the Udaya, resumed their role as mawlay makers.[23]

---

[21] "Shah-Sewan," EI[1], vol. 4, pp. 267-68.

[22] Only 15 of the 89 amirs were imperial slaves in 1629; see Minorsky, *op. cit.*, pp. 16-18 and 30-36.

[23] "Morocco," EI[1], vol. 3, pp. 586-87; "Makhzen," *ibid.*, pp. 166-71; "'Alawi," EI[2], vol. 1, pp. 355-58;

Meanwhile, in the declining Ottoman Empire of the seventeenth and eighteenth centuries, praetorianism had become a favorite pastime of the once impressive Janissary (*Yeni Çeri* or new force) Corps. The Janissaries were originally a product of a carefully elaborated program of recruitment and training that had made the Ottoman Empire the most professionally administered state of the day. The recruits were enslaved Christian youngsters, either captured in the newly conquered districts (chiefly of southeastern Europe) or later periodically conscripted there. As slaves of the sultan, they were first Turkified and Islamized and, after several stages of screening, the ablest were enrolled in special palace schools where they received intensive instruction for periods of two to eight years in Islam, designated crafts, and military skills. The graduates passed immediately into the imperial service: the central administration, the sultan's workshops, or the elite units of the armed forces. Most of the last were destined to become Janissaries. The Janissaries thus constituted at the time the most literate, best trained, and carefully screened military force in the world, and they were intensely loyal to the crown and to the dynasty. Their commander sat in the imperial council as the principal military adviser to the sultan and as police chief of the imperial capital.[24]

Murad III (1574-95) debased the Janissary units by doubling their size mostly with untrained free-born Muslims. Before the mid-seventeenth century the conscription of Christian youngsters and the palace schools were gradually abandoned. From elite troops the Janissaries were swiftly reduced to a privileged force of scarcely any military value. The Janissary commander, however, was almost invariably involved in the conspiracies for the making and breaking of sultans. Under the first ten Ottoman sultans, who ruled for some 270 years, the crown passed in vertical succession from father to son. The next twenty sultans, from Selim II (1566-74) and Mahmud II (1808-39), reigned for a total of 273 years, and the crown passed in each generation horizontally from brother to brother. In this period eight sultans abdicated, almost all forcibly, and half of these were murdered. In the conspiracies that led to the coups d'état the princes who were designated sultans did not participate.[25]

The practical resolution of the succession problem in the Muslim dynastic states, it is clear, varied with the structure of the army. In the later European imperial and even postimperial periods, the differences between tribal and nontribal armies also had a bearing on military politics, particularly on the rate and direction of attempted military-political modernization. But these are matters that lie beyond the range of the present paper.

"'Abd Allah b. Isma'il," *ibid.*, p. 47; "Djaysh: III, Muslim West," *ibid.*, vol. 2, pp. 509-11; "Hasani" *ibid.*, vol. 3, pp. 256-57; and Eugene Aubin, *Morocco of Today* (New York, 1906), pp. 143-47.

[24] "Ghulam" EI^2, vol. 2, pp. 1085-91; "Devshirme," *ibid.*, pp. 210-13; "'Adjami Oghlan," *ibid.*, vol. 1, pp. 206-7; Gibb and Bowen, *op. cit.*, vol. 1, part 1, pp. 56-66; and Barnette Miller, *The Palace School of Muhammad the Conqueror* (Cambridge, 1941).

[25] See, for example, Gibb and Bowen, *op. cit.*, vol. 1, part 1, p. 38; and Roderic H. Davison, *Reform in the Ottoman Empire, 1856-1876* (Princeton, 1963), pp. 16-19.

THE BATTLE BETWEEN MARDUK AND TIAMAT

THORKILD JACOBSEN
HARVARD UNIVERSITY

THE BATTLE BETWEEN MARDUK AND TIAMAT is a crucial and decisive event in the Babylonian epic of creation, *Enuma elish*. The older powers, led by Tiamat, threaten to attack and annihilate the younger ones, the gods, and the latter, greatly frightened and disturbed, choose young Marduk as their champion. When the opposing forces meet Marduk challenges Tiamat to single combat, and the fight is on (IV.93-103):

"Tiamat and the expert of the gods, Marduk, engaged,
were tangled in single combat, joined in battle.
The lord spread his net encompassing her,
the tempest, following after, he loosed in her face,
Tiamat opened her mouth to devour—
he drove in the tempest lest she close her lips,
the fierce winds filled her belly,
her insides congested and she opened wide her mouth,
he let fly an arrow, it split her belly,
cut through her inward parts and gashed the heart,
he held her fast, extinguished her life."

Marduk's victory saves the gods and opens the way for him to fashion the cosmos, order it, and to create man to be servant and labourer of the gods.

Thus far *Enūma elish*. Asking further about the meaning of the myth, which realities may be thought to underlie it, we are led to consider more closely what the two combatants represent and stand for.

In the case of Tiamat there can hardly be any question; her ultimate identity as a personification of the sea and its powers can not be in doubt. The name Tiamat is the common word for sea in Akkadian, *ti'amtum*, later *tâmtum*, as it appears in the absolute state without case-ending and mimation, a form frequent with common nouns used as proper names. That she is, in fact, the sea can be seen from the opening lines of the epic where it is said that she and the sweet waters, Apsû, mingled their waters together, and from the fact that some copyists of *Enūma elish* write *tâmtum*, the normal form of the word for "sea," for Tiamat. This would hardly have been possible if her identity with the sea had not been clearly felt by the copyist and his readers.[1]

Less easy to establish is the identity of Marduk, whose name, unlike that of Tiamat, is not immediately transparent. The traditional writing of it, ^{d}AMAR-UD, can be traced back as far as to the Second Early Dynastic Period[2] and would seem to be ideographic in nature. The earliest syllabic renderings we have are Akkadian, they date from Oldbabylonian time and give a form *marutuk*.[3] Still later, from the Cassite Period and onwards, are Akkadian syllabic and Hebrew alphabetical writings giving the variant forms *mar(u)duk* and *m(a)rodakh*.[4]

In attempting an interpretation one will obviously be guided by the oldest evidence, ^{d}AMAR-UD and *marutuk*. Together these different kinds of writing suggest that we are dealing with a Sumerian name consisting of two components, m a r, written with the value m á r of AMAR, and u t u k, a genitive form contracted from u t u - (a)k, written with the value u t u of UD. The final k of the genitive is not expressed in the standard writing, as is normal for such a k in Sumerian orthography when it closes a syllable. As for meaning, we clearly have in the element m a r the Sumerian word m á r "son" since that is the only meaning given by the lexical texts for AMAR with reading m á r.[5] In the element u t u of u t u - (a)k we may see a longer, older, form with *t* for *d* of the Sumerian word for "sun," "day," "storm," u(d). This longer, older, form, which varies between u t u and u t a, is preserved in the divine name U t u or U t a of the sun-god,[6] and in the divine epithet U t a - u l u "south-storm" of Ninurta.[7] In its meaning "day," "storm" it also shows variants with d for t[8] such

---

[1] Note also that Berossos was fully aware of Tiamat's identity with the sea. Speaking of the primeval woman, whom he calls Omorka, he says: "This in Chaldean is *thamte*, meaning in Greek 'the sea'." See Heidel, The Babylonian Genesis, pp. 66 f.

[2] See the inscription published by Ferris Stephens in YOS IX.2, which on epigraphical grounds should date to E. D. II.

[3] See 3N-T.299.16 ⌈d⌉A s a l : *Ma-ru-tu-uk* followed by 17 ⌈d⌉A s a l - l ú - h e : *A-sa-lu-úh* and 3N-T.408.9 ^{d}AMAR-UD : *Ma-ru-tu-x* where *x* may represent an incomplete *uk*.

[4] Of Cassite date is the writing ^{d}*Mar-duk* found in Peiser, Urkunden aus der Zeit des dritten Babylonische Dynastie nos. 132.2, 11 and 140.16. For later examples and for the writings ^{d}*Ma-ru-duk* see Deimel, Pantheon no. 2078.2. For LXX *Marodakh* and the Massoretic text's *M^{e}rodakh* see the Hebrew dictionaries. The loss of the first *u* suggested by the writing *Mar-duk* does not seem to have become general as indicated by the forms ^{d}*Ma-ru-duk*, *Marodakh*, and *M^{e}rodakh* in which this *u* is either preserved or restored. It is therefore perhaps worth considering whether one should not in general Assyriological usage replace the form Marduk with Merodakh or perhaps with the Oldbabylonian Marutuk.

Besides the forms here mentioned, all of which seem to go back to a form without case-ending and mimation, there are the variant forms ^{d}*Ma-ru-tu-uk-ku*, and ^{d}*Ma-ru-du-uk-ku*, *Enuma elish* Tablet VI Kish (OECT VI) 113 and Assur (KAR 164) 13, and *Mar-du-ku* in Strassmaier A. V. 5134 which appear to go back to an original form with case-ending and mimation **Marutukkum*.

[5] See Deimel, ŠL 437.4.

[6] Compare u$_4$ - t u - e - t a u$_4$ - t u - š u - š e "from sunrise to sunset" Poebel, ZAnF III p. 162, ú - t u : UD MSL II 156a. ù - t u - d i - i q - q[u . . .] corresponding to ^{d}U[D-d] i - ⌈k⌉ u$_5$ - g a l Falkenstein ZAnF XI p. 15 l. 13, ú - t u : MIN : " " : 4(= ^{d}UD), V R 37.41 (= á : A : *nâqu* II$_4$ 168), ú - t ú : UD : ^{d}UD CT XXV.25.4 with ú - t a : UD : ^{d}UD á : A : *nâqu* III$_3$ (Reading ú - t a from photo by B. Landsberger) *ú-ta* : UD S^{a} I.131 (MSL III p. 23). The variation may indicate that the final vowel was midway between *u* and *a* as is e. g. the vowel in English not, odd, (ɔ).

[7] Deimel, ŠL 381.209, Falkenstein ZAnF XV p. 147 and XXI p. 53.

[8] u$_4$ - d u : *u$_4$-mu* SBH 9 obv. 34-35, u$_4$ - d a - n e - e : *ina u$_4$-mi an-ni-i* IV R 28 1 rev. 9-10, u$_4$ - d a : *u$_4$-um* *ibid.* rev. 20-21.

as occur in the variants *(u)duk* and *odakh* of *Mar(u)duk* and *M(a)rodakh*.

We arrive thus at a name m a r - u t u - (a)k which could denote, depending on the shade of meaning of its last component, either " Son of the sun " or " Son of the storm." To see which of these two possible meanings fits the nature of the god best we must turn to the picture of him presented to us in the epic.

Since there is abundant evidence in Oldbabylonian proper names to show that a newborn child was frequently greeted as " my sun(-god)" by delighted relatives, not too much weight can be accorded the fact that Anu in the epic dotes on his newborn grandson in just such terms: " My son, an Utu, my son, an Utu, my son, my sungod, my sungod of the gods!"[8a] especially since this statement by Anu is elucidated later on in the epic (Tablet VII.122) as looking to Marduk's figuratively brightening the life of the gods by creating man and thus relieving them of menial toil. Rather more telling are numerous passages that show Marduk to be a power creating and controlling atmospheric phenomena, lightning, storms, clouds.

Thus, when Marduk arms himself for the battle with Tiamat he makes lightning precede him and fills his own body with searing flame (IV.39-40). The words used to describe him at his birth: " fire flared when he moved his lips " (I.96) would also seem to have reference to lightning, lightning preceding the voice of thunder. Marduk owns and controls the winds, the Southwind, the Northwind, the Eastwind, the Westwind; they were given to him at birth by grandfather Anu (IV.41-44 and I.105 ff.) He himself produces further storms, he engenders the tempest, the whirlwind, the hurricane, the fourfold wind, the sevenfold wind, the duststorm, the wind not to be equaled (IV.45-46), and his great weapon is the " cyclone " or " flood-storm " *(abūbu)* (IV.49). He rides to battle in " the chariot of the storm, the unopposable, the terrible " (IV.50 cf. II.118) and the word for " storm " here used is *ûmu*, the exact rendering of the Sumerian u t u or u t a in his name. Finally, when Marduk has created the present world out of Tiamat's body it is the atmospheric phenomena he keeps for himself as his own proper domain: " to raise the storm, let coolth rain, let the rainstorm shower down,[9] spread in layers her foam (the snow?), he assigned to himself, took it in hand " (V.50-52).

The picture given is unmistakably that of a god of storm, rain, lightning, and thunder, rather than of a solar figure, and we may accordingly give preference to the translation " Son of the storm," " storm-son " as the most appropriate one for M a r - u t u (-a)k, *Marutuk, Mar(u)duk*, or *M(a)rodakh*.[10]

If we must thus conclude that the battle between Marduk and Tiamat described in *Enūma elish* is a battle of the elements, of forces in nature, a battle between the thunderstorm and the sea, it will naturally occur to one that such a battle is well known from elsewhere in the Ancient Near

[8a] For the reading of this line see Poebel AJSL 51 (1935) p. 172, note 41.

[9] We believe Jensen's old translation of *imbāru* as " Wetterwolke " to be preferable to the now generally accepted rendering " fog " proposed by Schott in ZA 44.170 ff. Our reasons are:
(1) Sargon (TCL 3.261) tells that he let the smoke from burning enemy dwellings rise (*ušatbīma*) and lay hold of (*ušaṣbit*) the face of heaven (*pan šamē*) like an *imbāru*, which suggests that *imbāru* denotes a cloud in the sky, not fog hugging the ground.
(2) The frequent use of *zanānu* " to rain " with *imbāru* and the passage 4 R 54 rev. 1.19 *na-an-hu-us di-im-ta ki-ma im-bar-ri ú-šá-az-nin* " a store of tears he let rain down like an *imbāru* " suggests " rainshower," not " fog " as the meaning of *imbāru*.
(3) The heavy impact of the tear-like drops rained down by the *imbāru*, its capacity for beating down, is indicated by its frequent use with the verb *sahāpu*, which denotes the falling down upon something and flattening it as would a net (*sapāru*) or a bird-trap (*huhāru*). Consonant with this is the meaning *assukku* " slingstone " besides *imbāru* of Sumerian IM-DUGUD, which might even suggest " hailstorm " as a possible facet of the meaning of *imbāru*. The awkwardness of the translation " fog " comes out clearly in passages such as Sennacherib, Bavian 44 (OIP 2 p. 83) *ki-ma ti-ib me-he-e a-ziq-ma ki-ma im-ba-ri as-hu-up-šu* (var. *šú*) for which CAD vol. 7 p. 107 offers the translation: " I rushed in like the onslaught of a storm, and like a fog I overwhelmed him (*sic*! Correct to " it "; the reference is to the city of Babylon)." For an Assyrian scribe to compare Sennacherib's descent upon Babylon with the gentle envelopment in a fog, rather than with the harsh beating down of a rainstorm or hailstorm would surely be anticlimactic.

[10] The argument for considering Marduk a god of thunderstorms, closely related in nature to Adad and the Westsemitic Ba'al, whose name he shares in the form Bêl, has been held to a minimum. A few further points may be mentioned. In the discussion of the name Marduk (^{d}AMAR-UD) in *Enuma elish* Tablet VI. 123 f. the god is termed *šá-kin mi-ri-ti u maš-qí-ti mu-dah-hi-du ú-ri-šun* " establisher of pasture and

East. It is described in a myth[11] from Ras-Shamra, ancient Ugarit, in which the sea, prince Yamm, sends messengers to El demanding that Ba'al, the god of thunderstorms and "rider of the clouds," be surrendered to him to be his slave. El grants the request, but Ba'al himself has no intention of surrendering peacefully. He is helped by Kothar wa Hasis, who gives him two clubs—clearly thunderbolts—to use against the sea:

> "I tell thee, O prince Ba'al
> I declare, O Rider of the Clouds
> Now thine enemy, O Ba'al
> Now thine enemy wilt thou smite
> Now wilt thou cut off thine adversary
> Thou'lt take thine eternal kingdom
> Thine everlasting dominion."

The first pair of clubs do not prove efficient enough so Kothar wa Hasis gives Ba'al a second pair, and they are up to the task:

> "The club swoops in the hand of Ba'al
> Like an eagle from between his fingers
> It strikes the pate of Prince Yamm
> Between the eyes of Judge Nahar
> Yamm collapses,
> He falls to the ground;
> His joints bend
> His frame breaks
> Ba'al would rend, would smash Yamm
> Would annihilate Judge Nahar"

but at the intercession of Ashtoreth he relents and is satisfied to take Yamm captive.

To find the same mythological motif: a battle between the god of thunderstorms and the sea from which the god of the thunderstorm emerges victorious, both in *Enuma elish*—composed in Babylonia around the middle of the Second Millennium B. C.—and in an Ugaritic poem written down on the coast of the Mediterranean at roughly the same date naturally raises the question whether we are dealing with a case of independent invention, or with a motif that has wandered from East to West or from West to East.

Assuming first—for the sake of argument—that we are dealing with separate cases of independent invention it is obviously not difficult to see why such a motif should have taken form in Ugarit on the shore of the Mediterranean. The common sight of a thunderstorm attracted to, and spending its fury as it moved out over, the sea laid to hand a mythopoeic rendering in terms of a battle between the power in the thunderstorm and the power in the sea. In Mesopotamia, in Babylon, on the other hand, all incentive for such form-giving must seem absent. The sea is far away to the South behind extensive sweetwater marshes and reed-thickets. It is no part of the basic everyday experience of the common man, plays no part in his world as he knows it of own experience. That he should independently have thought up a myth about a battle between the thunderstorm and the sea and should then have made the myth central in his cosmogony is exceedingly difficult to imagine, and common sense must exclude it as a probable possibility.

This leaves us, then, with the alternative that the motif originated on the coast of the Mediterranean, where it fits in with the environmental context, and spread from there to Babylonia. Such an assumption is far more easy to accept, for—as we have seen—the chief god of Babylon, Marduk, was from the oldest times a god of thunderstorms so that a story told about a victory of the god of thunder would naturally be met with interest and readiness of acceptance. We tend therefore to assume that the story of the battle between the god of thunderstorms and the sea originated on the coast of the Mediterranean and wandered eastward from there to Babylon.

A final question is: "when?", and here we are left essentially to conjecture. The story may have been brought in by the Akkadians from an earlier western home, or it may have entered later during the time Old Akkadian was spoken, i. e. down to the beginning of the Isin/Larsa Period. For this period the name Tiamat would cause no difficulties

---

watering places, who makes their ranges abundant," tasks which belong to a god of rain. As a god of (rain-fed) rivers and of rains he is described in the prayer to him published by W. G. Lambert AOF XIX p. 61 line 5 following. Note especially line 9: [*mu-šá-a*]*z-nin na-al-ši ina ṣer-ret ša-ma-mi* "who makes showers rain down from heaven's udders." Note also the mention of "the raging winds and lightning of Marduk" in Shurpu VIII.5, cf. *ibid.* 13. The most frequent other name of the god, ᵈA s a l - l ú - h e "Asal the drenching man" is also, quite clearly, that of a rain-god. He shares his epithet l ú - h e "the drenching man" with Iškur/Adad, god of thundershowers and rain, who is also ᵈI š k u r - l ú - h e in Bernhard and Kramer, Enki und die Weltordnung, Wissenschaftliche Zeitschrift der Friederich-Schiller-Universität Jena IX 1959/60 Heft 1/2 page 237 line 314. Significant is also that Iškur/Adad shares his name Addu with Marduk *Enuma elish* Tablet VII.119-122 as thunderer and provider of rain.

[11] Translation of Ginsberg in Pritchard, Ancient Near Eastern Texts pp. 129 ff.

whatever, it is the normal, not yet contracted, name for the Sea.

The possibility of still later arrival of the story is, however, not excluded; the uncontracted *ti'amtum* "sea" is still fully alive in Old Babylonian, and one cannot help thinking of the Western Semites that founded the First Dynasty of Babylon, the Dynasty of Amurru as the Babylonians themselves called it. Which word these invaders used for "sea" is not known, but there is nothing to exclude the possibility that they used the term *tihāmatum*—in status indeterminatus for use as proper name: *Tihāmat.* The occurrence of *tehōm* in Hebrew and *tihāmat* in Arabic shows that it is entirely possible—one can only hope that new evidence will one day allow us to see more clearly on this point. Until then our personal preference is for assuming that the motif was brought to Babylon late, with the Amorites.

THE "BABEL OF TONGUES": A SUMERIAN VERSION

SAMUEL NOAH KRAMER
UNIVERSITY OF PENNSYLVANIA

IN HIS MEMORABLE CONTRIBUTION TO BIBLICAL CUNEIFORM RESEARCH, the Anchor Bible *Genesis*, E. A. Speiser analyses with characteristic acumen, learning, and skill the Mesopotamian background of the "Tower of Babel" narrative, and comes to the conclusion that it "had a demonstrable source in cuneiform literature" (pp. 74-76). This paper will help to corroborate and confirm Speiser's conclusion by bringing to light a new parallel to one of the essential motifs in the "Tower of Babel" theme—the confusion of tongues.

Oxford's Ashmolean Museum still has in its tablet collection thirty-odd unpublished cuneiform tablets and fragments dating from the early post-Sumerian period inscribed with Sumerian literary works, some of which were no doubt composed during the Third Dynasty of Ur.[1] The majority of the pieces come from the Anglo-American excavations in Kish (1923-1932); the remainder form part of the Weld-Blundell collection purchased from antiquity dealers.[2] All are now being copied by the Oxford cuneiformist, Oliver Gurney, and will be published in due course with an introduction by the writer.

Some ten of the Ashmolean tablets and fragments are inscribed with hitherto unknown compositions.[3] The rest are of considerable importance for the restoration of broken parts of compositions long known.[4] One of these is a fragmentary tablet of 27 lines, copied by Gurney, that helps to restore a "Golden Age" passage known in part for the past quarter century, and provides us with a Sumerian version of the "Babel of tongues" motif.[5] This passage consisted of 20 lines, but

[1] For the dating of the Sumerian literary material, cf. e. g. Falkenstein, *SAHG* 11 ff.; Kramer, *The Sumerians* 168 ff., and Hallo, *JAOS* 83: 167 ff.

[2] The texts from both sources have been published primarily in the *OECT* volumes.

[3] Among the more noteworthy of these are (1) a collection of four letters: the first is from a king to one of his officials; the second is a letter to the god Utu from some important individual in Larsa, depicting the bitter suffering of the city at the hands of Elam, Subir, and the Su-people, and pleading for deliverance; the third is a letter to Rim-Sin lamenting the destruction of Larsa; the fourth is a letter probably addressed to the goddess Ninisinna, pleading for the welfare of Larsa and its king Sinidinnam; (2) a hymnal prayer to Ninisinna for Larsa and Sinidinnam; (3) a collection of prayers for Iddin-Dagan addressed to the gods Ninisinna, An, Enlil, and Ninlil (in that order; by far the longest is the prayer to Ninisinna), each ending in the obscure phrase a-mu-zu (cf. *UET* VI[1] pp. 93-94 for a collection of prayers for Šulgi that end in the same phrase).

[4] Among these are: (1) Three school-practice letters of the type described in *UET* VI[2] pp. 3-4 (comment to Nos. 173-183); (2) a tablet inscribed with lines 65-119 of the "Lamentation Over Sumer and Ur" (cf. for the present *UET* VI[2] p. 1 comment to Nos. 124-134); (3) a four-column tablet inscribed with the Nidaba hymn published in *OECT* I plates 36-39 (cf. *SAHG* No. 7 and *Bi Or* XI 172); (4) the lower half of a rather poorly preserved four column tablet inscribed with the "Instructions of Šuruppak" (cf. for the present *UET* VI[2] p. 3, comment to Nos. 169-171).

[5] This passage is part of the epic tale "Enmerkar and the Lord of Aratta" that I published in 1952 as a University Museum Monograph. The poem is concerned with a struggle for power between the Sumerian hero Enmerkar, and an unnamed ruler of the as yet unidentified city-state Aratta, situated somewhere in

only the first 14 lines were well preserved, and these read as follows: [6]

136. Once upon a time there was no snake, there was no scorpion,
There was no hyena, there was no lion,
There was no wild(?)[7] dog, no wolf,
There was no fear, no terror,
140. Man had no rival.
In those days, the lands Šubur (and) Hamazi,
Harmony-tongued(?) Sumer, the great land of the decrees of princeship,
Uri, the land having all that is appropriate(?),
The land Martu, resting in security,
145. The whole universe, the people in unison(?),
To Enlil in one tongue.. . . .
Then a-da [8] the lord, a-da the prince, a-da the king,
Enki a-da the lord, a-da the prince, a-da the king,
a-da the lord, a-da the prince,[9] a-da the king. . . . .

The meaning of the first eleven lines of this passage was quite clear; they portrayed those happy golden days of long ago when man, free from fear and want, lived in a world of peace and prosperity, and when all the peoples of the universe, as represented by Šubur-Hamazi, Sumer, Uri (the later Akkad), and Martu, worshipped the same god, the leading deity of the Sumerian pantheon, Enlil. To be sure, the verb in line 146 was missing, but it was not unreasonable to surmise that it was something like "gave promise" or "spoke." However, this line contained the phrase "in one tongue" that was tantalizingly ambiguous; it could be taken literally, in which case the meaning would be that all the peoples of the universe spoke the same language, or it could be regarded as a figurative expression for unanimity, that is, all mankind was "of one heart" in acknowledging the supremacy of Enlil. Moreover lines 147-149 that concerned Enki, the Sumerian god of wisdom, were left hanging in mid-air, altogether unintelligible in the context, since the remainder of the passage was largely destroyed.

All this is now cleared up by the Ashmolean tablet [10] that provides us with the missing verb in line 146—it turns out to be "spoke" rather than "gave praise" as I had surmised [11]—and fills in virtually all of lines 150-155, so that the second part of the "Golden Age" passage (lines 147-155) can now be meaningfully translated as follows:

147. Then a-da the lord, a-da the prince, a-da the king,

Iran. The "Golden Age" passage is part of an address to the en of Aratta designed to persuade him to let himself become a vassal of Enmerkar, and to have his subjects bring down gold, silver, and semi-precious stones in order to build for him sundry shrines and temples, and especially the Abzu-temple of Enki's city, Eridu.

[6] The line numbering is that of the "Enmerkar and the Lord of Aratta" monograph.

[7] More literally, perhaps, "the princely dog," or perhaps even "the Sumerian dog" (as contrasted with ur-nim "the Elamite dog"); for ur-SÈ=ur-gi$_4$(r) cf. now Gordon in *JCS* 12: 72 ff. and Falkenstein in *ZA* 57: 81, comment to line 23.

[8] This enigmatic word was translated (with some qualms) by "father" in the monograph, that is as if a-da stood for ad-da. But as has been pointed out to me verbally by several scholars, this rendering is quite unjustified and it is preferable to leave it untranslated for the present.

[9] The Ashmolean text has the variant -e for NE in this line, which indicates that en-NE is to be read en-ne and nun-NE is to be read nun-ne; that is, the two complexes consist of a noun followed by the subject elements -e (in a-da-lugal-la, where the final -a is presumably for -àm, there is no subject element since -àm cannot be followed by a grammatical element). Note, however, that the combination of a final n and the subject element is regularly written with the sign NI rather than NE.

[10] The indications are that this was an exercise tablet written by a student who was not yet overly proficient in the scribal art. Thus, for example, in line 4 (=line 139 of the Enmerkar monograph) he writes ŠUL for the expected SU in the complex su-zi-zi-i; in line 5 he writes ZU for SU in gaba šu-gar; in line 6 he writes ZU-bir$_4$ for su-bir$_4$. In all these cases there is a bare possibility that some dialectal phonetic or orthographic variant is involved, but certainly nothing but carelessness and incompetence is involved in the writing of NA for KI following ZU-bir$_4$ (line 6), or KI for NA in nam-nun-na(!)-ka (line 7) or U for KUR in kur(!)-me-te-gál-la (line 8), or KI for NA in gi$_6$-ù-na(!)-ka (line 26).

[11] The verb is ḫé-en-na-da-ab-dug$_4$ (the nuance intended here by the infix -da- remains uncertain for the present).

[12] The Sumerian for these lines can now be restored to read:

147. u$_4$-ba a-da-en a-da-nun a-da-lugal-la
^{d}en-ki a-da-en a-da-nun a-da-lugal-la
a-da-en-e a-da-nun-e a-da-lugal-la

Ash. 1924.475

Obv.

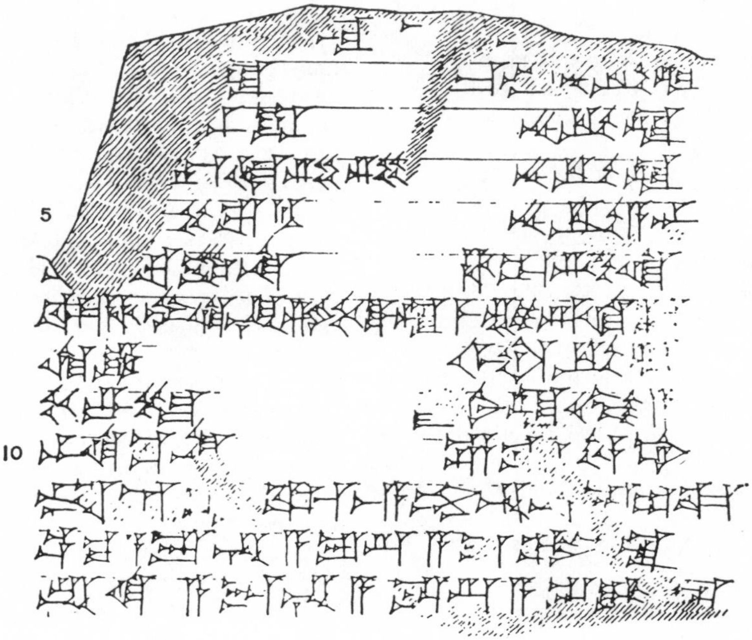

Rev.

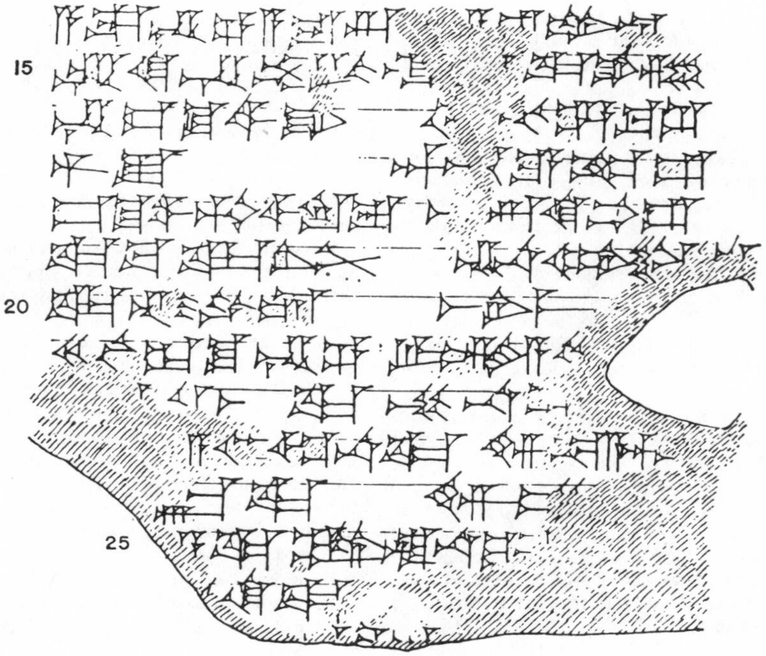

Copy by Oliver Gurney

Enki a-da the lord, a-da the prince, a-da the king,
a-da the lord, a-da the prince, a-da the king,
Enki, the lord of abundance, (whose) commands are trustworthy,
The lord of wisdom, who understands the land,
The leader of the gods,
Endowed with wisdom, the l[ord] of Eridu,
Changed the speech in their mouths, [brought(?)] contention into it,
Into the speech of man that (until then) had been one.[12]

Our new piece, therefore, puts it beyond all doubt that the Sumerians believed that there was a time when all mankind spoke one and the same language, and that it was Enki, the Sumerian god of wisdom, who confounded their speech. The reason for this fateful deed is not stated in the text; it may well have been inspired by Enki's jealousy of Enlil and the universal sway over mankind that he enjoyed.[13]

Turning now to Genesis 11:1-9, the first verse reads (in Speiser's translation): "The whole world had the same language and the same words," that is the Hebrew redactors of the Bible, like the Sumero-Akkadian mythographers, believed that there was a time when all men spoke the same tongue. Moreover, to judge from the second verse: "As men migrated from the east they came upon a valley in the land of Shinar and settled there," they were of the opinion that the inhabitants of Sumer, (or Sumer-Akkad)[14] originally spoke one and the same language, a view which no doubt goes back to cuneiform literary sources. On the other hand the Biblical explanation of the confuson of tongues that interprets the sky-reaching ziggurat as a product of man's deep-rooted hybris and as a threat to the gods, is quite different from our Sumerian version, and is undoubtedly a product of the Hebrew religious imagination and moralistic temperament.[15] Even so, the central motif was probably the same in both versions, that is, the "confounding" of tongues came about as the result of rivalry, except that in the Sumerian case this was between god and god, and in the Hebrew, between god and man.[16]

---

150. ^{d}en-ki en-ḫé-gál-la-[du]g_4-ga-zi
en-geštug-ga ig[i-g]ál-kalam-ma-ke_4
mas-su-dingir-re-e-ne-ke_4
geštug-ge-pà-da e[n]-eridu^{ki}-ga-ke_4
ka-ba eme ì-kúr en-na mi-ni-in- . . .
eme-nam-lú-lu_6 aš ì-me-[a]

To be noted is the following: For the obscure a-da (lines 147-150), cf. note 8. For the variant -e (for -ne) in line 149, cf. note 9. In line 150, text C (plate XIV of the Enmerkar monograph) has only one dug_4. In line 151, the restoration igi-gál was suggested by Hallo. In line 164, the crucial en-na has nothing to do with the en-na that is usually rendered "as long as"; it is the en-na which is found as a parallel to nu-še-(ga) in line 131 of the Enḫeduanna hymnal prayer (cf. *UET* VI[2] pp. 10-11, comment to Nos. 107-110; a definitive edition of the text prepared by Hallo and Van Dijk is soon to appear as a publication of the Yale University Press), and in line 17 of the reverse of *BE* XXIX No. 4. Finally, the new text makes it clear that there was one line too many in the restored text on p. 14 of the Enmerkar monograph, that is, there are only 5 lines between lines 150 and the line there numbered as 156, but which is actually 155.

[13] For the assumed rivalry between Enki and Enlil, cf. my comment in *Aspects du Contact Sumero-Akkadian* p. 276 and note 22. Note, too, that in the Išme-Dagan hymn *TRS* XV 9 line 7, the initial complex ^{d}en-ki-^{d}en-ki parallels the initial ^{d}a-nun-na-ke_4-ne of the preceding line; it is not unlikely, therefore, that ^{d}en-ki-^{d}en-ki stands for the *Igigû* (usually written nun-gal-e-ne). If so, we may surmise that in the time of Išme-Dagan there was current a myth revolving about a struggle between the Enki-gods (that is, the *Igigû*) and the An-gods (that is the *Anunnakû*, who are specifically stated to be the children of An) in which the *Igigû* were victorious. This might explain why in later days, the *Igigû* were at times considered as the heaven-gods while the *Anunnakû* (or at least some of them) became Nether-World gods. For different views and for the difficulties, complexities, and ambiguities involved in the *Anunnakû-Igigû* problem, cf. Von Soden, *CRRA* XI 102-111; and Falkenstein and Kienast in *Studies in Honor of Benno Landsberger*, 127-158.

[14] For the etymology of Shinar, cf. Poebel, *AJSL* XLVIII 26.

[15] The Biblical story-teller was no doubt inspired to invent his moralistic explanation by the two-fold aspect of the Babylonian ziggurat: (a) the high-rise; sky-reaching appearance of the structure in its prime, that could be interpreted as a threat to the gods and their power, and (b) its melancholy and pathetic appearance when in a state of disrepair and collapse (which was not infrequent), that could be viewed as a punishment by the angered gods (or Jahweh) for man's over-reaching ambition. The Mesopotamian, on the other hand, far from viewing the ziggurat as an outgrowth of man's rivalry with, and antagonism to, the gods, actually deemed it to be a bond between heaven and earth, man and god, and attributed its ruin and decay to the inscrutable will of the gods and their incontestable decisions.

[16] A tiny fragment in the University Museum very recently identified provides the missing last signs of line 154 as -gar-ra (presumably for -gar-ra-àm); the rendering "brought" should read "set up."

SESAM IM ALTEN MESOPOTAMIEN

F. R. Kraus

Leiden

I. Sesam im alten Mesopotamien?

Ein anspruchsloser Versuch, die bisher wenig beachteten und oft missverstandenen altmesopotamischen Nachrichten über Sesambau besonders aus altbabylonischer Zeit richtig zu deuten, war fast abgeschlossen, als Landsberger mich auf eine neue Theorie des Palaeo-Ethnobotanikers Helbaek aufmerksam machte. Sie besagt, in Helbaeks eigenen Worten, das Folgende: ". . . . . search as we will, paleoethnobotany is unable to point to one single find of a sesame seed anywhere in the Near East. Now, the nutritional equivalent to sesame, linseed, is found everywhere from the very beginnings of agriculture, also in Sumerian, Babylonian and Assyrian sites—but no name for linseed as a food element can be described as commonly occurring, if occurring at all. . . . . . Here is a discrepancy which can hardly be explained otherwise than by the assumption that the early Oriental name translated as sesame actually applied to linseed. And that the name was transferred to *Sesamum* when, about a thousand years ago, that commodity was introduced, replacing linseed as an important element in Near Eastern cooking." [1]

Die Theorie beruht auf zwei palaeo-botanischen Feststellungen,

1) Sesamkörner aus altmesopotamischer Zeit sind nicht gefunden worden,

2) dagegen ist Leinsamen in Mesopotamien seit Beginn des Ackerbaus nachweisbar,[2]

und einer ergänzenden Feststellung,

3) " Since sesame for cooking oil was introduced from India by Early Islamic trade, linseed has gone out of native production in the Near East," [3] von welcher nicht mitgeteilt wird, ob sie aus archaeologischen Funden oder literarischen Nachrichten oder etwa aus beiden resultiert. Der aus diesen Feststellungen gezogene Schluss ist philologischer Natur und zweiteilig,

4) das internationale Wort " Sesam " hat im Laufe seiner Existenz seine Bedeutung gewechselt, und zwar

5) ist es vor etwa tausend Jahren vom Leinsamen auf das Sesamkorn übertragen worden.

Dieser Vorstoss auf sein Gebiet fordert den Philologen geradezu zur Stellungsnahme heraus. Die Feststellungen 1) und 2) des Palaeo-Ethnobotanikers nehme ich dabei als gegeben an, doch steht es mir frei, 1) unverbindlich zu modifizieren: " Sesamkörner aus altmesopotamischer Zeit sind noch nicht gefunden worden." Feststellung 3) verstehe ich zunächst positiv dahin, daß Sesam seit der frühislamischen Periode im Vorderen Orient bezeugt ist. Da ich mir der Tatsache voll bewusst bin, " that the plants are never mentioned with specific descriptions and that consequently the correlation of the Sumerian or Babylonian names with the specific Latin ones may be difficult to the philologist who has mainly etymological criteria for guidance," [4] versuche ich keine botanische Deutung des bisher als " Sesam " aufgefassten sumerischen und babylonischen Wortes, schliesse aber die hier nicht untersuchte Möglichkeit einer indirekten Identifizierung der Pflanze auf Grund der unten, Abschnitt III, erörterten Nachrichten über ihren Anbau usw. nicht aus. Somit ausserhalb der assyriologischen Grenzen operierend, muss ich mich mit Erwägungen allgemeiner Art begnügen. Zu Theorie 4) vom Bedeutungswechsel des Wortes Sesam ist zuzugeben, dass er prinzipiell denkbar ist. Betrachten wir jedoch das griechische σήσαμον, " Samen oder Frucht der Sesampflanze "; (= σησάμη), " Sesampflanze," [5] so liegen über die so benannte Pflanze

[1] In: Mallowan, Nimrud and its remains 2 (1966), S. 618 3. Absatz.

[2] Eine Präzisierung dieser Angabe auf S. 616 4. Absatz, " It appears sporadically in finds of the early 8th millennium, but only after introduction of controlled irrigation, presumably about 5000 B. C., did it attain real importance."

[3] S. 616 4. Absatz.

[4] Helbaek, s. o., Anm. 1.

[5] Z. B. Liddell—Scott [9] (1966), S. 1595 links.

und ihren Samen aus dem klassischen Altertum seit Theophrast (372-287 v. Chr.) reichliche Nachrichten vor,[6] welche botanisch verwertbar zu sein und ihre Identität mit unserem Sesam (*Sesamum indicum,* aus der Gattung Pedaliazeen [7]) zu sichern scheinen. Die in 5) angenommene Namenübertragung könnte demnach nicht erst vor tausend Jahren erfolgt sein. Es scheint mir aber auch ausgeschlossen, dass das bereits bei Alkman (um 650 v. Chr.) und Solon (um 600 v. Chr.) vorkommende σήσαμον gerade in den zwei Jahrhunderten vor Theophrast auf den Sesam übertragen worden sein sollte; ich muss deshalb annehmen, dass das von Herodot (I 193) um 450 v. Chr. in Babylonien gesehene und als einzige Ölfrucht des Landes bezeichnete σήσαμον Sesam war.[8]

Ein von der Bedeutungskonstanz des Wortes σήσαμον, "Sesam," von Herodot bis heute unabhängiges zweites philologisches Argument gegen den von Helbaek angenommenen Bedeutungsübergang des "early Oriental name" des Sesams in frühislamischer Zeit liefert dieser Name selbst. Griechisch σήσαμον; aramäisch *šumšəmā*; *šūšəmā*; hebräisch *šumšum*; *šumšəmīn*; arabisch *simsim*; koptisch *semsēm*; *simsim* usw., die alle seit Jahrhunderten den Sesam bezeichnen, hängen sprachlich offenbar miteinander zusammen.[9] Da wenigstens zwei von ihnen, der griechische und der syrische Name, schon seit vorislamischer Zeit sicher bezeugt sind, hätten sie nach Helbaeks These denselben Bedeutungswandel unabhängig voneinander durchmachen müssen, was unvorstellbar ist.

Meines Erachtens gilt dieses Axiom, auch wenn der wahrscheinlich höchst komplexe Sachverhalt von Entlehnungen und vielleicht Rückentlehnungen des "early Oriental name" des Sesams sich heute noch keineswegs übersehen lässt. Eine Umschau und Umfrage bei hilfsbereiten Kollegen nach seinem Vorkommen in verschiedenen Sprachen ergab im Augenblick das Folgende. Vorislamische Stellen für arab. *simsim*, um die auch J. Brugman sich freundlichst vergebens bemüht hat, waren nicht nachzuweisen; man wird Sesam im alten Arabien ja auch wohl kaum erwarten dürfen. Stricker schreibt mir, dass ohne nähere Untersuchung auch sicher vorislamische koptische Belege nicht aufzuzeigen sind. Andererseits konnten P. A. H. de Boer und T. Jansma den vorislamischen hebräischen Vorkommen in der Mišna (s. Löw, Flora 3, S. 1 f.) und den aramäischen des babylonischen und Jerusalemer Talmuds keine Belege aus der Zeit nach 1000 n. Chr. gegenüberstellen, was zu befürchten war. Für das Syrische aber zitieren sie aus Brockelmann, Lex. syr. ² (1928), S. 767, die folgenden datierbaren schönen Belege: 1) vorislamisch: Übersetzung eines pseudogalenischen Buches von Sergios von Rēš ʿAinā (um 530 n. Chr.; zeitgenössisches MS): (*sic*!) ܣܐܣܐܡܘܢ ܕܐܝ ܬܘܗܝ ܫܘܫܡܐ, "sesamon d.h. Sesam," in einer Paragraphen-Überschrift; im Text dann korrekt ܫܘܫܡܢܐ (ZDMG 39 [1885], S. 295 Z. 10); 2) nach 1000 n. Chr.: Chronographie des Elija bar Šinaja († nach 1049), Jahr 396 (neuere Ausgabe von Brooks, Corpus Script. Christ. Orient., Scr. Syri, Series III, Tomus VII [1910], S. 224 Z. 10 mit Übersetzung S. 110 Z. 6); Bar Hebraeus († 1286) in Budge, Laughable stories (1896), S. 99 Z. 2-3 mit Übersetzung S. 123.

Eine lexikalisch—kulturgeschichtliche Untersuchung über den "early Oriental name" des Sesams im Vorderen Orient und der klassischen Antike, die ebenso mühsam wie lohnend zu werden verspricht, sei hiermit als Desideratum angemeldet.

Das gleiche Axiom gestattet uns, die soeben

---

[6] Steier in Pauly—Wissowa, 2. Reihe 2. Band (1923), Sp. 1849-1853, besonders Sp. 1850, 21 ff.

[7] Vgl. die einschlägigen Handbücher, auch über die Probleme der Systematik, die hier nicht zur Diskussion stehen.

[8] *sesamum* in Mesopotamien hat später, im 1. Jhdt. n. Chr., auch Columella gesehen nach Löw, Flora der Juden 3 (1924), S. 1.

[9] Direkte bzw. indirekte Entlehnung aus dem babylonischen *šamaššammū* vermutet Zimmern, Akkad. Fremdwörter (1915), S. 56, ergänzt von Löw, Flora 3, S. 4 5. Absatz. Dazu verweist mich T. Jansma noch freundlichst auf je einmal vorkommendes ugaritisches und phönizisches *š š m n*: C. H. Gordon, Ug. textbook (1965) 3 Nr. 2496; Donner und Röllig, Kanaan. und aram. Inschriften 3 (1964), S. 25 rechts, und auf mandäisches *šušma*: E. S. Drower and Macuch, Mandaic dictionary (1963), S. 458. Entlehnung ist wahrscheinlich trotz der gegen Gleichklangetymologie gebotenen Vorsicht, zu welcher in diesem Falle ägypt. *š m š m . t* mahnt, nach Keimer, Gartenpflanzen im alten Ägypten (1924), S. 134 f., vgl. Hild. von Deines und Grapow, Wörterbuch der äg. Drogennamen (1959), S. 493, nicht Sesam, sondern Hanf (*Cannabis sativa*); für den Hinweis auf beide Werke danke ich H. B. Stricker.—Übrigens sucht Keimer den Sesam im ägypt. *ʾ k y* >koptisch ⲟⲕⲉ (saʿīdisch); ⲁⲕⲉ (achmīmisch); vgl. ⲫⲁⲕⲓ (memphitisch).

verteidigte Bedeutungskonstanz des "early Oriental name" noch weit über die Zeit des Herodot hinaus ins zweite Jahrtausend v. Chr. auszudehnen. Auch mykenisch-griechisches *sa-sa-ma*,[10] vielleicht mit *σήσαμα* bei Hipponax (6. Jhdt. v. Chr.), übrigens einem Kleinasiaten wie Alkman, zu verbinden, dürfte mit babylonisch *šamaššammū* zusammenhängen und könnte in diesem Falle nicht nach Entlehnung aus dem Akkadischen den gleichen hypothetischen Bedeutungswandel wie *šamaššammū* durchgemacht haben. Diesen anzunehmen besteht aber kein Grund mehr, wenn Herodot in Babylonien Sesam gesehen hat, wie ich glaube; Feststellung 1) rechtfertigt dann nämlich Zweifel am Vorkommen des Sesams im alten Mesopotamien nicht.

Das positive Element in der Schlussfolgerung 5), die Ablösung des Leinsamens als Ölfrucht durch den Sesamsamen und die Übertragung seines Namens auf diesen bzw. des Namens des Flachses (*Linum usitatissimum*) auf den Sesam, ist mit der schriftlichen Überlieferung gänzlich unvereinbar. In Griechenland ist, wiederum seit Alkman und auch bereits im mykenischen Griechisch,[11] der Leinsamen, *λίνον*, bezeugt[12] und vom Sesamsamen, *σήσαμον*, verschieden, aber das Leinöl wird nie erwähnt,[13] übrigens ein indirekter Beweis dafür, dass Herodot nicht über Flachs und Leinöl in Babylonien sprechen kann. Auch Columellas *sesamum*, s. o., Anm. 8, kann kein Flachs gewesen sein. In altmesopotamischen Texten selbst besteht keine Beziehung zwischen dem vielbezeugten Flachs[14] und dem Sesam; Leinöl wird meines Wissens dort nicht genannt.

Die hier vorgebrachten Argumente konvergieren und zwingen mich, Helbaeks Theorie abzulehnen. Ich glaube also weiterhin an die bisher ohne viel Nachdenken allgemein als selbstverständlich hingenommene Annahme, *šamaššammū* und die mit ihm zusammenhängenden Wörter anderer Sprachen bezeichneten den Sesam. Das Ausbleiben von Funden an Sesamkörnern, deren lange Haltbarkeit Plinius erwähnt,[15] Frau Kraus aus praktischer Erfahrung heraus aber energisch bestreitet, bei Ausgrabungen kann ich mir nicht erklären und muss die Palaeo-Ethnobotaniker um eine neue Theorie darüber bitten.

II. Der babylonische und der sumerische Name des Sesams

Die zu erwartende Kernstelle aus ḪAR . r a = *ḫubullu* kann ich nicht beibringen. Das "praktische Vokabular" aus Assur bietet
Z. 38. ŠE.GIŠ.Ì = *šá-maš-šam-me*, "Sesam"
39. ŠE.GIŠ.Ì.BÁR.GA = " *ḫal-ṣu-ti*, "ausgepresster Sesam,"[16] eine andere Version(?), in CAD Ḫ (1956), S. 50 rechts unten, zitiert,
(Z. 38. . . . . = MIN *nuppuṣūti*), "gedroschener Sesam"
39. š e . g i š . ì . b a r a₂ . g a = *šá-maš-šam-me*[17] *ḫal-ṣu-ti*.

Das dort zu letzterer Stelle erwähnte, nicht eingeordnete Fragment aus Ḫḫ 24 lautet nach freundlicher Mitteilung Landsbergers
š e . g i š . ì = *šá-maš-šam-mu*
š e . g i š . ì. d ú b . d ú b . b u = *nu-up-pu-ṣu-tum/tú*
[š e . g i š . ì] . b á r . g a = *ḫal-ṣu-tu*.

Interessant wegen ihrer graphischen Varianten sind folgende sekundäre Stellen aus Ḫḫ,
m u . u n . d u (š e .) g i š . ì = " (= *šu-ru-ub-tum*) (1)/(2)/(3)/(4),
wobei (1) = *šá-maš-šam-me*; (2) = *šá-maš-sam-mu*; (3) = UD(= *šamaš*)-*šam-mu* (4) = *šam-šam-[me]*;[18]
u ḫ . š e . g i š . ì = " (= *kal-mat*) (1)/(4)/(5),
wobei (1) und (4) wie oben und (5) = *šam-šá-me*.[19]

Das sowohl für die Pflanze als auch für ihren Samen gebrauchte akkadische Wort, das ausserhalb der Vokabulare selten phonetisch geschrieben wird—altbabylonisch *ša-ma-ša-mi* (Akkusativ);[20] altassyrisch *ša-ma-[š]a-mì* (Genetiv);[21] ältere Vorkommen mir nicht bekannt—ist nach den Vokabularbelegen und vielen anderen Stellen

[10] Nach freundlichem Hinweise von F. B. J. Kuiper. Als Beleg zitiere ich, was ich zur Hand habe: Palmer, Mycenaean Greek texts (1963), S. 271 Nr. 166, 3.
[11] Geschrieben *ri-no*, s. Palmer (vgl. Anm. 10), S. 453 links Glossar.
[12] Olck, "Flacks," in Pauly-Wissowa 6. Band (1909), Sp. 2435-2484, s. Sp. 2449, 2 ff.
[13] Sp. 2483, 52 ff.
[14] Vgl. etwa AHw, S. 495 rechts *kitû*, für das Babylonische.
[15] Steier (s. o., Anm. 6), Sp. 1851, 4-6.
[16] Landsberger und Gurney, AfO 18 (1957-1958), S. 328 rechts.
[17] So nach freundlicher Mitteilung Landsbergers statt "-*ni*."
[18] Ḫḫ 1 Z. 162: MSL 5 (1957), S. 20 mit Anm.
[19] Ḫḫ 14 Z. 259: MSL 8/2 (1962), S. 29 mit Anm.
[20] UET 5 (1953) Nr. 73 Z. 8.
[21] BIN 6 (1944) Nr. 84 Z. 20.

eindeutig Pluraletantum, was oft übersehen worden ist. Bereits das spricht gegen die oft wiederholte Erklärung als "Ölkraut,"[22] stärker freilich noch der Umstand, dass vermeintliches **šaman šammim/šammī* doch nur mit "Kräuteröl/fett" übersetzt werden könnte, was kein Pflanzenname sein kann.

Nicht viel besser steht es mit unserem Verständnis des—soweit ich sehe, erst seit der Zeit der III. Dynastie von Ur zu belegenden—sumerischen Wortes še . giš . ì, dessen Lesung meines Wissens nicht überliefert ist und dessen grammatisches Regime ich nicht kenne. Die Bezeichnung, wiedergegeben mit "corn of the oil tree"[23] und neuestens mit "oil-wood barley,"[24] passt nicht einmal für den Samen, weil še, "Gerstenkorn," nicht als allgemeine Benennung von Samen verwendet wird, geschweige denn für die Pflanze; ein "oil tree," * giš . ì kommt nicht vor; Sesam (aber ebenso wenig auch irgendeine andere eventuell mit še . giš . ì zu identifizierende Ölpflanze) ist kein "Baum" oder "Holz," wenn er auch nach Herodot in Babylonien "baumhoch" wuchs; moderne Sorten in Indien und Indonesien variieren zwischen 25 cm und 1,5 m Höhe, werden aber allgemein als krautartig beschrieben; Sesam ist eine einjährige Pflanze.

Bereits die Schreiber der in Mari gefundenen Briefe scheinen sich Gedanken über das Ideogramm gemacht zu haben; sie schreiben es ŠE.Ì.GIŠ, aber auch ŠE.Ì.GIŠ.Ì.[25]

Die letzterhobenen beiden Einwände sind auch gegen die Auffassung von ì . giš, mir gleichfalls unbekannten Regimes, als "Baumöl" zu erheben, die aber durch

NI $^{i\text{-}mi\text{-}eš}$GIŠ [26]

und besonders durch die reguläre Entsprechung im Emesal,

u_5-mu = ì . giš = [*el-lu*],[27]

gestützt zu werden scheint.

Es ist vielleicht nicht zu gewagt, einen Anklang von * š e g̃ i š i an *šamaš(š)ammū* zu konstatieren. Er liesse sich begreifen als Folge der Entlehnung eines nicht rekonstruierbaren Wortes aus einer dritten Sprache ins Sumerische und ins Akkadische unter gleichzeitiger Eindeutung, die naturgemäss hier und dort zu verschiedenen Formen geführt haben müsste.[28] Ob auch * i g̃ i š als eingedeutetes Fremdwort mit oder ohne Beziehung zu dem hypothetischen Urtyp des Wortes für Sesam in Anspruch genommen werden dürfte, weiss ich nicht.

III. Sesambau im alten Mesopotamien

In der Erkenntnis, dass nur eine gewisse Einsicht in den modernen Sesambau dem Assyriologen einige Hoffnung auf richtiges Verständnis des über antike Sesamkultur Überlieferten geben kann, habe ich mich seinerzeit durch Vermittlung meines Wageninger Kollegen, des Agrarhistorikers B. H. Slicher van Bath, an den Lektor für tropische Ackerbaupflanzenzucht an der Landwirtschaftshochschule zu Wageningen (Niederlande), Herrn Ingenieur G. B. Bolhuis, gewandt mit der Bitte um Auskünfte über modernen Sesambau, welche die babylonischen Ausdrücke "Sesam(feld) glattstreichen," "Sesam ausreissen," "x des Sesams umpflügen," "Sesam ausklopfen" verständlich machen sowie Saat- und Erntezeit des Sesams ermitteln helfen können. Ermutigt durch die evidente Zweckdienlichkeit der Mitteilungen, für die ich Ir. Bolhuis auch hier bestens danke, habe ich die neuerworbenen Kenntnisse auch im Hinblick auf zusätzliches babylonisches Material noch etwas zu erweitern getrachtet durch Konsultieren einiger Fachliteratur, zu der mir Herr Verwer, der Leiter des Auskunftsdienstes der Leidener Universitätsbibliothek, dankenswerterweise aufs eifrigste verholfen hat.[29] Ich glaube, nunmehr die

---

[22] Z. B. Ungnad, NRVU Glossar (1937), S. 151; Ebeling, Glossar z. d. neubabyl. Briefen (1953), S. 227; vgl. Thompson, DAB (1949), S. 101 f. 7.; von Soden, AnOr 33 (1952) § 59 a. Vorsichtiger z. B. Torczyner, ATR (1913), S. 131 rechts שמשם; Mullo Weir, LAP (1934), S. 323 ("etym. uncertain"). Für sonstige etymologische Versuche s. Przyluski und Régamey, BSOS 8 (1935-1937), S. 706-708; den Hinweis auf diesen Artikel verdanke ich F. B. J. Kuiper.

[23] Thompson, *l. c.* (s. Anm. 22).

[24] Sollberger, Texts from cuneiform sources 1 (1966), S. 130 links unten.

[25] S. Bottéro und Finet, ARM 15 (1954), S. 263 und S. 85 (367) *128**.

[26] SLT (1929) Nr. 11 II' 4', nach Zitat von Goetze, LE (1956), S. 25 Anm. 2.

[27] Emesal-Vokabular 2 Z. 177: MSL 4 (1956), S. 23.

[28] Nur in dieser Hinsicht berührt meine Vermutung sich mit der These von Przyluski und Régamey, s. o., Anm. 22.

[29] Naturgemäss habe ich hauptsächlich holländische Literatur über den hinterindischen Archipel (die Sunda-Inseln) und englische über Indien eingesehen. Wer sich in anderen Ländern über den Gegenstand informieren will, wird andere Handbücher und Veröffentlichungen benutzen. Die sparsamen Literaturhinweise sollen denn auch in erster Linie als Belegstellen für das von mir Mitgeteilte dienen; sie stammen aus den Artikeln "Sesam of Widjen-cultuur" von Tromp de Haas in der

Grundzüge der babylonischen Sesamkultur im gröbsten herausstellen zu können.

A. *maḫāḫum*, "einweichen," Objekt: Sesam(körner). Beleg:[30] **1)** TLB 4 (1965) Nr. 65 (LB 1879) ^{1} ŠE.GIŠ.Ì *a-di šu-ku-dam ta-ma-ru* ^{2} *la ta-ma-ḫa-aḫ*, "Weiche den Sesam nicht ein, bevor du den Sirius gesehen hast!". Ich nehme an, dass es sich nach Analogie von Ungnad, VAB 6 (1914) Nr. 267 Z. 6-8, s. AHw (2) (1966), S. 577 rechts N, um Saatgut handelt, und kombiniere das Einweichen mit der Bemerkung des Theophrast, *h. pl.* VIII 6, 1, dass Sesam schwer keimt.[31] Mein Leidener Kollege H. Gloor bestätigte mir freundlichst, dass man schwer keimende Samen, z. B. gewisse Hülsenfrüchte, vor dem Stecken höchstens drei Tage lang in Wasser aufquellen lässt. Zu der Zeitbestimmung s. u., H.

Es handelt sich hier also um eine unmittelbar vor der Aussaat vorzunehmende Behandlung des Sesamsaatguts.

B. *sapānum*, "glattstreichen."[32] Belege,[30] teilweise nach Oppenheim, JNES 11 (1952), S. 136 rechts zu ARM 2 (1950) Nr. 87, und nach Aro, StOr 22 (1957), S. 90. Objekt: **a)** Feld für Sesam: **1)** OECT 3 (1924) Nr. 78[33] ^{12} a̤ . [š à *-lam*] *a̤-na* ŠE.GIŠ.Ì *li-is-pu-nu*, "das Feld sollen sie für den Sesam glattstreichen"; **2)** *ib.*[33] ^{14} b [ù r i k u a . š] à *-lam a-na* ŠE.GIŠ.Ì ^{15} [x x x] x *l*[*i*]-*i*[*s*]-*pu-nu*, "Ein Feld (von) 1 *bur* sollen sie für den Sesam [. . . . .] glattstreichen!"; **3)** UM 1, 2 (1919) Nr. 49 (Kassitenzeit) $^{17'}$ *ù* [*a-na*] ŠE.GIŠ.Ì *lu-da a-sa-pa-an*, "ferner werde ich das . . . . . . -Feld für den Sesam glattstreichen";[34] **4)** TCL 17 (1933) Nr. 7 ^{8} 10 b ù r i k u a . š à *-am as-sà-pa-ma-an*, "so hätte ich 10 *bur* Feld glattgestrichen," hierher nach b) 2), s. u., worauf es folgt und wozu es gehört. **b)** Sesam: **1)** TCL 17 Nr. 1 ^{27} 4 b ù r i k u ŠE.GIŠ.Ì *as-sà-pa-an*, "ich habe 4 *bur* Sesam glattgestrichen"; **2)** TCL 17 Nr. 7 ^{4} 5 b ù r i k u ŠE.GIŠ.Ì *i-na* . . . . (Ortsname) ^{5} *i-na sà-pa-ni-im ga-me-er*, "5 *bur* Sesam sind in . . . . fertig glattgestrichen"; **3)** YBT 8 (1941) Nr. 173 ^{1} 3 b ù r i k u a . š à . . . . ^{6} *a-na* ŠE.GIŠ.Ì *sà-pa-nim ù* š e *e-re-ši* . . . . . ^{8} *ú-ši-ṣi*, "Ein Feld (von) 3 *bur* hat NN gepachtet, um (darauf) Sesam glattzustreichen und Gerste zu drillen"; **4)** UM 1, 2 Nr. 49 (Kass.) $^{14'}$ *aš-šu* ŠE.GIŠ.Ì *be-lí sa-pa-na* [. . . .], "Was den Sesam betrifft, hat mein Herr Glattstreichen [*befohlen*]"; **5)** *ib.* $^{21'}$ ŠE.GIŠ.Ì *li-is-pu-nu*, "sie sollen den Sesam glattstreichen." **c)** Objekt nicht angegeben: **1)** UM 1, 2 Nr. 47 (Kassitenzeit) $^{16'}$ 9 *ma-ṣa-al-la i-na* š à a . š à *ša* ŠE.GIŠ.Ì $^{17'}$ *a-na sa-pa-ni ki-i iš-ku-nu*, "Als man neun . . . . .[35] auf dem Sesamfelde zwecks Glattstreichens anbrachte"; **2)** BE 17 (1908) Nr. 65 (Kassitenzeit) $^{7'}$ *li-is-pu-nu*, "man soll glattstreichen," ohne Kontext, aber Z. 5' ŠE.GIŠ.Ì.

Dazu Ir. Bolhuis: "Sesam wird gesät, und zwar entweder mit dem Pflanzstocke in Pflanzloch oder Furche[36] oder breitwürfig mit der Hand. Da Sesamsamen klein sind, muss die Furche rein und zerkrümelt sein. Das Glattstreichen, wahrscheinlich mit einem Brett oder Pfahl, wird wohl dazu gedient haben, die nach dem Pflügen noch vorkommenden Erdschollen so viel wie möglich zu zerkrümeln." Damit wären die Belege unter a) erklärt. Tromp de Haas, S. 392 letzter Absatz, schreibt für die Sunda-Inseln vor: "Die Saatkörner dürfen nicht tief unter den Grund gesät werden, weshalb es genügt sie nach dem Säen etwas anzudrücken"; das könnte sehr wohl an den Stellen unter b) gemeint sein. Allerdings ist mir nicht klar, ob a) und b) wirklich verschiedene Vorgänge bezeichnen.

Zeitschrift Teysmannia 14 (Batavia, 1903), S. 384-394; "Widjen" von van der Veer, 30 (1919), S. 263-272, beide hier nur mit dem Namen des Autors angedeutet, und aus "The Imperial gazetteer of India. The Indian Empire," vol. III, Economic. New edition (1907), hier in "Gazetteer" verkürzt.

[30] Altbabylonisch, falls nicht anders vermerkt; Vollständigkeit nicht angestrebt.

[31] Steier (s. o., Anm. 6), Sp. 1851, 6-8.

[32] Vgl. Landsberger und Theo Bauer, ZA 37 (1927), S. 216 Anm. 4, woher auch Zitate a) 3); b) 4) und 5) stammen.

[33] Nach eigener Kollation.

[34] Soweit sich dem lückenhaften und nicht fehlerlos kopierten Texte entnehmen lässt, scheint die Aussaat des Sesams dem "Glattstreichen" des . . . . .-Feldes (*lu-da*) zu folgen: $^{23'}$ *me-re-eš* ŠE.GIŠ.Ì A^{ki} $^{24'}$ *a-di* u$_4$ 14. k a m *il-la-ak ù me-re-eš* ŠE.GIŠ.Ì $^{25'}$ u r u B^{ki} *a-di* u$_4$ 10 . k a m *il-la-ak*, "Die Sesamaussaat von A wird bis zum 14. (des Monats) und die Sesamaussaat von Ortschaft B wird bis zum 10. (des Monats) dauern." Mit der AHw, S. 646 links 1), auch für unsere Stelle angenommenen Bedeutung "bestelltes Feld" des Wortes *mērešu* kommt man hier nicht aus. Bedeutung "dauern" von *alākum* fehlt in beiden Wörterbüchern, vgl. aber AHw, S. 34 links (Š) 4).

[35] AHw, S. 619 rechts, als *ma-ṣa-al-la⟨-ti⟩ sub maṣallu*, "Schlafstätte (für Hirten usw.)," was hier aber inhaltlich nicht überzeugt.

[36] Im alten Mesopotamien entspricht dem die *erēšum* genannte Art des Säens (Drillens), s. CAD E (1958), S. 285 rechts 1., welche in Anm. 34 auch für den Sesam nachgewiesen ist.

C.. *nasāḫum,* "ausreissen," Objekt: Sesam. Belege[30] (ausser den unter D angeführten, s. u.) teilweise nach meinem SD 5 (1958), S. 131 6.: **1)** VS 9 (1909) Nr. 22 [8] 150 e r i m [9] *na-si-iḫ* ŠE.GIŠ.Ì, "150 Mann Sesam-Ausreisser"; **2)** UM 7 (1915) Nr. 99 [12] *aš-šum* ŠE.GIŠ.Ì *na-sa-ḫi-im* . . . . . [15] PA.TE.SI. m e š *il-li-ku-nim,* "Um den Sesam auszureissen . . . . . , sind die Staatspächter hergekommen"; **3)** YBT 5 (1919) Nr. 95 [2] *aš-šum* ŠE.GIŠ.Ì *na-sà-ḫi-im*; **4)** ARM 3 (1950) Nr. 34 [13] *i-n[a]-an-na a-na* ŠE.GIŠ.Ì . . . . . [15] *na-sà-ḫi-im qa-tam aš-ku-un,* "Jetzt habe ich mich an das Ausreissen des Sesams . . . . gemacht"; **5)** Sumer 14 (1958), Pl. 9 Nr. 14 [16] ì r é . g a l - *lim* [17] *ù* d u m u . m e š u r u . k i *ša i-ba-aš-šu-ú* [18] *šu-ta-aṣ-bi-it-ma* [19] *li-is-su-ḫu-ú,* "Versammle Palastpersonal und Städter, die sich finden, und sie sollen ausreissen"; folgt Zitat F 2), s. u.

Dazu Ir. Bolhuis: "Sesam wird nicht gemäht, sondern meist geschnitten und gebündelt. Natürlich kann das Ernten auch so erfolgen, dass die ganzen Pflanzen herausgezogen und gebündelt werden." Gazetteer, S. 38: "It is best to harvest the plants by uprooting them," wozu wieder Tromp de Haas, S. 391 unten: "Der Sesam ist ein an der Oberfläche wurzelndes Gewächs."

D. *maịārī maḫāṣum,* "umpflügen,"[37] Objekt: *nisiḫ* ŠE.GIŠ.Ì. Belege[30] nach Landsberger, JCS 9 (1955), S. 130 links, wo aber mit "to hoe away the stubbles" übersetzt:[38] **1)** MAH 16180: JCS 5 (1951), S. 90 [16] *ni-si-iḫ* ŠE.GIŠ.Ì-*šu-nu* [17] *ma-ia-ri i-ma-aḫ-ḫa-ṣú-ma* [18] *a-na be-el* a . š à *i-na-ad-di-nu*; zur Übersetzung s. u.; **2)** eine mit 1) Z. 16 f. fast identische Stelle bei Landsberger, *l. c.* An allen von Landsberger, MSL 1 (1937), S. 161 1) für *maịārī maḫāṣum* zitierten Stellen ausser der letzten sowie in den neueren Belegen BIN 7 (1943) Nr. 56 Z. 7 f.; 177 Z. 15; 197 Z. 8 geschieht *m. m.* an einem Felde und an der von Landsberger, JCS 10 (1956), S. 39 rechts zu P. 130 a, herangezogenen schwierigen Stelle TCL 11 (1926) Nr. 236 Z. 4 bezieht sich *ni-sí-iḫ* ŠE.GIŠ.Ì der letzten Spalte auf ein in der ersten Spalte eingetragenes Feldareal. Deshalb muss auch *nisiḫ* ŠE.GIŠ.Ì unserer beiden Belege ein Feld sein: 1) "Ihr (Feld, auf dem der) Sesam ausgerissen (ist)/abgeerntetes Sesam(feld) werden sie umpflügen und dem Besitzer des Feldes übergeben," d. h. ihm gepflügt zurückgeben. Eine genaue Parallele hat diese Ausdrucksweise in der Bezeichnung eines Feldes als *mi-ḫi-iṣ ḫa-ar-bi-šu-nu,* "ihr umgepflügtes (Feld)," an der von Landsberger, AfO 3 (1926), S. 171 15. mit Anm. 3, erklärten, aber CAD Ḫ, S. 97 rechts (1) (b), wieder missverstandenen Stelle VS 8 (1909) Nr. 74 Z. 4.

Das Umpflügen des abgeernteten Sesamfeldes beschliesst die Anbauperiode.

E. *napāṣum,* "ausklopfen," Objekt: Sesam. Belege: **1)** OECT 3 Nr. 63 (mit eigener Kollation) [5] *aš-šum* ŠE.GIŠ.Ì . . . . . [7] ᴾNN . . . . . [8] *li-iḫ-mu-ṭa-am-ma* [9] *li-ip-pu-*ZU*-nu-ti,* "Was den Sesam betrifft, ... NN . . . . . soll ihn schnell ausklopfen!"; **2)** *ib.* [15] ᴾNN *ma-di-iš* [16] *nu-i-di-iš-šu ù i-na [na]-p[a-ṣ]i-im*[39] [17] *li-ig-mu-ur* [18] ŠE.GIŠ.Ì *ša-mu-ú* [19] *la i-ka-ša-da-am* [20] *ša na-pa-ṣi am-ri,* "Den NN instruiere genau, auch soll er fertig ausklopfen! Den Sesam soll der Regen nicht treffen! *Kontrolliere* (*das Resultat*) des Ausklopfens!"; **3)** TCL 17 Nr. 5 [4] 90 g u r ŠE.GIŠ.Ì *ib-ba-šu-ú* [5] *la-ma ša-mi-e-em* 40(?) g u r(?)-[*š*]*u*(?)-*nu*(?) *ap-pu-uṣ* [6] *ša-mu-ú-um ú-ul ik-šu-da-aš-šu-nu-ti,* "(Es) sind 90 Kor Sesam geworden. Vor (Beginn des) Regen(s) habe ich *40 Kor davon* ausgeklopft, der Regen hat ihn nicht getroffen"; **4)** ARM 2 Nr. 87 [17] *ù* ŠE.Ì.GIŠ [. . . . .] [18] *ú-ul na-ap-[ṣú]* . . . . . [20] *ù* ŠE.Ì.GIŠ *i-na-ap-pa-ṣú,* "Ferner ist der Sesam nicht ausgeklopft. . . . . . .[40] Ferner wird man den Sesam ausklopfen"; **5)** und **6)** zwei Vokabularstellen (1. Jahrtausend v. Chr.), s. o., Abschnitt II.

Dazu Ir. Bolhuis: "Sesam blüht während einer ziemlich langen Zeit von unten nach oben. Die ersten Früchte (Kapseln) sind infolgedessen schon reif, wenn die letzten noch kaum entwickelt sind. Deshalb frühe Ernte und Nachreifen in Bündeln oder Garben auf dem Felde. Nach Ernte und Nachreifen werden die Bündel über einer Plane umgedreht, wobei die reifen Samen aus den

---

[37] Vgl. Landsberger, MSL 1, S. 161 ff.

[38] Ob inhaltlich auch OECT 3 Nr. 63 Z. 12 f. (woraus Zitate E 1) und 2)), g u d . ḫ i . a . . . . . *ša ma-a-a-ra-am im-ḫa-ṣú,* "die Ochsen . . . . . , welche umgepflügt haben," hierher gehört, ist nicht auszumachen, da hier offenbar das der Sesamaussaat vorhergehende Umpflügen gemeint und nicht bekannt ist, ob auf dem betreffenden Felde auch vorher Sesam angebaut war, s. u. I 3.

[39] Nach geringen Spuren fast frei ergänzt.

[40] Das hier übergangene, mir unklare Sätzchen [19] g i š . ḫ i . a *šu-ur-pa-am i-le-qú-[ni]m* scheint nichts mit dem Ausklopfen des Sesams zu tun zu haben, sich vielmehr auf eine frühere Bemerkung im Briefe zu beziehen, die jetzt verloren ist.

von selbst aufgesprungenen Kapseln fallen. Darauf wird mit Stöcken geschlagen, um die nachgereiften Früchte zu öffnen und auch diesen Samen (meist zweiter Güte) zu sammeln." Dass Regen der Reife bzw. Nachreife unzuträglich ist (Zitat 2), versteht sich von selbst; van der Veer, S. 268 unten: "Man beschützt die Garben gegen Regen, indem man sie mit Blättern von Pisang oder Kokospalme abdeckt" (Sunda-Inseln).

F. *šumqutum/maqātum*, "herausfallen lassen"/"herausfallen," Objekt/Subjekt: Sesamkörner. Belege:[30] **1)** UET 5 Nr. 73 [7] *wa-ar-du-um* [8] *ša-ma-ša-mi ú-ša-am-qá-at*,[41] "Der Sklave wird die Sesamkörner herausfallen lassen." Hierin ist nach den Bemerkungen zu E. der allgemeinste Ausdruck für die Gewinnung der Sesamkörner zu sehen. Anders **2)** Sumer 14 Nr. 14 [19] ŠE.GIŠ.Ì *šu-nu* [20] *i-ma-qú-tu-ú-ma* é . g a l-*lum* [21] *it-ti-ka i-ta-wu-ú*, "Wenn besagter Sesam ausfällt, wird der Palast mit dir sprechen,"[42] folgt auf Zitat C 5), s. o. Dieses Ausfallen bezieht sich offenkundig auf Verlust von Körnern durch unvorsichtige Behandlung der ausgerissenen Pflanzen mit schon teilweise reifen Samenkapseln, die von selbst aufspringen, s. Bemerkungen zu E. Tromp de Haas, S. 393: "Man darf den Sesam nicht zu reif werden lassen; noch ehe die Früchte aufspringen, werden die Stengel . . . . abgeschnitten." Auch eine Mitteilung, dass in Indien die ausgerissenen Sesampflanzen mit grösster Behutsamkeit vom Felde auf die Tenne gebracht werden, wo später das Ausklopfen stattfindet, habe ich irgendwo gelesen, aber leider die Stelle zu notieren versäumt.

G. *nuššubum*, "ausblasen," Objekt: Sesam(körner). Beleg:[30] **1)** ARM 1 (1950) Nr. 21 Rs. [20′] 1 a n š e ŠE.Ì.GIŠ *uḫ-ḫu-*[. . . .] [21′] *li-na-ši-bu-ma* [22′] *ar-ḫi-iš* [23′] *a-na a-ka-li-ia* [24′] *šu-bi-lam*, "1 *homer* Sesam *ist* verspätet, man soll ihn ausblasen! Schick ihn mir dann schleunigst zum Essen!". Das "Ausblasen" des Sesams wie das der Gerste, *na-ša-bu šá* š e, CT 35 (1920), 3 Z. 34′, ist nach dem oft bildlich gebrauchten Ausdrucke "wie Spreu wegblasen"[43] eine Scheidungs- und Reinigungsprozedur bei der gedroschenen Gerste und beim ausgeklopften Sesam, das Worfeln. Es ist in Indien üblich, Gazetteer, S. 38: "The winnowing is done by wind in the ordinary way." Nach unserem Zitat beschliesst es den Produktionsprozess.

H. Vegetationsdauer des Sesams

Während heute in Indien sowohl Frühjahrs- als auch Herbstaussaat des Sesams, einer einjährigen Pflanze, vorkommt (Gazetteer, S. 37) und in manchen Gegenden zweimal im Jahre geerntet wird (Tromp de Haas, S. 392 5. Absatz), ist Sesam im modernen Iraq eine Sommerfrucht und wird es wohl auch im Altertum gewesen sein. Indirekte Angaben über Saat- und Erntezeit des Sesams enthalten die Belege A 1) und E 2) f. Nur letztere hatte ich Ir. Bolhuis unterbreitet mit der Frage, ob damit der Herbstregen gemeint sein könne, der im Iraq jetzt im September oder Oktober einsetzt. Die Antwort lautete: "Säen kann man gegen Ende der Regenzeit bei genügend hoher Temperatur—Sesam braucht als Ölpflanze viel Wärme—also wohl Ende März—Anfang April. Das Wachstum dauert vier bis sechs Monate, im September kann die Ernte also beendet sein." Dazu passt freilich Beleg A 1) nicht gut, den ich damals nicht berücksichtigt hatte. Hier wird als Termin für das Einweichen des Sesam(saatgut)s das Erscheinen des Sirius vorgeschrieben, welches in Mesopotamien auf den 12. Juli fällt, nämlich drei Wochen nach der Sommersonnenwende.[44] Wegen totaler Unkenntnis der Materie kann ich die Fragen nicht erörtern, ob Sesamaussaat um den 15. Juli überhaupt im Bereiche der Möglichkeiten liegt—erste Aussaat von Gerste im Juli ist schlecht bezeugt[45]—und ob allenfalls um den 15. Juli gesäter Sesam vor Beginn der Herbstregen schon geerntet sein könnte. Nach Angaben über Vegetationsdauer auf den Sunda-Inseln (drei bis vier Monate, Tromp de Haas, S. 390 unten) und in Indien (ungefähr hundert Tage, van der Veer, S. 268 vorletzter Absatz; aber: vier Monate bei Herbstaussaat, Gazetteer, S. 38) scheint es zur

[41] Den Brief, BM 131228 = 1953-4-11,63, hat Sollberger freundlichst für mich kollationiert; leider ist damit der auf das Zitat oben folgende Satz noch nicht ganz geklärt, [9] *ù e-la-am* GA *la*(?) *ka*|*am* [10] *i-na-di-ku-um*, "ferner wird er dir das . . . . . Öl übergeben."

[42] Schon AHw, S. 91 rechts *awûm* Gt 2) a), mit Goetze, LE, S. 124: § 50 Ende, verglichen. Der Satz enthält eine Drohung des Absenders an den Adressaten.

[43] Z. B. Dossin, Syria 33 (1956), S. 65 Z. 16; G. Meier, Maqlû (1937), S. 36 V 57; 42 VI 33.

[44] S. A. Sachs, JCS 6 (1952), S. 105 links; 113 links 28. und S. 109 Fig. 3, Spalten "Summer Solstice" und "Sirius Rising" (mit babylonischen Daten).

[45] Landsberger, JNES 8 (1949), S. 284.

Not möglich, falls sie auch für Mesopotamien gelten. Dass in E 2) wirklich der Beginn der Herbstregen gemeint ist und nicht irgendwelcher bei Abfassung des betreffenden Briefes gerade drohender Regen,[46] möchte ich aus der Mitteilung folgern "Ist die Pflanze abgeblüht und nähert sich dem Ende ihres Wachstums, so verlangt sie Trockenheit," Tromp de Haas, S. 391 2. Absatz.

I. Zusätzliche Nachrichten über Sesamkultur

1) Weisser Sesam, neubabylonische Belege bei Ebeling, Glossar zu. d. neubab. Briefen, S. 227. Nach den Handbüchern unterscheiden sich die heute angebauten Sesamsorten u. a. durch die Farbe der Sesamkörner; nach van der Veer, S. 268, kommen in Indien weisse, schwarze, rotbraune vor, noch mehr Farbnuancen nennt Tromp de Haas, S. 386, nach welchem jetzt gelblichweisser Sesam als ölreichster der meistbegehrte ist.

2) Gemischter Anbau. Gemeinsamer Anbau von Gerste, Senf und Sesam, den Ungnad, NRVU Glossar, S. 151 unten, aus dem im Jahre 486 v. Chr. abgefassten Kontrakte VS 5 (1908) Nr. 110 Z. 23, übersetzt NRVU (1935), S. 462 oben (Nr. 522), herausliest, würde heutigem Brauche in Indien (Gazetteer, S. 38) und auf den Sunda-Inseln (z. B. Tromp de Haas, S. 391 4. und vorletzter Absatz; van der Veer, S. 268 3. Absatz) entsprechen.

3) Fruchtwechsel. Die in Indien übliche Abwechslung von Sesamanbau mit dem anderer Pflanzen, z. B. Baumwolle (Gazetteer, S. 38), ist vielleicht für die altbabylonische Zeit im Briefe BIN 7 Nr. 56 bezeugt. Das dort zur Sprache kommende Feld ist zwar in Z. 4 als a . š à *ne-pé-še-et* ŠE.GIŠ.Ì bezeichnet, was "Anbauflächen von Sesam" bedeuten könnte,[47] aber gegen Landsberger, JNES 8, S. 279 rechts Anm. 104, wird Gerste von ihm geerntet, *i-na še-im* [. . . . .], Z. 12. Sinngemäss ist Z. 4 deshalb anscheinend zu verstehen als "Feld, auf dem in Parzellen Sesam angebaut war," *scil.* in der letzten Saison.

4) Ertrag. CT 43 (1963) = mein AbB 1 (1964) Nr. 33 [16] X i k u a . š à-*am* ŠE.GIŠ.Ì *i-ri-iš-ma* [17] 7 g u r ŠE.GIŠ.Ì *ú-ša-li-a-am* [18] ŠE.GIŠ.Ì *ki-ma a-da-ri-im ar-ra-ku* [19] *ù ma-di-iš dam-qú*, "Ich habe x *iku* Feld mit Sesam besät und 7 Kor Sesam eingebracht. Die Sesamkörner sind so lang wie (die Samen des) . . . .-Baum(es) und auch (von) sehr gut(er Qualität)." Die Stelle enthält eine Angabe über den Ertrag einer bestimmten Fläche, ist aber leider unbrauchbar. Denn nach eigener Kollation steht vor i k u, Z. 16, weder b ù r der Kopie ("achtzehn" in meiner Übersetzung, S. 29, ist ein Versehen, wie die korrekte Umschrift X, S. 28, zeigt) noch überhaupt ein normales Zahlzeichen, sondern ein langer kräftiger Strich, in mittlerer Höhe beginnend und in leichtem Bogen (mit dem Scheitel nach unten) bis an den oberen Zeilenrand gezogen. Z. 18 beziehe ich nach brieflichem Vorschlage Landsbergers jetzt auf die Sesamkörner; denn selbst wenn ein Vergleich der Sesampflanzen mit gewissen "Bäumen," den ich in AbB 1 unter dem Eindrucke von Herodots "baumhoch" ohne viel Überlegung hier angenommen hatte, sachlich möglich sein sollte (vgl. oben, II., S. 115), wäre eine Mitteilung über die Höhe der Pflanzen nach Abschluss der Ernte nicht mehr aktuell und deshalb kaum zu erwarten. Die indirekte Grössenangabe für die Sesamkörner, welche Z. 18 nach der neuen Auffassung enthält, sagt uns leider nichts, solange der *adārum* genannte "Baum" nicht identifiziert ist.

[46] Regen kann jetzt im Iraq vom September bis zum Juni fallen bei höchstens fünf bis sechs Regentagen im Monat.

[47] *nēpeštum* kann ich allerdings sonst nicht als *nomen loci* belegen, was es immerhin seiner Form nach ist.—Bis zum Abschluss des Manuscripts am 8.III.1967 waren von den Wörterbüchern erschienen CAD A/1; B; D; E; G; Ḫ; I/J; Ṣ; Z; AHw, S. 1-664.

THE QUEST FOR THE COUNTRY OF *UTÛM [1]

JØRGEN LAESSØE
UNIVERSITY OF COPENHAGEN

FEW ASSYRIOLOGISTS, if any, have contributed more significantly than E. A. Speiser towards exploring the ancient geography of the country east of the Tigris, in the north-eastern regions of Iraq —in what is to-day Iraqi Kurdistan. The journey which he undertook, in 1927, into an area which at the time was virtually virgin country from the archaeological point of view, produced a great deal of new evidence which was published soon afterwards in his monograph, *Southern Kurdistan in the Annals of Ashurnasirpal and Today* (*AASOR* 8 [1928], pp. 1-41). This was the country where ethnic groups like the Gutium, the Lullubum and the Turukkum were at home, and it was the country where the Hurrians, whose language Speiser did more than anyone else to recover from oblivion, gained strength before launching their combined assault into northern Mesopotamia, a concerted effort which resulted in the creation of the Kingdom of Mitanni.

The discovery of the Mari archives added innumerable toponyms to the geographical picture of northern Mesopotamia in antiquity. Many place names remain to be identified with the names of sites which, to-day, betoken ancient occupation. In some cases we may point with a reasonable degree of certainty to areas where, in general terms, ancient sites which we know only by name should be looked for; in other cases, the evidence from the ancient texts is inconclusive, and further archaeological investigation will be necessary before a clearer pattern may emerge.

One such site, the name of which occurs a number of times in the Mari archives and in the letters excavated at Tell Shemshāra, has so far defied attempts at identification: the " country of *Utûm."

The problems surrounding the town of Uta and the country of *Utûm (*māt Utêm*) have been summarised most recently by M. Birot in *ARM* 9, 357 f.[2] By reference to the Mari letter published as *ARM* 4, 20, however, Birot is inclined to think that the town of Uta was under the jurisdiction of the viceroy at Mari (" Or, la ville d'Uta était, d'après [*ARM*] *IV*, 20, sous le contrôle du viceroi de Mari " [p. 357]). The letter is unquestionably addressed to Jasmaḫ-Adad by his elder brother, Išmē-Dagan, and may be read, partly between the lines, as a treaty which the latter invites his brother to enter into. With regard to the town of Uta, Išmē-Dagan has the following to say:

(ll. 10-12)
a-lam^{KI} *Ú-ta ša i-na qa-ti-ka*
ta-ṣa-ab-ba-tu sa-li-im-šu
e-le-eq-qé

" As for the town of Uta, which you will take into your hand (*i. e.*, of which you will take charge), I will accept peaceful relations with it." As far as I can see, this passage cannot be used as evidence to show that Uta belonged to the jurisdiction of Mari; the present/future tense used in *taṣabbatu* would indicate that the author is referring to an event which is about to happen, but has not yet taken effect. The letter *ARM* 4, 20, is clearly datable to a period immediately fol-

[1] *Utûm is a reconstructed form. The geographical name is attested only in genitive connexions, *viz.*, *māt Utêm*; from these occurrences it has been assumed that the nominative form is **Utûm*.
Abbreviations used in this article are as follows:

AASOR	Annals of the American Schools of Oriental Research
ARM	Archives Royales de Mari
AS	Assyriological Studies (University of Chicago. Oriental Institute)
IM.	Iraq Museum, Museum Number.
SH.	Precedes field catalogue number of antiquities excavated by the Danish Dokān Expedition.
Sh. T.	Jørgen Laessøe, *The Shemshāra Tablets. A Preliminary Report* (Arkaeologisk-kunsthistoriske Meddelelser udgivet af Det Kongelige Danske Videnskabernes Selskab, Bd. 4, nr. 3 [Copenhagen, 1959]).

[2] *Utûm is featured with an asterisk throughout this article because the name so far has been found only in genitive constructions.

lowing the disappearance of Šamši-Adad from the Assyrian scene, Išmē-Dagan having inherited the throne; the situation at Mari must have been precarious, and Jasmaḫ-Adad was presumably about to pull out. I have previously suggested, in *Sh. T.*, p. 76, that there may have been a plan for Jasmaḫ-Adad to take over the responsibilities for Assyrian control with the eastern provinces, *i. a.*, the town of Uta; the proper interpretation of the present/future (*taṣabbatu*) would seem to corroborate this assumption, and would lend itself to doing away with the difficulty that Uta might have to be looked for in the neighbourhood, or within the immediate horizon, of Mari. Indications suggesting that Uta should in fact be looked for in the foothills of the Kurdish mountains, not too far from Tell Shemshāra, have been compiled in *Sh. T.*, p. 58.

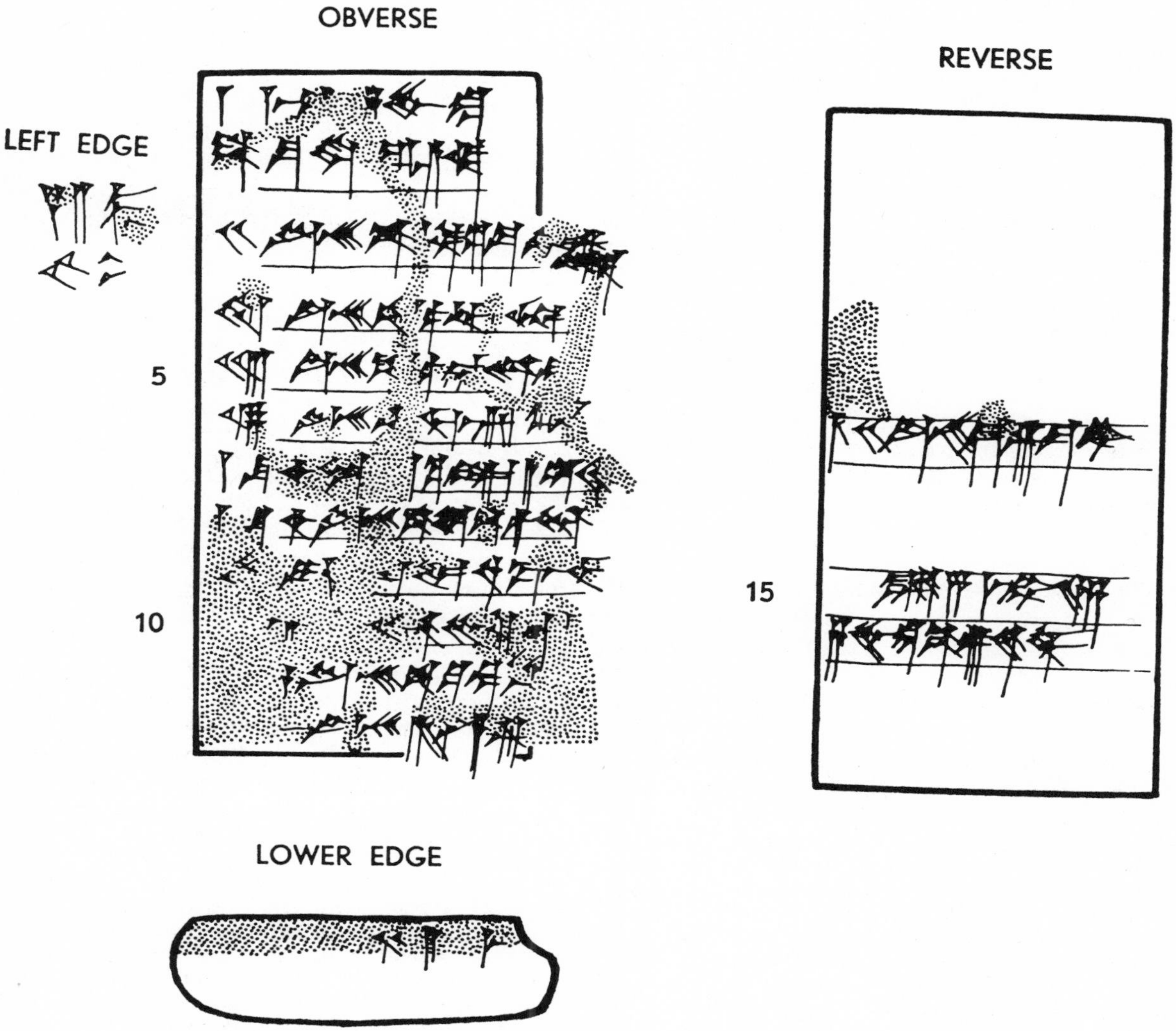

SH. 825

The "country of *Utûm" (*māt Utêm*) is mentioned in one instance in the Mari correspondence, in the letter *ARM* 1, 5 (24 ff.), where it is reported that Lidaja, a commander of an army of Turukkaeans, frightened by the din created by the Assyrian army under Išmē-Dagan, has abandoned

Burullum,[3] his city, whereupon Išmē-Dagan has conquered Burullum and the entire country of *Utûm. This would certainly suggest that Burullum was a town located in the country of *Utûm, and A. Finet suggested, reasonably, that Burullum was the capital of that country (*ARM* 15, 123).

Evidence with regard to the whereabouts of the country of *Utûm, of a somewhat clearer description, has been recovered from the Shemshāra archives. In the letter SH. 812 (= IM. 62091), published in *Sh. T.*, pp. 78 ff., when writing to Kuwari, the governor of Šušarrā, a certain Šepratu encourages him to leave his army in garrison if there is a danger that Šamši-Adad may turn against the city, "so that it may protect the country of *Utûm and the city of Šušarrā" (line 50: *ma-at Ú-te-em ù* URU.KI *Šu-šar-ra-e*^{KI} *li-ṣur*). In another letter, SH. 827 (= IM. 62100), published in *AS* 16 (1965), 191 ff., the same correspondent advises Kuwari to establish friendly relations with the kings of Lullum (Lullubum; Lullumû) so that they may be counted upon to act favourably towards the country of *Utûm and the city of Šušarrā and the *ḫarrānum* [4] (ll. 25-27: *sa-li-im-šu-nu le-qé ki-ma a-na ma-at Ú-te-em ù* URU.KI *Š[u-š]ar-ra-e*^{KI} *ù a-na* KASKAL *i-ṭà-bu*).

The passages so far quoted would seem to indicate that there is a close relationship, although no synonymity, between the terms "country of *Utûm" and "city of Šušarrā"; [5] their interests in political developments seem to be parallel, and what is useful to the country of *Utûm seems to be equally advantageous to the city of Šušarrā.

An administrative document excavated at Tell Shemshāra, now published in my article entitled *Det første assyriske imperium. Et aspekt* (*Festskrift udgivet af Københavns universitet i anledning af universitetets årsfest november 1966* [Copenhagen, 1966]), p. 104, and reproduced here on p. 121, may contain a further clue to the location of the country of *Utûm. The document in question, SH. 825, is a list of troops recruited from various places at and around Šušarrā. I shall not attempt to give a transliteration of the entire list in this context, but shall confine myself to pointing out that ll. 1-2 enumerate "100 troops from Šušarrā" (1 *me-a[t ṣ]a-bu-um ša Šu-šar-[r]a-a*^{KI}), an entry which must be regarded as having been included in the total figure given in l. 15 of the reverse of the tablet. The rev., ll. 14-16, reads as follows:

90 LÚ.MEŠ *ma-ru ma-tim*
ŠU.NIGIN 5 *me-tim* 26
ṣa-bu-um ša Ú-te-em

"Ninety men (who are) citizens.[6] Altogether five hundred and twenty-six troops from *Utûm." It would seem, therefore, that Šušarrā—the city itself, and the surrounding country (*māt Šušarrā*)—was part of the country of *Utûm, a subordinate territory in a larger state which also encompassed the city of Burullum, and most likely other towns and cities as well. The site of Burullum has not yet been identified. Šušarrā is identical with Tell Shemshāra, a mound on the right bank of the Lower Zāb in the Rānia Plain (Dasht-i-Bitwain). General inference would tend to indicate that Burullum is to be looked for in the same area, and it would seem to be a safe assumption that, in antiquity, the Rānia Plain was part of the country of *Utûm.

[3] Cf. references to Burulliwe and Šimerrini, Sumer 16 (1960), 15 f.

[4] *ḫarrānum*, in *AS* 16, 193-195, interpreted as "expeditionary force," may perhaps refer to the roads (the lines of communication), which in these parts were assuredly as uncertain then as they are to-day.

[5] The "city of *Šušarrā*" (*Šu-šar-ra-a*KI) also gave its name to the surrounding country; witness the frequently occurring term *māt Šušarrā* (*ma-a-at/ ma-at Šu-šar-ra-a*KI).

[6] *mārū mātim.* "Sons of the country," tentatively rendered as "citizens." The rendering seems to be warranted by comparison with the Code of Hammurapi, § 280, 84, where special privileges are accorded to persons who are clearly Babylonian citizens, and described as *mārū mātim.* See also G. R. Driver and J. C. Miles, *The Babylonian Laws*, 2 (1955), 281, with references to earlier literature on the matter.

LITERARY STYLE IN FIRST MILLENNIUM MESOPOTAMIA

W. G. LAMBERT
UNIVERSITY OF BIRMINGHAM

STUDENTS OF THE LATE E. A. SPEISER often speak of his feeling for literaure, which he disseminated in his teaching perhaps even more than in his publications. It is fitting, then, that this paper, composed in his memory, should be concerned with style. The term 'literary style' must be qualified for ancient Mesopotamia, since the cumbrous writing system restricted literacy to a highly trained corps of professional scribes, and any 'literary' composition would inevitably be comprehended with the ears, rather than the eyes, by most who made its acquaintance. Indeed, there is every reason to assume that 'literature' began entirely orally, and that when writing was invented and texts were written down the oral aspects of it continued exactly as before. We are in no position to be more specific, but a mention of this presumption is called for.

The first literary texts from Mesopotamia are Sumerian and date from the middle of the Third Millennium, from the sites of Fara and Tell Salabih mainly.[1] Too little of them is understood to permit any study of style, but they are the earliest witnesses to a development in Sumerian which was not finally exhausted until about 1,000 B. C. The development of Akkadian literature may well have been stimulated by the Old Akkadian dynasty (c. 2,300-2,200 B. C.), which made use of Semitic in royal inscriptions and generally seems to have provoked a cultural ferment. However, too little from this period remains in the way of Akkadian literature, and the next blossoming of culture, under the Third Dynasty of Ur, was, perhaps as a reaction, distinctly Sumerian. The break-up of this dynasty under the immigrating Amorites c. 2,000 B. C. was the time when Akkadian literature really began to develop, and three basic influences on its style can be traced. The first was the every-day language, Babylonian, known to us from many letters. The syntax of this dialect was largely Sumerian, with the verb at the end of its clause or sentence. But its Semitic connexions are unknown, since it differs widely from Old Akkadian, but shows no real Amorite influence. The second influence is the formal Sumerian style. The phraseology of royal inscriptions, to take the clearest example, was largely traditional and had been Sumerian in the first place. It remained Sumerian during the Isin-Larsa period, but starting with Hammurabi the inscriptions were generally issued in both Sumerian and Babylonian versions, which normally correspond almost word for word. In this way Akkadian absorbed Sumerian syntax, phraseology, and nuances. The same happened in other spheres. Much Sumerian religious language passed over into Akkadian in quite literal renderings. The third influence on style in the development of Akkadian literature was that of Old Akkadian. What had been ordinary language in that dialect was employed as high falutin by Old Babylonian *literati*. This applied particularly to vocabulary and to certain endings, especially the locative *-um* and the 'adverbial' *-iš*, which were no longer current in the Old Akkadian uses. Whether Old Babylonian poetic line patterns were taken over from the Old Akkadian period cannot yet be ascertained for lack of evidence. It does seem that behind the Old Babylonian poetic scene there is the influence of a Semitic poetry, like that from Ras Shamra, employing a short line. Both the Sumerian and the Old Akkadian influences helped to remove literary productions away from every-day speech, but hymns show these influences much more than epics.

As the Second Millennium passed the impact of all three sources of influence on style lessened. The development of academic learning resulted in a rejection of ordinary language forms as a suitable medium for literature. Old Akkadian had given what it could, and it could give nothing more. Sumerian was still a living tradition in the sense that texts were being composed in it, but it was increasingly under the influence of literary Akkadian. Thus the development of literary style in the second half of the Second Millen-

[1] See M. Civil and R. D. Biggs, *RA* 60 1-16.

nium could no longer depend on its old sources of inspiration and the tradition became inbred, relying on scholarship to create effect with abstruse words and archaisms (real or invented).

In the First Millennium the traditional style continued with amazing vigour. Assyrian royal inscriptions from the time of Sargon II onwards, and the royal inscriptions of Nabonidus are the best known and largest blocks of material, but no doubt there are many literary compositions belonging to this period which simply cannot be dated with certainty. At the best this style is immensely varied in expression despite the very few neologisms permitted, and the hankering for rare words and archaisms is less marked than before. At the worst it is a stock of hackneyed phrases and clichés. However, alongside the traditional style, a new kind of literary writing developed, though comparatively few texts reflect it, and they have been little studied. Three good specimens are the so-called Love Lyrics (*JSS* IV 1 ff.); *STT* 360; and Sumer XIII 119-121 (praise of Nabû and Tašmētum). In these and similar texts there is a clear break with tradition and often a certain lyricism enters them. Since the purpose of the present article is chiefly to present two First Millennium texts in the traditional style, this 'art noveau' will not be pursued further. Indeed, it made little headway, unless perhaps it was related to suspected developments in Aramaic which have not survived. The traditional style was amply maintained.[2]

The first text given here dates from the unsettled period of Babylonian history in the first half of the eighth century B. C. either from, or just after the reign of Nabû-šum-iškun. It was written at the command of Nabû-šum-imbi, commander (*šākin ṭēmi*) of Borsippa, to record his rebuilding of a storehouse in the Ezida complex. The concluding rubric informs us that this was an inscription in the wall of Ezida. The text we have is in two columns written around a solid clay barrel. It first names Nabû with abundant epithets (Col. Ia), and then moves to the appointment of the city commander and his decision to rebuild the storehouse (Ib 1-15). However, work was interrupted by an attack on the city by Arameans and the inhabitants (also Aramean?) of Dilbat, in which the city commander offered stout resistance (the rest of Ib and IIa). In the gap in column II no doubt victory over the enemy and the completion of the building were described, so that the final section of the inscription is reserved for the traditional request to the gods concerned (in this case Nabû and Tašmētum) for a blessing on their benefactor.

The importance of this text from a literary point of view lies in the evidence it offers for the continuity of literary effort during the dark ages when the Arameans were troubling the country. The city commander of Borsippa could put out a competent piece of writing loaded down with conventional phraseology. It shows no particular striving for special effect, but the use of *dušmû* "slave" in Ib 11 was surely conditioned by a desire to avoid the usual *ardu*, a word used on the streets.

Historically the inscription is of equal importance, showing a city commander close to Babylon, yet fighting his own war and writing his

[2] This persistence of tradition makes dating by style, except in a very general way, extremely hazardous. The recent attempt of I. M. Diakonoff (*AS* 16 343-349) to reassert his previous dating of a text to the lifetime of Merodach-baladan II to a large extent on the basis of phraseology must be considered unsuccessful. The argument is that a large number of technical terms in the *Advice to a Prince* either first or only occur in the royal inscriptions of Sargon and Sennacherib. However, on looking through the list of examples, it appears that quite a few of the words and phrases are poetic or literary, and not technical terms, e. g. *mūrnisqu* for "horse" and *katrû* "present." It has long been known that Assyrian royal inscriptions from the time of Sargon II and onwards suddenly introduce a large amount of poetic phraseology (von Soden, *ZA* 40 174[3]), and the lack of many of these terms in earlier Assyrian inscriptions merely illustrates this fact, but provides no criterion for dating *per se. tupšikka zabālu* is quoted as first occurring in Sennacherib, but it has just appeared in the second line of the Old Babylonian *Atra-ḫasīs* (*CT* 46 1 i 2). The risks of such arguments from silence need no underlining. Also some of the evidence is forced. As a parallel to *dekūt ummān māti* in the *Advice, dekūt māti* is quoted from one passage in Sennacherib. Apart from the problem of creating a technical term from one known example, it would be equally relevant to quote *dakūt ummānātiya* from Shalmaneser I (*KAH* I 13 i 30), more than 500 years earlier! Of the actual technical terms, that are not just timeless poetic language, on Diakonoff's own evidence the first occurrences are long before Sargon II, e. g. *šatam ēkurri* occurs in a text from the reign of Nabû-mukîn-apli c. 950 B. C. (*BBSt* p. 68 31), and again in a text from c. 750 of Nabû-šum-iškun (*VAS* I 36 iii 9, not ii 18 as given; the passage from Marduk-zākir-šumi given, *RA* XVI 125 ii 28, is irrelevant, as it has *šatammu* alone, not *šatam ēkurri*).

own quasi-royal inscription. The idea that he was a nominee of Assyria (last repeated by A. R. Millard, *Iraq* XXVI 30) is based on nothing more than a misreading of his father's name Ēda-ēṭir as Aššur! The commander is also named, with the same title and parent, in the only other major document from this generation, and also from Borsippa, *VAS* I 36 iii 6.[3] It is not certain that the cylinder edited here is a contemporary document, as assumed by J. Brinkman, *JCS* 16 100. It could perfectly well have been copied from the wall by some one with antiquarian interest under the Late Babylonian empire. Its orthography does not always agree with the certainly original text, *VAS* I 36. There the suffixed *-ma* is always so written, but in our text it is normally written *-mi*, as in other Late Babylonian documents. The barrel form does not necessarily mean that it was buried at the corner of the building, since there are one or two Late Babylonian examples of barrels of purely religious content.

The text was first made known by S. A. Strong in *JRAS* 1892 350-368, in an edition quite acceptable for the time, though far from adequate for today. Hugo Winckler also began to make a copy while in London, but was forced to leave before he had finished it. Nevertheless he published an edition of as much as he had copied, in *Altorientalische Forschungen* I 254-263, declaring (quite wrongly) that there was nothing of consequence after the point at which he broke off, and omitting a whole line (IIa 8) by *homoeoteleuton*. Accordingly a new edition is given here, based on the prism itself, collated by permission of the Trustees of the British Museum, so that in quite a number of points the text given differs from those of Strong and Winckler. Signs marked with an asterisk are no longer preserved on the original.

BM 33428 = Rm III 105

Column Ia

1 [xxxxx(x)]-*ni-šu kabtu*(idim) *šar-ḫi* ^{d}*mu-dùg-ga-*sa_4*-a šá-qí-i e-tel-*⌈*li*⌉

2 [xx] ^{d}*nin-*sig_5*-ga ka-nu-ut* ^{d}*ištarāti*(mùš)^{meš} *be-let da-ad-mi šá-ga-pu-ur-ti i-lat* [*p*]*aṭ gim-ri*

3 [^{d}*ut*]*-*u_x*-lu bēlu gaš-ri šá i-na ma-ḫar ilāni*^{meš} *kal-šú-nu il-la-ka ḫar-*⌈*ra*⌉*-ni*

4 [xx] *ilāni*^{meš} *gít-ma-li šu-pu-ú na-ram* ^{d}*nin-ši-kù*

5 [xx *n*]*é-me-qí ù ši-tul-ti muš-ta-bi-li te-re-e-ti*

6 [xx(x)]x *šarru-ú-ti mu-ma-ʾ-ir gim-ri na-din* ^{giš}*ḫaṭṭi* ^{giš}*kussî u palê*^{e} *a-ge-e šarru-ú-ti*

7 [xx(x)]x ^{d}*nu-nam-nir gít-ma-li māru kun-nu-ú i-lit-ti ru-bat ilāni*^{meš} ^{d}*e-ru-*u_8*-ú-a*

8 [xx(x)]x *é-sag-íl bēl gim-ri šit-lu-ṭu na-ram* ^{d}*marduk*

9 [xx ^{d}*as*]*ar-re aplu*(ibila) *reš-tu-ú a-šá-red a-lik maḫ-ri šá it-ti a-bi a-li-di-š*[*ú* . . .]xxxx*-ti*

10 [xxx *d*]*ayyān ilāni*^{meš} *šàr ilāni*^{meš} *rabûti*^{meš} *šá i-na ṣi-taš u šil-la-an šu-*[*pu-ú* . . .

11 [xx *ilā*]*ni*^{meš} *ma-lik rama-ni-šú le-qu-ú un-ni-ni še-mu-ú tés-li-ti rap-šú uz-*[*ni* . . .

12 [*ša a-na u*]*r-ti-šú ka-bit-ti* ^{d}*í-gì-gì ap-pi i-lab-bi-nu-šú* ^{d}*a-nun-na-ki* x[. . .

13 . . .] *melammi*(me.lám) *ellūti*^{meš} *ḫa-lip na-mur-ra-ti šá pul-ḫa-a-ti ma-lu-*[*ú* . . .

14 . . . -*š*]*u*? *i-šak-ka-nu šip-ṭu u* ^{d}*sibitti*(imin.bi) *la i-šak-*[. . .

15 . . . -*s*]*u-ú a-la-li ina qar-ba-a-ti mu-al-lid* AN x[. . .

16 . . .]x*-ti šá-ki-nu nuḫši*(ḫé.nun) *ṭuḫ-da u meš-re-e a-*[*na* . . .

17 . . .] x x [x] x x *ilāni*^{meš} *rabûti*^{meš} [. . .

18 . . .] *ú-šam-mi-ḫi ú-*[. . .

19 . . .]x *la iš-šá-an-na-n*[*i* . . .

20 . . .] ti ma x x x [. . .

[about twenty lines missing]

[3] A hitherto unnoticed fragment from the same generation and Borsippa is the part of an inscribed agate eye, L. Delaporte, *Musée du Louvre, Catalogue des Cylindres Orientaux* II, A 829. Cf. its reverse with *VAS* I 36 iii 19.

Column Ib

1 x x x [. . .
2 *šu-te-šur ni-š*[*i* . . .
3 *a-na* bàd.si.ab.b[a . . .
4 *i-šad-di-ḫi ú-ru-u*[*ḫ* . . .
5 *áš-ruk-ka-ti šu-a-ti* [. . .
6 *ú-raš ta-na-da-a-ti* si/ḫab* ma* [. . .
7 *šá áš-ruk-ka-ti šu-a-ti i*-na** x*[. . .
8 *i-qu-pu-ú-mi i-ni-šu* i[l xxxxxx] en [. . .
9 *šá ul-tu* u_4*-mi pa-ni ul-tu ul-la-nu-*⸢*ú*⸣*-a* ^{lú}*šākin ṭēmi* (gar umuš) ^{lú}*qé-pi* b[àd.si.ab.ba]
10 *la i-pu-šu šip-ri šu-a-ti ia-a-ši* ^{md}*nabû*(nà)*-šùm-im-bi mār* ^{m}*ēda-ēṭir*(aš.s[ur])
11 ^{lú}*ì-šak-ki* ^{lú}*ērib bīt* (ku_4 é) ^{d}*nabû* ^{lú}*šākin ṭēmi bár-síp*^{ki} *du-uš-mu-ú pa-liḫ ilu-ú-ti-šú*
12 *ra-bi-ti na-an-za-az maḫ-ri-šu re-du-ú mut-nin-nu-ú*
13 ⸢*šá*⸣ *a-na pa-ra-aṣ* ^{d}*nabû bēl mātāti*(kur.kur) *bēl i-lì pu-tuq-qu sa-an-tak*
14 *šip-ri šá-a-ši ú-qa-a-a-an-ni-mi ú-šad-gil pa-ni-ia*
15 *šip-ri šá-a-ši ú-šar-ri-i-mi e-pe-šú aq-bi iš-šá-ak-na-a-mi*
16 *i-na bár-síp*^{ki} *āl kit-ti ù mé-šá-ri e-šá-a-ti dal-ḫa-a-ti si-ḫi*
17 *ù saḫ-ma-šá-a-ti i-na palê*^{e} ^{d}*nabû-šùm-iš-kun šarri mār* ^{m}*da-ku-ri*
18 ^{lú}*bābilā'a*(din.tir$^{\text{ki.meš}}$) ^{lú}*barsipā'a*(bár.síp$^{\text{ki.meš}}$) ^{uru}*du-te-e-ti kišād* ^{íd}*puratti*^{ki}
19 *gab-bi* ^{uru}*kal-du* ^{lú}*a-ra-mi* ^{lú}*dilbatā'a*(dil.bat$^{\text{ki.meš}}$) *ūmī*^{meš} *ma-'-du-ú-ti*
20 *a-na lìb-bi a-ḫa-meš* ^{giš}*kakki-šú-nu i-še-el-li a-ḫa-meš ú-ra-sa-a-pu*
21 ⸢*ù*⸣ *it-ti* ^{lú}*barsipā'a*(bár.síp$^{\text{ki.meš}}$) *i-na muḫḫi eqlēti*^{meš}*-šú-nu ip-pu-šú ṣu-la-a-ti*
22 [x(x)]xxx ^{md}*nabû-šùm-iddina*(sì^{na}) *mār* ^{m}*aqar-*^{d}*nabû* ^{lú}*ērib bīt* ^{d}*nabû* ^{lú}*šà-tam é-zi-da*
23 [xxx]xxx *i-na rama-ni-šú i-na muḫḫi* ^{md}*nabû-šùm-im-bi mār* ^{m}*ēda-ēṭir* ^{lú}*šākin ṭēmi bár-síp*^{ki} *iš-kun*

Column IIa

1 *i-na šat mu-ši ki-ma šar-ra-qí-iš nak-ri a-ḫa* ^{lú}*ḫa-*[*za-an-ni* . . .
2 *za-ma-nu-ú lem-nu-ú-ti su-ku-ku-ú-ti la še-mi-ia-ma eg-*[*ru-ti* . . .
3 *a-na é-zi-da ú-tir-mi é-zi-da ù bár-síp*^{k}[^{i} . . .
4 *iṣ-ba-tu-mi muḫḫi āli ù é-kur ri-ig-mi ù ši-s*[*i-ti*]
5 *iš-kun-ú-mi ip-pu-šú ṣu-la-a-ti ù bīt* ^{md}*nabû-šùm-*[*im-bi mār* ^{m}*ēda-ēṭir*]
6 ^{lú}*šākin ṭēmi bár-síp*^{ki} *i-na mu-ši-šú-mi* ^{lú}*barsipā'a*(bár.síp$^{\text{ki.meš}}$) *ù* ^{lú}x[. . .
7 *šá a-na re-ṣu-ut a-ḫa-meš iz-zi-zu il-mu-ú-mi ina til-pa-na u* ⸢^{giš}⸣x[. . . *ul-tu li-la-a-ti*]
8 *adi na-pa-ḫi* ^{d}*šamši*^{ši} *ip-pu-šú ta-nu-qa-a-ti ul-tu li-l*[*a-a-ti*]
9 *a-di na-pa-ḫi* ^{d}*šamši*^{ši} ^{md}*nabû-šùm-im-bi mār* ^{m}*ēda-ēṭir* ^{lú}*šākin ṭēmi bár-s*[*íp*^{ki} . . .
10 . . .]x-*ti ú-ṣal-li* ^{d}*nabû* x x x-*ú-a ia-'-nu* [. . .
11 . . .] x x x ba [. . .

[about thirty lines missing]

Column IIb

1 . . .]x-*šú-nu* x[. . .
2 . . .] (vacat) [. . .
3 . . .]xxx[xx]x *iṣ-ru-pu* xx[. . .
4 . . .]x-*si nu-uḫ-ši* ⸢*ù a-na*⸣ x[. . .
5 . . .]x ú x-*ra-a-nu áš-ruk-k*[*a-ti* . . .
6 . . . ^{m}]^{d}*nabû-šùm-im-*⸢*bi*⸣ *mār* ^{m}*ēda-ēṭir* ^{lú}*šākin ṭēmi* [*bár-síp*^{ki}]

7 . . . *p*]*a-li-ḫi-šú n*[*a*]*-an-za-az ma*[*ḫ-ri-šú* . . .
8 . . . *ilu-ú*]*-ti-šú ra-bi-ti liq-bu-*[*ú* . . .
9 . . .]x *lim-gur sa-li-mi dumqi*(sig$_5$) x[. . .
10 [*a-na ši-rik-ti liš*]*-ruk-šú ù a-na qiš-ti* [*li-qis-su* . . .
11 . . .]x^{meš} ^{d}*be-let* ^{d}*ištarāti*(iš.tar)^{meš} [. . .
12 . . .] AN *il-ti reme-né-ti ba-na-*[*at* . . .
13 . . .]x *mit-gu-rat a-mat-si ṣi-i*[*t pi-i-šá*]
14 [*la ut-tak-ka-ru l*]*a in-nen-nu-ú qí-bi*[*t-si* . . .
15 ⸢*i-na ma-ḫar*⸣ [xxx]x *pa-ri-is purussî šamê*^{e} *ù* [*erṣetim*^{tim} . . .
16 *mār* ^{d}*en-lí*[*l ilāni*^{meš}] ⸢*u*$_4$⸣*-mi-šam lit-tas-qar a-bu-*[*ti* . . .
17 *lu-ú-uṣ-ṣib* [xxxx] ⸢*u*$_4$*-mi*⸣(?)^{meš} *rūqūti*(sù)^{meš} *šanāti*(mu)[^{meš} . . .
18 *ba-laṭ na-mar* [xxxxxx] *a-na ši-rik-t*[*i* . . .
19 *pir'u*(nunuz) *lu-ú-*[xxx(x) *na*]-⸢*an-na-bu*⸣ x[. . .
20 *i-na ēkal* [xxx(x)]x *lu mit-gu-rat a-mat-si* x[. . .
21 *it-ti é-z*[*i-da ù*] *bár-síp*^{ki} *li-ku-un re-*⸢*é*⸣*-*[*us-su* . . .
22 *li-ṭi-ib* [*at-m*]*u-šú eli šàr ilāni*^{meš} *bēl bēlē*(en.en) *tal-lak-t*[*i* . . . *é-zi-da*]
23 *ù bár-síp*[^{ki} *i*]*-na ma-ḫar* ^{d}*nabû u* ^{d}*na-na-a ilāni*^{meš} *šur-bu-t*[*i* . . .
24 *liš-ba-a lit-t*[*u-tu*] *i-na šá-áš-mi qab-li tāḫazi dan-nu ù a-lak* [*ṣēri* . . .
25 *ša-a-ši pir'u-*[*šú* x(x)]xx*-šú re-ṣu-us-si a-la-ki šum-qut* x [. . .
26 *nuḫšu*(ḫé.nun) ma x[x(x)] *ḫegalla*(ḫé.gál) *ma-'-da li-ma-al-la-a qātā*^{II}*-šú i-n*[*a* . . .
27 *ù i-na* [x]x ^{d}*èr-ra šal-ba-bi mār* ^{d}*en-líl ra-a-mi ga-á*[*š-ru*(?) . . .
28 *pat-ri šip-*[*ṭi*] *la iṭeḫḫi*(te)*-šú šá-lim-ti lu šá-ak-na-si a-a-bi-šú lem-nu-ú-*[*ti* . . .
29 *bul-l*[*a-šu*]*n ki-ma la-'-mi ilu-ú-ti-ku-nu ù nar-bi-*[*ku-nu lid-lul*]
30 *a-na* [*ni*]*šī*^{meš} *dar-ka-a-ti at-ta-mi bēlu lu tuk-la-šu* NAB[. . .
31 *i-bi šu-uš-šú a-na u*$_4$*-mi da-ru-ú-ti ta-nit-ti-*[*ku-nu* . . .
32 *ik-ri-bi u ṣu-le-e šá* ^{md}*nabû-šùm-im-bi* ^{lú}*šākin ṭēmi bár-síp*^{ki} ^{d}*nab*[*û* . . .

---

33 *musarû*(mu.sar) *šá áš-ruk-ka-ti šá du-ru é-zi-da*

Column Ia

1 [To . . . .]. . the venerable, the magnificent, Muduggasa'a, the lofty, the noble,
2 [spouse of] Ninsigga, the favoured one among the goddesses, mistress of human habitations, the warrior, goddess of the whole of everything,
3 Utulu, the mighty lord, who pursues his way before all the gods,
4 the supreme [. .] of the gods, resplendent, beloved of Ninšiku,
5 [endowed with] wisdom and counsel, who controls ordinances,
6 [. . .]. of kingship, who directs everything, who gives the sceptre, throne, mace, and royal tiara,
7 supreme [offspring] of Nunamnir, the favoured son, child of Eru'a, the lady of the gods,
8 [. . .] of Esagil, lord of everything, the victor, beloved of Marduk,
9 [. .] of Asare, firstborn heir, the foremost, he who goes in front, who, with the father who begat him [. . .]. . . . .
10 [. . .], judge of the gods, king of the great gods, who in East and West is resplendent [. . .
11 [. . of the] gods, his own counsellor, who accepts prayer and hearkens to petitions, of great intelligence [. . .
12 [at whose] solemn ordinance the Igigi express submission and the Anunnaki .[. . .
13 . . . clad in] a pure aura, robed in terror, filled with fearfulness [. . .
14 . . .]. establishes judgment and the Sibitti do not .[. . .

15 . . . who has] the work song sung in the fields, who begets . .[. . .
16 . . .]. . who establishes abundance, prosperity and wealth for [. . .
17 . . .]. .[.]. . the great gods [. . .
18 . . .] made prosperous .[. . .
19 . . .]. is not equalled [. . .
20 . . .]. . . . .[. . .

[about twenty lines missing]

Column Ib

1 . . .[. . .
2 to direct the people aright [. . .
3 to Borsippa [. . .
4 who goes in procession on the road [. . .
5 this storehouse [. . .
6 a praiseworthy structure . .[. . .
7 of this storehouse in .[. . .
8 which was weak and falling down .[. . . . . .].[. . .
9 which (task) no commanding supervisor of [Borsippa] from time immemorial, from before my era,
10 had done, to me Nabû-šum-imbi, son of Ēda-ēṭir,
11 city-governor, privileged to enter the temple of Nabû, commander of Borsippa, the slave who reverences his great
12 godhead, who stands at his service, the pious soldier
13 who constantly heeds the decrees of Nabû, Lord of the Lands, lord of the gods,
14 he entrusted that task and made me responsible.
15 I put that task in hand and commanded that it be done. In Borsippa,
16 the city of truth and justice, there came upon me troubles and disturbances, revolt
17 and acts of violence. In the reign of king Nabû-šum-iškun, of the Bīt Dakkuri tribe,
18 the Babylonians, the Borsippeans, (the people of) Dutēti on the bank of the Euphrates,
19 all the Chaldeans and Arameans and the people of Dilbat for many days
20 hurled their weapons against each other and slaughtered each other.
21 They also engaged in hostilities with the Borsippeans over their fields
22 [. .]. . . Nabû-šum-iddina, son of Aqar-Nabû, privileged to enter the temple of Nabû, provost of Ezida,
23 [. . .]. . . by himself he . . Nabû-šum-imbi, son of Ēda-ēṭir, commander of Borsippa.

Column IIa

1 By night the enemy, the foreigner, the mayor (?) [. . .
2 the evil, deaf foe, who did not obey me, perverse (?) [. . .
3 I turned to Ezida and Ezida and Borsippa [. . .
4 They seized and set up a hue and cry over the city and the temple
5 as they engaged in hostilities. By night the Borsippeans and the men of .[. . .]
6 who were there to help each other, surrounded the house of Nabû-šum-[imbi, son of Ēda-ēṭir],
7 and with javelins and . .[. . . from evening]
8 up to day-break they were howling. From [evening]
9 up to day-break Nabû-šum-imbi, son of Ēda-ēṭir, commander of Borsippa [. . .

10 . . .]. . prayed, "Nabû, my . . . . are no more! [. . .
11 . . .]. . . .[. . .

[about thirty lines missing]

Column IIb

1 . . .]. their .[. . .
2 . . .] [. . .
3 . . .]. . .[. .]. burnt . .[. . .
4 . . .]. . abundance and to .[. . .
5 . . .]. . . . . . the storehouse [. . .
6 . . .] Nabû-šum-imbi, son of Ēda-ēṭir, commander of [Borsippa . . .
7 . . .] who reverences him, who stands at [his] service [. . .
8 . . .] of his great [godhead], let them speak [. . .
9 . . .]. may he hear. Peace, divine favour .[. . .
10 [may he] grant him [as a gift] and [donate to him] as a donation [. . .
11 [May . . .]. . . mistress of goddesses [. . .
12 . . .]. the merciful goddess, creatress [of . . .
13 . . .]. whose word is favourable, whose utterance
14 [cannot be changed], whose command cannot be altered [. . .
15 in the presence of [. . .]., who issues decrees concerning heaven and [underworld . . .
16 son of the Enlil [of the gods], may she daily take my part [. . .
17 may I have increase of [. . . .] distant days, [far off] years [. . .
18 health of shining [. . . . . .] for a gift [. . .
19 offspring, may I [. . . .] descendants .[. . .
20 In the palace [. . . .]. may her word be favourable .[. . .
21 Together with Ezida [and] Borsippa may [his] shepherding be secure [. . .
22 may his words be acceptable to the king of the gods, the lord of lords; [may his] walk [. . . Ezida]
23 and Borsippa in the presence of Nabû and Nanai, the great gods [. . .
24 may he reach a ripe old age. In warfare, strife, mighty battle and campaigning [. . .
25 he, [his] offspring, his [. .]. . to go to his aid, to fell the .[. . .
26 may he fill his hands with abundance . .[. .] and much wealth . .[. . .
27 and at the [stroke] of Erra, the wise, beloved son of Enlil, the mighty (?) [. . .
28 his .[.]. . dagger, may peace be established for him/it. [May he succeed] in extinguishing
29 the wicked enemies like a flame, [may he praise] your godhead and greatness
30 to future generations. You, lord, be his help .[. . .
31 exalt him that [he may sing your] praises for the days of eternity [. . .
32 the prayers and petitions of Nabû-šum-imbi, commander of Borsippa, Nabû[. . .

33 Inscription relating to the storehouse, from the wall of Ezida.

Philological Notes

Ia 2 Ninsigga occurs again in *RA* 41 36 19, in the middle of a list of Gula names. For the meaning of *šagapu/iru* note *Malku* I 30: *ša-ga-pi-ru* = *qar-ra-du* (*JAOS* 83 425).

Ia 4 For the reading Ninšiku, not Ninigiku, see the forthcoming edition of *Atra-ḫasīs* by the present writer and A. R. Millard, note on I 16.

Ib 6 Of the meanings of *urāšu* (see Meissner, *AS* 4 no. 11) at least three are conceivable here: "house," "garden," and "an official." However, in the lack of more context the first of these seems preferable, cf. *Malku* I 257: *ú-ra-šú* = *bi-i-tu* (*JAOS* 83 429).

Ib 12 *rēdû* here seems strange, and elsewhere a phrase *rēšu mutninnû* occurs (*BWL* 331 note on rev. IV 21), but only substantial emendation will secure that here.

IIa 1 6 Note both *kīma* and *-iš*, and similarly both *ina* and *-šu* (for *-šum*) with *ina mūši-šumma*. This pleonastic use of "hymno-epic" endings is at least as old as the Code of Hammurabi, cf. *ina balûm*.

IIb 24 *littūtu* is explained as reaching 90 years in *STT* II 400 47: 90 = *lit-tu-tum*.

IIb 28 Cf. *Erra* V 58 (*Iraq* 24 124).

The second text given here is in many respects unique. It was found at Khorsabad by the expedition of the Oriental Institute of the University of Chicago in 1932, yet it is in Babylonian script and is a private document. On each side there is a prayer, followed by a rubric and instructions to recite it twice. The obverse has an eleven line prayer to Marduk, the reverse one of ten lines to Nabû. Both specify Nabû-ušebši, an otherwise unknown private person, as the one on whose behalf the prayer to Marduk asks for offspring, and that to Nabû for long life. It seems that the prayers represent private literary activity done on commission, or by the author for himself. They are quite different from the many short incantation prayers which served for private persons, and they have a range of vocabulary not ordinarily expended on a personal item. This extends even to the instruction to recite the prayers twice (note *miḫiltu* "inscription"). As to date, the ranking together of Marduk and Nabû strongly supports a first millennium date, and with this the stylistic sophistication agrees. This consists in substituting learned words for their ordinary equivalents. "Slave" is *dušmû*, not *ardu*; "heaven and underworld" is *ašru u kigallu*, not *šamê u erṣetim*; "life" is *šaṭāpu*, not *balāṭu*. The instruction on recitation is a learned but most clumsy circumlocution. The tablet is published here by kind permission of Professor I. J. Gelb.

Khorsabad 1932, 26

Obverse

1	*šá-áš-ši abbē*^{meš}*-šú mut-lel-lu-ú*	*e-tel-lu* ^{d}*asar-re*
2	*na-din* u_4*-mu ru-qu-ú-tu*	*et-pe-šú te-le-ʾ-e*
3	*bu-ul-lu-ṭu šu-ul-lu-mu*	*i-tuk-ka ba-a-šu*
4	*ú-šar-ba-a ba-ʾ-ú-la-a-tú*	*šùm-ka as-mu*
5	⸢*ú*⸣*-la-la u dun-na-mu-ú*	⸢*ú*⸣*-paq-qu ka-a-šá*
6	[*še-ma-t*]*a ik-ri-*⸢*bi*⸣*-šú-n*[*u*]	*ta-*[*na*]*m-din li-i-pu*
7	*u*[*š-tab*]*-ra-a nišī*^{meš} *māti*	*t*[*a-ni*]*t-ta-ka* u_4*-me-šam*
8	*ši-kin na-piš-ti ú-ša*[*r-ra-ḫa*]	*zi-kir-ka ṭa-a-bi*
9	*a-na* ^{md}*nabû*(nà)*-ú-šeb-ši re-e-*[*ši m*]*u*[*t-ni*]*n-ni-i*	*lib-ba-ši ṣu-lu-lu*
10	*ši-mat nišī*^{me} *li-ir-šá-a*	*na-an-na-bu ki-si-it-ti*
11	*pi-ir-ú-šú a-na ma-ti-ma*	*lil-bu-ru ma-ḫar-ka*
12	11 *šumāti*^{meš} *e-liš za-ra-a là šakna re-eš mi-ḫi-il-ti*	
13	*ù qí-it mi-ḫi-il-ti a-na šini-šú iš-šá-as-su-ú*	

Reverse

1	*šá-nu-du ti-iz-qa-ru*	[*b*]*u-kúr* ^{d}*asar-re*
2	*na-a-bi kal mim-ma šum-*[*šú*	*še-m*]*u-ú su-pe-e*
3	*bu-nu nam-ru-ti*	*ma-l*[*i-k*]*u abbē*^{meš}*-š*[*u*]
4	*ú-šum-gal-lum la ma-ḫar*	[*api*]*l*([ibil]a) ^{d}*nu-dím-*[*m*]*u*[*d*]
5	*ú-su-um* ^{d}*í-gì-gì be-el* [*né-me-q*]*í*	*ḫ*[*a-mi-m*]*u gi-mir uz-ni*
6	*šip-kát áš-ru u ki-gal-*[*lu*	*qa-tuk-k*]*a kun-nu*
7	⸢*ši-mat dum-qí ta-šá*⸣*-mu*	^{d}[*na-b*]*i-um e/si-nu-ú*
8	[*a-na* ^{md}*nabû*(nà)*-ú-š*]*eb-ši du-uš-m*[*i*]*-ka*	*šu-ru-uk šá-ṭa-pa*
9	[*ba-la-ṭa liš-b*]*a-a*	*lik-šu-du lit-tu-tú*
10	[x x x x *ku*]*-ul-la-tu*	*lid-lu-lu qur-di-ka*

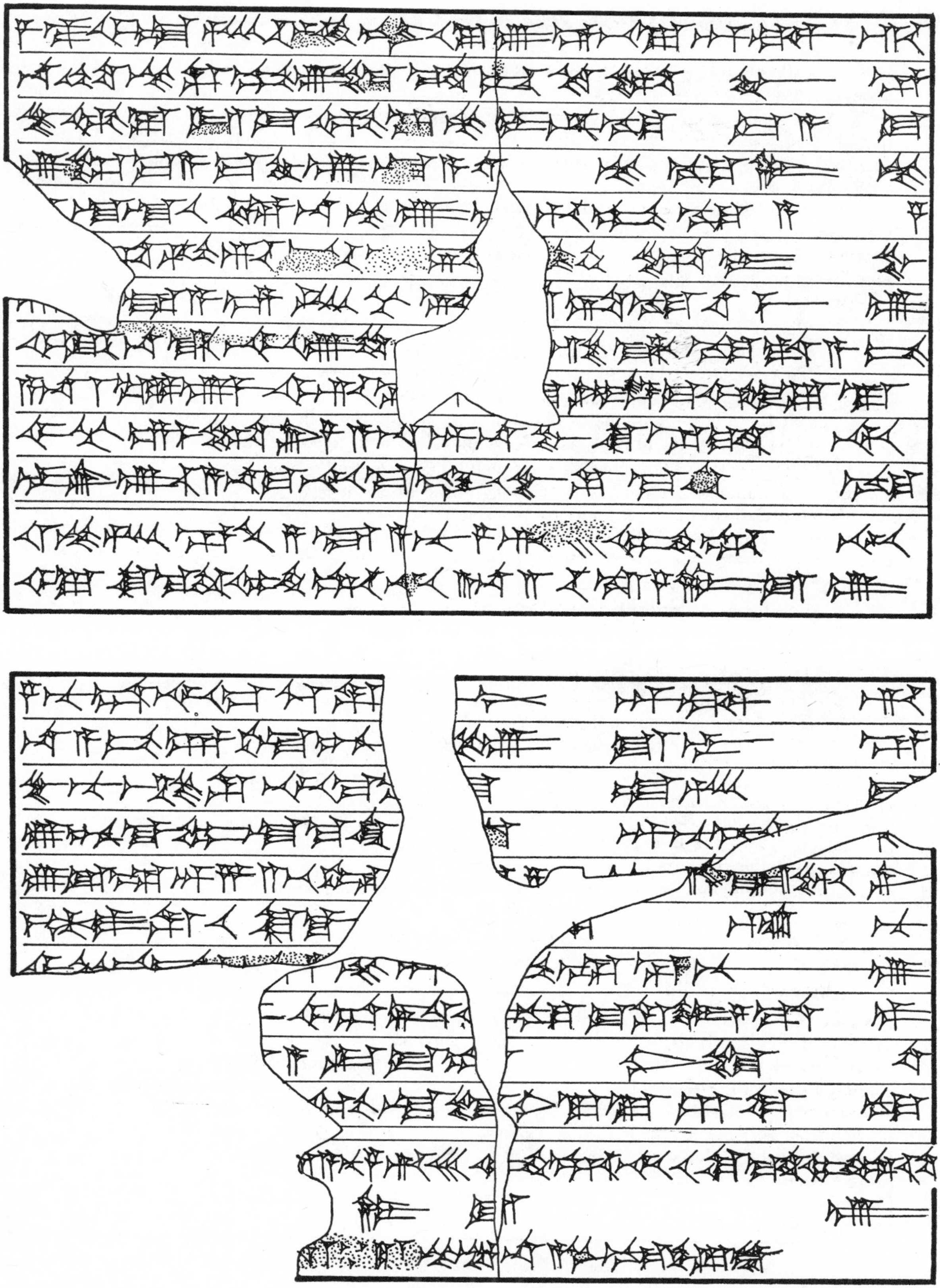

Khorsabad 1932. 26

11 [10 *šumāti*^{meš} *e-liš za-r*]*a-a là šakna re-eš mi-ḫi-il-ti u qí-it mi-ḫi-il-tú*
12 [*a-na šini-šú iš-šá*]*-as-su-ú*

Colophon

13 . . .] x x ⌜^{d}*nabû*⌝ (nà) ?-*šùm-iddina*(sì-*na*) *mār*(a) ^{lú}*ka-nik bābi*

Obverse

1 Sun of his fathers, exalted, the noble Asare,
2 The giver of length of days, skilled, learned,
3 It is in your sphere to keep alive and to preserve,
4 Mankind extols your fitting name.
5 The afflicted and the oppressed heed you,
6 You [heed] their prayer, you grant offspring,
7 The peoples of the land persist every day in praising you,
8 All living creatures magnify your sweet name.
9 Let there be protection for Nabû-ušebši, the reverent supplicant,
10 That he may get progeny and descendants, as is decreed for the peoples,
11 That his seed may be established before you for ever.

---

12 Eleven lines lacking . . . . . The beginning of the inscription
13 and the end of the inscription shall be recited twice.

Reverse

1 Hero, lofty, son of Asare,
2 Creator of everything that exists, hearer of prayer,
3 Of shining countenance, counsellor of his fathers,
4 Irresistible autocrat, heir of Nudimmud,
5 Most fitting of the Igigi, lord of [wisdom], who [comprehends] all learning,
6 The fashioning of heaven and underworld is established in your [hand],
7 You decree a favoured destiny, O . . . Nabû,
8 Give long life [to Nabû]-ušebši, your slave,
9 That he may enjoy [good health] and reach a ripe old age,
10 That all [. . . . .] may praise your prowess in war.

---

11 [Ten lines] lacking [. . .]. . The beginning of the inscription and the end of the inscription
12 [Shall be] recited [twice].

Colophon: . . .] Nabû (?)-šum-iddina, son of the Doorman.

Philological Notes

Obv. 1 *šašši abbēšu* as a title of Marduk results from exegesis of his name ^{d}amar.utu "bull-calf of Utu." The tortuous process is explained in the author's forthcoming *Babylonian Creation Myths.*

Obv. 9 For *rēši mutninnû* see the note on BM 33428 Ib 12 above.

Obv. 11 On first millennium tablets *lilbur* "grow old" and *libūr* "be established" interchange, but the phenomenon has not yet been adequately explained.

Obv. 12, rev. 11 This further example of *zarû* in colophons (the others are given in *CAD* under *zarû* B) at least proves that this is not only an Assyrian scribal term, though the meaning is still unknown.

THE THIRD TABLET OF THE SERIES EA A NÂQU

BENNO LANDSBERGER *
ORIENTAL INSTITUTE, UNIVERSITY OF CHICAGO

H. S. Schuster, who assisted me most efficiently in the reconstruction of the lexical series during the years 1932-1936, gave an account of this and related vademecums of the scribes in his doctoral dissertation, "Die nach Zeichen geordneten sumerisch-akkadischen Vokabulare" (ZA 44, 217-270 [1938]). He devotes pp. 238-263 to Ea (this is the abbreviation which CAD uses), and á-A (or simply A), its explicit version, also called "the *pirsu*'s" as against the "*ṭuppu*'s" of Ea.

To anybody who is not familiar with this branch of Assyriology, the study of Schuster can serve as an introduction. However, since its appearance, the following new developments have to be registered:

a) Sch. 238 f., "Vorläufer," the precursors of Nippur have been reconstructed by me, with few lacunas left, in MSL II (1951) and III (1955), under the name Proto-Ea. Further additions have now appeared in MSL IX 113 ff.

b) Sch. 257. Tablet IV and the first part of V has been edited by Hallock as AS 7 (1940).

c) Both the condensed and the explicit version, as well as the 'reciprocal' (Sch. 262 f.), have been reconstructed by me, in cooperation with Hallock. They are available in manuscripts and currently quoted in CAD.

d) The seventh tablet, still in a fragmentary state, was edited by me JCS XIII 128-132 (1959); its fourth *pirsu* by Goetze (*ibid.*, 120-127).

e) After having presented III here, the following state of preservation emerges for the whole series:

I, II, IV, complete;
V first half complete, second half and VI poorly preserved,
VII see above; VIII: little of Ea preserved, but three of the four *pirsu*'s almost complete.

* Deceased April 26, 1968.

Ea III

I acknowledge gratefully the help of colleagues Sollberger, Civil, and Sachs for making available to me the British Museum sources.

Sources

A = Ist. Ni. 10287 (copy of F. R. Kraus), Cassite period. 16-23a, 155-173, 223-241

B = K 8436 (CT 11, 28, photo). Sign-name column completely lost. 16-23a, 69-78

C = Assur, from Photo Konst. 494/5, where identified with excavation photo 21601(?). 94-114, 168-185

C_1 = probably part of C. VAT 14262 (photo). 69-77

D = BM 34950 (CT 12, 30, photo). 161-179, 237-252

E = BM 47467 (photo). 44-66, 112-130, 196-215

F = BM 47024 (photo)[1]. 1-8, 257-267

School-tablets:

S_1 = BM 46282 (photo) 36-39
S_2 = BM 37616 (photo) 116-121
S_3 = BM 33755 (photo) 118 f.

Excerpt = VAT 9541 r. III/IV (photo); only l. 1, 3 lines KAxX, 4 lines DUB and ll. 206 f., 213 partly preserved; not used for our compilation.

[1] Colophon in two lines
first line: a) catchline not preserved, but hardly room for the expected [[ka-na = KÁ = *ka-an-ka*]]-[*an-nu*] = [*ba-a-bu*]
b) [x x]-*ú* IM (= *ṭuppi*)
initial wedge a= A = *a-u* = *n*[*a-a-qu*]
second line: [*ša* PN *iš-ṭ*]*u-ru-*⌜*ma*⌝ *i* AN.KU.DUG.ḪA.*x* [*y z*]; not comprehensible, *x* is a vertical.

á-A, incipits

á-A	first *pirsu*	ga-da	= GAD	= qí-tu-ú	á-A III	1
	second	[gi-in]	= GIN_4	= ki-ma		2
	third	ù	= UD	= UD-mu		3
	fourth	mu-u	= MU	= šat-tum		4
	fifth	du-ub	= DUB	= la-mu-u		5
	sixth	ni-im	= NÍG	= šá UR.NÍG gir-ru		6

Sources

á-A III_1 A = VAT 9543 (copy Ehelolf), from Assur, according to subscript "Copy of Nippur," from the "Library of Tiglath-Pileser I," written by [Marduk-balāṭ]su-īriš, son of [Ninurta-uballiṭ]su ṭupšar šarri (Weidner, AfO 16, 202 f.).
Commentary = VAT 545 (photo) (NB), almost completely preserved, but hardly readable.

á-A III_2 VAT 10664 (photo) from Assur.
Commentary = BM 40745 (photo)

á-A III_3 A = BM 93037 (CT 12, 6 f., photo), called "Copy of Barsip" written by Nabû-kuṣuršu.
B = Rm. 341 (CT 11, 39), first half.

á-A III_4 A = BM 92692 (CT 12, 8 f.)
Same colophon as A of III_3.
B = same as B of III_3.

á-A III_5 A = 47760 (CT 12, 16 f.), likewise "Copy of Barsip," written by Lūṣâ-ana-Marduk.
B = K. 10072 (CT 11, 38).
C = VAT 11922 (Assur) (photo), only catchline preserved.

á-A III_6 A = Rm. 995 (copy B. L.)
B = K. 7661 (CT 11, 33) } parts of
B_1 = Rm. 910 (CT 11, 33) } same tablet
C = VAT 14393 (Assur), copy of Matouš.

I wish to express full appreciation and gratitude for collations, made in the British Museum, to W. G. Lambert, and wish to thank Mme. Çığ for collations of text A.

In presenting a continuous text with only *one* lacuna (lines 79-83, part of section KA with signs inscribed), we have to admit a great deal of unevenness; lines 36-45 (SAG × X) could not be filled, and even the number of lines not determined; no parallel could be found for 249-252 and 256-268.

Our numbering of lines was, however, made possible by the source E, where the end of columns I and II, as well as the beginning of IV are preserved. Judging also from external evidence, our average of 65 lines per column cannot be overrated; if underrated, the 'inner balance,' i. e., the correctness of the relative position of lines, is still guaranteed.

A check on the correctness of our numbers is allowed with the help of D and A: in D, ll. 165 and 238 are adjacent (column length of 72), a slight unevenness. A shows line 21 adjacent to line 74. This shortness can only be explained partially by the fact that some complicated sign names as e. g., 36, required two lines in A. It reveals an essential deficiency in the 'not authentic' part 25-35, 40-45 (hardly 67/8). Though I have to concede this, I still do not have to defend my efforts of many decades to reconstruct coherent texts of lexical sources, where any possibility is in sight. I do not go into arguments anymore about the desirability of this endeavor, but only deplore the fact that so little of the composed texts is published, so that the quotations of CAD's lexical sections cannot be checked by the users.

As to Ea III, presented here, the following degrees of certainty must be distinguished:

A: concerns whole lines or "items."

a) full authenticity, no brackets;
b) if the parallel-running *pirsu* is preserved, the only risk of the reconstruction is the possibility that we took into our edition lines omitted in the short version, either with full line numbering or like 31 a-d;
c) if not preserved, and we had to put up with what we know from S^b, Proto-Ea, and other sources, we face the danger of omission of lines. For example, nobody could guess at the lines 50-52, 56-59, 256-258, if these parts of Ea III were not preserved.

B: concerns lines only partly preserved. We have introduced [ ] for "from parallel source," but [[ ]] for "free restoration."

Other innovations:

(a) Cases where (4) has double entries, only one line is counted. This applies to 12, 22, 52, 71, 176, 181(?), 183, 213, 214, 222, 239, 240, 241, 244(?), 245.

(b) (3), sign-name column remains unfilled, unless fully or partly preserved in Ea III proper.

REMARKS

"Adab" is the abbreviation for Ist. Adab 753 = MSL II 152-154. Ist. stands for Ist. Ni. 10280 (copy Geers); it is part of a tablet also represented by Penns. 29-13-644 (abbreviation: Penns.), belonging to the Cassite period, archaic writing.

VAT 9523 (photo), from Assur, is an exercise in paleography.

11 a-c. á-A III 1, 20-22 with duplicate Diri I 226-228, uru-ak-a, uru-ul-la, uru-ka-duḫ-a = GAD + TAK$_4$ + GIŠ = ŠU.KI.

12a. á-A III 1, 27 has at least one more value of GAD + TAK$_4$ + ÙR.

16. (4) A: [*x*]-*ik*-[*y*]; B: [*xxy*]-*z*; *z* like edition CT 11 28, *tum* possible (collated).

18. Fills two lines in B because of complicated sign name, requiring two lines. (4) From B; A only [*š*]*u-mu-ut*-[*tum*].

19-19a. VAT 9523 line a3 preserves only *maš-ka-nu*.

20a. Only in B.

21. VAT 9523 offers instead lu-gu-ud = LAGARxŠE.SUM = *x-gu-u, x* like *te-*.

23a. A preserves (3) short sign, ending in vertical; (4) *t*[*a-x y*]. B preserves only end of (4) [*x x-t*]*a*-⌜*nu*⌝-*u* (not collated).

30. (4) Rests on an emendation of Rec. Ea A II 21, cf. note to S^b; furthermore attested by Nabnitu O 156, quoted AHw 541, from CT 19 26.

31. (1) From commentary VAT 545 to á-A III 1: readable end of reverse: ki-li-im = GIxGI = *íp-pi-ri* . . . = *nap-la-ku* . . . = *dim-mu-šat*. Cf. Ḫḫ VIII 168: gi-gilim = *ki-lim-bu*, and AHw 476 *kilimbu*.

36-40. Our placing of S_1 at the head of the sequence of KA × sign inscribed is arbitrary.

36. Parallel: Adab r. 13′: [x]y = SAGxA = *la-ša-š*[*u*] (!).

Note: this verb is not otherwise attested, but well known is the verbal adjective derived from it; it was confused in AHw 539 with the verb *laššu* = "not to have," or "not to exist," which does not occur in any literary text nor can form an adjective. Here is the textual evidence for the adjective *laššu*:

OB Lú B III 42-45, duplicates Ist. Ni. 10529 and Jena 1878:

lú.ir.ús.sa = la-aš-[šum]
lú.ir.ús.sa = la-ab-ṣu
lú.ir.gig = la-aq-qù
lú.ir.gar = la-aš-šum

Cf. KAR 24, 12 (quoted AHw) with duplicate AfO 16 296:

ir.uš bar.dag.dag.gi = *la-áš-šu-tu mut-ta-gi*-[*šu-tu*] (of the seven demons). This parallel, however, cannot be used for restoring our line, since such a rare item, whose survival into late tradition is doubtful, cannot have two more graphical variants (line 37 f.). Discussed sub 37-45.

37-45. Possibilities of restoration:

a) sa-an-du = SAGxDU = *qaqqadu*, to be presupposed for S^b I 245, cf. Deimel, ŠL I^3, No. 195; Schneider, AnOr XII 300. VAT 9523: [sa]g-du = [SAGxDU] = [*qaq-q*]*a-du*.

a$_1$) Ist. line 1′: [ ] = [SAG]xDU = *a*-[ ].

b) di-li-ib = SAGxDUB = *uruḫḫu* S^b I 246, also Proto-Ea 301, written SAGxŠID in NA (Kraus, TBP index to DILIB).

b$_1$) di-li-ib = SAGxGIR Proto-Ea 299

b$_2$) di-li-ib = SAGxX Proto-Ea 300.

c) gu-ṭu = SAGxUR = *qarradu* S^b I 248.
gu-ud = " Proto-Ea 296.
" = " = *qarradu* Adab r. 15′, VAT 9523 line 5b, and Ist. line 3′.

c$_1$) [ ] = SAGxX = *qarradu* Adab r. 14′.

d) ka-an = SAGxMI = *adāru, adirtu* S^b I 249 f.
ga-na = " = *idirtum* VAT 9523 line 5a, missing in Proto-Ea.

e) ḫu-sag = SAGxDAM Proto-Ea 298 (MSL III).

f) SAGxNUN Adab r. 16′.
g) SAGxLA[M] Adab r. 17′.
h) SAGxUŠ Adab r. 21′.
i) SAGxSAL Adab r. 22′.
j) [x]-šu-ul = SAGxEZEN = *si*-[*xy*] Ist. 3′.

[**REMARKS continued below, p. 144.**]

						á-A III/1	S^b	Proto-Ea	Others
F	1	ga-da	GAD	ma-nu-t[il-lu-u]	[qí-tu-ú]		I 228	166	Ea II Excerpt Catchline
F	2	[ ]	[GAD + TÙ]N	ga-da-tùn-n[u-u]	[šu-ku-su ša GAD.TÙN]	8	m	m	
F	3	[ ]	[GAD + TA]K$_4$	ga-da-t[a-ka-ku]	[tuk-ku]	9	m	n. p.	
F	4	[aš-šá]	[GAD + TA]K$_4$	" ["]	[ri-ig-mu]	10	229	m	Rec. Ea A V 21
F	5	[ ]	[GAD + TA]K$_4$	" ["]	[ši-si-tu]	11	m	m	Excerpt
F	6	[ ]	[GAD + TA]K$_4$	" ["]	[ta-nu-qa-tu]	14	m	m	
F	7	[aš-ta]	[GAD + TA]K$_4$	" ["]	[ik-kil-lu]	15	m	m	Rec. Ea A V 22
F	8	[ak-ki-il]	[GAD + TAK$_4$]	" ["]	["]	16	m	n. p.	diri I 229
br	9	["]	[GAD + TAK$_4$ + SI]		["]	17	232	m	nabn. B 140
	10	["]	[GAD + TAK$_4$ + GIŠ]		[kak-ka-bu]	18	m	n. p.	
	11	[si-iq-qa]	[GAD + TAK$_4$ + GIŠ]		[ur-ru-ú]	19	230	m	nabn. L 85
	12	[um-bi-in]	[GAD + TAK$_4$ + ÚR]		[ú-ba-nu]	23		n. p.	
					[ṣu-up-ru]	24	231		
	13	[ši-ni-ig]	[GAD + NÁG]		[bi-i-nu]	n. p.	233	MSL II 93 l. 5	diri II 244
	14	[ki-in-da]	[GAD + GAR] [GAD + GAR]		[gal-la-bu]	n. p.	234	n. p.	
	15	[la-ga-ar]	[LAGAR]		[la-ga-ru]	n. p.	235	165	
B$_I$ A$_I$	16	[ ]	[[LAGAR + x]]	[ ]	[x]-ik-[y]-z	n. p.	m	m	
B$_I$ A$_I$	17	[du-ú]	[LAGAR-gunû = DU$_6$]	[ ]	[š]u-ub-tum DU$_6$	n. p.	236	162	
B$_I$ A$_I$	18	[šu-mun-da]	[DU$_6$ DU$_6$]	[ ]	ša DU$_6$ SAR šu-mut-tú	n. p.	m	m	diri IV 5
B$_I$ A$_I$	19	[su-ú]	[DU$_6$]xŠE	[ ]	maš-ka-nu	n. p.	237	164	diri IV 244
B$_I$ A$_I$	20	[su-ul]	[DU$_6$]xŠE	[ ]	"	n. p.	238	m	
	a	[ ]	[[DU$_6$xŠE]]	[ ]	"	n. p.			
B$_I$ A$_I$	21	[lu-gu-ud]	⌜DU$_6$xŠE.SUM⌝	[ ]	ra-ḫi-ṣu	n. p.	239	m	
B$_I$ A$_I$	22	[su-ḫi-rim]	DU$_6$xŠE.SUM	[ ]	maš-ka-nu ša ŠE.IN.NU (= tibni)	n. p.	240	m	
B$_I$ A$_I$	23	[e]	[D]U$_6$ + DU	[ ]	ša-ra-am-mu e-lu-ú	n. p.	241	163	diri I 199
B$_I$ A$_I$	a	see note							
	24	[zi-i]	[ZI]		[na-piš-tu]	135	280	452	
	25	[su-um]	[ZI over ZI]		[ ]	n. p.	280a	453	
	26	[zu-ku-um]	[ZI over ZI + LAGAB]		[kib-su]	281	n. p.	456	
	27	[šu-ub]	[ZI over ZI + LAGAB]		[šub-ba-tum]	282	n. p.	454	
	28	[nu-mu-un]	[ZI over ZI + LAGAB]		[el-pe-tum]	n. p.	283	455	

							á-A III/1	S^b	Proto-Ea	Others
		29	[gi-i]	[GI]		[qa-nu-ú]	n. p.	284	460	
		30	[gi-e]	[GI-gunû]		[[la-mu-ú]]	n. p.	287	461	
		31	[ki-li-im]	[GIxGI]		[[e-ge-ru]]	see note	285 f.	m	
		31a	[gi-ib]	[GIxGI]		[pa-ra-ku]	227	m	m	
		31b	[gi-il]	[GIxGI]		[e-ge-ru]	229	m	m	
		31c	[gi-e]	[GIxGI]		[še-e-tu]	230	m	m	
		31d	[ ]	[GIxGI]		[še-e-nu]	239	m	m	
		32	[gi-in]	[GIM]		[ki-ma]	240 catch-line	291	530	Rec. ea A II 27 emended (Schuster, ZA 44, 263[6])
		33	[di-im]	[GIM]		[[ba-nu-ú]]	á-A III/2 n. p.	292	531	
		34	[ši-di-im]	[GIM]		[[i-tin-nu]]	n. p.	m	533	
		35	[sa-ag]	[SAG]		[a-me-lu]	n. p.	244	292	
S_1		36	[ ]	[SAGxA]	šá sa-an-ga-ku a-a i-du	[ ]	n. p.	m	m	
S_1		37	[ ]	[SAGxX]	[" x] y "(= idu)	"	n. p.			
S_1		38	[ ]	[SAGxX]	[" x] y "	"	n. p.			
S_1		39	[ ]	[SAGxX]	[" xy] "	x[ ]	n. p.			
br		40	[ ]	[SAGxX]	[" xy "]	[ ]	n. p.			
		41	[ ]	[SAGxX]	[" xy "]	[ ]	n. p.			
		42	[ ]	[SAGxX]	[" xy "]	[ ]	n. p.			
		43	[ ]	[SAGxX]	[" xy "]	[ ]	n. p.			
	E_I	44	[ ]	[SAGxX]	[" xy "]	["]	n. p.			
	E_I	45	[ ]	[SAGxX]	[" xy] "	["]	n. p.			
	E_I	46	[mu-ḫu-um]	[SAGxUB]	[" xy] "	mu-u[ḫ-ḫu]	n. p.	m	297 (MSL III)	
	E_I	47	["]	[SAGxKAK]	[šá sag-ga-ku] qaq-qa i-du	"	n. p.	247	m	
	E_I	48	["]	[A + SAG]	a-a-sag-ga-ku	"	n. p.	m	m	diri III 141
	E_I	49	[ú-gu]	[A + SAG]	a-a-sag-ga-ku	"	n. p.	m	m	
	E_I	50	[ ]	[PAP + SAG]	pa-ap-sag-ga-ku	ma-a-šú	n. p.	m	m	
	E_I	51	[ ]	[PAP + SAG]	" "	"	n. p.	m	m	
	E_I	52	[ ]	SAG SAG	sag-min-na-bi	ma-a-šú tu-'a-mu	n. p. n. p.	m m	m m	
	E_I	53	[ki-ši]	SAG-nutillû (= KIŠI₄)	sag-nu-til-lu-ú	mut-ta-tum	n. p.	234	295 (MSL III)	
	E_I	54	[ku-uš]	[SAG-gunû]	sag-gu-nu-ú	a-na-ḫu	n. p.	m	293 (MSL III)	
	E_I	55	[su-mu-ur]	[SAG-gunû]	" "	ez-zu	n. p.	252	294 (MSL III)	
	E_I	56	[ ]	[SAG-gunû]	" "	ṣu-lu-lu	n. p.	m	m	
		57	[ ]	[SAG-gunû]	sag-gu-nu-ú	"	n. p.	m	m	
	E_I	58	[ ]	[SAG-gunû]	" "	"	n. p.	m	m	
	E_I	59	[ ]	[SAG-gunû]	" "	"	n. p.	m	m	
	E_I	60	[[a-lam]]	[SAG-gunû]	" "	ṣal-mu	n. p.	m	m	

								á-A III/2	Sb	Proto-Ea	Others
E_I			61	[ka-a]	[KA]	ka-a-gu	pu-ú	n. p.	253	303	
E_I			62	[pi-i]	[KA]	"	"	n. p.	m	309	
E_I			63	[gi-ir]	[KA]	ka-a-gu	ap-pu	n. p.	254	305	
E_I			64	[[mi-li-ib]]	[KA]	"	a-la-tu	n. p.	m	m	
E_I			65	[i-nim]	[KA]	["]	a-ma-tum	n. p.	m	306	
E_I			66	[zu-ú]	[KA]	["]	ši-in-nu	n. p.	255	304	
br					End of column I in E						
	C_1		67	[[ ]]	[[KA]]		[[ ]]	n. p.	m	m	
	C_1		68	[[ ]]	[[KA]]		[[ ]]	132?	m	m	
	C_1	B_{II}	69	⌈du⌉-⌈ú⌉	KA		[qa-bu-ú]	133	m	306	
	C_1	B_{II}	70	da-ag	KA		"	141	m	m	
	C_1	B_{II}	71	e	KA		"	146	m	m	
							[tu-kul-tu]	147	m	m	
	C_1	B_{II}	72	gu-u	KA		r[i-ig-mu]	n. p.	m	307	
	C_1	B_{II}	73	ka-a	KA		KA.K[A.SI.GA]	n. p.	m	m	
			C_1 ———								
	C_1	B_{II}	74	e-me	KAxME		li-ša-[nu]	n. p.	259	322	Adab 16
	C_1	B_{II}	75	nu-un-du-un	KAxNUN		šap-[tu]	n. p.	260	321	Adab 17 Penns. 8
	C_1	B_{II}	76	su-un	KAxSA		zi-i[q-nu]	n. p.	262	319	Adab 18 Penns. 9
	C_1	B_{II}	77	mu-un-su-ub	KAxX		li-[[e-tu]]	n. p.	m	m	
		B_{II}	78	ú-su-ug	[KAxÚ]		[ú-suk-ku]	n. p.	m	m	see note
				GAP A: ± 15	KAxX						
	C		94	[tu-u]	[KAxLI]		[šip]-tum	n. p.	263	326	
	C		95	[uš]	[KAxLI]		["]	n. p.	m	325	Rec. ea A V 3
	C		96	[mu-ú]	[KAxLI]		["]	n. p.	m		Rec. ea E 7. cf., MSL VIII/1, 21 to 158.
	C		97	[uš]	[KAxBAD]		[i]m-tum	Comm. 1′	264	328	Adab 12 and r. 7
	C		98	[še-e]	[KAxŠID]		[šá]-ga-[mu]	2′	265	m	
	C		99	[šu-du]	[KAxŠU]		[i]k-ri-[bu]	3′	266	329	Adab r. 11
	C		100	[kur-ku]	[KAxX]		nu-uḫ-[[šu]]	4′	m	m	
	C		101	[pu-[[u]]	[KAxGÁN-t]enû		ša t[[il-te]]	6′	m	m	
	C		102	[ka-an]	[KA]xGÁN-tenû		a-da-[ru]	n. p.	m	320	
	C		103	[pu-zu-ur]	[KAxGÁN-tenû]		pu-zu-[ru]	n. p.	267	333	diri I 48
	C		104	["]	[KA]xGÁN-tenû + ŠA		"	n. p.	m	m	VAT 9523, 7b
	C		105	[ ]	[KA]xGÁN-tenû + ŠA		ṭí-e-[mu] ša ì-[[lí]]	n. p.	m	m	
	C		106	[bu-un]	KAxIM		nap-pa-[ḫu]	n. p.	269	324	
	C		107	[ ]	KAxIM		la-ta-[[ku]]	n. p.	m	m	
	C		108	[gu]-⌈ú⌉	KAxGAR		a-ka-[lu]	n. p.	256	311	Adab 1
	C		109	[[ni-g]]a	KAxGAR		ú-kul-[tum]	n. p.	256a?	m	
	C		110	[ša-ga-ar]	KAxGAR		bu-[ú-ru]	n. p.	m	312	
	C		111	[na-ag]	KAxA		ša-t[u-ú]	n. p.	257	314	
E_{II}	C		112	im-[mi-in]	KAxA		ṣu-ú-m[u]	n. p.	m	313	
E_{II}	C		113	"	KAxUD		"	n. p.	268	m	
E_{II}	C		114	e-me-i[n-gi]	KAxME.GI		šur-pu-[u]	Comm. r. 4	m	m	

							á-A III/2	Sb	Proto-Ea	Others
		E_{II}	115	im-mìn-te	[KAxME.TE]	kal-k[al-tum]	r. 6	m	m	
	S_2	E_{II}	116	tu-kur	[KAxŠE]	[ka-sa-su]	m., but cf. 117b	276	315a (MSL III, 174)	Adab 14
S_3	S_2	E_{II}	117	zu-gu-uz	K[AxLUM]	[ga-ṣa-ṣu]	r. 9	m	m	
S_3	S_2	E_{II}	118	ṣu-ub	KAxGA	[na-ṣa-bu]	r. 11	273	318	
S_3	S_2	E_{II}	119	ma-a	KAxKU	[qa-mu-ú]	n. p.	271	316	cf. Adab 13
S_3	S_2	E_{II}	120	mu-ú	KAxS[AR]	[ḫa-šu-ú]	n. p.	272	317	Adab 15
	S_2	E_{II}	121	mur-gu	KAxNE	[lib-ba-a-tum]	n. p.	m	323	Adab 7, Penns. 12
		E_{II}	122	ni-ig-ru	KAxLÙ	[a-ši-pu]	n. p.	m	m	LÚ-ša IV 153
		E_{II}	123	ir-ḫa-an-đi	KAxKIB	[ ]	n. p.	m	m	
		E_{II}	124	ne-ḫa-an-di	KAxKIB	[ ]	n. p.	m	m	
		E_{II}	125	ga-za	KA[xKIB]	[ ]	n. p.	m	331 (MSL III 199)	
		E_{II}	126	i-bi-ra	KA[xKIB]	[tam-ka-ru]	n. p.	m	m	
		E_{II}	127	zu-ku-ra	KA[[xTAR]]	[ ]	n. p.	m	m	
		E_{II}	128	"	K[AxX]	[ ]	n. p.			
		E_{II}	129	ši-lig	K[AxŠI]	[ša-ga-pu-ru]	n. p.	265a	m	
		E_{II}	130	ḫu-ur	K[AxX]	[ ]	n. p.	m	m	
End of column II in E										
			131	[ ]	[KAxX]	[ ]				
			132	[ ]	[KAxX]	[ ]				
			133	[u-gu]	[U + KA]	[mu-uḫ-ḫu]	n. p.	274	310	diri III 144
			134	[ù]	[UD]	[U_4-mu]	á-A III/3 1	II 79	151	
			135	[ug]	[UD]	"	22	m	m	
			136	[ú]	[UD]	[šá til-tum]	23	m	m	
			137	[ḫu-ud]	[UD]	[el-lum]	25	m	154a	
			138	[u-ud]	[UD]	[U_4-mu]	30	m	m	
			139	[ ]	[UD]	[el-lu]	38			
			140	[[ta-am]]	[UD]	[e-le-lum]	41	m	152	
			141	[za-la-ag]	[UD]	[eb-bu]	57	m	153	
			142	[[sa-la-aḫ]]	[UD]	[šá KI.UD maš-ka-nu]	63	m	m	
			143	[ba-ab-bar]	[UD]	[pe-ṣu-ú]	65	m	157	
			144	[bi-ir]	[UD]	[ka-la-ṣu]	74	m	154	
			145	[ḫa-ad]	[UD]	[el-lum]	82	m	156a (MSL III)	cf. diri I 111
			146	[da-ag]	[UD]	["]	88	m	m	103
			147	[ra-a]	[UD]	["]	91	m	m	104
			148	[la-aḫ]	[UD]	[šá SA.UD sa-[la-ḫu]]	96	m	m	
						[a-ba-lu]	103			
			149	[aḫ]	[UD]	["]	104	m	156	
			150	[e]	[UD]	["]	105	m	m	
			151	[a-a]	[UD]	["]	106	m	155	
			152	[[ḫa]-a]	[UD]	["]	107	m	m	

								á-A III/3	Sb	Proto-Ea	Others
			153	[ḫi-eš]	[UD]		[UD.KI]	113	m	m	diri I 136
			154	[ḫa-aš]	[UD]		[UD.KI]	114	m	m	diri I 137
		A_{III}	155	[pi-ṣi-it]	[UD]		[UD.KI]	115	m	m	diri I 138
		A_{III}	156	am-[na]	[UD]		[ᵈUD]	119	m	m	
		A_{III}	157	[ul]	[UD]		[na-ba-ṭu]	118	m	m	
		A_{III}	158	ú-[ta]	[UD]		[ᵈUD]	120	m	157a	
		A_{III}	159	ša-m[a-aš]	[UD]		["]	121		—	
		A_{III}	160	[uḫ]	[UD + NANGAR + DIŠ (= ÚḪ)]		[ru-'-tum]	137	II 83	160	
D_{III}		A_{III}	161	ak-ša-a[k]	[" "]		[[ŠU.URU]]	144	m	m	
D_{III}		A_{III}	162	qa-ru	[" "]		[ ]	143	m	m	
D_{III}		A_{III}	163	e	[UD + DU]		[a-ṣu-ú]	145	82	159	diri I 149
D_{III}		A_{III}	164	a-ra	UD[+ DU]		[nam-rum]	188	m	m	188
D_{III}		A_{III}	165	sag-uš	UD[+ DU]		[ka-a-a-nu]	190	m	m	191
D_{III}		A_{III}	166	bi-eš-bi-eš	UD[+ UD]		[na-ba-ṭú]	134	m	m	193
D_{III}		A_{III}	167	ú-ti-ma	UD[+ MI]		[e-ṭu-tum]	215	m	m	
D_{III}	C_{III}	A_{III}	168	a-ra-aḫ	UDxEŠ (= ITU)		a[r-ḫ]u	204	m	m	
D_{III}	C_{III}	A_{III}	169	i-ti	["]		["]	205	84	161	
D_{III}	C_{III}	A_{III}	170	"	[ITUxBAD]		"	206	85	m	
D_{III}	C_{III}	A_{III}	171	ú-zu	U + UD	giš-[pu-ut-ta-ku]	e-reb ᵈŠam-ši	208	80	158	
D_{III}	C_{III}	A_{III}	172	nin + gi-in	U + UD	" ["]	ku-ú-bu	210	m	m	
D_{III}	C_{III}	A_{III}	173	"	U + UD + KID	' [ut-ta-kit-ta-ku]	"	211	m	m	195
							ku-um-mu	212			
D_{III}	C_{III}		174	mu-ru	$MURUB_4$	i-ti-[gu-nu-u]	qab-lum	216	86	n. p.	
D_{III}	C_{III}		175	ni-sag	$MURUB_4$	" ["]	ni-qu-ú	218	87	n. p.	
			C								
D_{III}	C_{III}		176	mu-ú	MU	mu-[ḫal-dim-mu]	šat-tu	á-A III/4 1	I 300	171	
							šu-mu	3	m	172 (MSL III)	
D_{III}	C_{III}		177	gu-ú	MU	["]	[[ia-ú]]				
D_{III}	C_{III}		178	su-uḫ	MU	"	ta-ḫu-ú	n. p.	m	173	
			a	see note							
D_{III}	C_{III}		179	m[u-ḫal-di]m	MU		nu-ḫa-ti-mu	n. p.	301	174 (MSL III)	
	C_{III}		180	[da-aḫ]	MU MU		a-ṣa-[bu]	n. p.	302	175	
	C_{III}		181	[ú-du-un]	[U + MU]		ú-tu-[nu]	n. p.	II 93	176	
	C_{III}		182				ki-ir-[[ṣu]]	n. p.			
			C								
	C_{III}		183	[ši-ka]	[LA]		ḫa-aṣ-bu	61	m	180	
							[iš-ḫil-ṣu]	62		—	
	C_{III}		184	[la-a]	[LA]		la-lu-[ú]	63	I 204	179	
			C								

						á-A III/4	Sb	Proto-Ea	Others
C_{III}	185	[ne-e]	[PIRIG]		e-mu-[qu]	66	208	571 (MSL III)	
	186	[u-ug]	[PIRIG]		[U₄-mu]	67	m	m	
	187	[“]	[UG]		[nu-rum]	77	207	574	
	188	[pi-ri-ig]	[PIRIG]		[ni-e-šu]	n. p.	205	572	
	189	[[ ]]	[[PIRIG]]		[[šá-ra-ḫu]]	n. p.			ea III excerpt K 8503 (CT 11, 28)
	190	[az]	[PIRIGxZA = AZ]		[a-su]	n. p.	206	576 (MSL III)	
	191	[ ]	[ ]		[ ]				
	192	[ ]	[ ]		[ ]				
	193	[ ]	[ ]		[ ]				
	194	[ ]	[ ]		[ ]				
	195	[ku-šu]	[U + PIRIG]		[bu-lum]	n. p.	210	577 (MSL III)	
			[End of column III in E]						
E_{IV}	196	[ ]	U + PIRIG	giš-pu-pi-rig-ga-ku	šá-a-qu	n. p.	m	m	
E_{IV}	197	[ki-ši]	“	“ “	pi-a-zu	n. p.	m	m	Rec. ea, A III 21
E_{IV}	198	[si-i]	[SI]	[si]-su-ú	*PI[read ma]-lu-ú	n. p.	II 175	181	
E_{IV}	199	di-ri	SI + A	si-ia-a-ku	at-ri	231	176	182a (MSL III)	diri I 1
E_{IV}	200	[su-u]	[SI-gunû] + A	si-i-gu-nu-*ú-a-a-ku	sa-a-mu	222	177	183	
E_{IV}	201	[du-ub]	[DUB]	du-ub-bu	la-mu-ú	á-A III/5 1	113	188	
E_{IV}	202	[še-en]	[DUB] (URUD)	“	šu-uḫ-tum	10	m	m	
E_{IV}	203	[ú-ru-du]	[DUB] (URUD)	“	e-ru-ú	11	112	190	
E_{IV}	204	[me-en-bulug]	[DUB] (?)	“	pal-lu-uk-ku	12	m	m	
E_{IV}	205	[su-mug]	[DUB] (UM)	“	šu-lum	23	cf. 114	193	MSL II 94 II 5
E_{IV}	206	[sa-ma-ag]	[DUB] (UM)	du-ub-bu	um-ṣa-tum	25	m	m	MSL II 94 II 6
E_{IV}	207	[“]	[DUB (UM) xLAGAB]	du-ub-la-gab-ba-ku	“	26	115	194 (MSL III)	
E_{IV}	208	[di-iḫ]	[DUB] (UM)	du-ub-bu	li-ʾ-bu	13	m	185	
E_{IV}	209	[ú-um]	[DUB] (UM)	du-ub-bu	ṭup-pu (error for *um-mu)	2	116	184	
E_{IV}	210	[um-me-da]	[DUB (UM) + ME]	“ me-mu-u	ta-ri-tum	27	117	186	
E_{IV}	211	[me-ès]	[DUB (MES)]	du-ub-bu	eṭ-lum	17	118	187	
E_{IV}	212	[ki-ši-ib]	[DUB (MES)]	[“]	rit-tum	20	119	189	

								á-A III/5	Sᵇ	Proto-Ea	Others
E_{IV}			213	[ku-u]	[KUD]	si-lu-ú	pe-tú-ú šá A.MEŠ	29	m	195	
							[[na-ka-su]]	cf. 33	—	—	
							ba-ta-qa	38	—	—	
							pa-ra-su	53	—	—	
E_{IV}			214	[ḫa-aš]	[KUD]	["]	še-be-ru	103	m	196	
							[[ḫa-ṣa-bu]]	104	—	—	
E_{IV}			215	[ta-ar]	[KUD]	["]	[šá]-⌜a⌝-[lum]	105	m	197	
			216	[si-la]	[KUD]		[su-ú-qu]	170	302	198	
			217	[su-lu]	[KUD]		["]	179	m	m	
			218	[qu-ud-ma]	[KUD]		[ᵈKUD]	184	m	m	
			219	[qa-ad-ma]	[KUD]		["]	185	m	m	
			220	[ni-im]	[GAR]		[šá UR.NÍG gi-ir-ru]	186 (á-A III/6, 1)	m	208	
			221	[ni-in-da]	[GAR]		[a-ka-lu]	n. p.	I 12	210	
			222	[ ]	[GAR]		[ša-ka-nu]	34	m	209	
							[na-da-nu]	35	m	—	
		A_{IV}	223	[ ]	GAR		šu-ku-l[u]	n. p.	m	—	
		A_{IV}	224	[ ]	GAR		"	n. p.	m	—	
			225	[šu-tug]	PAD		šu-tuk-ku	n. p.	m	m	diri IV 232 Ḫḫ IX 368
		A_{IV}	226	[šu-ku-un]	PAD		ku-ru-ma-tum	60	15	211	
		A_{IV}	227	[ku-ru-um-ma]	PAD		"	n. p.	m	213	
		A_{IV}	228	[pa-a]d	PAD		ka-sà-pu	n. p.	16	212	
		A_{IV}	229	[ ]	PAD		na-sà-qu	n. p.	m	—	
		A_{IV}	230	[ ]	PAD		ŠU	n. p.	m	—	
		A_{IV}	231	[šu-ur]	ŠUR		ṣa-ra-rum	90	10	214	
		A_{IV}	232	[bu-ur]	BUR		nap-ta-nu	n. p.	14	215	
							ap-lum	n. p.	13	—	
		A_{IV}	233	[ku-u]	KÙ		kàs-pu	n. p.	II 107	218	
		A_{IV}	234	[a-za-ag]	KÙ		ŠU	n. p.	108	cf. 137a	
		A_{IV}	235	[e]	⌜E⌝		ka-a-t[a]	n. p.	242	216	cf. MSL IV 272, 278, 279.
		A_{IV}	236	[i-ig]	⌜E⌝		i-ku	n. p.	m	217	
	D_{IV}	A_{IV}	237	[ba-ra]	[KISAL]		šu-pár-ru-rum	n. p.	m	m	
	D_{IV}		238	[pa-ar]	[KISAL] (= par_4)		[šá SA.PÁR sa]-par-ri		m	219	
	D_{IV}	A_{IV}	239	[ki-sa-al]	KISAL		ki-sal-lu		229	220	
							pu-úḫ-rum		m	—	
	D_{IV}	A_{IV}	240	[e]	[É]	[bi-tu]	bi-i-tum		230	222	
	D_{IV}	A_{IV}	241	[[e]]	[É]	["]	"		—	—	
	D_{IV}		242	[[e]]	É	"	"		—	—	
	D_{IV}		243	[ar-ḫuš]	[ÉxSAL]	[šá bi-tak-ku mu-nu-sa i-du]	i-pu			226	MSL II 94 II 9 cf. ea IV 254
							ri-e-mu		cf. 316		

						á-A III/6	Sb	Proto-Ea	Others
D_{IV}	244	[uš]	[ÉxSAL]	[" "] "	i-pu		cf. 314	225	rec. ea V 8 f.
				[" "] "	si-li-tú		cf. 315		
D_{IV}	245	[a-ma]	[ÉxSAL]	[" "] "	maš-ta-ku		cf. 313	224	MSL II 94 II, 7, 8
									diri V 288
									ea IV 255
D_{IV}	246	[i-ti-ma]	[ÉxMI]	[" gik-ki-g]a "	ki-iṣ-ṣu		cf. 312	228	diri V 289
									ea IV 263
D_{IV}	247	[ ]	[ÉxGAR]	[" nin-da] "	mil-ku	n. p.	—	—	
D_{IV}	248	[ga-al-ga]	[ÉxGAR]	[" "] "	"	n. p.	cf. 321	223	ea IV 257
					ṭ[é-e-]mu	n. p.	—	—	ea IV 258
D_{IV}	249	[ ]	[ÉxX]	[" xy] "	[x (y)]-tum	n. p.			
D_{IV}	250	[ ]	[ÉxX]	[" xy "]	[x (y)]-tum	n. p.			
D_{IV}	251	[ ]	[ÉxX]	[" xy "]	[xy]-ba-ku	n. p.			
D_{IV}	252	[ ]	[ÉxX]	[" xy]	["]	n. p.			
					pa-aš-ku	n. p.			
		small gap possible							
	253	[e-sag]	[ÉxŠE]	[" še-a "]	[qa-ri-tum]	n. p.	cf. 317	227	diri V 286
									ea IV 237
	254	[e-sag-tur]	[ÉxŠE.TUR]	[" še-a tur-ra"]	[is-ru]	n. p.		m	diri V 287
									ea IV 241
	255	[a-ra-aḫ]	[ÉxŠE]	[" še-a "]	[ar-ḫu]	n. p.		m	m
									ea IV 239
					[na-aš-pa-ku]	n. p.		—	—
									ea IV 240
		small gap possible							
	256	[ ]	[ÉxX]	[" xy "]	[ ]	n. p.		m	
F	257	[ ]	[ÉxX]	" [" "]	[ ]	n. p.		m	
F	258	[ ]	[ÉxX]	" " ["]	[ ]	n. p.		m	
F	259	[ ]	[ÉxX]	" " ["]	[ ]	n. p.		m	
F	260	[ ]	[ÉxŠU]	" šu-šá-a ["]	[ ]	n. p.		m	
F	261	[ ]	[ÉxŠU]	" " ["]	[ ]	n. p.		m	
F	262	[ ]	[ÉxSI]	" si-sa-a ⌜"⌝	[ ]	n. p.		m	
F	263	[ ]	[ÉxKU]	" tu-kul-la ⌜"⌝	[ ]	n. p.		m	
F	264	[ ]	[ÉxGAN-tenû]	" ga-na te-na ["]	[ ]	n. p.		m	
F	265	[ ]	[ÉxGAN-tenû]	" " ["]	[ ]	n. p.		m	
F	266	[ ]	[ÉxGAN-tenû]	" " ["]	[ ]	n. p.		m	
F	267	[ ]	[ÉxGAN-tenû]	" " ["]	[ ]	n. p.		m	
		End of tablet							

k) x-gu-u[r] = SAGxKUD = *x*[*y* *z*] Ist. 4′. (x of (1) ends with vertical, *x* of (3) like *e*.).

l) Sign inscribed not preserved or not deciphered: Adab r. 18′-20; Ist. 2′.

We have reserved in our reconstruction (see above) nine lines for SAGxX; a-d above may be substituted "almost certainly"; no decision is possible for the other candidates; the poor remainders of sign names in 37-8 do not exclude a); in this case (3) of 38 ["a-ra-gub-b]a"; (4) ⌜*ú*⌝-[*ru-uḫ-ḫu*].

37. (3) remainders defy interpretation.

38. (3) y ends with vertical.

39. (4) x = *si* or *ma*[*r*.

44f. (3) Restoration is based on blank space.

47. (3) It is not explicable why E writes out this column, instead of writing " qaq-qa ".

49. Repetition of (3) makes this line suspect; we do not dare to emend to U + SAG, which is badly attested for *muḫḫu*: VAT 9523 6b: ú-gu = U + SAG = *mu-ḫu*; furthermore; if U + SAG were treated here, the line 251 of S^b I would be expected here.

56-59. (1) [du-ul], [an-dul] with phonetic variants, cf. Proto-Ea 141 and 141a; and CAD Ṣ 242 *ṣulūlu,* first section.

60. For this archaic orthography cf. Gelb, MAD III 244 f.

64. (1) This value can be gained by comparing KAxLI = *alātu,* discussed in notes to 79-93.

68. á-A III 2 (VAT 10664) offers, before 69, one line separated by division lines [ ] = [KA] = [*na*]-*du-u šá* GIŠ.X, X like A[L].

69-71. C_1 preserves only (3) and first sign of (4).

69. (1) B collated: possible but not clear, because of a wrongly joined little fragment.

71. B offers two identical lines with (1)e, which must be considered an error.

74–130. Sources for KA-compounds additional to Ea, S^b, and Proto-Ea:

a) Adab-Vocabulary MSL II 152-4, 1-24, and r. 1′-12′ revised: 19 (3): *ḫi-il-*[*tum*]; r. 3: gu = KAxGU = *ri-*[*ig-mu*] (Penns. 5). r. 4: gú-uk-ri = KAxGIŠ.SAR = *ša* [*ki-ri-im*].

(1) ex gù-kiri: Facsimile of Proto-Ea 330, source C favors KAxGIŠ.SAR; collations of other sources (MSL III 199) are advisable. r. 5: (2) correct to KAxBALAG.

b) Penns.
After break:

1)	a-gal	= KAx[X]	= [ ]	
2)	a-gal	= KAxGAL	= [ ]	
3)	u-gal	= KAxUŠ	= [ ]	
4)	a-lá	= KAxA.[LÁ]	= [ ]	
5)	gu-u	= KAxGU	= [ ]	Adab 3.
6)	pa-x	= KAxX	= [ ]	x like ŠIŠ.
7)	gu-šu-di	= KAx⌜BALAG⌝	= [ ]	Proto-Ea 332.
8)	nun-du-um	= KAxNUN	= š[a-ap-tum]	Ea III 75.
9)	su-ul	= KAxSA	= zi-[iq-nu]	Ea III 76
10)			sa-[ap-sa-pu]	
11)			dar-rum	
12)	mu-ur-gú	= KAxNE	= uz-[nu]	Ea III 121.
13)	tu-uk-r[i]	= KAxGILIM	= ka-[sa-su]	cf. Ea III 116.
14)	not deciphered break		= te-[ ]	

c) VAT 9523

7b.	pu-zu-ur	= KAxGÁN-tenû.ŠA	= pu-zu-ru	Ea III 104.
7c.	[ ]	= KAxŠA	= n[i-x x].	
8b.	gi-ri	= KAxLI	= ḫa-na-bu	
8c.	[ ]	= KAxKAK.GA	= [ ]	faulty

d) UET VI 354

1.	aš	= KAxAŠ	= ú-pu-um-tum
3.	mi-li-ba	= KAxLI-ba	= ḫa-la-tum

76. Another KAxSA, later written separately zú-sa, with variant KAxEŠ (three horizontals slanted to the right); explicitly treated in my "Date Palm and its By-products" p. 20, chapter K.

77. (2) C_1 preserves vertical wedge as end of x. [T]E may be proposed.

78. For archaic sign KAxÚ see Falkenstein, Gudea-Grammatik 32; written separately: ú-su-ug = Ú.KA = *mu-su-uk-[ku]*, Diri IV 44 with Proto-diri 185; furthermore, Ú.KA = *ú-su[k-ku]*, Izi E 255; also Ú.KA = *ú-suk-ku* LÚ = ša III col. IV 1 h; ká.gal Ú.KA = " (= *abul*) *mu-su-ka-tim*, Kagal I 4. Meaning first suggested by me DLZ 1928, 2101.

79-93. Filling of gap:

a) All signs KA with sign inscribed of S^b are found in the preserved part of Ea III, with the exception of 260, the second KAxA, with (1) still not established, but probably identical with Proto-Ea 315. It would be expected after our l. 111 and, since missing here, was not included in Ea.

b) From the KA×-signs of Proto-Ea, besides 315, the following are not in the preserved part of Ea III: 327, 330, 332.

c) Adab 2, 3, 4(?), 5, 6, 19-21, 22, 23, r. 1, 2, 4, 5, 6, 8-10, 12 are not contained, as well as Penns. 1-7, 13 (a graphical variant to Ea III 116).

d) Archaic signs KAxX not included in Proto-Ea:

KAxSA = zusa,	see note to line 76.
giš. KAxGÍR	Gudea, Cyl. B 14, 2.
KAxZI	LAK 335.

With the kind permission of M. Civil, from Penns. CBS 11318:

	Pronunciation	Sumerian	Akkadian
II 5′	bu-gu$_4$ bu-udu	KAxGUD KAxUDU	ri-gi$_4$-im GUD-im
			ri-gi$_4$-im UDU-im
	bu-šáḫ bu-anše	KAxŠÁḪ KAxANŠE	ri-gi$_4$-im ŠÁḪ
			ri-gi$_4$-im ANŠE
	uru-a še-da-da	uru KAxBALAG-da	[i-n]a a-lim
			ša-⸢sa⸣-a

Note: Compounds of KA may be suggested for Rm. 597 (CT 19 34) left column; with (4): " (= *rigmu*) *šá sinništi, kalbi, šaḫê, sinništi, šaḫê, sinništi, eṭli.*

We regret that this category of vocabularies, "complicated signs," was never treated with the exception of my contribution WO I 362-368.

The only safe conclusion to be drawn as to the filling of the gap concerns lines 93 f.:

93.	[mi-li-ib]	[KAxLI]	[a-la-tu]
94.	[me-li]	[KAxLI]	[ma-'-la-tu]
			[ne-im-lu-u]

Line 93 restored from UET VI 354 (above d), cf. Adab 19 (with variant of inscribed sign) and Ea III 64 (for simple KA). Line 94 restored from Proto-Ea 327 and Ḫh XV 31 b-c uzu$^{(me\text{-}li)}$ KAxLI = *ma-'-la-[tum], nim-lu-ú*; cf. Adab 20 f. with variants of inscribed signs.

We can hardly expect, in one line of the lacuna, the sign KAxBALAG, because it was replaced by KAxŠID, line 98. We have discussed this sign in line 332 of Proto-Ea in MSL II, and again MSL III 199; furthermore, in discussion to S^b I 265 (MSL III), where [še-e] now can be supplied safely in (1) from Ea III 98 and Penns. CBS 11318 (see above notes to 79-93).

We now add to our discussion in MSL III 19: To a): gu-šudi and variants continue to be compounds of gù "noise" and our root; gù replaced by bu in Penns.

To b): The value $še_x$ (with variant $ši_x$) has to be established for SIG_4.

To c): Reading ara was erroneous; this will be demonstrated in a forthcoming contribution of M. Civil.

94-96. Also in Adab 9-11, but (1) and (3) broken.

98. (1) From Commentary to á-A, replaces

KAxBALAG, just discussed. Also Adab 4, but (1) and (3) broken.

99. (1) From Commentary.

100. (1) From Commentary, which devotes two lines to this entry, but all but (1) broken. For Sumerian kurku: Sjöberg AS 16, 65-70, but (4) is not reconcilable with any meaning proved by Sjöberg; *agû* "flood," *tazzimtu* "desire," *šitammuru* "self-praise."

101. (1) pu-[x] preserved in commentary. (2) inscribed sign partly preserved in C. (4) *ša tēlti* reading of KA.KA.SI.GA, cf. my contribution to the 23rd Congress of Orientalists (Proceedings 124b).

This Akkadian value *pù* was registered in von Soden, Syllabar, first edition as Number 17 beside *-bum, -pum,* and *bù* (? B.L.); by Gelb, MAD II^2, as Number 17. The u-a-i-Syllabary, RA 9 80, lists IV 2′-5 KAxGÁN-*tenû* (= pù), pa, pi, but I 9: bu, ba, [bi].

It is remarkable that this obsolete sign was still preserved (last occurrence: ḫa-pù-da CAD Ḫ 86 *ḫapūtu*), but likewise remarkable that its Sumerian existence was forgotten; otherwise, the entry *pu(-u) = KAxGÁN = *na-sa-ḫu* should be included. See, ultimately, Falkenstein, Iraq 22 146, note 8, and Römer, Königshymnen 188.

102. Graphical variant of SAGxGÁN-*tenû*, see above notes to 31-45 sub d).

105. No exact parallel, but see Diri I 52-55: [ ] = [KAxGÁN-*tenû* + ŠA] = [*te*]-*me-qu*, [*t*]*e-ni-nu, te-er-tum, zu-zi-lum,* which suggests zuzil for (1). No correspondants in Proto-diri!

109. (1) Traces of the last sign in C unmistakable. ni-ga ex nì-gu$_7$-a = *ukultu* passim; on the other hand, ni-ga ex nì-gu$_7$-a = *marû* MSL IV 13 to line 90. S^b I 256a (1) to be corrected.

113. (2) Inscribed sign in C archaic: von Soden, Syllabar^1, number 227.

113a. Commentary to á-A III 2 (BM 40705 r. 1) inserts a line: [ ] = KAxSAL = *ṣa-a-ḫu*.

114. (1) E: e-me-i[n-]; Commentary: e-mi-in-gi. (2) C and Commentary. (4) From C; Commentary: *šu-ur-pi,* both for *šurubbû*.

115. (1) E and Commentary. (2) Commentary. (3) C and Commentary.

116. (1) E and S_2.

117. (1) E, S_2, and Commentary. (2) From Commentary. (4) From Commentary: zú-guz = *gaṣāṣu ša šinni*; parallels listed CAD G 52 first section: *gu-uz* = LUM = *ga-ṣa-ṣu*. Note: Quotation from Antagal D (line 6 to 10) has to be deleted. It rests on a faulty restoration in my manuscript. The MIN in question is *kakku*.

117a. Commentary has between 117 and 118: tu-ug = KAxÚ = *ga-ṣ*[*a*]-*ṣ*[*u*]. It looks like a faulty replacement of 116, but (2)KAxÚ is attested as a variant of KAxŠE by 3N-T924h (MSL III 197).

118. (1) From E, S_2. But S_3 and Commentary: zu-ub. (2) Inscribed sign given in archaic shape by S_3 and Commentary; otherwise not preserved.

119. (1) From E, S_2, S_3. (2) Preserved in S_3.

120. (1) From E, S_2. (2) Partly preserved in E.

121. (1) From E; S_2: mur-ga. (2) Preserved in E. Parallels: K 8503 (excerpt from Ea), published CT 11 28 IV 2: [m]ur-gu$_4$ = KAxNE = *lib-ba-a-tu*; Penns. 12 (above to 78-130), 12: mu-ur-gú = KAxNE = *uz*-[*zu*]. Adab 7 with (1) and (3) broken.

122. (2) Clear in E. Parallel: LÚ-ša IV 153, represented by VAT 9558 and 10386 (without gloss):

(ni-ig-ru) KAxAD + KÙ = " (= *a-ši-pu*).

123-125. Part of the body KAxKIB in forerunners of Ḫḫ XV from Susa (quoted MSL III 199 and edited MSL IX); Kraus, TDP 24 r. 2: *ana* GIŠ.KAxKIB *ili u šarri is-su* (= *id-šu*) *ú-bal,* listed with double emendation CAD A/1 19b line 4-6.

123. No exact parallels, but the god Ir-ḫa-an-gul, one of the six sons of the god Ne-si$_4$ (Lisin), CT 24 26 116; and the river Ir-ḫa-an, Fauna 61 note 1 (last two quotations may be deleted).

125. Parallel from Proto-Ea: ga-sa = KAxKIB.

126. Parallels: Nabnitu IV 270: (i-bi-ra) KAxKIB = *dam-ka-rum*; LÚ-ša IV 263; KAxKIB (ti-bi-ri) = *tam-ka-ru*;

A = VAT 9558 (faulty): URUD.NAGAR (ti-bi-ra) = *tam-ka-*[*ru*].
B = VAT 9717: (ti-bi-ra) KAxKIB = *tam-ka-ru*.
C = VAT 10386, only part of (1) preserved, not clear.

127. Compound of zú tooth and kur$_5$; for (4) there may be considered: *baṣāru* CAD B 134; hardly *našāku,* "to bite," for which E. Gordon,

Proverbs 186, proposes reading zú-kur$_5$, whereas the traditional pronunciation is zú-kud (Ḫḫ XIV 102; CT 16 20 120, KAR 54, 5).

131f. Gap may be longer.

144a. á-A III 4, 79: pa-ar = UD = KA.KA. SI.GA (*ša tēlti*).

144b. pi-rig = UD = *nam-rum*.

147a. á-A III 4, 93: a-ra = UD = *ša* UD.DU. BU.MUŠEN (= *arabû*).

147b. *ibid.* 94: la-a = UD = *ša* UD.UD.AK. KI.URU (= *Larak*).

152a. á-A III 4, 112: gal = UD = *ša* KI.KAL (read: KI.UD) = *a-pi-ti*.

152b. *ibid.* 113: al = UD = *ša* KI.KAL (read: KI.UD) = *ka-gal-lu*.

157. All that is left of this line in A is a blank space in (1), indicating that this value consists only of one sign.

162. (1) From D; A (and á-A): ga-ru.

163. Omitted in A.

165. Omitted in A.

166. (1) From A; D: peš-peš (á-A: pi-eš-pi-eš).

167. (1) A and D; á-A: i-ti-ma.

168-185. C preserves only (4); part of (2) only in line 173.

171. (1) From D; A: u$_4$-šú (á-A not preserved, S^b: ú-šú, Proto-Ea: ú-šu (with variants)).

172. (1) From D; A: ni-ga (á-A: ni-gi-i[n]).

177. Omitted in C.

178a. Position of MIN (sign name) in D favors double entry in (4).

196. Cf. Ea VII 299 (JCS 13 130) = á-A VII 4, 136 (*ibid.* 126): šu-ku-um = LUL = *šá-a-qu* (var: *šu-ú-qu*). Not clear!

200. Short remarks about the Sumerian equivalents of *sāmu* and *barmu*:

"red" in older Sumerian is si-a, rarely SI-*gunû-a*, to be pronounced: sü (Umlaut)-a; very rare: su$_4$-a (CAD Ḫ 246); late exclusively: SI + A, where si-a or sü-a are contracted to sā (artificial value); gu-nu (gùn) is not si-gunû (entry á-A) but, in old writing, not distinguished from dar; not yet derived from sign ḪU; it is listed in Proto-Ea as line 761 (MSL III); *barmu* is old gùn-a (= gūna), but late gùn-gùn-nu. (2) Sign A written apart from SI. (3) -ú-incomplete.

237-8. We proceed according to the degree of certainty:

a) KISAL = par$_4$ is well attested as (Akkadian) *ša tēlti*: von Soden Syllabar[1], Number 149 from u-a-i-lists; also Kızılyay, Zwei Schulbücher p. 61, Nr. 82 (plate Va); MSL II 129 13 must, with von Soden, be corrected to *par$_4$-ṣum*.

b) sapar is still usually written sa-KISAL, in OB Sumerian texts, e. g., Hymn to the Hoe 77 (ed. Civil).

c) On the other hand, the difference between bàr and dag in archaic writing, as presented in Syllabar[1], Number 151, cannot be maintained; in the Gudea Cyl. A XIV 20 the reading -dag-dag is more probable; the slight difference between this passage and Cyl. B XII 21 must be considered as a free variant. Therefore, "schon im Altbab. zusammengefallen" is not valid.

d) If anything, the sign KISAL should be considered as the precursor of bàr or bara(g)$_3$. But there is no attestation, with the exception of our line 237. It is probable that par$_4$ (above a, b) and a constructed *bara(g)$_4$ are one and the same.

e) The passages bara(g) "to spread" show unanimously the sign DAG. So Proto-Ea 236 f. (with MSL III 138, Text f., later Ea IV 15 f.) and the passages adduced by Falkenstein, Gudea-Grammatik I 24, where the reading ba-ra is proved by parallels; lately Römer, Königshymnen 189.

237. (4) A; D preserves only [ ]-*ru*.

238. Missing in A.

239. (4) From A; D: [ŠU//*p*]*u-uḫ-ri*.

240-242. We assume three different archaic forms of sign É, the third almost completely preserved in D.

240. (3) From D; A: [b]i-tum.

NOTES SUR LE PANTHÉON HOURRITE DE RAS SHAMRA

E. Laroche
University of Strasbourg

Le secteur de l'orientalisme où l'activité du regretté E. A. Speiser s'est déployée avec le plus d'ampleur et de perspicacité, c'est assurément le domaine hourrite. Afin d'honorer la mémoire de l'auteur de l'*Introduction to Hurrian,* nous présenterons ici quelques observations sur les listes divines hourrites révélées par la 24ème campagne de fouilles à Ras Shamra—Ugarit; le détail technique sera publié dans les *Ugaritica,* tome V.

Il s'agit d'une demi-douzaine de tablettes en hourrite alphabétique, qui décrivent des cérémonies du culte urbain et qui énumèrent des offrandes aux dieux, dans un ordre pratiquement invariable. On possédait déjà, en langue ougaritique, des documents fragmentaires de rédaction et de destination analogues; le fait nouveau, c'est l'apparition de leur réplique en langue hourrite, c'est-à-dire dans l'idiome de l'autre composante ethnique du petit royaume syrien. Mais—et cela est significatif—les scribes utilisent à cette fin l'alphabet local, au lieu du cunéiforme syllabique international que l'on était en droit d'attendre. Ils l'ont en effet pratiqué, comme leurs voisins et contemporains hittites, pour des besoins scolaires d'érudits: témoin la grande quadrilingue S[a], et la collection, encore inédite, de recettes magiques découvertes un peu plus tôt sur le même site.

Nous laisserons donc de côté, dans le cadre du présent article, les divers schémas dans lesquels s'insèrent les listes d'offrandes, et nous nous contenterons d'extraire des six versions parallèles une sorte de panthéon canonique.[1] En regard de chaque nom alphabétique, figure la lecture syllabique procurée par les autres sources hourritisantes, essentiellement Boğazköy, puis la "traduction" du nom en termes fonctionnels. La consonne *-đ* qui s'attache à la fin de chaque théonyme est le suffixe *-da* du datif-directif, équivalent du *l-* sémitique; *-n-* = -(*n*)*ni-* est l'article. Ces notes s'adressant à l'historien des religions plus qu'au linguiste, nous avons banni délibérément toute discussion d'ordre philologique concernant la graphie, la transcription et l'interprétation phonétique de l'alphabet ougarito-hourrite.

[1] Dans ces six tablettes est compris le fragment antérieurement étudié par Virolleaud et Hrozný (*Corpus* No 172). Les trouvailles de la 24ème campagne ont l'avantage de fournir des copies en excellent état, complètes et lisibles.

1.	*enšln-d*	= *eni šalanni-da*	"dieu le *šala* (?)"
2.	*enatn-d*	= *eni atta-nni-da*	"dieu le père"
3.	*el-d*	= **Eli-da*	"El"
4.	*tšb-d*	= *Tešuba-da*	Tešub = Adad = Ba'al
5.	*šušk-d*	= *Šauška-da*	Ištar
6.	*kmrb-n-d*	= *Kumarbi-ni-da*	"le Kumarbi"
7.	*kšǧ-d*	= *Kušuḫa-da*	dieu Lune
8.	*ey-d*	= *Eya-da*	dieu Ea
9.	*aštb-d*	= *Aštabi-da*	Aštabi, dieu guerrier
10.	*enardn-d*	= *eni arde-ni-da* ?	?
11.	*enḫmn(n)-d*	= *eni ḫumunni-da*	dieu Ḫumunni ?
12.	*'nt-d*	= *'Anata-da*	déesse 'Anat
13.	*šmgn-d*	= *Šimegi-ni-da*	dieu "le Soleil"
14.	*nbdg-d*	= *Nubadiga-da*	dieu Nubadig
15.	*pžžpḫn-d*	= *Pišašapḫi-ni-da*	"le (dieu) de Piša(i)šapa"
16.	*ḫbt-d*	= *Ḫebata-da*	déesse Ḫebat
17.	*užḫṙ-d*	= *Ušḫara-da*	déesse Išḫara
18.	*aln-d*	= *Allani-da*	déesse "la Dame"
19.	*ḫdn-št ḫdlr-št*	= *Ḫudena Ḫudellurra*	déesses du destin

20.	*nnt-d klt-d*	= *Ninatta Kulitta*	Ninatta et Kulitta (servantes d'Ištar-Šauška)
21.	*dqt-d*	= *Dakita-da*	Dakiti, la "petite (?)"
22.	*adm-d kbb-d*	= *Adamma-da Kubaba-da*	Adamma et Kubaba
23.	*nwrw-n-d*	= *Nawarwi-ni-da*	la (déesse) Nawarwi
24.	*ağršḫ-n-d*	= *aḫrušḫi-ni-da*	"l'encensoir"
25.	*ḫbršḫ-n-d*	= *ḫubrušḫi-ni-da*	"la terrine"
26.	*kld-n-d*	= *keldi-ni-da*	"la santé"

Les variantes portent sur l'ordre des Nos 16 et suivants, ainsi que sur la fin. En effet, deux des tablettes ajoutent encore:

Les autres items n'apparaissent chacun que sur une seule tablette.

L'intérêt premier et immédiat de la liste sacrificielle (ci-après texte A) est de permettre une meilleure lecture et une interprétation plus correcte du document sur lequel reposaient jusqu'alors toutes nos conceptions, à savoir RS 1929, 4 (ci-après texte 166).[2] On constate, en effet, qu'à la différence de A, 166 débite *sans ordre* des litanies à divers dieux, et que ces divinités y sont parfois groupées par paires. Ainsi, 166 § IV invoque *eykžğ*, que A 7-8 résout aussitôt en *ey-kžğ* "Ea *et* Kušuḫ." Par voie de conséquence, 166 § II *elkmrb*, dont on avait tiré l'équation *El* = *Kumarbi*, devient "El *et* Kumarbi," associant les deux dieux différents de A 3 et 6 (cf. infra).

Le plan de 166 n'apparaissait pas, et pour cause, car la succession des §§ I-XVII ne répond à aucun *système* religieux connu. La place accordée à la déesse *Ḫebat*, la dernière (§ XVII), est d'autant moins admissible qu'elle fait suite au § XVI déjà conclusif: "les dieux masculins (et) les dieux féminins." En A 16, Ḫebat ouvre le cortège des déesses, comme il convient à l'épouse parèdre de Tešub.

Le principe de A est assez clair dans l'ensemble, parfois surprenant dans le détail: d'abord les dieux en ordre d'importance décroissante (1-14), ensuite les déesses (16-23), dans l'ordre même que leur imposent les listes hourro-anatoliennes. La place d'*Ištar-Šauška* parmi les dieux (N° 5) s'explique en partie parce qu'elle est la titulaire de la cérémonie, en partie par son caractère bi- ou a-sexué, en partie parce qu'elle est la soeur combattante de Tešub (N° 4). Seule la cananéenne *'Anat* se glisse en intruse parmi les dieux.

Comme en Asie Mineure, A clôt le défilé des déesses à l'aide d'objets du culte soudain divinisés; on y retrouve sans surprise, associés comme à Boğazköy, les *aḫrušḫi-ḫubrušḫi*, le *keldi* et d'autres.

Si l'on voulait pousser plus loin l'analyse, et tirer toutes les conséquences du nouvel état de choses, il faudrait, à ce point, faire intervenir trois autres éléments de comparaison (dont deux inédits):

1) d'une part, les listes parallèles de Boğazköy, c'est-à-dire les "*kalutis*" du Kizzuwatna, sous leurs diverses variantes.[3] On y décèlerait des sous-groupes tels que *Išḫara—Allani, Ḫudena—Ḫudellurra, Ninatta—Kulitta, Adamma—Kubaba*. On y constaterait un accord fondamental dans la distribution des divinités selon leur sexe, celle-là même qui commande l'agencement du sanctuaire impérial de Yazilikaya. On y pourait aussi, en contre-partie, isoler les divergences les plus frappantes: l'absence de dieux syriens en Anatolie (*El, Dadmiš, 'Anat, Dakiti*, les énigmatiques *en-šln, en-ardn* et *en-ḫmn*); l'absence de dieux anatoliens à Ugarit (*Šarrumma, Ḫisui, Ḫatni, Ciel* et *Terre, Šerri* et *Ḫurri*, etc.); le déplacement imprévu de divinités majeures, telles que *el-atn* "dieu le père," *Šimegi* le soleil, *Nubadig*.

2) d'autre part, le panthéon "sémitique" d'Ugarit sous ses deux formes, syro-cananéenne et suméro-akkadienne (ci-après P).[4] Il y aurait, là encore, matière à commentaires instructifs. En tête vient "dieu le père" (A 2), là où P 1 nomme *el-eb* = DINGIR *a-bi*. Entre *Tešub* et *Kušuḫ-Ea*, A 6 insère *Kumarbi*; P 2-4, de son côté, énumère *El—Dagan—Ba'al du Ḫazi/Ṣapôn*. Cela nous ramène à 166 §§ II-III: *El—Kumarbi—Tešub Ḫalbaḫi*, et nous invite à en conclure que *Kumarbi* = *Dagan* et que *Tešub Ḫalbaḫi* n'est pas le dieu

[2] D'après le numéro qu'il porte chez A. Herdner, *Corpus des tablettes alphabétiques*, Paris, 1963.

[3] En dernier lieu, voir le tableau synoptique dressé par H. G. Güterbock, *RHA* XIX, 68, 1961, p. 3 sqq.

[4] D'après une copie aimablement communiquée par J. Nougayrol, qui publiera et commentera ce texte dans *Ugaritica*.

d'Alep, mais celui de "Ḫalba du Ḫazi/Ṣapôn," conformément à une notice précédemment connue.[5] Que *Kumarbi* soit le *Dagan* des Hourrites rouvre tout le dossier de ce dieu: alors *Šalaš*, épouse à la fois de Dagan et de Kumarbi, reprend un sens; alors Kumarbi dieu "grain" (cf. *Dagan*) explique le dieu à l'épi de Yazilikaya, entre un Tešub et le dieu Ea; alors *Ba'al* est "fils de Dagan" comme *Tešub* est celui de Kumarbi, d'après la tradition mythologique.

L'insertion de dieux "cananéens" dans le panthéon A, celle de dieux "hourrites" dans le panthéon P, sont un signe éclatant de syncrétisme théologique et de symbiose ethnique. Du coup, l'*Iršappa* de 166 § XII se révèle comme une adaptation pure et simple du nom de *Rešef* = *Nergal* (cf. P 26).

3) enfin la Quadrilingue S[a], qui, à la fin du verso, fournit plusieurs équations suméro-akkado-hourro-cananéennes du plus haut intérêt. Par exemple, le fait que *Šimegi-ni* "le Soleil" (A 13) soit identique à *Šamaš* = *špš* (P 21) et aussi à [d]UTU et *Šapšu* (Quadrilingue) montre que les Hourrites—ou leurs théologiens—ne retiennent que le nom de la déesse syrienne; ils le traduisent dans leur langue sans genre grammatical, alors que le Šimegi = Šamaš des Hourro-Anatoliens est assimilé à *un* Soleil bien masculin, celui de Yazilikaya, de Malatya et d'ailleurs. L'équation *Enlil* = *Kumarbi* = *Ilum* de la Quadrilingue contredit celle de Kumarbi = Dagan, mais atteste une tradition différente, profondément marquée de babylonisme.

Chacun de ces faits méritera un examen approfondi. On peut déjà faire observer, en guise de conclusion, que l'apparition fortuite de la tablette 166, de loin antérieure à celle de A et P, devait dérouter les meilleurs exégètes du panthéon hourrite: exemple typique de ces malchances archéologiques qui, pour de longues années, tracent des pistes trompeuses et suscitent des spéculations mal fondées.

[5] *Corpus* No 71, 50; cf. Aistleitner, *Wörterbuch* Nr. 1031.

A CONTRIBUTION TO THE HISTORICAL GEOGRAPHY OF THE NUZI TEXTS

HILDEGARD LEWY *

HEBREW UNION COLLEGE—JEWISH INSTITUTE OF RELIGION, CINCINNATI

AMONG THE MANY THOUSANDS of cuneiform texts at present available there is no single group which is as inseparably connected with E. A. Speiser's name as are the texts from Nuzi. He was among the first to explore the site, he found the texts, he read them and he published and discussed many of them. He penetrated more deeply into the complexities of the Ḫurrian language than any scholar had done before him. Since, moreover, Speiser traveled not only in the Nuzi region itself but also in the territory east of Nuzi toward the Bazian Pass, and since his detailed description of this journey [1] contributed considerably to the knowledge of that mountainous country, it seemed appropriate to dedicate to his memory an investigation into the historical geography of the Nuzi texts. Dozens and dozens of cities and towns are mentioned, and frequently it is impossible to understand the context or to make use of the historical implications of a passage without knowing where the city or town in question was situated. An attempt will therefore be made in the following pages to establish the location of at least some of the places mentioned most frequently in the Nuzi texts.

An inscription of king Tiglat-Pileser I of Assyria published about ten years ago [2] contains a brief account of his capture of the territory between the Lesser Zâb and the River Taûk named by the ancients Radânu. In one of the versions of this text, the region is described as being comprised between [âl]*Túr-ša-an ša e-ber-ta-an* and the city of Lubdi.[3] Both of these cities are mentioned

* Deceased October 9, 1967.

[1] See AASOR VIII, 1926-27, pp. 1-41.

[2] See E. Weidner, Archiv für Orientforschung XVIII (1957-58), pp. 347 ff., text No. II, variant B of l. 37.

[3] See ibidem, pp. 350 f. with note 37.

frequently in the Nuzi texts. As both occur in contexts referring to warlike actions,[4] it is reasonable to conclude that, even as in the day of Tiglat-Pileser I, they were located near the border of the territory which, more than three hundred years prior to the great Assyrian king, depended upon the city of Nuzi as administrative capital. As regards the location of Turšan or, as it is more frequently called in the Nuzi texts, Turša,[5] the evidence provided by the Assyrian royal inscription that it was located "on the opposite bank" (*ebertan*), which obviously means on the non-Assyrian, or southern bank of the Lesser Zâb, agrees well with the evidence provided by the Nuzi texts: as was pointed out elsewhere by the present writer,[6] prisoners, or rather hostages, taken by the Assyrians in a raid on Turša were brought to Qabra. Qabra is known to have stood on the northern bank of the Lesser Zâb near the point where the highway linking Arrapḫa (modern Kerkûk) with Arbela (modern Erbîl) crossed the river.[7]

Some more precise information about the location of Turša can be derived from the text AO 10887,[8] where a piece of real estate is said to have been situated [6]*ina âl Ap-za-ḫu-ul-lu-uš-ši ina šu-pa-al* [7]*ina ḫarrâni rabîte ša âl Túr-*[*š*]*a*, "in the town of Apzaḫullušši, below (it), [7]on the highway (lit. "the great road")[9] of Turša." Combined with the evidence previously derived from Tiglat-Pileser's inscription, this passage makes it clear that Turša stood on the south bank of the Lesser Zâb at a point where a highway, named the "highway of Turša," crossed the stream. Since, according to all the evidence available, the Lesser Zâb is easily crossed only at the site of present-day Altın Köprü, "The Gold Bridge," which, in turn, is identical with the point where medieval sources locate the town of al-Qanṭarah, "The Bridge," it appears that Turša and Qabra faced each other across the river, Turša standing on the southern and Qabra on the northern side of the river crossing of Altın Köprü.

Some passages in our texts show that the territory belonging to the city of Turša extended for some length along the river bank. In the exchange document N III 281, two orchards located in Turša[10] are described as *iṣkirû* [7]*ša mârê*meš [*mWarad*]*-te-ia i-na ú-sal-li* . . . . , "the orchard [7]of the sons of [Warad]-teia (is located) in the valley," and 2 *iṣawiḫâri iṣkirâ* [13] *i-na* ***aš-ra-nu-ma*** *i-na ú-sal-li-im-ma*, "2 awiḫâri of orchard [13]in the same locality, likewise in the valley." In N V 525, in turn, it is stated (in l. 61) that a man from Turša was seized by the Assyrians *ina ú-sal-li ti-ki*, "in the valley of the river-bank."[11] A further feature of Turša to which A. L. Oppenheim called attention years ago[12] is revealed by a passage of the exchange document N III 246.[13]

---

[4] As regards Turša(n), see, e.g., the texts N V 525 and N VI 670 discussed in Orientalia 28 (1959), pp. 5 ff. With respect to Lubdi see, e.g., H XIV 174, ll. 7 ff.: *šu-un-du iṣnarkabâte*<*meš*> [8]*i-na âlLu-um-*[*ti*] [9]*ú-ri-bu* (!); H XIV 523, ll. 20 ff.: *šu-un-du narkabâte*meš [21]*i-na âlLu-ub-ti* [22]*ta-ḫa-za i-ip-pu-šu*. Besides the spellings *Lu-ub-ti* and *Lu-um-ti* there also occurs a variant *âlNu-um-ti* (H XIV 132, l. 7).

[5] By far the most frequent spelling is *Túr-ša*; see, e.g., N III 239, l. 30; N III 246, l. 5; N III 256, ll. 6 and 20; N III 272, l. 6; N III 276, l. 4. Variant spellings are *Túr-šá* (e.g., N IV 397, l. 4); *Tù-ur-ša* (e.g., N 24, l. 6); *Tù-ur-šá* (e.g., H IX 23, l. 4); *Tu-ur-ša-an* (e.g., N II 121, l. 20); *Túr-ša-an* (e.g., N 44, l. 4).

[6] For the evidence see Orientalia 28 (1959), p. 8 with note 1 and pp. 24 ff.

[7] On the location of Qabra see Die Welt des Orients II (1959), p. 441, note 3.

[8] This text which comes from the royal administrative archive frequently referred to as "archive of Teḫiptilla," was published by G. Contenau in Rev. d'Ass. 28 (1931), pp. 33 f.

[9] A highway is mentioned also in N VI 623, l. 14 (*i-na ḫarrâniⁿⁱ rabîti*).

[10] To be sure, in l. 42 the name of the town where the document was written is broken. However, the three sons of Warad-teia who were one of the contracting parties recur in the exchange document N VI 617 where it is especially stated (in l. 16) that their possessions were located in Turša. That the two contracts were written in the same city becomes apparent from the fact that they are witnessed by the same persons part of whom are said in each of the two texts to have measured the property. Hence they are local people.

[11] In the Nuzi texts the term *tikku*, which usually means "neck," is a synonym of *âḫu*, "river bank." This is shown by a group of interrelated documents comprising the texts N 36; N 56; N IV 323; N IV 351, N IV 390 and N IV 395. A piece of irrigated land which Ka(w)inni, the son of Ḫulukka, had assigned to Teḫip-tilla as his inheritance share is said in N 56, l. 6 to have been located *i-na a-aḫ a-tap-pí ša mPu-ḫi-še-en-ni*, whereas in N IV 395, l. 12 (cf. N IV 390, l. 17) its site is described as *i-na ti-ik-ki ša a-tap-pí ša mPu-ḫi-še-en-ni*. Our term, therefore, must be compared with *kišâdu* which likewise means "neck," "throat," as well as "river bank."

[12] See Rev. d'Ass. 35 (1938), p. 146, note 1. However, his interpretation was incorrect.

[13] This text was partially transliterated and translated by E. Chiera and E. A. Speiser in JAOS 47 (1927), p. 45 (ll. 10 and 16-28 were omitted).

There the site of the houses involved in the transaction is described as [7]*i-na* [8]*libbi*[bi] *âl Túr-šá-ma i-na âli ša pa-pa-nu*.[14] Papanu being an adjectival derivative of the Ḫurrian term *pap-*, "mountain,"[15] it follows from this passage that there was a "mountain-town" within the city of Turša. Accordingly, the territory of Turša appears to have stretched some five miles southward from the river bank along the highway so as to comprise the site today called Gök Tepe. The ruin mound so named rises abruptly out of the plain and is described by modern travelers as a most unusual sight.[16]

Turša was not the only town exposed to Assyrian raiders. Evidence to this effect is contained in H XVI 393 which, after some broken lines, states: "[2]Ar[ru]mpa, the servant of [ ], [3]es[caped] from Turša; [5]he entered [4]the town of Kiparrapḫi. [6]Thus (said) Ḫapurḫe: [7]'Zizza, my servant [. . . . .], [8]fle[d] from Turša; [10]he entered [9]the town of Kiparrapḫi, too.' [11]Thus (said) Turar-Tešup: [12]'Ṣilla-Kubi, my servant, [13]fled from the town of Ka<ra>na; [14]he is staying in the city of Ašš[ur]. [15]Ipšaḫalu, the servant of [16]Teḫipšarri from the town of Natmani,[17] they took from [ ]-kašše; [17]he is staying in the house of Adad-[ ] in the city of Aššur.' . . . . . . [22]Thus (said) [. . . . . .]-pali from [the town of]: 'My brother, Paitilla, [24][went] [23]without [my] (consent) [24]to the town of Natmani [25]and Aš[šur-iqi]šani [entered] the houses [26]and now . . . .'" As the town of Kiparrapḫi is known from N V 525, ll. 30, 33, and 56 and H XVI 328, l. 11 to have been in Assyrian territory not too far from the border, this passage shows that also the towns of Natmani and Kana (or Karana?) were located close enough to the Assyrian frontier to make it easy for a servant from one of these towns to slip across the border in order to gain his freedom from his master. The Assyrians, by the same token, obviously did not find it too difficult to kidnap some men from these towns and take them to Assyria.

In so far as Natmani is concerned, further evidence to the same effect comes from N V 552,[18] a text which records the purchase by Teḫiptilla's father, Puḫišenni *mâr* Turišenni, of an estate of one hundred *imêr* of land worth one shekel of gold in the town of Natmani.[19] It is significant that this purchasing contract is witnessed (l. 24) by a person bearing the Assyrian name Taribatu and being designated as *malaḫu*, "the sailor." For the presence of a sailor at Natmani makes it reasonably certain that the town was located on a navigable stream which, in view of the proximity to the Assyrian frontier, must be identified with the Lesser Zâb.[20] The land holdings of the family were, to all appearances, supplemented by subsequent purchases of adjoining land; for in N V 492, ll. 7 ff., one of Puḫišenni's great-grandsons, Wur-Tešup *mâr* Akiptašenni, speaks of *i-na dimti ša* [m]*Pu-ḫi-še-en-ni* [8]*ù i-na dimti ša* [m]*Te-ḫi-ip-til-la a-bi-ni* [9]*ša* [âl]*Túr-ša*. As the contract N III 297 mentions (in ll. 10-13) a road linking Turša and Natmani, it thus appears that the estate of the Teḫiptilla family extended along this road, on the one hand, and along the Lesser Zâb, on the other.

In fact, the family shared with the other inhabitants of the Assyrian border region the sad fate of seeing some of its members kidnapped and deported to Aššur. Evidence to this effect is provided by several texts in the possession of the Musée d'Art et d'Histoire (hereafter abbreviated as MAH) at Geneva.[21] The first of the pertinent

[14] An *âlu ša pá-pá-nu* without reference to Turša is mentioned in N VI 615, l. 9.

[15] On this term see E. A. Speiser, Introduction to Ḫurrian, AASOR XX (1940-41), p. 38, sub (e).

[16] See, for instance, Carl Ritter, Die Erdkunde von Asien, VI. 2, 3 (Berlin 1840), p. 639. A sketch of the mound was published by E. A. Speiser, p. 41 of the work quoted above, note 1. Olmstead, JAOS 37 (1917), p. 183, note 37 proposed to identify Gök Tepe with the city known from Neo-Assyrian sources as Arzuḫina or Urzuḫina and fom the Nuzi texts as Azuḫinni. For the reasons outlined below, p. 162, this identification is untenable.

[17] This Teḫipšarri was obviously identical with Teḫipšarri mâr Akiia who heads the list of witnesses of the sales contract N V 553 which, according to ll. 25 f., was written at Natmani.

[18] On this text see, e. g., H. Lewy in JAOS 59, 1939, p. 119; P. M. Purves in Am. Journal of Sem. Lang. and Lit., 57, 1940, p. 165.

[19] See l. 11. This is one of the rare instances of a town name in a Nuzi text being written without the determinative.

[20] Carl Ritter, op. cit., vol. VI, 2, 3 (Leipzig 1840), pp. 638 f. describes the valley of the Lesser Zâb as it presented itself in the early 19th century when conditions are not likely to have differed materially from those of the Nuzi period. He reports that the river was navigable by "Kelek" from Köy Sanjak down to its junction with the Tigris.

[21] The permission to study and use these texts was given to the writer in 1960 by the then curator of the collection, Dr. Edmond Sollberger. I wish to express to

documents, MAH 16026, runs as follows: *um-ma* ^{f}*Ti-i-eš-na-a-a-m*[*a*] ^{2}*mârat* ^{m}*Te-ḫi-ip-til-la* ^{3}*amtu* ^{f}*Wi-la-ri-i ù wardu*[22] ^{4} ^{m}*Ut-ḫa-ap-ta-e an-nu-*tu_4 ^{5}*ša sisê uṣ-ṣu-ri-ma ù ia-ši* ^{6}[*š*]*a* [*i*]*-din-nu ù i-na-an-na* ^{7}[*amta* ^{f}*W*]*i-la-ri-i a-na mâri-i*[*a*] ^{8}*a-na* ^{m}*Tup-ki-ia at-ta-din* ^{9}*ù warda* ^{m}*Ut-ḫa-ap-ta-e a-na* ^{10}*mârti-ia a-na* ^{f}*Ti-iš-nu-ur-ḫé* ^{11}*at-ta-din-mi mâri-ia* ^{m}*Tup-ki-ia* ^{12}*ù mârti-ia* ^{f}*Ti-iš-nu-ur-ḫé* ^{13}[*a-n*]*a qât ummi*^{meš}*-ia a-na* ^{f}[*Ḫi-in-zu*]*-ri na-ad-nu* ^{14}[*ù*] *a-na pa-ni ummi*^{meš}*-ia* ^{15} ^{f}*Ḫi-in-zu-ri i-ra-ab-bu šu-nu-ti* ^{16}[. . . . .] *a ù š*[*um*]*-ma* [. . . . .] (the lower edge is broken off) rev. ^{1*}[. . . . . . *i-r*]*a-ab-bu-ú im-ma-ti-*[*me-e*] ^{2*}[*mâri*]*-ia ù mârti-ia ir-ta-bu-ú* ^{3*}*amta Wi-il-la-ri-i* $^{4*[m]}$*Tup-ki-ia il-te-qì* ^{5*}*ù warda* ^{m}*Ut-ḫa-ap-ta-e* ^{6*} ^{f}*Ti-eš-nu-ri il-te-qì* ^{7*}*ù ši-mu ša sisê a-na* ^{f}*Ḫi-i*[*n-zu-ri* . . . .] ^{8*}*maḫar A-kap-*[*t*]*a-e mâr Ma-ṣi-ili* ^{9*}*maḫar* Gi_5*-m*[*e*]*-la-dá mâr Zu-me* ^{10*}[*maḫar* . . . .]*uz-zi* ^{11*}*maḫar Ur-ḫi-ia mâr Ú-*[*ṣ*]*u-ur-m*[*e* . . .] ^{12*}*maḫar Ki-pá-a-a mâr Ili-ab-ri* ^{13*}*maḫar A-*ka_4*-wa-til mâr Mu-uš-Te-šup* ^{14*}*maḫar Tup-pí-ia mâr Nu-ri-ia* L. E. ^{15*} ^{aban}*kunuk* ^{m}*Gimil*(Šu)-^{d}*Adad* ^{aban}*kunuk A-*ka_4*-wa-til* ^{16*} ^{aban}*kunuk Ur-ḫi-ia* Left edge [^{aban}*kunuk A*]*-kap-ta-e* $^{ab[an}$*ku*]*nuk* ^{m}*Ili-ia.* "Thus (said) Tiešnaia,[23] ^{2}the daughter of Teḫiptilla: ^{3}'The maid servant Wilarî and the male servant ^{4}Utḫaptae, the ones ^{5}who marked the horses, (it was) to me ^{6}that he gave (them). And now ^{7}[the maid-servant W]ilarî to my son, ^{8}to Tupkiia, I have given; ^{9}and the male servant Utḫaptae to ^{10}my daughter, to Tišnurḫe, ^{11}I have given; and my son, Tupkiia, ^{12}and my daughter, Tišnurḫe, ^{13}[int]o the hand of my mother, to [Ḫinzu]ri, have been given. ^{14}[And] under the supervision of my mother ^{15}Ḫinzuri they will grow up. ^{16}[. . . . .] and i[f . . . .] (edge broken) ^{1*}[. . . . they will g]row up. As soon as ^{2*}my [son] and my daughter are grown up, ^{3*}the maid-servant Wilarî ^{4*}Tupkiia will take ^{5*}and the male servant Utḫaptae ^{6*}Tiešnuri (sic) will take. ^{7*}And the price of the horses to Ḫin[zuri . . . . . .']." Ll. 8*-14*: 7 witnesses; lower edge and left edge: 5 seals and the names of their owners.

The document represents a declaration before witnesses on the part of Teḫiptilla's daughter,[24] Tiešnaia, by which she appointed her mother, Ḫinzuri, guardian of her two children. Her two servants, a man and a woman, she assigned to the two children who were to take possession of them as soon as they had reached the age of maturity. The declaration does not state why Tiešnaia did not raise the children herself and did not make use of the services of the two domestics. Yet the very fragmentary text MAH 16114 indicates that a sister of Tiešnaia named Zilimnaia did a very similar thing. She sent two men, Kiparrapḫi and Akkulinni, as messengers to her brother, Ennamati, informing him that she assigned to him all her male and female servants together with their offspring. She ended her message by stating that she assumed full responsibility for these servants in case claims should be raised against them. The explanation of this strange behavior of the two daughters of Teḫiptilla comes from the text MAH 15864 which reads as follows: *um-ma* ^{m}*Ur-ḫi-ia-ma* ^{2}*um-ma* ^{m}*It-ḫi-til-la-ma* ^{3}*um-ma* ^{m}*Ḫé-šal-la-ma* ^{4}*ù um-ma* ^{m}*Be-li-ia-ma* ^{5} ^{f}*Zi-li-im-na-a-a* ^{6}*mâr*(sic) *Te-ḫi-ip-til-la* ^{7}*iš-tu* ^{mât}*Aš-šúr* ^{8}*a-na* ^{m}*En-na-ma-ti* ^{9}*ì-iš-pur-a-ni-in-ni* ^{10}edge *um-ma šu-ú-ma-mi* rev. ^{11}[ ] *um-ma-a-mi* ^{12} ^{f}*A-ba-ba-al-ṭi* ^{13}*i-na qâti*^{ti}*-ka-mi pí-qí-is-sú-mi* ^{14}*ù a-na ḫa-ša-ar-te-en-na* ^{15}*ša me-li-is-sú-ú-mi* ^{16}*im-ma-ti-me-e a-ša-pá-ra-ak-ku* ^{17}[*še*]*-bi-i-la,* ^{18}*aban* ^{m}*Ḫé-šal-la*[25] ^{19}*aban* ^{m}*Ur-ḫi-ia.* "Thus (said) Urḫiia, ^{2}thus (said) Itḫitilla,

him my warmest thanks for his kindness and cooperation and I trust that the present authorities of the Musée d'Art et d'Histoire do not object to the use of some of their texts in the present study. [These texts have now been fully published by E. R. Lacheman, Genava 15 (1967), pp. 5-23. Ed.]

[22] It should be noted again that the local scribes of the Nuzi region still pronounced the initial w as shown by spellings such as ^{m}*Wa-ra-ad-ku-bi* N II 213, ll. 2; 18; 22; ^{âl}*Wa-ar-dì-Iš-tar-*[*we*] and the like. An Assyrian scribe, however, will write his name ^{m}*Ú-ra-aš-še-ru-a* (H XIX 53, left edge) instead of Warad-šerua and *urki šuduti* (H XIX 58, l. 14), whereas a Babylonian scribe writes *ar-*ka_4*-nu* (H V 32, l. 6).

[23] The pronunciation of this and related names such as ^{f}*Ti-iš-nu-ur-ḫé* (ll. 10 and 12 of the present text) or ^{m}*Ti-e-eš-ur-ḫé* (e. g., H XIV 92, l. 6; variant ^{m}*Ti-eš-ur-ḫé* H XIV 130, l. 7) is still uncertain. Since the name of Takku's son, the last member of the Teḫiptilla family, appears also in the variants ^{m}*Ti-a-aš-ur-ḫé* N III 310, ll. 5 f.; ^{m}*Te-eš-ur-ḫi* N V 433, l. 39; and ^{m}*Ti-iš-ur-ḫé* H XVI 109, l. 4 it is impossible to decide whether one or two vowels are intended, or whether the various spellings are meant to render a vowel which had no counterpart in Akkadian and hence no sign in cuneiform script.

[24] That she is a daughter of the prominent Nuzi personnage, Teḫiptilla *mâr* Puḫišenni and not of one of the numerous other persons bearing the name Teḫiptilla follows from the name of her mother, Ḫinzuri who is known as Teḫiptilla's spouse; see, e. g., N VI 655, ll. 5 f.: ^{f}*Ḫi-in-zu-ri aššat*^{at} ^{m}*Te-ḫi-*[*ip*]*-til-la.*

[25] The seal which is identified as Ḫešalla's is known as that of Ḫešalla *mâr* Zume; see Edith Porada, AASOR 24 (1944-45), plate 32, No. 643.

[3]thus (said) Ḫešalla, [4]and thus (said) Beliia: [5]Zilimnaia, [6]the daughter of Teḫiptilla, [9]sent me [26] [7]from Assyria [8]to Ennamati. Thus she (said): '[11][ ] thus: [12]Ababalṭi [13]has been entrusted to your hand; [14]and as a *ḫašartenna* (it is) [15]that you shall surrender her; [27] [16]as soon as I send you a message, [17]cause her to be brought there!'" It is not stated in the text in which relation Ababalṭi was to Zilimnaia; however, since in MAH 16114 the various male and female servants are not mentioned by name, it is possible that she was one of the female servants who had reached the age of maturity and was to assume the function of a *ḫašartennu*. At any rate it is learned from Zilimnaia's message why she handed over all her domestics to her brother Ennamati: she was in Aššur and obviously was not in a position to make use of her servants. Whereas Zilimnaia's messages to Ennamati leave it open whether she voluntarily deprived herself of the services of her domestics, the fact that her sister, Tiešnaia, was unable to bring up her own children makes it clear that the two sisters had been taken by force to Aššur, and, contrary to the usual practice, could not be redeemed by their families.

Whereas the question as to whether Natmani was located upstream or downstream from Turša is not directly answered by the texts at present available, the connection of Natmani with the Teḫiptilla family suggests that it was downstream, which means, fairly close to Nuzi. For as those members of the family who were public officials—notably Teḫiptilla, the *ḫalṣuḫlu*, and Tiešurḫe, the *šakin mâti* [28]—had their archives and hence probably their offices in Nuzi, easy communication between the family estate and the city of Nuzi would appear to have been a necessity. Some pertinent information can also be derived from the fact that the "road to Natmani" is repeatedly mentioned in contracts dealing with property in the town of Tentewe.[29] As all the contracts involving Tentewe were written at Turša, it is apparent that Tentewe was too small a town to have a scribe of its own; whence the parties who needed a written record had to proceed to the nearest city where the services of a scribe were available. As they proceeded to Turša, it is apparent that Tentewe was located close to Turša. On the other hand, it can be inferred from the Tentewe contracts concerning the landholdings of Itḫišta's descendants that this town was a road junction; because their fields are described not only in relation to the road to Natmani but also to the road to Bûr-Adadwe (N II 212, ll. 5-7). One must therefore look for Tentewe in the region of the modern town of Madrana, some 7½ miles as the crow flies downstream from Altın-köprü-Turša; at this point a small affluent falls into the Zâb River,[30] and a road first follows this affluent and then bifurcates, one branch running southeast toward Nuzi whereas the other one runs due east to join the highway Arrapḫa-Turša. Natmani then would have been located still further downstream, possibly near modern Melisa or at the point today called Mahud, some 25 miles, as the crow flies, from Turša. Mahud appears to be the site of an ancient town.[31]

As regards Bûr-Adadwe [32] which was linked by a road with Tentewe, it recurs in the list H XV 124 together with at least six other places of which it is said in ll. 11 f.: *an-nu-tù alâni ina nakrûti*[meš] *gab-ba*(?) *nu-a-n*[*a*](?), "these towns

---

[26] Thus under the assumption that the form intended was *išpuranni* (the masc. instead of the fem. is common in the Nuzi texts).

[27] *melissumi* seems to be intended as the imperative of *mallu'um* "to make full, to pay" (usually *malli*; see, e. g., KTS 13[a], l. 24). In the Nuzi texts *mallu'um* is not infrequently used with reference to persons; see, e. g., Gadd 22, l. 9: 5 ÌR[meš] *umalla*[meš] *la*.

[28] To all appearances he was both *šakin mâti* and *ḫazannu* of the city of Natmani.

[29] These contracts are N 68 (transliterated and translated by C. H. Gordon, Le Muséon 48, 1935, pp. 120 ff.) where Tentewe is to be restored in l. 10; N IV 415, ll. 8 and 12; N VI 603, ll. 7 and 11. All three concern the holdings of a family consisting of the brothers Šarra-šaduni, Akiia, and Ḫišmeia, the sons of Itḫišta, and Ḫišmeia's wife, Uššennaia; two further texts belonging to the records of this family are N II 101 and N II 212.

[30] See the map below (p. 161) which is based on the map 1 : 400000 issued in 1917 by the German General Staff.

[31] Thus according to a map issued in 1954 by the Directorate General of Antiquities in Baghdad; it spells the name Mahuz and dates the ruins to the Parthian period. It does not indicate, however, whether underneath the Parthian ruins remains of older occupation are traceable.

[32] The spelling of this town name [âl]*Bu-ra-dá-ad-we* which recurs in N II 212, l. 7, makes it clear that, at least in so far as the people of Nuzi are concerned, the name of the weather god was pronounced Adad; sometimes the final d was assimilated to the following consonant; see, e. g., *A-da-aš-še-ia* (N III 288, l. 3) which is the phonetic spelling of [d]IM-*še-ia* (N IV 408, l. 2; N IV 359, l. 2). As the present writer pointed out in CAH I[2], 1966, fasc. 53, p. 41, the pronunciation Adad is also traceable in Old Assyrian.

are devastated [33] by enemy action." Accordingly, Bûr-Adadwe and the other towns in its vicinity—among which we mention War(ad)-Tišpaki and Puḫišenniwe [34] *ša šupali*—were close enough to the frontier to be reached by Assyrian invaders even though, as shown by the afore-cited passage N II 212, ll. 5-7, the road from Tentewe to Bûr-Adadwe ran in a southerly direction, which means away from the Assyrian border.

The names of some further towns in the immediate vicinity of Natmani are revealed by H XVI 394 which, after two broken lines, states: "[3][x men] from [4][the town of Ta]inšuḫwe, [5][y men] from the town of Ḫalmaniwe, [6][x men] from the town of Katiriwe, [7][x_2 do]mestics from [8][the to]wn of Karanna, [9]altogether 47 persons; [10]these are men from (surrounding) towns; [11]they are staying in the city of Natmani." Among these towns, Karanna (l. 8) is most likely to be identical with the town from which, according to the afore-quoted text H XVI 393,[35] a servant with the Assyrian name Ṣilla-Kubi had fled to Aššur. Katiriwe,[36] on the other hand, is also known from the two interrelated texts N IV 326 and N IV 353 [37] to have been in the immediate vicinity of Natmani. In both records Teḫiptilla accused the neatherd of the town of Katiriwe [38] of having slaughtered cattle without the owner's permission; the defendant, on the contrary, retorts that the cattle was slaughtered not by him but by the butcher [39] of Natmani (N IV 353, ll. 7-8) who, however, denied the accusation. It is learned from this case not only that Katiriwe was close to Natmani but also that not only the Teḫiptilla family but also another one of the prominent aristocratic families of the Nuzi region had its private estate in the Natmani region. This tends to indicate that the best land available in the proximity of Nuzi was in and around Natmani, in the valley of the Lesser Zâb.

As regards Ḫalmaniwe, another one of the towns citizens of which, according to the afore-cited document H XVI 394, were staying at Natmani, it was, to judge by H XVI 237, located right in the center of the grain-producing country near Natmani. The text lists various amounts of seed grain taken by a person named Warad-Ištar (probably an official) from the grain storage (*magrattu*) of the town of Ḫalmaniwe. The proximity of Ḫalmaniwe to Natmani is further suggested by H XV 72, a list of towns from which trucks (*ereqqâtu*) had been received. Here Ḫalmaniwe is listed immediately after Natmani (ll. 6 f.).

In discussing the town of Ḫalmaniwe it is not without interest to mention that the afore-cited report of Tiglat-Pileser I [40] about his campaign against Babylonia mentions not only Turša(n) but also a city of Arman located in the same general region. In consideration of the frequent interchange between l and r in the language of the Nuzi people [41] we need not hesitate in identifying this city of Arman with Ḫalmaniwe even though the Nuzi material provides no clue to the identity of the city of Sa-lum in the surroundings of which Arman is said in Tiglat-Pileser's inscription to have been situated.[42] In referring to ^{âl}*Ar-ma-an ugar* ^{âl}*Sa-lum*, Tiglat-Pileser appears to quote from the Synchronistic History the passage describing (col. I, l. 30) the borderline between Assyria and Babylonia as established by Adad-narâri I in his peace treaty with

[33] Thus on the assumption that the verb is a II, 1 permansive of *nawâ'um*.

[34] As is well known, the Nuzi people usually named towns for their founders and first residents, in the present case Warad-Tišpak and Puḫišenni, respectively.

[35] See above, p. 152.

[36] Katiri, the founder of the town of Katiriwe, is the ancestor of one of the prominent Nuzi families. The successive generations are represented by Katiri's son, Akkuia, Akkuia's son, Zigi, and several sons of the latter; for numerous documents concerning this family see Speiser in AASOR 10, 1928-29. That it is actually the ancestor of this family for whom the town is named is indicated by N IV 326, l. 26 where Katiri's son, Akkuia, is listed as witness in the town of Katiriwe.

[37] Both texts were transliterated and translated by C. H. Gordon, Orientalia 5, 1936, pp. 326 ff.

[38] The defendant in both lawsuits is a certain Tillia *mâr* Taia; he is designated in N IV 353 as *rê alpê*^{meš} *ša* ^{m}*Teḫiptilla* and in N IV 326 as *rê alpê*^{meš} *ina âl Katiriwe*.

[39] For *urparinnu*, "butcher," see Leo Oppenheim in Revue Hittite et Asianique 26 (1937), pp. 65 f., note 13.

[40] See above, p. 150 with note 2.

[41] Many examples can be added to those given by M. Berkooz, The Nuzi Dialect of Akkadian, Language Dissertations No. 23, 1937, pp. 59 f., sub G; e. g., the very frequent name *Na-iš-gi-el-pi*, father of Piru (e. g., N I 1, ll. 25 and 29; N I 2, l. 26 and passim appears as *Na-iš-gi-ir-pi*, father of Piru in N 80, l. 12; other instances: *Ku-ur-mi-ia mâr Gi-li-ia* N V 492, l. 34 and *Ku-ul-mi-ia mâr Gilia* H XIII 6, l. 14; *E-wa-ar-ka*$_4$*-ri*, father of Uḫḫi-Tešup N IV 358, l. 31 and *E-wa-ar-ka*$_4$*-li* f. of Urḫi-Tešup H XIII 122, l. 2.

[42] H XV 18 mentions, in l. 27 a town named *ša-al-lu*; as the nature of the sibilant cannot be determined, it is uncertain whether it is the precursor of Sa-lum.

Nazimaruttaš. This frontier, running from the Tigris via Arman *ugar* Salu to the land of Lullume must have been approximately identical with the line which, in the post-Teḫiptilla period, separated Assyria from the province the administrative capital of which was the city of Nuzi.

Another town which, to judge by H XVI 394, was located close to Natmani was Tainšuḫwe.[43] This place must have been particularly exposed to enemy raiders, because in the document H XV 1 a proclamation by the king of Arrapḫa has been preserved in which he advised the city-ruler (*ḫazannu*) of Tainšuḫwe to communicate to his fellow *ḫazannu*-officials as well as to the *dimtu*-holders (*bêlê dimâti*) that they would be held responsible for any losses in human beings as well as in property caused by enemy raids.[44] This text appears to belong to one of the short periods when the Nuzi region and the Zâb Valley depended upon the small kingdom of Arrapḫa rather than upon the powerful kingdom of Ḫanigalbat.

Leaving the valley of the Lesser Zâb and proceeding in a south-easterly direction along what our texts call *ḫarrânu rabîtu ša âl Turša*,[45] one reaches the city of Arrapḫa. Whereas the identification of this city with modern Kerkuk cannot be questioned,[46] it must be emphasized that, contrary to the view expressed by some modern scholars, *âl Arrapḫi* is not the same as *âl ilâni*. Proof to this effect is now furnished by H XIV 63 which lists, in ll. 1-8, what is described in ll. 9-10 as "this is the distribution which was given to the queen of the city of Arrapḫe." The following lines (ll. 11-16) list items summarized as "this Ḫekru took for the queen of *âl ilâni*" (ll. 17-19); in ll. 20 ff., finally, the corresponding items given to the queen of Nuzi are listed. Thus there is no room for any doubt that this text lists three different distributions of grain products to the queens of three cities, *âl Arrapḫi, âl ilâni*, and *âl Nuzi*.

In attempting to locate *âl ilâni*, it must be taken into consideration that it was a twin city consisting of one part called *âl ilâni* and another one called *âl Tašeniwe*. The two towns, to all appearances, had the *êkallum*, or administration building, in common as is indicated by the numerous texts listing distributions of food for the *nîš bîti*[47] *ša âl Tašeniwe u ša âl ilâni*.[48] It is equally characteristic that some persons are described sometimes as being *ša âl ilâni* and at other times *ša âl Tašeniwe*.[49]

If one ventures an explanation of the name *âl Tašeniwe*, he will remember that a term *ta-še-e-ni-e-we* occurs in the Tušratta letter (I, ll. 91, 99) which is usually interpreted by modern scholars as "for sacrifice."[50] If this is the meaning of the city name, it is easy to understand that it was part of a complex the other part of which was *âl ilâni*, the temple city; for the latter appears to have been a community where all the sanctuaries of the gods worshipped in Arrapḫa were located.[51] As regards the location of Tašeniwe, Speiser tentatively suggested in 1938 to identify it with the site today called Tisʿîn which is located two miles north of Kerkuk.[52] Gelb, on the other hand, suggested a site named Tešʿin southwest of Kerkuk.[52a] This is probably the locality marked as

[43] The following are some variant spellings of this name: *âl Ta-in-šu-uḫ* N VI 643, l. 6; *âlTa-i-šu-uḫ-we* N I 23, ll. 5, 6, (31); *âl Ta-šu-uḫ-ḫé-w*[*e*] H XV 1, l. 1.

[44] A most unfortunate attempt at rendering parts of this text is found s. v. *ḫazannu* in CAD vol. 6, Ḫ. The transliteration is full of errors and unnecessary emendations, and the "translation" has little in common with the text.

[45] See above, p. 151.

[46] For the evidence see especially C. J. Gadd in Rev. d'Ass. 23 (1926), p. 64.

[47] *nîs bîti* is usually spelled *ni-eš* É$^{tu}_4$.

[48] See, e. g., H. XIV 617, ll. 51-54; H XVI 55, ll. 5-6; particularly characteristic is H XVI 12; it lists first a distribution to the *nîš bîti* of Nuzi, then one to those of Zizza, and then (in ll. 8-10) one to those of *âl* [*ilâni*] and *âl Tašeniwe*.

[49] The text H XIII 161 is said in ll. 50 f. to have been written *i-na âl ilâni*meš. The first witness with the rare name Nikmiia *mâr* Alkiia (see ll. 36 and 53) also heads the list of witnesses of Gadd 50 (see l. 36). Also the witness Turari who sealed H XIII 161 (see l. 52) appears as a witness in Gadd 50, l. 37. Now the first seven witnesses including Nikmiia are identified in H XIII 161, l. 43 as men from *âl ilâni* and the text is said to have been written in *âl ilâni*; Gadd 50, however, is said to have been written in *âl Tašeniwe*.

[50] See, e. g., F. Thureau-Dangin, Syria 12 (1931), p. 255.

[51] According to the present writer's collation (made in September, 1938), the text No. 309 of the collection of the Musée du Cinquantenaire in Brussels has, in l. 6, the interesting variant *âlu bît ilâni*meš. In the "copy" of this text published by L. Speleers in 1925, the line is unrecognizable. On the function of *âl ilâni* in juridical proceedings see the present writer's remarks in The Nuzian Feudal System, Orientalia 11 (1942), p. 30, note 5 from p. 29.

[52] See JAOS 58, 1938, p. 463, note 8.

[52a] See Gelb, Purves and MacRae, Nuzi Personal Names (Chicago, 1943), p. 263.

Tājiān on the afore-quoted map of the German general staff; it is situated 2½ miles SW of Kerkuk. The latter location is more likely, because, according to the evidence of our texts, the sanctuaries of *âl ilâni* served both Nuzi and Arrapḫa.

Proceeding from Arrapḫa in a southwesterly direction one reaches, after a ten-mile ride, Nuzi, the city which the kings of Ḫanigalbat chose as the administrative capital of the region. Much as the cities of Tašeniwe and *âl ilâni* were twin cities, Nuzi appears to have been one half of a metropolitan complex of two settlements. The other component was named âl Anzukallim.[53] The close link between the two cities is suggested by passages such as the short letter H XV 222 addressed by a Šurkitilla to the *^awel^ḫa-za-an-nu* ²*ša âl Nu-zi* ³*ù ša âl An-zu-ká*[*l-lim*]. This letter suggests that, at least in certain periods, the two cities had one and the same city ruler. The text H XVI 43 makes it clear (in ll. 2 f.: *še'ati*^meš^ *ti eš-še-ti ša âl Nu-zu* ³*ù ša âl An-zu-kál-lim*) that the two cities had a common grain storage facility; the text then deals with a distribution of new barley from the two cities amounting, according to l. 26, to 18 *imer* 30 *qa*. In ll. 26 f. it is added: "[Fr]om ²⁷the city of Anzukallim (came) ²⁸11 *imêr* 50 *qa* ²⁷[o]f ²⁸(this amount)."

In order to decide which of the numerous ruin mounds[54] surrounding the city of Nuzi was the site of Anzukallim it is not without importance to note that several texts dealing with real estate in Nuzi mention an *atappu*, sometimes called *atappu nirašše ša âl Anzukallim*, "the canal" or "very good[55] canal of the city of Anzukallim." There also was, as is quite natural, a "road to Anzukallim" in the city of Nuzi.[56] It may be remarked in this connection that the mention in the Nuzi texts of this and numerous other canals and natural watercourses as well as their names which praise them as givers of abundance[57] contradicts the assertion of Starr that the inhabitants of the Nuzi region did agricultural work "without artificial irrigation" and were "not dependent for moisture on the changing whims of a meandering watercourse."[58] Now the map of the German general staff actually shows a watercourse running past Nuzi and joining the Kasa Çay which, in turn, runs through Arrapḫa and thence, in a southerly direction, toward what is called today Tase Hurmatly. Yet neither one of Starr's maps shows a trace of this watercourse. Carl Ritter quotes Ker Porter as having seen this watercourse when he traveled from Tuz Hurmatly via Taûk and Taze Hurmatly to Kerkuk.[59] However, he adds that no other traveller mentions it. The explanation of this seeming contradiction is suggested by Ritter's description of the Taûk Çay as "ein wild tosender Strom" in winter; then "er wird in mehrere Canäle zur Irrigation verteilt. . . . . . Im Sommer liegt er oft ganz trocken, weil er zur Irrigation der anliegenden Aecker und Wiesen verbraucht wird." It seems therefore reasonable to assume that the "canal of Anzukallim" in Nuzi was either a branch of or identical with the watercourse shown on the map near Nuzi. If this assumption is correct, one has to look for Anzukallim upstream, or WNW from Nuzi, which means exactly in the direction in which Starr marks on his map the large ruin mound of Viran Şehir, 2½ miles from Nuzi.

One further site in the immediate vicinity of Nuzi can be identified with a good degree of certainty. In N VI 662, a field is described as follows: ⁹3 *imêr eqla i-na ú-ga₅-ar ša âl Nu-zi* . . . . . ¹¹*i-na il-ta-na-an eqlâti*^meš^ *ša âl Ar-we* . . . . . .

---

[53] In most instances this city name was written *âl An-zu-kál-lim*; in some rare cases (as, e. g., N III 233, l. 7) the spelling is *âl An-zu-ka₄-al-en*. As always in the Nuzi script, the sibilant is uncertain.

[54] See R. F. S. Starr, Nuzi, II (Cambridge, 1937), plan I and vol. I, p. XXX.

[55] Nirašše is not, of course, a personal name as assumed by some scholars (see, e. g., Akkad. Handwörterbuch, p. 86ᵇ, s. v. *atappu*) but a Ḫurrian adjective consisting of *nir-*, "good" and the augmentative ending *-aš* (for *nir-* see, e. g., E. Laroche, Rev. d'Ass. 54, 1960, p. 188; for the ending *-aš* cf. Speiser, Introduction to Hurrian, p. 132 f., sub (6)).

[56] *girru* or *ḫarrânu ša âl Anzukallim* is very frequent in the description of fields; in N II 152, l. 8 and N II 194, l. 8 it is certain that the "road to Anzukallim" was in Nuzi.

[57] Besides the *atappu nirašše* we mention the *na-aḫ-li ap-ta nu-uḫ-ši*, "the stream 'hole of abundance'" in AO 10888 (Rev. d'Ass. 28, 1931, pp. 35 and 28 f.), ll. 5-6 (it is perhaps not superfluous to mention that, in spite of the misleading title "Tablettes de Kerkouk du Musée du Louvre" not only AO 10887 referred to above, p. 151 with note 8 but also the other seven texts published together with it come from Nuzi). Cf. also N V 483 where (in l. 4) a field is said to have been located *ina šapat iarru*, being the Ḫurrian term for water which eventually passed into Akkadian; cf. col. VI, l. 46 (*ia-ar-ri ma-ar-ti*) of the Nebukadnezzar inscription VAB IV, No. 15. Cf. further the name *ra-ḫi-um* of a canal shown on H X 1.

[58] Op. cit., I, pp. XXX and XXXI.

[59] Op. cit., pp. 549 f.

[14]*it-t*[*a-d*]*in*. This implies that the environs (*ugaru*) of Nuzi were immediately north of the fields of the town of Arwe. Starr marks on his map a ruin mound named Barghût, 2 miles south of Nuzi. Both Viran Şehir and Barghût are described by him as being from the Nuzi period.[60]

Anzukallim as well as Arwe were linked by roads with the city of Zizza.[61] Since, accordingly, the traveller coming from Zizza reached Arwe before he came to Nuzi, and since, as we have seen, Arwe lay south of Nuzi, it is obvious that one must look for Zizza still further south. This conclusion is well in line with the evidence that Zizza, a city very frequently mentioned in our material, was, in the latest period attested, under siege and temporarily occupied by an enemy. H XV 40, for instance, lists numerous officers with their men who lost their horses and therefore did not go to Zizza (left edge).[62] Significant in this respect is H XV 43 which contains these lines: [11]*napḫar 38 awîlê*[meš] [12]*a-lik ṣêri* (EDIN.NA) *i-na* [13][*â*]*l Zi-iz-za* [14][*is-ru*] *šum-ma awîl nakru* [15][*i-na â*]*l Zi-iz-za* [16]*ú-ši-bu* [17][*x* +]*10 awîlê*[meš] *ša âl A-pè-na-aš* [18][*i*]*-na âl Zi-iz-za is-ru*, "[11]altogether 38 men, [12]footsoldiers, [14]were [taken prisoner] [12]in [13]Zizza [14]when the enemy [16]stayed [15][in] Zizza. [17][x +]10 men from Apenaš [18]were taken prisoner in Zizza." However, the enemy who, according to this passage, captured Zizza and imprisoned its defenders, was driven from the city. This follows in the first place from the date formula preserved in H XIV 131, ll. 9-11: *šu-un-du*$_4$ [10]*nakru*[meš] *i-na âl Zi-iz-za* [11]*aš-bu*; another date formula, this one preserved on two tablets[63] reports a royal visit to Zizza, possibly made in order to pay tribute to the defenders after the city's liberation. From the point of view of the present discussion the letter H XIV 14, to all appearances written right after the liberation of Zizza, is of special interest. It is addressed by the king to Šar-Tešup, administrator of the armor.[64] He advises the official to send messages to Zizza and Apenaš about the preparations for a festival; even though this is not stated, it is likely that the festival was to celebrate the liberation of Zizza by men from Apenaš who, as evidenced by the afore-quoted lines from H XV 43, had been active in the defense of Zizza.

Who was the enemy who attacked Zizza? Since, as we have seen before, Zizza was located south of Nuzi and since, on the other hand, it is known that in the Tiešurḫe period the relations between the Nuzi region and Assyria were cordial,[65] and since it is further known that the Babylonians eventually destroyed the city of Nuzi,[66] it is a priori likely that the enemy in this case was the Babylonian. This conclusion is well in line with two passages which, by listing Zizza together with Lubdi[67] show that it was located close to the Babylonian frontier. For Lubdi is generally assumed, on good reasons, to have stood at, or near, modern Taûk,[68] about 21 miles SE of Nuzi. A closer link than to Lubdi, however, appears to have existed between the cities of Zizza and Apenaš. This conclusion imposes itself not only because, as was seen before, the defenders of Zizza came from Apenaš but also because, in H XIII 417, a road to Apenaš within the city of Zizza is mentioned. Since, on the other hand, H I 14 mentions in ll. 5 f. a road to Apenaš in Nuzi, this city must have been located between Zizza and Nuzi, though not on a straight line. When trying to locate Apenaš it is further important to know that it served as a point of refuge and retreat for the troops who had defended Dûr-ubla when this city was attacked and, to all appearances, occupied by the Babylonians. Evidence to

[60] See op. cit., I, p. XXX. On the other hand, he mentions a ruin mound named Alwan which he defines as prehistoric. It would be very surprising if this name did not perpetuate the ancient name Arwe. Other occurrences of âl Arwe are the following: H IX 43, l. 13; H XIII 72, l. 15; H XIII 428, l. 29; H XV 72, l. 36. H XIV 171 deals with a situation in which Ḫanigalbataean war chariots were stationed at Arwe and Arnapuwe, the latter being a town which occurs also in H XV 72 together with Arwe.

[61] For the "road to Anzukallim" in Zizza see N III 244, l. 5; N III 250, l. 10; N V 439, l. 5; for the "road to Arwe" in Zizza see H XIII 363, l. 57.

[62] The comparative date of the text can be determined since Tiešurḫe is mentioned (in l. 15) as one of the officers. The action must have taken place when he was a young man, which means long before he became *šakin mâti*.

[63] H XIV 42, ll. 8-11; H XIV 53, ll. 22-25.

[64] In l. 1 of the letter here under discussion, Šar-Tešup is designated as *šatammu* (ideogr. ŠATAM, Labat, No. 355); H XV 6, obviously referring to the same person, speaks in ll. 17 f. of a *awêlša-tam sà-re-*[*e*] *ša* [m]*Ša-ar-Te-*[*šup*]. On *sariam*, "armor," see Speiser in *JAOS* 70 (1950), pp. 47 f.; cf. L. Oppenheim, *JCS* 4 (1950), p. 192.

[65] See Orientalia 28 (1959), pp. 9 ff.

[66] Ibidem, p. 22.

[67] H XIV 119, ll. 12-15; H XV 235, ll. 8-13.

[68] See J. J. Finkelstein, JCS 9 (1955), pp. 1 f.

this effect is contained in H XIV 175 (cf. H XV 264, ll. 12 f.) according to which Tiešurḫe, the *šakin mâti*, brought food to the men from Dûr-ubla then staying in Apenaš. From H XV 264 it further follows that this siege and occupation of Dûr-ubla took place at the same time when Telipirra and Irḫaḫḫe were under Babylonian siege,[69] which means toward the very end of the period covered by the Nuzi texts. Now Dûr-ubla can be located with a fair degree of precision in view of the tablet H X 1. As will be remembered, this tablet shows a map on which the points of the compass are marked; and in the NW corner of this map, the ancient scribe made a circle and inscribed it with the name Maškan-Dûr-ibla. Meek who edited and discussed this tablet which dates from the Old Akkadian period identified this site with the town of Dûr-ibla of the Nuzi period. Further information about the site can be gleaned from the fact that immediately north of Maškan-Dûr-ibla, the map shows what Meek described as "a large body of water" from which several arms of a stream emerge and unite further south. Thus one shall not fail in identifying the "large body of water" with the great swamp along the western shore of which the Kasa Çay flows southward and receives several auxiliaries from the swamp. Dûr-ubla then must be looked for south of the swamp near the point where the Matar Dere leaves the swamp and joins the Kasa Çay. Immediately west of the Kasa Çay run two roads on which, to judge by the map, numerous ancient tells are located. The road more to the west runs almost straight to the Tigris which it reaches between Tekrît and Samarra. The one further to the east follows the course of the Kasa Çay up to and beyond its junction with the Taûk River. The two roads join some 8 miles north of the swamp, and it is in this region, near the present day village of Kara Tepe, that one must look for Zizza. If the Babylonians chose either one of these two roads as invasion routes to the Nuzi region, they came first to Dûr-ubla and then to Zizza; as the men of both of these cities took refuge in, and received help from, Apenaš, this city, in turn, must have been located further north on the same road. For the location of Apenaš it is also significant that, whenever land in this community is mentioned in the texts, it is designated as "irrigated land."[70] This definitely points to a site where natural irrigation is plentiful. If it is further taken into consideration that Apenaš was located in a strategically important position because, according to H XV 32, ll. 25-28, it had a garrison of soldiers from Ḫanigalbat,[71] Taze Hurmatly or its immediate vicinity is the logical place to look for Apenaš. Taze Hurmatly is located on the east bank of the Kasa Çay and on the western bank of a smaller stream, the Ḫôr Dere. It is further situated at the junction of the highway Taûk-Kerkuk (or, in antiquity, Lubdi-Arrapḫa) with the road described previously running on the western shore of the swamp.

A further city of some importance for which one must look south of Nuzi near the Babylonian frontier was Temtena or Temtenaš.[72] A tentative conclusion as to its location can be derived from the fact that the city is frequently mentioned in the archive of the family of Gurpazaḫ, the son of Ḫilpišuḫ who bears a Kassite name as do several members of his family.[73] More positive information about the location of Temtena can be derived from the mention of a "road to Lubdi"[74] as well as of a "road to Matka"[75] in texts dealing with real estate in Temtena. For these two city names bring us in the immediate vicinity of present-day Taûk,[76] Lubdi being, as was repeatedly mentioned before close to the site of Taûk but probably located on the bank of the Taûk Su.

[69] See the present writer's remarks in Orientalia 28 (1959), pp. 21 f. and cf. H XV 279 and H XIV 238.

[70] See, e. g., N I 5, l. 5; N I 71, l. 7; N I 94, l. 6; N II 202, l. 6.

[71] On the reading and interpretation of the pertinent line see H. Lewy and M. Mayrhofer, Orientalia 34, 1965, pp. 30 f.

[72] This name must not be confused with that of the city of Tentewe discussed above, pp. 154 f.

[73] To this archive belong, inter alia, the following texts: N I 87; N II 204; N II 124; N III 255; N III 311; N III 315; N III 320; N IV, 331; N V 478; N VI 604; N VI 645. That Gurpa or Kurpa and zaḫ are Kassite name elements was pointed out by Gelb, Purves, and MacRae, Nuzi Personal Names, Chicago 1943, p. 195. Gurpazaḫ's brother was named Punniia or Punni-ḫarpa for which name see ibidem, pp. 246 f.; Gurpazaḫ's cousin, Ianzi-mašḫu, the son of Ḫilpišuḫ's brother, Aiittara, also bears a Kassite name; cf. ibidem, p. 219.

[74] See N II 204, l. 5 (on this text see Orientalia 9, 1940, pp. 362 f.); N III 255, l. 20.

[75] N I 29, ll. 8-9.

[76] As early as 1938, Leo Oppenheim (Rev. d'Ass. 35 p. 152) called attention to the proximity of Temtenaš and Lubdi.

Matka, in turn, can safely be identified with the modern town of Matika,[77] 2½ miles SSW of Taûk. It is further important to keep in mind that Temtena was located on a stream; for N III 315 describes a field in Temtena as being situated *ina šapat naḫli*. It is possibly due to this supply of water that, as suggested by N II 124, N II 204, N VI 604 and other passages, a good part of the land holdings of the Gurpazaḫ family which, as was mentioned before, were all located in Temtena, were orchards. Even in modern times, the region around Taûk produced rich vegetation before it was devastated by the Kurds. Ritter (op. cit., pp. 548 f.) quoted an early French explorer, Olivier, as describing the approaches to Taûk being planted with orchards in which date palms, lemons, and other fruit trees grew and produced fruit. Later travellers saw no more vegetation around Taûk.

In view of the wealth of this region it is not surprising that "the enemy," which means the Babylonians, undertook raids and made efforts to seize Temtena. One such attempt is alluded to in H XIV 238; this text deals with the food ration of 25 men who, coming from Nuzi, drove the enemy from Temtena, captured his war chariots and took them to Irḫaḫḫe and Telipirra.

Besides the two roads already mentioned—that to Lubdi and the one to Matka—a third one, leading to Azuḫinni ran through, or started at, Temtena. Evidence to this effect comes from H XVI 387 and the parallel text, H XVI 398, the former of which runs as follows: "^{f}Unammi, [2] ^{f}Tuppilenna, [3] ^{f}Ištar [78]-ummi, [4] ^{f}Allainaia,[79] [5] ^{f}Iamaštui, [6] ^{f}Tuwurnaia: [7]these 6 women [8]from the military district of Azuḫinni [9]with their belongings [80] [10]Ḫupita [13]caused to return [11]to the hand of [12]Akiptašenni, the governor. [14](At the time) when [81] the women [16]returned [15]from Temtena. [17]Seal of Akiptašenni, the governor." Since two texts preserved in the palace at Nuzi deal with the return of these women to their home at Azuḫinni and since the governor himself acknowledged their safe arrival by sealing the document, it is obvious that they were very important personalities.[82] As Temtena probably was not the point of departure of the six women but merely the last stop on their way back to Azuḫinni, the text makes it clear that a road ran from Temtena to Azuḫinni. Some further information with regard to this road can be derived from H XIII 36, a message sent out by Akiptašenni *mâr* Ennamati, the governor of Azuḫinni who sealed and dispatched the text H XVI 387 just discussed. H XIII 36 runs as follows: "Thus (spoke) Akiptašenni, [2]the governor, the son of Ennamati: [3]The king sent a message as follows: 'When [83] [4]they send [Ḫ]ašimaru,[84] [5][then] Akiptašenni

[77] As was intimated above, p. 158, note 60, some of the geographical names of the 15th pre-Christian century appear to have survived in the Nuzi region in spite of all the changes in the population. As Lacheman pointed out (BASOR 81, 1941, p. 12), the modern town of Tarkhelan, less than 2 miles NE of Nuzi, is likely to have preserved the name of the Ḫurrian town of Tarkulli. If this identification is correct, it should be possible to locate also the city of Ulamme not far from Nuzi; for from H XVI 397 it is learned that the *ḫalṣu* of Ulamme comprised the towns of Tarkulli and Til Duri. On the other hand, H XIV 118 would seem to suggest that Ulamme was closer to the Assyrian frontier, because the king stayed there obviously in order to receive an Assyrian visitor; cf. Orientalia 28 (1959), pp. 9 ff.

[78] Lacheman transcribes the name as ^{f}*An-nu-um-mi*; however, the parallel text, H XVI 398, gives in l. 3 this woman's name as ^{d}*Ištar-um-mi*.

[79] Lacheman transliterates ^{f}*Al-la-i-ta-a-a*; in the parallel passage H XVI 398, l. 6, he offers ^{f}*Al-la-i-na-a-a*. As this name recurs (with n) in H XIII 209, l. 15, the latter reading is more likely.

[80] The parallel passage is more explicit; it reads: [7]6 *sinnišâtu*^{meš} [*an*]-*nu*-[*tu*$_4$] [8]*ša ḫal-ṣí* [^{âl}*A-zu-ḫi-in-ni it-ti* [9]6(?) *ṣubâti-šu-nu* 5 *ḫu-bur*-[*ni-šu*]-*nu* [10][*mašaksu*]-*ḫu*-[*up*]-*ti-šu-nu* [11][*it-ti pa-ḫu-uz*]-*zi-šu-nu* [12]*ù it-ti ḫa-aš-ta-ri-šu-nu*, "[7][th]es[e] 6 women [8](are) from the military district of [Azuḫinni; with] [9]6(?) clothing-outfits of theirs, 5 foodcontain[ers of t]heirs, [10]their [s]hoes, [11]with their [*paḫuz*]*zi* [12]and with their sandals(?) . . . ."

[81] *šum-ma* is not infrequently used in the Nuzi texts in the sense of "at the time when;" see, e. g., H XIII 63, ll. 5 and 13; H XV 43, l. 14; H XV 84, l. 8, etc.

[82] The function of the women is perhaps somewhat elucidated by H XV 120 which lists first one woman belonging to Akiptašenni, obviously the governor, and a second one belonging to the *êntu*-priestess (NIN.DINGIR.RA) of Azuḫinni. Accordingly, the city must have been a cult center of some importance if it had a priestess of this rank. If the women were priestesses, they may well have been taken to some out-of-town place in order to officiate at a festival as did the priestesses of Apenaš according to the afore-quoted text H XIV 14 (see above, p. 158; NIN.MEŠ in l. 10 of this text is obviously an error for NIN.DINGIR.RA.MEŠ; for it is known from H XV 120, rev., l. 7 that Apenaš had an *êntu*-priestess).

[83] See above, note 81.

[84] The name Ḫašimaru recalls, of course, the name of mount Ḫašimur which, as Weidner pointed out (AfO 9, 1933-34, p. 97), designates a mountain in the chain today called Ḥamrîn. Hence it is obvious that Ḫašimaru

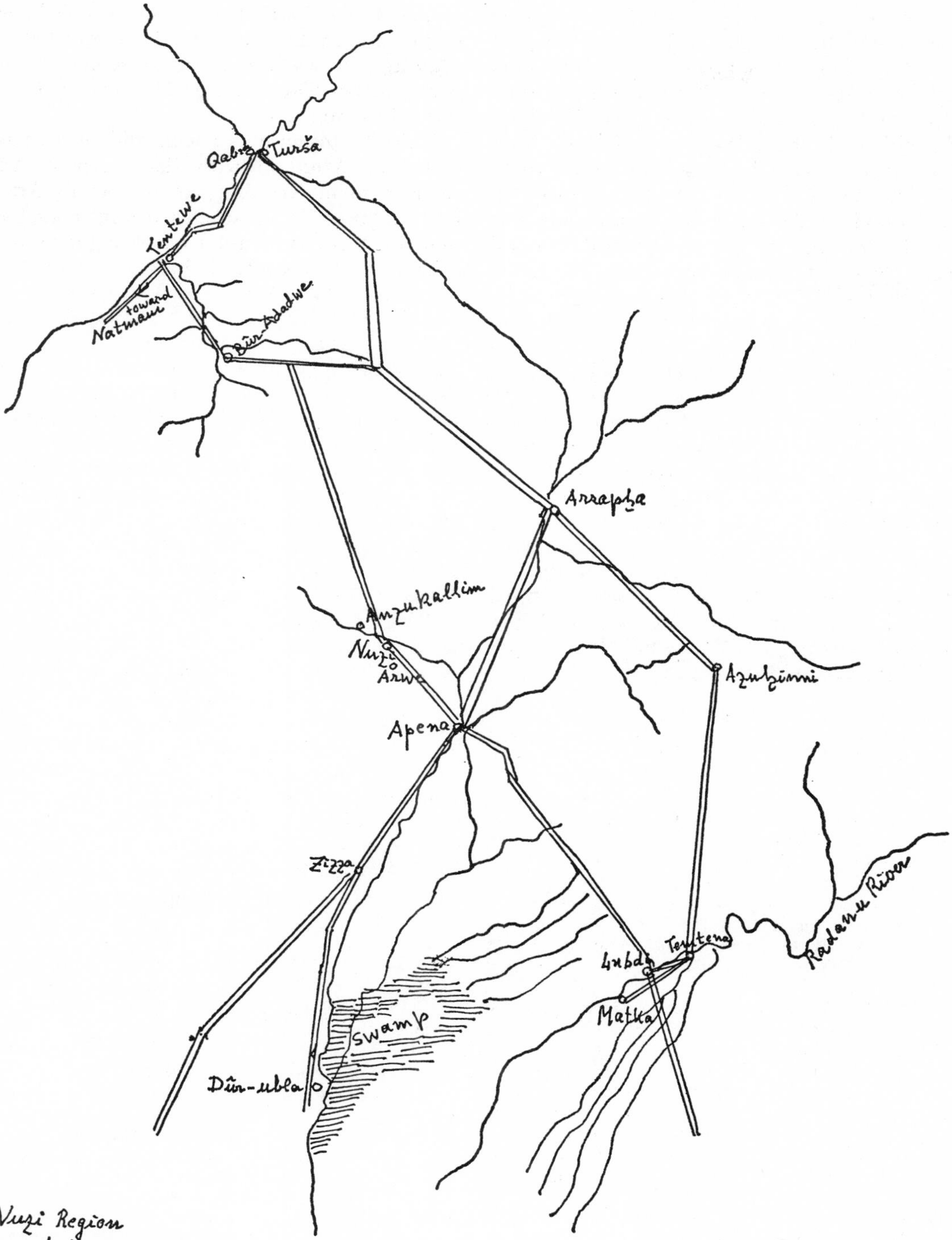

Nuzi Region
1:400000

[6]shall give (him) [5]into [6][the han]ds of 3 men and [7]they will bring (him) [t]o the country of Nullu; [8]they will watch (him) and return him. [9]When they bring (him) up,[85] these 3 men [11]shall stay [10]in Azuḫinni [11]and 3 (other) men [12]Akiptašenni [14]will send [13]with Ḫašimaru. But if [17]they kill [15]Ḫašimaru [17](or) he flees [15]within the country of [Kuššu]ḫe[86] (or) [16]in the country of Nullu, [20]he (i. e., the king) will not in any way send [18]Akiptašenni [19]to the river ordeal [21]or kill (him).' [22]Seal of Akiptašenni, [23]son of Ennamati." Ḫašimaru was, to all appearances, a diplomatic envoy who travelled to Nullu via Azuḫinni. As he came from Babylonia,[87] he travelled via Temtena to Azuḫinni on the same road on which the six women dealt with in the texts H XVI 387 and H XVI 398 returned to their home. Yet as we learn from H XIII 36 that this road continued beyond Azuḫinni to the country of Nullu, we are in a position to define the location of Azuḫinni, a provincial capital which played a considerable rôle at the time covered by the Nuzi material as well as in the Neo-Assyrian period. Nullu, the country called in the Neo-Assyrian sources either Lullu or Zamua, is the region east of the Bazian Pass. Since accordingly Azuḫinni lay on the road leading from the region of Taûk-Lubdi

is a name derived from a geographical name as were Dûr-ubli (H XIX 85, l. 35), Arrapḫari, Arzizza, and others.

[85] Which means, when they return him from Nullu to Azuḫinni.

[86] Lacheman restores Arrapḫe. However, this restoration is untenable, in the first place because the spelling of the latter name with *ḫé* instead of *ḫi* is very rare, whereas it is the usual spelling in the name Kušuḫḫe. In the second place, and this is more important, the context requires a foreign country in which, even as in Nullu, Akiptašenni, the governor of Azuḫinni, could not guarantee the safety of Ḫašimaru. In his own province, he was of course responsible for whatever happened to Ḫašimaru; and in an adjoining province of Ḫanigalbataean territory he could, and was expected to, make arrangements to protect the travelers.

[87] Mount Ḫašimur for which he was named (see above, note 84) was, of course, located in Kassite territory. As the present writer pointed out in Orientalia 28 (1959), pp. 8-15, the Assyrian envoy who came to Nuzi territory in order to establish friendly diplomatic relations between Assyria and Ḫanigalbat was the governor of the Assyrian province north of the Lesser Zâb. To judge by the name Ḫašimaru, the Babylonians adhered to a similar practice, sending a man from a near-by province as envoy to Nullu.

to the Bazian Pass, it obviously occupied the site of present-day Leilan from where, still today, one road leads to the Bazian Pass, a second one southward toward Taûk and a third one NW toward Kerkuk-Arrapḫa.

This conclusion does not invalidate the identification of Azuḫinni with the provincial capital referred to in Neo-Assyrian sources as Arzuḫina or Urzuḫina. To be sure, as was intimated above, note 16, this city is usually looked for by modern authors at or near Kerkuk,[88] merely on the evidence that the Assyrians had to cross the Lesser Zâb in order to reach it. Yet a Neo-Assyrian letter published in 1958[89] makes it clear that the southern boundary of the province of Urzuḫina was the Radanu, which is, in present-day terminology, the Taûk Çay. This makes, of course, good sense for the province centering around Leilan. It may be added that this result agrees well with the route through Arzuḫina outlined in the Neo-Assyrian text K. 4675 (= ADD II, No. 1096). The traveler who kept this record proceeded in one day from ${}^{\text{âl}}$*Ba-kar-ri* (l. 1) via ${}^{\text{âl}}$*Sa-re-e* (ll. 1^{b}-2) and ${}^{\text{âl}}$*Ár-zu-ḫi-na* (ll. 2^{b}-3) to Tell *Ár-zu-ḫi-na* (l. 3^{b}). On the next day, he travelled to Dûr-Atanate (l. 5).[90] From there he reached Dûr Talite in one day and the Bazian Pass after another short march. In other words, as Arzuḫina and Tell Arzuḫina can be assumed to have been located at a short distance from one another,[91] the region of Arzuḫina was situated slightly more than two travel-days from the Bazian Pass. The distance from Leilan to the Bazian Pass is $32\frac{1}{3}$ miles as the crow flies, which means actually slightly more than two day-marches, the average traveler covering approximately 15 miles in a day.[92]

[88] See, e. g., E. F. Weidner, AfO 21 (1966), p. 42b.

[89] See H. W. F. Saggs, Iraq 20, 1958, No. XLI (pl. XXXVIII and pp. 187 ff.; cf. Saggs' remarks ibidem, p. 209.

[90] On the reading of this name see Speiser, p. 16, note 25 of the study quoted above, note 1.

[91] Probably Arzuḫina was, at some time in its history, destroyed either by an enemy or by a natural catastrophe such as a conflagration and was then reconstructed not exactly on the same but on a near-by site.

[92] As regards *âl Sa-re-e* from where the traveler of K. 4675 proceeded to Arzuḫina, it occurs as *âl Sa-a-ra* in H XIII 428, l. 36; however, no conclusion as to its location can be reached from this occurrence except that it was located south of Arrapḫa.

KING LISTS OF THE OLD BABYLONIAN PERIOD AND BIBLICAL GENEALOGIES

ABRAHAM MALAMAT

THE HEBREW UNIVERSITY, JERUSALEM

BIBLICAL GENEALOGIES—especially the ethnographic tables in Genesis and the tribal genealogies assembled mainly in the first nine chapters of 1 Chronicles—represent a unique historiographical genre within the literature of the ancient Near East.[1] Only at the start of the Islamic period did Arab chronographers create such broad genealogical tables, encompassing northern and southern Arabian tribes, dwarfing in extent even their biblical archetypes.[2]

An extraordinary document containing the full genealogy of the Hammurapi dynasty (henceforth GHD), recently published by J. J. Finkelstein,[3] prompts a reassessment in this field. The Old Babylonian king list, together with the upper part of the Assyrian King List (henceforth AKL),[4] now provides further insights into the essence and structure of biblical genealogies. Moreover, examination of lineage systems among present-day primitive tribal societies, which have been the subject of intense anthropological study in recent years, may give a clearer picture of genealogical patterns in the ancient Near East, in spite of the different historical and sociological contexts, and especially as those societies are of an entirely illiterate nature.[5]

We should note, *a priori*, the parallel and the divergent features in the genealogical schemes of the Bible and the Mesopotamian king lists, for they define the possibilities of comparative discussion. Whereas the king lists are of an obvious vertical construction, biblical genealogies are spread out on a horizontal plane as well, exemplified for instance by the twelve tribes stemming from Jacob. Only the latter, a two-dimensional pattern, can form a true family tree, revealing a genealogical panorama of a single tribe or of an entire group of peoples. The Bible, followed by the Arabian genealogists, often resorts to accomodating female elements, wives or concubines, mothers or daughters, elements which naturally have no place in strictly vertical lineages of societies basing on agnatic descent.

[1] On genealogies in the Bible in general, see the biblical dictionaries s. v.: e. g., *The Interpreter's Dictionary of the Bible* II, 1962, pp. 362 ff. (R. A. Bowman); *Encyclopaedia Biblica* III, 1958, cols. 663 ff. (Y. Liver; in Hebrew), with bibliographical references there. For the various interpretations of Israelite tribal genealogies, see W. Duffy, *The Tribal-Historical Theory on the Origin of the Hebrew People,* 1944. Cf. also L. Ramlot, Les généalogies bibliques, *Bible et Vie chrétienne* 60 (1964), pp. 53 ff.

[2] The basic treatment of these genealogies in relation with their biblical antecedents is still W. Robertson Smith, *Kinship and Marriage in Early Arabia*², 1903. Cf. also the most recent studies on Arabian genealogies: J. Obermann, "Early Islam," in *The Idea of History in the Ancient Near East,* 1955, especially pp. 242 ff. and 290 ff.; W. Caskel, Die Bedeutung der Beduinen in der Geschichte der Araber, *Arbeitsgemeinschaft für Forschung des Landes Nordrhein-Westfalen,* Heft 8, 1953; idem, *Ǧamharat an-nasab—Das genealogische Werk des Hišām ibn Muḥammad al-Kalbi* I-II, 1966.

[3] The Genealogy of the Hammurapi Dynasty, *JCS* 20 (1966), pp. 95-118 (hereinafter cited by page number only); for specific points see also the bibliographical references there.

[4] The first real comprehension of the upper portion of AKL was achieved by B. Landsberger, Assyrische Königsliste und "Dunkles Zeitalter," *JCS* 8 (1954), pp. 33 ff. and 109 ff. (hereinafter cited only by page number); for two subsequent comprehensive investigations, cf. F. R. Kraus, Könige, die in Zelten wohnten, *Mededelingen der koninklijke Nederlandse Akademie van Wetenschappen* (Afd. Letterkunde, N. R. 28, No. 2), 1965; H. Lewy, Assyria (2600-1816 *B. C.*), CAH I, Ch. XXV (rev. ed.), 1966, pp. 17 ff. For the two full copies of AKL extant, cf. I. J. Gelb, *JNES* 12 (1954), pp. 209 ff.

[5] However, a conclusive study of this facet must be left to a combined effort with modern anthropology, for within the present discussion only casual steps have been taken in this direction. Illuminating comparative material may be gleaned from investigations of, for instance, African peoples; cf., *inter alia,* E. E. Evans-Pritchard, *The Nuer,* 1940 (especially Ch. V); M. Fortes, *The Web of Kinship among the Tallensi,* 1949 (Chs. I and II); I. Cunnison, *The Luapula Peoples of Northern Rhodesia,* 1959 (Ch. IV). Cf. also L. Bohanan, A Genealogical Charter, *Africa* 22 (1952), pp. 301 ff.; and E. Peters, The Proliferation of Lineage Segments in Cyrenaica, *Journ. Royal Anthr. Inst.* 90 (1960), pp. 29 ff.

Vertical, one-dimensional patterns record only "genealogical depth" and sequence of generations, while the two-dimensional pattern forms points of segmentation; that is, it encompasses nodal eponyms from which stem several descendants who in turn may act as founding ancestors of peoples, tribes and clans, such as Terah, Abraham, Isaac, Jacob, and his twelve sons, in the Bible. This segmentation, with its wide range of primary and secondary lineages, is the foremost concept in the genealogical positioning of the individual and in the ascertaining of kinship, whether on a broad ethnographic plane or within a more restricted tribal circle. Hence, the king lists are particularly relevant to the study of only the vertical genealogies in the Bible. However, superimposition of the two diverging Mesopotamian lineages, Babylonian and Assyrian, renders a somewhat two-dimensional picture, thus enabling us to approach the other genealogical patterns as well.

It is now evident that the vertical genealogical compositions in the Bible stem from archetypes current among West Semitic tribes from the Old Babylonian period (and possibly earlier), antedating those of the Bible by hundreds of years. The Babylonian king list under discussion dates to the reign of Ammiṣaduqa (1646-1626 B. C., according to the middle chronology used in the present paper), the penultimate ruler of the Hammurapi dynasty. But Landsberger (pp. 109 ff.) has convincingly shown that even the upper part of AKL, preserved only in the final redaction of the list as a whole, is the work of scribes of the Old Babylonian period, more precisely of the West Semitic dynasty of Shamshi-Adad, an older contemporary of Hammurapi. Moreover, these royal genealogies were composed in a technique similar to that known in the Bible, of fictitiously linking historical personages to earlier eponyms in fact representing names of an artificial character, such as tribes or geographical entities—as demonstrated by Finkelstein concerning GHD, and Kraus for AKL.

What is more, comparison of the Babylonian and Assyrian king lists, headed by essentially identical putative eponyms, indicates a common genealogical tradition, whether historically based or of mere scribal deduction—one most likely shared by early West Semitic tribes in general. A similar consciousness of common ancestors is evident in the genealogical tables of Genesis, many of the peoples living along-side Israel being assigned within the same family tree as Israel itself. The external evidence now lends support to the assumption that the genealogical traditions contained in Genesis reflect beliefs actually current among these peoples, notions which consciously upheld their common ancestry and not the products of fancy or the pride of Israelite scribes. The self-centered Israelite approach is apparent only in its tendency to place the Israelite line at the center of the family tree, whereas the other peoples derive from it as secondary branches. (The Table of Nations in Genesis 10, which does not include Israel at all, is a matter for separate consideration.)

The upper part of AKL is divided into three sections, the first two of which will concern us in the present paper. At the start, seventeen names are given with the concluding formula "total of 17 kings who dwell in tents," followed by ten names summarized by the phrase "total of 10 kings who are ancestors." As Landsberger has proved (pp. 33 f.), this latter group is to be regarded as the "Ahnentafel" of king Shamshi-Adad. In contrast, GHD lists the generations in an uninterrupted line; at the end of the list of fictitious and historical kings, however, three *palû*'s (i. e. "eras" or "dynasties") are given by name (in historical sequence, reading): the *palû* of the Gutians, the *p.* of the Haneans, and the *p.* of the Amorites—to which all the generations listed are to be distributed, as demonstrated by Finkelstein (pp. 103-113).

Yet, to arrive at the very nature of these genealogies and to derive the most instructive lesson for the parallel biblical patterns as well, a structural analysis is called for, comparing the two king lists, Babylonian and Assyrian. Such analysis reveals four successive groups, distinct in their historiographical character and functional aim, which we may here term: (a) the genealogical stock, i. e. the common antecedent generations; (b) the determinative line, i. e. the specific descent of a people or dynasty; (c) the table of ancestors, the actual pedigree of (d) a concrete historical line or dynasty. These, in principle, accord with the structure of the biblical genealogies, yet such segments are not formed into a single continuous line, but are scattered in the Bible.

The genealogical stock

Group (*a*) includes the names at the top of the two royal lists which derive from a common basis, as Finkelstein has attempted to demonstrate. The two texts differ in order of names and in several major or minor textual variants, which are, in part, the result of faulty transmission. Moreover, the cumbersome names of the first three lines of GHD prove each to be compounded forms of two originally separate names corresponding to pairs of names in AKL. Accepting Finkelstein's analysis, the first nine to eleven names are common to both lists.[6] This is the genealogical depth of many lineages in ancient times, even as in some modern tribal societies.[7]

This genealogical stock is an apparently artificial composition of personal names (such as Adamu) and appellatives or even tribal names (the most obvious examples are Ḫanū/Ḫeana and Dit/dānu) and toponyms (such as possibly Madara and Namzū), presented as putative eponyms. Most have definite affinities, whether ethnic or geographical, or even linguistic (especially the GHD forms), with the West Semitic peoples. Such lists may have been transmitted orally among these tribes as mnemotechnic accounts, such as parallelled in modern tribal genealogies; they could even have been some sort of desert chant, as suggested by Finkelstein concerning the first six names (p. 112). The fictitious stock could have easily been absorbed into the general genealogical scheme, mainly because of the fluidity in usage of personal names, tribal names and toponyms, a universal phenomenon especially frequent among West Semitic peoples in the Old Babylonian period.[8] In order to lend an authentic ring to this putative list, it was built around approximately ten generations, as a sort of retrojection of the optimal ten-generation pattern of real lineages, as found in the " Ahnentafeln " of the Babylonian and Assyrian kings, appearing later in both AKL and GHD (see group [c], below).

The character and make-up of this group immediately brings to mind the scheme of the Hebrew line (*tōlᵉdōt*) from Shem to Terah or Abraham (Gen. 11:10-26), surely to be regarded as the genealogical stock of the people of Israel, which was held in common with several other related peoples. Quite a separate matter is the genealogy from Adam to Noah (Gen. 5), comprising the universal ancestors of the antediluvian generations, beyond the realm of actual history. The compiler of GHD was also aware of an earlier era (*palū*), but he saw no need to enter its generations into his list (cf. line 32), they being of no relevance for the historical reality of the West Semitic tribes. Interestingly enough, the biblical name of the progenitor of mankind, Adam, is parallelled by the second name in AKL,[9] and possibly the fourth in GHD. This name may have actually been borrowed from early West Semitic genealogical concepts and applied in the Bible at the beginning of the primordial line, out of etymological considerations; for in Hebrew *'ādām* is also the generic term for "man," there being a play on the word *'ᵃdāmā* "ground" in Gen. 2:7—"And the Lord God formed man (*'ādām*) of the dust of the ground (*'ᵃdāmā*)." The ante- and postdiluvian lines (i.e. Adam and of Shem, respectively), symmetrically arranged to a ten-generation depth, are undoubtedly the product of intentional harmonization and in imitation of the concrete genealogical model (cf. Mishnah Aboth 5:2).

Though according to the Massoretic version the line from Shem to Abraham embraces ten generations, there are various indications of pos-

---

[6] In AKL, the problematic entries are Emṣu and ḪARṣu (Nos. 7-8) which seem to be variants of a single name corresponding to Namz/ṣū of GHD (No. 8); and Zu'abu and Nuabu (Nos. 11-12), which may or may not be equated with Zummabu and Namḫū of GHD (Nos. 10-11) (see Finkelstein, pp. 98-99). As the last equation (Nuabu-Namḫū) seems especially doubtful, the latter names are possibly to be ascribed to group (b), and would then reveal a standardized pattern of ten generations in the genealogical stock (see below).

[7] For a 10-generation depth among the Bedouin east of Damascus, cf. Caskel, *Die Bedeutung* . . . (above, n. 2), p. 7; for a constant 11 generations among the Bedouin of Cyrenaica (though their history may be traced as far back as the 11th century A.D.), cf. M. Gluckman, *Politics, Law and Ritual in Tribal Society*, 1965, p. 272 (citing Peters, *op. cit.* [above, n. 5]), and pp. 271-275 for African (quoting several works mentioned above, n. 5) and other tribal lineages of 10- to 12-generation depth.

[8] J. R. Kupper. *Les nomades en Mésopotamie au temps des rois de Mari*, 1957, pp. 215 ff., gives several examples including Numḫā (compare Namḫū, GHD No. 11), a West Semitic tribal and geographical name, as well as an element in personal names.

[9] As alluded to by A. Poebel in the initial treatment of AKL: *JNES* 1 (1942), p. 253. For the personal name Adamu in the Old Akkadian period, see I. J. Gelb, *Glossary of Old Akkadian*, 1957, p. 19, and in the Old Babylonian period, C. J. Gadd, *Iraq* 4 (1937), p. 35.

sible minor fluctuations in the original scheme of this group.[10] On the one hand, Shem or Abraham, or possibly both, were not initially included within the genealogical stock. The former may have been appended as a heading to join the Hebrew line to the Table of Nations and the primordial accounts in Genesis, Arpachshad having originally headed the list. We may also assume that the list in fact concluded with Terah, to whom the Bible ascribes a line (*tōlᵉdōt*) of his own (Gen. 11:27), whereas his three sons, Abraham, Nahor, and Haran, the father of Lot, were conceived of as the founding ancestors of individual lineages. On the other hand, the Septuagint (cf. also Luke 3:35) inserts an additional link between Arpachshad and Shelah—Kenan, a tradition also reflected in the Table of Nations in the Book of Jubilees (8:1 ff.).

Moreover, the name Arpachshad is linguistically and ethnographically puzzling, and differs from the other names in Shem's line, which are short and comprised of a single name element. We most likely have here a fused form of two names, just as with the initial entries in GHD, the parallel becoming even more obvious if we assume that Arpachshad once stood at the head of the line. Indeed, already in ancient times (cf. Jubilees 9:4; Josephus, *Antiquities* I, 6:4) there was a tendency, shared by modern exegetes, to identify the second element in Arpachshad with Chesed, the Chaldeans.

Like its Mesopotamian archetype, the line of Shem also contains a mixture of appellatives, tribal names, and toponyms, all in the guise of patriarchal eponyms. Among the appellatives we may include Shem, for its meaning in Hebrew, as in the Akkadian cognate, is simply "name," or "reputation," "posterity."[11] Most likely appellative, too, is Peleg, "a division," at least on the basis of the etymology given in the Bible—"for in his days was the earth divided (*niphlᵉgā*)" (Gen. 10:25), though there has been an attempt to relate the name with *Phalga* on the middle Euphrates, a place name known from Hellenistic times. The outstanding tribal name is Eber, a personification derived from the gentilicon *'ibrī*, "Hebrew" (see below, n. 14), and surely not the other way around. Another possible tribal name is Reu, a compound form of which, Reuel, constitutes a sub-tribe in the genealogy of Edom (Gen. 36 passim), as well as of Midian (Num. 10:29; LXX Gen. 25:3).[12]

The three last links in the line of Shem—Serug, Nahor and Terah—stand out as topographical entries, all three signifying locations in the Balikh region and attested in neo-Assyrian documents as Sarūgi, Til-Naḫiri, and Til-(ša)-Turaḫi.[13] Only the city Nahor/Naḫur was known as an important political center already in the 19th-18th centuries B.C. in texts from Cappadocia, Chagar Bazar and, above all, in the Mari documents, where it appears as a focal point of West Semitic tribes, as well. The proximity of the three sites to Haran associates these eponyms with the ancestral home, according to biblical tradition, of the Hebrews; this is the special significance of their insertion within the genealogical stock.

As with the Mesopotamian parallel, here too, putative compilation was facilitated by onomastic and toponymic affiliation; that is, identity of personal, clan or tribal names, and of geographic locations, a phenomenon common enough in the Bible, as well. Thus, the name Eber, which in the Israelite mind had a geographic connotation associated with *'ēḇer hannāhār*, "beyond the river," where "in days of old your fathers lived" (Josh. 24:2), is found in the Bible also as a clan or personal name (Neh. 12:20; 1 Chron. 5:13; 8:12, 22). Again, Nahor serves both as the eponym of the Nahorites (Gen. 22:20-24), and as the name of the "city of Nahor" (Gen. 24:10). Moreover, this phenomenon is clearly dis-

[10] For particulars on this line, which is attributed to the P source, like most of the Pentateuchal genealogical records, cf. the commentaries, especially O. Procksch, *Die Genesis*[2-3], 1924, pp. 492 ff.; B. Jacob, *Genesis*, 1934, pp. 304 ff.; and U. Cassuto, *From Noah to Abraham*, (English ed.), 1964, pp. 250 ff.

[11] The suggested derivation of Shem from Shumer (with the final syllable silent), reintroduced by S. N. Kramer, *Studia Biblica et Orientalia* III (Analecta Biblica 12), 1959, pp. 203 f., does not seem plausible.

[12] In the latter connection, W. F. Albright, *CBQ* 25 (1963), pp. 5 f., has shown that Reuel is the Midianite clan-name of Hobab, and not the name of his actual father.

[13] Cf., in addition to the commentaries mentioned in n. 10 above, W. F. Albright, *From Stone Age to Christianity*[2], 1957, pp. 236 f., and R. de Vaux, *RB* 55 (1948), pp. 323 f. On Nahor, in the cuneiform sources as well as in the Bible, see A. Malamat, *Encyclopaedia Biblica* V, s.v. cols. 805 ff. (Hebrew). The component *Til-* in these and other place-names of the Neo-Assyrian period, may be an Aramean-Assyrian appendage to older names of sites which had been re-established in this period.

played in the account of the genealogy of Cain, relating of the founding of the first city, that Cain "called . . . after the name of his son, Enoch" (Gen. 4:17). But Enoch is also the name of a clan in the tribe of Midian (Gen. 25:4), as well as in the tribe of Reuben (Gen. 46:9). The same is true in many other instances, such as the name Dan, which is eponymic, tribal and topographic, in the last instance applied to the town of Laish after its conquest by the Danites: "And they called the name of their city Dan after the name of Dan their father, who was born unto Israel" (Judg. 18:29).

However, comparison of the Mesopotamian and the biblical genealogical stocks is of special interest concerning the respective eponyms Ḫanū and Eber, both representing actual historic entities well-known even to the later redactors of the lists. The insertion of these eponyms among the antecedent generations undoubtedly represents a prevailing attitude on the antiquity of these tribes, as GHD actually indicates in ranking "the *palū* of the Haneans" earlier than "the *p.* of the Amorites," and implies an awareness of putative relation with subsequent entries. However, this latter does not necessarily have bearing on true ethnic kinship of subsequent generations, as GHD may serve to show. Whereas the Shamshi-Adad dynasty of Assyria in effect likely stemmed from the Hanean tribal association, this does not hold for the Babylonian dynasty, which was closely related with the Amnānu and Yaḫruru tribes, as indicated in its determinative line in GHD (group [b]) and various other sources. Yet, these latter tribes, as is evidenced in the Mari documents, were part of a tribal association other than the Haneans: their oftimes rivals, the Yaminites (see below note 17).

Thus, the mention of the eponym Ḫeana (Ḫanū) in the lineage of the kings of Babylon conflicts with actual ethno-historic reality. But the compilers of GHD took no objection to this obvious discrepancy, indicating the actual contrast only by accomodating the determinative Babylonian line (group [b]) within the *palū* of the Amorites, as against the *palū* of the Haneans, which embraces the latter part of the genealogical stock (group [a]), from Ḫeana on.

The above conclusions are instructive concerning the relation between the eponym Eber and the concept "Hebrew." Eber, too, may have in reality been linked with only this branch or that, and did not necessarily envelop *all* the generations following it. Indeed, the empiric use of the term "Hebrew" (which occurs some thirty times in the Bible) is of a definite ethnic nature, applying only to the people of Israel, as has rightly been noted by several scholars dealing with this problem.[14] Moreover, as widely recognized, this term is specifically used to denote the Israelites as such in their confrontation with other peoples (thus against the Egyptians, Philistines and Canaanites). Hence, anyone assuming that the biblical term "Hebrew" embraces a circle wider than the Israelites alone, a view based mainly on the appearance of the eponym Eber six generations prior to Abraham, must bear the *onus probandi.*

The other descendants of Eber, such as the Nahorites or even the "sons" of Lot, were not necessarily considered as actual Hebrews, whether by self-definition or otherwise. The direct grafting to Eber of far-away tribes of the South Arabian region, represented by Joktan and his descendants in the Table of Nations (Gen. 10:25 ff.), is elusive. The only eponym expressly bearing the designation "Hebrew" is Abraham. Much has been speculated regarding the precise meaning of the phrase "Abram the Hebrew" (Gen. 14:13), but even with all the shades of meaning attributed to this phrase,[15] its major intent is obviously to single out Abraham as the founder of the determinative line (group [b]) of the Israelite genealogy. There is no indication that any other people related to Abraham but not of the direct Israelite line was "Hebrew" (i.e. the "sons" of Keturah, the Ishmaelites and the Edomites).

---

[14] Among others, B. Landsberger, *Kleinasiatische Forschungen* 1 (1930), pp. 329 ff.; de Vaux, *op. cit.* (above, n. 13), pp. 337 ff.; and especially M. Greenberg, *The Hab/piru*, 1955, pp. 91 ff. The various proposed etymologies of the term *'ibrī*, and its even more intricate relationship with Ḫab/piru-'Apiru (cf. the bibliography in the last mentioned work), are beyond the scope of the present paper.

[15] The two most recent major studies are W. F. Albright, Abram the Hebrew, *BASOR* 163 (1961), pp. 36 ff., regarding *'ibrī*, like Egyptian *'Apiru*, as a 'donkey driver,' 'caravaneer'; and especially N. A. van Uchelen, *Abraham de Hebreeër*, 1964, which reviews the history of interpretation of our passage, from LXX on, van Uchelen himself stressing the military aspect of the term here, typifying Abraham as a warrior-hero. This same facet is interestingly also often found in the term Ḫana of the Mari documents. E. A. Speiser regards Gen. 14 as a Hebrew adaptation of an Akkadian source, seeing in Abraham a Ḫabiru warrior; see his *Genesis*, 1964, pp. 102 ff.

This state of affairs is similar to the Mesopotamian context: Shamshi-Adad was regarded as a Hanean in contrast to the kings of Babylon, just as the rulers of the local dynasty at Mari actually adopted the titulary "king of Ḫana," while the rulers of the Old Babylonian dynasty at Uruk were apparently referred to as kings (of the tribe) of Amnānu, as attested in regard to two of them.[16] Thus finds expression the concept of the specific determinative line. We cannot be far off in assuming that, had we possession of the genealogical tables of the two latter dynasties (i. e. of Mari and Uruk), Ḫanū would most likely be found among the earlier eponyms (group [a]) in both, in spite of the ethnic affinity of the Uruk dynasty. Another parallel use of the terms "Hanean" and "Hebrew" is revealed in their application in a geographical-territorial context, signifying the main areas of ultimate sedentation of these originally nomadic tribes. Thus, the Mari documents refer to the middle Euphrates region as "the land of Ḫana" (*māt Ḫana*), whereas in the Bible the land of Canaan (or a part thereof) is once called "the land of the Hebrews" (Gen. 40:15).

The further genealogical line

Group (b): The determinative line.

We include in this group the generations bridging the common genealogical stock with the tables of ancestors; in the Mesopotamian lists these determine the pedigrees culminating in the founders of the West Semitic dynasties in Babylon and Assyria (i. e. Sumuabum and Shamshi-Adad, respectively). Finkelstein has convincingly shown that, while the pedigree of Sumuabum actually starts with Ipti-yamūta (No. 14), the latter's two "ancestors," Amnānu and Yaḫruru (Nos. 12 and 13), serve to determine the national affiliation of the Babylonian line (pp. 111-112). As already noted, these latter were West Semitic, basically nomadic tribes; thus, if we were to label the Babylonian lineage up to Ipti-yamūta, in terms employed by AKL, the phrase "total of 13 kings who dwell in tents" would be most appropriate.

The determinative Babylonian line may illuminate the controversial subject of the origin and meaning of the term DUMU.MEŠ-*yamina*, i. e. "sons of the South," found in the Mari documents, and there only, as a designation for a broad tribal confederation, the Amnānu and Yaḫruru comprising its main elements.[17] The grafting of the Babylonian table of ancestors to the latter tribes indicates that Yaminite groups had become entrenched in southern Mesopotamia already long before Yaḫdunlim (c. 1825-1810 B. C.) and Shamshi-Adad (c. 1815-1782 B. C.)—the respective founders of the West Semitic dynasties in Mari and Assyria. In Babylon the Yaminites achieved political independence some three generations prior to the above rulers, namely, in the days of Sumuabum (c. 1894-1881 B. C.), whereas at Uruk the special ties of the Amnānu with the ruling dynasty go back to the time of king Sīnkāshid (c. 1865-1833 B. C.; see above, n. 16). Thus, it would seem that the term DUMU.MEŠ-*yamina*, used by the Mari authorities and perhaps even coined by them, may have been applied originally to these tribal units for they had already become a decisive historical factor in the regions to the *south*, from the viewpoint of Mari.[18]

---

[16] I. e., Sīnkāshid and one of his grandsons (either Sīngāmil or Ilumgāmil); see A. Falkenstein, *Baghdader Mitteilungen* 2 (1963), pp. 22 ff. Moreover, an obscure passage in a letter of king Anam of Uruk to Sīnmuballiṭ of Babylon (col. III, l. 40—*ibid*., pp. 58, 62, 70) evidently points to a special connection between Uruk and the Amnānu. However, Falkenstein has raised doubts as to whether the Uruk dynasty truly stemmed from the Amnānu, or for that matter whether it was West Semitic altogether. Cf. also the review of the above by F. R. Kraus, *Bi Or* 22 (1965), pp. 287 ff.

[17] On this tribal association and its sub-groups, see Kupper, *op. cit.* (above, n. 8), ch. II: Les Benjaminites. It should be noted that Amnānu and Yaḫruru together are explicitly designated as Yaminites only in *ARM* III, 50, ll. 10-13 (and not in the oft-quoted passage in *ARM* I, 42, ll. 30-31), as is the former alone in Yaḫdunlim's Foundation Inscription, col. III, ll. 6 ff. (in ll. 17 and 21 DUMU-*mi-im* surely represents an abbreviated form of the term Yaminites). See my 'Aspects of Tribal Societies in Mari and Israel,' *XVe Rencontre assyr. internat.*, Université de Liège, 1967, p. 137, n. 1, for the various readings of DUMU.MEŠ-*yamina*.

[18] Admittedly, the Yaminites as such are referred to throughout the Mari documents as being only in the regions to the north and west of Mari, where they were still pursuing a (semi-)nomadic life. In contrast to important groups of urbanized Yaminites to the south, these gained mention in the documents through their continual conflict with the Mari authorities. On the other hand, A. Parrot, in *Abraham et son temps*, 1962, pp. 45 f., has doubtfully suggested that the name Yaminites indicates that this tribal grouping originated in southern Mesopotamia, from whence it penetrated northward at an early period. The DUMU.MEŠ-*sim'al*, i. e. 'sons of the north,' were, of course, always located

As for AKL, the determinative genealogical line embraces, according to our present analysis, the names from Abazu to Apiashal (Nos. 13-17); that is, the last five generations of "the 17 kings dwelling in tents." In contrast to the parallel section in GHD, the names here in AKL are obscure and not of a tribal character, but rather seem to be proper names. They are unknown from any other source, except for the name Ushpia (No. 16), mentioned in late Assyrian royal inscriptions as an early Assyrian king who founded the national sanctuary in the city of Ashur.[19] It is doubtful whether Ushpia was inserted in the list, as suggested by Mrs. H. Lewy, in order to indicate the transition from nomadic life to permanent settlement in Ashur, for he is definitely included among the "kings dwelling in tents," and he is not even the last of these. More probably, an early historical Assyrian king was purposely inserted here in the determinative line of AKL in order to lend it further authenticity.

Group (c): Table of ancestors

While in GHD the table of ancestors may be deduced only indirectly, on the basis of the seeming authenticity of the personal names preceding Sumuabum, in AKL this group appears as a separate section concluding with the rubric "10 kings who are *ancestors*" (see above, p. 164). In the latter list, however, the generations are given in reverse order; that is, in ascending generations. In reality, we should detach the first generation from this table, i. e. Apiashal (son of Ushpia), whose name is not West Semitic, in contrast to all the other names in this group, for he also appears earlier in the genealogical list (No. 17) and is repeated here only to tie up with the former section. Shamshi-Adad should then be appended at the end of the table of ancestors as the tenth name, for this pedigree, beginning now with Ḫalē (No. 18), is actually his (see the Table at the end of this article).

Of special note is the fact that the parallel group in GHD, i. e. from Ipti-yamūta to Sumuabum (Nos. 14-23), also includes exactly ten entries. Thus we may assume that the ideal pattern of an "Ahnentafel" was based on a constant genealogical depth of ten generations. From the viewpoint of the genealogical pattern, it was immaterial whether this aim was achieved by means of integrating even fictitious names (such as, possibly, the pair of rhymed names Yakmesi-Yakmeni, Nos. 22-23 in AKL), in the lack of fuller knowledge of actual ancestors; or by means of entries such as Aminu (AKL, No. 26), evidently Shamshi-Adad's brother, not father (who is definitely known as Ila-kabkabu, both from a remark in AKL proper and from other sources), though Aminu apparently preceded Shamshi-Adad to the throne (Landsberger, p. 34).

The nine ancestors of Sumuabum and of Shamshi-Adad, who lived in the 20th and 19th centuries B. C. at places unknown to us,[20] were tribal chieftains who may even have adopted the title "king," like those in the middle Euphrates region mentioned in the inscriptions of Yaḫdunlim from Mari: "7 kings, fathers (*abū*) of Ḫana" (Disc Inscription, col. I, ll. 15-16); and three Yaminite "kings" named with their regal cities and tribal territories (Foundation Inscription, col. III, ll. 4-10). The actual rulers who reigned in the city of Ashur proper during the period of Shamshi-Adad's forebears were accomodated by the compiler of AKL between Aminu and Shamshi-Adad. The first of these, Sulili, is listed as Aminu's son, a seemingly fictitious linkage with the previous section. These kings, most of whom are attested in other sources, should be regarded as a line more or less synchronous with the "Ahnentafel" of Shamshi-Adad, and thus not to be included within his actual pedigree (and consequently omitted in the Table at the end of this article).[21]

much farther to the north, namely in the upper Habur and Balikh valleys.

[19] See Landsberger, p. 109, n. 206. According to H. Lewy, *op. cit.* (above, n. 4), pp. 18 f., Ushpia reigned before the mid-third millennium B.C., but the dating of this king to the end of the Third Dynasty of Ur or thereabouts seems preferable; cf. W. W. Hallo, *JNES* 15 (1956), pp. 220 f.

[20] Only the immediate predecessors of Shamshi-Adad can be assumed to have ruled in the city of Terqa near the confluence of the Habur river; see Landsberger, p. 35, n. 26. This same city may have also been the ancestral home of the Mari dynasty, as indicated by a letter to king Zimrilim urging that the *kispu* rites honoring the manes of his father Yaḫdunlim be performed there (*ARM* III, 40); cf. A. Malamat, Prophecy in the Mari Documents, *Eretz-Israel* 4 (1956), p. 76 (Hebrew).

[21] For an attempted reconstruction of the two parallel lines, cf. Hallo, *op. cit.* (above, n. 19), p. 221, n. 9, which we may accept with some reservation: Apiashal and Sulili, respectively opening and closing the Ahnentafel of Shamshi-Adad (Hallo's left-hand column) should be removed to the top of the line of 'real' kings of Ashur (Hallo's right-hand column), following Ushpia

The above analysis clarifies the underlying structure of the royal Mesopotamian genealogies. Tables of ancestors containing ten generations were appended to the universal stock by means of transitional links—our determinative line. Here, the difference in span of the respective determinative lines is highly instructive, five entries in AKL as against two in GHD (or six as against three if the eponyms Nuabu and Namḫū, respectively, are to be detached from the genealogical stock and joined to the following section; see above, n. 6).

This difference of three generations is not, evidently, incidental but rather the outcome of the structure of the genealogical scheme as described, and reflects the true chronological gap existing between the foundation of the two West Semitic dynasties, in Babylon (start of 19th cent. B. C.) and in Assyria (end of 19th cent. B. C.). As Finkelstein has already demonstrated (pp. 109 ff.), the two dynastic lists, in spite of the artificiality of many of the names, rely on chronological-historical traditions and on more or less reliable calculations of generations. The surprising chronological harmony between the two lists is evident from the fact that Shamshi-Adad and his Babylonian contemporary, Sīnmuballiṭ the father of Hammurapi, both occupy the same respective numerical positions, that is, the twenty-seventh. However, we have noted above (p. 168) concerning the two dynastic founders, that Sumuabum (No. 23) preceded Shamshi-Adad by some three generations (though he was the fourth king before Sīnmuballiṭ). Now, if the respective scribes of the two lists began their reckoning from one and the same common stock, and since the table of ancestors of the dynastic founders was based on a constant ten-generation depth, the cancelling out of the above chronological discrepancy was achieved by means of appropriate additions to the Assyrian determinative line.

The royal genealogies of Israel

In dealing with the generations subsequent to the basic stock, comparative treatment of the data in the Bible and the Mesopotamian archetypes is a more complicated matter, forcing us, *inter alia*, to reconstruct the biblical lineages from scattered materials, sometimes even resorting to sources of a narrative nature. The determinative lineage defining the people of Israel comprises the series of the three Patriarchs—Abraham, Isaac and Jacob, whereas, e. g., Abraham-Isaac-Esau specifies the Edomites, and the eponyms Haran and Lot, the Ammonites and the Moabites, respectively. But intramural Israelite usage demands an additional eponym following the basic patriarchal scheme, representing one of the twelve tribes, such as Judah, Benjamin, etc., to complete the determinative line. Ultimately, these four generations determine each and every Israelite lineage.

However, these individual lineages, which are to be regarded as the "tables of ancestors," are of a problematic character. On the one hand, the initial generations represent, as a rule, a graduated, intra-tribal classification—sub-tribe, clan, family. On the other hand, the lineages are normally selective, telescoping generations here and there similar to modern tribal genealogies, and thus depriving them of true chronological value.[22] A case in point is the lineage of Moses (third generation from Levi—Ex. 6:16-20) as against that of his younger contemporary Joshua (ninth, or possibly tenth, generation from Joseph —1 Chron. 7:22-27).

For sake of comparison with GHD and AKL, we must ascertain as closely as possible the ideal genealogical model within the corpus of biblical genealogies. There seems to be no more suitable parallel than the lineage of David, founder of the venerable dynasty of Judah, which was surely compiled and transmitted with the utmost care.[23] Whereas David's line of successors is given in 1 Chron. 3, his "table of ancestors" may easily be recognized as a distinct entity among the many branches of the tribe of Judah (see 1 Chron. 2:5, 9-15). The same "table of ancestors" has been

(cf. Landsberger, p. 33). Mrs. Lewy's conjecture (*op. cit.* [above, n. 4], p. 20) that Shamshi-Adad's Ahnentafel is in fact to be ascribed to Sulili is hardly acceptable.

[22] See the recent pointed remarks of D. N. Freedman, in *The Bible and the Ancient Near East* (ed. G. E. Wright), 1961, pp. 206 f., and K. A. Kitchen, *Ancient Orient and Old Testament*, 1966, pp. 54 ff., both citing various examples, especially from the Exodus-Numbers cycle.

[23] A similar practice is found among modern tribal lineages, e. g. the Luapula of Rhodesia where the royal line is preserved at a 9-generation depth, as against the telescoped commoner lineages which embrace only 4 to 7 generations; cf. I. Cunnison, History and Genealogies in a Conquest State, *American Anthropologist* 59 (1957), pp. 20 ff. (especially p. 27).

appended to the Book of Ruth as well (4:18-22).[24] Both of these sources seemingly derive from an earlier genealogical document, as implied also in the heading "Now these are the line ($t\bar{o}l^ed\bar{o}t$) of Perez" (Ruth 4:18) to the lineage: Perez (the son of Judah)-Hezron-Ram-Amminadab-Nahshon-Salmon (Salma)-Boaz-Obed-Jesse-David.

It is most interesting that, here again, a "table of ancestors" contains exactly ten generations, even though this depth is much too shallow to fill the time-span between the "Patriarchal period" and the time of David.[24a] This discrepancy is also apparent from the fact that Nahshon son of Amminadab is placed in the fifth generation before David, whereas according to biblical tradition he was a tribal head of Judah in the days of the Exodus (cf. Ex. 6:23; Num. 1:7; 2:3; 1 Chron. 2:10), some two hundred-fifty years before David. Moreover, in keeping with the abovementioned principle of gentilic classification, the compiler of this table resorted in the first two or three generations to eponyms personifying well-known tribal groups within Judah (Perez, Hezron and possibly also Ram).

In short, David's table of ancestors is largely an artificial construction formed on an ideal, traditional model, as befitting a royal lineage. David's lineage (group [c]) links up with the eponym Judah in the determinative Israelite line (group [b]), which in turn is tied to the genealogical stock (group [a]), i. e., the line of Shem. Indeed, the entire reconstructed genealogical line, like the continuous Mesopotamian king lists, is brought forth in the New Testament, within the pedigree of Jesus, which was traced back through David (from Abraham to David in Matthew 1:3-6, and from David to Adam, in ascending order, in Luke 3:31-38).

As with the Davidic dynasty, the Bible gives the genealogy of the house of Saul, the first Israelite king, of the tribe of Benjamin. Yet Saul's "table of ancestors" has been preserved only in an incomplete form, and then in two conflicting traditions. His immediate ancestors are included in an appendix to the genealogy of the tribe of Benjamin in 1 Chron. 8:29 ff., with a duplicate, but slightly tampered-with version in 1 Chron. 9:35 ff.[25] The latter gives the line as: Jeiel ("the father of [the city of] Gibeon")-Ner-Kish-Saul. The linkage of the house of Saul with the Israelite settlement in Gibeon is strange in itself, for Saul's family stemmed from the city of Gibeah of Benjamin. This tie is seemingly artificial, as evidenced also in the Massoretic text of 1 Chron. 8, an apparently more reliable version where Ner is lacking among the sons of the "father of Gibeon" (v. 30). Ner appears only in v. 33, at the head of Saul's line.

Another genealogical tradition, fuller and more revealing, opens the cycle of the Saul stories in I Sam. 9:1.[26] Unlike the genealogical lists, and as in narrative and historiographical usage, the sequence of generations here ascends, like the table of ancestors of Shamshi-Adad; that is, "Kish (father of Saul), son of Abiel, son of Zeror, son of Bechorath, son of Aphiah, son of a (Ben)-jaminite." Here, the name of Ner, father of Kish and grandfather of Saul, has been omitted, as against the list in Chronicles and the fragment of the family record of Saul (1 Sam. 14:50-51).[27] It is also difficult here to draw the dividing-line between Saul's actual ancestors and the fictitious eponyms personifying sub-tribal groups within Benjamin. Yet it is almost certain that Bechorath, the fifth generation (including Ner) before Saul, already represents Becher, one of the major Benjaminite clans (Gen. 46:21; 1 Chron. 7:6, 8: and cf. 2 Sam. 20:1).[28] However, Bechorath's father

[24] See the commentaries on Chronicles by J. W. Rothstein-J. Hänel, *Das erste Buch der Chronik*, 1927, pp. 18, 44; W. Rudolph, *Chronikbücher*, 1955, p. 16; J. M. Myers, *I Chronicles*, 1965, pp. 13 f.; and on Ruth by W. Rudolph, *Das Buch Ruth*, 1962, pp. 71 f.

[24a] But note some 20 generations from Levi to Samuel, David's older contemporary, in the fuller, though suspicious, genealogy of Heman in I Chron. 6:18-23 (= 33-38 in the English version).

[25] See the commentaries on Chronicles in the previous note: Rothstein-Hänel, pp. 165 ff.; Rudolph, pp. 80 f.; Myers, p. 62.

[26] In addition to the references in n. 25, where the relation between the two traditions is dealt with, see S. R. Driver, *Notes on the Hebrew Text of the Books of Samuel*², 1913, pp. 68 f.; M. Z. Segal, *The Books of Samuel*, 1956, p. 65 (Hebrew).

[27] This last passage can only read as translated in the King James Version and rightly interpreted by Rudolph, *Chronikbücher* (above, n. 24), p. 81: 'And the name of the captain of his (i. e. Saul's) host was Abner, the son of Ner, Saul's uncle; and Kish was the father of Saul; and Ner the father of Abner was the son of Abiel.' That is, Abner (and not Ner) was Saul's uncle and the brother of Kish, and Abner and Kish both were sons of Ner and grandsons of Abiel. Any other interpretation would require textual emendation.

[28] Thus already B. Luther, *ZAW* 21 (1901), p. 55; and Segal, *loc. cit.* (above, n. 26). One of Becher's sons,

COMPARATIVE STRUCTURAL TABLE OF ROYAL GENEALOGIES

	BABYLONIA	ASSYRIA	ISRAEL	
	(Sumuabum)	(Shamshi-Adad)	(David)	(Saul)
	(GHD)*	(AKL)		
Group (a) Genealogical Stock	Ara(m/Ḫarḫar) (1)	Ṭudiya (1)	Shem	
	Madara (2)	Adamu (2)	Arpa//chshad	
	Tu(b)ti(ya) (3)	Yangi (3)	(Kenan)	
	(Y)amuta/Atamu (4)	Sa/i/uḫlamu (4)	Shelah	
	Yamqu (5)	Ḫarḫaru (5)	Eber	
	Suḫ(ḫa)la(m)ma (6)	Mandaru (6)	Peleg	
	Ḫeana (7)	Emṣu (7)	Reu	
	Namz/ṣū (8)	ḪARṣu (8)	Serug	
	Ditānu (9)	Didānu (9)	Nahor	
	Zummabu (10)	Ḫanū (10)	Terah	
	Namḫū (11)	Zu'abu (11)		
		Nuabu (12)		
(Group (b) Determinative Line	Amnānu (12)	Abazu (13)	Abraham	
	Yaḫrurum (13)	Bēlū (14)	Isaac	
		Azaraḫ (15)	Jacob	
		Ušpiya (16)		
		Apiašal (17)		
			Judah	Benjamin
Group (c) Table of Ancestors	Ipti-yamūta (14)	Ḫalē (18)	Perez	—
	Buḫazum (15)	Samanu (19)	Hezron	—
	Su-malika (16)	Ḫayanu (20)	Ram	X (a Benjaminite)
	Ašmadu (17)	Ilu-mer (21)	Amminadab	Aphiah
	Abi-yamūta (18)	Yakmesi (22)	Nahshon	Bechorath
	Abi-ditan (19)	Yakmeni (23)	Salma	Zeror
	Ma-am(?)-x-x-x (20)	Yazkur-ēl (24)	Boaz	Abiel
	Šu-x-ni(?)-x (21)	Ila-kabkaku (25)	Obed	⟨Ner⟩
	Dad(banaya [?]) (22)	Aminu (26)	Jesse	Kish
	Sumuabum (23)	Shamshi-Adad (27)	David	Saul
Group (d) Historical Line	(Sumula'ē) (24)	(etc.)	(etc.)	(etc.)
	(Zābium) (25)			
	(Apil-Sīn) (26)			
	(Sīn-muballiṭ) (27)			
	(Ḫammurapi) (28)			
	(etc.)			

*(Cf. Finkelstein, p. 114).

Aphiah, who is otherwise unknown, could hardly be the immediate link with the eponym Benjamin. The unusual formulation "Aphiah, son of a (Ben)jaminite (*ben îš yemînî*)" would indicate that at least one antecedent (the unnamed "Benjaminite") is missing before reaching the determinative line.

A comparative table of the parallel genealogical structures underying the Israelite and Mesopotamian royal lines [29] is given on page 172.

Abijah (1 Chron. 7: 8), is possibly to be identified with the abovementioned Abiel (with an exchange of the theophoric element).

[29] Another interesting point in GHD possibly bearing on the Bible can only be noted here. Finkelstein has shown that the final passage in GHD, dealing with mortuary offerings for the manes of royal ancestors, etc., gives the raison d'être for the entire document. The text seems to have been inherently involved in the *kispu* ceremonies honoring the past generations of the royal line, held on the day of the new moon (pp. 113 ff., 117). In 1 Sam. 20, it is related that Saul held a feast on the new moon (vss. 5, 18 ff.), while David was to have returned to Bethlehem, his home, to participate in family sacrifices (vss. 6, 29). Could these gatherings, held at ancestral homes, have been the occasion on which genealogical accounts were employed to invoke the names of dead ancestors, as has been assumed for the *kispu* ritual held by the Babylonian and Assyrian dynasties?

"THE EYES OF THE LORD"

A. L. OPPENHEIM
UNIVERSITY OF CHICAGO

THIS PAPER DISCUSSES several literary expressions of wide distribution in and beyond the ancient Near East, and investigates the concepts behind them, as well as their basis in actual experiences.

I begin with the expressions "the eyes of the king" and "the ears of the king" as designations of certain important royal officials.

The earliest references to officials called "eyes" and "ears of the king" come from Egyptian sources datable to the second half of the second millennium.[1] Next in time are a number of passages in Greek texts which describe or refer to certain institutions of the Persian empire. I quote here a few lines from Xenophon's Cyropaedia in the translation of Walter Miller (from Loeb Classical Library, Cyropaedia Book 8 ii 10 ff.):

"Moreover, we have discovered that he (Cyrus) acquired the so-called 'king's eyes' and 'king's ears' in no other way than by bestowing presents and honours; for by rewarding liberally those who reported to him whatever was to his interest to hear, he prompted many men to make it their business to use their eyes and ears to spy out what they could report to the king to his advantage. As a natural result of this, many 'eyes' and many 'ears' were ascribed to the king. But if anyone thinks that the king selected one man to be his 'eye,' he is wrong; for one only would see and one would hear but little; and it would have amounted to ordering all the rest to pay no attention, if only one would have been appointed to see and to hear. Besides, if people knew that a certain man was the 'eye,' they would know that they must beware of him. But such is not the case; for the king listens to anyone who may claim to have heard or seen anything worthy of attention. And thus the saying comes about, 'The king has many ears and many eyes'; and people are always afraid to say anything to the discredit of the king, just as if he himself were listening; or to do anything to harm him, just as if he were present."

In this moralizing interpretation of an institution foreign to the Greek social climate, Xenophon contradicts what he says later on in the same book (Book 8 vi 16) about the high Persian official called "the eyes of the king" and what Herodotus had already indicated in Klio 114. Our author thinks of a sort of royal secret service making use of a large number of paid informers rather than of a special official in an elevated position, if not belonging to the entourage of the king himself. We seem to have here an old confusion between informers paid for incidental services, and a high official charged with specific duties.[2] Both are likely to have existed in the

[1] See simply Ägyptisches Wörterbuch sub *jr . t* (p. 107) and *'nḫ* (p. 205).

[2] This is confirmed by Plutarch (12, 1) in his biography of Artaxerxes II. For other passages from Greek

Persian empire as the evidence to be presented later in this paper (see p. 178) will show.

From India, similar institutions are reported in texts beginning with the second century A. D.[3] A late work speaks with characteristic exaggeration of as many as five imperial "censors" referred to as the "five senses of the government." From China may be adduced the designation "ear-and-eye-official" (*erh-mu kuan*) for a censor of the seventh century A. D.; earlier references of that provenience are likewise known.[4]

When we turn toward Mesopotamia (to fill the gap in documentation between Egypt and Persia) we find no direct evidence for these picturesque titles. We encounter, however, in texts dating from the final century of the Assyrian empire, an idiomatic use of the two verbs *amāru* and *šemû*, "to see" and "to hear," which suggests similar practices. In the letters of the kings of the Sargonid dynasty (721-627 B. C.) we often encounter such commands as *mala tammara u tašemma' šuprani* "write me whatever you see and hear!" (ABL 831 r. 3 f., also ABL 472: 3 f., and passim), and such assurances of the loyal servants of the king as *mīnu ša ammaruni ša ašammûni ana šarri bēlija aqabbi* "I will report to the king, my lord, everything I see and hear" (ABL 317: 8 ff. and note the parallels ABL 211: 11 f., 288: 12 f., 1166 r. 8 f., and passim). We know these are not empty words because certain passages in administrative documents that define expressly the duties of the king's servants employ a similar phraseology. Thus the text of the loyalty oath for officials preserved in ABL 656 states that *mannu ša memeni išammûni ina pan šarri la iqabbûni* "anybody who does not report to the king everything he hears" (r. 20 f.) has to account for this dereliction of duty. This is corroborated by the text of the treaty between King Esarhaddon and his vassals, the Median chieftains. There it is demanded of them—obviously as part of their obligations as subjects of the Assyrian king—to report whatever they have heard about disloyal and hostile acts, and not to conceal any such information (see lines 73 ff., also 108 f., 149, etc.).[5]

The *amāru-šamû* references come exclusively[6] from the Assyrian court of the first third of the first millennium B. C. and are therefore much earlier than the Persian institution of the "eyes and ears" of the kings. In time, they are followed by passages from later sections of the Old Testament which I will discuss presently. This distribution raises a number of interesting but difficult problems; while one could assume that all Eastern (i. e., Indian and even Chinese) parallels came about under the influence of the court practices of the Persian empire which reached from the Mediterranean Sea into India, the relationship between the Persian and the earlier Assyrian empire to the west of it remains uncertain. Tentatively one could suggest the following explanation: it is not always realized that the Assyrian imperial administration represents with its techniques and attitudes something novel if not alien within the Mesopotamian bureaucratic traditions of governing an extensive territorial state from a capital. It is therefore conceivable that a sort of secret information service was one of the features of the novel method. We might, one day, find that the kingdoms of Northern Syria, and even of Urartu, had, at times, exercised considerably more influence on the Assyrian court in matters military, diplomatic and artistic than we are wont to assume, and that the new Persian Empire was likewise receptive to Western influences. However, the situation underlying the concept we are dealing with in this paper is much too involved for simple explanations, as will become evident presently.

---

sources (Aischylos, Aristophanes and Aristotle) see simply H. H. Schaeder, "Das Auge des Königs" in Iranica I (Abhandlungen der Gesellschaft der Wissenschaften zu Göttingen, Philologisch-Historische Klasse, Dritte Folge No. 10, 1934) pp. 3 f.

[3] I owe the following references to my colleague David Pingree: for the occurrences in the 2nd century A. D. see Manusmṛti 9,256 (ed. Bombay, 1946), also Matsyapurāṇa, Viṣṇudharmottarapurāṇa, etc.; for the Mahābhārata see Udyogaparvan 34,32 (Critical Edition, vol. 6, Poona 1940), for the 5th and 6th centuries see Kāmandaka, Nītisāra 13, 19, 28 ff. (ed. ASS, vol. 2, Poona 1964, pp. 286 ff.). For the five imperial censors see Epigraphia Carnatica, vol. 7, Shikarpur Nos. 102 + 123.

[4] Hsin T'ang Shu, ch. 116, p. 4a, in Po-na Pen ed. I owe this reference to my colleague Edward J. Kracke.

[5] The article by R. Follet, S. J., "'Deuxième Bureau' et information diplomatique dans l'Assyrie des Sargonides, quelques notes" in RSO 32 (1957) pp. 68-81, is not pertinent, in spite of its title.

[6] It might not be an accident that a similar expression appears in an Amarna letter addressed to the Pharoah (RA 19 104 AO 7094: 21) *ina ūmi ašmi u ammaru ipiš nukurti* "the very day I hear or see an evil deed (the king shall know it)."

The expressions discussed so far characterize these officials as extensions, so to speak, of the dreaded presence of the ruler because through his "eyes" and his "ears" the king achieves godlike omnipresence and, hence, omniscience. They keep him constantly informed and aware of every hostile or disloyal act the very moment it is committed. It also shows that the king's subjects well realized the extent and effectiveness of the essential part of the governmental machinery that relentlessly searches for the enemies of the ruler. Secrecy, of course, is the prime requisite for these servants of the king so that unexpectedly and swiftly his arm can strike those who fail in what the king considers their duty, or those who act directly against his interests. The traumatic effect produced by the activities of such a "secret service" provides the psychological basis for the concepts behind these expressions.

The Old Testament passages do not speak of the "ears" but only of the "eyes," and they do this in connection with God rather than with the king. Nearly all of these passages can be found in the intriguing visions of the late prophet Zechariah. Their variety and especially their intensity lead one to suspect that they are the expression of some specific personal experience of the prophet, perhaps a clash with the Persian "secret service" since Zechariah was in fact a contemporary of Darius I Hystaspes. Let me begin by quoting what the prophet said he saw: "a candlestick all of gold, with a bowl upon the top of it, and his seven lamps thereon, and seven pipes to the seven lamps, which are upon the top thereof" (iv 2). An angel of the Lord offers the following in answer to the prophet's query: "They are the eyes of the Lord, which run to and fro through the whole earth" (iv 10). At each side of this miraculous "candlestick"[7] stands an olive tree with golden pipes directing the oil of its fruits into the lamps (iv 12), patently a rather sophisticated device to maintain the lamps burning without refilling and to achieve thus a constant surveillance of the entire earth by these "seeing" lamps which apparently have to be lighted in order to "see." What visual experience—apart from the "candlestick" in the temple (Ex. xxv 31 ff.) —could possibly have prompted the prophet to conceive of such a "modern" piece of machinery, instead of using the doubtlessly well-known *topos* of the ever-moving "eyes of the Lord"?

We know of these "eyes of the Lord" from a passage in 2 Chron. xvi 9 which is quite explicit about their working and their purpose: "for the eyes of the Lord run to and fro throughout the whole earth, to shew himself strong in the behalf of them whose heart is perfect towards him." The "eyes" have, as the seer Hanani points out here to Asa, king of Judah, discovered the king's wrongdoing and now God is to punish him on the basis of the information the "eyes" have relayed to him. There is a certain discrepancy in this passage from the second book of Chronicles which I would like to underline for reasons that will become evident later on. The "eyes of the Lord" seem to have a double function: on one hand they act in accordance with what the "eyes of the king" are supposed to do, namely, to spot misdeeds, report them to the authority and bring about swift punishment of the culprit; on the other hand, they are spoken of by the seer as if their purpose were rather to bring comfort to the pious and as if they were charged with his protection.

Evidently, the Old Testament passages for the "eyes of the Lord" represent a transfer of a political institution to a theological level. From the subject's constant awareness of a dangerous and invisible royal "secret service," ready and eager to report on him and to hurt him, we have moved toward the religious conviction of the presence and nearness of God, and his intense interest in the pious.

This primary religious experience of being under immediate divine surveillance and protection was rather crudely "mythologized" by Zechariah in a number of passages found in the collection of his visionary experiences. I have already mentioned the fantastic apparatus in which seven ever-burning oil lamps magically scan the entire earth for the purpose, we may assume, of reporting to God on mankind. But the prophet's imagination seems to have been sparked by several heterogeneous concepts and images.[8]

[7] Bible passages in this article are given according to the King James Version.

[8] It is perhaps worthy of note that the concept of an angel serving as an "accuser" was also known to the prophet Zechariah who speaks, in iii 1, of the "accuser" standing at the right hand of the angel of the Lord. Note in this context the strange expression "children of Belial" which denotes the accuser and informer in the Naboth story of 1 Kings xxi 10 and 13. For Belial

Of another of these concepts we get an inkling from the just quoted words of the angel: "the eyes (which) run to and fro throughout the whole earth." The explanation for divine omnipresence offered in this characteristic expression seems to be on a more "rational" level than that of the "candlestick," as I plan to show by following up the concept of the permanent restlessness of these "eyes."

The traumatic effect of the secret surveillance of the individual exercised by either king or god seems to be ascribed here to the continuous, ceaseless motion of these "eyes." With uncanny speed they roam, unseen, among the terrified subjects. Specific references to this phenomenon appear in two other visions of the prophet Zechariah, each time in a somewhat different mood. The prophet seems to think of these spying "eyes" in terms of somewhat ill-defined demonic riders or charioteers, i. e., messengers provided with a rapid means of transportation. He uses the following words: "I saw by night and behold a man riding on a red horse, and he stood among the myrtle trees that were in the bottom; and behind him were there red horses, speckled and white" (i 8). The mysterious rider explains his task as follows: "These are they whom the Lord has sent to walk to and fro through the earth" (i 10). The next verse tells us quite explicitly what these mysterious night-riding spies of the Lord are supposed to report: "We have walked to and fro through the earth, and, behold, all the earth sitteth still, and is at rest" (i 11). In another vision, Zechariah sees these men not on horseback but on chariots and he elaborates on their activities and appearances in a clearly mythological vein. Four such chariots are coming out "between the two mountains of brass" in which we have to see the entrance to heaven, the same cosmic locality characterized by two mountains between which, in Mesopotamian and related cosmologic representations, the Sun god comes forth and enters heaven every day. "These are the four spirits of the heavens, which should go forth from standing before the Lord" (vi 5). Order is given them: "Get hence, walk to and fro through the earth" (vi 7). This they do on their chariots drawn by horses of different colors, each toward one point of the compass. It seems that these riders and charioteers start their rounds at night and are to roam the earth until morning when they report on what they have seen, standing again before the Lord.

We have tried to trace the recurring allusions to the restlessness of these ever observant demonic or celestial beings, the "eyes" of the Lord. This search is bound to bring to one's mind the familiar passages from the Prologue to the Book of Job. When the "sons of God" come before the Lord, and when Satan is asked "Whence comest thou?" he answers: "from going to and fro in the earth, and from walking up and down in it" (i 7 and ii 2). This Satan does in the service of the Lord and for the explicit purpose of watching over people—in fact, he is supposed to know them by name—and he seems even to have had the power of manipulating the events which happen to them. In the instance of Job, he is expressly given permission by God to make misfortunes of all kinds befall Job and the members of his family, his cattle, possessions, etc. He is, admittedly, enjoined from taking Job's life, but this restriction on his influence on the fortunes of individuals may well be considered a concession to the monotheistic attitude of the poet while utilizing popular demonological concepts.

Much has, of course, been written on Satan and I have no intention to reopen any discussions or even to review the literature. For the rather limited purposes of this paper, it should suffice to point out three more or less recent articles which run, to some extent, parallel to my investigation: H. Torzcyner "How Satan Came into the World," (Bulletin of the Hebrew University, Jerusalem; No. 4, January 1937, pp. 14-20), A. Brock-Utne "Der Feind—Die alttestamentliche Satansgestalt im Lichte der sozialen Verhältnisse des nahen Orients," (Klio 28, NF 4, 1945, pp. 220 and 227), and A. Lods "Les origines de la figure de Satan, ses fonctions à la cour céleste," (Mélanges syriens offerts à M. R. Dussaud 2, 1939, pp. 649-66). The interpretations offered in these papers, and in the earlier literature, range from "secret agent," "*agent provocateur*" to "public accuser," and thus move distinctly along lines which are quite similar to the characterization of the "eyes" and "ears of the king" pointed out in the present investigation. Yet, it may well be said that none of these or similar proposals fits all known passages for the word *sāṭān* or its Greek correspondence: *diabolos*, lit.: the accuser, in the Old and New Testaments. It is *a priori*

see simply the pertinent article by T. H. Gaster in The Interpreter's Dictionary of the Bible.

unrealistic to expect any one acceptable and defensible rendering in English of such an elusive "functionary" as Satan. The evidence available to us in the Hebrew and Greek texts represents but a quite accidental selection and therefore can hardly be made to furnish any striking insights into the function and the internal development of the concept of Satan. There must have existed several distinct shades of meaning of this designation throughout the extended periods in which this and similar demonic figures are mentioned in the texts that constitute the Bible. Each such meaning is by necessity embedded in a specific social and literary context but the contexts reflected in the few accidentally preserved passages are of the kind that is either beneath the threshold of what is admitted by literary conventions or—more often—suppressed by the editors of the sacred text. Thus essential phases of the "prehistory of Satan" remain forever beyond our reach. Yet, much of the subsequent development and the crucial impact of the idea of Satan must have had roots in this submerged phase of his history.

The following bears on the problem of "demonization." By this I mean the process I have just described in which a human being, typically an official, is changed into a demon, a malevolent supernatural being. We have seen this happen to the officials called "eyes (and ears) of the king" and have tried to outline the stages in this development. The same holds true not only for officials of the king but also for informers motivated by greed or hatred. In the unique instance of Satan, the demon eventually became highly individualized, was provided with specific characteristic features and finally changed into an evil power of cosmic import. This "demonization" of the informer, secret agent, spy or overseer of the king was in the ancient Near East the direct consequence of the mentioned psychological impact of his very existence on the common man. To stress this point, I am offering here two more parallels for the "demonization" of royal officials, this time taken from cuneiform sources.

When one glances through the names given in Mesopotamian texts to those supernatural powers now usually and summarily identified as "demons," one discovers an intriguing array of designations. Some refer to diseases of all kinds; others to the spirits of the dead and similar manifestations which we are at a loss to name in English; many remain still quite unintelligible. "Demonology" as a topic of research in the field of the ancient Near East has fallen completely out of fashion. Today's Assyriologists prefer lines of approach to Mesopotamian religion that are dominated by their own religious interests and inclinations. Nevertheless, demons and their activities, their powers and the ways to deal with them have constituted one of the main concerns of man for the longest part of his intellectual history. For the understanding of the religious experience of Mesopotamian man, demons are perhaps more important than gods.

Two names point directly at the topic under discussion: *šarrabdû* (s á r . r a . a b . d ù) and *rābiṣu* (Sum. m a š k i m). Both words not only denote demons but also are titles of specific officials. The reason these two officials appear also as demons must have been that the nature of their activities was so specific and so obnoxious or hated as to release the process of "demonization." It is difficult, however, to find any pertinent indication in cuneiform documents. The persons with these designations do not belong in the category of the occasional informer for whom we know in Akkadian several names such as *munaggiru, ākil karṣî, mubbiru* and *bātiqu*.[9]

As a matter of fact, there does not seem to have existed in Mesopotamia an institutionalized "accuser" before the Neo-Babylonian period. There, we find, mainly in tablets from the temple administrations, references to food rations paid

[9] As to the distribution of these terms in time and region, note that *munaggiru* (first pointed out by B. Landsberger in JCS 9 (1955) 123 ff.) is restricted to the Old Babylonian period, in fact to the Codex Hammurapi, while the *bātiqu* appears in Neo-Babylonian texts (once in a Neo-Assyrian letter, see CAD s. v.). The Code regulates the remuneration for the *munaggiru*-informer (§ 26: 10) who is shown there as denouncing those who failed to do service for the king or hired a substitute for that purpose. The *bātiqu*, on the other hand, is typically mentioned beside eye-witnesses in cases of theft. The term *mubbiru* is restricted in the Code (§ 1: 31, 44, 55) to the person who accuses another (*ubburu*) of witchcraft. In a late copy of an earlier, probably Old Babylonian, description of a release of debts (*mīšaru*), contained in the "prophecy" CT 13 50 K. 7861 recently presented by A. K. Grayson in JCS 18 16: 12, the *mubbiru* seems, however, to have acted as informer in times of an economic depression. The expression *ākil karṣi* (CAD s. v.) is much less opprobrious and is restricted to literary texts and to situations outside the court of justice, to denunciations, jealousies at court, etc.

out to persons called *muraššû*, cf. Nbn. 546:27, 915:23 and GCCI 1 210:9, 255:7, the last two from Uruk. The official bearing this name appears in the series LÚ which enumerates names of professions, crafts, human types, etc., in III i 30 f. as follows: EME$^{e\text{-}me\text{-}tu\text{-}ku}$TUK = ŠU-*ú* (i. e., *emetukû*), *mu-ra-šu-ú*; he is listed between the *ākil karṣī* "accuser" and *dābibu*, the one who likes to complain and to quarrel. The meaning of *muraššû* is based on the verbs *ruššû* and *ruteššû* (see Diri I 289 f. and A VI/1:105 f. for Sum. hi.bi.is) and seems to be confirmed by the syllabic Sumerian spelling of the designation *muraššû* as LÚ.E(!).ME.TUK in a contemporary Neo-Babylonian text, Nbn. 362:4.[10] The proposed translation for *muraššû*—against that of F. R. Kraus in ZA 43 106 (to p. 92 i 32′) "Zänker"—is required by the above cited passages which indicate that this individual had an official position and function. As such the *muraššû* is an "accuser" and "informer" or "inspector," while in the omen passage discussed by Kraus the designation "slanderer" or the like seems more adequate. It should be noted that though *muraššû* as a word for the "accuser" is known only from late texts, its appearance in the lexical series attests to its existence in the second millennium B. C., although one cannot tell whether or not this specific connotation was then known.

A special case seems to occur in the Persian empire, as an isolated reference on an Aramaic papyrus found in Elephantine (Upper Egypt) suggests. There an official called, in Aramaic, גושכיא, which is said to render the Old Persian word **gaušaka* (see the literature cited on p. 5 f. of the book by H. H. Schaeder cited in note 2), is mentioned in the papyrus beside the judges and another Persian official who happens to reappear in the Book of Daniel iii 2 and 5 where the King James Version renders his title as "counselor." Now **gaušaka* means "listener" and the word was taken over into Armenian as *gušak* meaning "informer." It seems rather obvious that we have here an "ear" of the king at work not as a high dignitary of the realm nor as a paid informer (see above p. 177 f.) but rather as some kind of public functionary.

Let us return now to the names of the two officials—and demons—the *sarrabdû* and the *rābiṣu*.

What do we know about them? We may easily dispose of the *šarrabdû*; he is quite rare as an official.[11] We find this strange and unintelligible designation only in texts of the Third Dynasty of Ur where the *šarrabdû* appears as a minor functionary, some kind of overseer. As a demon, he is listed only once, among the infernal host of Nergal, in the story of the conquest of the netherworld by this god, preserved in only two copies, one found in Egypt (Amarna), the other in Upper Syria (Sultan Tepe).[12]

Far more interesting is the case of the *rābiṣu*, among the officials on earth as well as in the world of the demons. With the Old Babylonian period the official of this name disappears from legal and administrative texts coming from Mesopotamia proper. He continues to be mentioned in texts from the West: in Old Assyrian texts, in the Amarna correspondence and in the archives from Ugarit and Boghazkeui. Up to the end of the Mesopotamian civilization, literary texts in cuneiform continue to use his name in connection with the celestial court, etc. As for his role in the early legal and administrative texts, the *rābiṣu* (m a š k i m) is perhaps best characterized as a subaltern official acting mainly as the representative of an authority. The traditional translation "commissary" or "bailiff" seems often too narrow because under certain circumstances the *rābiṣu* can wield considerable authority and be charged with important responsibilities.[13] This seems to have been the case in the West; according to the Amarna letters, the officials of the Pharoah were given that title, and, in the Ras Shamrā and Boghazkeui texts,[14] the *rābiṣu* was in charge of important towns. From literary tablets we gather furthermore that the god Išum was the *rābiṣu* of the great gods, and the Sun god himself is called in a late text *rābiṣ*

[10] This syllabic writing is not without parallels in administrative and legal texts of the Neo-Babylonian period. The relationship between the word *muraššû* and the animal of apparently the same designation (see Landsberger Fauna 87 n. 1) will not be discussed here. It is much too facile a method of lexicography to establish relationships by means of semantically vague translations suggested (consciously or not) by etymological considerations.

[11] See CAD sub *ababdû*.

[12] See A. Falkenstein Gerichtsurkunden No. 214: 11, also Oppenheim Eames Collection p. 130.

[13] See A. Falkenstein Gerichtsurkunden p. 53, n. 3, with earlier literature.

[14] See J. Nougayrol MRS 6, index p. 235, E. Ebeling EA Vol. 2 index p. 1495 and H. Otten Baghd. Mitt. 3 p. 94. For the readings of MAŠKIM in the West see G. Buccellati, Oriens Antiquus 2 (1963) pp. 224-8.

dingiruggê ina qereb Aralli "the *rābiṣu* of the Dead Gods within the Netherworld," for whom he has to provide the cool water the dead need.[15] None of these contexts is specific enough to characterize clearly the position and nature of the office of the *rābiṣu* or to yield any clue as to why this designation was used for a dangerous demon.[16]

Passages in cuneiform texts which deal with demons either describe their dangerous activities or prescribe prophylactic and apotropaic magic meant to help those who are threatened or affected by the demons. Both types of passages contain references to the *rābiṣu* but these are rather uncharacteristic. The demon is usually grouped with the malevolent spirits of the dead, those who are uncared for and therefore turn into dangerous ghosts, and, as such, imperil the living. One might note in this connection a certain amount of atypical specialization: a *rābiṣ urḫi*, i.e., one who attacks people on the roads (e.g., Labat TDP 182:40), a *rābiṣ musâti* "of the lavatory" (e.g., AMT 77,1 i 10), and a disease called *qāt rābiṣi* or *miḫiṣ rābiṣi*.

Since the word *rābiṣu*[17] is an active participle, the underlying verb should provide a suggestion as to the typical activity of the demon—and of the official. The verb *rabāṣu* denotes in most of its occurrences the lying down of animals for sleep or rest, normally the crouching down of quadrupeds, but is said also of snakes. In a few instances, *rabāṣu* (Sum. ná), in combination with the preposition *eli*, describes the lying and waiting in ambush of evil spirits prying upon human beings (a.lá.ḫul lú.ra ná.a PBS 1/2 116:16 f., and see CAD sub *alû* A). This expression has a parallel in the well-known passage "sin lieth at the door" from Genesis iv 7 which uses the Hebrew *rōbeṣ* in exactly the same way. As H. Duhm, Die bösen Geister des Alten Testaments (1930) p. 62, suggests, this refers to an evil demon instigating envy and the wish to murder in Cain. The lurking of demons and even of angels acting for the Lord is also indicated in the designation *m^{e}'ar^{e}ḇīm* in 2 Chron. xx 22 as proposed by S. Grill, "Synonyme Engelsnamen im Alten Testament" (Theologische Zeitschrift 18, 1962, p. 241). From all this we might learn that the Akkadian *rābiṣu* official must have had—at least in the specific situation in which his name was coined—the hated function of spying on people in order to report on them. This is nowhere stated but then neither the legal nor the administrative documents in which he is mentioned can be expected to reflect the thoughts and the feelings of those unfortunates who were directly affected by the activities of the *rābiṣu*. The transformation of this official into a demon came about for exactly the same reasons the "eyes of the king" became "demonized." Those who felt spied upon by unseen or hidden agents, those who suffered from the actions of the king brought about by these secret informers, gave the names of their enemies to demons.

There is a further point to be made in connection with this "demonization." In the description of Mesopotamian demons, stress is put again and again on their facelessness and their speed. These demons have hardly any of the nightmarish quality inherent in the fantastic and exaggerated features we know so well from other demonologies.[18] With hooded faces, uncertain body features, working swiftly at night and in uncanny and unclean localities, the Mesopotamian demons attack with devastating speed. Here is the *tertium comparationis* which identifies hated officials of the type shown in this paper with dreaded demons.

The demonic figure of the *rābiṣu* is actually much more complex. A number of passages differentiate between two contrasting types of *rābiṣu* demons, one benevolent, called *rābiṣ šulmi* (e.g., YOS 10 53:30, BE 8 4:8, etc.) or *rābiṣ dumqi* (AMT 101,2 r. i 6), and one evil, *rābiṣ lemutti* (AfO 12 365:35) or *rābiṣ lumni* (AMT 101,1 r. i 6). Such differentiation reminds one of other demonic figures such as the *šēdu* and the *lamassu*, each likewise considered to have two contrasting functions or, rather, natures. As I

---

[15] See A. Falkenstein UVB 15 p. 36:9: sag.tuku.dingir.ug$_5$.ga.àm šà.ga aralli.ke$_4$: *ra-bi-iṣ dingiruggê ina qereb Aralli*.

[16] Note also the curious commentary passage in Kraus Texte No. 24 r. 5 which explains that when a man has hairy underarms (*ammātušu šarta laḫma*) he is said to have *rābiṣu* hands. Note also DIŠ *qaqqad ra-⌈bi⌉-[ṣi* GAR] "if he has the head of a *rābiṣu*" ibid. 2a r. 28′.

[17] I cannot accept the proposal of A. Poebel, AS 14 55 f., who separates *rābiṣu* "overseer," which he connects with an Arabic *rabaṣa* "to wait for someone," from the Akkadian verb *rabāṣu* "to lie down (said of animals)" for which he adduces an Arabic *rabaḍa* "to lie down."

[18] The "demons" Pazuzu and Lamaštu form an exception, their features being quite specific, apparently individualized for the purpose of creating apotropaic representations.

have tried to show in my *Ancient Mesopotamia* (pp. 200 f.), such pairs of demons are thought to accompany, unseen, the individual, dispensing to him either fortune or misfortune. I have explained this phenomenon (well-known from other civilizations) in terms of "external souls" which accompany the individual to the fulfillment of his own nature or—what amounts to the same thing—his own destiny.[19]

In the light of what has been suggested here about the demonic "servants of the Lord" who roam the earth at night, observe or spy on its inhabitants, help the pious, check on their acts, nay even—as the case of Job shows—on the motivation for their overt behavior, one can well see a similar role for the Mesopotamian m a š k i m or *rābiṣu*, i. e. a role which is characteristically ambivalent: beneficial as well as demonic. Since we have, of course, no direct proof we can only point out parallelisms between the ever-lurking *rābiṣu* and the swift-moving, demonic "eyes" of the Lord and, eventually, the Satan, the "accuser . . . which accused them before our God day and night" (Rev. xii 10).

In the present investigation, we have ranged over a wide area and have cut across many boundary lines separating periods and civilizations. This was necessary to gather the evidence for a rather specific social practice and its institutionalized *modus operandi.* Informers, accusers, internal spies, censors, secret agents and their like form, in all these civilizations, then as well as today, an effective and often unobtrusive web, that with constant vigilance and demonic effectiveness directs, controls and coerces the individual in his social setting. The documentary sources at our disposal hardly mention the day-to-day doings of that host of ever present and interfering "eyes" and "ears." We learn more about them when their activities are transferred to a supernatural level and they appear either as evil demons, as the swift messengers and servants or the "Eyes of the Lord."

[19] A further point of parallelism between the *rābiṣu* and the *šēdu* is that the former serves as protector and guardian of the entrance to the palace (YOS 10 25: 62), also of the *bīt tākulti* (see Frankena Tākultu p. 109 No. 186) just as the latter does (see CAD sub *aladlammû*).

DEUTERO-ISAIAH AND CUNEIFORM ROYAL INSCRIPTIONS *

SHALOM M. PAUL
JEWISH THEOLOGICAL SEMINARY OF AMERICA

MOST SCHOLARS TODAY are in basic agreement that chapters 40–48 of Deutero-Isaiah are a self-contained literary unit consisting of prophecies written in Babylonia during the earliest part of that anonymous prophet's career,[1] and it is precisely within this complex that analogies to the language and phraseology of cuneiform royal inscriptions have been found. Kittel,[2] already in 1898, drew attention to similarities between Deutero-Isaiah and Cyrus' proclamation, and concluded that both were dependent on what he called "the Babylonian court style." Though other scholars expanded the field of research to include both royal and hymnic inscriptions,[3] their

* This paper is dedicated to the fond memory of my teacher Professor E. A. Speiser. It was my great privilege to be the last doctoral student to complete a dissertation under his supervision in the study of cuneiform and biblical literature, two of the fields in which he made so many outstanding contributions.

[1] For the latest study of these chapters, see M. Haran, *Between RI'SHONÔT (Former Prophecies) and ḤADASHÔT (New Prophecies). A Literary-Historical Study in the Group of Prophecies Isaiah XL-XLVIII*, Heb. (Jerusalem, 1963), and "The Literary Structure and Chronological Framework of the Prophecies in Is. XL-XLVIII," *SVT* 9 (1963), pp. 127-155.

[2] R. Kittel, "Cyrus und Deuterojesaja," *ZAW* 18 (1898), pp. 149-164. Cf. also his comments in *Geschichte des Volkes Israels*, Vol. III/1 (Stuttgart, 1927), pp. 210 ff.

[3] E. Sellin, *Studien zur Entstehungsgeschichte der jüdischen Gemeinde nach dem babylonischen Exil.* Vol. I: *Der Knecht Gottes bei Deuterojesaja* (Leipzig, 1901), pp. 131-135; L. Dürr, *Ursprung und Aufbau der israelitisch-jüdischen Heilandserwartung* (Berlin, 1925), pp. 146-152; F. Stummer, "Einige keilschriftliche Pa-

studies were mainly limited to the neo-Babylonian period, and hence they did not take into consideration that many of the formulaic expressions current in the documents of that period could be traced back to earlier prototypes.

The purpose of this paper is to point out several as yet unrecognized analogues to the language, phraseology, and ideology of royal inscriptions in the writing of the prophet who, more than any of his predecessors, was so strongly influenced by this literary genre. The examples, moreover, are culled from various sections of the book of Deutero-Isaiah and are not limited to the first nine chapters.

A familiar motif from Sumerian times on is the predestination and designation of the king's legitimacy by a divine call.[4] In a study of Mesopotamian royal titles, Hallo[5] assembled the various epithets compounded with a divine name such as "called by the god by name" Sum. mu.pàd.da DN; "named with a (good) name by the god" Sum. mu.(du_{10}).sa_4.a DN; "beloved of the god" Sum. ki.ág DN; "favorite of the god" Sum. še.ga DN; "servant" Sum. $arad_2$; and "shepherd" Sum. sipa.

Now all of these epithets are also found in the later cuneiform royal inscriptions where the king is the one whose "name had been called or designated" by the gods, Akk. *šumšu/zikiršu/nibīssu/nibīt šumišu nabû* and *šumšu/zakār šumišu/nibīt šumišu zakāru*,[6] expressions which are exactly identical to the calling of Cyrus and the "servant" in Deutero-Isaiah: קראתי בשמך "I have called you by your name" (43:1),[7] and הזכיר שמי "He designated my name" (49:1).[8] The Akk. phrases *narām ili* "the beloved of the god," *migir ili* "the favorite of the god," and *itût* (*kūn libbi*) *ili* "the chosen/selected of the god," correspond, moreover, to the Heb. אהבי "my beloved" (41:8)[9] and בחירי רצתה נפשי "my chosen one whom I desire" (42:1).[10] And last, but not least, the cognates of Akk. *rē'ûm* "shepherd" and *wardum* "servant" both appear in Deutero-Isaiah, the former when Cyrus is called רֹעִי (Is. 44:28) and the latter throughout the famous עבד passages of that prophet.[11]

Another way of expressing the divine legitimation and selection of the king is by the use of Akk. *kēniš* "truly, favorably"[12] with such verbs as *naplusu* and *naṭālu* "to look at," *ḫašāḫu* "to desire," *uttû* "to select," *banû* "to create,"[13] *rēšam ullû* "to elevate."[14] Two other verbs employed with this adverb are *zakāru* and *nabû*.[15]

rallelen zu Jes. 40-46," *JBL* (1926), pp. 171-189; H. Gressmann, *Der Messias* (Göttingen, 1929) = *Forschungen zur Religion und Literatur des Alten und Neuen Testaments* 19, pp. 59-61; A. Jeremias, *Das Alte Testament im Lichte des alten Orients*, 4th Ed. (Leipzig, 1930), pp. 601, 684-690; J. W. Behr, *The Writings of Deutero-Isaiah and the Neo-Babylonian Royal Inscriptions* (Pretoria, 1937); I. Engnell, "The 'Ebed Yahweh Songs and the Suffering Messiah in 'Deutero-Isaiah'," *BJRL* 31 (1948), pp. 77 ff.; M. Smith, "II Isaiah and the Persians," *JAOS* 13 (1963), pp. 415-421. Many of the examples adduced in these studies, with the exception of the monograph by Behr, are quite general and not altogether convincing. Cf., on the other hand, the comparison between the prism inscription of Sennacherib V: 67-69) and Is. 59: 17 made by E. A. Speiser in *The World History of the Jewish People*. Vol. 1: *At the Dawn of Civilization*. Ed. E. A. Speiser (Tel-Aviv, 1964), p. 120.

While Behr attributes the similarities between the royal and prophetic writings to a common Babylonian cultural environment, Smith is of the opinion that the parallels between Deutero-Isaiah and Cyrus' proclamation are due to Persian political propaganda put out in Babylonia by Cyrus' agents before the conquest.

[4] Cf. E. Dhorme, *La religion assyro-babylonienne* (Paris, 1916), pp. 150 ff.; R. Labat, *Le caractère religieux de la royauté assyro-babylonienne* (Paris, 1939), pp. 40 ff.; H. Frankfort, *Kingship and the Gods* (Chicago, 1948), pp. 238-240.

[5] W. W. Hallo, *Early Mesopotamian Royal Titles: A Philologic and Historical Analysis* (New Haven, 1957) = *AOS* 43, pp. 132-142.

[6] Cf. M-J. Seux, *Épithètes Royales* (Paris, 1967), pp. 176-9, 370 f.

[7] Cf. 42: 6; 45: 3, 4; 48: 12 (מקראי); 49: 1.

[8] Found only here with this precise meaning.

[9] Cf. 43: 4; 48: 14.

[10] Cf. 41: 8, 9; 43: 10, 20; 44: 1, 2; 45: 4; 49: 7; 65: 9, 15, 22.

[11] Cf. 41: 8; 42: 1; 43: 10; 44: 1, 21; 45: 4; 49: 5; *et al.* Many of these examples, with the corresponding cuneiform expressions, have already been noted by Behr, *op. cit.* For the neo-Babylonian equivalent of the Sum. mu.du_{10}.sa_4.a DN "named with a good name by the god," cf. Neriglissar's inscription in S. Langdon, *Die neubabylonische Königsinschriften* (Leipzig, 1912) = *VAB* 4, p. 214, l. 20: *šú-um ṭa-a-bi lu-ú im-ba-an-ni*.

[12] Akk. *ṭābiš* and *ḫadiš* occasionally alternate with *kēniš*. For the former, see the inscription of Šamaš-šumukin cited below in the text, and for the latter, see *VAB* 4, p. 142, col. I, l. 14.

[13] For selected references, see W. von Soden, *Akkadisches Handwörterbuch*, Vol. 6 (Wiesbaden, 1965), p. 480.

[14] R. Borger, *Die Inschriften Asarhaddons, Königs von Assyrien* (Graz, 1956) = *AfO Beiheft* 9, p. 40, l. 11.

[15] von Soden, *loc. cit.*

Of Nabonidus it is said *šú-um-šú ki-ni-iš iz-ku-ru* "they favorably designated his name,"[16] and of Esarhaddon *zi-kir šumi-ia ke-niš im-bu-ú* "they favorably called my name."[17] Now in Hebrew the interdialectal functional equivalent of Akk. *kēnu/kēniš* is צדק[18]/בצדק, and this is precisely the very word employed in the selection and call of the designated servant in 42:6 אני ה' קראתיך בצדק "I, YHWH, have graciously called you," an expression which verifies and legitimizes the divine call of this individual alone.[19]

In the royal inscriptions after the king is called and selected by the gods, he is then given a task to fulfill. A similar sequence of events is found in Deutero-Isaiah where the designated servant is called upon to fulfill his unique twofold mission (42:6). Then in 42:7 he is bidden:

לפקח עינים עורות להוציא ממסגר אסיר
מבית כלא ישבי חשך

"to open blind eyes, to liberate prisoners from confinement, (and) dwellers in darkness from prison."[20] Here the expression "to open blind eyes" is a metaphor for the releasing of the imprisoned or "dwellers in darkness" from their dungeons. Similarly in cuneiform inscriptions Sargon declares: *apli Sippar Nippur Bābili ù Barsip ša i-na la an-ni-šu-nu i-na qir-bi-šu ka-mu-ú ṣi-bit-ta-šú-nu a-bu-ut-ma u-kal-lim-šu-nu-ti nu-ru* "The people of Sippar, Nippur, Babylon, and Borsippa who, through no fault of theirs, have been kept imprisoned in it (i.e., the conquered city of Dur-Yakin), I destroyed their prison and let them see the light" (i.e., "I set them free").[21]

The equation in Hebrew of "opening one's eyes" with freedom and liberation explains, furthermore, a lexical innovation of Deutero-Isaiah, for in 61:1 the prophet announces that he was sent by God לקרא לשבוים דרור "to proclaim liberty to captives" ולאסורים פקח־קוח "and to prisoners freedom" (lit. "opening of eyes").[22]

When the prophet comes to describe the future tribute that will be brought to Jerusalem by the various nations of the world, he makes specific reference in one instance to the valuable wood which will be used to rebuild and redecorate the Temple (Is. 60:13):

כבוד הלבנון אליך יבוא
ברוש תדהר ותאשור יחדו
לפאר מקום מקדשי
ומקום[23] רגלי אכבד

"The glory of the Lebanon shall come to you,
ברוש תדהר ותאשור יחדו[24]
To adorn the site of My sanctuary,
And the site[23] of My feet shall I glorify."

The "glory of the Lebanon" is none other than the precious cedar whose wood supplied the neces-

[16] *VAB* 4, p. 234, l. 15.

[17] Borger, *op. cit.*, p. 80, l. 18.

[18] Cf. the corresponding names of the two kings *Šarru-kēn* (Sargon) and מלכיצדק (Gen. 14:18; Ps. 110:4) "the king is legitimate."

[19] This clause is then followed in the text by another phrase characteristic of Deutero-Isaiah—ואחזק בידך "I grasped your hand" (cf. 41:9, 13; 45:1) whose cuneiform analogue is found in l. 12 of the Cyrus cylinder, where it is stated that Marduk searched for a just ruler *šá it-ta-ma-aḫ qa-tu-uš-šú* "whom he could grasp by the hand," F. H. Weissbach, *Die Keilinschriften der Achämeniden* (Leipzig, 1911) = *VAB* 3, p. 2. Note the use of Akk. *tamāḫu* here and its Heb. cognate תמך which is employed in the same context in 41:10 and 42:1. (Cf. also Ps. 73:23.) For a similar expression in a Hittite text, see Jeremias, *op. cit.*, and Stummer, *op. cit.* The grasping of an individual's hand by a deity is a scene often depicted on cylinder seals.

Another correspondence between the royal inscriptions and Deutero-Isaiah is the motif of divine help (Akk. *tukkulu*, Heb. עזר). Cf. 41:10, 13, 14; 44:2, and M. Streck, *Assurbanipal und die letzten assyrischen Könige bis zum Untergange Niniveh's*, Vol. II (Leipzig, 1916) = *VAB* 7, p. 70, l. 59: *ilAššur ša ú-tak-kil-an-ni*; p. 100, l. 32; p. 108, l. 68; p. 110, l. 2; *et al.*

[20] According to Y. Kaufmann, *The Religion of Israel*, Vol. 8, Heb. (Jerusalem, 1956), p. 125, this mission was to be performed by God and not by the servant. Cf. 49:9.

[21] H. Winckler, *Die Keilschrifttexte Sargons*, Vol. I (Leipzig, 1889), pp. 122-124, ll. 134-135; cf. pp. 58-60, ll. 359-360. See also W. G. Lambert, "Three Literary Prayers of the Babylonians," *AfO* 19 (1959), p. 66, l. 8: . . . *ša ina bīt ṣi-bit-ti na-du-ú tu-kal-lam nu-ur* ". . . you show light (i.e., "liberate") to those who have been thrown into prison." Cf. p. 54, ll. 212-213, and Stummer, *op. cit.*, p. 180.

[22] Heb. פקח־קוח refers to the "opening" of the eyes and not as E. J. Kissane, *The Book of Isaiah*, Vol. II (Dublin, 1943), p. 274, suggests to the opening of bonds or prisons. The verb פקח is used throughout the Bible only of the opening of the eyes or the ears (Is. 42:20).

[23] Elsewhere throughout the Bible (Is. 66:1; Ps. 99:5; 110:1; 132:7; Lam. 2:1; I Ch. 28:2) the word employed in this expression is Heb. הדום "footstool."

[24] Heb. יחדו is occasionally found in Deutero-Isaiah at the conclusion of a series of nouns or verbs; cf. 41:19 (identical to 60:13), 20, 23; 45:21.

sary timber for the building of the First Temple.[25] Cuneiform sources likewise mention the bringing of cedars (Akk. *erēnu*) taken from the Lebanon as tribute to the king for the construction of palaces and temples.[26] Nebuchadnezzar reports that the kings *iṣerēnimeš dannuti ul-tu šadLa-ab-na-nim a-na maḫāzi-ia Bāb-iliki i-ba-ab-ba-lu-nim* "brought me mighty cedars from the mountains of Lebanon to my city of Babylon."[27]

In the Hebrew text there then follows a triad of trees[28] whose wood is to be used for the construction and adornment of the future Temple. Whereas the identity of the first tree, Heb. ברוש, cognate to Akk. *burāšu*, has been established as "juniper,"[29] a tree which also grows in the Lebanon[30] and was employed along with the cedar in both the building and decoration of the Israelite First Temple[31] and the palaces and temples of Mesopotamian rulers,[32] the other two trees, תדהר ותאשור, have been subject to various conflicting interpretations.[33] It would seem likely, in view of the above, that their identity should be sought in the following manner: trees which grow in the Lebanon (or anti-Lebanon), are associated with the cedar and juniper, and whose wood is used for construction purposes. It is then interesting to note that in many cuneiform records of trees brought as tribute to the Assyrian kings, a favorite recurrent combination found in the inscriptions of Aššurnasirpal II,[34] Sargon,[35] and Sennacherib[36] is *erēnu* "cedar," *burāšu* "juniper," *šurmēnu* "cypress,"[37] and *duprānu* (or *daprānu*) another variety of "juniper";[38] e.g., *gušūrē erēni šurmēni daprāni burāši lu akkis* "I (Aššurnasirpal) felled (in the Amanus) logs of cedar, cypress, *duprānu* and *burāšu* junipers."[39] Hence these two trees, *šurmēnu* and *duprānu*, which also grow in the Lebanon and are often cited in connection with palaces and temples,[40] seem to fill the exact same slots as Heb. תאשור and תדהר. A further clue to the identity of the former may be found in the Talmud where תאשור is equated with שורבינא[41] (cognate of Syr. *šarwainā* and Arab. *šerbīn*)[42] "cypress," and שורבינא, in turn, has been independently related to Akk. *šurmēnu*.[43] If this Talmudic tradition can be relied upon, it would give further support for the identification of Heb. תאשור with Akk. *šurmēnu*, and it would then stand to reason that תדהר is none other than the interdialectal equivalent of Akk. *duprānu*.

In addition to precious trees, men and women, silver and gold, and cattle and sheep are all frequently mentioned in the lists of tribute brought to the Mesopotamian monarchs. Many inscriptions include, furthermore, *narkabāti* "chariots," *ṣumbī* "wagons," *sīsê* "horses," *parê* "mules," and *gammalē* "camels."[44] Now in Isa. 66:20 there

[25] Cf. the manifold references in II Ki. 6–7.

[26] For references, see *CAD*, Vol. 4, pp. 274-276.

[27] *VAB* 4, p. 148, col. III, ll. 15-18. The Hebrew cognate to Akk. *erēnu*, ארן, appears as a *hapax legomenon* in Is. 44:14.

[28] Cf. also 41:19.

[29] I. Löw, *Die Flora der Juden*, Vol. 3 (Wien, 1924), pp. 33-36, and *CAD*, Vol. 2, p. 328. Cf. also von Soden, *Handwörterbuch*, Vol. 2, p. 139, and M. Zohary, *IDB*, Vol. 2, p. 293.

[30] See the article ברוש in *Encyclopedia Biblica*, Vol. 2, Heb. (Jerusalem, 1954), pp. 339-341. For the occurrence of cedar and juniper trees in the Lebanon and anti-Lebanon, cf. Is. 37:24 and the statement of Salmanezzar III in E. Michel, "Die Assur-Texte Salmanassars III," *WO* 2 (1964) p. 40, ll. 17-18: *a-na šadḪa-ma-ni e-li iṣgušūrēmeš iṣe-ri-ni iṣburāši a-ki-si* "I went into the Amanus and cut timber of cedar (and) juniper trees."

[31] I Ki. 5:22, 24; 6:15, 34; 9:11.

[32] See *CAD*, Vol. 2, p. 327.

[33] Cf. the standard commentaries and lexica.

[34] E. Schrader, *Sammlung von assyrischen und babylonischen Texten* (Berlin, 1889) = *KB* I, p. 109, l. 89.

[35] Winckler, *Sargon*, p. 70, l. 419; p. 90, l. 72; p. 128, ll. 158-159; p. 144, ll. 31-32.

[36] D. L. Luckenbill, *The Annals of Sennacherib* (Chicago, 1924) = *O.I.P.* II, p. 110, ll. 36-37.

[37] Löw, *op. cit.*, p. 29, and Zohary, *op. cit.*, p. 292. Cf. also A. Malamat, "Campaigns to the Mediterranean by Iahdunlim and Other Early Mesopotamian Rulers," *Studies in Honor of Benno Landsberger* (Chicago, 1965), pp. 368-369.

[38] *CAD*, Vol. 3, pp. 189-190.

[39] *KB* 1, p. 108, ll. 88-89.

[40] For *šurmēnu*, e.g., *iṣšurmēnu e-ri-šu ṭa-bu ša ki-rib šad!Si-ra-ra* "sweet fragrant cypresses from Sirara"; *iṣgušūrēmeš iṣeri-nu ù iṣšurmēnu ṣi-ru-tu tar-bi-tu šadḪa-ma-nu ù šadLab-na-nu* "logs of tall cedars and cypresses which grow in the Amanus and Lebanon"—*VAB* 7, Vol. 2, p. 170, l. 46, and p. 246, ll. 58-60.

For a similar reference to *duprānu*, see n. 34 above, and for the juxtaposition of the *šurmēnu* and *duprānu* trees, see the additional examples cited in von Soden, *op. cit.*, Vol. 2, p. 162. The *dprn* tree now appears in Ugaritic texts; see C. H. Gordon, *Ugaritic Textbook* (Rome, 1965), p. 386.

[41] *Talmud Bavli*, *Rosh Hashanah* 23a and *Baba Batra* 80b.

[42] Löw, *op. cit.*, pp. 26-29.

[43] *Ibid.*, p. 29.

[44] Cf. *VAB* 7, Vol. 2, p. 46, l. 61; p. 327, n. 8 (Aššurbanipal); Winckler, *op. cit.*, p. 42, l. 253; p. 48, l. 280; p. 76, l. 440; p. 132, ll. 183-185 (Sargon); and Luckenbill, *op cit.*, p. 24, l. 25; p. 25, ll. 51-52; p. 28, ll. 20-21; p. 33, l. 25; and esp. p. 51, l. 29: *iṣnarkabātimeš iṣṣu-um-*

is a description of the return of the diaspora when the distant nations shall come to Jerusalem to pay homage to God by bringing back the scattered exiles of Israel. The prophet then describes this return as a מנחה "tribute" in terms familiar from the tribute lists of inscriptional literature. The children of Israel shall be brought on סוסים, Akk. *sīsê* "horses," רכב, Akk. *narkabāti* "chariots," צבים, Akk. *ṣumbī* "wagons," פרדים, Akk. *parê* "mules,"[45] and finally כרכרות, the only unknown element in the list. It is precisely at this point[46] in the cuneiform royal inscriptions that camels are mentioned.[47] This sequence then would help to equate Heb. כרכרות as a semantic equivalent of Akk. *gammalē,* and thus lends further support to one of the traditional interpretations[48] which identifies the word as a synonym for "dromedaries."[49] That Deutero-Isaiah knew of camels brought as tribute is attested to by 60 : 6 :

שפעת גמלים תכסך
בכרי מדין ועיפה

"A multitude (or "a dust cloud")[50] of camels
shall cover you,
Young camels of Midian and Ephah."

Note also that the prophet employs in this passage another synonym for camel, Heb. בכר, the etymon of Akk. *bakru,* which appears only in late Babylonian times[51] and is mentioned as tribute in the inscriptions of Tiglat-Pilessar III: *a-na-qa-ti a-di* ^{imēr}*ba-ak-ka-ri-ši-na am-ḫur* "I received (as tribute) female camels with their young."[52]

For my last example I wish to return to the motif of divine predestination and selection. A theme which occurs in the inscriptions of seven kings starting with Aššur-rēš-iši I (1130-1113) down to Nabonidus (556-539) is the designation of the king while yet in the womb of his mother:[53]

1. *Aššur-rēš-iši* I (1130-1113):[54]

^{m}*Aš-šur-rēš-i-iši* . . . *ša* ^{il}*A-nu* ^{il}*Enlil ù* ^{il}*Ea ilāni*^{meš} *rabûti*^{meš} *i-na libbi agarinni ki-niš iḫ-šu-ḫu-šu-ma a-na šu-te-šur māt Aš-šur bēlu-šu ib-bu-ú* "A. whom Anu, Enlil, and Ea, the great gods, truly desired (while still) in the womb of his mother, and decreed his rule in order to guide Assyria on the right path."

2. *Sennacherib* (705-681):[55]

^{il}*Be-lit ilāni*^{meš} *be-lit nab-ni-ti i-na šasurri a-ga-ri-in-ni a-lit-ti-ia ki-niš ippalsa-an-ni-ma ú-ṣab-ba-a nab-ni-ti* "Bēlit-ili, the goddess of procreation, looked favorably upon me (while still) in the womb of my mother, who bore me, and created my features."

3. *Esarhaddon* (681-669):[56]

. . . *ilāni*^{meš} *rabûti*‹^{meš}› *šàr māti e-li-tum ù š*[*ap-lîtum* . . . *ina*] *šasurri a-ga-ri-in-ni a-lit-ti-*

---

bi sīsê^{meš} *parê*^{meš} *imērē*^{meš} *gammalē*^{meš} *imērud-ri* ("camels") (Sennacherib). The complete list of items appears only in this last citation. The *sīsê* are usually combined with the *narkabāti,* and the *parê* with the *ṣumbī*; cf. F. Delitzsch, *Assyrisches Handwörterbuch* (Leipzig, 1896), p. 558 (*ṣumbu*), and Is. 66: 20.

[45] The etymological equivalent of Akk. *parû* is Heb. פרא; Heb. פרד is its semantic equivalent. In the cuneiform inscriptions mules and donkeys (Akk. *imērē*) usually appear one after the other.

[46] I. e., after Akk. *parê* and *imērē.*

[47] See above, n. 44 for the reference to Sennacherib.

[48] This interpretation found in the commentaries of Kimchi and Abarbanel is the most popular one cited in translations commentaries, and lexica. It first appears, I think, in Saadya when he translates the Heb. כרכרות by Arab. אלעמאריאת "dromedaries." See Y. Derenbourg, *Tafsir of the Book of Isaiah,* Heb. (Paris, 1936), *ad. loc.*

[49] Though one must be extremely wary in listing support from Arabic which abounds in its number of synonyms for "camels," it should be noted at least in passing that *kirkirat*^{un} is "the callosity, or callous protuberance, upon the breast of the camel which, when the animal lies down, touches and rests upon the ground, projecting from his body like a cake of bread," Lane, *Arabic-English* Lexicon, Vol. 1[7] (London, 1885), p. 2601. It is most unlikely, however, that the two words are related.

In the Qumran scroll of Isaiah (IQIsa) the word is spelled כורכובות.

[50] N. H. Tur Sinai, *The Book of Job,* Heb. (Tel-Aviv, 1954), p. 205.

[51] Cf. von Soden, *op. cit.,* Vol. 2, p. 97, and *CAD,* Vol. 2, p. 35.

[52] P. Rost, *Die Keilschrifttexte Tiglat-Pilesers III,* Vol. 1 (Leipzig, 1893), p. 26, l. 157; cf. also D. J. Wiseman, "A Fragmentary Inscription of Tiglat-Pileser III from Nimrud," *Iraq* 18 (1956), p. 126, l. 21.

[53] This motif also appears in the stele of King Pianchi of Egypt (751-730): "It was in the belly of your mother that I said concerning you that you were to be ruler of Egypt; it was as seed and while you were in the egg, that I knew you, that (I knew) you were to be lord." See M. Gilula, "An Egyptian Parallel to Jeremiah I 4-5," *VT* 17 (1967), p. 114.

[54] E. Weidner, *Die Inschriften Tukulti-Ninurtas I. und seiner Nachfolger* (Graz, 1959) = *AfO,* Beiheft 12, p. 54, ll. 1-3. Cf also R. Borger, *Einleitung in die assyrischen Königsinschriften* (Leiden, 1961) = *Handbuch der Orientalistik* V/1, p. 103.

[55] Luckenbill, *op. cit.,* p. 117, l. 3.

[56] Borger, *Asarhaddon,* p. 115, Text 82, ll. 7-10. Cf. p. 119, Text 101, ll. 10-15, esp. l. 13. See also Luckenbill, *Ancient Records of Assyria and Babylonia,* Vol. 2 (Chicago, 1927), p. 223, Text 571.

i[a . . .] be-lu-ú-te(!) ša(!) ka-la mātāti^{meš}*-ma [. . .] lìb(?)-bi* ^{il}*Aš-šur ú-zak-ki-ru-ma* ". . . The great gods designated (me) king of the upper and l[ower] lands . . . (while yet) [in the] womb of my mother who bore me . . . for rule of all the lands (in accordance with) the will(?) of Aššur."

4. *Aššurbanipal* (669-632?):[57]

a-na-ku ^{md}*Aššur-bān-apli bi-nu-tu* ^{il}*Aššur u* ^{il}*Bēlit . . . ša* ^{il}*Aššur ù* ^{il}*Sin bēl agî ul-tu ûmê*^{meš} *rūqūte*^{meš} *ni-bit šumi-šú iz-ku-ru a-na šarru-ú-ti ù ina libbi ummi-šu ib-nu-ú ana re'û-ut* $^{\text{māt il}}$*Aššur*^{ki} . . . "I, Aššurbanipal, am the creation of Aššur and Bēlit . . . whom Aššur and Sin, the lord of the crown, already in the distant past[58] had called by name for ruling, and who had created him in his mother's womb for the shepherding of Assyria."

5. *Šamaššumukin* (652-648):[59]

. . . a-šar nab-ni-it um-mi a-lit-ti-ia a-na e-nu-ut nîšê šu-mi ṭa-bi-iš lu-ú ta-am-bi šar-rat ilāni^{meš} ^{il}*E-ru-u-a* ". . . in the place of forming (= womb) of the mother who bore me, Erua, the queen of the gods, favorably called my name for lordship over mankind."

6. *Nebuchadnezzar* (605-562):[60]

iš-tu ib-na-an-ni bēl ^{il}*Ir-u-a* ^{il}*Marduk ib-ši-mu na-ab-ni-ti i-na um-mu e-nu-ma al-da-ku ab-ba-nu-ú a-na-ku* "After Erua had created me (and) Marduk formed my features within my mother, when I was born (and) created."

7. *Nabonidus* (556-539):[61]

a-na-ku ^{il}*Na-bi-um-na-'-id . . . šá* ^{il}*Sin ù* ^{il}*Nin-gal i-na libbi um-mi-šu a-na ši-ma-at šarru-ú-tu i-ši-mu ši-ma-at-su* "I, Nabonidus, . . . whose fate Sin and Ningal (while yet) in the womb of his mother had destined for dominion."

This motif occurs in the Bible in Jeremiah's dedication scene:[62]

בטרם אצרך בבטן ידעתיך
ובטרם תצא מרחם הקדשתיך
נביא לגוים נתתיך

"Before I had created you in the womb, I chose you,[63]
And before you were born, I set you apart;
I appointed you prophet to the nations"
(Jer. 1:5).

And it is often repeated in chapters 41–49 of Deutero-Isaiah, e. g.,

ה' מבטן קראני
ממעי אמי הזכיר שמי

"YHWH called me while yet in the womb;
While yet in my mother's womb He designated my name" (49:1).

ועתה אמר ה' יצרי מבטן לעבד לו

"And now said YHWH, who created me even in the womb to be His servant" (49:5).

Thus this exilic prophet had two main sources from which he drew: inner-Biblical, i. e., Jeremiah, and extra-Biblical, i. e., royal inscriptions. Of the two, however, Jeremiah proved to be the far more influential and inspirational in the development of Deutero-Isaiah's thought,[64] for he adopted not only the theme of predestination from Jeremiah, but also that prophet's very phraseology—and then reinterpreted the message in the light of his own religious genius.[65] In Jeremiah it is written:

אצרך . . . נביא לגוים נתתיך

"I have created you . . . (and) designated you a prophet to the nations" (Jer. 1:5).

---

[57] *VAB* 7, Vol. 2, p. 2, ll. 1-5. Cf. pp. 252-254, ll. 1-6.

[58] Akk. *ultu ûmê*^{meš} *rūqūte*^{meš} "in the distant past," *ina ṣeḫērišu* "in his childhood," (KB, Vol. 1, p. 188, l. 2; p. 190, l. 1—Adad-Nirari III), *ultu ṣeḫērišu* "from his childhood" (*VAB* 7, Vol. 2, p. 2, l. 3—Aššurbanipal), and *ultu ûmê*^{meš} *ṣeḫērišu* "from the days of his childhood (Borger, *Asarhaddon*, p. 12, ll. 13-14—*Esarhaddon*) are other expressions for the early choice of the king by the gods. Cf. H. Lewy, "Nitokris-Naqî'a," *JNES* 11 (1952), p. 264, n. 5.

[59] C. F. Lehmann, *Šamaššumukin König von Babylon* (Leipzig, 1892), p. 7, ll. 6-8. This is a bilingual text (the Sumerian version is on p. 6), and the difficult Akkadian grammatical construction is most likely due to its Sumerian prototype. For several different translations of the Akkadian text, cf. Lehmann, *loc. cit.*; *KB*, Vol. 3/1, p. 198, ll. 6-8; and Dhorme, *La religion assyro-babylonienne*, p. 153.

[60] *VAB* 4, p. 122, ll. 23-27.

[61] *Ibid.*, p. 218, ll. 1-5.

[62] For an earlier example of pre-natal designation, see Jud. 13:5.

[63] Cf. the similar phraseology, "I chose you," lit. "I knew you," in n. 53 above.

[64] However, the specific motif of being "called" while yet in the womb is a feature which Deutero-Isaiah shares only with his Mesopotamian prototypes.

[65] This was illuminatingly pointed out to me by Prof. H. L. Ginsberg.

Deutero-Isaiah, in turn, employs these same two verbs (יצר . . . נתן) in his description of the creation and mission of Israel:

אצרך ואתנך לברית עם לאור גוים

"I have created you and appointed you a covenant people, a light to the nations" (42:6).

יצרי מבטן . . . ונתתיך לאור גוים

"He who created me in the womb . . . (said) 'I will make you a light to the nations'" (49:5-6).

ואצרך ואתנך לברית עם

"I have created you[66] and appointed you a covenant people" (49:8).

However, even though the phraseology is borrowed from Jeremiah,[67] Deutero-Isaiah completely transformed and transcended that prophet's original message. For whereas the call in Jeremiah was to an individual, here it is expanded to encompass all of Israel—the entire people was created and chosen from the very beginning to fulfill a divine task. And while Jeremiah was to become נביא לגוים "*a prophet to the nations*," i.e., to announce to all nations (including Israel) their present and future fate, Israel in Deutero-Isaiah was to be a *prophet nation* (49:2-3; 51:16; 59:21) whose mission it was to spread the teaching of God to all humanity (42:1-4) and to recount God's glory (43:21), and thus to become לאור גוים (lit. "a light of nations"), that is to say, to bring God's blessing (ישועה, lit. "deliverance, salvation") to the ends of the earth (49:6). Israel, as God's witnesses,[68] becomes the source and the instrument whereby His benificence will spread throughout the entire world (45:22-24).[69] Israel's mission is not one of *world conquest*, as in the Mesopotamian inscriptions,[70] nor one of *world prediction*, as in Jeremiah, but rather one of *world salvation*.

[66] The constant juxtaposition of these two verbs, which ultimately derives from the prophecy in Jeremiah, proves that the stem of אצרך is יצר "create" and not נצר "preserve."

[67] The influence of Jeremiah upon the phraseology and ideology of Deutero-Isaiah will be studied in a future paper.

[68] A theme which appears in 43:10, 12 and 44:8.

[69] Cf. 55:4.

[70] See above n. 59. Cf. also *VAB* 7, Vol. 2, p. 382, l. 8.

THIRTY PIECES OF SILVER

ERICA REINER
UNIVERSITY OF CHICAGO

IN THE RECENTLY PUBLISHED Sumerian poem "Curse on Agade,"[1] we read in line 107, in Falkenstein's translation: "achtete er das g i g u n a (von Nippur) nur dreissig Sekel wert," i.e., "he deemed the g i g u n a (of Nippur) only thirty shekels' worth." The biblically schooled mind discovers here a parallel to the thirty pieces of silver of Matt. 26:15 and 27:3 ff.[1a]

Then one of the Twelve, the man called Judas Iscariot, went to the chief priests, and said, "What are you prepared to give me if I hand him over to you?" They paid him thirty silver pieces. (Matt. 26:14-15)[2]

I propose here to trace the motif of the thirty pieces of silver.

The traditional way of looking at this phrase is to look for a socio-economic interpretation, and to seek in the thirty shekels received by Judas the price of some marketable item, usually the valuation of a slave's life.[3] In view of the Sumerian documentation of this phrase now available, I would like to assume that the "market value" explanation is, and was perhaps already in Biblical times, a secondary rationalization.

Of the three Sumerian attestations of e š e . g í n . . . a k a, literally "to do (as/for) thirty shekels" (all cited by Falkenstein, loc. cit. p. 94, and previously by Kramer, AS 10 59 f. and again in AS 12 89), the most literal is found in the poem

[1] Published by A. Falkenstein, ZA 57 (1965), pp. 43 ff.

[1a] This parallel, based on all three Sumerian passages here discussed, was first noted by P. René Follet, "'Constituerunt ei triginta argenteos' (ad Mt 26,15)," *Verbum Domini* 29 (1951), pp. 98-100.

[2] *The Jerusalem Bible* (Doubleday, Garden City, N.Y., 1966). Remaining Old and New Testament quotations also come from this edition.

[3] Roman B. Halas, *Judas Iscariot* (The Catholic University of America Studies in Sacred Theology, No. 96) (Washington D.C., 1946), pp. 77 f.

on Gilgameš and the Huluppu-Tree (Kramer, AS 10, p. 9:90). The poem describes how Gilgameš put on armor weighing fifty minas (i. e., ca. 50 lbs.), ninnu.ma.na.àm eše.gín ba.ši.in.aka, "he *considered* the fifty minas as (a mere) thirty shekels." The second reference to eše.gín ... aka is from the Lamentation Over the Destruction of Ur (Kramer, AS 12, p. 44:244): "The Sutians and the Elamites, the destroyers, considered it (i. e., the Egišnugal of Ur) only thirty shekels' worth." For both these, and the third reference (cited below), Kramer proposed the meaning "to hold in light esteem," "to treat with contempt," and Falkenstein's translation moves along the same line of thought, since evidently the "thirty shekels" represent an idiomatic phrase.[4] The third text, the Curse on Agade, describes the destruction of Agade by the Gutians, attributing it to Enlil's revenge for the destruction of his temple Ekur in Nippur by Naram-Sin of Akkad. Lines 104-107 of this poem read, in Falkenstein's translation:

Wie ein Starker, der zu hoher Kraft geschaffen ist,
machte er gegen das Ekur . . . . ;
wie ein Läufer, der zur Körperkraft . . . . . ,
achete er das giguna (von Nippur) nur dreissig Sekel wert.

The Sumerian text of these lines runs:

á.tuku kisal(!).maḫ.šè ku$_4$.ku$_4$.gim
é.kur.šè šu.kéš ba.ši.in.aka
du$_{10}$.tuku lirum.šè gam.e.gim
gi.gun$_4$.šè[5] eše.gín ba.ši.in.aka

I would propose the following translation for these lines, keeping Falkenstein's translation for the last line since the latter is the subject of this article:

Like a strong man (preparing) to enter the large courtyard,[6]
he organized (his troops) against the Ekur;
like a runner bending down(?) ready for the race,
he considered the giguna a mere thirty shekels' worth.

My translation differs from that of Falkenstein in the interpretation of šu.kéš...aka (Akkadian *kaṣāru*) as "to make ready," and of lirum as "contest, race" (Akk. *abāru*, usually in combination with *umāšu*, translated as "wrestling, athletics, fights" in CAD 1/2 (A) s. v. *abāru* B); the verb gam "to bend, in connection with the runner (du$_{10}$.gam) in line 106, seems to me to refer to the position from which the runners start, well known in sports.[7]

While in the first reference (from Gilgameš), "to consider as thirty shekels" (i. e. half a pound) can be taken literally as referring to weight, the other two references where temples are named are not easy to explain. Undoubtedly, however, eše.gín was a set phrase in Sumerian which could be used in such similes and did not express any actual weight or value; in fact, this phrase is never used in its concrete sense, since thirty shekels, in legal, economic, and administrative texts, is normally written as one-half mina.

The phrase "thirty shekels" in a literary context next appears in the Old Testament book of Zechariah, which is cited in Matt. 27:9-10; to this occurrence we shall return presently. If, however, we follow a chronological sequence in the attestation of the phrase "thirty shekels," we must note two references, both from the West Semitic area, which name this amount, but these are in non-literary contexts and denote actual monetary compensation. One of the occurrences, usually cited in connection with Matt. 26:15, is Ex. 21:32, where thirty shekels are specified as the compensation to be paid for a slave gored to death by an ox. Among the corresponding Mesopotamian laws which are often cited in this connection (see, e. g., Goetze, LE p. 139 f.), § 251 of the Code of Hammurapi gives the same amount (but stated, as expected, as one-half mina of silver) as the compensation for a free man gored to death, while in the Eshnunna Code the amounts to be paid as compensation differ. Exodus and the Code of Hammurapi are the first, and indeed the only known occurrences of thirty shekels of silver as "blood money"; another occurence from a similar cultural setting—this time as ransom—

[4] Damit heisst die Redewendung "für das giguna machte er (nur) dreissig Sekel (als Preis) fest." Falkenstein, ZA 57 (1965), p. 94.

[5] Vars. gi.gun$_4$.na, gi.gun$_4$.na.bi, gi.gun$_4$.na.aš, kindly communicated to me by M. Civil.

[6] Translation based on the reading kisal!.maḫ instead of šu.maḫ, collated for me by M. Civil.

[7] This kneeling posture called *Knielauf*, represented in Mesopotamian iconography mostly in the figure of the so-called "master of animals," also appears in Greek art, where "the kneeling pose was endowed with a new connotation, that of swift motion." For a discussion of the *Knielauf* in Mesopotamian and Greek iconography, see H. J. Kantor, JNES 21 (1962), pp. 104 ff., especially pp. 109 f.

is in the Amarna letter EA 292, written by ^{d}IM.DI.KUD, prince of Gezer (his name is read Addu-dâni by Knudtzon, and Ba'lu-šipṭi by Albright) to the "king" (i. e., to Akh-en-aton), lines 49 ff.: "A man is ransomed from the mountain (region) for 30 (shekels of) silver, whereas from Peya for a hundred (shekels of) silver (only)" (for a recent translation, see Albright, ANET 489 f.).

I have intentionally discussed these two references separately from the Zechariah passage, since in the latter thirty shekels denote neither blood money nor ransom, but "wages." This is the enigmatic passage Zech. 11: 12-13:

> And they weighed out my wages: thirty shekels of silver. But Yahweh told me, "Throw it into the treasury, this princely sum at which they have valued me." Taking the thirty shekels of silver, I threw them into the Temple of Yahweh, into the treasury.[8]

There are several philological difficulties in these verses, especially the Hebrew words for "lordly price" and "treasury"[9] for which the Syriac and Greek versions give differing translations. Many emendations and interpretations have been proposed, and still these verses are not satisfactorily translated; see, e. g., the remarks by B. Otzen, *Studien über Deuterosacharja* (Copenhagen, 1964), p. 156.[10]

There is, however, no doubt that it is this passage that is meant by the prophecy of "Jeremiah" which, Matthew says, came true when Judas cast the thirty pieces of silver into the treasury:

> The words of the prophet Jeremiah were then fulfilled: "And they took the thirty silver pieces, the sum at which the precious One was priced by children of Israel, and they gave them for the potter's field just as the Lord directed me." (Matt. 27: 9-10)

It is usually assumed that Matthew attributed the prophecy to Jeremiah instead of to Zechariah on account of the story of the purchase of a field in Jer. 32: 6-15 and of Jeremiah's visit to the potter's house in Jer. 18: 2 ff. However this may be, there is no mention of a sum of thirty shekels of silver in Jeremiah, and consequently the New Testament exegetes have explained the blood money paid to Judas as representing the value of a slave as stated in the passage Ex. 21: 32 referred to above.[11]

This prosaic interpretation is in sharp contrast with the story of the thirty pieces of silver in medieval apocrypha and legends. According to the legend of Judas[12] that can be dated to the late 12th century, the most generally known version of which is found in the Golden Legend, Judas betrayed Jesus for thirty pieces of silver in order to compensate himself for the "tithe"—the amount he used to appropriate for himself from the monies he kept—that he would have embezzled, had the costly perfume that Mary, sister of Martha, poured over Jesus' feet in Bethany (John 12: 3-6) been sold for 300 pieces of silver instead:

> Dolens vero tempore dominicae passionis, quod unguentum, quod trecentos denarios valebat, non fuerat venditum, ut illos etiam denarios furaretur, abiit et dominum triginta denariis vendidit, quorum unus quisque valebat decem denarios usuales et damnum unguenti denariorum recompensavit; vel, ut quidam ajunt, omnium, quae pro Christo dabantur, decimam partem fureabatur et ideo pro decima parte quam in unguento amiserat, scilicet pro triginta denariis, dominum vendidit.[13]

A tradition also exists, attested in early apocrypha and in the Fathers of the Church, according to which Joseph was sold by his brothers not for twenty shekels (Gen. 37: 28), but for thirty,[14] a tradition consonant with the view that

[8] Note the commentary of the "Bible de Jérusalem": Un gouverneur a droit à une rétribution . . . Ici, celle qui est donnée allégoriquement par les classes dirigeantes au prophète (figurant Yahvé) est dérisoire, le prix d'un esclave, Ex 21.32. Bref, on se moque de Yahvé!—Mt 27.3-10 a appliqué les vv. 12-13 au Christ, dont le prophète, tenant la place de Yahvé méprisé, apparaît comme le type.

[9] For יוצר in Zech. 11: 13, see Gösta Ahlström, VT XVII (1967), 1 ff.

[10] I am indebted to Professor Gösta Ahlström, University of Chicago, for supplying me with references concerning the mentioned Zechariah verses.

[11] Krister Stendahl, *The School of St. Matthew and Its Use of the Old Testament* (Uppsala, 1954), p. 196 f., does not dwell on the amount of money Judas received, except to suggest that in Matt. 26: 15 "the exact number could be an adaptation to the prophecy." For a comparison of Matt. 27: 9-10 with Zech. 11: 12-13, see ibid., pp. 120-126.

[12] Paull Franklin Baum, "The Mediaeval Legend of Judas Iscariot," *Publications of the Modern Language Association of America,* 31 (1916), pp. 481-632.

[13] Jacopo da Voragine, *Legenda aurea,* chap. xlv, ed. Graesse, pp. 183-188; cf. Wilhelm Creizenach, *Judas Ischarioth in Legende und Sage des Mittelalters,* Separatabdruck aus den *Beiträgen zur Geschichte der Deutschen Sprache und Literatur,* Band II, Heft 2 (Halle, 1875), p. 2.

[14] Benjamin Murmelstein, "Die Gestalt Josefs in der

Joseph was the prefiguration of Christ.[15] However, it is not only the exact number of the silver pieces that has found such legendary or exegetical explanation,[16] but the concrete, physical existence as well. Rudolph Hoffman, *Das Leben Jesu nach den Apokryphen* (Leipzig, 1851), in § 77, "Judas Ischarioth," gives a summary (p. 333) of the story of the "Silberlinge," the thirty pieces of silver; Murmelstein, loc. cit., p. 54 n. 4, cites Hoffman's summary, which narrates the peregrinations of the thirty pieces of silver from the sale of Joseph to Judas. Creizenach,[17] in his summary, takes the story back to Terah, the father of Abraham; Abraham is said to have used the thirty pieces of silver for the purchase of the cave of Machpelah as a burial site (cf. Gen. 23:7-16). Terah's coining of these pieces for Abraham appears in the Syriac *Book of the Bee*, ed. E. A. W. Budge (Oxford, 1886), chap. xliv (English translation pp. 95 f.).[18]

Of the western medieval versions of the legendary story of the thirty silver pieces, the poetic version by Godfrey of Viterbo, *Pantheon*, chap. xx, is the fullest I have been able to find in its original form (as quoted in Du Méril, *Poésies populaires latines du moyen âge* (Paris, 1847),[19] pp. 321-24. It begins:

Denariis triginta Deum vendit Galilaeus,
quos et apostolicus describit Bartholomaeus,
unde prius veniant, quis fabricavit eos.

Fecerat hos nummos Ninus, rex Assyriorum,[20]
et fuit ex auro Thares fabricator eorum;
cum quibus instituit rex ninivita forum.

Godfrey then narrates how Abraham received the coins from Thares (i.e., Terah), and bought a field with them from the people of Jericho; Joseph was also purchased with them ("*his etiam Joseph est emptus ab Ismahelitis*"); then they came into Pharaoh's treasury, and then into the treasury of the Queen of the Arabs, who gave them to Solomon. When Nebuchadnezzar pillaged the Temple, he took them along to Babylon, where they were given as pay to the soldiers of the kingdom of Saba; the kings of Saba sent them with the three Magi as a gift to Jesus. During the Flight into Egypt, they were hidden in a cave (according to the German version of the legend, they were lost on the way to Egypt), and then found by an Armenian astrologer, who gave them to the Temple:

Denarios triginta Deo quos inde tulerunt,
in gazam templi, Jhesu mandante, dederunt;
quos Judam pretio post habuisse ferunt.

Godfrey concludes by arguing—or rather, invoking the authority of St. Bartholomew to prove—that the coins were gold rather than silver.

We see then that, by the Middle Ages, the thirty shekels of silver had taken on an independent, and indeed indestructible, existence, going about on peregrinations of their own—from Assyria to Canaan to Egypt to Arabia to Babylon to Persia and back to Palestine—a route, with perhaps some extra detours, strikingly like that of the motif itself.

On the sole basis of these traditions, which nowhere connect the thirty pieces of silver with the price or value of a slave, I would be ready to suggest that we follow their poetic interpretation rather than the rationalistic view which hangs everything on the thirty shekels of Ex. 31:32. I would like, therefore, to suggest that we take as starting point the idiomatic meaning of "thirty shekels' worth" as attested in Sumerian, namely "a trifling amount." In my opinion, this idiom, i.e. an expression whose meaning cannot be predicted from the meanings of its component parts,

Agada und die Evangeliengeschichte," *Angelos* 4 (1932), pp. 51-55; for this tradition, Murmelstein cites the Testament of Gad 2, in Kautzsch, *Apokryphen* 2, p. 493 (also edited R. H. Charles, *The Apocrypha and Pseudoepigrapha of the Old Testament* [Oxford, 1913], 2 p. 340), and ". . . Joseph, ille qui distractus est triginta argenteis . . ." Origenes, Homily to Ex. 1:6 ff., ed. Baehrens, 1, p. 149. See also H. A. Brongers, *De Jozefsgeschiedenis bij Joden, Christenen en Mohammedanen* (Waegeningen, 1962), pp. 52 f.

[15] Cf. "Vides alibi viginti, alibi viginti et quinque aureis, alibi triginta invenimus emptum Joseph; quia non omnibus unius aestimatione pretii valet Christus." Ambrosius, De Jos. Pat., p. 647, cited Murmelstein, loc. cit., p. 54 n. 3. Murmelstein believes that the altering of the purchase price for Joseph was influenced by Ex. 31:32, and strengthened by the parallel in Zech. 11:12-13, and thus was upheld in the tradition against the actual twenty shekels of Gen. 37:28.

[16] Note also, as recently as 1932, an explanation advanced—one wonders how seriously—on the basis of *gemmatria* (number symbolism) by Murmelstein, loc. cit. p. 54: the numerical value of the letters y, h, w, d, h (10 + 5 + 6 + 4 + 5) that make up the name of Judas (in Hebrew) equals 30.

[17] loc. cit.; see note 13 above.

[18] The Syriac version omits the price paid for Joseph from the narrative.

[19] Reference from Creizenach, op. cit. p. 3 n. 2.

[20] Ninus is the eponymous founder of Nineveh in Greek mythology.

underwent a curious development: it lost its idiomatic meaning and reassumed its literal meaning, that of a specific amount (or weight) of silver. Such a de-idiomatization must have occurred, as is often the case, in connection with a change in linguistic or cultural setting. In the absence—probably fortuitous—of an Akkadian link between the Sumerian idiom and its reappearance in Hebrew, it can only be tentatively suggested that it is through translation into some Semitic language that the Sumerian idiom ultimately—but not necessarily immediately—lost its idiomatic meaning. I would however venture to suggest that the idiomatic meaning of this expression is not restricted to the Sumerian passages cited, but may still be considered present in the Zechariah [21] and Matthew passages under discussion. The situation in which the words quoted in Matt. 26 : 15 were spoken, when the high priests offered Judas thirty pieces of silver, may well have expressed the contempt of the priests, who would have meant "we will give you no more than a farthing," or the like.

This view is strengthened, I believe, by the Joseph story as told in the Koran. There no actual figure is mentioned concerning the sale of Joseph; the Koran simply says (Sura 12 :20), "They sold him for a trifling price, for a few pieces of silver. They cared nothing for him." (Transl. of N. J. Dawood, *The Koran* [The Penguin Classics L52, 1956], p. 39 f.). In the translation of A. J. Arberry, *The Koran Interpreted* (London, 1955), "Then they sold him for a paltry price, a handful of counted dirhams; for they set small store by him." While the Koran commentators knew of traditions according to which the "few pieces of silver" were twenty or twenty-two dirhems, the wording of the Koran indicates that the actual amount in the transaction was not what mattered, but its idiomatic meaning: a trifling, paltry price. Thus, we may perhaps best use the words of the Koran for an idiomatic translation of the Sumerian poem with which we began: "he (Naram-Sin) set small store by the g i g u n a of Nippur."

But, I believe, we can proceed one step farther in determining the meaning of the Sumerian idiom e š e . g í n, the "thirty shekels" which, so to speak, are the root of all evil. It is rather unexpected to find, as an expression for a "trifling sum," the figure thirty; one expects something in the semantic range of a fraction: a farthing, a "halfpennyworth." [22] As a matter of fact, the Sumerian word read e š e is written with the EŠ-sign, which represents the figure 30, but which, in the reading b a - a, means "half"; the relationship of the two values for the same sign is evident from the sexagesimal notation wherein 30 is not only 30 but also half of the next higher unit, cf. English *fifty-fifty*, i. e., "half-half." Sumerian ba-aEŠ, i. e. the sign 30 with the reading b a - a, is equated with the Akkadian words *mišlu, muttatu, zūzu,* and *bamtu,* all meaning "half." Of these, *zūzu,* etymologically "fraction," then "the (first) fraction," became specialized in the meaning "half shekel" and was borowed into Aramaic as *zūzā*, see CAD 21 (Z) p. 170. Indeed, the Syriac term for the silver pieces in the Book of the Bee (see above, p. 189) is *zūzā*, but obviously is used there simply as a monetary unit, and has shed all its etymological connotations.

We have seen various attempts at interpreting the thirty pieces of silver: from the positivistic slave-price interpretation to their legendary transcendental individualization, and even an attempt at attributing to them a cabbalistic value through *gemmatria*. As a philologist, I have tried to approach the question by examining the relevant textual evidence, semantic probability, and etymology. These show that Gilgameš considered the fifty-mina armor "as light as a feather," and the enemies of Sumer considered its temples a mere "halfpennyworth," to use the appropriate idiomatic English equivalent. The ambiguity of the number system gave rise to the literal interpretation "thirty shekels" which maintained itself up to modern times, when Sumerologists correctly guessed the contextual, external meaning without analyzing the internal composition of the idiom. No wonder that the ancient *literati*, while similarly interpreting the idiom correctly, likewise rendered it, in their own language, with the incompatible literal equivalent "thirty shekels." [23] It is perhaps due to the unusual number contained in the idiom that so many legendary—as well as scholarly—interpretations were necessary to explain "*unde prius veniant*," the origin of the thirty pieces of silver.

[21] Note the comment of the Bible de Jérusalem cited above n. 8: "Bref, on se moque de Yahvé!"

[22] Cf. also Hungarian *egy félkrajcárt sem ér*, "not worth half a penny."

[23] Not connected with "half" since the Hebrew mina, unlike the Sumerian and Babylonian, was divided into fifty, not sixty, shekels.

TWO KASSITE VOTIVE INSCRIPTIONS

EDMOND SOLLBERGER
THE BRITISH MUSEUM, LONDON

I. INTRODUCTION

The first of the two inscriptions published here was inscribed, in Sumerian, on the back of a terra-cotta dog[1] by one Ninurta-rēṣūšu, *šatammu*[2] of the E-u-gal under King Nazi-Maruttaš. The second was inscribed, in Akkadian, by the same gentleman at a later stage in his career—he was then *nēšakku*[3] of Enlil—, on a clay quadrangular prism.[4] The dog, dedicated to Gula, is poorly preserved but enough to show it to be of the same type as the clay dog from Sippar published by Scheil, Une saison de fouilles à Sippar p. 91 fig. 15. It may indeed come from Sippar too: Ninurta-rēṣūšu's other inscription, the clay prism, belongs to a collection registered as coming from Abū Ḥabba. The prism is dedicated to Adad whose three-pronged thunderbolt[5] is represented on the top and twice on one side (A). On side D, in the blank space between lines 29 and 30, there is a deep depression apparently made by a thumb.

In the prism inscription, the author gives only his name and title and the name of his father, UD-Delebat.[6] In the dog inscription, however, the father's title is given as *nēšakku* of Enlil, the son being only *šatammu* of the E-u-gal. Also named are an ancestor, Enlil-bānī, *rabānum* (i. e., 'mayor')[7] of KUR.TI;[8] and an even remoter ancestor, Amīlatum, *šandabakku*[9] of Nippur.

Enlil-bānī is undoubtedly the same official who is mentioned on a clay *kudurru*[10] as the *nēšakku* of Enlil under Kuri-Galzu I. As such, he was certainly also *šandabakku* of Nippur in the early part of the latter's reign, as aptly suggested by K. Balkan.[11] That in addition (or before) he was *rabānum* of KUR.TI, as Dūr-Kuri-Galzu was known before its 'foundation' by Kuri-Galzu I,[12] is chronologically consistent.

Enlil-bānī's successor, both as *šandabakku* of Nippur and *nēšakku* of Enlil, Ninurta-nādin-aḫḫē, was still in office under Burna-Buryaš II.[13] It is quite likely that he was Enlil-bānī's son or at least a member of the family. He was succeeded by his son, Enlil-kidinnī, whose tenure covered the three following reigns.[14] Under Nazi-Maruttaš, however, the situation was obviously different: the offices of *šandabakku* and *nēšakku* were held by different persons, the former by Nazi-Enlil,[15] the latter by UD-Delebat whose son, Ninurta-rēṣūšu, seems also to have been only a *nēšakku*. The *šandabakku* Ninurta-apla-iddina[16] may well have been his contemporary.[17]

---

[1] BM 81-7-1,3395, length 34 cm., diameter of body 10 cm.

[2] The translation 'bishop' has recently been proposed by B. Landsberger; see his Brief des Bischofs von Esagila an König Asarhaddon (Amsterdam 1965), especially pp. 58 ff.

[3] Cf. Landsberger Brief p. 59.

[4] BM 92699 = 82-7-14,4460, 16 × 9 × 9 cm. Described (under a wrong BM number and rather inaccurately) by Budge, Guide 1922 p. 91 no. 159.

[5] See Unger RLA 2 p. 56 f., van Buren AnOr 23 pp. 67 ff.

[6] This PN, known from other Kassite sources, is read as Nūr-Ištar by Clay YOR 1 p. 114; for UD (or ZALAG) = *nūr*, see Stamm Namengebung p. 151. Aro Glossar zu den mB Briefen (= StOr 22) s. v. *nakāru* D, reads mZALAG-dDIL.BAT.

[7] Cf. Krückmann RLA 1 p. 445 § 3. For the title *rabiānum* MAR.TU, see Kupper Nomades pp. 192 f., Edzard Zwischenzeit p. 37, Sollberger UET 8 p. 12 ad 65.

[8] See below, fn. 12.

[9] Cf. Landsberger Brief pp. 75 ff.

[10] King BBSt 1 (= Winckler ZA 2 p. 309). Spelled d*en-lil-ba-ni*.

[11] Belleten 12 p. 746.

[12] Cf. Poebel AS 14 p. 1 ff., especially pp. 6-10. For the reading of the GN, see now Lambert AfO 18 pp. 396 f., and Moran Orientalia 29 pp. 103 f.

[13] Balkan Ankara Üniversitesi Dil ve Tarih-Coğrafya Fakültesi Dergisi 2 p. 50, Belleten 12 p. 746; Landsberger Brief p. 77. For the double title, see Hilprecht BE 1 33 lines 11-12.

[14] Balkan Ankara . . . Dergisi 2 p. 50, Belleten 12 p. 747 fn. 72; Landsberger Brief p. 77.

[15] Balkan Ankara . . . Dergisi 2 p. 50, Belleten 12 p. 748 fn. 77; Landsberger Brief p. 77.

[16] Balkan Ankara . . . Dergisi 2 p. 50, Landsberger Brief p. 77.

[17] From Kadašman-Enlil II to Kaštilyaš III, as observed by Landsberger Brief p. 77, the two offices are again held by one man, the king himself, though a *šandabakku*, Amīl-Marduk, is found under Kudur-Enlil and Šagarakti-Šuryaš (Balkan Ankara . . . Dergisi 2 p. 50, Belleten 12 p. 755; Landsberger Brief p. 77). Later on the offices seem to be split again: under Adad-šuma-uṣur the *šandabakku* is Enlil-šuma-imbī while the

It would thus appear that whereas Amīlatum's lineage managed to retain the office of *nēšakku* of Enlil, that of *šandabakku* of Nippur had, under, or just before, Nazi-Maruttaš, passed into other hands. The foregoing remarks may be tabulated as follows:—[18]

before Kuri-Galzu I	Amīlatum	šN	[nE]
Kuri-Galzu I, Kadašman-Enlil I, Burna-Buryaš II	Enlil-bānī	[šN]	nE
	? Ninurta-nādin-aḫḫē	šN	nE
Burna-Buryaš II, Kara-Hardaš, Nazi-Bugaš, Kuri-Galzu II	Enlil-kidinnī	šN	[nE]
Nazi-Maruttaš	ᴜᴅ-Delebat		nE
	Nazi-Enlil	šN	
Nazi-Maruttaš or after	Ninurta-rēṣūšu		nE
	Ninurta-apla-iddina	šN	

II. THE TEXTS[19]

1. BM 81-7-1,3395.

^{d}gu-la
nin maḫ-di
ama diğir-re-é-ne-er
nin-a-ni-ir
^{m} ^{d}*nin-urta-re-ṣú-šu*
šà-tam é-u-gal
šà-tam lugal(a) ^{d}en-líl-le
dumu ^{m}ᴜᴅ-^{d}*dele-bat*
nu-èš ^{d}en-líl
šà-bal-bal ^{m} ^{d}*en-líl*-ᴅù
ra-ba-nu-um ᴋᴜʀ.ᴛɪ^{ki}
nunuz-bal ^{m}*a-mi-la-tum*
$ša_x$-dub-ba(!)-a nibru^{ki}
n[am]-ti-la
[^{d}na-z]i-ma-[r]u-ut-ta-aš
[lugal] šár(a)
[lugal-l]a-ni-ir
[alam(?)] ur x-x-ni
gú i_7]ᴜᴅ.ᴋɪʙ.ɴᴜɴ^{ki}-gé
[i_7] dağal-la-na
[é-mu]-pà-da
[é ki-á]ğ-ğá-ni
[nam-ti-l]a-a-ni-šè
[ù nam-ti-la k]alam-ma-šè
[ḫu-mu-u]n-dí[m]

1–4 To Gula, the sublime lady, the mother of the gods, his mistress:—

5–13 Ninurta-rēṣūšu, *šatammu* of the E-u-gal, royal *šatammu* of Enlil, son of ᴜᴅ-Delebat, *nēšakku* of Enlil, descendant of Enlil-bānī, mayor of ᴋᴜʀ.ᴛɪ, scion of Amīlatum, *šandabakku* of Nippur,—

14–16 for the life of Nazi-Maruttaš, king of the world, his master,

nēšakku is his father Dayān-Marduk (King BBSt 3 i 44 ff., iii 6 f., et passim).

[18] šN = *šandabakku* of Nippur, nE = *nēšakku* of Enlil.

[19] Both inscriptions are very worn and fairly difficult to read. The copies offered here are the result of several months of scrutinizing the texts under varying lighting conditions. The signs are reproduced as faithfully to the originals as possible, except that variations in sharpness have been ignored. No photographs are published as they would have been practically illegible.

18–25 did fashion an image(?) of her . . . dog, on the bank of the Euphrates, her wide river, in the E-mupada, her beloved temple, for his life and for the life of the land.

2. BM 92699 = 82-7-14,4460.

[*a-na*] ^{d}IM
[*m*]*u-di-im*
3 DUMU *an-nim*
[*b*]*e-lí-šu*
^{d}*nin-urta-re-ṣú-šu*
6 NU.ÈŠ ^{d}en-líl
DUMU UD-^{d}*dele-bat*
a-na ma-aš-ri ba-la-a[*ṭ*] *ša-la-mi-šu*
9 *i-na* KISAL é-mu-pà-da
šub-ti ni-ṣir-ti
ša ^{d}nin-urta
12 *ù* ^{d}gu-la
be-lu gi-im-ri
ša URU *ḫi-il-pi*^{ki}
15 *ša* GÚ
^{i_7}UD.KIB.NUN^{ki}
a-na
18 PA.DINGIR.RA *im-qí*
[*a-na*] *pu-ḫi*
[*i*]*d-di-ma*
21 *i-na* ŠE.NUMUN
ù ḫir-ṣa-ti
qut-ri-nam
24 *ú-ša-aq-ti-ir*
a-[*na*]
^{d}[IM]
27 *a-n*[*a*]
PA.DINGIR
im-qí
30 *a-na*
^{d}IM
a-na
33 PA.DINGIR
im-qí

1–4 For Adad, the wise, the son of Anu, his master:—
5–7 Ninurta-rēṣūšu, *nēšakku* of Enlil, son of UD-Delebat,—
8 for his riches (and) healthy life,—
9–16 in the forecourt of the E-mupada, the precious(?) dwelling of Ninurta and Gula, lords of the universe, which is in the town of Ḫilpu on the bank of the Euphrates,
17–24 he libated to the Thunderbolt(?); he established it as a substitute and, from seeds and . . .-roots, he caused incense to go up in smoke.
25–34 For Adad, he libated to the Thunderbolt (?). For Adad, he libated to the Thunderbolt(?).

III. NOTES TO THE TEXTS

1. BM 81-7-1,3395.

This text presents a certain number of grammatical 'irregularities' often found in Kassite inscriptions. Note the redundant dative suffix in line 3; -e for -a(k) in line 7; -ani for the genitive in line 18 and for the locative in line 22. The dative (-r) in line 17, instead of the expected directive (-šè), occurs also, in a similar context, in an inscription from Uruk (also Nazi-Maruttaš!), Falkenstein UVB 12-13 p. 43. For -e in line 19, cf. gú ^{i_7}e-ki-iš-tum(a)-gé, Hilprecht BE 1 33 line 19.—The apparent AŠ at the end of line 20, however, is in all likelihood an accidental scratch.

2-3.—Neither of these epithets is listed in Tallqvist Götterepitheta as directly applied to Gula. Their occurrence here can easily be explained by the identification of Gula with one of the great goddesses to whom they normally apply; see Tallqvist Götterepitheta p. 22 (*ummi ilāni*) and p. 96 (*tizqartu*).—In line 3, note the spelling -é- for -e-.

6.—The name of Enlil's temple at Dūr-Kuri-Galzu means certainly 'house of the great lord.' I have nevertheless retained the reading é-u-gal because both u and umun are given for U = *bēlu* (see CAD s. v.), and also because of the variant spelling é-u$_4$-gal (references in the articles by Lambert and Moran quoted above, fn. 12). It should be noted, however, that, as observed by Moran *loc. cit.,* é-u$_4$-gal is not necessarily a mere variant spelling: we may, in fact, have two different temples, one of Enlil (u) and one of Adad (u$_4$); cf. also the Adad temple é-u$_4$-gal-gal (CḪ iii 66).

7.—The phrase is unusual: the normal construction is šatam + temple (or city) name. Note, however, that šà-tam lugal(a) is listed between [šà]-tam and šà-tam é-gal(a) in the early vocabulary Chiera OIP 11 109 ii. I understand the title in our text as a more emphatic restatement of the preceding line.

BM 81-7-1, 3395

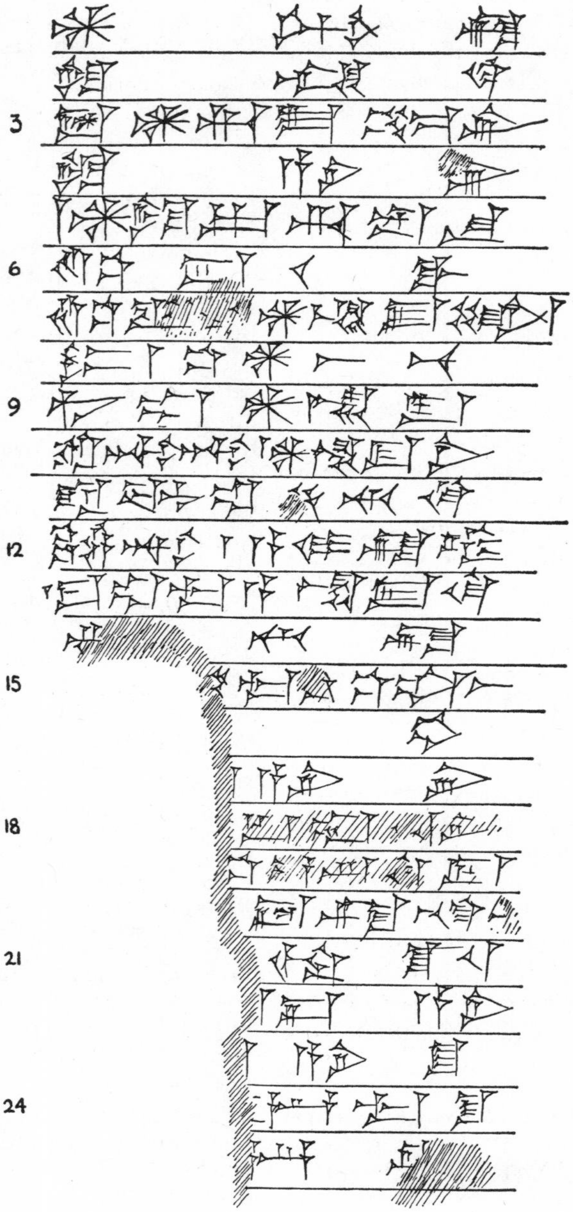

10.—šà is written over an erasure.

12.—nunuz-bal, which does not seem to be attested elsewhere, is probably a cross between šà-bal-bal = *liblibbi* (AHw *līpu*(*m*) 2) and nunuz = *līpu* (AHw s. v.) and *pir'u* (ŠL 394.7).

13.—Although the third sign is unequivocally MA it is difficult to see how else the line could be read.

16.—For [lugal] šár(a)[20], see, *e. g.*, Kuri-

[20] This restoration, rather than [lugal ki]-šár(a), is certain, in spite of lugal ki-šár-ra in the Uruk text quoted above.

Galzu: LUGAL ŠÁR, Delaporte Catalogue Louvre A. 819 (Akk.); Nies & Keiser BIN 2 15 (Sum. or Akk.); Nazi-Maruttaš: LUGAL ŠÁR.RA, Scheil MDP 2 pl. 16 ii 27 (Akk.), but *ibid.* i 2 has LUGAL KIŠ; on the same *kudurru*, the '2e médaillon' (Akk., time of Marduk-apla-iddina) has LUGAL ŠÁR. See also Seux RA 59 p. 6 f.

18.—I can offer no suggestion for the signs following ur. Neither ur-gi$_7$, as on a clay dog dedicated to Meme (= Gula),[21] nor ur kin-ge$_4$-a, as in the case of a dog dedicated to Nin-tin-uga (= Gula),[22] seems acceptable.

19 ff.—See below, **2** 9 ff.

2. BM 92699 = 82-7-14,4460.

2.—This epithet is not recorded by Tallqvist Götterepitheta p. 249 among those extolling Adad's wisdom (*apkallu, eršu,* etc.).

8.—The phrase is rather unusual but may be compared to the MB seal inscription Langdon RA 16 p. 89 no. 44, quoted CAD *balāṭu* s. 1 c 1′. *balāṭ šalāmišu* seems parallel to the well-attested *balāṭ napšātišu*: cf. CAD *ibid.* 1 c 2′ and Deller Oientalia 35 p. 305.

9.—One could also read É é-mu-pà-da 'the temple E-mupada': cf. É é-babbar, É é-gal-maḫ, É é-maḫ (CḪ ii 30, ii 54, iii 69). This temple name is otherwise unknown to me.

10.—Cf. É *niṣirti* 'treasury,' in NA inscriptions: AHw *bītu(m)* B 17; cf. also URU *niṣirti,* said of Babylon, Langdon VAB 4 p. 116 27, p. 136 viii 34. Unless *niṣirtu* be taken here as 'secret, mystery, arcane'; see Bezold Glossar p. 204a, CAD *bārûtu* 3.

13.—Neither Ninurta nor Gula is listed as *bēl(et) gimri* in Tallqvist Götterepitheta.

14-16.—I know of no other reference to a town of this name. The site of Ḫilpu is obviously to be sought along the (ancient) course of the Euphrates, somewhere between 'Aqar-Qūf (= Dūr-Kuri-Galzu; cf. above, **1** 6) and Abū Ḥabba (= Sippar) where the inscription was found.

18, 28, 33.—The translation of PA.DINGIR(.RA) as 'thunderbolt' (*birqu*) is, of course, only a guess but, I think, a plausible guess ('staff of the god'). The usual value of PA.DINGIR, garza = *parṣu,*[23] would leave the RA in line 18 unexplained, besides being rather difficult to fit into the context. Note that the thunderbolt is actually represented thrice on the prism and that three libations to the PA.DINGIR(.RA) are mentioned in the text.[24]

18, 29, 34.—*imqī* is for *iqqī,* from *naqû.* The only alternative reading materially possible, *imkī,* from *mekû* 'to neglect, be negligent,' is ruled out by its meaning. Although I cannot quote any direct evidence for the passage *-nq-* > *-mq-,* one may perhaps adduce phonetic variations of the *inamdin* type. See, for example, Aro Studien zur mB Grammatik (= StOr 20) p. 35 ff.; von Soden Grundriss § 32.[25]

19-20.—A thunderbolt (probably in metal) must have been placed in the temple as a symbol of, and therefore a substitute for, Adad. A similar event is apparently referred to in the year-name Abī-ešuḫ k (Morgan MCS 4 p. 47 no. 434 f.).

21.—For ŠE.NUMUN in this context, see CAD *zēru* s. 1 c 2′.

22.—Cf. CAD *ḫirṣu* B, where only lexical occurrences are cited.

[21] Scheil Sippar p. 90 fig. 13.

[22] F. A. Ali ArOr 34 p. 292. The dog in question bears a name, tu$_6$-ni-lú-sa$_6$, reminiscent of those of some of Gula's officers; see Tallqvist Götterepitheta p. 317.

[23] It is certainly so to be understood in the Burna-Buryaš inscription Hilprecht BE 1 33 (line 3).

[24] The translation 'thunderbolt' should perhaps also be considered for AN.PA.AN-ka (or ^{d}PA.DINGIR-ka) ba-ra-an-sum-mu-uš in the text of the Kuri-Galzu statue from 'Aqar-Qūf (A v 6-8, see Kramer Sumer 4 pl. I and pp. [5] and [21] note 13).

[25] Incidentally, the term 'palatale Nasal $\mathring{n}$' used there is not a very happy one since a palatal *n* would be similar to Spanish *ñ*, i.e., [ny], whereas the consonant in question (appropriately symbolized by von Soden as $\mathring{n}$) is in all probability a velar nasal. The phrase 'französ. nasalen *n*' is an obvious lapsus calami.

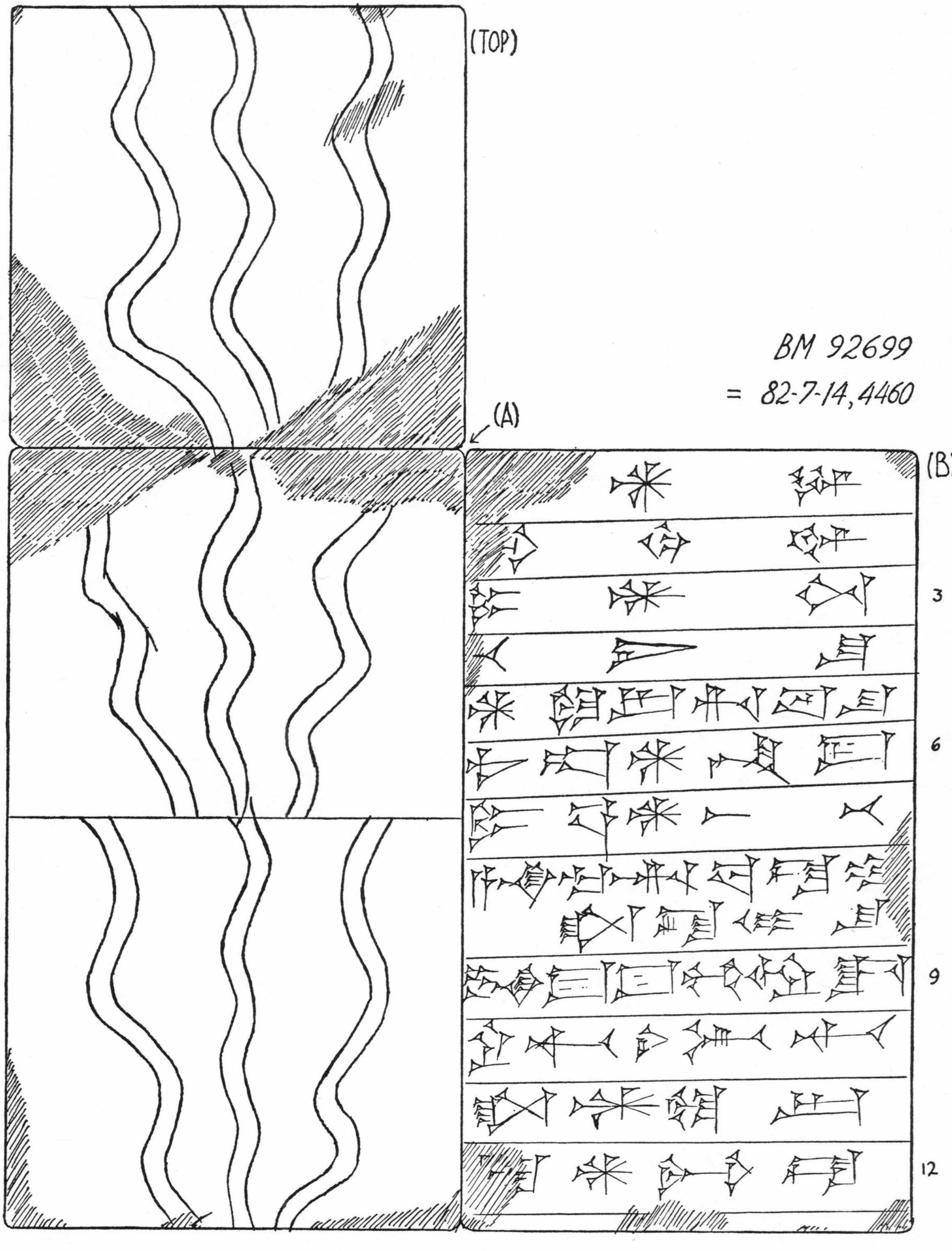
(TOP)
BM 92699
= 82-7-14,4460
(A)
(B)
3
6
9
12

BM 92699 (cont.)

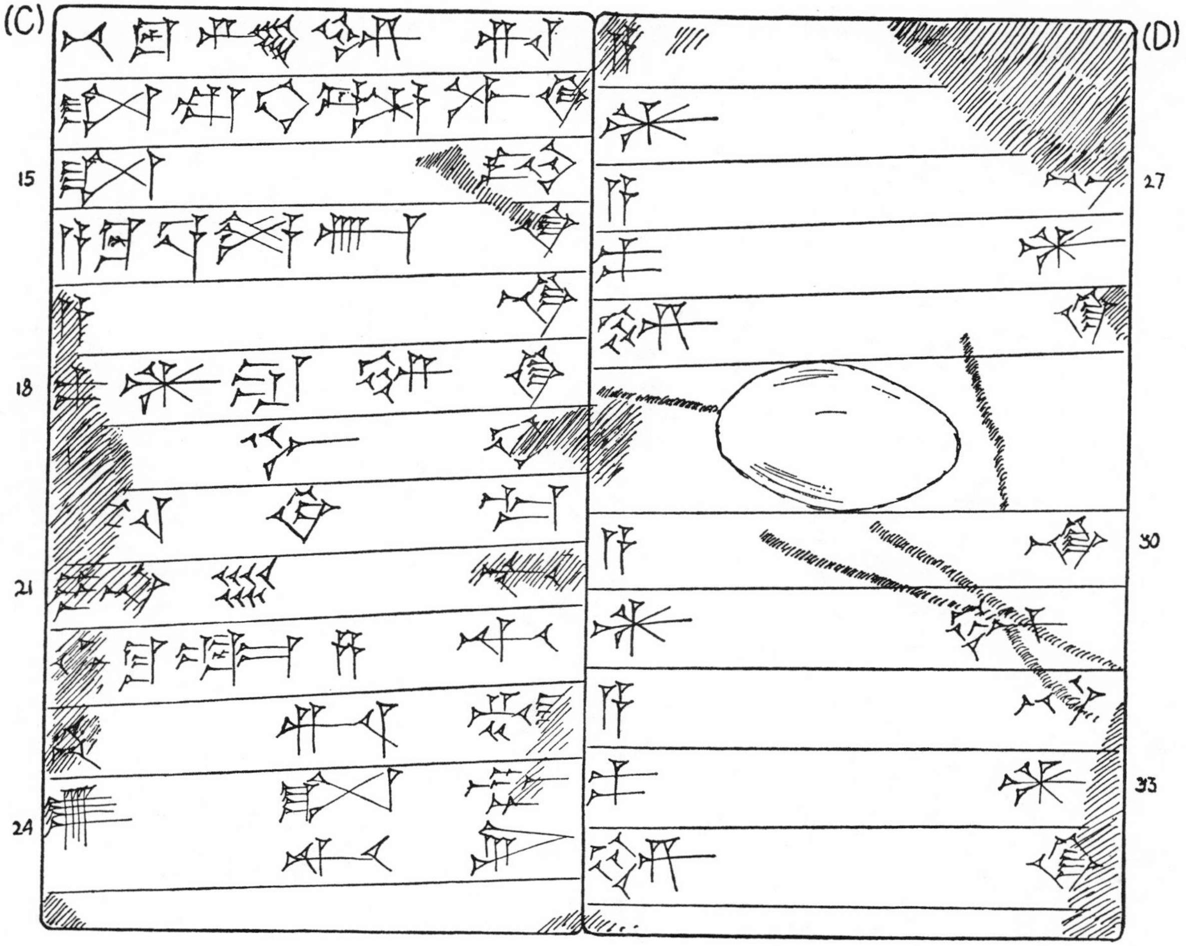

INDEX

Compiled by Barry L. Eichler

DN = divine name GN = geographical name PN = personal name RN = royal name TN = temple name